79.50

READING RATE

READING RATE

A Review of Research and Theory

Ronald P. Carver

School of Education
University of Missouri–Kansas City
Kansas City, Missouri

ACADEMIC PRESS, INC.
Harcourt Brace Jovanovich, Publishers
San Diego   New York   Boston
London   Sydney   Tokyo   Toronto

Copyright © 1990 by Academic Press, Inc.
All Rights Reserved.
No part of this publication may be reproduced or transmitted in any
form or by any means, electronic or mechanical, including photocopy,
recording, or any information storage and retrieval system, without
permission in writing from the publisher.

Academic Press, Inc.
San Diego, California 92101

United Kingdom Edition published by
Academic Press Limited
24–28 Oval Road, London NW1 7DX

Library of Congress Cataloging-in-Publication Data

Carver, Ronald P.
    Reading rate : a review of research and theory / by Ronald P.
Carver.
        p.   cm.
    Includes bibliographical references.
    ISBN   0-12-162420-X   (alk. paper)
    1. Reading–Research. 2. Reading comprehension. 3. Rapid
reading.   I. Title.
LB1050.6.C37   1990
428.4'3–dc20   90-32574
                                                                       CIP

Printed in the United States of America
90   91   92   93   9   8   7   6   5   4   3   2   1

To Mary Lou

CONTENTS

PREFACE

What do we know about reading rate? This book is a long answer to that question.

Prior research on reading rate has had little impact on current research or practice in reading, probably because there has been no organizing conceptual framework. Reading rate typically has been viewed as peculiar to the situation, rather than lawful. In this book, I have reviewed 100 years of reading rate research, including such areas as eye movements, silent speech, comprehension, word recognition, oral reading, textual presentation, automaticity, and speed reading. A theoretical framework has been used to organize and interpret this research. Contrary to the prevailing view, I have found reading rate to be highly lawful and predictable.

Chapter 1 contains an overview of the research reviewed in Chapters 3–20. Chapter 2 contains the theoretical foundation necessary for comprehending the lawfulness underlying all of this research. Chapter 21, the last chapter, is a summary of my findings.

The book is for all those who want to learn what science can tell us about reading rate. Therefore, it should be of interest to researchers in reading, language arts, psychology, and education, as well as teachers, clinicians, college study skills specialists, lay persons, and those who teach speed reading courses to people in business.

Reading rate has been a favorite research interest of mine during the past 25 years. I have long wished that someone would review all the research that has been conducted on this topic, but always found excuses why I should not be the one to do it. About five years ago, I finally gave in to my sense of duty and requested a research leave for one semester to start on this task. When the University of Missouri–Kansas City (UMKC) actually granted my request for leave, I had mixed feelings. I greatly appreciated their gift of time but there were no excuses left. I could no longer avoid this laborious and time-consuming task.

After I started reviewing articles, I was surprised to find I actually enjoyed it. The research data were not very difficult to organize and made a great deal of sense from my theoretical framework. I became engrossed in the wealth of empirical data collected by researchers over the years, many of whom are now dead. My hat goes off to all those persons who understand that the scientific method only works when our theories, ideas, and hypotheses are tested by collecting data, facts, and empirical evidence.

I could never have written this book without the patience and support of my wife, Mary Lou. Besides her, UMKC, and hundreds of researchers, I must acknowledge the help I received from colleagues who criticized draft chapters. Fortunately, I have good friends who will tell me when I have food on my face and *faux pas* in my manuscript. They know that the manuscript would never have been published if they had not given me their best advice. They are as follows: Ed Coleman, Mark Condon, Donald Doehring, Donna Emery, Linda Gambrell, Arthur Graesser, Frank Greene, Martha Haggard, Mark Jackson, George Klare, Patricia Koskinen, Betty Ann Levy, Michael Masson, George McConkie, Larry Mikulecky, and Edward Sipay.

A great deal of credit also goes to Suzan Murphy, Betty Jean Green, Lois Nesbit, and Felicia Stewart. They typed and corrected the manuscript innumerable times over the past few years. They were able to take my messy handwritten pages and make them bookworthy; I am grateful.

During the time I spent working on this book, I think I increased my knowledge about reading rate one hundred-fold. I hope those who read it can do the same.

Part I

The First Part

This book contains a review of research and theory relevant to reading rate; it is divided into five parts. Part I, which follows, contains two introductory chapters. Chapter 1 describes how research studies on reading rate were selected for review, and how the entire book is organized. Chapter 2 introduces the reader to the essentials of reading rate; it contains the prerequisites for understanding the remaining chapters.

1

INTRODUCTION

Reading rate has been of great interest to researchers at least as long ago as Huey (1908) who considered reading rate to be ". . . of the greatest importance practically and pedagogically . . ." (p. 170). One purpose of this book will be to review the research literature and summarize what we have learned about reading rate since Huey. This review will be organized around the theoretical framework afforded by rauding theory (Carver, 1981). After the research has been reviewed, methodological techniques will be recommended for designing future research.

The readers of this book are no doubt expecting to find that prior research on reading rate has been reviewed with great thoroughness. They should not be disappointed. However, they may be surprised when they find out how closely the research has been related to theory. The readers may also be surprised when they find that the content extends well beyond reading rate into how all future research on reading could be conceptualized, designed, and interpreted. For example, an attempt has been made to clarify the concept of reading comprehension; ways of measuring it are also made more explicit.

The readers will find numerous reanalyses of previously collected data, providing new results and interpretations that are sometimes completely counter to conventional wisdom. For example, good readers generally do not change their rate with the difficulty level of material—as Woodworth (1938) contended. And, good readers generally do not change their rate from moment to moment with the difficulty of words or phrases—as Just and Carpenter (1980) have suggested.

Research on reading rate has not been given much attention in recent years. Many researchers seem to treat reading rate as a nuisance that can be safely avoided; for example, reading rate is hardly mentioned in the

Handbook of Reading Research (Pearson, 1984). Perhaps this is because rate is generally considered to vary with purpose, difficulty, and a host of other variables in unpredictable ways. One purpose of this book is to explicate the lawfulness of reading rate, showing that it can be predicted with surprising accuracy under most experimental conditions. An attempt will be made to demonstrate the importance of reading rate when theorizing, designing, and analyzing, even when the focus is on reading comprehension. Rate is an inextricable dimension of what happens during comprehension; the accuracy of comprehension can be increased by decreasing rate, and rate can be increased by decreasing the accuracy of comprehension.

The present investigation was initiated by ordering a computer search of three data bases: Educational Resources Information Center (ERIC), PsycINFO (formally known as Psychological Abstracts), and Language and Language Behavior Abstracts (LLBA). English language articles were selected that had "reading rate" or "reading speed" as a key word descriptor. From printouts containing over 600 citations, about half were eventually disregarded. Citations were almost always disregarded if they were in any of the following categories: (a) duplications; (b) dissertations; (c) foreign language journals; (d) newsletters; (e) regional, state, or local journals; (f) convention presentations or proceedings; (g) technical or progress reports; (h) unpublished papers; (i) involved special problem students such as blind, deaf, stutterers, learning disabled, and foreign language; (j) primarily involved speech production; (k) involved reading graphs, tables, and visual displays; and (l) were focused on nonreading factors such as body movements, shyness, hypnosis, coronary-prone, and transcendental meditation. Also excluded were articles that measured time instead of rate unless: (a) it was possible to calculate rate from other information given, or (b) the article was uniquely important for some other reason.

Dissertations have not been reviewed for the following reasons: (a) they are not published research that has successfully withstood the rigors of review by editors and researchers in that area, (b) the higher quality dissertation data are ordinarily published, and (c) dissertation studies are not regarded as being on the same level of quality as published research in most fields of science. Certainly, some exceptions may be found; however, there is little reason to expect that omitting dissertation data constitutes a systematic bias.

A review of the selected articles led to other relevant cited articles which were obtained and also reviewed. In addition, some articles were located from prior reviews of the literature (Berger, 1966; Hanson,

1968; Harris, 1968; D. Miller, 1966) and various annotated bibliographies (Berger, 1967; 1968b; Berger & Peebles, 1976).

The above sources, plus others personally collected through the years, were sorted into common topics, and a chapter has been devoted to each topic. In the following chapter the case will be made for separating reading activities into five basic processing types prior to reviewing reading rate. Chapter 2 contains the essentials for understanding much of the material contained in the remaining four parts of this book.

Part II will focus on such fundamental factors as effects of context, individual differences, tasks, and materials (Chapter 3); silent speech (Chapter 4); and eye movements (Chapter 5).

Part III will review research relevant to the five basic reading processes—scanning and skimming (Chapter 6); rauding (Chapter 7); learning and memorizing (Chapter 8)—and then relevant theory will be treated in more detail (Chapter 9).

Part IV covers factors influencing reading rate, that is, flexibility (Chapter 10); growth (Chapter 11); word recognition and cognitive speed (Chapter 12); rauding (Chapter 13); oral reading (Chapter 14); textual presentation (Chapter 15); comprehension (Chapter 16); automaticity and practice (Chapter 17); and rapid reading training (Chapter 18).

Part V, the last part, is a miscellaneous collection of three chapters. Chapter 19 is a review of research on speed readers; Chapter 20 contains recommendations about methodology; and Chapter 21 contains conclusions drawn from all the theory and research reviewed.

After the last chapter, Appendix A contains a short article by E. B. Coleman that is relevant to Chapter 5 on eye movements, and Appendix B contains a table for converting reading rate into grade equivalents. Then a glossary has been provided. Finally, the references for all chapters are presented.

The term "rauding" is a new term for many readers (see Glossary). In its simplest form, rauding means reading with comprehension. More precisely, rauding means to attend to each consecutive word and understand the complete thoughts in the successive sentences of passages. In rauding theory, mentioned earlier, rauding rate plays a prominent role (Carver, 1981). Rauding rate is the fastest rate at which the rauding process can successfully operate on relatively easy material. Throughout the remaining chapters, rauding theory will provide a framework for reviewing the research on rate. This theoretical framework will make it easier to organize results so as to answer many important questions. A list of such questions is presented next; these questions will be answered in the last chapter.

1. Do most individuals read at a relatively constant rate?
2. Is silent speech—covertly talking to oneself—harmful to reading, and does it slow down reading rate?
3. Is reading done by looking at each word, or can reading rate be increased by skipping the less informative words with no loss in comprehension?
4. When individuals read at their typical, normal, natural, or ordinary rate, is that their most efficient rate?
5. Is there only one reading process, or are there several different processes that can all be legitimately called reading processes?
6. What determines how fast individuals typically read?
7. Are good readers also flexible readers in that they automatically adjust their rate to the difficulty of the material and to their purpose for reading?
8. Is there more growth in reading rate each year during the early grades of school as compared to the later grades?
9. To what extent is rauding rate influenced by word recognition speed?
10. What is the relationship between the rate of comprehension during reading and the rate of comprehension during auding?
11. What is the relationship between oral reading rate and rauding rate?
12. Can the rate at which the rauding process operates be increased by grouping the words in passages into more meaningful units or phrases?
13. What is the relationship between rate and comprehension?
14. What does automaticity have to do with rauding rate?
15. Does rapid reading training increase rauding rate so that individuals can increase their rate of comprehension on passages without any loss in their accuracy of comprehension?
16. Are there individuals who can successfully operate their rauding process at rates greater than 600 words per minute, or stated differently, are there speed readers or super readers who have rauding rates greater than 600 words per minute?

The following 20 chapters contain research and theory relevant to the above questions. Approximately 500 articles and books have been cited, and over 250 research studies have been summarized in considerable detail. After reviewing this research, the last chapter answers the above questions and summarizes the most important conclusions relevant to reading rate.

2

READING RATE ESSENTIALS

INTRODUCTION

The concepts and constructs discussed in this chapter are essential for understanding the review of research and theory presented in the remaining chapters. There is a great deal of lawfulness associated with rate, but it is apparent only to those who are willing to deal with the complexities involved. The prerequisites for dealing with these complexities are explained in this chapter.

Reading rate is a concept that refers to how fast words are covered while reading. Ordinarily, the words are in the form of sentences that make up paragraphs or passages. Ordinarily, reading means nothing more precise than looking at the words from beginning to end in approximately serial order. So, reading rate can be measured quite simply by counting the number of words in the passage that have been covered during the length of time that a reading process has been operating. For example, if 300 words were covered in 2 minutes, then one way to express reading rate would be 300/2 or 150 words per minute (wpm). However, reading rate has also been measured in other ways, such as syllables per minute and letters per second. Much of the lawfulness of reading rate does not become apparent unless reading rate is measured in standard length words. So it is essential that the reader understand standard words and how they are measured.

Another essential idea required for understanding rate is that reading can involve more than one process. These processes have been divided into five basic types called scanning, skimming, rauding, learning, and memorizing. The rauding process is the one that operates normally, but individuals are often induced to shift out of this process by the instructions, the objective consequences, and the relative difficulty of the materials used in an experiment. The concept of shifting gears from one basic process to another is also essential to understanding reading rate.

Since the most important reading rate is that associated with the rauding process, it is essential that the existing constructs and laws associated with that process be introduced. The concept of reading rate will be refined into several precise constructs of rauding theory, and then the laws interrelating these constructs will be presented in the form of mathematical equations.

The following sections contain more detailed explanations of measuring reading rate, the five basic reading processes, shifting gears from one process to another, and the relevant constructs and laws of rauding theory. Unless the traditionally global concepts of reading rate and reading comprehension are precisely defined using several theoretical constructs, the lawful nature of reading rate will continue to elude us. Furthermore, successfully dealing with the complexities presented in this chapter is essential for understanding the empirical data reviewed in the remaining chapters.

MEASURING RATE

Introduction

Reading rate can be measured in many different ways. A common metric is needed so that research that, for example, measures rate in words per minute can be compared to research that measures rate in syllables per minute. Standard length words are used to provide a common metric. Formulas are given for converting from one metric to another. Then, normative data is presented which indicate what reading rate can be expected for students in each grade of school.

Standard Length Words

Most studies that measure reading rate do so by counting the actual number of words covered, as noted earlier. The word and its length are basic units in reading (e.g., see Friedrich, Shadler, & Juola, 1979). However, easier material has shorter words on the average (see Carver, 1976). Therefore, 150 words on passages at the first grade level of difficulty represent less material covered than 150 words on passages at grade level 12 in difficulty. One solution to this problem would be to count syllables and report rate in syllables per minute. For example, there may be 225 syllables in the 150 words of a grade 1 passage and 275 syllables in the 150 words of a grade 12 passage. However, syllables are difficult to count and even more difficult to count accurately.

The number of syllables per word is closely related to the number of letters per word (Coleman, 1971), and it is more convenient and more accurate to count character spaces—*using six character spaces as a standard length word* (Carver, 1977). For example, there may be 120 standard length words in the 150 actual words of a grade 1 passage and 152 standard length words in the 150 actual words of a grade 12 passage. Hereafter, a standard length word will be capitalized, such as Word, to keep it separate from an actual word. Actual words per minute will be symbolized using the uncapitalized "wpm" and standard words per minute will always be symbolized using the capitalized "Wpm."

Rate Formulas

The equations given later in this subsection allow rate to be estimated in standard length words per minute (Wpm) when it has been reported in other units, such as actual words per minute (wpm) or letters per second. This technical information will be extremely useful when interpreting some of the data reviewed in later chapters. However, some readers may prefer to skim this subsection now, and then refer back to it later when the information is required in later chapters.

The equations below are based on those given by Carver (1976). The formulas used material difficulty levels expressed in whole grade equivalent (GE) units, such as GE = 9. Since the middle of the ninth grade is more traditionally expressed as 9.5, the relevant formulas have been revamped so as to handle GE units to the nearest tenth of a grade level, with 0.5 representing the middle of each GE unit. Also, in those previously published equations the difficulty level in GE units was symbolized as G_d indicating grade level of difficulty; that symbol will be replaced by D_L indicating difficulty level.

Equation (2.1), presented below, provides an estimate of the difficulty level of the material in GE units given a count of the number of characters per word (cpw):

$$D_L = 13.28 \text{ (cpw)} - 66.4 \tag{2.1}$$

For example, if a passage had 609 character spaces from beginning to end (the number of keystrokes needed to type the material if it were all typed on one line with one space after each word and two spaces after every sentence), and there were 98 words (the number of words defined as the number of character strings between blank spaces with the exception that two words separated by a hyphen is counted as two words), then cpw would be 609/98 = 6.2. Substituting 6.2 for cpw in Equation (2.1) yields the estimate that $D_L = 15.9$, or that this material is at the fifteenth grade level of difficulty, GE = 15.9.

Equation (2.1) can be solved for cpw to yield Equation (2.2) given below:

$$\text{cpw} = 0.0753D_L + 5.0 \tag{2.2}$$

In this equation, the number of characters per word (cpw) in a passage can be estimated from the grade level difficulty of the passage. For example, if a passage has been estimated to be at the sixth grade level of difficulty, then 6.5 can be substituted into Equation (2.2) for D_L to give cpw = 5.5.

In some cases, it is more accurate or convenient to work with the average number of letters per word (lpw) instead of characters per word (cpw). Therefore, given below are the corresponding equations expressed in lpw instead of cpw:

$$D_L = 12.71(\text{lpw}) - 48.5, \text{ and} \tag{2.3}$$
$$\text{lpw} = 0.0787D_L + 3.82 \tag{2.4}$$

Carver (1976) has also given an equation for estimating cpw when lpw is known:

$$\text{cpw} = 0.957(\text{lpw}) + 1.342 \tag{2.5}$$

Also given below is Carver's earlier equation for estimating Wpm when wpm is known and cpw can be estimated:

$$\text{Wpm} = (\text{wpm})(\text{cpw}/6) \tag{2.6}$$

Two other conversion formulas will be given for estimating rate in Wpm, one involving syllables and the other involving printer's units in ems. When rate is given in syllables per minute (spm), it can be converted into Wpm using the following equation:

$$\text{Wpm} = \text{spm}/1.66 \tag{2.7}$$

Equation (2.7) was derived from the research of Coke and Rothkoff (1970) who presented equations for relating letters per word to syllables in passages. The value of 1.66 syllables per Word, obtained from Coke and Rothkoff, is similar to the 1.64 syllables per Word obtained from Morton (1964). Morton also reported data indicating 1.62 syllables per Word for zero to eighth order approximations to English.

As for the printer's unit of ems, I. H. Anderson (1937) reported that there were 2.3 characters per em, so 6.0 characters per Word would give the following conversion formula:

$$\text{Wpm} = (\text{ems/min})/2.6 \tag{2.8}$$

After rate has been estimated or measured in Wpm, it can be transformed into standard length sentences per minute (Spm) using the following formula:

$$Spm = Wpm/16.7 \qquad (2.9)$$

This equation has been based on the estimate that sentences are around 16 words in length. A standard length sentence was set at 100 character spaces which is $100/6 = 16.7$ standard words per standard sentence. If an individual reads a passage at 300 Wpm, then $Spm = 300/16.7 = 18$ standard sentences per minute. Standard length sentences will be signified by capitalization, e.g., Sentences, so that Spm means Sentences per minute.

Normative Data

Taylor (1965) measured the reading rate of 12,359 students in each of grades 1 through 12 plus college, and then reported their average rates in each grade. His results are presented in Table 2.1. Notice that

Table 2.1

Taylor Rates in wpm for Each Grade in School and Corresponding Rates in Wpm Estimated by Empirical Formula

Grade	Taylor wpm[a]	Taylor Wpm
1	80	68
2	115	99
3	138	121
4	158	141
5	173	156
6	185	169
7	195	181
8	204	192
9	214	204
10	224	216
11	237	234
12	250	248
13		263
14		278
15		294
16		309
17		324
18		340

[a] From Taylor (1965).

the average fifth grader reads at 173 wpm. Another column in Table 2.1 presents the same rates in standard words per minute; notice that the average rate of fifth graders was 156 Wpm. The rates in Wpm were estimated using Equations (2.2) and (2.6) for converting wpm into Wpm when the difficulty level of the material is known. For example, the sixth graders read at an average rate of 185 wpm and the material being read was at the sixth grade level of difficulty. So, cpw was estimated to be 5.5 from Equation (2.2) using D_L = 6.5. And, Wpm was estimated to be 169 from Equation (2.6) using cpw = 5.5.

Taylor reported a college rate of 280 wpm. This rate was considered as being at the middle of grades 12–16, and thereupon converted into 286 Wpm. Then, the 248 Wpm at grade 12 and the 286 Wpm value at the center of grades 12–16 were used to form a straight line from whence the Wpm values from grade 13 to grade 18 in Table 2.1 were extrapolated. Notice that college freshmen have been estimated to have an average rate of 263 Wpm and college seniors have been estimated to have an average rate of 309 Wpm.

Taylor reported that the passages he gave to students in each grade were at an equivalent grade level of difficulty; for example, fifth grade students were given passages at the fifth grade level of difficulty. Taylor asked two short questions after each passage was read; the students did not know ahead of time what the questions were about, and Taylor did not report that he emphasized to the students the importance of answering these questions. It seems reasonable to infer that these students were reading at their typical or normal rate under these conditions. Thus, Taylor's college students averaged 280 wpm or 286 Wpm when engaged in ordinary, typical, or normal reading.

In later chapters, the reading rates found in research studies for students in a certain school grade will be compared to the rates in Table 2.1. For example, if college freshmen are found to be reading at an average rate of 115 wpm, it is questionable whether they were reading at their normal or typical rate since this is the average rate of students in grade 2.

THE READING PROCESSES

Introduction

The concept of reading rate has been applied to a wide range of processes, all of which are called reading. These processes are often as qualitatively different as apples and oranges. Apples and oranges are different types of fruit; they have different attributes and their juices have quite different effects upon the taste buds. Similarly, skimming and learning from prose involve different types of reading processes; they have different attributes and they have different consequences, outcomes, or results. Since there are several different reading processes, we are likely to learn more about reading rate if we distinguish among the different processes involved.

The basic reading processes to be reviewed (a) are used to achieve different goals, (b) involve different steps or component parts, and (c) produce different results. For example, during one reading process, called scanning, the goal may be to find a certain topic, such as "teacher." The words may be looked at for only enough time to recognize this topic or target word. If the target word is detected during this process, the process is immediately terminated. This scanning process is quite different from memorizing. When memorizing, the goal is to be able to recall freely the words, ideas, or thoughts at a later time. The components of this latter process often involve lexically accessing words, semantically encoding them, sententially integrating them, learning what the thoughts mean, and rehearsing them for later recall. The memorizing process is only terminated when the results satisfy a criterion for memorization.

To think that we have learned some generalizable property about reading rate, or *the* reading process, by investigating a memorizing process may be just as dangerous as thinking that we have learned some generalizable property about the sweetness of fruit by studying lemons. It seems to be misleading to refer to "reading rate" or "the reading process" because it suggests that there is a single process that can be studied. (Note: Use of the phrase "the reading process" goes back at least as far as Pintner, 1913.) It seems better to acknowledge that there are as many different reading rates as there are different types of reading processes. Therefore, it will be helpful to categorize the different types of reading processes into basic types so that we can better organize our knowledge about reading rate.

Each of the basic reading processes differ from each other in terms of their component parts. The idea that a reading process involves component subprocesses is not new (e.g., see Kieras, 1981, or Spache, 1963). Also, the idea of basic reading processes is not new. In 1928, Yoakam argued for ". . . at least four well recognized types of reading when considered according to the rate at which words are recognized: (1) scanning or skimming; (2) rapid reading; (3) normal reading; and (4) careful reading, which includes assimilative and analytic reading" (p. 64). In 1981, Carver advanced five types of reading processes: scanning, skimming, rauding, studying, and memorizing. These latter five types have been modified, refined, and improved; the results of these changes will be presented next.

Table 2.2

Typical Rates and Processing Components for the Five Basic Reading Processes

Five basic types of reading processes	Typical rate for a college student		Processing components involved	Gear
	Wpm	msec/ Word		
A model scanning process	600	100	Lexical accessing	5
A model skimming process	450	133	Semantic encoding	4
The rauding process	300	200	Sentence integrating	3
A model learning process	200	300	Idea remembering	2
A model memorizing process	138	433	Fact rehearsing	1

Five Basic Processes

As mentioned earlier, the five basic reading processes used to organize the following review of reading rate research will be called scanning, skimming, rauding, learning, and memorizing. These five basic processes involve different processing components that may be employed when an individual encounters a prose passage, which is defined as a set of coherently related sentences. Table 2.2 contains a listing of these five processes along with the typical rate at which college students execute these processes; the rates are expressed in standard words per minute (Wpm) and milliseconds per standard word (msec/Word). These rates represent best estimates for college students, and would vary with individual differences in ability. Also presented in Table 2.2 is a column containing the culminating processing component involved in each of these five processes that are listed; for example, a model skimming process involves lexical accessing plus the culminating component called semantic encoding.

It will be convenient to think of these five basic processes as different gears that operate at different rates and at different levels of power, from first gear to fifth gear. For example, fifth gear refers to a model scanning process that is executed by typical college students at a rate around 600 Wpm (or 100 msec/Word), and it involves a processing component called lexical access. Each of these five basic reading processes will be discussed in turn.

A Scanning Process

Fifth gear, scanning, is the fastest of the five basic reading processes. There are many processes that might be reasonably referred to as scanning, so a model scanning process will be operationally defined. In this model scanning process, an individual is searching for a target word by looking at each consecutive word of a prose passage. Only the processing component called lexical access (see Perfetti, 1985) is involved because the individual only has to recognize each consecutive word so as not to miss the target word. In later chapters, evidence will be presented that college students typically need to average only about 100 msec on each Word (600 Wpm) in order to execute this model scanning process successfully.

A Skimming Process

Fourth gear, skimming, is the second fastest reading process. Since there are many processes that might reasonably be called skimming processes, a model skimming process will be operationally defined. In this model skimming process an individual is searching a prose passage to find two adjacent words whose order has been reversed or transposed. This process illustrates the use of lexical access plus a semantic encoding component (see Perfetti, 1985). The individual must attach a contextually relevant meaning to each word in order to determine whether two words are out of order.

In later chapters, evidence will be presented that college students typically need to average about 133 msec/Word (450 Wpm) to execute this model skimming process successfully. Semantic encoding involves recognizing or identifying each word, called lexical access, plus the additional requirement of recognizing what the word means as it is used in the context of the sentence and the passage. Since this latter requirement involves a component, or subprocess, that is additional to that required by scanning, the model skimming process takes about 33 msec per Word longer than the scanning process. Since this model skimming process involves a component additional to scanning that facilitates the achievement of a more difficult goal, it is said to be a more powerful process than scanning. Stated differently, fourth gear is more powerful than fifth gear.

The Rauding Process

Third gear, the rauding process, is the predominantly used gear. It is utilized in situations where an individual is looking at each consecutive word of a prose passage in order to comprehend the complete thought contained in each sentence. In contrast to the other five basic processes, there is only one rauding process so it will be referred to as "the" rauding process. Sentence integrating is the culminating component involved in the rauding process because the words in each sentence must be integrated into the complete thought the author intended to communicate when the prose passage was written.

The rauding process also involves the lexical accessing component of the model scanning process and the semantic encoding component of the model skimming process. It would be impossible to integrate each word into the complete thought of the sentence without identifying the word and its meaning within the sentence. So, sentence integrating also involves lexically accessing and semantically encoding each word.

The rauding process is slower than the model skimming process because there is the additional requirement that the meaning of each word be integrated into the meaning of the sentence, thus building the complete thought represented by the sentence. Also, the thoughts in sentences are not completely isolated but are related to the thoughts in the previous sentences of a passage. This building of complete thoughts by relating them to prior thoughts is an additional requirement that involves the additional hierarchical component of sentential integration.

The rauding process for college students typically takes about 200 msec per Word, or 300 Wpm—about 67 msec per word longer than the model skimming process described above. The rauding process is representative of what is often called natural, normal, typical, or ordinary reading. It will be elaborated upon in much more detail in later chapters. (Note: In later chapters, evidence will be presented that the rauding process does represent typical or normal reading.) It is said to be a more powerful process than skimming because it involves an additional component or step that helps accomplish a goal that requires more effort to achieve. Stated differently, third gear is more powerful but slower than fourth gear.

A Learning Process

Second gear, a learning process, is slower but more powerful than the rauding process. In the model learning process, the individual's goal is to know the information contained in the passage. This goal can be accomplished by adding another component to the reading process, called idea remembering. This component involves continuous checks to determine whether the ideas encountered are likely to be remembered later. Obviously, it takes additional time when the thoughts not only must be understood but also must be remembered. This learning process is slower than the rauding process and more powerful because it can be used to gain knowledge from material that is likely to be remembered later.

Besides this model learning process, there is another commonly encountered learning process that has as its goal the understanding of the thoughts contained in relatively hard material. If individuals are operating their rauding process because their goal is to understand the complete thoughts in sentences but they are not successful in accomplishing this goal, they will likely shift down to a learning process. They shift down to Gear 2 by adding a time consuming component that helps them solve the problem of understanding by regressing. They go back over the words in the sentences in an effort to figure out what thoughts the writer is trying to communicate. This is an example of another type of learning process.

A Memorizing Process

First gear, a memorizing process, is the slowest and most powerful of the five basic reading processes. Again, many processes could be referred to as memorizing processes, so a model will be operationally defined. In this model memorizing process, the individual not only is engaged in remembering ideas but also is engaged in the rehearsal of facts so as to increase the likelihood of being able to recall specific facts later. This means that the individual does a great deal of regressing and repeating because this type of rehearsal is necessary in order to be successful at remembering the words and thoughts at a later point in time. So, this model memorizing process requires the most time of all, typically operating at 433 msec/Word (138 Wpm).

GEAR SHIFTING

Introduction

To facilitate communication, the five basic processes presented in Table 2.2 were referred to earlier as Gears 1 through 5. Just as an automobile driver gears down to a more powerful first gear to accomplish the more difficult task of reaching the top of a steep hill, similarly, a reader gears down to a more powerful first gear to accomplish the more difficult task of memorizing the information contained in prose passages. Just as an individual can travel at faster speeds in the higher gears of an automobile, similarly an individual can read at faster speeds in the higher gears. Gear 5 can operate at 600 Wpm for a college student whereas Gear 1 operates at 138 Wpm. Each gear operates at different rates depending on which components are involved in that particular reading process.

Gear 3 is the normal, typical, natural, or ordinary reading process. Individuals shift up to the faster gears, 4 and 5, when their goals can be accomplished without the time consuming requirement of sentential integration. Individuals ordinarily shift down to the slower gears, 1 and 2, when their goals can only be accomplished by adding the time consuming components associated with these gears.

Notice that the goal of the reader, in terms of desired results or consequences, usually determines which gear or basic reading process will be selected. So, gear shifting depends upon goals. During a research study, the reading goals of an individual are ordinarily determined by the instructions, the objective consequences, and the relative difficulty of the material, each of which will be discussed in turn.

Instructions

To illustrate the effect of instructions, Table 2.3 contains various instructions that have been or may be given in a reading research study.

Table 2.3
Instructions Likely to Produce Three of the Five Basic Reading Processes

Rauding process	1. Read the material once as you normally read. There will not be a test on what you read.
	2. When you finish reading each passage, you will be asked to rate how easy or difficult it was to understand.
	3. Read the material once, carefully.
	4. Read carefully because there will be a few questions on what you read later.
Learning process	5. Read as you normally would but if you do not understand something, try your best to figure it out before you continue.
	6. Read as rapidly as you can and still learn the essential elements of the text.
	7. Read each passage carefully enough to comprehend it and do well on a comprehension test that will be administered afterwards.
Memorizing process	8. Read very carefully because you will be asked to remember the details as well as the important information.
	9. Read the material carefully because you will be asked to recall everything that you can remember about each sentence you read.
	10. Comprehend what you read very well because later you will be asked to write an essay on the contents of the passage.
	11. Read carefully because you will be asked to write down everything you can remember when you are finished.

Notice that the instructions have been ranked from top to bottom in terms of how likely they are to activate the rauding process, with each instruction categorized with respect to the most likely process to be activated. For example, if subjects are told to read the material once as you normally read and they are also told that there will be no test on what they read (No. 1 in Table 2.3), then it is highly likely they will execute their rauding process. If subjects are told to read as they normally would but if they do not understand something, they should try their best to understand it before continuing, then they will probably engage in a learning process (No. 5 in Table 2.3). If subjects are told that they should read the material carefully because they will be asked to recall everything they can remember about each sentence they read, then they are likely to execute a memorizing process (No. 9 in Table 2.3). It appears to be extremely important to look carefully at the instructions used in a research study because they influence the basic reading process selected by the readers, as will become more apparent in later chapters.

Objective Consequences

During an experiment, subjects are usually asked to do things after they have finished reading a passage, such as answer questions. These objective consequences will also have a major impact upon which basic process the reader will choose to operate. Table 2.4 contains the goals, components, objective consequences, and rates for each of the five basic processes and their models, as they were presented and discussed earlier. The only new information contained in Table 2.4 is in the column headed Objective consequences. For example, the first row in Table 2.4 contains the gear, process, goal, components, objective consequences, and rate for a model scanning process, Gear 5.

For this Gear 5, one objective consequence of this process would be the correct identification of a target word. For example, suppose individuals are given a passage and instructed to search for the word "horse" contained in the passage. This word could be underlined, for example, thus giving an objective indication of the successful operation of this process. The goal of the individual, derived from the instructions and objective consequences, would be to find this target word. To satisfy this goal, the lexical accessing component of the reading process could be used on the passage starting with the first word and continuing with each successive word until the word "horse" was encountered and underlined. It would be expected that college students could successfully operate this process on passages at average rates around 600 Wpm.

For Gear 4, the model skimming process, an objective consequence would be the correct identification of a pair of transposed words. For

Table 2.4
The Five Basic Reading Processes with Goals, Components,
Objective Consequences, and Typical Rates for College Students

Gear	Process	Goal	Components	Objective consequences	Rate (Wpm)
5	Scanning (model)	Find target word	Lexical accessing	Correctly iden-tify target word in passage	600
4	Skimming (model)	Find anomalous words	Lexical access-ing, semantic encoding	Correctly iden-tify anomalous words in passage	450
3	Rauding	Understand the complete thoughts the writer in-tended to communicate	Lexical access-ing, semantic encoding, sentence integrating	Correctly iden-tify incomplete thoughts or anomalous sentences	300
2	Learning (model)	Know the information	Lexical access-ing, semantic encoding, sen-tence integrat-ing, idea remembering	Answer multiple-choice questions on the passage	200
1	Recalling (model)	Recall the facts	Lexical access-ing, semantic encoding, sen-tence integrat-ing, idea remembering, fact rehearsing	Write down exact words or facts from passage	138

example, the two words at the end of the following sentence have been transposed: "The plants have watered been." One way to objectively investigate the model skimming process would be to give college students passages with transposed words and then find out how fast they can locate and underline them. It would be expected that they could successfully operate this process at average rates around 450 Wpm.

For Gear 3, the rauding process, an objective consequence would be to identify anomalous sentences. Passages could be administered containing sentences that do not make sense. A key word could be changed so that the word would make sense grammatically within the sentence but the complete thought represented by the sentence would not make sense in the context of the prior sentences in the passage. This type of objective consequence should be successfully fulfilled by college students reading at rates around 300 Wpm. For example, the word "college" in the preceding sentence could be replaced by the word "elementary" and the readers of this book who have been operating their rauding process should be able to detect that the sentence does not make sense in the context of this chapter.

For Gear 2, the model learning process, an objective consequence would involve giving students several passages to read, and requiring them to answer multiple-choice questions on each passage as soon as they finished reading, such as one question on each sentence of the passage. Average rates around 200 Wpm would be expected for college students in this situation.

For Gear 1, the model memorizing process, an objective consequence would be to require individuals to write down as many exact words, or facts, as they could recall after they finished reading each passage. When college students realize that this is their goal, this particular reading process is likely to be operated at rates around 138 Wpm.

As stressed earlier, it will be helpful to organize our knowledge about reading rate in terms of the five basic processes. The particular process we are dealing with in an experiment depends on the instructions and objective consequences that were administered. The experimenter can manipulate the instructions and objective consequences to produce different goals. In turn, these goals induce different reading processes involving different components that require more or less time to operate successfully. So, if we want to understand reading rate, it seems best to try to determine which basic process was likely to have been operating, given the instructions and objective consequences administered by the researcher.

Relative Difficulty

Gear selection, i.e., shifting up or down from the rauding process, is also likely to be affected by the relative difficulty of the material being read. For example, suppose subjects are asked to read normally and then they are given a passage that is very hard for them to understand. They may shift down to a learning process. On the other hand, if the subjects are subsequently asked very easy questions on the material, they may shift back up to their rauding process.

If the material is relatively easy, if the instructions are to read normally, and if the objective consequences do not distract from the normal comprehension of complete thoughts in sentences, then the rauding process is likely to be operating in a research study.

Concluding Comments

When discussing these five basic processes in later chapters, it should be remembered that Gear 3 will be referred to as "the" rauding process whereas the other four gears will be referred to as "a" certain process, e.g., a learning process. This distinction helps to focus on the notion that typical reading involves a process with component parts that vary little between individuals or within individuals on different occasions or conditions. However, scanning, skimming, learning, and memorizing are likely to contain components that vary more when executed by different individuals and to vary more within individuals on different occasions or conditions. A model scanning process has been described as one example of a range of processes that will be called scanning, and similar models have been described for skimming, learning, and memorizing.

As discussed several times earlier, these distinctions among the five basic processes will help make sense out of the research on reading rate that will be reviewed later. By analogy, it is not very helpful to report that a farmer raised a piece of fruit that was 5 inches in diameter unless we are also told whether it was a grapefruit or a lemon. Similarly, it is not very helpful to report that a group of college students averaged 350 words per minute (wpm) if we do not know whether they were engaged in the rauding process or a skimming process; 350 wpm may be fast for the rauding process but slow for a skimming process. The remainder of this review of research and theory will be organized around these five basic processes with the bulk of the attention paid to the rauding process.

The research to be reviewed has not been designed within the framework of these five basic processes. Therefore, the information relevant to instructions, objective consequences, and relative difficulty will often be conflicting. For example, a researcher may ask college students to read normally (which should produce the rauding process that typically operates around 300 Wpm), but then the researcher may provide objective consequences (such as writing down everything that can be remembered) which require these students to shift to a recalling process operating around 100 Wpm in order to be successful. In conflicting situations such as this, the student might operate a learning process, Gear 2, as a compromise for responding to instructions that would ordinarily induce Gear 3 and objective consequences that would ordinarily produce Gear 1.

The studies reviewed later will often be forced into one of the five basic processes, even when the reports about instructions, objective consequences, and relative difficulty are vague or conflicting. In the future, researchers may find it helpful to coordinate the instructions to the subjects, the objective consequences, and the relative difficulty of the material being read so that it is more likely that a particular basic process will be operating. For example, if the researcher wants to investigate a learning process: (a) the materials can be selected to be relatively hard, (b) the students can be instructed to read carefully so they can answer most of the test questions correctly, and (c) the multiple-choice questions can be designed so that they are not easily answered without shifting down to Gear 2.

It will be helpful to try to categorize existing research into the five basic processes, even if the fit is often forced and questionable. The most important reason for categorizing research this way is to make sure that lawful research results involving the rauding process are not contaminated by results associated with other processes. Results that seem to conflict may not be conflicting at all but may represent different basic processes instead.

CONSTRUCTS AND LAWS

Introduction

The constructs and laws of rauding theory apply specifically to the rauding process. As noted earlier, the most important reading rates are those associated with the rauding process. Therefore, some of the constructs and laws of rauding theory that are especially relevant to rauding rates will be presented in this section. The theoretical constructs will be described and explained in great detail first. It will become apparent that the traditional concepts of reading rate and reading comprehension have been refined into more exact constructs. In turn, these constructs will be lawfully related so that an individual's accuracy of passage comprehension can be predicted using the precision of mathematical formulas.

Constructs

The primary constructs in rauding theory are refinements on the traditional concepts of material difficulty, reading rate, comprehension accuracy, and efficiency of reading. The primary constructs are symbolized as D_L, A, R, E, A_r, R_r, E_r, A_L, R_L, E_L, and $A_L - D_L$, where D stands for difficulty, L stands for level, A stands for accuracy, R stands for rate, E stands for efficiency, and r stands for rauding. Table 2.5 contains a listing of these constructs and their symbols, along with their related traditional concepts. For example, rauding accuracy level is symbolized as A_L, and it is a theoretical construct that is similar to the traditional concept of reading level or instructional level. This table can be used now as a pre-

Table 2.5
Constructs from Rauding Theory with Symbols and Related Traditional Concepts

Symbol	Construct	Related traditional concept
D_L	Difficulty level	Readability
A	Accuracy of comprehension	Percent comprehension
R	Rate of comprehension	Average rate or reading time
E	Efficiency of comprehension	Reading efficiency
A_r	Rauding accuracy	Comprehension during reading process
R_r	Rauding rate	Rate of reading process
E_r	Rauding efficiency	Efficiency of reading process
A_L	Rauding accuracy level	Reading level or instructional level (also measured by vocabulary tests)
R_L	Rauding rate level	Reading rate (measured by standardized rate tests)
E_L	Rauding efficiency level	Reading comprehension (measured by standardized tests)
$A_L - D_L$	Relative difficulty	Easiness of material

view and later as a reference. These constructs dealing with difficulty, accuracy, rate, and efficiency will be explained in detail using the context of realistic examples.

Consider first the example passage given below, taken from the 330 passages sampled from curriculum materials by J. R. Bormuth (see Carver, 1984c).

> A plant, in order to live, must have water, light, the right kind of soil, and enough heat or cold to suit its needs. One of the worst enemies of plants is dryness. Plants that live in places that are dry much of the time, such as the desert or a prairie country, have many ways of getting and keeping water to live on.
>
> The cactus has many ways of storing up and saving moisture. The inside of its body is just like a sponge. A sponge, you know, can hold much water. The plant gets the moisture to fill this sponge by putting down long roots which run deep into the ground.

The above passage, Bormuth ID No. 024, has been rated at the fifth grade level of difficulty (see Carver, 1984c) by use of the Rauding Scale of Prose Difficulty (Carver, 1975a). The difficulty level of passages in GE units ranging from 1 to 18 was symbolized earlier as D_L; therefore $D_L = 5$ for the example passage above.

There are many possible measures that can be used as indicants of D_L, such as the traditional readability measures, e.g., Dale–Chall formula, Fry readability graph (see Klare, 1984). However, the most valid of all these indicants seems to be the Rauding Scale mentioned above (see Carver, 1975a).

A correlate of D_L is a measure of difficulty, or readability, that does not use GE units, such as the Degrees of Reading Power (DRP) formula (see Carver, 1985c) or the Flesch (1949) formula. The DRP uses units from about 20 (the easiest prose) to about 80 (the hardest prose), and the Flesch uses units from 100 (the easiest prose) to 0 (the hardest prose). These two correlates of D_L have been subsequently rescaled into GE units; therefore, both can also be expressed as indicants of D_L when their GE units are used (see Carver, 1985c; Flesch, 1949).

To summarize, D_L is a theoretical construct in rauding theory representing the difficulty level of prose in GE units from 1 to 18. Indicants of D_L have the same GE type of units as D_L, but vary in terms of their validity, with the Rauding Scale appearing to be the most valid at present. Correlates of D_L do not have the same units as D_L but correlate highly with indicants of D_L that do use GE units. Henceforth, it will be helpful to continue to distinguish among: (a) theoretical constructs, such as D_L, (b) the most valid indicants of a construct, such as the Rauding Scale, (c) other indicants that have the same units, such as the GE scores using the Dale–Chall readability formula, and (d) correlates of a theoretical construct, such as measuring readability with the DRP scale which has its own DRP units.

Besides difficulty level, D_L, the length of a passage is also important. The actual number of words in the example passage is 113, and the actual number of sentences is 7. The total number of character spaces from beginning to end is 582, counting letters, punctuation, one space after each word, and two spaces after each sentence. The number of standard length words in the example passage is 582/6 or 97.0; a standard word was defined earlier as 6 character spaces. (Remember, an actual word will not be capitalized but a standard word will be capitalized as Word.) The number of standard length sentences in the example passage is 582/100, or 5.82 Sentences; this is because 100 character spaces, or 16.7 Words, was defined earlier as comprising a standard sentence. (Remember, a standard sentence will be capitalized as Sentence.)

The rauding theory constructs of D_L, Words, and Sentences have now been defined using the example passage. The remaining constructs will be defined using attributes of a hypothetical male, called Subject 1, and a hypothetical female, called Subject 2.

Suppose Subject 1 is given the example passage presented earlier and asked to read it normally, called Situation 1. After 12 seconds, or 0.20 minutes, he is told to stop reading. Then, he is asked to estimate the number of complete thoughts, or sentences, in the passage that he comprehended. Suppose this judgment of Subject 1 was 4. The estimated number of thoughts comprehended (T_c) by Subject 1 during the time (t) allowed for reading would be 4. The total number of thoughts in the passage will be symbolized as T_p. In this situation, an indicant of T_p would be 7 because there are seven sentences in the example passage.

The accuracy of comprehension of a passage will be symbolized as A, and defined as the proportion T_c/T_p. In Situation 1, an indicant of A would be 4/7 or 0.57. Expressed as a percentage instead of a proportion, this indicant of A would be 57%. So, the accuracy of comprehension, A, is similar to the more traditional concept of percentage comprehension.

The rate of comprehension of a passage will be symbolized as R, and defined as T_p/t. In Situation 1, an indicant of R would be 7/0.20 = 35 thoughts per minute.

The efficiency of comprehension of a passage will be symbolized as E, and defined as T_c/t. Or, E can be defined alternatively as the product of A and R. In Situation 1, an indicant of the efficiency of comprehension, E, would be 4/0.20, or 20 thoughts per minute. Alternatively, E would be the product (0.57)(35), or 20.

In prior research, Sentences have been used as valid indicants of T_p (Carver, 1982). Also, subjects have been asked to provide estimates of the percentage of a passage that they comprehended, or understood, and this has provided a valid indicant of A (Carver, 1982). Suppose our hypothetical Subject 2 is subjected to a reading condition similar to that of Subject 1, called Situation 2. Suppose Subject 2 was also allowed 0.20 minutes of reading time, and then she estimated that she understood 30% of the example passage. In Situation 2, the relevant indicants would be $A = 0.30$, $R = 5.82/0.20 = 29.1$ Spm, and $E = (0.30)(29.1) = 8.7$ Spm.

Rate expressed in Wpm instead of Spm would be a perfect correlate of R; using Equation 2.9, a correlate of R in Situation 2 would be 485 Wpm. Notice that 485 Wpm, or 29.1 Spm, is the average rate of comprehension, R, for the passage. This means that the average rate at which the reading process was operating on the entire passage was 485 Wpm, or 29.1 Spm. The accuracy of comprehension, A, was estimated to be 0.30 at this rate, and the efficiency of comprehension, E, was estimated to be 8.7 Sentences per minute. In this situation, Sentences were used as an indicant of complete thoughts so that R was indicated in Spm, and a correlate of R was given in Wpm. An indicant of the accuracy of comprehension of the passage was obtained from a judgment made by the subject. An indicant of the efficiency of comprehension, E, was calculated from the product of the indicants of A and R.

It should not go unnoticed that R is a refinement of the concept of reading rate. It is the average rate that a passage has been presented for reading, in Sentences per minute. It may also be considered as the rate of comprehension in the sense that the comprehension process operated at this average rate for the entire passage.

In the example above, it is obvious that R is not an estimate of the typical or actual rate that Subject 2 read the example passage. Subject 2 probably was stopped prior to completing the passage. Suppose we ask Subject 2 to read the passage once at her normal reading rate, and then we measure the time, t, that it took her to complete the passage. Let's say that t was measured to be 0.50 minutes, and the subject's judgment of her accuracy of comprehension of the entire passage was 0.80. Now, the rate of comprehension, R, in this situation becomes an indicant of the individual's rauding rate, symbolized as R_r. Now, the accuracy of comprehension, A, which accompanied the rauding rate, R_r, becomes an indicant of rauding accuracy, A_r. Now, the product of A_r and R_r becomes an indicant of rauding efficiency, E_r. In this example, the indicant of rauding rate, R_r, is $5.82/0.50 = 11.6$ Spm (a correlate of R_r is 194 Wpm). The indicant of rauding accuracy, A_r, is 0.80. So, the indicant of rauding efficiency, E_r, is $(0.80)(11.6) = 9.3$ Spm.

Of the three above constructs, the most important is rauding rate, R_r; it is defined as the highest rate, R, that an individual can accurately comprehend ($A > 0.75$) relatively easy material. (Note: The traditional 75% criterion has been used to define what it means to comprehend accurately.) Rauding rate, R_r, is theorized to be a constant rate across varying levels of material difficulty as long as the material is relatively easy for the individual (Carver, 1981). It may be noted that an individual's rauding rate, R_r, is a construct that is similar to the traditional concept of reading rate measured in wpm. However, the constructs of R_r and R are refinements upon the concept of reading rate—R_r represents a more precisely defined attribute of the individual, and R represents the average rate at which a passage is presented for reading.

In rauding theory, a *reader* is an individual who is operating one of the five basic reading process, and a *rauder* is an individual who is operating his or her rauding process. The ability of the rauder, or rauding ability, is reflected by three additional constructs: rauding accuracy level (A_L), rauding rate level (R_L), and rauding efficiency level (E_L). These three constructs will be discussed next.

Rauding accuracy level, A_L, represents the highest difficulty level, D_L, of material that an individual can accurately comprehend ($A > 0.75$) when reading at the rauding rate, R_r. As mentioned earlier, A_L is a construct that is similar to the traditional concept of reading level or instructional level. For example, suppose Subject 2 is able to comprehend material accurately up to the tenth grade level of difficulty when reading at 194 Wpm, her rauding rate. Therefore, Subject 2 would have an accuracy level of 10, or $A_L = 10$, because $D_L = 10$ was the most difficult material that could be accurately comprehended at this rate.

A standardized test has been developed to provide an indicant of A_L, and it is appropriately called the Accuracy Level Test; it appears to provide a valid indicant of A_L in GE units that are criterion-referenced (Carver, 1987c). A correlate of A_L is provided by the Degrees of Reading Power (DRP) test, which is purported to reflect the most difficult material that the individual can accurately comprehend; it contains passages that vary in difficulty from very easy to very difficult (using the DRP formula discussed earlier) so that the scores vary from about 20 to about 80 in DRP units. This DRP test appears to provide scores that are highly valid as a correlate of A_L (Carver, 1990d). This same DRP test also has been rescaled into GE units that appear to be highly valid as indicants of A_L (Carver, 1990f).

A case has been made that traditional standardized vocabulary tests also provide excellent correlates of A_L (Carver, 1990b), and there is empirical evidence that the vocabulary measure on the Iowa Test of Basic Skills (ITBS) provides a highly valid indicant of A_L (Carver, 1990d). However, it should be noted that the GE units from the ITBS are norm-referenced and probably less valid for estimating absolute levels of A_L. In summary, rauding accuracy level, A_L, is the most difficult level of material that an individual can accurately comprehend when the material is read at the individual's own rauding rate, R_r, and indicants of A_L can be obtained from such measures as the Accuracy Level Test, the DRP test, and the ITBS Vocabulary Test.

Rauding rate level, R_L, is a measure of rauding rate, R_r, in GE units. It represents the average rauding rate, R_r, of individuals at a particular level of A_L. For example, if the average rauding rate, R_r, of individuals at $A_L = 6.0$ is 170 Wpm, then $R_r = 170$ Wpm may also be expressed as the $R_L = 6.0$.

A standardized test has been developed to provide an indicant of R_L, and it is called the Rate Level Test. It has been designed to provide valid indicants of rauding rate level, R_L, in GE units. Suppose Subject 2 was administered the Rate Level Test, and obtained a rate level score of 8.1. This would be interpreted as indicating that Subject 2 has a rauding rate, R_r, equal to the average R_r for all readers at $A_L = 8.1$. The Rate Level

Test also provides a correlate of R_L in Wpm units. In this example, Subject 2 who has an 8.1 GE score as an estimate of R_L would have a 200 Wpm correlate of R_r (see Carver, 1987a). Another correlate of R_L, for example, would be the Rate score on the Nelson–Denny Reading Test, but it is not a very reliable or valid correlate (Carver, 1990d). Measures used in earlier years that would probably provide valid correlates of R_L are the Tinker Speed of Reading Test and the Chapman Cook Reading Test because they reflected how fast individuals could read relatively easy materials.

Notice that R_r is a theoretical construct that can be estimated more than one way. In the situations given for Subject 2, above, the Rate Level Test provided an indicant of R_L in GE units (8.1), and a correlate of R_r in Wpm (200). Another indicant of R_r in Wpm was given earlier (194), and it came from having Subject 2 read a relatively easy passage ($D_L = 5$) once at her normal reading rate. The most valid ways of estimating R_r would be those that reflect the fastest rate that relatively easy materials can be accurately comprehended.

Rauding efficiency level, E_L, is the most difficult level of material that an individual can accurately comprehend when it is read at a rate commensurate with that same level. For example, suppose that Subject 2 has $A = 0.80$ when a passage at $D_L = 9$ is presented at a rate equivalent to $R_L = 9$. However, when the difficulty level is increased to $D_L = 10$ and rate is correspondingly increased to $R_L = 10$, then her accuracy drops to $A = 0.60$. In this situation, $E_L = 9$ because that is the highest level of difficulty, $D_L = 9$, that Subject 2 can accurately comprehend ($A > 0.75$) when the material is presented at a rate, R, that is comparable in R_L units to D_L.

An indicant of E_L is provided by the Rauding Efficiency Level Test (RELT); it appears to provide a valid indicant of rauding efficiency level (Carver, 1987b). A valid correlate of E_L appears to be provided by the Comprehension score on Nelson–Denny Reading Test, NDRT (Carver, 1990d). The most valid indicant of E_L appears to be an average of the GE scores on the Accuracy Level Test and the Rate Level Test (Carver, 1990d), which comprise the Reading Efficiency Level Battery (Carver, 1987f). For example, these two hypothetical scores given for Subject 2 earlier were 10.0 and 8.1, respectively, and their average would be 9.0; so $E_L = 9.0$, as an indicant of rauding efficiency level for Subject 2.

Most traditional measures of reading comprehension are timed tests that reflect both rate and accuracy, so these measures are also correlates of E_L. Thus, this new construct, called rauding efficiency level, is a refinement of what has been measured by traditional standardized tests of reading comprehension and often referred to as general reading ability.

One final construct needs to be defined. The relative difficulty of material refers to the difference between the ability level of the individual and difficulty level of the material. More precisely, relative difficulty is defined as $A_L - D_L$, the difference between the rauding accuracy level of the individual and the rauding difficulty level of the material. If the rauding accuracy level of the individual is higher than the rauding difficulty level of the material, $A_L > D_L$, then the material is said to be relatively easy. If the rauding accuracy level of the individual is lower than the rauding difficulty level of the material, $A_L < D_L$, then the material is said to be relatively hard. Passages at $A_L = D_L$ are defined as neither easy nor hard, and are said to be at "matched difficulty."

In the previous example, Subject 2 was estimated to be at $A_L = 10$, and the example passage was estimated to be at $D_L = 5$, so the relative difficulty of the material for this individual was $10 - 5 = +5$. This passage was estimated to be relatively easy for this individual. Passages with positive relative difficulties are defined as relatively easy, passages with zero relative difficulties are defined as matched difficulty, and passages with negative relative difficulties are defined as relatively hard. In practice, when indicants of A_L and D_L are being used for an individual, which ordinarily have an error of about 1 GE unit associated with them, it is probably best if matched difficulty is not defined so precisely as $A_L - D_L = 0$, but allowed to be extended beyond 0 to at least $+1$ and -1.

The primary constructs of rauding theory—D_L, A, R, E, A_r, R_r, E_r, A_L, R_L, E_L, $A_L - D_L$, Wpm, and Spm—have now been defined. This subsection will be summarized by listing the values of the constructs given earlier for the example passage and the hypothetical female in Situation 2:

$D_L = 5$: Difficulty level in GE units, as indicated by various readability techniques and formulas, such as the Rauding Scale of Prose Difficulty, Dale–Chall, Fry, etc.

$A = 0.30$: Accuracy of comprehension of a passage expressed as a proportion, as indicated by percentage comprehension scores on a multiple-choice test, percentage comprehension judgements, etc.

$R = 29.1$: Rate of comprehension of a passage in thoughts per minute, as indicated by Sentences per minute, Spm. Also, can be measured using a correlate such as 485 Wpm. The average rate at which a passage is presented for reading.

$E = 8.7$: Efficiency of comprehension of a passage in complete thoughts per minute, as indicated by the number of Sentences per minute, Spm, that were comprehended.

$A_r = 0.80$: Rauding accuracy of an individual for a particular passage. Accuracy of comprehension, A, that accompanied the rauding rate, as indicated by percentage comprehension judgements, for example, after an entire passage has been read once at the normal reading rate.

R_r = 11.6: Rauding rate of an individual in thoughts per minute, as indicated by the number of Sentences in relatively easy material that were covered per minute during normal reading. Also, can be expressed as a correlate, such as 194 Wpm. The fastest rate at which relatively easy material can be accurately comprehended.

E_r = 9.3: Rauding efficiency of an individual for a particular passage. Efficiency of comprehension, E, that accompanied the rauding rate in thoughts per minute, as indicated by the product of A_r and R_r.

A_L = 10.0: Rauding accuracy level in GE units, as indicated by the Accuracy Level Test, for example. The score on most standardized vocabulary tests provide a correlate of A_L. The most difficult level of material that can be accurately comprehended.

R_L = 8.1: Rauding rate level in GE units, as indicated by the Rate Level Test, for example. The Rate score in wpm on Nelson–Denny Reading Test provides a correlate of R_L. The fastest rate at which an individual can accurately comprehend relatively easy material expressed in GE units.

E_L = 9.0: Rauding efficiency level in GE units, as indicated by the Rauding Efficiency Level Test or the Reading Efficiency Level Battery, for example. Other indicants and correlates come from traditional standardized tests of reading comprehension, such as the Comprehension score on the ITBS. The most difficult level of material that can be accurately comprehended when it is presented at a rate level comparable to the difficulty level.

$A_L - D_L$ = +5: Relative difficulty of the material in GE units as indicated by the difference between an indicant of accuracy level (such as provided by the Accuracy Level Test) and an indicant of difficulty level (such as provided by the Rauding Scale).

Laws

Next the three laws of rauding theory (Carver, 1981) will be discussed in turn. Then the theoretical equations will be given expressing the lawful nature of the relationships among the constructs defined earlier.

Law I is that *individuals attempt to comprehend thoughts in passages at a constant rate, called the rauding rate, unless they are influenced by situation-specific factors to change that rate.* This means that ordinarily, $R = R_r$, or that the rate of comprehending a passage is the rauding rate. When individuals are reading as they typically do, their rate of comprehension of a passage, R, is ordinarily the same as the fastest rate at which they can accurately comprehend relatively easy passages, R_r. It is true that an individual may shift to another reading process so that R is no longer equal to R_r, such as when (a) the instructions request slow or fast reading, (b) the objective consequences require more or less than simply comprehending the complete thoughts in the sentences, or (c) the material is relatively difficult ($A_L < D_L$). It is also true that the rate of comprehending, R, is often not equal to the rauding rate, R_r, in research situations where the individual is not allowed to finish reading the passage or is given unlimited time to study a passage.

Law II is that *the efficiency of passage comprehension depends upon the accuracy of passage comprehension and the rate of passage comprehension*. More specifically, Law II is that:

$$E = AR, \tag{2.10}$$

as was mentioned earlier. This means that the efficiency of comprehension, E, is the product of the accuracy of comprehension, A, and the rate of comprehension, R.

Law III is that *the most efficient rate of comprehending thoughts in a passage is the rauding rate*. More specifically, when $R = R_r$, then $E_{max} = E_r$. When the rauding process is operating on an entire passage at the rauding rate, then the efficiency which accompanied this rate was the maximum possible efficiency. In other words, if the passage is covered at any other rate besides R_r, so that R is not equal to R_r, then the resulting efficiency of comprehension, E, will be less than E_r, or $E < E_r$. Stated in yet another way, the rauding rate, R_r, is the optimal rate because the efficiency of comprehension, E, at any other rate is lower.

There is a great deal of empirical evidence supporting the above three laws (e.g., Carver, 1982, 1983, 1984b, 1985a, b), most of which will be reviewed in detail in later chapters of this book. Next, the empirically validated equations of rauding theory (Carver, 1981) will be presented.

Reading rate, in the form of R and R_r, along with rauding accuracy A_r, determine the accuracy of comprehension of a passage, A. When the time allowed for reading is *less* than the time needed to finish the passage once at the rauding rate, R_r, then the equation for determining the accuracy of comprehension is as follows:

$$A = A_r R_r (1/R) \tag{2.11}$$

When the time allowed for reading is *more* than the time needed to finish the passage once at the rauding rate, R_r, then

$$A = (1/R)/[(1/R) + i] \tag{2.12}$$

where

$$i = (1/R_r)[(1/A_r) - 1] \qquad (2.13)$$

In the equations above, $1/R$ is the average time for reading each thought in the passage, such as minutes per thought or minutes per Sentence. The time required to finish reading the passage once can be determined by dividing the number of Sentences in the passage by R_r. There is a great deal of empirical support for the theoretical relationships expressed in Equations (2.11), (2.12), and (2.13) (Carver, 1977, 1984b, 1985a, b).

It should not go unnoticed that in rauding theory R_r, A_r, and $1/R$ completely determine the accuracy with which a passage will be comprehended, A. The value of R_r for an individual can be estimated from the Rate Level Test, as discussed earlier. An indicant of R is simply the number of Sentences divided by the time allowed to read the passage. An indicant of A_r (which is rauding accuracy and should not be confused with accuracy level, A_L) depends upon the relative difficulty of the material, $A_L - D_L$. The relationship between A_r and $A_L - D_L$ was empirically determined by Carver (1990e) to be as follows:

$$A_r = 0.03951(A_L - D_L) + 0.6446 \qquad (2.14)$$

The predictive power of these relationships expressed in Equations (2.11), (2.12), (2.13), and (2.14), can be illustrated using the example passage and Subject 2, from the preceding subsection. Subject 2 read the example passage, $D_L = 5$, for 0.20 minutes. We want to predict the accuracy of comprehension, A, so we need to have values of R, R_r, and A_r. R was estimated to be 29.1 Spm, R_r was estimated to be 11.6 Spm, and A_r was estimated to be 0.80. The time needed to finish reading the passage once at the rauding rate would be 5.82/11.6 or 0.50 minutes (30 sec), so from Equation (2.11),

$$A = (0.80)(11.6)(1/29.1) = 0.32. \qquad (2.15)$$

This means Subject 2 would be predicted to comprehend 32% of the example passage at $D_L = 5$ when given only 12 seconds to read it. Remember, Subject 2 provided another indicant of A by her judgment that she comprehended 30%.

The predictive power of the equations given earlier will now be illustrated using a hypothetical class of sixth graders. Suppose a new history textbook is being considered. Its difficulty level has been estimated to be 5.8 using the DRP technique, $D_L = 5.8$, and its length has been estimated to be 3000 Sentences. Suppose the class has been administered the Accuracy Level Test and the Rate Level Test, and the resulting average estimates were $A_L = 7.6$, $R_L = 7.1$, and $R_r = 11.1$. From the passage length and R_r it can be estimated that it would take the students 3000/ 11.1 = 270 minutes, or 4.5 hours to finish reading the book once at their normal rate. The relative difficulty, $A_L - D_L$, would be $7.6 - 5.8 = +1.8$. From this 1.8 value, rauding accuracy, A_r, can be estimated from Equation 2.14 to be 0.72. So, it can be estimated that typical students in this class would take 4 1/2 hours to read this history book once, and they would comprehend 72% of it.

It can further be estimated that if this group was encouraged to read the book twice ($R = 3000/540 = 5.56$), then

$$i = (1/11.1)(1/0.72 - 1) = 0.035 \qquad (2.16)$$

from Equation (2.13), and

$$A = (1/5.56)/(1/5.56 + 0.035) = 0.84 \qquad (2.17)$$

from Equation (2.12). So, it would be predicted that, on the average, this class would comprehend 84% of this textbook if they read it twice, taking 9 hours.

Given the constructs, laws, and equations of rauding theory, plus the empirical techniques for measuring these constructs, it is evident that the accuracy of comprehension of a passage can be predicted quite precisely. Reading rate, as reflected by R and R_r, are very important determinants of the accuracy of comprehension, A, along with D_L and A_L. As the average time allowed for reading a passage increases ($1/R$ increases), then an individuals' accuracy of comprehension also increases as long as everything else (D_L, A_L, R_r) stays constant. As individuals are found who have higher rauding rates, R_r, then their accuracy of comprehension will also be higher as long as everything else (D_L, A_L, R) stays constant. As individuals are found who have higher rauding accuracy levels, A_L, then their accuracy of comprehension will also be higher as long as everything else (D_L, R_r, R) stays constant. As passages, or textbooks, are found that are at lower levels of difficulty, then accuracy of comprehension will be higher as long as everything else (R_r, R, A_L) stays constant.

In summary, the accuracy of comprehension of a passage, A, can be predicted quite precisely from valid estimates of the following: (a) the length of the passage in Sentences, (b) the difficulty level of the passage, D_L, (c) the rauding accuracy level of the individual, A_L, (d) the rauding rate of the individual, R_r, and (e) the time allowed to read the passage, expressed as $1/R$.

Concluding Comments

The concept of reading rate has been refined in rauding theory. The concept has little meaning without first specifying which one of the basic reading processes was likely to be operating. When the rauding process is operating, then it is helpful to refine the concept of reading rate further into R, R_r, and R_L. The rate of comprehension, R, is the average rate at which the passage was covered or the rate of comprehension for the passage; an indicant of R is the number of Sentences in the passage divided by the time allowed for reading in minutes. Wpm is a correlate of R. Rauding rate, R_r, is the fastest rate at which the rauding process can operate and still be successful in accurately comprehending the complete thoughts in the sentences; an indicant of R_r can be obtained from the Rate Level Test. Rauding rate level, R_L, is simply rauding rate, R_r, expressed in GE units. So, R measures the average rate at which a passage was presented for reading, R_r measures the ability of the reader in terms of the fastest rate at which the individual can successfully operate the rauding process, and R_L also measures the same ability as R_r expressed in GE units. In typical reading situations, $R = R_r$, because individuals ordinarily read an entire passage at their rauding rate.

The above constructs help refine the concept of reading rate, and the other constructs of rauding theory help refine the concept of reading comprehension. The comprehension that occurs during the operation of the rauding process is one of the most important aspects of reading comprehension. Using the construct, A, helps to clarify reading comprehension because it refers specifically to the accuracy of comprehension of a passage, keeping this aspect of reading comprehension separate from the construct, E, which is the efficiency of comprehension of a passage. Using the construct, A_L, also helps to clarify reading comprehension because some standardized tests that purport to measure reading comprehension actually are correlates of E_L more than A_L because reading comprehension tests ordinarily reflect rauding rate level, R_L, about as much as they reflect rauding accuracy level, A_L.

When the material being read is relatively easy, $A_L > D_L$, it is highly likely that individuals will operate their rauding process on passages at their own rauding rate, R_r, measured in Wpm, unless there is something unusual about the situation. For example, in research situations individuals may be induced to shift out of their rauding process by the time limits allowed, the instructions given, the objective consequences, or by the administration of relatively hard passages ($A_L < D_L$). In any reading situation involving the comprehension of sentences in passages, the efficiency, E, will be equal to the product of the accuracy, A, and the rate R. Furthermore, the rate, R, at which the passage can be comprehended with the highest efficiency, E, will be the rauding rate, R_r.

Reading rate and reading comprehension need to be refined and clarified by using the constructs of rauding theory—D_L, A, R, E, A_r, R_r,

E_r, A_L, R_L, E_L, A_L – D_L, Spm, and Wpm—so that some of the lawfulness of reading rate can become apparent. Again, the empirical evidence
relevant to this lawfulness will be reviewed in later chapters.

CONCLUSIONS

Researchers report reading rate in actual words per minute, wpm, syllables per minute, spm, and various other units. Whenever possible,
reading rate will be transformed into standard length words per minute,
Wpm, because the latter is more accurate and lawful in representing the
amount read per unit of time. The data collected by Taylor (1965) will
be used to estimate rates in grade equivalent units. From these estimates
it will often be possible to make reasonable guesses about what type of
reading process is being used whenever the ability level of the individuals
is known.

Five basic types of reading that involve different processes—scanning,
skimming, rauding, learning, and memorizing—will be used to organize
the research on reading rate. Each successive process in this list operates
slower than the one before because of the additional time required to
operate the additional components involved. The rauding process, called
third gear, is the most important of all the reading processes because it
is the process that individuals use most often when they are reading; the
rauding process is the process involved in "typical reading," "normal
reading," "natural reading," or "ordinary reading." Individuals typically
use the rauding process because their normal goal is to comprehend the
complete thoughts that the author intended to communicate when the
successive sentences were written. Ordinarily, individuals will shift up to
a faster gear when the goal can be accomplished with less components
and they will shift down to a slower gear when the goal requires the
additional components of these more powerful processes.

In reading research, the goals of the individual are primarily manipulated by the instructions and objective consequences administered by the
researcher. This means that it will often be possible to infer which basic
reading process was being operated by the individuals in a research study
from a knowledge of the instructions and objective consequences. Another factor that is often important for inferring whether individuals
have shifted up or down out of third gear, the rauding process, is the
relative difficulty of the material.

It is now possible to make some rather precise predictions about reading rate. For example, suppose a researcher presents relatively easy material to college freshmen and asks them to read it at their normal reading rate. Then when they have finished reading, they are asked to simply

rate the material on a scale from 1 to 5 in difficulty. In this situation, it would be inferred that these individuals would operate their rauding process at a mean rate of 263 Wpm, using the data from Table 2.1. Given the instructions, the objective consequences, and the relative difficulty of the material used in research, it is possible to infer which basic reading process is operating. If that process is the one that individuals ordinarily operate, called Gear 3 or the rauding process, then the mean reading rate can be estimated from normative data.

Precise predictions of an individual's accuracy of comprehension of a passage can be made using Equations 2.11, 2.12, 2.13, and 2.14. These predictions require estimates of the difficulty level of the passage, D_L, the accuracy level of the individual, A_L, the rauding rate of the individual, R_r, and the time allowed for reading, $1/R$.

There appears to be a great deal of lawfulness associated with reading rate, as long as the essentials presented in this chapter are not disregarded.

Part II

Fundamental
Factors

In this part of the book, theory and research fundamental to any study of reading rate will be reviewed. Chapter 3 examines the effects of context, individual differences, tasks, and materials on reading rate. Chapter 4 contains a review of the research on silent speech, which accompanies reading rate. Chapter 5 reviews basic research on eye movements, another factor that is fundamentally involved in reading rate.

3

CONTEXT, INDIVIDUAL DIFFERENCES, TASKS, AND MATERIALS

INTRODUCTION

A case has been made by Jenkins (1979) for the influence of four inter-acting factors on the results of any information gathered during the col-lection of research data: context, individual differences, experimental tasks, and materials. Context includes variables affected by the labora-tory, classroom, work setting, and own-time situations. Individual differ-ences include age, grade, or ability level. Experimental tasks include variables affected by instructions, procedures, and criterion measures. Materials include variables affected by the use of nonsense words and varying difficulty levels. These are examples of the kinds of factors likely to influence reading rate.

Some of the research studies to be reviewed later, in this chapter as well as subsequent chapters, have shown reading rate to vary with certain characteristics of the study, such as instructions, tasks, and difficulty of the material. In contrast, other research studies have shown reading rate to be constant. Order can often be achieved where inconsistencies seem to reign by using some of the essentials discussed in Chapter 2, especially the framework afforded by rauding theory. Indeed, rauding theory predicts that (a) rate varies between individuals due to differences in ability, (b) rate will be relatively constant within individuals whenever the situation is conducive to the rauding process, and (c) rate will change whenever the situation is conducive to gear shifting between reading processes, such as when the objective consequences associated with the tasks vary.

The effects of context, individual differences, tasks, and materials upon reading rate will be addressed (a) by applying some of the theory covered in Chapter 2, and (b) by reviewing relevant research.

CONTEXT

If the reading rate of students is studied in the context of a laboratory experiment, will the results of that research generalize to reading at home, at school, at work, or at the library? In research on reading rate, there is always concern for external validity, i.e., the degree to which our results will generalize to situations beyond the context of the research and into the real world of interest.

The results from rate research involving scanning a word list to find a target word may generalize to the rate of scanning a phone book to find a name or scanning a magazine article to find out if a certain subject is discussed. Rate results from skimming a book in an experimental study may generalize to a work situation where an executive must have limited knowledge about many different departmental reports. The rate results from rauding experimentally selected passages may generalize to normal, typical, or ordinary reading in the real world. Rate results involving learning from experimental passages may generalize to real world situations where professionals try to keep up with the latest knowledge in their field or where adults try to educate themselves on difficult subjects. Rate results from memorizing may generalize to some academic situations where students must recall textbook material in order to do well on essay tests.

In the real world beyond the laboratory, there is little doubt that many adults and most college students do engage in all of the five basic types of reading processes. However, there is also little doubt that most of the reading that goes on in this world involves the rauding process. Relevant empirical evidence comes from Sharon (1973), who surveyed adults and found that less than 1% of the reading done involved reading difficult materials.

The difficult materials encountered by students in academic situations represents only a fraction of the population of reading situations involving adults and children, so that the learning and memorizing processes used by students probably occupy less than 10% of the total time spent reading in the population of readers. Scanning and skimming combined also probably occupy less than 10% of the total time spent reading in the population of readers. It would seem reasonable to estimate that the rauding process would be used about 90% or more of the total time spent reading during any given week for all readers in the world. Therefore, from a sheer frequency standpoint, rauding rate would seem to deserve the most attention from researchers. Given the importance of gaining knowledge by studying, it would seem that rates associated with learning processes should be given the next priority. Finally, given the infrequent usefulness of scanning, skimming, and memorizing, research on these processes would seem to deserve the lowest priority in terms of time and effort.

For most individuals, the most important context is the normal or typical one which is conducive to the rauding process. For the population of readers, the bulk of the reading time during a week is likely to be spent in the rauding process at a rate which varies with the level of ability of these individuals. On rare occasions, individuals may read at a slower rate because they are trying to remember the information covered using a learning process, or they may read at a faster reading rate because they are scanning or skimming.

In the so-called real world, the context influences reading rate because the goals associated with the context stimulate individuals to switch from one process to another depending upon whether they are (a) looking up a phone number for a friend, (b) skimming a newspaper editorial that is somewhat relevant to the upcoming election, (c) rauding a magazine article on a sports personality, (d) reading an article to gain knowledge about gardening, or (e) studying material so as to be able to recall the facts well enough to present them orally to a supervisor. The individual's goal forces shifts among the different reading processes so as to better accomplish the goal.

Most of the time, for most individuals, the goal is to understand the complete thoughts the writer intended to communicate by the sentences placed on the page. Goodman (1966) expressed the idea this way: ". . . the extent to which his reconstructed message agrees with the writer's intended message is the extent to which he has comprehended" (p. 188). When this is the goal, then the rauding process ordinarily will be operating. And the rauding process will continue to operate unless the goal changes to remembering the information being read, in which case a component will be added that involves idea remembering. If the goal is to satisfy some specific external criterion, such as passing an especially difficult test, then a memorizing process may be used. If the goal is to find one or more specific words embedded within many words, then a scanning process may be used. If the goal is to get an overview, or get the "gist," of an article, report, passage, or book, then a skimming process may be used.

The goal associated with the context can influence reading rate in the real world because some types of reading processes are inherently faster than others, i.e., less time consuming components are needed to achieve the goals. Therefore, when conducting research on reading rate, it becomes important to scrutinize carefully the demand characteristics of the research to determine which processes are probably being used so that generalizations to real world reading are more likely to be valid.

It may be noted that the concept of context is being used here in a slightly different way than Jenkins (1979). For Jenkins, context included a recognition of the difference between real world situations and laboratory situations. Here, context also applies to varieties of real world situations that influence the goals of the individual which in turn result in the choice of different reading processes to meet the situation. The laboratory is not necessarily a different context from this standpoint but a contrived and controlled situation with tasks designed to mirror real world situations closely enough to be able to make valid generalizations about them.

In summary, the context of real world reading situations affect reading rate because the context usually influences the goals which in turn influences which reading process will be used. In research studies, the context is ordinarily manipulated by the experimenters through their choice of instructions, objective consequences, ability level of subjects, and difficulty level of materials.

INDIVIDUAL DIFFERENCES

Most researchers would probably agree that there are large individual differences in reading rate. This section will contain data relevant to the theory that R_L, rauding rate level, is an important construct relevant to reading rate. Furthermore, since the construct E_L, rauding efficiency level, involves rauding rate, then its contribution also deserves attention.

In Chapter 2, the most important individual differences in reading were purported to be reflected by rauding ability, that is, rauding accuracy level, A_L, rauding rate level, R_L, and rauding efficiency level, E_L. This section on individual differences will focus on the empirical evidence relevant to the theory that (a) individual differences in reading rate are most succinctly explained by reference to R_L, (b) individual differences on traditional vocabulary tests are most succinctly explained by A_L, and (c) individual differences in what is measured by traditional reading comprehension tests are most succinctly explained by E_L.

Evidence relevant to individual differences in A_L, R_L, and E_L was collected by Carver (1972c). He factor-analyzed various reading measures from several tests: the Nelson–Denny Reading Test (NDRT), the Davis Reading Test (DRT), the Tinker Speed of Reading Test, and the Chunked Reading Test. For the college students involved ($N = 41$) two factors were found: an accuracy factor and a rate factor. These two factors accounted for 75% of the variance, and were correlated 0.56. When a single factor fit was forced upon variables, the result was readily interpreted as an efficiency factor. For example, the Comprehension score on the NDRT was obviously reflecting an Efficiency factor (0.83 loading) more than an Accuracy factor (0.67 loading) or a Rate factor (0.27 loading). Reading comprehension tests are highly likely to be correlates of rauding efficiency level (E_L) because they are timed tests that often reflect speed as much as accuracy. These data collected by Carver provided support for the constructs of A_L, R_L, and E_L as the primary individual difference factors in reading.

The above research was extended and replicated by Carver (1990d). The Nelson–Denny test was administered to 64 college students, along with the Accuracy Level Test and the Rate Level Test that were mentioned in Chapter 2. In the 1972 study discussed above, the Vocabulary section of the NDRT was not given. In this later research, it was purposely included because the size of vocabulary was expected to be a very good correlate of rauding accuracy level (A_L). Again, two factors resulted from the factor analysis, and they were readily interpreted as an Accuracy factor and a Rate factor, which is more support for A_L and R_L being primary factors. These two factors accounted for 74% of the variance, and they correlated 0.41. When a single factor fit was forced upon the data, it was readily interpreted as an Efficiency factor, more support for E_L being the primary factor that encompasses both A_L and R_L. Again, the Comprehension score on the NDRT loaded higher on the Efficiency factor (0.79) than it did on the Accuracy factor (.076) or the Rate factor (0.54) which is more support for traditional reading comprehension tests primarily being correlates of E_L. The Vocabulary score of the NDRT loaded higher on the accuracy factor (0.92) than it did on the Rate factor (0.42) or the efficiency factor (0.83) which is support for traditional vocabulary tests being primarily correlates of A_L. The Rate score on the NDRT loaded higher on the Rate factor (0.65) than it did on the Accuracy factor (0.35) or the Efficiency factor (0.58), more support for traditional rate measures being correlates of R_L. The Accuracy Level Test and the Rate Level Test were found to provide highly valid indicants of A_L, R_L, and E_L; the Accuracy Level Test loaded 0.90 on the Accuracy factor, the Rate Level Test loaded 0.91 on the Rate factor, and the Efficiency Score (which is derived from both tests) loaded 0.87 on the Efficiency factor. These data again provide strong support for A_L, R_L, and E_L being the most important individual difference factors in reading, with R_L reflecting the primary individual difference factor in reading rate.

Another part of the research described above (Carver, 1990d) involved three factor analyses of 354 students in grades 3–8 who took the Iowa Test of Basic Skills (ITBS), the Rauding Efficiency Level Test (RELT), and the Degrees of Reading Power (DRP) test. For all three of these analyses, a single factor resulted which was readily interpreted as an Efficiency factor; this is more support for traditional reading tests primarily being correlates of E_L. When two factors were forced upon these data, one was readily interpreted as an Accuracy factor and the other a Rate factor, more support for A_L and R_L being the primary subfactors in reading. The measures that were expected to provide highly valid indicants or correlates of A_L, i.e., Accuracy Level Test, DRP test, and ITBS–Vocabulary, consistently loaded high on the Accuracy factor. The Rate Level Test consistently loaded the highest of all the variables on the Rate factor. The Reading Comprehension section of the ITBS consistently loaded higher on the Efficiency factor than it did on the Accuracy and Rate factors. And, the Efficiency Score from the Accuracy Level Test and the Rate Level Test loaded the highest of all the variables on the Efficiency factor in all three factor analyses involved. These data further support A_L, R_L, and E_L as the primary individual difference factors involved in reading, with R_L being the primary individual difference variable involved in reading rate.

The above data (Carver, 1972c, 1990e) strongly support the theory that traditional standardized tests of reading comprehension are correlates of rauding efficiency level (E_L) and therefore involve rauding rate (R_L). These reading comprehension tests require the ability represented by the construct called rauding accuracy level (A_L) and they also require the ability represented by the construct called rauding rate level (R_L).

Further evidence to support the explanatory power of these three constructs, A_L, R_L, and E_L, comes from an investigation by Palmer, MacLeod, Hunt, and Davidson (1985). They presented correlations among eight variables representing scores on several reading and listening comprehension tests. These measures were readily classified into correlates of A_L, R_L, and E_L. Their data have been reanalyzed using the same type of factor analyses described earlier. This study and the measures involved will be described first, and then the results will be presented.

Palmer *et al.* administered a large number of standardized tests and experimental measures to 91 sophomores and juniors in college.

Two variables that can be considered as correlates of A_L were (a) the vocabulary score taken from the Washington Pre-College test, called Washington-Vocab, and (b) the listening comprehension score taken from administering the Davis Reading Test as a listening test, called Davis-Listening. In Chapter 2 it was noted that vocabulary measures ordinarily provide excellent indicators or correlates of A_L. Individual differences in the listening test scores were also reflecting accuracy of comprehension because listening rate was held constant at 200 wpm.

The three variables that were considered to be correlates of R_L came from (a) the Rate score on the Nelson–Denny Reading Test, called Nelson–Denny-Rate, (b) the score on the Minnesota Speed of Reading Test, called Minnesota-Rate, and (c) the rate score on an experimental speed of reading test, called Experimental-Rate. The score on the Minnesota test required individuals to cross out as many irrelevant phrases as possible, in 5 minutes, from 36 short paragraphs. The experimental reading speed test required students to mark the line they were reading when told to stop after 45 seconds. Palmer *et al.* converted all three of these rate scores into time measures, e.g., milliseconds per word, prior to analysis.

The three variables that were considered to be correlates of E_L were (a) the comprehension score on the Nelson–Denny Reading Test, called Nelson Denny-Comprehension, (b) the comprehension score on the Davis Reading Test, called Davis-Comprehension, and (c) the comprehension score on the Washington Pre-College test, called Washington-Comprehension. All three of these measures required answering comprehension questions on passages during a fixed length of time.

Palmer *et al.* reported the correlations among the eight variables in their Table 12. These correlations were used to conduct a new principal components factor analysis of these variables. Two factors resulted which correlated 0.44 and accounted for 76.7% of the variance. The 16 factor loadings, obliquely rotated, are presented as Analysis 1 in Table 3.1. Also in the table are the loadings that resulted from a single factor forced upon the data, called Analysis 2.

In Analysis 1, Factor 1 appears to be an Accuracy factor since the two highest loadings on this factor came from the two Accuracy correlates, Washington-Vocab, 0.87, and Davis-Listening, 0.92. Factor 2 appears to be a Rate factor since the three highest loadings on this factor came from the three rate correlates, Nelson–Denny-Rate (0.92), Minnesota-Rate (0.86), and Experimental-Rate (0.77). The two resulting factors were readily interpreted as an Accuracy factor and a Rate factor, which is exactly as predicted from the A_L and R_L constructs in rauding theory.

Table 3.1

Factor Loadings from Two Factor Analyses of the Palmer[a] Data
Involving Eight Measures of Rate and Comprehension

Variables	Analysis 1[b]		Analysis 2[b]
	Factor 1: Accuracy	Factor 2: Rate	Factor 1: Efficiency
Accuracy correlates			
Washington-Vocab	"0.87"	0.32	0.81
Davis-Listening	"0.92"	0.35	0.86
Rate correlates			
Nelson–Denny-Rate	0.40	"0.92"	0.64
Minnesota-Rate	0.32	"0.86"	0.55
Experimental-Rate	0.62	"0.77"	0.75
Efficiency correlates			
Nelson–Denny-Comprehension	0.86	0.55	"0.88"
Davis-Comprehension	0.87	0.44	"0.85"
Washington-Comprehension	0.84	0.36	"0.79"

[a] From Palmer *et al.* (1985).
[b] Quotation marks indicate loadings predicted by theory to be highest.

These data from Analysis 1 provide additional support for the theory that A_L and R_L represent the most important differences among individuals in rauding ability.

When a single factor was forced upon the data in Analysis 2, the highest loading was on the Nelson–Denny-Comprehension variable (0.88), which is a correlate of E_L. This single factor from Analysis 2 appears to be an Efficiency factor. Notice that in all of these prior factor analyses of the Nelson–Denny test, the Comprehension score has consistently been interpreted as reflecting an Efficiency factor, additional support for E_L as a primary factor. The other two correlates of E_L, i.e., Davis-Comprehension and Washington-Comprehension, also loaded highly on the Efficiency factor, 0.85 and 0.79, respectively. However, these latter two variables loaded slightly higher on the Accuracy factor than they did on the Efficiency factor. The reason that these latter two Efficiency correlates did not load higher on the Efficiency factor probably indicates that these two tests were more power tests than rate tests. If the time limits for these two tests were shortened, then their loadings on the Accuracy factor would probably go down and their loadings on the Efficiency factor would probably go up.

In Table 3.1, notice that quotation marks have been placed around one loading out of the three for each variable. This one loading was predicted from theory to be the highest of the three. For all five of the accuracy and rate correlates, this prediction was correct. For example, notice that the highest of the three loadings for the Washington-Vocab variable was 0.87 (compared to 0.32 and 0.81), and it was the loading on the Accuracy factor as was predicted from theory. It should also be noted that only one of the three predictions was correct for the three efficiency correlates. Again, missing two out of the last three predictions is not absolutely crucial for the theory since it is possible to increase or decrease these loadings on reading comprehension tests by changing the time limits. The longer the time limit, the more the test reflects accuracy; the shorter the time limit the more the test reflects rate and efficiency.

Palmer *et al.* drew the following conclusions at the end of their 30-page research article: (a) reading speed and comprehension should be treated as distinct abilities rather than being combined into a single reading score, (b) reading comprehension ability is highly related to listening comprehension ability, and (c) reading speed and listening comprehension are not highly related. From the standpoint of the constructs of rauding theory, and the data presented in Table 3.1, these three conclusions can be refined.

When Palmer *et al.* refer to reading speed, we can substitute rauding rate level (R_L). When they refer to reading comprehension, we can substitute E_L because their measures of reading comprehension reflect E_L both theoretically and empirically. When they refer to listening comprehension, we can substitute A_L because their measure of listening comprehension reflected A_L from both a theoretical and empirical standpoint. Therefore, their first conclusion is that reading speed (R_L) is a distinctly different ability from comprehension (E_L). This conclusion is questionable because rauding rate level (R_L) is inherently included in rauding efficiency level (E_L). It would not seem to be fruitful, from a theoretical standpoint, to look for a consistent degree of relationship between traditional standardized tests of reading comprehension (correlates of E_L) and measures of reading rate (correlates of R_L) because (a) E_L is partly composed of R_L, and (b) the time limit on the reading comprehension test probably determines the degree to which these two variables will be correlated.

The second conclusion of Palmer *et al.* is that reading comprehension ability (a correlate of E_L) and listening comprehension ability (a correlate of A_L) are highly related. With the advantage of rauding theory, this conclusion is predetermined since A_L is an inherent part of E_L.

The third conclusion of Palmer *et al.* is that reading speed (a correlate of R_L) and listening comprehension (a correlate of A_L) are not highly related. Note that theoretically R_L and A_L are inherently different constructs, but empirical indicants of these two variables seem to be moderately correlated; the two factors correlated 0.44. Furthermore, in the data reviewed earlier, the A_L and R_L factors were so highly correlated for elementary students that only a single E_L factor resulted. With the college students involved in the three studies that have been reviewed (Carver, 1972c, 1990d; Palmer *et al.*, 1985), the A_L and R_L factors correlated 0.56, 0.41, and 0.44 respectively. Contrary to the conclusions of Palmer *et al.*, it appears that individual differences in the most important factor involved in reading rate, R_L, are substantially related to individual differences in the most important factor involved in comprehension, A_L.

This reanalysis of the Palmer *et al.* data provides strong empirical support for the rauding theory constructs of A_L, R_L, and E_L. The correlations among the eight measures administered by these researchers were readily explained by an Accuracy factor (A_L) and a Rate factor (R_L). The correlates of A_L loaded highly on the Accuracy factor, and the correlates of R_L loaded highly on the Rate factor. The reading comprehension measures involved both rate and accuracy, in varying degrees, probably depending upon the time limit for the test.

In summary, there seems to be no doubt that there are large and important individual differences with respect to reading rate and reading comprehension. Individual differences relevant to reading rate appear to be explained best by a theoretical construct called rauding rate, R_r, or rauding rate level, R_L. Individual differences relevant to vocabulary measures appear to be explained best by a theoretical construct called rauding accuracy level, A_L. Individual differences relevant to measures of reading comprehension appear to be explained best by a theoretical construct called rauding efficiency level, E_L. Factors that reflect R_L in college students correlated about 0.50 with factors that reflect A_L, and these two factors were so highly related in elementary students that only one factor was needed, E_L. In the future, it will probably be helpful to (a) use the constructs of rate of comprehension, R, rauding rate, R_r, and rauding rate level, R_L, when investigating reading rate, (b) use the construct of rauding rate level, R_L, whenever individual differences in reading rate are important, and (c) recognize that measures purporting to reflect individual differences in reading comprehension are ordinarily reflecting rauding efficiency level, E_L, and therefore are also reflecting both rauding rate level, R_L, and rauding accuracy level, A_L, in varying degrees.

TASKS

In Chapter 2, the importance of instructions and objective consequences were stressed, and these aspects of the experimental situation are directly relevant to the task factor noted by Jenkins (1979). The tasks used in research studies on reading rate can affect reading rate because different tasks may force the individual to execute different reading processes to meet the demands of the task, and these processes operate at different rates. In order to successfully accomplish the task, a certain gear from 1 to 5 may be required, and the choice of this gear directly affects reading rate.

The effect of tasks will be illustrated using a series of experiments conducted in the early 1970s by McConkie and associates. These researchers were concerned about the lack of reader flexibility found by earlier researchers (e.g., Herculane, 1961; Hill, 1964; Letson, 1959; Rankin, 1970). They experimentally manipulated the tasks required of the reader in an effort to find evidence of reading rate changes associated with different tasks. With the benefit of hindsight, these data will be interpreted as providing evidence that readers can shift down from Gear 3 to Gears 1 and 2 in response to experimental task demands; these data do not seem relevant to variations in rate during the execution of the rauding process, Gear 3.

In the research of McConkie and Rayner (1974), the rate of reading under seven different conditions was investigated. College students were asked to read seven different 500-word passages from *Scientific American* with 10 questions given after each passage. The tasks involved the presence or absence of (a) questions immediately after each passage, (b) payoff for meeting criterion, (c) clarity of payoff instructions, and (d) emphasis on payoff criterion. These *Scientific American* articles contained topics such as set theory and biosphere, and were likely to include many thoughts that college students cannot understand at first encounter. Every condition involved short written answers to 10 questions that tested retention of specific details; answering the questions probably took considerably more time than reading the 500-word passage. There was one recall type question on each 50 words. There is little doubt that these tasks would result in some form of a learning or memorizing process being executed. Indeed, the mean reading rates for the seven conditions ranged from 151 to 234 wpm with a grand mean of 188.2. This average rate of 188 wpm is well below the average rauding rate of college students as estimated earlier by Taylor (1965) to be 280 wpm, and is typical of sixth graders (see Table 2.1); these rates were in the range of the model learning process rate of 200 Wpm (see Table 2.2). McConkie and Raynor concluded from their research that ". . . the students exhibited a considerable amount of flexibility in their reading, changing their rate in accordance with the demand characteristics of the reading task given them" (p. 16).

The above-mentioned data can be interpreted another way. The most important finding seems to be that the variation in rate was not exceptionally large, from a mean of 151 wpm to a mean of 234 wpm. This amount of variability was achieved after using payoff conditions (money) that rewarded speed or comprehension in an extreme fashion that may never be approached in the real world. The variations in rate found by McConkie and Raynor were not likely to be relevant to how much individuals change their rates when switching from one basic type of reading process to another, but instead were more relevant to how much individuals change their rates within various types of learning and memorizing processes. The objective consequences were conducive to Gears 1 and 2 of the five basic processes. From the vantage point of over 10 years of hindsight, these researchers appear to have found (a) a mean learning process rate of 234 wpm for the fastest of seven conditions where speed was rewarded with money, and (b) a mean memorizing process rate of 151 wpm for the slowest. These data appear to indicate that rate can vary between Gear 1 and Gear 2 and within Gear 1 and Gear 2 by changing the objective consequences.

McConkie and Meyer (1974) replicated the McConkie and Raynor research described above. This time there were seven multiple-choice questions on each 325-word passage, and the questions were all "related to the higher levels of Bloom's Taxonomy . . . : comprehension, application, analysis, synthesis or evaluation" (p. 152). So there was one higher order type question about every 50 words. In this replication they used five different but similar conditions to investigate the influence of task demands upon reading rate. This time the mean rates ranged from 180 wpm for the control condition to 253 wpm for one of the task conditions that emphasized speed. The mean over all five conditions was 216.4, well below the average rauding rate for college students but within the range of a learning process rate. Again, these data may be interpreted as providing some idea of how fast individuals execute a learning process and how much their rate changes when they modify this process to meet the specific demands of a variety of experimenter-induced objective consequences.

Finally, a study by McConkie, Rayner, and Wilson (1973) will be reviewed. In their research, the variations in the tasks were primarily in terms of the type of criterion test questions used: higher order, factual, sequence, recognition, and number. There was no mention of instructions so it can be assumed that repeated experience with the objective consequences defined the goal of the reader. In this research, the passages were again 500 words in length but there were only five multiple-choice questions in four of the five types of questions. This was only one

question per 100 words. In the fifth type, recognition, it was only necessary to check which 10 of 20 phrases were in the passage. The mean rate
of all groups was 266 wpm. These college student subjects were members
of an introductory psychology class so it can be estimated that they were
mostly freshmen and sophomores with a rauding rate around 270 Wpm,
using Table 2.1. The fastest mean rate was 306 wpm for the "number"
condition. In this condition, the answers to all the questions were numbers. After having five passages in which to learn that the only thing they
would be asked about was numerical data in the passage, this group got
up to an average rate of 306 wpm. This would involve an unusual kind
of reading process because a scanning process could be used first to
locate the numerical information that would constitute the only kind
of information in the passage that needed to be recalled. The second
fastest rate was 286 wpm for the recognition questions; these were the
easiest questions and they produced rates almost exactly equal to the
average reading rate of college students (mean = 280). The slowest rate,
234 wpm, was for a "combined" group that received a combination of all
types of questions. It appears that these rates were all close to their estimated rauding process rate.

The preceding data, relevant to tasks and variations in reading rate,
provide evidence that rate can be manipulated by changing the task.
Tasks that are likely to induce a memorizing process, such as writing
answers to high-density questions, produce slow rates around 150 wpm
for college students; this is close to the 138 Wpm rate given for a model
memorizing process (Table 2.1). Tasks that required answering high-
density, higher-order, multiple-choice questions produced faster rates
(mean = 216); this is close to the 200 Wpm rate given for a model learning process (Table 2.1). And, tasks that required answering low-density,
multiple-choice questions produced faster rates (mean = 266 wpm) that
were close to the 280 wpm average rate of college students. These data
support the general idea of rauding theory that rate can be manipulated
experimentally by objective consequences. Furthermore, these college
student data may be interpreted as providing general support for the
five basic processes of rauding theory since (a) the objective consequences associated with a memorizing process produced rates around
138 Wpm, (b) the objective consequences associated with a learning process produced rates around 200 Wpm, and (c) as the objective consequences approached those of the rauding process, the rates approached
the typical reading rates of college students.

It should not go unnoticed that the above data can easily be interpreted as indicating that reading rates can be manipulated by using objective consequences that force individuals to change their goals. In turn,

these goals force shifts from the rauding process (Gear 3) to a learning process (Gear 2), or a memorizing process (Gear 1). However, these data do *not* provide any indication of how much rate varies within the rauding process, Gear 3.

In summary, it appears that the mean reading rate of college students can be predicted relatively accurately using the normative criteria presented in Tables 2.1 and 2.2, given a knowledge of whether the objective consequences of the task are conducive to a memorizing process, a learning process, or the rauding process.

MATERIALS

The difficulty level of the reading material has long been considered an important factor affecting reading rate. Is easy material read faster than difficult material? As the difficulty of the material increases does reading rate decrease?

Woodworth (1938) included a chapter on reading in his book, *Experimental Psychology*, and in a section on "Speed of Reading" he made the following comment, "The mere fact that easy material is read more rapidly than difficult . . ." (p. 715). The view that reading rate slows as the material becomes more difficult is a prevalent one. The effect of the difficulty level of materials on reading rate will be explored next by focusing on a series of experiments that were conducted in the 1970s.

Carver (1971a) reported on whether the size of the pupil in the eye could be used as an index of information processing load. The data he reported, which involved the reading rate of passages at different difficulty levels, would later emphasize a startling fact about reading rate. Carver used 4 of the 36 passages that had been studied earlier by G. R. Miller and Coleman (1967). Relevant to Woodworth's wisdom, Carver (1971b) reanalyzed the Carver (1971a) data, and found that reading rate in actual words per minute, wpm, did indeed drop steadily as the difficulty of the passages became harder. Figure 3.1 contains the data from two experiments. For example, in Experiment 1 the easiest of four passages (10) was read at about 240 wpm and the hardest (36) at about 140 wpm. However, Carver noticed that the easier passages were shorter than the harder passages even though they contained approximately the same number of words. He was also aware of some unpublished research of John R. Bormuth at the University of Chicago which indicated that one of the two highest correlates of cloze difficulty scores, out of 169 variables, was the average length of the words in the passages. Therefore, Carver reanalyzed his own data using the standard length word of

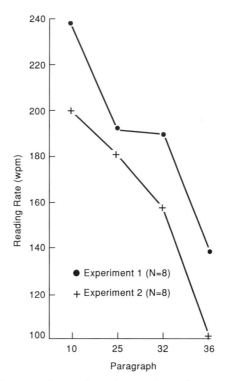

Fig. 3.1 Mean reading rates, in actual words per minute, for two experimental groups reading four of the Miller–Coleman paragraphs that vary from very easy to very difficult. (Fig. 1 from Carver, 1971b.)

six character spaces (see Chapter 2). He found that when he used standard words per minute (Wpm) the three easier passages were read at approximately the same rate. These data are presented in Fig. 3.2. He suggested that individuals may read most material at a relatively constant rate in terms of the progression of the eyes across the characters of a line but that this may change when relatively difficult material is encountered.

Sparks of controversy associated with the data in Fig. 3.2 ignited a series of definitive studies. The initial controversy was mostly semantic, dealing with the term "readability." As mentioned earlier, Carver had used four passages sampled from the 36 originally used by G. R. Miller and Coleman (1967) in a study of material difficulty. These 36 passages were later published intact by Aquino (1969), and were referred to by Aquino as the Miller–Coleman Readability Scale. Carver argued that if

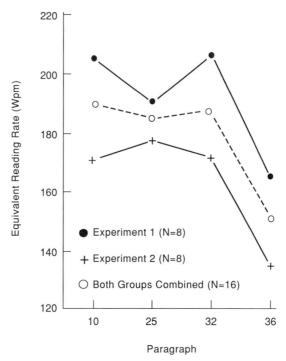

Fig. 3.2 Mean reading rates for the same data as presented in Fig. 3.1, with rate expressed in standard length words per minute, Wpm, instead of actual words per minute, wpm. (Fig. 2 from Carver, 1971b.)

passages along this scale of difficulty were read at the same rate, then it was misleading to call it a readability scale since these passages seemed to be equally readable.

G. R. Miller and Coleman (1971) not only responded to Carver but they also reported the results of a research study wherein they administered all of the 36 experimental passages to a total of 83 college freshmen. Miller and Coleman told the students to "read each passage carefully enough to take a test on it," but when the students finished ". . . they were told that the instruction to prepare themselves for a test had been given only to insure careful reading and that no test would be given" (p. 50). These instructions and objective consequences probably were not strong enough to induce a memorizing process or a learning process. Indeed, there would seem to be small likelihood that these students would shift out of a rauding process, so a rate of 263 Wpm would be predicted from Table 2.1. Miller and Coleman measured rate in letters per second which can be divided by 5 and multiplied by 60 to give an approximation of Wpm (see Chapter 2). Most of their 36 passages were read around 250 Wpm which is close to the predicted value of 263 Wpm. They concluded that their data ". . . show clearly that when reading speed is measured in a more finely grained unit such as letters, syllables, or morphenes, it is constant across a range of difficulty that extends from first-grade texts to the most difficult technical prose in the language" (p. 56).

The constant rate data from these two studies were inconsistent with the conventional wisdom expressed by Woodworth in 1938 that easier material is read faster than harder material. Carver had pointed out that this Woodworth type of wisdom seemed to be true (a) only if rate was measured in a way that did not control for word length, and (b) only if the material became exceedingly difficult. Miller and Coleman went one step further and concluded on the basis of their data that rate was constant across the whole range of material difficulty as long as rate was measured in syllables or letters instead of words.

Miller and Coleman also severely questioned Carver's finding that the most difficult passage was read more slowly. So, Carver (1976) reanalyzed the G. R. Miller and Coleman (1971) data using the GE scale of difficulty from the Rauding Scale (Carver, 1975b), discussed earlier in Chapter 2. He found that Miller and Coleman's data replicated his own 1971 data: when rate was measured in actual words per minute (wpm) rate dropped steadily from about 315 wpm for passages at GE levels 1–3, to about 200 wpm for passages at GE levels 16–18. But, when measured in standard words per minute (Wpm) the passages at GE levels 1–15 were all read at approximately the same rate, about 260 Wpm (closer to the predicted 263 Wpm), and rate dropped to around 220 Wpm for the passages at the relatively hard levels of 16–18. These data are presented in Fig. 3.3. (Note: Carver estimated Wpm two separate ways and both gave approximately the same results.) Carver suggested that individuals tend to read material that is equal to or below their own level of ability at approximately the same rate. As long as the material did not become relatively hard, the individuals appeared to operate their rauding process at a constant rate across a wide range of difficulty (from GE = 2 to GE = 14). However, when the material became relatively hard, they appeared to shift down to a learning process that operated at a slower but more powerful rate.

The above data from Carver (1971b), G. R. Miller and Coleman (1971), and Carver (1976) can now be reinterpreted from the framework of rauding theory. The mean rates that Carver (1971b) found varied from about 170 Wpm to about 210 Wpm for material that was relatively easy for college students. These rates are in the range of a learning pro-

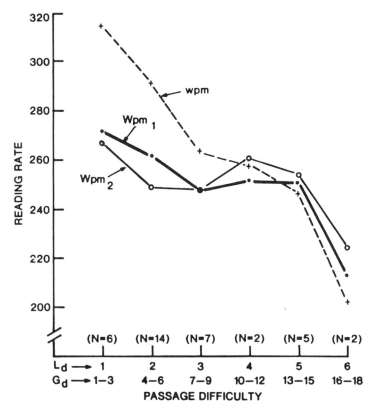

Fig. 3.3 Reading rate as a function of passage difficulty (G_d and L_d) using actual words per minute, wpm, and standard length words per minute, Wpm; there were two methods for estimating Wpm. Passage difficulty in grade equivalent units was symbolized using an older symbol, G_d, which means the same as difficulty level, D_L. (Fig. 2 from Carver, 1976.)

cess, and this could be predicted because Carver required his college students to take a cloze type of test on each passage when they finished reading. Thus, these data may be interpreted as indicating little change in the rate of a learning process when the material varies in difficulty but remains relatively easy ($A_L > D_L$). Rate did drop considerably, about 20%, for the most difficult passage which was probably relatively hard for these individuals. With respect to the G. R. Miller and Coleman (1971) data, they found rates around 260 Wpm, which is a reasonable rate for the rauding process to operate for college freshmen. Remember their instructions were to "read each passage carefully enough to take a test on it" but they gave no test. Furthermore, they reported that the

83 subjects came from freshman statistics classes so the word could have gotten around from one class to another that there would be no test. It appears reasonable to predict that the rauding process would be adopted from the instructions and objective consequences, and the rate for these 13th graders was almost exactly equal to the predicted rate. Carver's reanalysis of Miller and Coleman's data, presented in Fig. 3.3, shows the mean rates varying from about 250 Wpm to about 270 Wpm when the material varied in difficulty from about GE = 2 to about GE = 14; rate dropped about 15% for the two hardest passages at about GE = 17 difficulty. It seems reasonable to interpret these data as indicating that the rauding process ordinarily operates at a constant rate for college students when they read passages that are not relatively hard for them (Carver, 1978a). These data provide strong support for Law I of rauding theory, as described in Chapter 2. When the material becomes relatively hard, it is likely that the readers will shift gears to a learning process that proceeds at a slower rate.

In the span between 1971 and 1976, Coke, Rothkopf, and Coatney at Bell Laboratories appear to have been stimulated by the above-mentioned research of Carver, Miller, and Coleman. They expanded the investigation of the relationship between reading rate and material difficulty.

Coke (1974) reported the results of two experiments. In Experiment 1, 20 college students read orally 90 passages that were ordered in difficulty using the Flesch Reading Ease Score (Flesch, 1949): the passages ranged from very easy (100) to very hard (0), which is from easier than GE = 5 to more difficult than GE = 16 using the grade equivalents presented by Flesch (1949). Coke found that when oral reading rate was measured in actual words per minute (wpm) it steadily decreased from about 260 wpm for the easiest passages to about 140 wpm for the hardest passages. However, when oral reading rate was measured in syllables per minute, rate was approximately constant at about 320 syllables per minute across the entire range of difficulty. [Note: The value of 320 syllables per minute becomes 193 Wpm using Equation (2.7)]. For these 90 passages, Coke also reported that the time required to read aloud each passage correlated 0.94 with the number of syllables in the passage but only 0.72 with the number of words. Thus, when measured in syllables per minute oral reading rate was relatively constant.

In the second of Coke's two experiments, 32 passages were selected from the original 90 to represent the same range of difficulty. They were administered to 20 high school students in each of three groups. The Aloud-Pronounce group simply read the passage orally with their only task to judge how difficult the words were to pronounce when they finished a passage. The Aloud-Understand group also read the passages orally but they had to judge how difficult the passage was to understand when they finished; these instructions and objective consequences would be conducive to the rauding process. The Silent-Understand group read each passage silently and they also rated how difficult the passage was to understand when they finished. Coke found that all three groups of subjects ". . . read the passages at a relatively constant syllable rate" (p. 408), and the correlations between the number of syllables in passages and the time required to read them was 0.99, 0.98, and 0.94 for the three groups, Aloud-Pronounce, Aloud-Understand, and Silent-Understand, respectively. So, the earlier findings of Carver and Miller and Coleman that silent reading rate was constant across difficulty levels were replicated by Coke using different subjects, passages, instructions, and measures of material difficulty; this is more support for Law I of rauding theory. Unfortunately, Coke did not report any of the data from Experiment 2 in rate form so it was impossible to determine whether the subjects in the Silent-Understand group actually read at a rate predictable from the data in Table 2.1.

This research of Coke's was valuable in two other ways that may seem small but are important. First, it reinforced a connection between reading rate and speaking rate (see Carver, 1977) in that each seems to be tied to a constancy in terms of syllables articulated per minute. Second, an unannounced short-answer comprehension test was administered to the subjects when they finished reading all passages to find out if they were in fact comprehending. The same test was also given to a special control group which did not read the passages. This control group only answered an average of 1% of the questions correctly while the subjects who read the passages answered over 50% of the short-answer questions correctly. She concluded: "These findings rule out an explanation of the observed syllable rate constancy in terms of superficial processing. Subjects in this experiment were not simply pronouncing words without comprehension when reading aloud or were not simply glancing at the texts when reading silently" (p. 409).

A minor liability of the Coke (1974) study was that data were not reported in a form that helped to determine whether reading rate did or did not decrease when exceedingly difficult material was encountered. According to rauding theory (Carver, 1981), when individuals are given instructions and objective consequences that are conducive to the engagement of the rauding process, then reading rate will be constant because the individuals will read at their rauding rate (R_r), which is constant. However, when the material becomes relatively hard, then the individual is more likely to switch to a learning process. If individuals do shift gears to a learning process when the material becomes relatively hard, then reading rate will automatically drop. This theoretical viewpoint requires that more attention be focused on the details of the experimental conditions so as to be able to ascertain or predict which particular one of the five basic processes is most likely to have been activated. If the instructions and objective consequences are conducive to the rauding process, and if the material is not relatively difficult, then the rauding process is likely to operate at a constant rate predictable from the ability level of the individuals using Table 2.1.

Rothkopf and Coatney (1974) continued to investigate the effect of passage difficulty upon reading rate. Their particular purpose was to determine if reading hard material would result in a slower reading rate that would carry over to easy material read later. Or, conversely, would reading easy material result in a faster rate that would carry over into hard material read later? Their 92 college student subjects were told to ". . . read each text slide as rapidly as they could and still learn the essential elements of the content" (p. 680). When they finished reading, they were given a cloze type test. The most interesting aspect about the experiment was that the 1271-word passage on the geography and history of Thailand (Flesch = 51; GE = 12) was rewritten into a more difficult form (Flesch = 20; GE = 16+) and administered in either its easy or hard form. The passage was divided into half with some subjects getting one half of the passage in the easy form and one half in the hard form. From the instructions to "learn" from passages at GE = 12 and higher, and from objective consequences involving a cloze test, it would be predicted that a learning process would be operating.

The results obtained by Rothkopf and Coatney are presented in Table 3.2. They gave their original rate results in syllables per minute, but they have been converted here into Wpm using the 1.66 syllables per word conversion noted earlier [see Equation (2.7)]. (Note: They used a neutral term "inspection rate" instead of reading rate.) The mean rate over all conditions and subjects was 175 Wpm which was close to the 200 Wpm predicted for college students operating a learning process. Notice that the first two groups listed in the table, II-A and I-A, both received the easy passage first and their rates on this easy passage were comparable, 184 and 189 Wpm. The first group listed, II-A, received the hard version on the second half, and they decreased their rate, −4%. The second group, I-A, continued with the easy version and their rate increased, +14%. This slight increase may reflect a tendency for subjects to avoid the execution of the more difficult components of the learning process, when engaged in a lengthy task in which they are not highly motivated to excel. Thus, these data can be interpreted as evidence that a learning

Table 3.2

Learning Process Rates for Four Groups Reading the First and Second Half
of a Passage That Was Presented in an Easy and a Hard Form[a]

Group	First Half	Second Half	Rate Change
II-A	Easy: 184 Wpm	Hard: 176 Wpm	−4%
I-A	Easy: 189 Wpm	Easy: 216 Wpm	+14%
		Easy to Hard Net Change	−18%
I-B	Hard: 143 Wpm	Easy: 176 Wpm	+23%
II-B	Hard: 150 Wpm	Hard: 163 Wpm	+9%
		Hard to Easy Net Change	+14%
Mean	166.5 Wpm	182.8 Wpm	

[a] These results represent a reanalysis of data originally collected by Rothkopf and Coatney (1974).

process is sensitive to a shift in the difficulty of the material from relatively easy to relatively hard; the net change between the two conditions was − 18%.

The results obtained for groups I-B and II-B were similar to those discussed above for groups I-A and II-A. Both I-B and II-B read the hard first half at approximately the same rate, 143 and 150 Wpm. Group I-B increased their rate when they encountered the easy material on the second half, +23%. Group II-B received both halves in the hard form, and they went a little faster on the second half, +9%; this effect was similar to Group I-A who increased their rate by 14% on the second half even though both halves were easy. The net change for the latter two conditions was +14%.

These data from Rothkopf and Coatney provide evidence that this learning process, which operated at a slower rate than the rauding process, was somewhat sensitive to the difficulty of the material when it changed from relatively easy to relatively hard. The change from relatively easy to relatively hard netted an 18% drop in rate, and the change from relatively hard to relatively easy netted a 14% increase in rate.

Before leaving these data, it is important to point out that the above interpretation is somewhat different from the way Rothkopf and Coatney interpreted their own data. They concluded: "The results . . . provide substantial indications that the rate at which subjects inspect text depends not only on the reading ease of the materials with which they are currently confronted but also the reading ease of recently inspected text segments" (p. 682). It does not seem that this interpretation is the only one, or the best one. Instead, it seems that the differences in rate are almost completely dependent upon the relative difficulty of the material. If each of the second half rates are reduced by 16.3 to eliminate a practice effect and make them comparable to the first half rates, then the mean of the four easy conditions was 183 with an SD of 15 and the mean of the four hard conditions was 150 with an SD of 6. This is an increase in rate of 22% when shifting from hard to easy materials. Thus, there seems to be no compelling reason to accept Rothkopf and Coatney's explanation that their results are better explained by the hypothesis that subjects get into a set or habit and this accounts for the stability of rate found by Carver (1971b), G. R. Miller and Coleman (1971), or Coke (1974).

These findings of Rothkopf and Coatney can be interpreted as indicating that when college students are operating a learning process, Gear 2, on material that varies in difficulty from relatively easy (GE = 12) to relatively hard (GE = 16+), then a 15–20% change in rate can be expected. Indeed, this finding replicates the 20% drop in rate noted in the Carver (1971b) results reviewed earlier. However, it should not be forgotten that these data from research on Gear 2 are not relevant to the first law of rauding theory (from Chapter 2) that the rate at which the rauding process operates, Gear 3, is constant as long as the material is relatively easy and rate is measured in Wpm.

The final research to be reported from Bell Laboratories during this period was also conducted by Coke (1976). She surmised that the reason there has been a failure to find a relationship between the difficulty level of material and reading rate was because the earlier research ". . . used reading tasks that induced a very general set to understand the material" (p. 167). Thus, Coke was indirectly acknowledging that instructions and objective consequences inducing the rauding process would produce no relationship between reading rate and material difficulty but that instructions and tasks that activated more components in the processes might result in a relationship between reading rate and material difficulty. To test this hypothesis she asked 68 high school students to read 16 passages, ranging from 85 to 171 words in length. They were presented under eight conditions involving three dichotomous variables. First, one half of the subjects were given easy passages and the other half hard. Second, the subjects were asked after they had finished reading whether a short list of target words were in the passage; one half of the subjects were given word lists that were identical to words in the text and the other half were given lists that were only synonyms of words in the text. Third, one half were also given the words prior to the task, the Search Condition, and the other half did not know ahead of time which words they would later be asked about, the Memory Condition. After all passages had been read, a modified cloze type of test was administered to all groups. With the cloze test required along with the target search, some variant of a learning or memorizing process would be predicted.

Coke reported mean rates ranging from about 130 Wpm to about 190 Wpm (converting from letter spaces per minute to Wpm by dividing by 6), so the prediction was confirmed by these rates. She was successful in forcing these students to shift down from their rauding process, Gear 3, into more powerful processes such as learning, Gear 2, or memorizing, Gear 1.

Coke found little or no difference between the easy and hard passages under the Search condition, either with identical or synonym target words. This means that when the subjects knew ahead of time that they would be looking for certain target words while they were reading, they could do this task just as fast when the material was hard as when it was easy; i.e., no effect of material difficulty upon reading rate. (Note: These data are relevant to model scanning in Chapter 2.) However, when the subjects did not know ahead of time which target words they would be asked about later, then the hard material was read about 15% slower than the easy material, under both the identical and synonym target lists. Her original hypothesis was confirmed in that she obtained an interaction between task and difficulty with respect to their effects upon reading rate.

From the above study of Coke (1976), we did not learn anything directly relevant to the rate at which the rauding process operates (Gear 3) because her instructions and objective consequences were not designed to elicit the rauding process. We did learn that the rates of certain reading processes do change with the difficulty of the material and others do not. In this case, the goal that forced the subjects to look for certain words at the same time as they were engaged in all the components of the rauding process (a simultaneous combination of two of the five basic processes) did not result in any change in rate with difficulty level. So, we can see that adding a target word search component to the rauding process results in a lower reading rate but the rate did not get slower when switching from easy to hard materials because none of these components were affected by material difficulty. However, when the subjects did not know what the target words were while they were reading, their process slowed when they encountered the more difficult material. This is because they had to engage some of the components unique to learning, which rely on such subprocesses as repetition when encountering less frequently used words and concepts.

There is one more study to be reviewed from that era. Kintsch and

Keenan (1973) have provided data which may be interpreted by some as evidence against the constancy of rate across material of differing difficulty. They suggested that the difficulty of material could be measured by the number of propositions in the material. They found that reading rate varied with the number of propositions in a sentence even though the number of words remained constant. Ideally, they would have measured rate in syllables per second or standard length words per minute but it seems safe to assume that their results would not have changed drastically even if they had. So, it becomes important, over 15 years later, to try to explain how they could get results that appear to be drastically inconsistent with the constancy of rate found by Carver (1971b), G. R. Miller and Coleman (1971), and Coke (1974).

As was noted earlier, it is necessary to dissect the task, instructions, and objective consequences in order to reasonably infer something about the type of reading process used by their subjects. Kintsch and Keenan used isolated sentences as their experimental materials, in contrast to the prose passages used in all of the previously reviewed research. They asked their 29 college students to read 10 sentences that were about 16 words in length and had been selected from topics in classical history to ". . . hold the familiarity of the text to a minimum . . ." (p. 259). When they finished reading each sentence they were asked to write down the sentence they had just been presented to read. Their instructions ". . . emphasized that exact wording was not as important as the meaning of the sentence, and the subjects were asked to work as fast as possible, keeping in mind that the important thing was how much they remembered, not speed" (p. 261). The subjects were not likely to have attempted to use their rauding process, and even if they had it would have been impossible to use it in its described form since it requires understanding sentences in the context of other sentences, not isolated sentences. Their subjects probably used some type of memorizing process that was designed to maximize the exact recall of all of the important parts of a sentence.

By expecting a memorizing process, it would be predicted from Table 2.2 that reading rate would be around 138 Wpm. Their mean reading rates varied from about 65 wpm for nine proposition sentences to about 100 wpm for four proposition sentences. On the basis of hindsight, it seems obvious that generalizing these Gear 1 results to any of the more typical reading processes, such as the rauding process (Gear 3) or a learning process (Gear 2) would be dangerous. Typical reading rates for college students require one-fourth of a second per word, or less, yet the average time spent per word in this study was one full second or more.

It would appear that the processes used in this study by Kintsch and Keenan are as far removed from what we commonly call reading as is possible, without being embarrassed to say that reading or "reading rate" was being investigated. This Gear 1 research by Kintsch and Keenan is mostly irrelevant to whether the rauding process, Gear 3, operates at a relatively constant rate in Wpm as long as the material is relatively easy. These data of Kintsch and Keenan appear to provide results that are inconsistent with the constancy of rate data found earlier, but viewed from the framework of rauding theory they represent results specific to a Gear 1 memorizing process and are therefore not inconsistent with Gear 3 theory and data.

CONCLUSIONS

There are three main points to be made in this chapter. First, the rate at which the rauding process operates, Gear 3, varies with the ability level of the reader, and can be predicted using the normative data in Table 2.1. Second, the instructions and objective consequences associated with certain contexts and tasks can affect the goals of readers, often inducing them to shift out of Gear 3, which is natural, normal, and typical for most people; gear shifting affects reading rate because different gears have different components and operate at different rates. Third, changing the difficulty of material does not have an effect upon the rate at which the rauding process operates as long as the material is relatively easy; when the material becomes relatively hard, it is likely that the reader will shift to a lower gear with a slower rate. The data reviewed in this chapter also suggest that a learning process also tends to operate at a relatively constant rate across difficulty levels until the material becomes relatively hard.

The studies reviewed earlier from the 1970s left little doubt that reading rate does not change in normal, ordinary, or typical reading situations. The idea that reading rate decreases with increased difficulty of material was not supported by the evidence; the only changes in rate with difficulty seem to occur when there is a shift from relatively easy to relatively hard materials. The finding that actual reading rate, in wpm, decreased steadily as material difficulty increased turns out to be an artifact since the words become longer as the material becomes more difficult. This means that it is not valid to measure rate in actual words per minute (wpm) when comparing rates at different difficulty levels; rate needs to be measured in standard words per minute (Wpm) or some comparable measure that controls for word length. (Note: See Chapter 2 for more about the difference between wpm and Wpm.)

From the theory and research reviewed so far, the following conclusions have been drawn.

1. The most important individual differences in reading involve rauding ability, i.e., rauding accuracy level, A_L, rauding rate level, R_L, and rauding efficiency level, E_L.
2. Traditional vocabulary tests reflect individual differences in A_L, traditional rate measures reflect individual differences in R_L, and traditional reading comprehension tests reflect individual differences in both A_L and R_L which is called rauding efficiency level, E_L.
3. The rauding process ordinarily operates at a constant rate under a wide range of differences in material difficulty, as long as A_L is greater than the difficulty level of the material ($A_L > D_L$).
4. The reason that many researchers have found that reading rate does not change when material gets more difficult is that their instructions and objective consequences elicited a rauding process which operates at a constant rauding rate in syllables per minute, letters per second, or standard length words per minute; this rate averages around 260–300 Wpm for college students.
5. In those research studies where reading rate decreased when the materials became more difficult, the most likely explanation was that the material became relatively hard so that the subjects used processes that contained more time consuming components, such as shifting down from the rauding process, Gear 3, to a learning process, Gear 2.
6. Although reading rates varied within learning processes and within memorizing processes, these variations have not been especially large in size; these rate changes were often around 20–40 Wpm, or 10–20%.
7. Only one of the research studies reviewed in this chapter studied skimming or scanning processes, and it produced evidence that rate was not affected by the difficulty level of the material. Thus, ordinary skimming and scanning rates do not seem to be affected by material difficulty.

In summary, individuals tend to operate their rauding process at a constant rate that depends on individual differences in rauding ability, in accordance with Law I of rauding theory. The effect of context and tasks is primarily on shifting gears between one reading process and another, and this in turn sets reading rate at predictable levels, e.g., for college students, about 138 Wpm for memorizing processes, about 200 Wpm for learning processes, and about 260–300 Wpm for the rauding process. When the experimental conditions were conducive to the operation of the rauding process and the materials were relatively easy, there was no evidence that an individual's rate of operating the rauding process varied greatly. If the difficulty level of the materials shifted from relatively easy to relatively hard, then there was likely to be a shift down to a lower gear that operated more slowly. Using these concepts and constructs of rauding theory, it is possible to predict quite accurately the mean reading rate in a variety of experiments. If the ability level of the experimental subjects is known, and if the instructions, objective consequences, and relative difficulty of the material is conducive to the rauding process, then the rate can be predicted from the normative data for ability level given in Table 2.1. When the experimental subjects are college students and when the instructions and objective consequences suggest that a learning process or a memorizing process was operating, then the mean rate can be predicted from the estimates given in Table 2.2.

There appears to be evidence that rauding theory provides some order and lawfulness to rate data that previously was interpreted as disorderly and unpredictable. It appears that the effects of context, individual differences, tasks, and materials upon reading rate can be predicted using rauding theory by applying such concepts as basic reading processes, gear shifting, rauding ability, instructions, objective consequences, and relative difficulty.

4

SILENT SPEECH

INTRODUCTION

Does saying the words to yourself while reading slow you down? What is the relationship between silent speech and reading? Before attempting to investigate these questions by reference to the published literature, let us first deal with a semantic problem. Saying the words to oneself while reading has been referred to by a long list of different terms, such as silent speech, inner speech, inner articulation, subvocalization, internal talking, covert verbal behavior, implicit speech, covert oral language, phonemic encoding, speech recoding, acoustic recoding, implicit pronunciation, and speech–reading parallelism. When reviewing the research and theory of others, the term silent speech will often be used in place of the particular label used in the work cited.

Secor (1899) appears to have been the first to publish empirically collected data relevant to silent speech, but it is Huey (1908) who is ordinarily given credit for theorizing early and well about the role of silent speech and reading. He stated:

> The fact of inner speech forming a part of silent reading has not been disputed, so far as I am aware, by anyone who has experimentally investigated the process of reading. Its presence has been established, for most readers, when adequate tests have been made. . . . Purely visual reading is quite possible, theoretically; and Secor, in a study made at Cornell University, found that some readers could read visually while whistling or doing other motor tasks that would hinder inner speech. . . . it is perfectly certain that the inner hearing or pronunciation, or both, of what is read, is a constituent part of the reading of by far the most of people, as they ordinarily and actually read. (pp. 117, 118)

More than seventy-five years later, we still have no evidence that would refute this viewpoint of Huey's, and a large amount of data have been collected in support of it. Yet, acknowledging the fact that silent speech typically occurs during reading says nothing about whether it is helpful or harmful to reading. Does it slow down reading unnecessarily, so that if individuals could somehow purge themselves of this bad habit they could comprehend the same amount in less time? On the other hand, maybe silent speech is helpful so that if individuals were forced to get along without it, they would take longer to comprehend the same amount or they would comprehend less at the same rate.

There were a number of early advocates of the "harmful" thesis, such as Pintner (1913), McDade (1937), and Woodworth (1938). Probably the most influential spokesperson for the harmful thesis has been Buswell (1947) at the University of Chicago. He stated: "Since the neuromuscular processes of speech require more time than the silent process of thinking the meaning, subvocalization results in a slow rate of reading." (p. 190). "Completely silent reading is carried on without subvocalization or consciousness of words as words" (p. 193). Buswell was convinced that oral reading during early reading instruction was the major reason why silent speech was so common in the ordinary reading of college students and adults. In more recent times, the harmful thesis has been advocated by F. Smith (1972a). As late as 1975, we find Gibson and Levin stating that "adults reading silently to themselves bypass subvocalization and go directly to the abstract meaning . . ." (p. 476).

On the other hand, early on, Huey (1908) was able to discern that silent speech could be helpful. He stated that the subvocalization ". . . seems to help hold the word in consciousness until enough others are given to combine with it in touching off the unitary utterance of the sentence which they form . . ." (p. 146).

Edfeldt (1960) published an exceptionally thorough study of silent speech during reading, using electromyography (EMG), i.e., the recording of electrical potentials from active muscles. He carefully reviewed earlier research and followed stringent design procedures. His data provided support for the three hypotheses that guided his research: (a) good readers engage in less silent speech than do poor readers, (b) as the content of the text becomes more difficult, silent speech increases in all readers, and (c) the reading of a clear text results in less silent speech than does the reading of a blurred one. He concluded that "silent speech occurs in the reading of all people" (p. 151), and "it is . . . impossible to view silent speech as a habit detrimental to reading" (p. 152). So, the extensive research of Edfeldt indicates no support for the harmful thesis and does provide support for the helpful thesis.

In 1972, a translation of Sokolov's extensive research on silent speech was published. He studied EMGs from silent speech while reading to oneself, while listening to speech, during mental reproduction, and during the recollection of verbal materials. He concluded that the concealed articulation associated with silent speech was the principal mechanism of thought. Thus, to suggest that people would be able to read better without silent speech might be suggesting that people could read better and faster if they were somehow prevented from doing their best thinking, obviously an absurd proposition.

In the 1960s, McGuigan (see his review, 1970) conducted many studies of EMG (some of which involved reading) using surface electrodes instead of the needle electrodes used by earlier researchers such as Edfeldt (1960). During this same period, Hardyck, Petrinovich, and Ellsworth (1966) collected EMG data during silent reading, working under the supposition that it was harmful; they began by saying the "subvocalization is considered one of the most difficult problems to overcome in increasing reading speed" (p. 1467), and they ended by concluding: "This treatment resulted in immediate and long lasting cessation of the subvocalization ... [and] ... should prove valuable in treating some reading problems" (p. 1467). Methodological problems with their research were critiqued in the review by McGuigan (1970), mentioned above, who concluded elsewhere (1973) that ". . . covert oral behavior facilitates reading proficiency" (p. 362). [Note: McGuigan (1973) briefly sketched the results of an earlier study on reading rate that was reported in a paper read at a convention but there was not enough detail published to evaluate this unpublished research.]

The preceding background sets the stage for a review of the more recent research literature relevant to whether silent speech during reading is helpful or harmful, and how it affects reading rate. Cloer (1977) conducted such a review and concluded that the advantages of silent speech outweighted its disadvantages. The present review will concentrate on how silent speech affects the five basic reading processes, scanning, skimming, rauding, learning, and memorizing. However, some of the research on silent speech cannot be placed into one of these five categories. For example, in Experiment 1 of Levy (1977), short, easy, unrelated sentences were presented in sets of three, for 3 seconds at a time, and then performance was tested by administering a sentence which may or may not have changed the meaning; one experimental condition involved a shadowing task of counting from 1 to 10 as a means of disrupting silent speech. From the tests employed it might appear that a rauding process was likely to have been used, except the sentences did not form passages and the time allowed for reading sentences nine words long was much longer than necessary for a rauding process. This design of Levy's was replicated by Margolin, Griebel, and Wolford (1982) using an additional distraction task that did not involve silent speech; they presented results which called into question the interpretation that the disruption of silent speech accounts for poor performance during shadowing. As will be shown later, the results of relevant research form a pattern when categorized into the five reading gears, and future research will be needed to adjudicate whether the conflicting results coming from the hybrid research of Margolin *et al.* is significant or not.

To understand the relevant research literature that will be reviewed later, it will be necessary to introduce the concept of memory load in verbal short-term memory. Most theorists in this area have been convinced from prior research (e.g., Atkinson & Shiffrin, 1968) that individuals have a limited amount of storage capacity for immediate memory or short-term memory (STM) that affects some of the reading processes. For example, a sentence that is 50 words long will not affect the model scanning process reviewed from Chapter 2 because each new word in the long sentence can be discharged from memory as soon as it has been compared with the target word. However, a sentence 50 words long may be impossible to understand during the rauding process because each word must be stored in short-term memory until the end of the sentence is reached and the complete thought has been comprehended. Thus, the load on memory becomes increasingly crucial to operation of the processes associated with the lower and more powerful gears, and silent speech is an aid to the short-term memory required to use these processes successfully (see Levy, 1977).

With this introduction, the research relevant to each of the five basic reading processes will be presented in turn.

SCANNING PROCESSES

Most of the research that has been conducted on silent speech has involved lexical accessing, Gear 1. However, seldom has this research involved scanning prose for a target word which is the model scanning process described in Chapter 2. Instead, this research has involved how fast individuals can react to words, i.e., reaction time, when their silent speech has been suppressed or disrupted. Since the speed of scanning processes depends directly upon how fast words can be recognized, a few of these more recent reaction time studies will be reviewed to obtain some indication of their implications for the effect of silent speech upon scanning rate.

Klapp, Anderson, and Berrian (1973) conducted a series of experiments involving reaction times to words and pictures. They presented one- and two-syllable words, five letters long, to college students and measured the reaction time between the onset of the stimulus word and the time required to start its pronunciation. They found that it took subjects slightly longer to recognize two-syllable words. In a similar experiment, subjects did not have to pronounce the word, only to categorize it in their response as "animal" or "object." In this study, they found no difference between the one- and two-syllable words. They concluded that ". . . although implicit speech may sometimes occur during reading, it does not occur universally and is not necessary for reading comprehension" (p. 373). Their use of the term "reading comprehension" is exceptionally ambitious. To be more accurate, they could have concluded that they found no evidence that silent speech is either helpful or harmful to the rate at which isolated words are recognized.

D. E. Meyer, Schvaneveldt, and Ruddy (1974) had high school students respond yes or no to whether a pair of letter strings were words or not. The letter strings were made up of words and nonwords and also varied in terms of their graphic (COUCH–TOUCH) and phonemic (BRIBE–TRIBE) similarity. If the subjects always recognized the letter strings from their visual representations, without regard for rhyming, then they should not recognize the rhyming words any faster than the graphemically similar words. Instead they found that performance was worse when the pair was only graphemically similar. They concluded that ". . . the data are inconsistent with the graphemic-encoding hypothesis and indicate the involvement of phonological representations in visual word recognition . . ." (p. 315). A second experiment replicated the first under slightly different experimental conditions and further substantiated that silent speech is used during visual word recognition. They cautioned that ". . . our results do not prove that it is impossible to recognize printed words directly from their visual representations," but "it appears that visual word recognition is mediated at least part of the time through phonological representations" (p. 318). On the basis of their research, it seems unreasonable to argue that silent speech is harmful to the speed at which words are recognized since the data suggested that the use of the sounds of the words seemed to decrease the time needed for their recognition.

Kleiman (1975) conducted a lengthy investigation that involved three experiments. In the first two, he studied the reaction time to phonemically similar word pairs (TICKLE–PICKLE) and phonemically dissimilar word pairs (HEARD–BEARD) while college students were asked to repeat digits. This shadowing task disrupts or acts as suppressor of silent speech. From the pattern of results in the first two experiments, he concluded that there was ". . . strong evidence that speech recoding is not needed for retrieval of lexical information" (p. 322). So, according to

Kleiman, saying the words to oneself in some inaudible fashion is not required for recognizing the word, but this adds nothing to answering our original questions about whether silent speech is helpful or harmful. Just because it is "not needed" does not necessarily mean it is harmful or slows down the rate at which words are recognized.

The third experiment of Kleiman's was the only one found in the literature which studied silent speech during a scanning process. There were four types of decisions, two of which involved scanning. In the graphemic condition a target word was given (e.g., BURY) and the subject had to respond "true" or "false" to whether there was a graphemically similar word in a five-word sentence (e.g., YESTERDAY THE GRAND JURY ADJOURNED: True). In the phonemic condition, a target word was given (e.g., CREAM) and the subject had to decide if there was a phonemically similar word in a five-word sentence (e.g., HE AWAKENED FROM THE DREAM: True). All decisions were made with and without shadowing. Shadowing disrupted the phonemic decisions as would be expected but the graphemic decisions were affected to a much lesser degree. Therefore, it would appear that lexical access can be readily accomplished without silent speech. At least it appears that some scanning processes can operate just about as fast when silent speech is made more difficult as when it is free to operate normally. So, these data leave the original question in a stalemate position. During scanning, there is no strong evidence that silent speech is harmful to rate and there is no strong evidence that it is helpful to rate.

M. Martin (1978) conducted a brilliant study from the standpoint of both methodology and theory. It also helped make sense of the results from the earlier studies of word recognition rate. The Stroop (1935) interference task was used wherein subjects must respond to colors written in different words. For example, the word BLACK, might be presented on a card in red ink (Incongruent). It takes longer to sort those red cards into color piles than if only red X's are on the card (Control) or if the red ink is used for the word red (Congruent). A shadowing task of saying "bla" continuously was also used. If silent speech occurs during the recognition of these words, then shadowing should (a) be helpful when the color (e.g., red ink) and the word (e.g., BLACK) are incongruent, (b) be harmful when the words are congruent with the color, and (c) be neither helpful nor harmful in the control condition when only colors are on the card in the form of X's. Indeed, the pattern of results were exactly as would be predicted under the hypothesis that silent speech is occurring during word recognition.

Martin (1978) also conducted a second experiment that resulted in a "greater reduction in the Stroop effect when subjects were concurrently engaged in a phonemic rather than a graphemic task" (p. 113). Martin's results would not necessarily have told us much with respect to whether silent speech was helpful or harmful if she had not been able to compare the speeds of graphemic encoding, speech encoding, and color coding. With this design advantage, she was able to draw the following conclusions:

> Irrelevant articulation led to a decrease in the extent of the Stroop effect in both experiments, implying that skilled readers usually translate the visual representation of a word into a speech representation in order to access the meaning of the word, although readers may also use a slower graphemic route to lexical memory.
>
> In conclusion, the results of the two experiments provide support for the dual-encoding hypothesis . . . which states that reading involves converting a visual representation into a speech code, and that both visual and speech codes provide access to lexical memory. (p. 113)

Thus, the work of Martin allows us to conclude this section on scanning, Gear 1, in a way that explains why some earlier studies found that silent speech was helpful and others found that it was not necessary. Scanning ordinarily involves silent speech and it is usually helpful to word recognition but silent speech ordinarily accompanies word recognition whether it is helpful or not. If silent speech is disrupted, word recognition can still take place without it, even though it may proceed at a slower rate. This addition to knowledge is completely incompatible with Buswell's contention that silent speech slows reading rate but we could find Buswell to be correct as we move into the slower and more powerful gears.

SKIMMING PROCESSES

Baddeley, Eldridge, and Lewis (1981) conducted three experiments in what they called the role of subvocalization in "fluent" reading. In Experiment I, they presented sentences that were relatively long and complex, such as "she doesn't mind going to the dentist to have fillings, but doesn't like the pain when he gives her the injection at the beginning." Anomalous sentences were created by replacing a word such as "pain" above, with "rent." There were a total of 94 sentences, 32 of which were anomalous. As fast as possible after the sentence was presented, subjects pushed one button if the sentence was anomalous and another button if it was semantically acceptable. Under the condition of silent speech suppression, the subjects had to count repeatedly from one to six.

The above task would likely produce a model type of skimming process, as it has been described earlier. It is more than scanning because it requires more than lexical access. The task does not involve the rauding process, Gear 3, because it was not necessary that the entire sentence be understood or related to other sentences; the anomalous word could be detected without even finishing the sentence. Their task required semantic encoding of each word to see if its meaning was appropriate within the context of the sentence; i.e., a process that is involved in the model skimming task presented in Chapter 2.

Baddeley *et al.* found that the rates of classifying the *meaningful* sentences were exactly the same whether they were suppressed or not, when only the correct responses were analyzed. Similarly, they found that the rates of classifying the *meaningless* sentences (anomalous) were also exactly the same whether they were suppressed or not, when only the correct responses were analyzed. However, when the error rates were analyzed, they found that there were about twice as many errors in detecting the meaningless sentences when suppressed (about 18%) compared to unsuppressed (about 9%). So, they found that the rate at which this skimming process operated was not slowed by a disruption of silent speech but the process was much less effective because their subjects failed to detect the semantically incorrect words twice as often.

It seemed possible that the reason the subjects in the above research made more errors under suppression was because of the extra attention or memory demands created by the suppression task. So, in Experiment II they added a tapping condition to the suppression and nonsuppression conditions. They also changed the task somewhat. They selected short passages from real world material and reversed the order of pairs of words within some of the sentences. For example, the order of "learn" and "that" has been reversed in the following sentence: "We were to that learn he was a very honest person, even though he loved money." The task for the subjects was to circle the pairs of reversed words in the passage as fast as possible. Again, this is the model type of skimming task that requires semantic encoding. They found that the rate of reading the passages was the same under all three conditions, as in Experiment I. Again, they found an increase in errors under the suppression condition, but no increase in errors under the tapping condition which also competed for attention and memory.

They conducted Experiment III to rule out the role of acoustic interference in explaining their results. They used a task that was similar to the one in Experiment II, but they added conditions to determine if noise presented over a loudspeaker would have an effect; the noise conditions were provided by a tape of 15 different three-letter words which was repeated during the experimental period. They again replicated their findings. Speed of processing was not affected by suppression while accuracy was, but the effect of the noise condition did not produce this pattern of results.

Baddeley *et al.* (1981) summarized their findings as follows:

> Our results have shown unequivocally that preventing subjects from subvocalising substantially impairs their ability to detect semantically anomalous sentences whether the anomaly is produced by substituting inappropriate words or by changing word order within text. Our results suggest that it is extremely unlikely that this decrement stems from the general attentional demand of carrying out a secondary task since tapping at the same rate as subjects were required to subvocalise produced no decrement. The possibility that articulatory suppression may be affecting performance because of its auditory characteristics was explored by presenting irrelevant speech during the reading task. We obtained no evidence for a disrupting effect of concurrent irrelevant speech. It therefore appears likely that our effects are attributable to the tendency for suppression to interfere with the translation of print into an articulatory code. Since none of our studies show any tendency for articulatory suppression to influence speed of processing, it seems likely that the articulatory code is created in parallel with other processes in reading. (p. 452)

This research of Baddeley *et al.* (1981) seems to indicate that silent speech is helpful to a skimming process. It seemed to be helpful in an unexpected way, however. The research reviewed earlier seemed to indicate that lexical access was helped by silent speech because silent speech made lexical access faster. Since skimming relies upon lexical access, it is not clear why this skimming process operated just as fast when silent speech was suppressed. This is a logical inconsistency.

At this point, there is still no sound evidence that silent speech is harmful. In fact, it seems to be automatic and inevitable (see Tzeng & Wang, 1983). Silent speech may be helpful for recognizing some words that are known auditorily but not visually but most scanning and skimming involves words whose meaning can be lexically accessed and therefore the accompanying silent speech is neither helpful nor harmful to these processes. Therefore, silent speech is not harmful to the rate at which a scanning process or a skimming process operates.

RAUDING PROCESS

As explained earlier in Chapter 2, the rauding process involves lexical access, semantic encoding, plus sentence integration. The rauding process not only involves the understanding of individual sentences but also how they are related to understanding a larger body of material in the form of paragraphs or passages. Therefore, research that involves understanding isolated sentences is caught in an area between skimming processes and the rauding process. However, since there is so little research directly relevant to the rauding process and silent speech, this section will include those studies that involve the comprehension of the thoughts contained in isolated sentences.

The earlier discussed research of Kleiman (1975) will now be continued because there were two conditions in his Experiment III that are indirectly relevant to the rauding process. Subjects were asked to respond as quickly as possible as to whether sentences were meaningful (e.g., NOISY PARTIES DISTURB SLEEPING NEIGHBORS) or not meaningful (e.g., PIZZAS HAVE BEEN EATING JERRY); in this task, more than lexical access and semantic encoding are involved. There was also a kind of control condition that involved scanning plus semantic encoding; a target word was presented (e.g., GAMES) and the task was to decide whether or not a word appeared in the sentence that was in the same category as the target word (e.g., EVERYONE AT HOME PLAYED MONOPOLY: Yes). The shadowing condition considerably slowed the time required for the sentence acceptability task, by 28%, but it only slowed the word category task slightly, by 5%. Using the data and example sentences given by Kleiman, it was possible to estimate that the average reading rate for the acceptability task was 262 Wpm, a plausible rate for college students to operate their rauding process (see Chapter 2).

Kleiman interpreted his results as indicating that silent speech is an aid to memory and that is why the suppression of it slowed the acceptability task which depends on all the words in the sentence being stored prior to determining acceptability. Translated, these data of Kleiman's can be interpreted as indicating that silent speech is helpful to the rauding process because rauding functions much slower if silent speech is disrupted.

There are other aspects of Kleiman's findings that add to the inconsistencies noted earlier in connection with scanning and skimming. He suggested that his data indicate that visual coding without silent speech is faster for lexical access and that ". . . speech recoding is used only when necessary; that is, when the capacity of temporary storage for visually coded words gets overloaded" (p. 337). This puts him in conflict with D. E. Meyer et al. (1974) who concluded that the recoding of silent speech was faster than visual recoding. But, this puts him in agreement with Baddeley et al. (1981) who found that suppression of silent speech did not make a typical skimming process operate any slower. Kleiman says that it is an interesting possibility that ". . . while skimming the reader does not recode, since it is a time consuming process" (p. 337). This latter statement of Kleiman's is especially noteworthy for several reasons. First, he is suggesting that individuals do not use silent speech while skimming because silent speech would make skimming slower. The research reviewed earlier by Baddeley *et al.* (1981), reported 6 years after Kleiman (1975), found no change in skimming rate due to suppression. But the Baddeley *et al.* subjects were evidently using silent speech during this skimming process, otherwise there is no readily apparent explanation as to why their errors increased during suppression (remember several alternative hypotheses, such as attention, were considered to be ruled out by subsequent experiments). Second, Baddeley *et al.* (1981) did not consider their own research as an investigation of skimming; instead they called it fluent reading although they were aware that their data might not generalize to what they called "normal reading." Third, what Kleiman (1975) called skimming might be quite different from the typical skimming processes described herein. It might be helpful if some of the more precise definitions used in rauding theory were universally adopted to reduce confusions among terms such as normal reading, fluent reading, and skimming.

At this point, Kleiman's research seems to indicate that the memory storage requirements of the rauding process are helped by silent speech so that it cannot proceed as fast without silent speech. This means that the rauding process, Gear 3, is slowed when individuals do not use silent speech.

In 1977, Levy presented the results of a series of silent speech studies culminating in one experiment that very likely involved the rauding process. She asked college students to read passages each containing seven sentences. In the thematic condition, the sentences were presented in a meaningful order with a title. In the unrelated condition the sentences were presented in a randomized order. Each sentence was presented on a card for 2 seconds; using the two-example passages as representative of average sentence length, the average reading rate was estimated to be 233 Wpm. This rate is a plausible lower limit for college students to operate their rauding process but it is also a plausible rate for a learning process. The task for the subjects was to read each passage and then answer yes or no to whether a test sentence had appeared in the passage in an identical form. Some of the test sentences were not identical because a word had been changed that preserved the meaning and other test sentences were not identical because the meaning had been changed. This task (a) would not be conducive to skimming, (b) would not be likely to induce a learning process because the sentences would be easy for college students to understand, and (c) would not be conducive to a memorizing process because of the 2 second time limit to read each sentence. Given that this researcher was not attempting to design a study of the rauding process, *per se*, this study seems about as well designed for this purpose as it is reasonable to expect.

To investigate silent speech, Levy used a shadowing task consisting of counting ". . . softly from 1 to 10, repeatedly and as quickly as possible . . ." (p. 628). The results indicated that the accuracy with which subjects could identify changed sentences was better with the thematic passages as compared to the unrelated passages, as would be expected. The most important finding relevant to silent speech was that when it was suppressed by shadowing, accuracy dropped considerably. Silent speech seemed to help accuracy whether the test sentence involved a lexical change or a semantic change. Levy commented as follows:

> To summarize the present findings, Experiment I documented a reliable deficit in fluent reading when speech recoding was suppressed. This suppression decrement did not occur in an analogous listening task. Experiment II demonstrated that the speech interference is nontrivial, in that it does not succumb to practice effects, nor does it disappear when subjects are free to read at their chosen rate. Experiment III illustrated that this speech interference effect occurs even when meaningful passages are read. Meaningfulness aids reading in that it makes the material more memorable, but it does not lead to the by-passing or attenuation of speech processing, as evidenced by the occurrence of the suppression decrement. (p. 635)

Levy also related her research results to bottom-up, top-down, and interactive processes in reading. She suggested that her thematic effect is a top-down effect and the silent speech effect is a bottom-up effect. She concluded that "the present data clearly support an additive, rather than compensatory, relationship between speech and meaning processing" (p. 637).

Slowiaczek and Clifton (1980) conducted two experiments that appear to meet the requirement for involving the rauding process; only the second will be reviewed here. College students were given 2 seconds to read each sentence in passages that were 70 sentences long. There was also a comparable listening condition. The four passages used were relatively easy for college students, judging from the example sentences given, e.g., "The outgoing woman suggested a rendezvous." Each sentence was presented on a computer monitor for 2 seconds. From the shortest and longest sentences presented in the example, it could be estimated that the rates varied from 230 Wpm to 270 Wpm, again plausible lower rates for college students to operate their rauding process (see Table 2.2). The shadowing technique used was to say "colacolacola" continuously. The tests for accuracy of comprehension involved the presentation of sentences that either did or did not change the meaning of what was presented in the passage. For example, one test sentence was "The local girl suggested a rendezvous" and the correct answer was "yes" because this sentence did not change the meaning from what was stated in the passage. This kind of question was the easiest because it involved only the change of a single concept in a sentence. Other test sentences required the integration of information across sentences.

As for the results of Slowiaczek and Clifton, the test sentences that required the integration of information across sentences had much lower scores under the shadowing. They summarized their results as follows:

> In these experiments, reading for meaning was severely impaired when subvocalization was suppressed. Listening comprehension was also reduced by suppressing subvocalization, but the effect was much smaller.
>
> Our experiments demonstrated that although understanding individual concepts might be possible without subvocalization, combining concepts and integrating ideas does require subvocalization. (p. 580)

These data of Levy's, Kleiman's, and Slowiaczek and Clifton's indicate that the rauding process, Gear 3, is helped by silent speech. From the research of Kleiman, it appears that if the rauding process is forced to proceed at a certain average rate of comprehension that is reasonable for it to operate, then the accuracy of comprehension will be higher when accompanied by silent speech.

LEARNING AND MEMORIZING PROCESSES

As was mentioned earlier, it is easier to make a theoretical discrimination between learning processes and memorizing processes based upon real world activities than it is to make this distinction when confronted with experiments that were not designed with this distinction in mind. No experiments on silent speech were found that seemed to induce learning processes without also meeting the criteria for inducing a memorizing process. Therefore, the following research is all in the category of learning and memorizing processes.

Hardyck and Petrinovich (1970) argued that in the field of remedial reading, teachers are advised that they should help students eliminate their silent speech so they can attain a rapid reading speed. To investigate the helpfulness or harmfulness of silent speech, they asked college students in a remedial English class to read an easy essay, 3975 words long, and a difficult essay, 3443 words long, while samples of EMGs were being recorded. All subjects had been screened to eliminate habitual subvocalizers. One group read normally while the records were being taken.

Another group was given feedback designed to reduce or eliminate sub-vocalization. A control group received feedback based upon the amplitude of the forearm flexor instead of laryngeal. All groups were administered a 25-item multiple-choice test on the content of each essay when they finished reading it. It seems likely that this 25-item test would induce a learning or memorizing process in their readers.

They found that there was more silent speech for the difficult material than for the easy material for all three groups. However, the increase in silent speech due to reading was much less for the feedback group, indicating that feedback indeed reduced silent speech. However, this reduction in silent speech for the feedback group was accompanied by a notable reduction in comprehension test scores for the feedback group when they were reading the difficult material. For the easy material, there were no differences among the three groups on the test.

These investigators did not present any analyses of their reading rate data but they did present their mean reading times, in minutes, for each passage read by each group. The normal, feedback, and control groups read the easy passage at 173, 196, and 176 wpm, respectively, and the corresponding rates for the difficult passage were 141, 155, and 147 wpm. From the brief description of the passages, these rates were converted into Wpm (using the equations in Chapter 2) by assuming that the easy passage was at the eighth grade level of difficulty and the difficult passage at the fourteenth grade level; these corresponding rates were 162, 184, and 165 Wpm for the easy passage and 143, 157, and 149 Wpm for the difficult passage. Since these students were in a remedial English class, the predicted learning process rate of 200 Wpm should be adjusted downward so the rates of 162, 184, and 165 Wpm for the easy passages are quite compatible with expected rate. Also, the somewhat slower rates of 143, 157, and 149 Wpm are reasonable for a reduction in rate due to a shift from relatively easy to relatively hard material. The normal and control groups read the easy passage at approximately the same rates (162 and 165 Wpm) while the feedback group was induced to read about 13% faster (184 Wpm). The multiple-choice test on the easy material did not appear to be sensitive to this small increase in rate. For the hard material, the normal group slowed down their rate by 12%, the feedback group slowed by 15%, and the control group slowed down by 10%. Still, the feedback group was reading 10% faster than the control group. This means that the group that had their silent speech disrupted by feedback indeed read the hard material 10% faster than the control group but their accuracy of comprehension scores notably decreased.

In contrast to some of the earlier quoted comments made from papers that Hardyck authored (with others) that suggested that silent speech was harmful, the conclusion he drew from these results suggests otherwise. For example, his discussion of the above results was initiated by the following comment: "These results support the interpretation that subvocal speech as measured here is a useful stimulus input capable of mediating a cognitive response" (p. 651).

The above data may be interpreted as indicating that indeed silent speech slows certain learning and memorizing processes but the slowing down serves a useful purpose when the material is difficult because more can be comprehended. But what about the easy material? Reducing silent speech was accompanied by an increase in rate with no measured loss in recall. Could this mean that silent speech is harmful when studying easy material? This would be a dangerous conclusion. Nothing was reported about this 25-item multiple-choice test and it could easily be that the test was so easy that it was not sensitive to the losses associated with this small 10% increase in rate. Still, on the basis of these data alone, the most that it is reasonable to conclude is that silent speech was helpful when studying difficult materials and that rate seemed to increase slightly when silent speech was reduced.

P. M. Cunningham and Cunningham (1978) investigated the effect of unpronounceable words in reading passages to pass a test on their meaning. They created a passage that contained short paragraphs describing the characteristics of six fictitious fish. For one-half of the subjects, the names of the fish were pronounceable: doffit, dulmet, mintex, mastib, pontud, and pemtad. For the other half, the names were not pronounceable: dfofti, dlumte, mnitxe, msatbi, pnotdu, and pmetda. They reasoned that if fluent reading proceeds directly from print to meaning without silent speech then it should make no difference whether the words were pronounceable or not. An example paragraph from the passage is presented below:

> The pontud is a famous fish because of the way its body lights up when it falls in love with another pontud. Scientists have tried to figure out how to make flashlights work on the same chemical that the pontud has, but they have not succeeded. It is a beautiful sight to see two pontuds, swimming along blinking at each other. (p. 117)

Before reading the passage, all subjects had to be able to match the printed names of the fish correctly with their pictures, twice; this procedure familiarized the subjects with the orthographic irregularities of the printed words.

For this experiment, there was a graduate student group and an elementary student group. All subjects were told "to read the passage so that after reading they could point to the fish that had particular traits" (p. 118). This task and instructions would likely induce a learning process, and this inference was supported by the slow reading rates reported. Cunningham and Cunningham reported the time in minutes to read the passage, which they included, verbatim; it contained 356 Words so their times were converted into Wpm. The graduate students who read the pronounceable version had a rate of 185 Wpm and those who read the unpronounceable version had a rate of 156 Wpm, 16% slower. Not only was the unpronounceable version read more slowly but the mean number of the six fish correctly named after reading was only 2.7 for the unpronounceable group as compared to 4.3 for the pronounceable group.

These graduate students, who were studying passages that were easy for them, i.e., around 8th grade level in difficulty, were not only slowed 16% by the unpronounceable names of the fish but were also much less successful in learning which characteristics went with each fish, even with the extended time.

For the elementary students, the material was much more difficult relative to their ability. The rate for the subjects who were given the pronounceable passage was 159 Wpm and the rate for the subjects who were given the unpronounceable passage as 134 Wpm, again 16% slower. On the naming task, the unpronounceable group scored lower (1.7) than the pronounceable group (2.6). These results indicate that the unpronounceable names slowed elementary students and resulted in less learning.

These data indicate that silent speech is helpful not only to elementary students while engaged in a learning process, but it is also helpful to graduate students while engaged in a learning process. Even graduate students who are highly skilled readers benefit from silent speech during learning. Furthermore, these data indicate that when some of the words are made into a form that cannot easily be pronounced during silent speech, then reading rate is slowed somewhat, 16%, but performance on the criterion task for studying is drastically lowered.

These two studies, taken together with all of the other research, force the conclusion that silent speech is helpful to learning and memorizing processes. Furthermore, there is no compelling evidence that these processes could operate faster with the same positive effect if silent speech were somehow reduced or eliminated. Instead, it appears that the beneficial effects of an increase in the intensity of silent speech almost automatically means a slowing of the learning or memorizing processes. Yet, if the goal is a certain level of high performance on the criterion task, then this slowing of rate associated with a higher intensity of silent speech is probably the fastest way of achieving the criterion performance.

Riley and Lowe (1981) attempted to study the effects of enhancing vs. reducing silent speech during reading. They were interested in difficulty of the material, comprehension, and especially reading rate. From the description of the task it seemed likely that a learning process would be induced. Since the study seemed to be designed to produce results more relevant to learning process rates, it was enthusiastically scrutinized. Unfortunately, no data were presented, such as means or SDs; only the p values were made available from statistical significance tests of the differences among four groups of ten subjects each. The lack of statistical significance does not justify the conclusions of no differences, and the finding of statistical significance does not necessarily justify the conclusion of important differences (see Carver, 1978b). The publication of a research report without data, such as this one, is a scientific oddity that should be made even more rare in the future.

Waters, Komoda, and Arbuckle (1985) studied the effect of silent speech upon reading rate by using a shadowing task and statistically controlling for cognitive processing capacity. They contended that the shadowing effect found in previous research might have been artifactual. Since shadowing involves attention that might distract from general processing capacity, previous decrements associated with shadowing might be due to this factor rather than a disruption of silent speech. They investigated this hypothesis in four experiments involving many different experimental conditions. This review will focus upon their three most important experimental conditions, presented in Experiments 1 and 2.

Waters *et al.* asked college students to read 150-word passages that were graded for difficulty into easy, medium, and hard. After the subjects finished reading the passages that were projected on a screen, they were asked to write down as much as they could freely recall. From these instructions and objective consequences, it would be predicted that a memorizing process would be used. It should be noted that reading was a secondary task in these experimental conditions. Two primary tasks were tone tracking and shadowing. In tone tracking, the subject was to listen to tones and push one of three buttons depending upon the type of tone; this task involved neither verbal stimuli nor an articulatory response. In shadowing the subject was to listen to random digits and say them aloud; this task involved both verbal stimuli and an articulatory response. In a control condition, there was no tone tracking or shadowing. However, in all three of these conditions there was a third task involving reaction time to a dot appearing on a screen (using a foot pedal to respond). This third task allowed for statistically adjusting the mean reading rates (by ANCOVA) on the basis of a measure of cognitive capacity. The reasoning was that if shadowing was interfering with needed silent speech, then reading rate under the silent speech condition should be slower than the control condition but reading rate under the tone tracking condition should be equal to the control condition as long as rate was statistically controlled for differences in the cognitive capacity of the task.

The results of Waters *et al.* were mostly in accordance with the above hypothesis, as the data presented in Table 4.1 indicate. Notice that when the rates were averaged over the three difficulty levels, the mean rate under the control condition was 136 wpm which is very close to the 138 Wpm rate predicted in Table 2.2 for a memorizing process. Also notice that the mean rate for tone tracking was almost exactly the same as under the control condition (136 versus 134 wpm), and this indicates that tone tracking did not have a detrimental effect upon reading rate, when rate was controlled for cognitive capacity differences in the tasks. Most importantly, notice that shadowing did have a detrimental effect upon reading rate when compared to the control condition (115 versus 136 wpm), when rate was controlled for cognitive capacity.

These data of Waters *et al.* appear to provide strong support for the helpfulness of silent speech when a memorizing process is operating. However, it should be noted that Waters *et al.* presented their data in seconds, not wpm, and they did not average over the three difficulty levels from two experiments. Furthermore, and most importantly, Waters *et al.* came to the opposite conclusion. They concluded that shadowing was not different from the control condition, that shadowing does not interfere with reading, and that silent speech seems to play a minor role in skilled reading. This conclusion was based upon tests of statistical significance for each difficulty level of material. Elsewhere, Carver (1978b) has argued that statistical significance testing involves a

Table 4.1
Reading Rates, in wpm, under Three Experimental Conditions[a]

Passage difficulty	Control	Tone tracking	Shadowing
Easy (Exp. 1)	173	156	152
Medium (Exp. 2)	130	142	105
Hard (Exp. 1)	105	105	87
Mean	136	134	115

[a] From Waters *et al.* (1985).

corrupt form of the scientific method because (a) large, important differences may not be statistically significant, and (b) trivial, unimportant differences can be statistically significant. In the present situation, it seems reasonable to assert that the data of Waters *et al.* may be alternatively interpreted as providing strong support for the helpfulness of silent speech when a memorizing process is being used.

In summary, silent speech appears to be helpful to the operation of Gears 1 and 2, the learning and recalling processes.

CONCLUSIONS

Before drawing conclusions about silent speech and reading rate, the ideas expressed by Perfetti (1985) should be recognized. He argued for a speech activation continuum that ranges from zero, or resting level, up to overt speech. He contended that phonetic activation, a low level of speech activation, automatically accompanies lexical access. It facilitates comprehension by aiding immediate memory for what has been encoded in earlier words or sentences. According to Perfetti, this low level of speech activation will not show up in EMG activity because it is below the threshold for the motor components of speech. Above this threshold, at a higher level of speech activation is "subvocal speech." He argues persuasively that support for these ideas comes from such studies as the tongue twister research of McCutchen and Perfetti (1982) and from the research on backward visual masking of words by Naish (1980). Perfetti concluded that ". . . speech processes occur as support for memory and comprehension" (p. 67).

On the basis of the preceding research evidence relevant to silent speech and reading, the following conclusions have been drawn:

1. Silent speech is an aid to thought under almost any cognitive activity conceivable, especially during reading. The reason that silent speech is especially helpful to the more powerful reading processes, Gears 1–3, is that it facilitates short-term memory for building the complete thought from the first word in a sentence to the last.

2. Silent speech is involved in all reading processes in varying degrees of intensity. The more difficult the task for the reader, the more intense will be the involvement of silent speech with an accompanying reduction in reading rate and an accompanying improvement in performance.

3. The involvement of silent speech in many scanning and skimming processes, Gears 4 and 5, is at a low level of intensity and is thereby

often undetected. Silent speech will have less of an effect at the relatively high rates and low storage capacity requirements associated with these faster but less powerful processes.

4. Given the concept of varying intensities of silent speech, given that silent speech is more intense and detectable at slower rates, given that silent speech is an aid to memory, and given that reading rate slows with each lower gear of the reading process, then it is not surprising that: (a) there is little or no ambiguity about silent speech as an aid to the rauding process and to the more powerful processes of learning and memorizing, and (b) there should be little surprise that the role of silent speech during the faster and less powerful processes of scanning and skimming is still somewhat ambiguous and seemingly inconsistent.

5. There is no solid evidence that silent speech is harmful, or that it unnecessarily slows the rauding process, the most important of all reading processes. Instead, silent speech helps the rauding process proceed at its most efficient rate—in terms of most thoughts in sentences comprehended per the amount of time spent.

6. Efforts by educators to get students to reduce their silent speech will be potentially harmful to the rauding process, harmful to learning processes, and harmful to memorizing processes. Also, such efforts may even be harmful to scanning and skimming processes. Given the extensive amount of research supporting the helpful nature of silent speech to reading, any educational program or research based upon an hypothesis that it is harmful should justify the rationale for this hypothesis after reviewing these contrary hypotheses and their supporting research evidence.

Finally, to suggest that the rauding process, Gear 3, would operate faster if we could somehow eliminate silent speech appears to be similar to suggesting that airplanes could fly faster if we could eliminate their heavy wings. Wings help the airplane go fast, and silent speech helps the rauding process go fast.

5

EYE MOVEMENTS

INTRODUCTION

In a review of eye movement research, Tinker (1958) noted that ". . . some writers still adhere to the mistaken notion that training eye movements as such is an effective way to improve reading" (p. 229). Tinker's position is very much a part of conventional wisdom regarding the relationship between eye movements and efficient reading; however, eye movements do affect reading rate. Therefore, research on eye movements is fundamental to the focus of this review of research and to rauding theory.

At the outset, it will be helpful to review some basic concepts and terminology. When the eyes are moving, there is no clear vision for printed material. Words are only perceived when the eyes are not moving or are "fixated." The short jerky movements of the eye across a line of print are called "saccades." Saccades may be forward (left-to-right in English text) or backward (right-to-left). A saccade that moves the focus of clear vision to words previously encountered are called "regressions." The area around the fixation point, which is perceived in the fovia of the eye, is the most clearly perceived; the area around this point wherein information about words can be used during reading is called the "perceptual span."

Rate can be increased (a) by stopping the eye for a shorter length of time, i.e., shorter fixation durations, (b) by making longer eye movements, saccades, (c) by making fewer regressions, and (d) by increasing the perceptual span. With regard to the perceptual span, Woodworth (1938) assumed that ". . . the subject sees ten letters at each fixation" (p. 55), and this same assumption was made earlier by Judd and Buswell (1922). More recently, F. Smith (1972b), among others, has contended that individuals perceive groups of words such as phrases at a single fixation. Later, we will review more recent research relevant to the length of the perceptual span, fixation duration, saccades, and regressions as they impinge upon reading rate.

Some readers may be concerned about whether the reading that occurs while eye movements are being recorded will generalize to real world reading. However, this concern was dispelled for most researchers years ago when Gilbert and Gilbert (1942) found that reading in front of an eye movement camera was much the same as reading away from it.

This review will again be divided into the same five basic reading processes noted earlier: scanning, skimming, rauding, learning, and memorizing. Before starting those sections however, a lengthy and historically important eye movement study by I. H. Anderson (1937) will be reviewed because it is directly relevant to these basic reading processes.

ANDERSON DATA

Introduction

I. H. Anderson (1937) investigated the eye movements of university freshmen, separated into good and poor readers according to scores on the Iowa Silent Reading Test. Anderson investigated the effects of varying the difficulty of material and varying the purpose for reading upon eye movements and reading rate. The methods he used were patterned after a similar study conducted by Walker (1933) in the same reading clinic at the University of Iowa. Walker studied good readers and Anderson replicated the study using poor readers. Anderson's study will be reported upon in detail because it included the data from both the good and the poor readers.

Method

The good readers were 50 freshmen who scored in the top 10% on both the Iowa Silent Reading Test and the University of Iowa Qualifying Examination. The poor readers were 50 freshmen who scored in the bottom 25% on the Iowa Silent Reading Test. The passages read by both the good readers and poor readers were at three levels of difficulty: I, II, and III. Passage I was taken from an elementary primer, the elementary passage. Passage II was equal in difficulty to a college freshman textbook, the freshman passage. Passage III was taken from a very difficult advanced text, the graduate passage. These college students were instructed "to read the passage once, to make necessary regressions within any one line, but not to return to a previous line" (p. 4). The subjects were instructed to read as they "normally would read such material"

(p. 5), and this was called reading ". . . to obtain a moderate knowledge of the text" (p. 5). A test with four true–false questions on each passage was administered as a "modest comprehension requirement to insure a serious attitude toward the experiment" (p. 5). These instructions and objective consequences would likely induce the rauding process with a predicted rate of 263 Wpm (from Table 2.1) for average college freshmen reading the relatively easy material in the elementary passage. The rates in Wpm for both groups are given below:

Passage	Good readers	Poor readers
Elementary	292	191
Freshman	266	188
Graduate	215	175

These rates in Wpm were estimated from the rates given by Anderson in the printers units of ems per minute using the 2.6 ems per Word conversion factor (see Equation 2.8).

It seems reasonable to assert that these above average freshmen (good readers) were in fact using their rauding process on the elementary passage because their rate (292 Wpm) was above the rate predicted for average freshmen (263 Wpm). The freshman passages probably forced these good readers into a learning process part of the time and lowered their rate to 266 Wpm. For the relatively hard graduate passage, they would likely shift down to a learning process all of the time, and their rate of 215 Wpm is a reasonable learning process rate for above average freshmen. The poor readers changed their rates only slightly from a high of 191, to a low of 175. These poor readers may have adopted a learning process as their typical or normal rate no matter what the difficulty level, but this is speculation since there is no separate estimate of their rauding rate available. Later, in Chapter 9, a more detailed theoretical explanation will be given for the relatively low and constant rate of the Poor Readers.

Processing Types

The above results reported by Anderson were only ancillary to the main reason for reviewing this research. He and Walker also studied what was called "three silent reading attitudes." The term "attitudes" used by Anderson and Walker can be easily translated into what has been called "goals" since Chapter 2. Each of the three goals was applied to a different passage—all of comparable difficulty—Passages II, IV, and V. Notice that Passage II was the freshman passage noted earlier so all passages were college freshman textbook material. Passage IV was read "... to secure only the general idea of the contents" (p. 12)—General Idea Goal. Passage II was read to obtain a moderate knowledge of the text—Moderate Knowledge Goal. Passage V was "... studied to obtain a knowledge as complete and detailed as possible from one reading" (p. 12)—Detailed Knowledge Goal. Figure 5.1 contains a graphic depiction of the conditions under which the five passages were read. Notice that difficulty level increases from left to right while the goal stays constant, and the demand associated with each goal increases from top to bottom while the difficulty stays constant.

For the good readers, the General Idea Goal would likely elicit a skimming process at least part of the time so it is not surprising that the good readers had their highest rate under this condition, 339 Wpm for Pas-

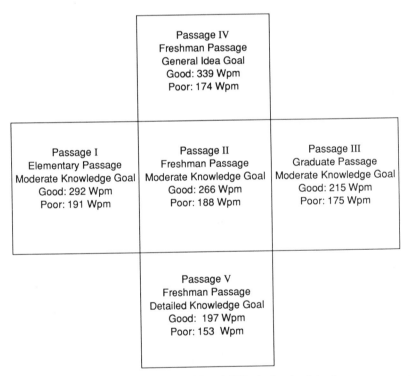

Figure 5.1 A graphic depiction of the goals and difficulty levels of the five passages used in I. H. Anderson's (1937) study of good and poor readers.

sage IV. The Moderate Knowledge Goal would involve a component that was less demanding in terms of outcomes, and rate dropped to the 266 Wpm value which is close to the typical rauding process rate for college students, as noted earlier. The Detailed Knowledge Goal would likely induce a learning process so the 197 Wpm rate obtained would be expected.

For the poor readers, the rates for the same three goals were 174, 188, and 153, respectively. Thus, the poor readers varied their rates very little compared to the good readers and may be faulted by some for not being flexible in their reading. Yet, it seems likely that this freshman textbook material could have been quite difficult for these poor reading freshmen so that the best they could do under any condition was operate their regular learning process, as hypothesized earlier, at its concomitant slow rate.

This research of I. H. Anderson's (1937) and Walker's (1933) appears to be the first on record indicating how different goals produce different reading processes in good readers, which in turn proceed at different rates. The good readers appeared to operate their rauding process on the relatively easy material (292 Wpm). They shifted down to a learning process when the material became relatively difficult (215 Wpm). They also shifted down to a learning process when the instructions were to obtain complete and detailed knowledge (197 Wpm). And, they shifted up to a skimming process when the instructions were to get only a general idea of the content (339 Wpm). Now, the eye movement data associated with these skimming, rauding, and learning processes will be scrutinized.

Eye Movements

Both the good and poor readers exhibited the most irregularity while reading Passage V, which was a freshman passage presented under the Detailed Knowledge Goal. The irregularity was described as ". . . an increased number of forward and regressive shifts of long and variable duration" (p. 17). Under this condition the individuals would likely be engaged in a learning process so they would be expected to pause longer and regress so as to better remember the ideas. They would be expected to fail to understand some sentences and regress to test hypotheses designed to solve the problem of integrating the words into the complete thoughts represented by the sentences.

Eye Movements of Good Readers

The fixation duration of the good readers increased as the difficulty of the passage increased and as the goal became more demanding. As the process shifts to lower and more powerful gears to accomplish the goal, the average time spent looking at each word increases.

The variability (SD) in the fixation durations for each individual increased as difficulty increased and as the goal became more demanding. This result suggests that as the process moves to a lower gear there are bigger differences between the shortest times spent on each word and the longest times spent on each word. Probably, the variability is almost entirely due to many of the fixation durations getting much longer, rather than many also getting shorter.

The mean length of the forward saccades decreased from 1.65 Words for the elementary passage to 1.56 Words for the graduate passage and it also decreased from 1.74 Words for the General Idea Goal to 1.50 Words for the Detailed Knowledge Goal. (Note: As mentioned earlier, Anderson measured this length in ems which were first transformed into characters by multiplying by 2.3 and then transformed into standard length words by dividing by 6.) This result suggests that as a reading process moves down to lower gears the eyes are thrown a bit less further down the line, on the average. However, since 1.74 Words is about 10 characters and 1.56 Words is about 9 characters, it can be seen that the difference between the longest saccades for the highest gear used in this research and the shortest saccades for the lowest is only 1 character space on the average—a small difference. Thus, it appears that these good readers tend to modify their process in a way that involves spending more time on each of the words they look at, rather than taking in more words with each fixation. In turn, this suggests that forward saccades had little to do with changes in rate since the distance the eyes moved forward remained relatively constant as rate increased.

The mean number of regressions per line increased from 0.44 for the elementary passage to 0.92 for the graduate passage and from 0.33 for the General Idea Goal to 1.02 for the Detailed Knowledge Goal. These data indicate that as the goal becomes more difficult to achieve there are more occasions where individuals need to reread something that was read before. Indeed, as the demands associated with the goals increase, then there are more occasions whereby the goal is not met and the individual must go back and try again. It should not be forgotten that these subjects were told to read the passage only once and not to return to a previous line.

These eye movement results for the good readers seem to indicate that their eyes move down a line in a rather habitual way for all the processes studied. As the individual shifts down to lower gears, more time is spent each time the eyes stop and there are more times that the words are reread. Stated differently, these individuals slowed their reading rate by spending more time looking at words and by rereading words more often; they did not increase their rate much by moving their eyes down a line further each time they moved them forward. Thus, forward eye movements *per se* had little to do with rate while backward eye movements (regressions) were a major factor influencing rate differences among these processes.

Eye Movements of Poor Readers

The results and generalizations for the poor reader group are not as easy to summarize as for the good reader group, above. The patterns for the three difficulty levels were exactly the same as for the good readers. However, the patterns were not the same for the three purposes because the poor readers read a freshman passage under the Moderate Knowledge Goal Faster than a freshman passage under the General Idea Goal (188 versus 174 Wpm). However, the four eye movement measures changed in parallel with the reading rate changes just exactly as they did with the good readers, with only one exception. Thus, it appears that the generalizations made earlier about eye movements and reading rate for good readers also apply equally well to the poor readers except the relationships are not as clear cut because there is less variability in rate for the poor readers. Probably, there was less variability in rate for the poor readers because they have adopted a learning process all the time even when the material is relatively easy and they are instructed to only obtain a general idea.

Concluding Comments

Although conducted about 50 years ago, this 1933 and 1937 research on eye movements has helped set the background for interpreting all subsequent research relevant to reading rate in general, and eye movements in particular. It appears that the instructions, the objective consequences, and the relative difficulty of the material influence the goals of the subject. These goals elicit different gears associated with reading processes. The more difficult the task is, the more time will be spent looking at the words, and the more often the words will be reread; the lower the gear used to achieve the goal the longer the fixation durations and the greater number of regressions. The slower rates associated with the more powerful processes are not associated with any important increase in forward saccade length thus suggesting that the eyes move across the line in a relatively constant pattern in terms of fixating upon almost every word no matter which one of these processes is being executed.

With this background, the stage is now set for interpreting more recent research relevant to each of the basic reading processes. However, the scanning process will not be reviewed because no eye movement studies were found which seemed directly relevant to a scanning process. After the selected eye movement studies relevant to the skimming, rauding, learning, and memorizing processes have been reviewed, this chapter will be closed by one section devoted to conclusions and another section devoted to implications.

SKIMMING PROCESSES

Walker (1933) conducted a major study of the effects of goals and difficulty, as was mentioned earlier. One small part of that study involved a condition which he called skimming. However, the details of the instructions were somewhat vague, and the rate was only 296 Wpm for college students. Walker himself devoted only one paragraph to the results and in that paragraph he noted that "the results seem to contradict the general meaning of the word 'skimming,' but only apply to this definition of skimming" (p. 112). His research has already been reviewed in connection with I. H. Anderson (1937), earlier. This research is being noted again mainly because it seems to be the first that purported to study eye movements during a skimming process.

Laycock (1955) studied the eye movements of 37 "flexible" reading college students and compared them to 35 "inflexible" reading college students. These two groups were selected from the extremes of a larger group of 492, which included freshmen, upper classmen, and graduate students. They were selected on the basis of whether they could read quickly when asked to do so; this was measured by the difference between (a) their rate when asked ". . . to read in order to answer simple questions afterwards" and (b) their rate when asked ". . . to read as fast as possible without missing important points" (p. 312). These two goal conditions were called "Normal" and "Advanced," respectively. After the two groups had been selected, the experimental situation was similar to the selection situation except eye movements were measured in the experimental situation.

The Normal Goal would likely produce a rauding process at least as long as the difficulty level of the material was not higher than the ability level of the subjects. The difficulty of the selection passages was described as easy material adapted from scripts used in a radio program. One passage was on little known foods and minerals in the ocean and the other was on earthquake research. These passages that were used to select the subjects were described as harder than the actual passages used in the research. There were comprehension questions given afterwards but nothing was stated about how many, what kind, or what scores resulted. Thus, it seems reasonable to assume that the questions were relatively insignificant. Under the Normal Goal, the flexible group read at 356 wpm and the inflexible group read at 322 wpm. From the instructions, objective consequences, and relative difficulty, it would be predicted that these students would adopt a rauding process so these rates of 356 and 322 wpm would not be unreasonable (see Chapter 2) given that many of them could be graduate students. Under the Advanced Goal, the flexible group increased their rate to 533 wpm (50% increase) and the inflexible group increased their rate to 428 Wpm (33% increase). Thus, it is reasonable to infer that the Advanced Goal induced a skimming process, Gear 4.

This research of Laycock's allows us to find out what happens to eye movements when subjects are induced to switch from the rauding process (Normal Goal) to a skimming process (Advanced Goal). The mean fixation duration decreased (10% for the flexible group and 4% for the inflexible group), and the mean number of regressions decreased (24% for the flexible group and 17% for the inflexible group). These changes are approximately equal for the two groups and there appear to be no differences between the two groups important enough to prevent them being treated as equal in the subsequent generalizations.

It appears that a switch to a skimming process with its accompanying 33–50% increase in rate was accomplished by drastically reducing, by about 20%, the number of times words are reread. There was also a 4–10% reduction in the time spent looking at the words when the eyes were stopped. The mean number of fixations decreased substantially, 17–24%, and this decrease was only partially accounted for by the lesser number of regressions. It can be estimated from these data that the forward saccade was lengthened by 23% and 14% in the two groups, respectively. So, it appears that the switch from the rauding process to the skimming process was mainly accomplished by increasing the forward saccades, i.e., forcing the eyes to move across the line a bit further, so it took fewer fixations to finish the passage. But, the increase in rate was also aided by spending less time fixating at each stop and by reducing the amount of rereading.

In general, these data are in accordance with the Anderson results discussed earlier except that the good readers in that research did not substantially change their saccade length. Perhaps the difference was related to the fact that their mean rates varied from 197 to 339 Wpm compared to 356 to 533 wpm in Laycock's research.

This research of Laycock's was the only research found which purported to provide evidence directly relevant to reading rate and eye movements during a skimming process.

RAUDING PROCESS

Seibert (1943) measured the eye movements of 60 eighth grade students who were given 300-word passages at the eighth grade level of difficulty. The passages were in six different subject matter areas: mathematics, biography, adventure, physical science, history, and geography. The only instructions reported were as follows: "The subject was told before reading the selection that he would be asked to answer questions on it" (p. 38). There were at least 14 and at most 24 questions on each of these six passages. Not enough information was given to be highly confident about which basic reading process would likely have been used. Since there appears to have been little or no direction given about how to read, this would likely induce a rauding process. On the other hand, the lengthy comprehension tests may induce a learning process. The mean reading rate over all 60 students and all six passages was reported to be 183 wpm, which is about GE = 6 for a rauding process rate according to the data presented Table 2.1. So, it appears that these eighth grade students may have been reading a little slower (183 wpm) than the typical rauding rate of eighth graders (204 wpm) but they were reading at a rate plausible for their rauding process.

As for Seibert's results, the mean rates for the six passages in six different subject matter areas only ranged from 175 to 194; the slowest of the six mean rates was only 10% slower than the fastest. This indicates that the rate at which these eighth graders operated their rauding process was almost perfectly constant across six widely different subject matter areas.

Seibert also reported upon the rates for the 1st, 2nd, and 3rd 100-words in these 300-word passages. The three means were 182, 184, and 188, respectively. These data indicate almost perfect constancy of rate within the parts of the passage. These data establish the relative constancy of the rauding process for junior high students (a) across different subject matter areas, and (b) across the beginning, middle, and end of a 300-word passage.

In 1951, Morse, Ballantine, and Dixon each published three lengthy and separate research studies on eye movements that were republished together 17 years later as a book (Morse, Ballantine, & Dixon, 1968). In this section, two of these three studies will be briefly reviewed. One involved fifth and seventh grade pupils and another involved university professors and graduate students. The remaining study dealt with age changes and will be reviewed later in Chapter 11 on growth in reading rate.

Morse (1951) studied the eye movements of 54 fifth graders and 54 seventh graders who were reading at the fifth grade level and seventh grade level, respectively, according to reading achievement tests (also see Morse *et al.*, 1968). The fifth graders were given 300-word passages at the third, fifth, and seventh grade levels of difficulty while the seventh graders were given 300-word passages at the fifth, seventh, and ninth grade levels of difficulty. The unit of measurement was ems, which was converted into Wpm using their suggested conversion of 2.6 ems per Word (see Equation 2.8).

These students were instructed to read each selection just as they would read a story in a book. There were 15 yes–no and factual recall questions on each passage. The instructions would likely induce the rauding process but the objective consequences might induce a learning process.

The results obtained by Morse were as expected in that the seventh graders read both the fifth and seventh grade passages faster than the fifth graders, with fewer fixations per word, fewer regressions, and smaller fixation durations. Contrary to his expectations, however, there was no important change in the eye movements for either group as the difficulty level of the material increased. Also, rate (the composite of eye movements) stayed constant no matter what the difficulty level. This constancy in rate across difficulty levels (D_L) is evident when their data are plotted graphically; see Fig. 5.2. Notice the constancy in rate for the students who scored at the same ability level. At the fifth grade level, $A_L = 5$, the three rates were 154, 149, and 163 Wpm for the passages at $D_L = 3$, 5, and 7, respectively. These three rates for fifth graders were also very close to the predicted rauding rates for the fifth grade level presented in Table 2.1, i.e., 156 Wpm. From Fig. 5.2, the constancy in rate is also evident for those students at the seventh grade level, $A_L = 7$; the three rates were 185, 195, and 194 Wpm for passages at $D_L = 5$, 7, and 9, respectively. These three rates were also very close to the rauding rates predicted for the seventh grade level, i.e., 181 Wpm.

These data suggest that these students stayed in the rauding process, Gear 3, for all three levels of difficulty. The fifth graders read the passages at the third and seventh grade levels almost exactly the same way, and the seventh graders read the fifth and ninth grade level materials almost exactly the same way in terms of eye movements. This result is relevant to the earlier research presented in Chapter 3 on the effect of material difficulty, and provides support for Law I of rauding theory (see Chapter 2). This eye movement research involving passages at various difficulty levels predated the Carver (1971b) research and the G. R. Miller and Coleman (1971) research, which initiated the flurry of studies reviewed in Chapter 3 that established the constancy of reading rate

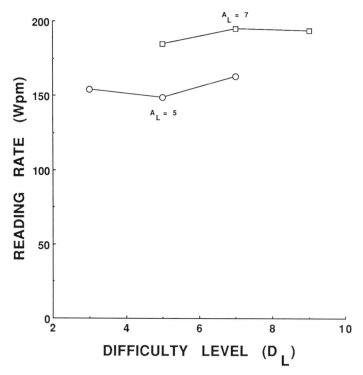

Figure 5.2 Reading rate, in Wpm, as a function of the difficulty level of the passage, D_L, for both fifth graders, $A_L = 5$, and seventh graders, $A_L = 7$. Data collected by Morse (1951).

across a range of difficulties. Those studies reviewed earlier did not involve any elementary or junior high students, however.

From this research of Morse it appears that there is evidence that children tend to adopt the rauding process under instructions to read normally, and this means that the eye movements do not change with changes in the difficulty of the material or with objective consequences that could induce a learning process.

W. R. Dixon (1951) wanted to find out if familiarity was a factor influencing eye movements and rate of reading (see also Morse *et al.*, 1968). He had two types of good readers, 16 professors and 16 graduate students in each of the departments of Education, Physics, and History; each was asked to read 200-word passages in the content areas of Education, Physics, and History. The passages were at about the eighth grade level of difficulty as measured by two readability formulas. He asked each subject to "read each passage through once as you normally would to understand the material" (p. 132). He administered five yes–no type questions on each passage. According to Morse *et al.* (1968), "the five questions on each passage were general rather than specific in nature, just enough to let the subject know that he was expected to read for meaning, but not enough to make him hyperconscious of the comprehension requirement" (p. 133). The instructions, the objective consequences, and the relative difficulty of the material appear to be optimal for eliciting the rauding process, Gear 3. Thus, it would be predicted that these exceptionally good readers would read in this situation at the estimated rate of graduate students, 324 Wpm from Table 2.1.

As for Dixon's results, there were two types of good readers in three departmental areas who were reading passages in three content areas, which yielded a total of 18 reading rate means. The lowest mean was 267 Wpm which was for graduate students in Physics reading an Education passage; the highest mean was 361 Wpm which was for Physics professors reading a Physics passage. The grand mean of the 18 means was 306 Wpm, which is close to the predicted rate of 324 Wpm. So, 300 Wpm seems to be about average for college seniors, university professors, and graduate students. There appears to be no question that these professors and graduate students should be among the best readers because they have chosen a career that involves reading and scholarship. Thus, the value of 300 Wpm that was chosen to represent the rate of college students operating their rauding process (see Table 2.2) seems to represent graduate students and college professors quite well. These data seem to indicate that there is a limit for rauding rate that does not increase with practice or age beyond that expected for a college senior.

Dixon found minor differences in rate associated with reading material in one's own field compared to other fields. The mean rate for subjects reading material *not* in their own field was 292 Wpm and the corresponding rate for subjects reading material in their own field was 13% higher at 334 Wpm. The results for eye movements generally paralleled those of rate with no important differences associated with type of material or the department of the reader. For example, all three of the professor groups made their fewest fixations and the fewest regressions on material in their own field.

The two preceding studies, first published in 1951 by Morse and Dixon, contain data that are in accordance with the earlier reported research that indicated that the rauding process operates at a relatively constant rate; these results extend this finding to elementary students, junior high students, graduate students, and college professors. These data also confirm that it is the relative constancy of eye movements that accounts for the constancy of reading rate for this particular process.

These data indicate that 300 Wpm is a reasonable rate for mature good readers to operate their rauding process since college professors and graduate students operated their rauding process at this rate. Also, there are no important changes in eye movements or rate when good readers such as university professors and graduate students read material in different areas of familiarity as long as they are executing their rauding process as they typically do when the material is relatively easy. Again, these data provide support for Law I of rauding theory (see Chapter 2).

Rayner (1975) gave 10 college students short paragraphs to read which contained 225 special sentences. These special sentences contained a critical word that was changed into other words or nonwords as the eye was in motion so the subjects could not perceive the change. The individuals were told that they would be asked to read a series of paragraphs to understand them. They were also asked ". . . not to skip lines as they read and to refrain from making long regressive movements," and ". . . not to reread any lines" (p. 73). When they finished the 15th paragraph of each block of paragraphs, they were given a set of 12 test sentences and asked to mark the ones which came from the paragraphs they had just finished reading. There was no other description of the test and no results reported from these scores so it may be assumed that the importance of doing well on the test was not impressed upon the subjects. The difficulty of the paragraphs was never mentioned but from the example sentence given it must be assumed that they would be easy for college students. The instructions, the objective consequences, and the relative difficulty would likely induce the rauding process, which should be around 260–300 Wpm for these college students.

It was noted that "the reading speed of the subjects was in the range of 200–400 wpm" but no indication was given as to how this was determined. Furthermore, no rate data were given. However, from the first figure presented, it could be estimated that the mean fixation duration was about 210 msec/word. Given the Tinker (1958) estimate that eye movements take about 93% of the time during reading, it can be estimated that reading rate was 266 wpm. Thus, this work of Rayner's appears to be appropriately categorized as rauding process research.

Rayner's most important finding was that changing the critical word into other words or nonwords had no effect upon the fixation durations until the word was 1–3 characters to the right of the character being fixated. If the word was 4–18 characters away into the periphery, then it seemed to have no effect. He summarized his results as follows: "These results failed to show any evidence that readers recognize that a letter string is not a word when they are fixating more than three or four character positions to the left of the beginning of that string (p. 77).

These data of Rayner's seem to indicate that during the rauding process, the eye must be fixating upon one of the letters of the word or it must be fixating 1–3 characters to the left of the word in order for any meaning to be obtained from the word. This may be interpreted as suggesting that there is no evidence that an individual can be fixating upon the middle letter of a five-letter word while engaged in the rauding process, and still be able to get the meaning of the next five-letter word to the right without fixating upon one of its letters during the next forward saccade. Thus, the word-recognition span appears to be quite small during the rauding process. This process appears to be pretty much a word for word process in that all the words are lexically accessed, semantically encoded, and sententially integrated into the complete thought by moving the fixation point of the eye to a position that is either on the word or within a few character spaces of it so that it can be perceived and processed.

It should be pointed out before leaving Rayner's research that he also found that these readers could pick up information about the shape of the word and the initial and final letters of words when fixating 7–12 character spaces before the word. Thus, gross visual characteristics of the next word in the periphery is obtainable even though the meaning of the word is not. Given this limited amount of information that a reader can pick up each time the eye stops during the operation of a rauding process, it is understandable that college students as a group are limited to a rauding process rate that averages around 260–300 Wpm. Since almost all the words must be fixated upon in order for all the components of the rauding process to have time to operate successfully, 200 msec per Word (which is 300 Wpm) seems to be the average amount of time college students require to make the process operate successfully.

Zuber and Wetzel (1981) conducted a study of reading rate and eye movements using the same G. R. Miller and Coleman (1971) passages that were described earlier in Chapter 3. These passages vary from about first grade to graduate school in difficulty level. Zuber and Wetzel wanted to monitor eye movements and see if they could replicate the results of Miller and Coleman who found no change in reading rate across this wide range of passages. Zuber and Wetzel did not use passage 36, the last and most difficult of all their passages, and the one that Carver (1971b, 1976) found to be associated with a drop in rate.

Zuber and Wetzel said that since they ". . . aimed at understanding the normal, mature reading process," their "subjects are typically drawn from the college population" (p. 199). They gave no information about what they instructed their subjects to do and there was no test or consequence of reading mentioned. It seems prudent to assume that they wanted their subjects to read normally, and there was no indication from their tasks or instructions that their subjects would do otherwise. Therefore, it seems safe to expect that they would have induced a rauding process for most of their subjects for most of the passages because there were only a few passages that might be difficult for college level readers (see Carver, 1976). Therefore, it would be predicted that these college students would read at a mean rate around 260–300 Wpm (see Chapter 2).

Zuber and Wetzel first measured rate in actual words per minute, wpm, and found that it dropped from about 360 wpm for the easiest passages to about 260 wpm for the hardest, a 28% drop. When these same data were converted into letter spaces per minute there was no similar drop in rate. Their letter spaces per minute can be converted into standard words per minute, Wpm, by dividing by six. The easiest passages were read at about 283 Wpm and the hardest were read at about 267 Wpm, only a 6% drop across the entire range of difficulty from about first grade level to college level. These rates were as predicted from a knowledge of the ability level of the readers, the instructions, the objective consequences, and the relative difficulty of the material.

Zuber and Wetzel summarized their eye movement findings as follows: "We feel that the present results justify the conclusion that virtually all eye movement parameters are essentially constant over the entire range of text difficulty studied" (p. 207). They also speculated that "the implication of this observation is that at some point in the information processing mechanism a constant rate of information flow is utilized" (p. 207). There were no important changes in the eye movements across a wide range of difficulty, i.e., mean fixation duration, number of fixations, number of regressions, and average size of forward saccades in letter spaces were all relatively constant. These results of Zuber and Wetzel's further replicate the constancy of reading rate under the rauding process across a wide range of difficulty (Carver, 1971b, 1976; Coke, 1974; G. R. Miller & Coleman, 1971; Morse, 1951). Again, this is strong support for Law I of rauding theory (see Chapter 2).

Rayner, Inhoff, Morrison, Slowiaczek, and Bertera (1981) investigated perceptual span by using a window and a mask. In Experiment 1, a window varying in size from 1 to 33 characters in width around the fixation point limited how much the reader could see with each fixation. In Experiment 2, a mask that varied in size from 1 to 17 characters blocked out what could be seen around the fixation point. In both experiments, the six adult subjects were given isolated sentences to read that varied in length from five to eight words. The sentences were all "easy to understand" and the subjects were asked to read normally and not to try to memorize the sentences. They were able to recall all the words in the sentences with 100% accuracy in the control conditions that involved no window and no mask as well as most of the other conditions. The rate of reading was given for the control conditions that involved no window and no mask, and those rates were around 300 wpm. This rate suggests that the subjects did in fact read normally and use a rauding process, as would have been predicted from the instructions, the objective consequences, and the relative difficulty.

As for the results, Rayner *et al.* found that reading was slowed to rates below 300 wpm for the window sizes of 25 characters and smaller. Saccade length was increased, up to about seven characters, as window size increased for the 29-, 33-, and no-window condition. Stated differently, these readers had an average saccade length of seven characters when the window extended 14 characters to the right of a fixation point. Smaller windows produced shorter saccades but larger windows did not. This means that information is being picked up to the right of the fixation point no further than about 14 characters; blocking out this information beyond 14 characters to the right of the fixation point will not slow reading rate but blocking it out seven characters to the right, for example, will slow reading rate.

As noted earlier, Rayner *et al.* also had a condition where they masked out letters at the center of a fixation, leaving the letters in the periphery. They found that the bigger the mask in the center of fixation, the more detrimental the effect on reading rate. Even the smallest mask (only one character at the fixation point was blocked out) had a disastrous effect upon reading rate. The mean rate without a mask was 295 wpm and the mean rate with a tiny one-character mask at the point of fixation reduced the reading rate to 160 wpm which is almost half as fast. When the mask was as large as five characters wide, about the size of a standard length word, rate had dropped to about 50 wpm, while the accuracy of sentence reproduction was still at 100%. This means that readers do not get very much information beyond the word they are looking at and blocking out even one letter of that word has a tremendous detrimental effect upon how fast they can read.

In conclusion, these results of Rayner *et al.* suggest that almost all of the information necessary for reading comes from the word or words that are within about three characters to the left and right of the fixation point. There is some helpful information obtained from the next word to the right of the one being fixated but beyond that one there is little or nothing being obtained. Again, these results are perfectly consistent with the word for word reading that is characteristic of the rauding process. (Note: This usage of the term "word for word reading" does *not* mean a perfect oral rendition of a passage; see Glossary.) The rauding process appears to be undisturbed if the reader is fixating upon a standard length word and the words beyond the next word in the periphery are never allowed to be seen. However, the rauding process appears to be greatly disturbed (rate cut in half) if even one letter is removed from each word that is being fixated upon, and if the entire word being fixated upon is blocked out then reading rate is reduced by 80%.

Rayner and Pollatsek (1981) conducted three experiments designed to investigate what factors control the eye movements during reading. The six adult subjects were given isolated sentences to read that were five to eight words in length and "were easy to understand" (p. 355). The subjects read while a window that varied in size and duration limited how much they could see and how long they could see it on each fixation. After each sentence the subjects were asked to ". . . report it verbatim or paraphrase it (they all reported it verbatim)" (p. 355). Using easy sentences would be conducive to a rauding process but having the subjects recall the sentences verbatim would suggest a memorizing process. However, the rate in one experiment when there was no experimental conditions in effect was reported as being around 340 wpm which would probably drop to around 300 Wpm for the easy material used. Therefore, the research is likely to be more relevant to the rauding process even though only isolated sentences were used. Probably the rauding process could be used on these sentences and the sentences still could be recalled verbatim because they were short and easy.

Rayner and Pollatsek interpret their saccade length, fixation duration, and reading rate results as supporting a model of eye control that is based on two factors. The first factor is a *cognitive* one relevant to the length of the fixation duration; the decision about when to move the eye forward depends upon whether "enough information has been understood to move on" (p. 369). The second factor is a *perceptual* one relevant to the length of the saccade; the decision about where to move the eye depends upon the location of "the first word that hasn't been processed" (p. 369). Notice that this model is completely in accordance with the rauding process in that the eye movements are programmed to perceive each word long enough to understand the sentence as it is being read word for word.

The above theoretical interpretations by Rayner and Pollatsek regarding the mechanisms underlying eye movements are indeed compatible with rauding theory. However, they are not specific enough to explain why college students operate their rauding process at a constant rate in standard length words per minute across widely different levels of material difficulty. On the basis of the two-factor model above—cognitive and perceptual—it might be expected that fourth grade material would be read faster than college level material, but it is not. Fourth grade words and thoughts might be expected to be understood faster than college level material so that fixation durations would be shorter under the cognitive factor. In any event, it seems important that models of eye movements attempt to account for the constancy of the rauding process across materials that vary widely in difficulty. It seems likely that another factor needs to be added such as a *silent speech* factor; this factor accompanying the other two could help account for this constant rate because the eyes would also be paced by a constant rate of silent speech in syllables per minute (see Carver, 1977).

McConkie and Hogaboam (1985) removed a passage from readers while they were reading and then studied the last word the subjects reported having read in relationship to the word at which their eyes were directly looking. A series of three experiments were conducted, each involving 10 or 11 undergraduates reading a passage on "gnomes" or "about backpacking." The subjects were "instructed to read and try to comprehend the passage" (p. 160). At random times during a saccadic movement, the text on computer screen would disappear and be replaced by a line of X's. Then, they would be asked to report the last word they were reading when the text disappeared. After reporting that word, they were asked to guess at the next word.

These subjects were probably using their rauding process. The text was probably relatively easy for college students given that the topics were gnomes and backpacking. The instructions were general enough to induce rauding (see guidelines presented Table 2.3). Also, the objective consequences were not likely to induce the subjects to shift out of their normal reading in third gear because the subjects were reported to be very successful in the primary task, i.e., 88–95% of the time the last word reported was in fact on the line they were reading. No information about reading rate, or fixation duration, was reported so it was impossible to check whether the predicted rate of 260–300 Wpm was accurate, thereby confirming that the rauding process was operating. Of course, it is possible that the subjects were engaged in a learning process. With the limited information given about the relative difficulty of the materials and the lack of reading rate data, it is impossible to be sure. Nonetheless, it seems most likely that these subjects would be operating their rauding process.

McConkie and Hogaboam found that the last word the subjects reported having read was most commonly the word fixated during the last fixation or the word to the right of it. These two words accounted for about 60–65% of the last words reported. Another 20–25% came from an earlier word than the one last fixated, and the remaining 10–20% was two or three words into the periphery. Given that short words occur quite frequently and often in pairs, such as "of the" or "in the" it is easy to understand that sometimes an individual could be fixating upon the last letter in a word right before "of the" and still be able to report the last word read as the one recorded as two words into the periphery, even though it is only the next standard length word into the periphery. Thus, it appears that it is virtually impossible for a reader to fixate upon the center of one standard length word and be able to report accurately another word that is further than one standard length word into the periphery during the operation of the rauding process.

By asking their subjects to guess at the next word beyond the last one they read, McConkie and Hogaboam were obtaining evidence relevant to how much information can be obtained about words from the periphery that might facilitate their perception. They reported that their subjects correctly guessed the next word, beyond the last one reported, about 24–31% of the time. This latter rate of correct reporting is exactly what would be anticipated from the redundancy of language using the data reported by Carver (1976). This means that it appears that the subjects picked up no helpful information from the periphery since they could guess the word beyond the last word read no better than college students who had absolutely no knowledge about the next word when they made their guesses. This interpretation is reinforced by McConkie and Hogaboam's report that "the last word read was reported with great confidence, whereas subjects felt that they had no information about the immediately following word and were making a poor guess" (p. 164). McConkie and Hogaboam (1985) interpreted their own results as follows:

> It has often been suggested that skilled readers form hypotheses and anticipations of upcoming text, and that these facilitate perception of the words (Goodman, 1976). Peripherally obtained information is assumed to facilitate this process by reducing the number of alternatives, thereby having relatively little further perceptual work to do when a word is brought into the fovea (Haber & Haber, 1981). If this were the nature of perceptual processing during skilled reading, we might have expected the readers in the studies reported here to make accurate guesses of upcoming words based on the peripherally obtained information, and to make such guesses quite readily when reading was terminated. (p. 170)

These data and interpretations of McConkie and Hogaboam appear to be relevant to the rauding process and further reinforce the theory that it is a word for word process that involves looking directly at each word in succession; looking directly at each word means that a fixation must be centered on one of its letters, or be within about four to five characters of the beginning of the word. There appears to be no evidence to support the idea that the redundancy of the words in the passage allows some words to be skipped without reducing the accuracy or rate of sentence comprehension. Instead, the rauding process appears to proceed on a rather rhythmic word by word basis. The eyes move across the line just fast enough for each word to be perceived, lexically accessed, semantically encoded, and sententially integrated with no words being skipped and the words being given equal time proportional to their length in character spaces or syllables.

Rayner (1986) extended his 1975 research on perceptual span to include elementary school students. In the earlier 1975 research, he investigated word recognition span as well as the entire perceptual span that included how far into the periphery individuals were getting information about beginning letters and word length. He did not investigate word recognition span in his 1986 research. Students in second, fourth, and sixth grades, as well as college students were given sentences to read while their eye movements were measured. There were four experiments. Again, these data are not directly relevant to the rauding process since they involve the reading of isolated sentences. However, the task produced reading rates comparable to expected rauding rates for these students so these data will be treated as indirectly reflecting upon the rauding process.

Rayner found that the size of the perceptual span for the college students was limited to about 14 character spaces to the right of the letter in the word being fixated; this means that it was limited to the word being fixated upon plus the next two words to the right. For sixth graders and fourth graders, perceptual span was limited to about 11 character spaces to the right, which is the word being fixated plus the next two words to the right. Second graders had a perceptual span about eight characters to the right, which is the word being fixated plus one word to the right. (Note: The preceding summary comes from an interpretation of the data given by Rayner (1986) in his Figures 1 and 3.)

It should not be forgotten that the span for word recognition is smaller than the perceptual span because perceptual span includes information about word shape and length. It does not appear that a smaller perceptual span can account for the fact that fourth graders operate their rauding process at a rate that is about one-half as fast as college students. Indeed, Rayner's data indicate that neither college students nor fourth graders pick up any useful information in the periphery beyond the next two words to the right of the one being fixated upon. Also, remember that college students cannot recognize any more than the word being fixated upon plus the next one to the right sometimes (see Rayner, 1975). So, it appears that the rauding process operates primarily upon the word being fixated upon with the qualification that the next one to the right can sometimes be recognized. Also, some information about where the eye should be thrown next can come from the letters and length of the first and second words to the right of the one being fixated.

In summary, these eye movement studies relevant to the rauding process seem to leave little doubt that this process operates on a word for word basis at a relatively constant rate for each individual. Ordinarily, readers move their eyes forward so they can fixate on the next word, unless they happen to be close enough on the previous fixation to perceive the word, in which case they may skip over the following word for their next fixation. This allows them to spend the time necessary during a fixation to lexically access, semantically encode, and sententially integrate each consecutive word into the complete thought of the sentence. The rauding process tends to be operated at a relatively constant rate for each individual because the eye movement components that influence rate, i.e. fixation duration, regressions, forward saccade length, and perceptual span, seem to be relatively constant even when the difficulty level of the material changes drastically.

LEARNING PROCESS

McConkie and Rayner (1975) studied the eye movements of six high school students who were ". . . identified as being among the best readers in their school" (p. 579). Being among the best readers in school probably made these individuals comparable in ability to college students. They were asked to read sixteen 500-word passages taken from a high school psychology text; none of the subjects had taken a course in psychology. No information was given about what instructions were given to the subjects or about the goal of their reading. However, the following details were given about the objective consequences:

> After reading all six pages of a passage, the subject came off the equipment and took a test for that passage. Prior to reading the next passage, the test was scored and he was informed of his score. In order to encourage subjects to put their emphasis on understanding and remembering the content of the passages, they were given 1 cent for each correct answer on the test. (p. 580)

These tests contained two questions on each page of the text; given six pages for each 500-word passage, this resulted in 12 questions per passage. No information was given about the nature of the test items.

It is not a simple matter to infer what reading process these subjects likely used. It is difficult to infer the goal because no information was given about the instructions, and not enough information was given about the objective consequences associated with the test items or their results. However, since there was such importance placed upon the scores on the tests through paying for correct answers, since the material was taken from an unfamiliar textbook, and since the expressed intent was placed upon "understanding and remembering," it seems reasonable to infer that a learning process would be induced. No rate data were reported, but reading time per 100 characters was given in the fifth figure they presented. Using the situation least affected by the special conditions of the experiment, it was possible to estimate average reading rate to be about 235 Wpm. This research has been categorized as representing a learning process, but this rate could also represent the rauding process for these students.

McConkie and Rayner were investigating the size of the perceptual span, during the operation of a learning process (or possibly the rauding process). They manipulated how much of the line a student could see on any particular fixation, varying the size of this window from 13 character spaces up to 45, and then no window at all. From the results of the second figure they presented, it is possible to note that 75% of all forward saccades were no more than one standard length word into the periphery. McConkie and Rayner (1975) concluded the following:

> Thus, it does not appear to be true that entire sentences are seen during a fixation. (p. 585)
>
> For the subjects studied here, saccades of median length carry the eye to a location just short of the furthest point where letter- and word-shape information tend to be acquired. (p. 586)

These data suggest that a learning process, like the rauding process, is primarily a word for word reading process. (Note: These results were essentially replicated by Underwood and McConkie, 1985, except the size of the span was found to be slightly smaller; changing four characters to the left of the fixation and eight to the right had little or no effect.)

Another reason for reviewing these important data collected by McConkie and Rayner was to focus upon what appears to be an inconsistency between the intent of the study and the design of the study, from the vantage point of hindsight. The authors stated in their introduction that "the research to be reported here is an attempt to develop a method for obtaining information about the size of the region from which specific types of visual information are obtained during fixations while the subjects are involved in reading a passage with as few constraints on their behavior as possible" (p. 579). In an earlier publication where they were discussing the same data collection effort (McConkie and Rayner, 1973), they stated that "an important goal for reading research is to develop techniques for studying the processes involved in reading as the person is engaged in the normal reading task, reading a passage for meaning, rather than having to depend so completely on other tasks which are thought to be similar to normal reading in certain ways" (p. 120). It can be seen from the preceding quotes that McConkie and Rayner wanted to study perceptual span during "normal" reading. For them, normal reading probably meant how students ordinarily read when they are involved in study reading. They seem to have investigated the size of the perceptual span in a situation that may be closer to involving a learning process rather than the rauding process which is more normal. To be more confident about inducing the rauding process, it is probably best (a) not to pay subjects on the basis of correct answers, (b) use relatively easy material, and (c) ask subjects to try to read as they normally would read. To study a learning process that is probably more similar to what college students or high school students engage in when reading a textbook, it is probably best to use subjects and materials that are at a comparable level of ability and difficulty, or use material that is relatively hard. For example, average high school students could be given an average high school textbook and then test questions similar to those a teacher or professor might ask could be administered. Again, on the basis of hindsight, it seems likely that regressions and fixation durations will be different during the operation of a learning process as compared to the rauding process.

Just and Carpenter (1980) published a theory of reading based upon the empirical data they collected on eye fixations. This lengthy work will require a lengthy review.

Just and Carpenter asked 14 college students to read 15 scientific texts without rereading even parts of them. They stated that: "Although the readers were asked to recall each passage immediately after reading it, they also were told to read naturally without memorizing" (p. 335). This instruction, together with the admonition that subjects not reread, seems to preclude a memorizing process even though the "recall" instruction and task would ordinarily make this process more likely. Nothing more was ever said about the recall—no description and no results—so it is impossible to evaluate further the probable effects of these objective consequences upon the process used. The difficulty of the scientific passages they used was assessed using Flesch's readability scale. No Flesch score was reported but the 17 words per sentence and the 1.6 syllables per word translates into a Flesch score of 55 and the eleventh grade level of difficulty (Flesch, 1949). Therefore, these 14 college students were asked to read scientific passages that were at the eleventh grade level according to a readability formula. They were also asked to "recall" what they read, in an unknown manner without memorizing while reading naturally. Some of these instructions would be conducive to the rauding process, such as reading naturally and not rereading (see Table 2.3). The objective consequences would seem to be more conducive to a memorizing process. Taking all of the above factors into account, plus the fact that the authors did acknowledge in the results section that "occasional rereading" did occur, it seems most likely that the subjects would engage in a lower gear than the rauding process and a higher gear than a memorizing process which leaves a learning process as most likely. The information given about reading rate confirms this inference. They reported in their results that the average reading rate was 225 wpm, which can be used to estimate Wpm as 220, using the GE = 11 difficulty level for the passages [see Equations (2.2) and (2.6)]. The 220 Wpm is close to the predicted 200 Wpm rate of a learning process for college students (see Table 2.2).

The results and theoretical inferences made from these data by Just and Carpenter need to be continually referenced to a learning process, and not the rauding process which is more typical, ordinary, and normal. This qualification need not detract from their work because the learning process is probably used most often by college students, if not most students, while engaged in academically related reading.

One of the main thrusts of Just and Carpenter's theoretical ideas is that there are wide variations in the fixation durations which are associated with the amount of processing required based upon the case role assignment or structural properties of the word. For example, they point out that an unknown word like "flywheel" is fixated upon for 1566 msec when their average fixation duration was 239 msec per word. Yet, this finding is specific to a learning process. Parenthetically, it may be noted that if one wants to make it very likely that the rauding process, Gear 3, is used, then scientific texts and unknown words would not be used.

Just and Carpenter used a regression model to predict gaze durations for each word using 17 predictors. For these predictors (a) 4 of the 17 were from the encoding and lexical processing stage, e.g., number of syllables, and whether or not the word was novel; (b) 11 were categorized as "case role assignment," e.g., verb or rhetorical word; and (c) 2 were interclause integration, e.g., last word in the sentence. They reported an R^2 of 0.72 and a standard error of estimate of 88 msec. They also reported regression weights in msec, the largest regression weight being a 802 msec value associated with the novel word variable. The lowest regression weight was 9 msec, and the highest one, excluding novel words, was 157. It can be seen from these data that their results probably would not generalize to the rauding process because during the execution of the rauding process there is no stopping for novel words, because there are no novel words involved during the operation of the rauding process in almost all situations wherein it is operating. Investigators of the rauding process should be careful to reduce the likelihood of including unknown words. In fairness to Just and Carpenter, they were often careful to restrict their generalizations. For example, the very first sentence in their abstract is as follows: "This article presents a model of reading comprehension that accounts for the allocation of eye fixations of college students reading scientific passages."

It should also be remembered that I. H. Anderson (1937) found that the amount of variability associated with fixation durations increased as the gears were shifted down from skimming through rauding to the learning process. This means that if the rauding process had been studied, the R^2 value of 0.72 probably would have been drastically reduced simply because the variability in fixation durations would be much smaller during the rauding process; correlations are almost automatically decreased when the variability is reduced.

This Just and Carpenter (1980) research may be quite typical for a learning process but quite atypical for the rauding process. Their findings are relevant to reading rate during the execution of a learning process. Their interpretations of their findings relevant to reading rate are given below:

> There is a common misconception that readers do not fixate every word, but only some small proportion of the text, perhaps one out of every two or three words. However, . . . our data . . . show that during ordinary reading, almost all content words are fixated. (p. 329)
>
> When readers are given a text that is appropriate for their age level, they average 1.2 words per fixation. The words that are not always fixated tend to be short function words, such as *the, of,* and *a.* The number of words per fixation is even lower if the text is especially difficult or if the reader is poorly educated. (p. 330)

Thus, eye movement research seems to leave no doubt that almost every word is looked at during the execution of a learning process and that the time spent looking at each word averages about 240 msec per word for the Just and Carpenter research, which translates into around 220 Wpm.

Before leaving this research of Just and Carpenter, there is one more important point to be made that is directly relevant to reading rate and requires extensive explanation. They not only analyzed their data on a word for word basis, but they also analyzed it by what they called "sectors," hereafter called "phrases." They reported that their prediction variable could predict the time to read the phrases with an R^2 of 0.94, thus leaving only 6% of the variance in time to read phrases unaccounted for by their 17 predictor variables. To illustrate how they used structural analysis to separate their 15 passages into phrases, they presented phrases for one of their passages in their Table 3; they also included the observed times to read all the words in each phrase plus the times predicted from their 17 variables via multiple regression.

The phrase data, noted above, have been reanalyzed by E. B. Coleman, and his results and interpretations have been published at the end of this book in Appendix A. His main point is that only one variable is needed to account for 95% of the variance in their example passage. That variable was letter spaces per phrase. Stated differently, if the number of standard length words is counted for each phrase and used to predict the times they reported to read each phrase, the correlation is 0.98 and $R^2 = 0.95$. It appears that the rate of reading phrases, in Wpm, was almost exactly constant for each phrase no matter what its place in their four-tiered hierarchy, going from a low level phrase which they called Detail to their highest level phrases which they called Topic. The findings discussed earlier that passages of widely different difficulty levels are read at a constant rate during the execution of the rauding process (Carver, 1976; G. R. Miller & Coleman, 1971; Morse, 1951; Zuber & Wetzel, 1981) and a learning process (Carver, 1971b) has now been replicated for a learning process. It appears that phrases at different hierarchical levels of structural analysis are also read at a constant rate in Wpm during a learning process. This finding, first noted by Coleman, has serious ramifications for the theoretical arguments of Just and Carpenter. Rather than requiring the detailed knowledge associated with their theoretically derived 17 predictor variables, it appears that there is some mechanism that makes the rate of reading phrases during the learning process relatively constant in terms of character spaces covered per unit of time, at least for units as large as phrases. When only 1 variable instead of 17 is needed to account for 95 % of the variance in phrase reading time, there seems to be a compelling need to use Occam's razor and eliminate these 17 variables in our theoretical thinking.

Kliegl, Olson, and Davidson (1982) attempted to replicate aspects of the Just and Carpenter (1980) research reviewed earlier. They gave six pages out of Camus' novel *The Plague* to six college graduates and told them that they "would have to answer a difficult questionnaire about the text afterward and, so, should remember as much detail as possible" (p. 290). Evidently, the subjects had no feedback so there was no opportunity for them to modify their process to be more successful on the performance measure. These pages in this novel were probably of college level difficulty, i.e., not relatively easy, and the instructions were definitely oriented toward a learning process. Therefore a learning process would be most likely and this was confirmed by the 219 wpm mean rate reported (see Table 2.2).

The thrust of this research by Kliegl *et al.* was to analyze the Just and Carpenter research and to point out "some statistical and theoretical problems with their use of simultaneous analysis of gaze duration measures. . ." (p. 287). For example, they noted that Just and Carpenter claimed that "their 'psycholinguistic' variables accounted for 72% of the variance in gaze durations" whereas their own results "revealed that most gaze duration variance was contributed by number of fixations . . ." (p. 287). The main reason for reviewing this research of Kliegl *et al.* was to present one of their explanations for why some of their results were different from Just and Carpenter. They noted that Just and Carpenter used "technical text paragraphs on flywheels in combustion engines, thermoaluminescence, staphylococci, and so on" (p. 294). Then Kliegl *et al.* (1982) argued that:

> This combination of technicality of reading material and frequent memory tests is very likely to have introduced different reading behavior compared to our study. After a few tests, their subjects may have realized that it was important to memorize the facts presented in the text. This might have caused them to very carefully examine words that carry main ideas. Usually, these words are less frequent and longer. (p. 294)

Notice that the above explanation proposes a different reading process to explain seemingly inconsistent results. Even though the two studies both involved a learning process, learning processes can be modified and tailored to be more successful for accomplishing somewhat different goals. Indeed, if readers are able to make these adjustments when reading at around 200 Wpm, it should not be difficult to concede that the results of these studies involving second gear will not necessarily generalize to normal or typical reading while operating in third gear (the rauding process). As was pointed out in connection with the earlier review of the Just and Carpenter research, when the rauding process is operating successfully as it ordinarily does in normal or typical reading situations, there is likely to be much less variance in gaze durations because subjects are not likely to spend over 1000 msec on a particular word since none of the words are unknown in typical reading situations. The main point is that this research of Kliegl *et al.* reinforces the admonition to refrain from generalizing about reading or "the reading process" when conducting research on a learning process, and it reinforces the theory presented in Chapter 2 that reading can involve different processes especially in research situations.

McConkie, Zola, Blanchard, and Wolverton (1982) studied the effect of changing letters in words in the periphery during saccades so that the subjects were not aware that changes were being made and so the researchers could determine what words were perceived in the periphery. They gave 16 undergraduates relatively easy sentences that made sense with any one of four words occupying a certain position. For example, see the following sentence: "Ruth's great aunt is definitely the most mushy/musty/gushy/gusty person she has ever met" (p. 280). Some of these sentences were preceded or followed by other sentences that made the text to be read longer. There was no mention of what instructions were given to the subjects about how they were to read. Immediately after reading each set of sentences the subjects were asked to mark which of the words they saw, e.g., mushy, musty, gushy, or gusty, while they were reading earlier. After a few trials, it seems likely that the subjects would develop a reading process that helped them be successful on this particular task. Since the materials to be read were relatively easy, it is possible that the subjects would operate a rauding process, but the focus of the task upon choosing a particular word could easily induce them to operate a learning process. McConkie *et al.* did not report any reading rate data. However, all their target words were five letters long and they did report the mean fixation duration for fixations on the target words for a control condition where none of the words were changed during saccades, i.e., 254 msec. In another article McConkie (1982) reported that normal saccades seven to nine characters long require 35 msec, so $254 + 35 = 289$ msec for a standard length word would be 208 Wpm. Therefore, it can be estimated that this research involved a learning process, not the rauding process, because 208 Wpm is the average reading rate of ninth graders (see Table 2.1).

From the results of the target words that subjects reported seeing in conjunction with what words were actually present in the periphery and during a fixation on the target word, McConkie *et al.* concluded that the target "words were being perceived during only one fixation, that on which the word was directly fixated . . ." (p. 277). They went on to point out that these results were in direct conflict with the Rayner (1975) results, reviewed earlier. Rayner found that information about word shape was obtained when fixating 7–12 character spaces before the word, and McConkie *et al.* noted that they could not replicate this finding. They discuss several possible reasons for the discrepancy and then conclude that "when a person is reading carefully, five-letter words which are relatively unconstrained are read only when directly fixated" (p. 279).

It should not go unnoticed that the reason that McConkie *et al.* obtained different results from Rayner could easily have been because Rayner's subjects were operating the rauding process, Gear 3, as previously indicated, and the subjects in McConkie *et al.* research were operating a learning process, Gear 2. The mean fixation durations reported by Rayner under unconstrained control conditions were around 200 msec while the corresponding mean for McConkie *et al.* was 254 msec. Yet, it is difficult to sort out for sure what we have learned about a learning process or the rauding process, without information about the ability level of subjects, the difficulty of passages, the instructions, the objective consequences, and the reading rate in Wpm.

From this research of McConkie *et al.* (1982), it appears that we have learned the following: when a learning process is operating whereby the subjects are reading relatively easy material in order to be able to recognize later a particular word they read earlier, they do not pick up any information about the words in the periphery but instead rely solely upon information they receive from fixations directly upon the words themselves. McConkie (1983) appeared to recognize the danger of generalizing from one basic reading process to another when he said "we need to take more care to recognize the diversity of tasks involving reading and the differences in perceptual processes that may be involved, thus being more careful not to overgeneralize, than has often been the case in the past" (p. 67). In this 1983 article, McConkie further cautioned that he would restrict his subsequent review of eye movement research to "careful reading." Since the McConkie *et al.* (1982) research, reviewed above, was referred to as careful reading, it could be inferred that McConkie only wants to generalize to the type of reading involved in learning processes. If so, then eye movement researchers may be divorcing themselves from generalizing about the rauding process, Gear 3, which is typically and normally used by most people, in favor of a learning process, Gear 2, which may be typical for college students but is atypical in terms of usage in the population of readers.

McConkie and Zola (1984) studied the importance of words as a perceptual unit by finding the position of the eye within a word at the end of a saccade as compared to where the saccade started. Most of their subjects were probably college students but the following brief description of the method left some ambiguity:

> As subjects have come into our laboratory to participate in other studies, we have typically had them read a 417-word passage taken from a high-school level encyclopedia. Its readability is estimated for 16-year-old students. Thus, it was relatively easy reading for the college students who participated in our research. However, they were told that they would be given questions after reading the passage, implying that they should read carefully. (p. 65)

The description of the readability of the passage as "16-year-old" is unorthodox but most likely it was at the tenth or eleventh grade level. For students at the college level of ability, it was probably relatively easy as the authors state and also conducive to the rauding process. Telling subjects that they would be given questions afterwards is too ambiguous to adjudicate between a rauding process and a learning process but "implying that they should read carefully" tips the evidence to a learning process in keeping with the earlier research by McConkie that involved "reading carefully." There was no information given about reading rate or fixation durations that would help categorize the type of process used. A close call decision was made to treat the research as involving a learning process rather than the rauding process.

McConkie and Zola reported that the average saccade length was 7.20 characters and the SD was 2.90, for around 9200 forward saccades. They presented frequency distributions of saccade lengths in characters that indicated that the second letter of a five-letter word was most likely to be fixated upon whether the saccade started three to four characters or five to six characters in front of the word. And, the third letter of a seven-letter word was most likely to be fixated upon when the saccade started five to six characters to the left. They also showed that a bimodal frequency distribution resulted when looking at the fixation point of saccades that started in the character position immediately in front of a five-letter word, with modes at 4 and 10 characters to the right of the beginning of the word. This distribution, as well as a similar pattern for seven-letter words, suggested that (a) if the word to the right of the initial fixation (where the saccade started) was identified and processed, then the saccade was 10 characters long to jump over the identified word to the next one, and (b) if the word to the right was not identified, then the saccade was only four characters long so that this word could be fixated upon, identified, and processed. They interpreted these results as indicating that words are important units and that "the eyes are simply sent to the next unidentified word while reading carefully" (p. 72).

In summary, the preceding results leave little doubt that most learning processes involve word for word reading wherein the eyes move down a line fixating upon almost every word and fixating close enough, within about three characters, of every word so that it can be perceived and processed. There are many more eye movement studies relevant to learning processes that could have been reviewed but the focus of this review of research and theory will remain upon the rauding process; reviewing the other basic processes helps place into context the research on the rauding process.

MEMORIZING PROCESS

Mehler, Bever, and Carey (1967) investigated the eye movements of forty college students (from Harvard and Radcliffe) while they were reading especially constructed passages that were short stories containing five sentences. The fourth sentence was always the target sentence. The target sentences each contained eight to ten words with a total of 37–40 letters. From the examples of partial sentences given, the material appeared to be very easy; e.g., "they gave her dog candies . . ." After reading, the task was to retell each story aloud. Even though the material would undoubtedly be exceptionally easy for those above average college students, still the task of retelling what had been recalled would likely induce a memorizing process unless there was some restriction about not rereading.

From the rate data given, there is no doubt that a memorizing process was employed. The sentences were presented one at a time every 5 sec. An average length of 38.5 letters per sentence and 9 words per sentence produces an average of 49.5 character spaces per sentence which yields 8.25 Words per 5 sec or 99 Wpm. With these objective consequences and this exceptionally low reading rate, 99 Wpm, there is no doubt that a memorizing process was induced.

The above researchers were investigating "which aspects of sentence structure affect the visual scanning pattern in reading" (p. 213). They manipulated the early sentences in a story so exactly the same words, e.g., they gave her dog candies . . . , meant that candies were given to her dog or that dog candies were given to her. They summarized their results as follows:

> A general eye-fixation rule predicts the pattern of adults' eye-fixations in a study of reading predictable sentences: "fixate on the first half of phrase structure constituents." (p. 213)

The authors appear to be aware that their results are not likely to generalize to other reading situations when they state: "In everyday reading, for example, we make far less than one fixation every .26 letters" (p. 217). Indeed, in the preceding research by Just and Carpenter (1980) they reported one fixation every 1.2 words which would be about one fixation every 6.0 letters instead of one fixation about 0.3 letters in this Mehler *et al.* research.

It appears that the results of Mehler *et al.* must be restricted to a memorizing process. From their data, there is absolutely no reason to expect a similar fixation pattern during the rauding process and probably not during a learning process. However, this kind of word by word grammatical analysis also formed the basis of the Just and Carpenter data. It should not be forgotten, however, that a substantial part of the Just and Carpenter data could easily be explained without resort to any grammatical or text structure variable.

There appears to be nothing in this study by Mehler *et al.* which has direct significance for generalizing about reading rate beyond a memorizing process. This research happened to be the only research study found which studied eye movements during the execution of this type of process. Perhaps the most important information to be gained from this research is that it is dangerous to take the results of a study like this and think it applies to reading in general. For example, on the basis of hindsight, it would have been better if Mehler *et al.* had stated their purpose for doing the research as follows: "Which aspects of sentence structure affect the visual scanning pattern while individuals are executing a memorizing process during reading?" Again the problem is that, by analogy, some reading researchers are investigating the taste of fruit and finding that fruit is sometimes bitter and sometimes sweet. If, instead, researchers would refrain from stating that they were investigating the taste of fruit and instead start stating that they were investigating the taste of a small yellow fruit (a memorizing process) and the taste of larger orange fruit (the rauding process) they would find more lawful relationships for the taste of each type of fruit (each basic reading process).

CONCLUSIONS

The eye movement data presented in this chapter seem to justify the following conclusions.

1. The goals induced by instructions and objective consequences can get readers to shift out of a rauding process, up to a skimming process or down to a learning process, whenever the material is not relatively hard (I. H. Anderson, 1937). Shifting up will result in less regressions, shorter fixation durations, and longer saccade

lengths (I. H. Anderson, 1937; Laycock, 1955). Shifting down will result in more regressions, longer fixation durations, and shorter saccade lengths (I. H. Anderson, 1937). However, shifting down has a relatively small effect on saccade lengths and fixation durations compared to relatively large effects upon regressions, i.e., shifting down to a learning process is mainly accomplished by regressing and rereading the words (I. H. Anderson, 1937). Shifting up also has a large effect upon regressions (I. H. Anderson, 1937; Laycock, 1955).

2. During the operation of the rauding process, there is little or no change in rate associated with large differences in material difficulty level (from grade 1 to college level) as long as college students do not read materials that are relatively hard for them (Zuber & Wetzel, 1981). Also, elementary and junior high students tend to operate their rauding process at a constant rate across a wide span of material difficulty (Morse, 1951). Junior high students read passages in widely different subject matter areas at almost exactly the same rate (Seibert, 1943). Even graduate students and university professors tend to read familiar and unfamiliar materials at the same rate, around 300 Wpm, as long as the material is relatively easy (W. R. Dixon, 1951). These data, from eye movement research, strongly support the conclusion that the rauding process operates at a constant rate across a wide range of difficulty levels and subject matter areas. These eye movement data provide strong support for Law I of rauding theory (see Chapter 2).

3. During the rauding process, reading proceeds on a word for word basis because readers fail to recognize a word unless they are fixating within three or four character spaces of the word (Rayner, 1975), and rate is slowed drastically if even one letter is masked in the center of a fixation (Rayner et al., 1981). Also, when the text is removed while reading, individuals can only accurately report upon the word they were fixating upon or the next one to the right (McConkie & Hogaboam, 1985). There is no evidence from eye movement research that individuals are making predictions based upon hypotheses about words in the periphery so that they can skip over or spend less time on unimportant or more redundant words during the operation of the rauding process.

4. During the operation of learning processes while reading, almost every word is fixated upon (McConkie et al., 1982) and some words are fixated upon for very long durations (Just & Carpenter, 1980).

5. Researchers investigating eye movements often do not report details about the ability level of the reader, the difficulty level of the

material, the instructions given to the reader, the objective consequences associated with the reading task, and the resulting reading
rate. Therefore, it is often difficult to ascertain whether typical
reading, the rauding process, is being investigated. Given the information reported, it can often be surmised that a learning process, Gear 2, is being investigated, and these results will not necessarily generalize to the rauding process, Gear 3.

IMPLICATIONS

It has been suggested that the amount of time spent on different words
in a passage provides an indicator useful in the study of language processes (McConkie, Hogaboam, Wolverton, Zola, & Lucas, 1979). Indeed,
this was the technique used in the Just and Carpenter (1980) research
reviewed earlier. It appears that this use of eye movements can be validly
used for the slower and more powerful reading processes involved in
learning and memorizing. However, this technique does not seem to
hold much promise for studying the normal, typical, or ordinary reading
process, Gear 3. In situations where each word must be processed to
form the complete thought involved in sentences, where the words are
all known words, and where the passages are relatively easy to comprehend accurately, there seems to be little likelihood that eye movements
can be used to study such things as the effects of verbs versus nouns.
Since college students tend to operate their rauding process on fourth
grade level material at about the same rate as they do on college grade
level material, it does not seem likely that it would be fruitful to study
the location or duration of fixations during the operation of this process.
For example, McConkie and Zola (1984) have pointed out that the word
"the" is fixated upon less per character than other words but even this
difference may evaporate if the research was restricted to the rauding
process.

Most reading research involving eye movements does not include a
measure of reading rate, and this is lamentable. Reporting reading
rates, along with information about the instructions, the objective consequences, and the relative difficulty of the material would provide an
indication of the type of reading process likely to have been used by the
subjects in the research. Also, it seems important that any theory purporting to explain eye movements account for the fact that reading processes often operate at a constant rate across widely different levels of
material difficulty.

In summary, eye movement research seems to hold promise for studying language processing during the execution of learning and memorizing

processes, Gears 1 and 2, but *not* during the more typical reading involving the rauding process, Gear 3. And, eye movement researchers investigating any reading process should consider reporting about the rate at which the process operated; more valid inferences could then be made about which basic process was actually being studied. Eye movement theorists and researchers might consider the challenge of explaining the fact that during typical or ordinary reading, rate is usually constant across levels of material difficulty and redundancy, as long as word length is controlled.

Part III

Reading Processes

This part of the book contains four chapters, three of which are reviews of research covering the five basic reading processes. Chapter 6 reviews scanning and skimming processes, Gears 4 and 5. Chapter 7 reviews the rauding process, Gear 3, the typical and most important of all reading processes. Chapter 8 reviews the two learning and memorizing processes, Gears 1 and 2. Then, Chapter 9 contains a theoretical analysis of these processes and the factors that causally affect reading rate.

6

SCANNING AND SKIMMING

INTRODUCTION

Scanning and skimming are reading processes that represent Gear 5 and Gear 4, respectively. Shifting up into these two gears can be helpful at times, and other times dangerous. Over 65 years ago, Judd and Buswell (1922) gave the following explanation which is still valid today:

> . . . let us consider an important type of reading which may or may not prove to be appropriate to the middle grades, namely, the type which is exhibited when a reader skims a page in search of a particular item or kind of information. There is no more useful practical ability than that of going rapidly over a page, omitting most of it in order to catch the small items which suits one's immediate purpose. Nor is there any more dangerous habit to acquire than that of skimming. (p. 152)

Shifting up into Gears 4 and 5 can be a dangerous habit for students if it replaces Gear 3 when the goal should be to comprehend the complete thoughts in sentences.

Scanning research and skimming research have already been reviewed in connection with the topics of the three preceding chapters. And, scanning and skimming research will continue to be reviewed in chapters following this one, for example, in Chapter 10 on flexibility. Since the focus of the present investigation is reading rate during typical reading, this review of scanning and skimming will be more illustrative than exhaustive. By making it perfectly clear what it means to shift into the higher gears of scanning and skimming, it will be more difficult to confuse these reading processes with the rauding process.

Research on scanning processes, Gear 5, will be reviewed first, and research on skimming processes, Gear 4, will be reviewed second.

SCANNING PROCESSES

As discussed earlier, scanning processes are those that primarily involve the lexical component, i.e., word recognition. Only the scanning processes that involve the recognition of words in sentences or passages will be reviewed. This eliminates all the research on letter scanning, for example (see Neisser, 1964). Again, the intent is to focus upon research that has some direct relevance for reading rate in words per minute.

Maxwell (1969a) summarized research findings on scanning and skimming improvement. She cited five studies: two were unpublished papers, one was an unpublished university report, one was in conference proceedings, and the fifth one was Laffitte (1963); the Laffitte article contained an overview which was enlarged in a later report (Laffitte, 1964) that will be reviewed in more detail in Chapter 18. It appears that there was not much research done on scanning processes prior to 1969.

Katz and Wicklund (1971) studied word scanning in isolated sentences for good and poor reading fifth graders. However, the sentences were only two words or three words long—not similar enough to prose to provide meaningful generalizations about reading rate.

Leslie and Calfee (1971) investigated the scanning rates of second, fourth, and sixth graders plus college students. They did not use prose passages. However, scanning for a target word embedded in a vertical list may involve rates similar to a model scanning process (described in Chapter 2). They used 17 ten-word lists which were constructed by random selection from 634 four-letter words selected from the cumulative vocabulary of a third grade basal reader. They measured reaction time between the onset of the list and the time the target word was spotted, as indicated by a switch being pressed by the subject. They reported search rates ranging from 3.3 words/sec for the second graders to 8.4 words/sec for the college students. These two rates are 198 wpm and 504 wpm, respectively. The words were all four-letter words, and a standard length word consists of five letters and a blank space, so these rates convert into 248 Wpm for the second graders and 630 Wpm for the college students. This rate of 630 Wpm is close to the 600 Wpm for the model scanning process for college students (see Table 2.2).

Fisher (1975) asked 36 college students to search prose passages for a target word. The passages were taken from the Nelson–Denny Reading Test. He varied type face (normal, capital, and alternating) and spacing (normal, filled, and no spacing). Altogether, there were 162 different target words used, 44 with five letters or less and 58 with eight letters or more. As would be expected, the fastest reading rate under these nine possible conditions was the one with normal type face and normal spacing between words. He did not give the nine rates but only the rates for the two separate main effects. However, he did report that there were no interactions so it was possible to calculate that the average scanning rate was approximately 556 wpm. This rate is close to the model scanning rate of 600 Wpm given earlier in Table 2.2. In another similar experiment, reported in the same publication, the group receiving normal spacing and normal type face was the fastest again; the rate was 600 wpm. These data of Fisher's appear to be the first to establish that college students can be expected to recognize each word in normal prose passages at an average rate of about 600 Wpm, or 100 msec per Word.

Fisher and Lefton (1976) reported scanning data for third, fourth, and sixth graders ($N = 216$ total) plus college students ($N = 72$). The elementary students were only selected if they were reading at their grade level or above. Passages were used that were equal in difficulty to the grade level of the students. These passages were searched for a target word which was a noun with "no particular distinctiveness", e.g., not capitalized or of any particular length. Various unnatural textual manipulations were studied along with a normal passage. Their scanning rates under normal typographical conditions were about 210, 410, 450, and 600 wpm for the third, fourth, and sixth grades, and college students, respectively. Given the estimates of the difficulty level of the passages, these rates can be converted into 184, 365, 406, 609 Wpm, respectively, using the equations given in Chapter 2. These data from college students support the 600 Wpm model rate in Table 2.2. The 365 and 406 Wpm rates for the fourth and sixth graders indicate that even children are capable of high scanning rates with relatively low error rates, 10 and 9% respectively. Again, this study reinforces the 600 Wpm model scanning rate for college students, and provides some indication of model scanning rates for above average readers in elementary school.

Coke (1977) asked college students to search easy passages (about GE = 6) and difficult passages (about GE = 13) for target words. Under eight separate conditions, she reported mean reading rates that varied from about 220 Wpm to about 290 Wpm. These are relatively slow scanning rates. However, she required that the subjects search for three target words and report the one word out of the three that was *not* in the passage. Therefore, it is understandable that her rates were considerably lower than the 600 Wpm model rate for scanning prose. Holding three targets in memory and scanning for all three would take longer. Coke also asked high school students to do a similar search except they were to look for synonyms of the target words. Their mean rates under the same eight conditions varied from about 110 Wpm to about 140 Wpm. Obviously, rate alone does not reflect which reading process is being used. Some search tasks involve scanning processes that are slower than the rauding process and equal to the model rate for the memorizing process. So, the major reason for including this research study is to illustrate the fact that some scanning processes can involve tasks with components that slow the process considerably below the model rate of 600 Wpm.

Maxwell (1978) gave 20 high school students 80 trials on a scanning task. They searched for phrases, such as "When you hear the buzzer." They were induced to scan a page at average rates faster than 800 wpm. For Maxwell, scanning was defined as ". . . the ability to locate specific facts and details quickly . . ." (p. 49). The data were analyzed for eight sessions of ten trials each. The mean time to find the target phrase varied from a high of 0.79 sec for Session 1 to a low of 0.57 sec at Session 6. Almost all of the gain in speed occurred between Session 1 and Session 2. The correlation between the scores on Session 1 and Session 8 was 0.78, indicating that the subjects who were the fastest initially were also the fastest after a great deal of practice. Furthermore, the mean search time for the 10 fastest scanners at Session 1 (0.67 sec) was lower than the 10 slowest scanners after 80 practice trials (0.72 sec). These data suggest the existence of a cognitive speed factor representing a limit for each individual. These data also suggest that a phrase can be located faster than a single word.

This research of Maxwell's was reviewed to illustrate the fact that some scanning processes can cover prose passages faster than 600 Wpm, which is the model rate for scanning prose for a single target word that is not readily distinguishable from the other words. This study also illustrates that there are other types of scanning, besides the model scanning task, that are just as relevant to real world scanning tasks, if not more relevant. In these real world tasks, there is a great deal of skipping over words mixed in with model scanning. Skipping can produce rates that are unlimited, i.e., approaching infinity if entire sections are skipped. Stated differently, scanning is also a general term that includes model scanning at 600 Wpm (see Chapter 2) plus unlimited amounts of skipping that can push the apparent reading rate to values considerably higher than 600 Wpm.

Fisher, Lefton, and Moss (1978) reported search rates for 112 college students under various normal and abnormal text conditions. The passages were at the college level of difficulty. Again, the fastest rate was obtained under the normal text condition, 666 wpm, thus providing another replication of the model prose scanning rate for college students.

In summary, it appears reasonable to conclude that college students can read prose passages at around 600 Wpm on the average when their only goal is the successful recognition of a single target word embedded in the material. Since 600 Wpm is 100 msec per Word, it appears that, on the average, standard length words need only about 100 msec to be lexically accessed by college students when the model scanning process is being operated. These data also suggest that even elementary students are capable of relatively high model scanning rates of around 300–400 Wpm. These data help to set the upper limit for reading rate. Other processes that require more than simply checking each word to see if it matches a target word would have to operate at slower rates on the average. And, a mixture of skipping and the model scanning process can result in reading rates that are almost unlimited; but these high speed processes are only effective in finding the targets when the targets are more readily distinguishable than an ordinary word embedded in an ordinary prose passage.

SKIMMING PROCESSES

Skimming is a term that has several possible meanings. The model skimming process described in Chapter 2 involves the semantic encoding of each word. This means that the word must be recognized *and* its meaning discerned within the context of the sentence. For example, passages may be given to subjects, some of which have had two words transposed and the task is for the subjects to find the transposed words as fast as possible. Compared to the model scanning process described in the previous section, it should take longer to operate the model skimming process because it involves more than the recognition of each word. Compared to the rauding process, it should take less time to operate the model skimming process because it does not require that the meaning of the words be integrated into the complete thought of the sentence within the context of the passage.

Obviously, processes quite different from the model skimming process described above are still called skimming. For Maxwell (1969a), skimming meant to locate the main idea of a selection quickly. Skimming is also a descriptive term that can be applied to reading situations that involve a great deal of skipping. Although both scanning and skimming may involve skipping, scanning is often used to describe a process whereby the goal is to locate a certain word, words, or ideas and all other information is totally irrelevant. Skimming is often used to describe the process used when the goal is to extract and remember gist, or the most important ideas representing the entire body of thoughts being covered.

It seems possible to get the gist of the passage in at least two distinctly different ways: (a) by processing every word as in model skimming, or (b) by executing model skimming until the decision is made to skip to a more promising sentence or to switch to a rauding process on sentences deemed to be highly important. Tinker (1965) defined skimming in the following way that would include both scanning and skimming as defined earlier:

> Skimming should be done with a definite purpose to acquire certain precise and accurate information or ideas or points of view. Thus the information sought might be just a single item such as the name of a person or place, a particular date, or a germaine fact. It might be a point of view developed in a magazine article, or a section of an article or book that is relevant to a problem at hand. (p. 45)

Now that the definition of skimming has been discussed, we are ready to begin the review of relevant research.

Whipple and Curtis (1917) began their article in the *Journal of Educational Psychology* with the following sentence, "This appears to be the first published experimental study of the process of skimming in reading" (p. 333). They reported mean reading rates for their six subjects (two undergraduates, two graduate students, and two instructors) when they read educational reprints from journals such as *School Review*. When they read these materials normally and silently, their rate was 231 wpm, and when they skimmed they read at 455 wpm. Given the difficulty level of journal articles, it is not too surprising that their "normal" rate was 231 wpm. The skimming rate of 455 wpm is roughly the model skimming rate given in Chapter 2. Whipple and Curtis listed 12 conclusions, three of which are quoted below:

> Skimming itself embraces at least five different varieties or modes. (p. 333)
>
> When readers are forced to skim at a prescribed and unusually high rate, reproduction becomes very poor and the whole process becomes disagreeable and flurried. (p. 333)
>
> Subject matter lying outside the reader's general range of information would undoubtedly be skimmed only with difficulty and poorly, since in successful skimming much is supplied by the reader's previous information or his interpretation of the writer's intent as gathered from the context. (p. 334)

The above quotations from 70 years ago captured the essence of skimming as a basic reading process, and show no sign of being out of date.

McClusky (1934) studied the effect of ". . . preliminary skimming on a normal reading of the same passage immediately following the skimming" (p. 521). His research involved an experimental group of 59 college sophomores who were given 15 minutes of practice in three types of skimming. His control group consisted of 59 matched pairs—matched on an intelligence test and a reading test. Both groups were asked to read normally a 611-word passage from sociology dealing with the topic of "Woman and Marriage." After reading, 21 "new-type objective questions" were administered. The experimental group was asked to skim the passage for 15 seconds before they read it "normally." The reading rate for the experimental group, including the 15 second "warm up," was 233 wpm; the rate for the control group was 211 wpm—9% slower. The experimental group was slightly faster and answered slightly fewer of the comprehension questions correctly—16.18 versus 16.37. It appears that asking these college students to shift up to a skimming process immediately prior to operating their "normal" reading process had little or no effect upon the rate or efficiency at which this lower gear operated.

Fleming (1968) conducted a review of skimming research with the following introductory comments:

> Despite the frequency with which skimming is mentioned as an important skill, there has been surprisingly little research on the nature of this skill. In fact, it would seem that skimming has been almost totally neglected as a subject for empirical research. A fairly careful review of the pertinent research literature has revealed only two major experimental studies of skimming, and these studies, both doctoral dissertations were conducted some years ago. . . . (p. 211)

Fleming appears to have missed the 1917 and 1934 publications, reviewed earlier. However, in the 50-year period between 1917 and 1968 there appears to have been only one published research study on skimming. After reviewing these two dissertations that he found, Fleming concluded that "an increase in our understanding of skimming is essential" (p. 218).

Maxwell (1972) presented a very brief overview of a study that involved four groups of college students, two of which received skimming instruction and two of which did not. No differences were found among the groups on the criterion measure of skimming improvement. This study has been mentioned only because of the paucity of research relevant to investigation of scanning and skimming improvement. It seems possible that the reason there is so little published research in this area, is because it is difficult, if not impossible, to teach people how to improve their ability to get the gist or to locate the most important information faster, as will be suggested by subsequent research.

Masson (1982) published a series of skimming studies that are exemplars of carefulness and control. This research will be described in detail. The research was introduced as follows:

A significant amount of processing of written text involves reading speeds in excess of the normal range of 200–300 words/minute. On many occasions a reader is interested in obtaining a specific piece of information or gist of a story in a short time without carefully reading each sentence. In these instances some sort of rapid reading technique, generally referred to here as *skimming*, is used which enables the reader to process a story at rates perhaps two or three times normal reading speed.

When skimming a story, however, a reader most likely misses a good deal of the information that could be extracted by a more careful reading. (p. 400)

In Masson's Experiment I, 72 college students were given ". . . four report-style narratives from *Reader's Digest*, of about 1,000 words each, and four wire service newspaper stories, each about 400 words . . ." (p. 402). In the normal rate condition, the subjects ". . . were instructed to read at the rate they would use to read a story for full comprehension and to try to comprehend the meaning of the stories," and in the skimming condition the subjects ". . . were told to read at the rate they would use to comprehend the gist of a story and were told to read each story for its gist" (p. 403). The subjects were also told that ". . . a test would follow, but reading for meaning rather than memorization was stressed" (p. 403). Practice was given so subjects had a good idea of what the questions required. There were three types of questions: gist, which they labeled macrostatements; detailed, which they labeled microstatements; and inference. They also gave their test questions to the members of a control group who had no opportunity to read the passages.

Masson reported the mean reading rate under the normal condition to be 232 wpm, which is well below the average rauding process rate of college students. Parenthetically, and with the clear vision of hindsight, it will be noted that if the purpose was to compare skimming to normal reading, i.e., the rauding process or third gear, then the instructions for normal reading could have been improved in the following ways: (a) by *not* asking the subjects to read for "full comprehension," and (b) by telling the subjects *not* to modify their normal reading habits just so they could improve their performance on the test questions. Possibly these modified instructions would have kept their subjects from using their learning process (Gear 2) on this relatively easy material. With respect to the skimming rate of 382 wpm, both groups of subjects reported on a questionnaire administered after the experiment that ". . . they read about as fast or slightly faster in the experiment than they normally would when reading for full comprehension or skimming" (p. 405). Thus, the results are probably representative of a typical skimming process. It may not be the model skimming process but it is proceeding at a rate somewhat comparable to the rate hypothesized for the model skimming process (450 Wpm given in Table 2.2.).

The results indicated that when subjects increased their reading rate and tried to get the gist, scores on all types of tests suffered approximately equally. There was no evidence that the subjects were able to find the more important or gist information so that gist and inference suffered less than detailed information. Stated differently, when their subjects speeded up their reading rates, switching from a process designed to produce "full comprehension" to a process designed to get the gist, scores on all types of test questions—inference, gist, and details— dropped equal amounts. This suggested that "increasing reading rate caused memory for (and perhaps comprehension of) important and unimportant information to suffer to the same degree" (p. 406). It appears that skimming simply resulted in sampling less of the information by skipping over parts of it without any evidence that the subjects were able to accurately predict which parts were more or less important.

In Masson's Experiment II, the design was similar to Experiment I except rates were manipulated by pacing subjects (a tone sounded when it was time to turn a page) and the total time was limited so that the average reading rates were 225, 375, and 600 wpm. As in Experiment I, the results were the same for both the narrative passages and the newspaper stories. There was no evidence that either of the two skimming groups (375 Wpm and 600 Wpm) were able to skip unimportant information and concentrate more on important information because performance on inference, gist, and detail questions all dropped equally as rate increased. The results were summarized as follows: "In the first two experiments, subjects were assigned the general task of extracting important, gist-relevant information from stories, and they showed little evidence of being able to sample this information selectively while skipping details" (p. 409).

In Masson's Experiment III, the design was similar to Experiment II except the reading material was changed. The 355-word passages could be read from two different perspectives, depending upon what title preceded the story. Half the subjects were given one of the two titles and told to try to derive from each story information relevant to the particular perspective indication by their title. The results were similar to Experiments I and II and were summarized as follows:

> . . . we consistently see subjects losing about equal amounts of important and unimportant or relevant and irrelevant information as reading speeds increase. This probably is a result of the fact that strategies such as reading the

first sentence of each paragraph or looking for key words do not adequately encompass the critical information in a text. Information contributing to the gist of certain types of passages can be lodged in very inconspicuous locations which readers using common types of skimming strategies would fail to explore. (p. 412)

In Experiment IV, the design was similar to Experiment III, except the material was different and the testing was different. There were seven 500-word passages taken from *Reader's Digest*. The subjects were told ". . . to read each story for its gist and that after reading a story they would be asked to recall everything they could, as completely as possible, from one paragraph" (p. 413). Again, the results replicated Experiments I, II, and III. Compared to the 225 wpm condition, the 375 and 600 wpm skimming conditions indicated less recall of both important and unimportant information.

For the total of 330 subjects who skimmed in the four experiments conducted by Masson, the quotation below appeared to summarize the findings best:

Readers do not seem to be able to skip over details and read only the important information. In most stories there rarely is an obvious basis for accepting a statement as important or rejecting it as unimportant, beyond reading at least part of the statement. Reading-time constraints seem to force readers to sample only certain portions of a text while completely missing other potentially important information. (p. 415)

Masson (1983) compared a traditional skimming process to RSVP (rapid sequential visual presentation of words) in a series of experiments. The materials presented for viewing on a computer monitor were passages taken from *Reader's Digest* articles which averaged 133 words in length. Under the traditional skimming condition the entire passage was presented. Under the RSVP condition only one word at a time was presented. In the first three experiments, involving rates from 375 to 700 wpm, Masson used various measures of the accuracy of comprehension, *A*, and he found that the RSVP condition was generally inferior to the skimming condition. For example, in Experiment 2, the traditional skimming condition had a higher score both at 375 wpm (0.36 versus 0.34) and at 500 wpm (0.32 versus 0.27) when the measure of comprehension involved writing a one-sentence summary. In Experiment 4, Masson presented each word for 100 msec and inserted 500 msec pauses at the end of sentences during the RSVP condition. He showed that performance under the RSVP condition improved so that it was almost exactly equal to traditional skimming. For example, at 500 wpm the difference was

0.39 versus 0.35 using general questions, and the difference was 0.22 versus 0.19 using specific questions.

These differences between traditional skimming processes and RSVP are quite small and might have evaporated completely if Masson had based his word presentation time of 100 msec on standard length words instead of actual words. For example, Masson would present the word "go" for 100 msec and he would also present the word "anniversary" for 100 msec. If Masson had instead based his word presentation times on standard length words per minute, i.e., 500 Wpm, then (a) the word "go" would have been presented for 60 msec and the word "anniversary" would have been presented for 220 msec, and (b) the word "go" at the end of a sentence would have been presented for 100 msec. This latter presentation condition would allow long words the time they need in proportion to the time needed for short words, and it would also allow an extra 40 msec at the end of each sentence. In any event, the supposed advantages associated with traditional skimming, such as being able to skip over unimportant words to better obtain the gist seem to be non-existent or trivial at best. Otherwise, presenting all the words in the RSVP condition—one word at a time with a pause at the end of sentences—would not have provided comprehension scores so close to the scores obtained from traditional skimming which supposedly involves skipping unimportant words or sentences.

Before leaving this skimming research of Masson's, it should not go unnoticed that his series of experiments involved rates of 375, 500, 600, and 700 wpm, with most of his conditions concentrated on 375 and 500 wpm. It can be seen that the model skimming rate of 450 Wpm presented in Chapter 2 is very close to the rates chosen by this researcher to study reading processes that he chose to call skimming.

From the skimming data reviewed in this section, it appears prudent to conclude that the 450 Wpm rate for model skimming is a reasonable value for Gear 2 to operate. The college students in Masson's 1982 research, Experiment I, chose to operate a reading process, which they themselves regarded as skimming, at a rate of 382 wpm. Thus, when college students choose to give up some comprehension and get the gist of a passage, they appear to do this at a rate somewhere between their typical rauding process rate of about 260–300 Wpm and their normal model scanning rate of 600 Wpm.

There appears to be no evidence that college students are able to speed up their reading rate by skipping over *unimportant* information. Instead, the evidence suggests that when they shift out of Gear 3 and operate at faster rates, they simply sample less of all types of information, such as gist versus detailed, important versus unimportant, or relevant versus irrelevant.

CONCLUSIONS

Introduction

The research reviewed up to this point will now be interpreted with respect to certain theory and practices relevant to scanning and skimming. These conclusions will be structured using six so-called "myths" about reading given by Maxwell (1969b). These myths supposedly prevent students from developing good scanning and skimming skills. The six myths are contained in a textbook/workbook designed to help students improve their skills and they appear to have been taken seriously by practioners (see Sherer, 1975).

Myth 1. I have to read every word   In her explanation of this myth, Maxwell argues that ". . . articles, redundant phrases, etc., can often be ignored by the reader, depending upon his purpose, without risking loss of comprehension" (p. 50). The research reviewed in earlier chapters, most of which came after Maxwell's writings, indicates that in fact one must read every word in order to understand the content of written material, at least during the operation of the rauding process, a learning process, or a recalling process. Operating in third gear, the rauding process, seems to be necessary for comprehending the complete thoughts contained in the sentences of passages and this requires the recognition and semantic encoding of each and every word. It is true that readers can skip over words and even sentences during skimming, but there is no evidence that college students can be taught to ignore the unimportant words such as articles or redundant phrases to their advantage. Maxwell does not refer to any research evidence which directly supports the belief that this is a myth and the more recent research (Masson, 1982) suggests that this myth is not a myth at all. Suggesting to students that they can learn to skip over unimportant words and thereby improve their reading rate without losing any comprehension has no basis in fact. Maxwell's Myth 1 is not a myth and probably does more harm than good when forced upon students. Given what we now know, it would make more sense to tell students that they should read every word when they are operating normally in third gear, but they may skip words when they shift into fourth or fifth gear to accomplish different goals.

Myth 2. Reading once is enough   The point of this myth is that some students supposedly think that reading a passage once is enough to remember it forever. Indeed, this does appear to be a myth. Shifting into the more powerful first and second gears may be required to understand and remember most textbook material. Also, using one of the reading processes that operates in these lower gears often requires that the words be read more than once, as the research on regressive eye movements indicated in Chapter 5.

Myth 3. It is sinful to skip passages in reading A careful reading of what Maxwell has written about this myth suggests that she is concerned that some students approach all reading situations with exactly the same word for word reading process and have not learned to scan or skim. Indeed, every college student should be capable of shifting out of Gear 3 into a skimming process when only the gist or an overview is the best goal in a particular situation. Maxwell's Myth 3 appears to be on target because it deals more with encouraging students to learn to shift up to Gears 4 and 5 when the goals require it.

Myth 4. Machines are necessary to improve my reading speed Indeed, there appears to be no evidence that machines are needed to teach people to shift into fourth or fifth gear which accomplish different goals, involve different components, and proceed at faster rates (see Berger, 1969).

Myth 5. If I skim or read too rapidly, my comprehension will drop The argument here is based upon a correlation between scores on comprehension measures and rate measures. It is true that the individuals who score the highest on measures of the accuracy of comprehension, A, tend to be the same individuals who read the fastest, and these data will be reviewed in much more detail in Chapter 16. Thus, Maxwell exhorts students to speed up their rate because she says rate can be increased without any loss of comprehension by extracting and retaining the important ideas.

Maxwell's Myth 5 is not a myth and must be rejected; this so-called myth is based upon one of the most pernicious pitfalls associated with reading rate. Just because certain measures of comprehension and rate are positively correlated *between* individuals does not mean that comprehension and rate are positively correlated *within* individuals. For example, there is generally a positive correlation between scores on a reading rate test and scores on a reading comprehension test because the students who read the fastest also tend to be the same ones who get the higher comprehension test scores. However, this is a between-individual positive correlation between comprehension and rate. This does *not* mean that if a particular student reads a passage faster that student will comprehend more of that passage. In fact, Masson's (1982) research indicates just the opposite; as a general rule, increasing rate automatically lowers comprehension.

In addition, the Masson research found no evidence that students could increase their rate during skimming and maintain their ability to locate important or gist information. Instead, the evidence indicated that increasing rate lowers every type of comprehension (gist, detail, inference) because the increase in rate simply reflects an indiscriminant skipping of all types of information with a subsequent loss of all types equally. In summary, Myth 5 of Maxwell's turns out to be a major truth instead of a myth.

It should not go unnoticed that the goal of skimming is *not* to comprehend the complete thought in each sentence, which is the goal of the rauding process. Shifting up to Gear 4, skimming, necessarily involves a lowering of the accuracy of comprehension, *A*, because dropping the sentential integration component is what allows skimming to go faster.

Myth 6. There is something about my eyes that keeps me from reading fast Under this myth, Maxwell tells students that it is their brain that slows them down, not their eyes, and that they need to break the habit of sounding out the words as they read. There is no known research that suggests that the primary cause of slow reading rate is a malfunction of the eyes (see Chapter 5 on eye movements), so there is no problem with this aspect of Myth 6. However, the research reviewed earlier on silent speech in Chapter 4 suggests that silent speech is not harmful. Saying the words to oneself during reading is not counter productive but instead is definitely helpful to the rauding, learning, and memorizing processes, and may be helpful to scanning and skimming processes as well. Therefore this 1969 advice given by Maxwell about the harmful effect of sounding out words appears to be wrong, given the research that has accumulated in the subsequent 20-year period.

With respect to Maxwell's six myths, some modifications are in order. Myth 1 needs to be drastically revised. Students do have to look at every word when engaged in Gears 1, 2, and 3 but not in Gears 4 and 5. The rauding process, a learning process, or a recalling process ordinarily require word for word reading but during a skimming process or a scanning process, words or sentences may be skipped. However, the accuracy or comprehension, *A*, will definitely drop during a skimming or scanning process; there is no evidence that students can learn to skip over the less important words or information without also skipping over the more important words or information. Maxwell's Myths 2, 3, and 4 appear to be acceptable but Myths 1, 5, and 6 need to be rejected or drastically revised.

The above conclusions have been given in the context of a review of Maxwell's myths because it is assumed that these myths are representative of the kind of misinformation still being given to college students since 1969. For example, Fry (1978) also suggested to students that they can skip and still be capable of locating the more important information, but to his credit he does acknowledge that adopting a skimming approach automatically means that the student must be willing to accept *lower* comprehension.

Summary

Prior theory and research on scanning and skimming have suffered from a failure to discriminate among the five basic reading processes, which have different goals, components, and consequences. Shifting into the two highest gears that involve scanning and skimming processes is necessary to achieve efficiently the goals associated with these faster reading processes. However, there is no evidence that students can learn to skip over unimportant words and thereby speed up Gear 3, the rauding process, without lowering the accuracy of comprehension, A. Also, there is no evidence that students can learn to avoid sounding out each of the words in sentences and thereby speed up their rauding process. Instead of claiming that students can be taught to operate their rauding process faster by skimming and scanning training, they could be taught when profitably to shift out of their normally operating third gear into their faster operating fourth and fifth gears.

It is important to recognize the distinctive differences between the rauding process and the faster reading processes of scanning and skimming. Operating in fourth and fifth gears allows more words to be covered in less time but readers should not expect to accomplish what the more powerful third gear accomplishes with its sentence integration component.

7

RAUDING

INTRODUCTION

The rauding process, Gear 3, is the most important of all the reading processes because it is the essence of most people's daily reading. When authors compose the sentences that form passages, they assume that most readers will use their rauding process so that each consecutive complete thought of the author will be comprehended. This process is used more frequently than any other reading process. As noted earlier, third gear seems to be the type of reading process operating when individuals are described as being engaged in ordinary reading, normal reading, natural reading, or typical reading. This process ordinarily operates slower than skimming processes, fourth gear, because it requires that the words in sentences be integrated into the complete thoughts they represent. This process ordinarily operates faster than learning processes, second gear, because there is no requirement that the ideas be remembered. Also, there are few regressions for rereading or rethinking about words or thoughts because they are typically understood on the first encounter.

The rauding process is most effective for understanding the thoughts contained in passages that are at a level of difficulty, D_L, that is below the level of ability of the individual, A_L. Most individuals, most of the time, read material that is not too difficult to understand ($A_L > D_L$). For example, it was noted earlier that Sharon (1973) surveyed a national sample of American adults and found that only about 1% reported having any difficulty with any material that they read; one interpretation that Sharon gave for this finding was that almost all individuals who find material hard to understand simply do not bother reading it. It appears that most individuals operate their rauding process close to its upper limit, integrating the thoughts in sentences just as fast as their thinking speed, or cognitive speed, will allow.

The parts of the rauding process involved in navigating through text can be likened to similar parts in the walking process involved in navigating through streets. In rauding and in walking, the eyes and the legs respectively seem to be automatically programmed to move across a line and over cracks at a comfortable rate that maximizes the distance covered per level of effort expended. By concentrating on the walking process, individuals can easily speed up their rate 10–15% but they will undoubtedly find that they will not be able to walk as long without fatigue as they would have at their normal walking rate. Similarly, individuals can probably speed up their rauding process rate by about 10–15% without any loss in the accuracy of comprehension, but they will probably not be able to read as long without becoming fatigued.

To support these general ideas about rauding, some of the details of the process that were described in Chapter 2 will be reviewed. During the operation of the rauding process, the individual fixates upon the first word in the sentence, recognizes it visually, and simultaneously recodes it into a form of silent speech. The word is semantically encoded and integrated with the prior words in the sentence. It is also stored in short-term memory, so it can be integrated with the subsequent words in the sentence and formed into the complete thought that is related to its context. The eye is then moved forward so that the subsequent word can be perceived and processed similarly. This process continues with each subsequent word until the last word in the sentence has been processed, at which time the complete thought in the sentence is understood in its context and then short-term memory of these words is cleared so as to be ready for the next sentence. When this process is operated on relatively easy material ($A_L > D_L$), there are few if any regressions. The fastest rate at which this process can successfully operate, i.e., $A > 0.75$, is called the rauding rate, R_r.

The rauding rate is also purported to be the optimal rate in the sense that other rates for operating the rauding process will result in fewer sentences, or thoughts, understood per minute. The rauding rate is the most efficient rate; when $R = R_r$, then E is at a maximum. For example, if the individual is presented the words in passages at a rate R that is higher than the rauding rate ($R > R_r$) such as the model skimming rate at 450 Wpm, then the accuracy A at which the thoughts are being understood will drop faster than the speed is being increased so their product, $A \times R$, will decrease. The product, $A \times R$, is called efficiency, E, and the efficiency that accompanies the rauding rate is symbolized as E_r.

Operating the rauding process at R_r represents the fastest rate at which an individual can successfully understand the complete thought in each consecutive sentence. The rauding rate is the individual's highest rate of comprehension whereby comprehension is relatively accurate; it is the highest rate at which the rauding process can operate and be relatively successful in that the accuracy of thoughts comprehended is greater than 75%. Thus, a person's R_r is also a threshold rate. Rates higher than R_r will not allow enough time for the components of the rauding process to function successfully. R_r is also a constant rate over varying levels of material difficulty. It operates at each individual's limit in terms of how fast the words can be perceived or recognized, internally articulated, semantically encoded, integrated into the partial thought of the sentence, and stored into a temporary memory buffer until the end of the sentence is reached, at which time the complete thought is understood. Then, the sentences are stored in the "Place Where Sentences Go When They Are Understood," all in accordance with the processes outlined by P. H. Gough (1972).

The rauding process is assumed to operate according to the principles outlined above. Stated differently, it is also assumed to operate according to three laws of rauding theory (Carver, 1981), which were also described earlier in Chapter 2. Law I is that individuals attempt to comprehend the thoughts in the sentences of passages at a constant rate, unless they are influenced by situation specific factors to change that rate $(R = R_r)$. This means that the rauding rate is the normal, ordinary, and typical rate that individuals read or operate their rauding process. For example, if you tap people on the shoulder, hand them a short, easy passage, and then ask them to "read" it, they are likely to engage their rauding process at R_r. Law II is that the efficiency of passage comprehension is the product of the accuracy of comprehension and the rate of comprehension $(E = AR)$, as was discussed earlier. Law III is that the most efficient rate of comprehending thoughts in a passage is the rauding rate (when $R = R_r$, then $E_{max} = E_r$), as was also discussed earlier.

In summary, the rauding process operates at a constant rate across different levels of material difficulty as long as the ability of the reader is higher than the difficulty of the material $(R = R_r$ when $A_L > D_L)$. R_r is also purported to be the optimal rate because efficiency is lower at other rates; this optimal characteristic of is not restricted to reading but also applies to auding (see Glossary).

Evidence relevant to the above properties purported to be associated with the rauding process will now be reviewed.

RESEARCH

In 1983, Carver reported a study of reading rates involving 435 students who were asked to read passages at the following grade levels of difficulty: 1, 4, 7, 10, 13, and 16. The students, ranging from grade 4 through college, were instructed to "read at the rate at which they normally read," and they were told that "there would be no test on what they read" because the purpose was ". . . to get an idea about their normal reading rate" (p. 195). These instructions and objective consequences are likely to induce most students to engage their rauding process. In accordance with the results reviewed earlier in Chapter 3, reading rate in wpm declined with each increasingly difficult passage. However, for all levels of reader ability, the rate in Wpm was relatively constant across different levels of difficulty, especially when $A_L > D_L$. For example, the rates at which the college level readers (called Ability Level 5) read the fourth, seventh, tenth, and thirteenth grade level passages were about 300, 310, 310, and 290 Wpm, respectively. These results are presented in Fig. 7.1. Notice that the same degree of constancy was exhibited by the other levels of reader ability, e.g., high school (Level 4), junior high (Level 3), and elementary (Levels 2 and 1), and this replicates the constancy of rate that Morse (1951) found for fifth graders and seventh graders (see Fig. 5.2).

The amount of change in rate between one level of difficulty and another was also calculated for each individual and averaged. For those situations involving relatively easy material, $A_L > D_L$, the mean percentage change values ranged from 12.0 to 14.4%. This means that there was

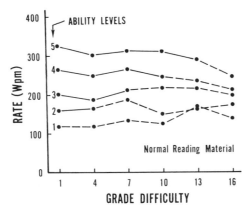

Figure 7.1 Reading rate in standard length words per minute, Wpm, as a function of the difficulty level, D_L, of the material for individuals at five levels of reading ability. The five levels of ability were as follows: Level 5, college; Level 4, high school; Level 3, junior high; Level 2, elementary; Level 1, primary. The long dashed lines indicate that the material was relatively difficult ($A_L < D_L$) because the ability level of the individual was lower than the difficulty level of the material (Fig. 4 from Carver, 1983.)

no tendency for individuals to speed up when they encountered easier material, as long as $A_L > D_L$, but individuals did vary their rauding process rate about 13%, on the average, from one difficulty level to another. These college students averaged about 300 Wpm, when $A_L > D_L$, and this means that typical college students can be expected to vary the rate of their rauding process from about 260 to 340 Wpm.

These 1983 data of Carver's plus those data reviewed earlier in Chapters 3 and 5 (Carver, 1976; Coke, 1974; G. R. Miller & Coleman, 1971; Morse, 1951; Zuber & Wetzel, 1981) leave little doubt that the rauding process operates at a relatively constant rate, ±13% within individuals across a range of material difficulties and across a range of ability levels. These data also indicate that the process is relatively constant but not perfectly constant since rate changed by about 13% either higher or lower, on the average, from one difficulty level to another. These data are also in accordance with the rauding process operating at an average around 260–300 Wpm for college students, as was hypothesized at the outset. These data also provide strong support for Law I of rauding theory as discussed earlier in this chapter.

In 1982, a year earlier than the above research, Carver reported upon a lengthy study of the effect of reading rate and auding rate upon the accuracy and efficiency of comprehension. Reading rate was manipulated by presenting passages at rates between 83 and 500 Wpm using motion picture film. Auding rate was also manipulated between 83 and 500 Wpm using time-compressed speech. The 108 college students involved were paid bonuses depending upon how well they did on the tests that they were administered on the 100-word passages. These bonuses could not indirectly induce students to shift to a lower gear since the students had little or no control over how the material was encountered. The following four grade levels of difficulty were used: 5, 8, 11, and 14, called Level 2 (elementary), Level 3 (junior high), Level 4 (senior high), and Level 5 (college), respectively. There were two types of objective tests. One type involved multiple-choice tests based upon paraphrases of the sentences in the passages. The other was a modified cloze type of test. Subjects were also asked to rate the percentage of each passage they thought they understood.

All three of the above indicants of the accuracy of comprehension, A, produced similar results. As rate increased, accuracy of comprehension decreased; this was true in all eight difficulty-mode conditions and is depicted in the eight graphs of Fig. 7.2. No matter which of the four difficulty levels, 5, 8, 11, or 14, and no matter whether the subjects were reading or listening, accuracy of comprehension, A, tended to decline as rate was increased. (Note: The symbol "L" in Fig. 7.2 has been used to designate a grouping of three grade levels, e.g., $L_d = 1$ means a grouping of first, second, and third grade levels of difficulty.)

The more interesting and relevant results of this Carver (1982) research, however, involved the effect of rate upon the efficiency of comprehension, E, which is $A \times R$ as noted earlier. For each of the eight difficulty-mode conditions, efficiency increased as rate increased, up to about 300 Wpm, and then further increases in rates were associated with decreases in efficiency. In other words, efficiency peaked around 300 Wpm for all four levels of difficulty under both reading and auding conditions. These results are presented in Fig. 7.3. (Note: The data for the two objective tests in Fig. 7.2 were averaged and presented as a composite in Fig. 7.3.)

Further data analyses indicated that the rate where efficiency was a maximum tended to be constant across difficulty levels for those college students reading at the college level of ability (Level 5) as well as those college students reading at the high school level of ability (Level 4). There was a tendency for the optimal reading rate to be slightly higher than the optimal listening rate but the difference was only about 10% or about 30 Wpm; this was interpreted as a trivial difference in this experiment. These latter results are presented in Fig. 7.4. For example, for those students scoring at the college level of ability, $L_a = 5$, the rate at which efficiency was a maximum (in sentences per minute) was about 20 for Level 2 materials, about 22 for Level 3 materials, about 20 for Level 4 materials, and about 20 for Level 5 materials; this means that these college students read material at the fifth grade level at the same maximum efficiency as material at the fourteenth grade level. For the students testing out at the high school level of ability, $L_a = 4$, the data tended to replicate the college level readers, $L_a = 5$, and the auding data tended to replicate the reading data. Both the high school and college level readers ($L_a = 4$ and $L_a = 5$) tended to have lower maximum efficiency scores for the college level of material difficulty ($L_d = 5$ or $GE = 14$ material), as indicated by the drop off in the four dotted lines in Fig. 7.4. However, the rate at which the maximum efficiency occurred tended to be constant across all four difficulty levels as indicated by the four relatively flat, solid lines in Fig. 7.4.

The above results of this study were summarized by Carver (1982) as follows:

> The empirical results of this research provide strong support for the existence of an optimal rate of reading prose and an optimal rate for auding prose. The optimal rate of reading prose tended to be approximately equal to the optimal rate of auding prose. The optimal rate for both reading and auding prose

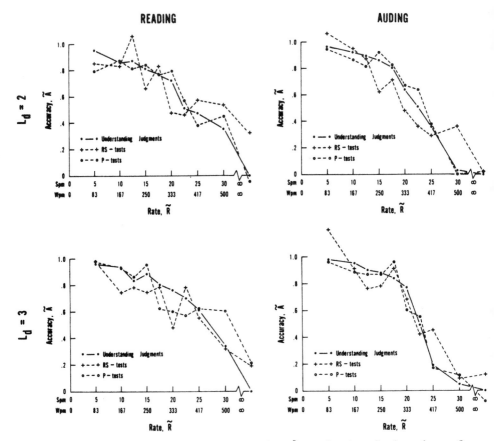

Figure 7.2 Estimated accuracy of comprehension, $\tilde{A}$, as a function of estimated rate of comprehension, $\tilde{R}$, when accuracy has been estimated using three different methods; there are eight graphs, for each of four different levels of difficulty and for both reading and auding at each level of difficulty. The difficulty levels were as follows: $L_d = 2$ is $D_L = 4, 5, 6$; $L_d = 3$ is $D_L = 7, 8, 9$; $L_d = 4$ is $D_L = 10, 11, 12$; $L_d = 5$ is $D_L = 13, 14, 15$. (Fig. 1 from Carver, 1982.)

tended to be a constant across a wide range of passage difficulty levels. The efficiency of comprehension for this group of college students tended to peak at an optimal rate of approximately 300 words per min when they were reading and when they were auding the passages. This same optimal rate of 300 words per minute held for passages at grade difficulties 5, 8, 11, and 14. The efficiencies associated with the optimal rates also tended to be equal across the two modes. In summary, the data indicate that there is an optimal rate that is constant across reading and auding and is also constant across prose difficulty levels. (p. 85)

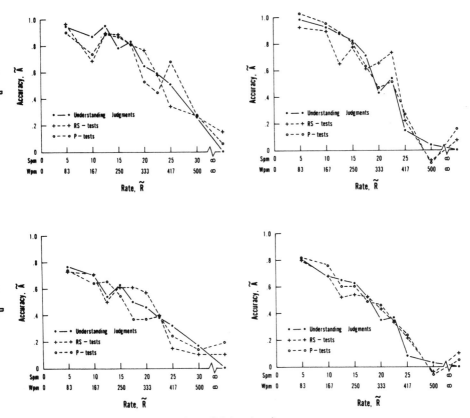

Figure 7.2 (*continued*)

CONCLUSIONS

The data reviewed above support the existence of the rauding process for college students that operates at a constant rate around 300 Wpm across material of varying difficulty levels and also across two modes of presentation, reading and auding. One reason why college students do not choose to operate their rauding process during reading at an average rate higher than 300 Wpm appears to be because their most efficient rate is at 300 Wpm. Forcing these college students to read at rates higher than 300 Wpm resulted in lower efficiency of comprehension. Another reason why college students do not choose to operate their rauding process at a higher rate, i.e., force their eyes to move faster, is that 300 Wpm

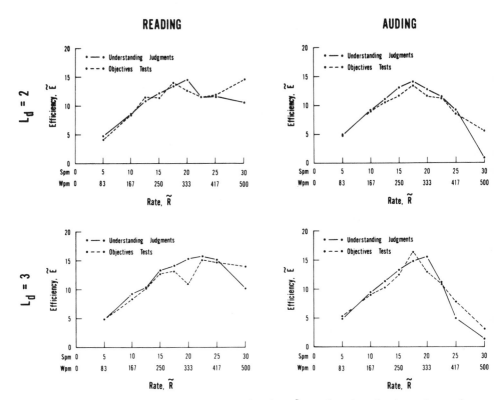

Figure 7.3 Estimated efficiency of comprehension, $\bar{E}$, as a function of estimated rate of comprehension, $\tilde{R}$, when accuracy of comprehension is estimated two ways, understanding judgments and an average of two objective tests. There are eight graphs, one for reading and one for auding at each of four levels of difficulty. The difficulty levels are as follows: $L_d = 2$ is $D_L = 4, 5, 6$; $L_d = 3$ is $D_L = 7, 8, 9$; $L_d = 4$ is $D_L = 10, 11, 12$; $L_d = 5$ is $D_L = 13, 14, 15$. (Fig. 2 from Carver, 1982.)

appears to represent a limit for operating the components of the rauding process. Otherwise, why was the optimal rate of reading the same as the optimal rate of auding? The factor limiting reading rate while trying to operate the rauding process successfully appears to have nothing directly to do with printed words or eye movements because there was no difference between the optimal rates during reading and auding. This means that it is very likely that the rauding process during reading is a print-driven process similar to the rauding process during auding which is a sound-driven process. Both involve the comprehension of the complete thoughts in sentences via lexical assessing, semantic encoding, and sentential integrating.

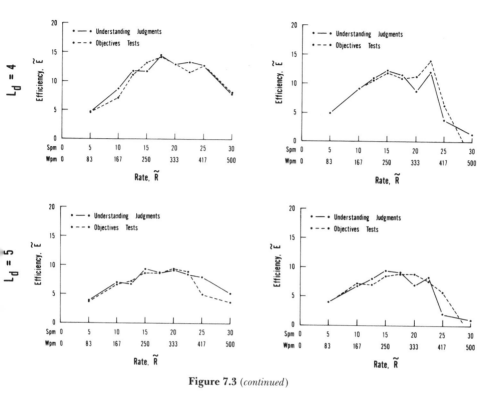

Figure 7.3 (*continued*)

IMPLICATIONS

If ordinary or normal reading is in fact best described as the operation of the rauding process, then the data reviewed in this chapter have important implications for reading and reading research. The constant rate of operation of the rauding process across difficulty levels and the constant rate across reading and auding suggests that accompanying eye movements and fixation durations are not likely to provide clues to higher cognitive processes. This is because it seems likely that eye movements and fixation durations act as a perceptual scoop for loading the printed words into a hopper and simultaneously converting them into silent speech. The same mechanism that allows us to comprehend the complete thoughts in auditorily presented prose also seems to be operating during reading. Once this translation is made into silent speech, all

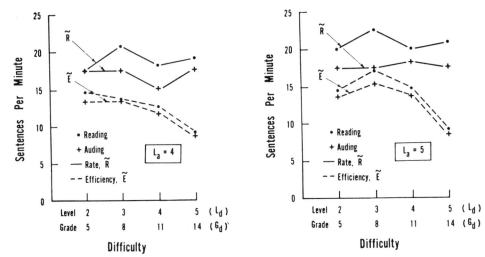

Figure 7.4   Estimated maximum efficiencies of comprehension, $\tilde{E}$, and the optimal rates associated with these maximum efficiencies, $\tilde{R}$, as a function of difficulty level (symbolized here as G_d instead of D_L) for college students reading at the high school level ($L_a = 4$ means $A_L = 10, 11, 12$) and at the college level ($L_a = 5$ means $A_L = 13, 14, 15$). (Fig. 7 from Carver, 1982.)

the other components such as lexical access, semantic encoding, and sentence integrating can proceed in an equally effective manner no matter whether the original stimulus was visual or auditory.

If Just and Carpenter (1980), for example, had been studying ordinary or normal reading (see Chapter 5), they would not have been able to predict variations in word fixation durations accurately for individual words. Instead of investigating the rauding process, they were investigating a learning process, as has already been discussed. They knowingly selected materials that contained unknown words, and there is nothing inherently wrong with this except their results probably will not generalize to the situation in which they seemed to be interested, i.e., ordinary reading.

In summary, knowledge about reading rate is almost useless unless the type of reading process involved is also known. The most important type of reading rate is that associated with the rauding process. The fastest rate at which an individual can operate the rauding process on relatively easy material is the rauding rate, R_r. This rate averages around 300 Wpm for college students reading at the college level of ability and it is systematically lower for lower levels of ability (see Table 2.1).

8

LEARNING AND MEMORIZING

INTRODUCTION

The learning and memorizing processes, Gear 2 and Gear 1 respectively, operate at a slower rate than the rauding process because they ordinarily involve all the components of the rauding process plus others. The additional components of these lower gears make them more powerful because they can be used to accomplish more difficult goals. In order to know the information contained in a passage, the idea-remembering component may be employed in the model learning process. The model memorizing process involves all the components of the learning process, plus the rehearsal component is also activated so that the words and thoughts are more likely to be freely recalled after the reading has been completed. Again, the main reason for reviewing research on learning and memorizing processes is to illustrate indelibly how these processes are distinctively different from the rauding process.

Before embarking upon the review of relevant research, the relationship between studying and these two basic reading processes, Gears 1 and 2, will be discussed. Studying usually involves an unspecified mixture of reading processes designed to accomplish a criterion task, such as passing a test. Studying may involve all five of the basic processes discussed in Chapter 2 plus others. Suppose a student is studying for a college course. A scanning process may be used to locate material relevant to a topic that is being researched for a term paper. Once a relevant source has been located by scanning, the material may be skimmed for the purpose of accumulating an overview while deciding how to organize the paper. The rauding process may be engaged whenever material is deemed highly relevant and the sentences are not too difficult to understand. A learning process may be engaged whenever the sentences are not being understood the first time they are read, or the accuracy of comprehension needs to be increased so that the probability of doing well on a midterm multiple-choice test is increased. A memorizing process also may be engaged, especially if the material is being studied for an essay exam or for an oral exam.

The studying literature has been reviewed by T. H. Anderson and Armbruster (1984). They note that reading passages more than once has been found to be an effective studying strategy. The model processes (see Chapter 2) have been presented in the context of reading the material once, except for regressions within sentences and occasional regressions to earlier sentences. Besides involving all five of the basic processes, studying is often accompanied by off-line behaviors that interrupt on-line processing, such as underlining, note taking, summarizing, questioning, and outlining. Thus, studying in the real world will ordinarily involve the five basic reading processes plus other nonreading processes that are supplementary. It may be irrelevant to measure reading rate during real world studying because reading processes are only involved part of the time.

Although studying in the real world may not be meaningfully described by measuring reading rate, or words covered per unit of time, research on studying can be so described. It is possible to separate and measure the reading rate that accompanies each of the five basic processes involved in studying. In fact, a great deal of existing reading research can be described as studying research because it often involves a criterion task that the subject is trying to accomplish by reading prose passages. This is the task demand aspect discussed earlier in Chapter 3. Researchers often intend to design an experiment to investigate normal reading, but because of the nature of their criterion task, they induce the subjects to engage in studying activities that are ancillary to the rauding process. For example, investigating "normal reading" by asking the same questions before and after the prose passages will likely induce studying kinds of activities such as scanning and skimming. These processes are used to locate the sentences in the passage directly relevant to the questions. Then, the rauding process, a learning process, and/or a memorizing process is engaged only on those sentences and none of the others.

Research on learning and memorizing processes will have a great deal in common with research on studying because they ordinarily involve a criterion task that induces the learning and memorizing processes. In the future, it will be helpful for researchers to be more explicit about which type of reading process they want to investigate. Danks (1969) seems to be one of the first experimentalists to have learned this lesson. He studied grammaticalness and meaningfulness in comprehension of sentences, and he concluded that "the learning and comprehension processes are not necessarily isomorphic and the variables identified as important in one situation may have a minimal effect in the other" (p. 696).

The ideal for researchers has been demonstrated by Aaronson (1976) who theorized that the processes associated with tasks that require comprehension were quite different from the processes associated with tasks that require verbatim memory. She then proceeded to collect data that in fact showed that individuals spent more time reading words at the end of phrases during a memorizing process whereas the reading times for words during a comprehension task were much lower and constant, and not higher at the end of phrases (Aaronson & Scarborough, 1976). Following that research, Aaronson and Scarborough (1977) concentrated on theory and data relevant to verbatim recall, i.e., a memorizing process, knowing full well that neither the theory nor the results would generalize to comprehension tasks. Stated differently, these researchers concentrated on reading times for a memorizing process expecting their results to be irrelevant to a learning process or the rauding process. The relevance of their theory and data to real world reading situations can be questioned, but the efforts to avoid generalizing across distinctively different reading processes should be applauded.

A learning process is used in the real world when we want to remember the information contained in a passage, or we want to understand the complete thoughts in difficult sentences. In this situation, we may do the following: (a) concentrate longer and harder on each word, (b) go back and reread phrases, (c) go back and reread prior sentences, and/or (d) make hypotheses about what it would take to make the sentences understandable. The model learning process described in Chapter 2 focused upon the idea-remembering component, when it is desirable to do well on a subsequent criterion task. However, it was also mentioned that a learning process is often used when we encounter sentences that we cannot understand during the operation of a rauding process. When we cannot successfully operate the rauding process, yet we are determined to learn what the author intended to communicate, then we often shift to a lower gear and try to solve this problem by hypothesizing what the meaning might be and then gathering data to test this hypothesis.

It may be relatively easy to describe how learning processes work, but it is not easy to find pure examples of research that can be used to demonstrate the existence of one of these processes. Asking multiple-choice questions is likely to induce a learning process. However, if the subjects learn that the questions are easy and few in number then the rauding process is more likely to be engaged. Or, multiple-choice questions will likely induce a memorizing process if the subjects learn that they are numerous and quite difficult to answer successfully unless they do a great deal of rehearsal on the factual details contained in the passage.

Next, research relevant to learning processes and memorizing processes will be reviewed, in turn.

LEARNING PROCESSES

Morasky and Willcox (1970) gave college students a 2000-word passage with questions immediately following each of the 21 paragraphs contained in the passage. The time required to read was measured separately from the time taken to answer the questions. The mean total time was 707.7 sec so the average reading rate was 170 wpm, which is close to the model learning process rate of 200 Wpm (see Chapter 2). Even this rate is not as accurate as desirable, since it includes the time taken on two graphs that were included with the paragraphs. Thus, the rate without graphical material would be expected to be slightly higher. One of the empirical purposes of this research was to compare the reading times of subjects who received the questions before the passages versus those who received them afterwards. With the advantage of hindsight, this research could be viewed as comparing the time taken by one group who used a learning process with another group who used a combination of scanning, skimming, rauding, and learning processes.

Graesser, Hoffman, and Clark (1980) gave 12 passages to college students from an introductory psychology course. Half of the 36 subjects were "... instructed to comprehend the passages well because they would later be tested by writing essays on the contents of each passage," and the other half were told that they would "later receive a multiple-choice test on the information" (p. 143). It could be predicted that the multiple-choice group would be induced to adopt a learning process and the essay group would be induced to adopt a slower memorizing process. Indeed, these researchers reported that "subjects in the essay condition generally read the material for a longer duration," (p. 143) and this supports the descriptions of the learning and memorizing processes. Unfortunately, they did not report the rates for each of the two groups. Instead they reported a combined rate of 158 words per minute. It seems possible that the rates for the multiple-choice group would have approached 200 Wpm and the rates for the essay group would have approached 138 Wpm, as would be predicted from theory presented in Chapter 2.

Graesser *et al.* seemed to agree with the main thesis of the five basic reading processes when they noted that "processing components that conceptually relate words and sentences are more demanding on resources and require more time to complete" (p. 135). However, they later commented that "researchers generally agree that reading is an active, flexible process that varies with the goals of the comprehender" (p. 142). This latter statement is worded in a way that blurs the distinctions among processes but does emphasize the goals that form the basis for shifting from one process to another.

The ambiguity noted above seems to reflect much current thinking which insists on studying "the" reading process as if there were one process. By analogy, many researchers seem to have a view of reading that is similar to an automatic transmission with no manual gear shifting while the thesis of this book has been a manual transmission with five gears. Since the five basic processes described in Chapter 2 involve different components or subprocesses, shifting from one gear to another is not simply a matter of shifting rates but of shifting goals, components, and outcomes. In keeping with the idea of a highly fluid process, Graesser *et al.* comment that the 158 wpm rate of their subjects was ". . . not substantially slower than the rate of casual reading (200–300 wpm)." This comment makes the conflict between their notions and the current focus upon five basic processes more apparent. Their observed rate of 158 wpm for college students is the rate at which students at the fourth grade level of ability operate their rauding process (see Table 2.1), and is not close to typical or normal reading for college students. They reference Tinker (1965) for this range of 200–300 wpm for casual reading but I scanned his 322 page book and could only find where he said that "the rate in normal reading would be 250 to 300 words per minute" (p. 20), which is much more in keeping with the rate assigned the rauding process in Table 2.2, i.e., 300 Wpm.

R. F. Lorch, Lorch, and Matthews (1985) asked 59 college students to read passages that were over 100 sentences long while measuring their reading times for topic and nontopic sentences. No measure of the difficulty level of the material was given. The sentences were presented one at a time on a computer screen; the students pressed the space bar when they were through reading a sentence and then the next sentence would appear. The students were told that (a) the purpose of the research was to investigate reading comprehension, (b) the computer would measure their reading times, and (c) "they should not rush their reading but read at a comfortable pace without stopping to rest" (p. 354). After reading one of these passages that contained around 115 sentences, the students were presented a "verification" task. This task involved answering true or false to 24 sentences, 12 of which were paraphrases of sentences they had just read (true sentences) and 12 contained information that contradicted the text (false sentences). From this information about the materials, individuals, instructions, and objective consequences it is not easy to be confident that these students would shift out of third gear into a learning process. However, from the reading times presented in seconds per sentence and the actual sentences presented in an appendix, it was possible to calculate the reading rate for the topic sentences (in Experiment 1) to be 147 wpm, and for the nontopic sentences it was 166 wpm. These rates also include reaction time for pressing the space bar so these rates would actually be higher, probably around the 200 Wpm for a model learning process. Therefore, it seems reasonable to categorize this research as an investigation of a learning process.

R. F. Lorch *et al.* interpreted their results as being relevant to a "general model of reading" and the role played in "the reading process" by on-line processing of topic structure; they noted that reading times were "considerably slower" for topic sentences than for nontopic sentences. There are two problems with this interpretation. First, the difference they found was between 147 and 166 wpm which is only 19 wpm or 11%, and it is possible to consider this difference to be small or relatively insignificant. Second, the rates of 147 and 166 wpm likely reflect a reading process that is quite different from the rauding process and therefore it is questionable whether the impression should be left that these results apply to a general model of reading.

It is crucial that results from research on learning processes not be interpreted as necessarily having relevance to other basic processes. Notice that some researchers might erroneously interpret the R. F. Lorch *et al.* data as being in conflict with rauding theory which holds that the rauding process ordinarily operates at a constant rate. If topic sentences are read slower than nontopic sentences then this would seem to provide evidence against this aspect of rauding theory. However, these rates of 147 and 166 wpm are comparable to the average reading rates of students in the fourth and fifth grades (see Table 2.1) and cannot be reasonably interpreted as representative of a normal or typical reading process for college students. In fact, if college students were induced to operate their rauding process in this research, it could be predicted that the 11% difference in rate between topic sentences and nontopic sentences would evaporate completely.

R. F. Lorch and Lorch (1986) studied the rate at which 77 college students read sentences in four passages when certain sentences were signaled as being summary sentences or important sentences. The difficulty level of the passages was not mentioned. There were three to five comprehension questions on each of the four passages. There was no information given about how the students were instructed to read the text, but the authors did report that they did not analyze the data from the comprehension tests because "the purpose of the tests was to encourage the subjects to read the texts carefully" (p. 492). These conditions were likely to elicit a learning process but that could not be confirmed because there were no rate data reported. From a regression analysis, the authors concluded that there were no effects of importance signals on the reading time of sentences but there were effects of summary signals. Unfortunately, it is impossible to determine the size of these effects on reading rate, or to determine what reading rates were involved, when the only data given were regression weights, standard errors, R's, df's, MS's, F's, and p values.

The four research studies reviewed in this section help to delineate research on a learning process. In the future, it would be helpful if researchers were more explicit about which basic reading process they wanted to study and then presented all the methodological information relevant to how they induced that process: individual ability, passage difficulty, instructions, and objective consequences. Most importantly, however, it would be extremely helpful if reading rate was reported in Wpm because this is crucial for adjudicating which basic reading process their subjects were actually operating.

MEMORIZING PROCESSES

There are many studies available for illustrating memorizing processes. Representative studies will be reviewed in chronological order.

Kintsch and Keenan (1973) conducted a study which superficially seemed to provide evidence against the constancy of reading rate across material of varying levels of difficulty. (Note: This same study was reviewed earlier in Chapter 3.) They gave college students sentences which were all the same length in words but varied in number of propositions from four to nine. They told their subjects that they should "work as fast as possible, keeping in mind that the important thing was how much they remembered not speed" (p. 261). The task was for the subjects to recall each sentence in writing, with the instructions emphasizing ". . . that exact wording was not as important as the meaning of the sentences. . ." (p. 261). This research appears to be designed so that a memorizing process would be induced. Therefore, it is not surprising that the average reading rates varied from about 65 wpm for nine propositions to about

100 wpm for four propositions. Clearly, it would be unwise to interpret these data as somehow relevant to reading rate during the rauding process. It may be that reading rate varies with the number of propositions during the execution of a memorizing process, but even this finding is suspect because only time was measured, not Wpm. It seems likely that the sentences with more propositions were also longer in both letters and syllables and this variable was not controlled, as it could have been by using Wpm.

Kintsch, Kozminsky, Streby, McKoon, and Keenan (1975) constructed special paragraphs based upon history and science texts and then asked college students to read and recall them. The subjects were instructed ". . . to read the paragraph at their own rate, making sure that they understand it well . . ." (p. 201), and then they were to write down whatever they could remember from what they had just read. They also reported that they emphasized that the subjects ". . . recall as much as possible and not worry about whether recall was verbatim" (p. 201). They reported reading time in seconds for short passages (21 + words) and long passages (68 + words) that contained few or many arguments in history and science, a total of eight means. They did not report reading rate in words per minute but they did give the median number of words in each of the eight conditions and they did give an example passage for each of the eight conditions. Therefore, it was possible to estimate wpm and then convert this into Wpm (using the equations given in Chapter 2) after counting all the character spaces in their eight example paragraphs. The eight means they reported ranged from 84 to 173 Wpm, which is close to the 138 Wpm reported for a memorizing process in Chapter 2. These rates could have been predicted on the basis of their instructions and objective consequences.

Kintsch *et al.* also repeated the experiment with average rate under the control of the experimenter instead of the subjects; they did this by presenting the passages auditorily and also for the same length of time visually. Their resulting rates were estimated in Wpm units, in the same manner as described above, and they ranged from 160 to 166 Wpm under all of the reading and listening conditions. They reported that "reading times were longer and recall was less for texts with many different word concepts . . ." (p. 196). Again, this generalization needs to be restricted to a memorizing process. It is possible that they would get similar recall results after the subjects had operated a rauding process but it is impossible to determine from these data. Therefore, these data collected during the operation of Gear 1 are ecologically invalid for generalizing to an ordinary or normal reading situation that involves the rauding process, Gear 3.

In the above research of Kintsch *et al.*, it is interesting that in one of the four comparisons between few and many arguments, the reading rate was actually faster with many arguments than it was with few arguments when rate was estimated in Wpm (145 and 143 Wpm, respectively). It is also interesting to note that the passages used by these researchers varied considerably in difficulty. The easiest passage was at grade level 1.0 and the hardest passage was at grade level 22.6, when passage difficulty was estimated from the number of character spaces per word (cpw) using Equation 2.1. Interpretations of research involving passages usually are facilitated by some estimate of grade level difficulty. Kintsch *et al.* did report that their history passages were ". . . constructed about widely known topics from classical history . . ." and were ". . . adapted from 'A Child's History of the World,' and were, therefore, easy reading material for college student subjects" (p. 197). However, the estimates of difficulty, D_L, for the four example passages were 1.0, 4.5, 17.8, and 22.6, which is quite a range for supposedly easy reading material. As has already been noted, it is helpful for researchers to report reading rate in Wpm and the difficulty of their passages in GE units.

B. J. F. Meyer (1975) asked 105 college students to read 500–600-word passages under two conditions, high and low content structure. She asked these students to read at their normal rate, which would seem to be conducive to producing the rauding process. However, her main purpose was to test her hypothesis that recall is better for passages with high content structure than it is for passages with low content structure. To test this recall hypothesis she asked the students to write down, in sentence form, everything they could remember about each passage they read. With this objective consequence, this research has to be classified as intending to induce a memorizing process. Evidence relevant to the success of this intention comes from the rate data she reported. Under the high content structure condition the mean reading rate was 124 wpm, and under the low content structure condition the corresponding rate was 127 wpm. These rates confirm that Meyer induced a memorizing process; her two rates were very close to the 138 Wpm model memorizing rate presented in Chapter 2. The recall scores for high content structure were about 11% higher than the scores for low content structure. It appears that when college students operate a memorizing process, content structure can have a small to moderate effect upon recall of the passages. However, it would be a serious overgeneralization to suggest that this effect involving Gear 1 also applies to the rauding process since the rauding process, Gear 3, and normal reading rates were in fact not investigated.

Britton, Holdredge, Curry, and Westbrook (1979) gave six passages to college students and asked them to ". . . read the material carefully so that they would be prepared to take a test on it . . ." (p. 265). The "learning test" consisted of the same passage with "5–11 important content words" deleted; the subject's task was to complete the missing words. The instructions and objective consequences in this investigation would seem likely to induce a learning process. However, the average passage length was 131.3 words and the average time to read the passages was 74 sec, so the average rate was 106 wpm; this rate suggests a memorizing process. Furthermore, a memorizing process seems likely from the fact that only 56% of the test items were answered correctly. Remember, the test consisted of almost the entire passage with only a few words missing, and the task for the subject was to fill in the exact word. Many subjects could undoubtedly get a number of these correct simply by reading the test, i.e., without reading the passage. Therefore, the only good reason for reading the passage was to try to increase the probability of recalling the exact word on the test. Given this task analysis, it is not surprising that the subjects adopted a memorizing process with its exceptionally low rate of 106 wpm. The stated purpose of their research was to investigate cognitive capacity, but they did not limit the interpretations of their results to a memorizing type of process even though it would seem prudent to do so.

J. R. Miller and Kintsch (1980) asked 600 college students to read and recall 20 passages that ranged from very easy to very difficult. Flesh scores varied from 8.7 to 80.6, which is from about GE = 6 to GE = 16+ (Flesch, 1949). Miller and Kintsch instructed their subjects ". . . to read the text at their own rate . . . ," and then they asked them ". . . to recall in writing as much of the paragraph as they could, although not necessarily verbatim" (p. 342). Given these instructions, it is understandable that they reported a mean reading rate of 68 wpm. Thus, the evidence seems overwhelming that a memorizing process was used, and that all generalizations about readability and reading processes should be restricted to this process. However, they contended that since Masson (1982) reported a good fit of his skimming data (reviewed earlier in Chapter 6) to their text structure model data (this was also a 1979 doctoral dissertation), they said that they ". . . believe that the reading processes were similar in both cases" (p. 350). Given that Masson's rates were manipulated to be 225, 375, and 600 wpm, it is highly questionable to contend that the reading processes involved in Masson's research could be similar to those involved when subjects read at 68 wpm in this Miller and Kintsch research. The only similarity between the two studies is that recall protocols were scored using the same propositional analyses. Thus, it seems easy to agree that concepts that are higher in the structure of a passage, by being more related to other concepts, would be better re-called than those lower no matter which reading process is used. How-ever, to infer from this type of result that the reading processes used are similar seems to be highly questionable. Again, the type of reading pro-cess used can be inferred best from the instructions, the objective con-sequences, and the relative difficulty of the material.

As a postscript to the above Miller and Kintsch study, it is especially disappointing that the reading times for the 20 passages were not con-verted into Wpm. Since the passages varied in length from 67 to 85 words and since the passages varied in difficulty from grade 5 to college, it seems questionable to use reading time as a major criterion variable without controlling for length in character spaces. If this conversion had been done, and it was then found that reading rate did not vary across a wide range of passage difficulty, then it could be argued more convinc-ingly that the reading process involved was similar to other reading pro-cesses such as the rauding process. However, there is no reason to expect that this result occurred. We already know that passage difficulty is re-lated to redundancy and word length (see G. R. Miller & Coleman, 1967), so we would predict that recall and rate in words per minute would be related to any measure dealing with conceptual difficulty. What would be of interest is whether these relationships would be sustained or would evaporate when length factors were controlled. As mentioned earlier, it seems important to measure and report rate using measures which control for word length, such as Wpm.

Britton, Glynn, Muth, and Penland (1985) studied the recall of 72 college students under three conditions: specific objectives, general ob-jectives, and no objectives. They told their subjects "your primary objec-tive is to read the text so that you can later write down, in complete sentences, everything you can remember from it" (p. 109). Obviously, these investigators wanted to study a memorizing process and the read-ing rates of their subjects confirmed that they were successful in inducing such a process. Under the control condition that involved no objectives, the rate was 154 wpm, close to the 138 Wpm for the model memorizing process presented in Chapter 2. The other two experimental conditions were read slower, 108 wpm for specific objectives and 135 wpm for general objectives. These researchers noted that reading time was cor-related with recall, so they surmised that reading time was reflecting ". . . rehearsal activity—that is, the activity of mentally repeating the con-tent to commit it to memory" (p. 110). These theoretical comments about rehearsal are in keeping with the description of the model memorizing process given earlier in Chapter 2.

Britton *et al.* concluded that their finding "provided additional empirical support for using specific instructional objectives to introduce chapters in content area text" (p. 112). However, it should not go unnoticed that these researchers investigated a memorizing process and then generalized about real world studying situations which are not likely to involve a memorizing process operating at 108 wpm. College students studying a college textbook do not have to write, in sentence form, everything they can remember about chapters in books. Therefore, it is unreasonable to expect them to be operating a memorizing process similar to this one during their study time. A learning process is more likely, and many students may be operating their rauding process. For Britton *et al.* to make the generalization they seem to want to make about recall, it would be better to ask students to read the text as they would normally read when they were studying for a test; these instructions would probably induce a learning process with higher rates around 200 Wpm. There seems to be a distinct advantage for researchers to focus upon which basic reading process is of interest, such as a learning process used by college students when they read their textbooks. Such a focus will help prevent the research from getting off track by investigating one reading process and generalizing to another.

In summary, there are numerous studies of memorizing processes and they are often regarded as reflecting upon "the" reading process even though the reading rates involved are around 100 wpm, about the reading rate of first graders. With the advantage of hindsight, it seems obvious that the results of these studies involving Gear 1 will not generalize to Gear 3 which is typical and ordinary reading.

CONCLUSIONS

For college students, there was no research found which provided evidence against the idea that learning processes ordinarily operate around 200 Wpm and the recalling processes ordinarily operate around 138 Wpm and lower. When subjects are required to give evidence that they can freely recall what they have read, they shift out of their ordinary reading process by adding remembering and rehearsal components. These components drastically slow down the rate to the model memorizing rate of about 138 Wpm (e.g., see Britton *et al.*, 1985; Kintsch & Keenan, 1973; Kintsch *et al.*, 1975; B. J. F. Meyer, 1975; J. R. Miller & Kintsch, 1980). If the subjects are not asked to recall, but to answer questions, then the process they adopt seems to depend upon the difficulty of the questions. As a rule of thumb, it seems likely that if the subjects learn that they can answer 75% or more of the questions by using a rauding process, then they will in fact use this process because it is the one they normally use in reading situations. If they cannot answer 75% of the questions by using a rauding process then they probably will shift to a lower gear and use a learning process. However, if the questions are very difficult, for example, less than 50% can be answered correctly using this process, then they will probably shift down again to a memorizing process, which is first gear.

IMPLICATIONS

The main implication underlying the research reviewed in this chapter is that the results obtained under one of the basic reading processes should not be generalized to another of these processes. More specifically, research results that involve a learning process or a memorizing process do not automatically generalize to the rauding process. There are many good reasons for investigating reading rate during studying situations that ordinarily involve learning and memorizing processes. However, the importance of these investigations for Gears 1 and 2 should not be allowed to cover up their irrelevance to ordinary or normal reading which typically involves only the rauding process, Gear 3.

One of the best sources of information relevant to which basic reading process was operating is reading rate measured in Wpm. However, the more recent research usually uses reading time (e.g., see E. P. Lorch, Lorch, Gretter, & Horn, 1987, or Tousignant, Hall, & Loftus, 1986), or msec per word (e.g., see Haberlandt, Graesser, Schneider, & Kiely, 1986, or Schmalhofer & Glavanov, 1986), often in ways that make the calculation of rate in wpm or Wpm either extremely difficult or impossible. It seems that some indicant of reading rate, such as reading time, is becoming a favorite dependent variable in current experimental research. However, there is no evidence that word length is being controlled when measuring reading time or reading rate. There seems to be no good reason to allow word length to contaminate our present day research results when this problem was recognized and solved over 50 years ago by I. H. Anderson (1937) and Walker (1933) who used the printer's unit of ems (see Chapter 2).

THEORETICAL CONSIDERATIONS

INTRODUCTION

This chapter will provide an extensive theoretical framework for reviewing the remaining research. In order to understand this framework, it will be helpful to provide an overview of prior concepts from rauding theory, first. Then, additional theory will be presented regarding the determinants of reading rate and the determinants of the rate at which the rauding process operates.

REVIEW OF RAUDING THEORY

The first attempts to theorize about the rauding process will be referred to as Rauding Theory I (Carver, 1977; 1981), and the more recent attempts to relate the theory to instruction and learning will be referred to as Rauding Theory II (Carver, 1990b). The primary ideas involved in Rauding Theory I dealt with the accuracy, A, rate, R, and efficiency, E, of comprehension, as were described earlier in Chapter 2. These constructs will be briefly reviewed so the reader will have them clearly in mind.

The product of A and R, is the efficiency of comprehension, E, which is the number of thoughts understood per unit of time. Suppose an individual is given a passage to read that contains ten sentences. Suppose the individual reads these sentences at 300 Wpm or 18 standard length sentences per minute. Suppose the individual understood eight of the ten sentences. In this situation, $A = 0.80$, $R = 18$ Sentences per minute, and $E = 14.4$ Sentences per minute.

In Rauding Theory I, the focus was upon the comprehension of passages and how the accuracy of comprehension, A, is affected by the time spent reading a passage, its difficulty level, and the ability of the individual. Equations were presented in Chapter 2 for predicting the accuracy of comprehension, A, under certain known conditions.

In Rauding Theory II, the focus is upon rauding ability and how it can be improved. Figure 9.1 contains an overview of the causal framework represented in Rauding Theory II. This figure will be used to help place rauding rate, R_r, into its larger context. Inside the circle on the far right side of the figure is E_L, rauding efficiency level. It represents the combined effects of the two attributes, A_L, and R_L, that were considered in some detail in Chapter 3. E_L is measured in grade equivalents, such as

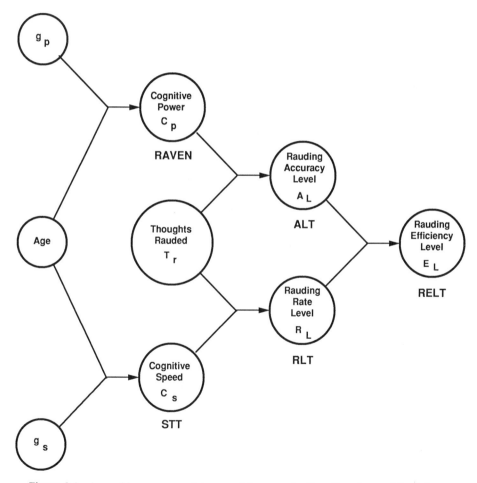

Figure 9.1 A graphic summary of the causal framework of rauding theory. (Fig. 1 from Carver, 1990b.)

E_L = 12, or twelfth grade level of rauding efficiency. Being at the twelfth grade level in rauding efficiency means that the individual is able to comprehend at least 75% (A_r = 0.75) of material at a difficulty level of D_L = 12 when reading it at a rate comparable to an average rate of individuals at a rauding accuracy level of A_L = 12. E_L is a single measure that reflects rauding ability in terms of how well individuals can operate their rauding process.

The two factors that determine E_L are rauding accuracy level, A_L, and rauding rate level, R_L. In order for individuals at E_L = 12 to reach E_L = 13, they need to be able to operate the rauding process on passages at D_L = 13 with an accuracy of 0.75 or higher ($A_r > 0.75$). This means that these individuals need to increase their rauding accuracy to a higher level, such as A_L = 13, so they can raud D_L = 13 material. Increasing A_L is one way to improve E_L and the other way is to improve R_r; as noted earlier in Chapter 2, when rauding rate is expressed in GE units, it will be symbolized as R_L and referred to as rauding rate level. Figure 9.1 shows R_L to be one of the two primary factors influencing E_L.

Reading ability is a term that can be applied to a wide range of reading-related attributes of individuals. For example, the so-called metacognitive skill of knowing when it is better to switch from the rauding process to a skimming process, or to a learning process, is one aspect of reading ability. Reading ability also encompasses skimming ability and various study skills. Rauding Theory II, however, focuses on rauding ability, which is the most important part of reading ability. Rauding ability is an umbrella term that will be used to refer to E_L and its two components, A_L and R_L.

Thoughts rauded, T_r, is shown in the middle of the figure as a primary factor influencing both R_L and A_L. For example, individuals who have an A_L at grade 9 could be given material to read at grade 9 difficulty, so that $A_L = D_L$. It has been theorized that operating the rauding process on materials at $A_L = D_L$ will improve A_L. It has also been theorized that operating the rauding process on relatively easy materials, $A_L > D_L$, will help individuals reach their highest R_L and maintain it there.

Notice that A_L is also influenced by a factor called cognitive power (C_p). It reflects the ability to solve more difficult intellectual problems without time limits. Notice also that R_L is influenced by a factor called cognitive speed (C_s). It reflects the ability to solve easy verbal problems quickly.

Figure 9.1 shows age as a factor influencing both C_p and C_s. As individuals grow older to maturity, C_p and C_s increase. C_p is also shown as being influenced by g_p, a general factor that accounts for individual differences in C_p. C_s is also shown as being influenced by g_s, a general factor that accounts for individual differences in C_s.

In Fig. 9.1, just below the circle that encompasses each causal factor, is the name of a test that can be used to measure each factor. E_L can be measured by RELT, the Rauding Efficiency Level Test (Carver, 1987b). A_L can be measured by ALT, the Accuracy Level Test (Carver, 1987c). R_r or R_L can be measured by RLT, the Rate Level Test (Carver, 1987a). C_s can be measured by the STT, the Speed of Thinking Test which is part of the Cognitive Speed Battery (Carver, 1988). C_p can be measured by the Raven Progressive Matrices Test, an instrument that is well known in the testing field because it has been considered to be the best measure of g, general intelligence (Jensen, 1982).

In summary, there are many different aspects of reading ability, the most important of which are those attributes that primarily influence the operation of the rauding process. The two attributes of individuals that primarily determine the operation of their rauding process are their A_L and their R_L. R_r is the most important aspect of reading rate because it sets the limits for the rate at which the rauding process can be successfully operated.

(Note: In some of the earlier publications dealing with rauding theory, different symbols and names were used for some of the concepts. The difficulty level of material, D_L, was symbolized earlier as G_d. The concept symbolized herein as A_L and called rauding accuracy level was symbolized in earlier publications as G_a and was referred to as "rauding ability." As noted earlier, the term "rauding ability" will be used henceforth as an umbrella term to refer to rauding accuracy level, A_L, rauding rate level, R_L, and rauding efficiency level, E_L.)

DETERMINANTS OF READING RATE

The primary factor that influences reading rate is the particular reading process an individual selects in order to accomplish a certain goal. Once this selection is made, then reading rate is limited by the time required to operate all of the components of this process successfully. Most of the variance in the range of reading rates can be accounted for by the particular process selected to accomplish a goal.

In the real world, as distinguished from research conditions, the primary goals are as follows: (a) locate a word, topic, or fact, Gear 5, (b) get an overview or gist, Gear 4, (c) understand each thought the writer intended to communicate when the sentences are relatively easy, Gear 3, (d) understand and remember new ideas even when the sentences are relatively difficult, Gear 2, and (e) be able to recall freely the thoughts later, Gear 1. Within each of these goals, the processes may vary somewhat and these variations may affect reading rate. The above five goals can be achieved by a scanning process, a skimming process, the rauding process, a learning process, and a memorizing process, respectively. A model process was proposed for the basic processes in Chapter 2, with rates of 600, 450, 300, 200, 138 Wpm, respectively, for college students (see Table 2.2).

Using the model processes and their rates, it can be seen that the reading rate of a college student can be about 4.5 times as fast when a scanning process is used as compared to a memorizing process. Ordinarily, a memorizing process cannot possibly operate successfully at 600 Wpm, and ordinarily a scanning process can be operated successfully at rates much higher than 138 Wpm. As noted earlier, the factor that accounts for most of the variance in reading rate is the type of process selected to accomplish a certain goal. Therefore, reading rate depends primarily upon which of the five basic processes individuals select to accomplish their goal.

There are two secondary factors that may influence reading rate after the process has been selected: the difficulty level of the material, D_L, and cognitive speed, C_s. These two factors will be discussed in turn.

Figure 9.2 contains a graphical illustration of the theorized interrelationships among reading rate, passage difficulty, and type of reading process for college students who are reading materials that are *not* relatively hard, $A_L > D_L$. For example, the rate at which the rauding process operates is theorized to be constant at 300 Wpm across a wide range of material difficulty from grade levels 2 through 14. A great deal of empirical evidence has been presented in earlier chapters supporting the constancy of reading rate during the rauding process (Carver, 1976, 1983; Coke, 1974; G. R. Miller & Coleman, 1971; Morse, 1951; Zuber & Wetzel, 1981). For college students this rate has tended to average around 300 Wpm, as depicted by the flat line in Fig. 9.2. However, the data are scanty supporting the constancy of the model scanning rates and the model skimming rates across this range of passage difficulty, as the flat lines in Fig. 9.2 also depict (see Coke, 1976). Yet, there do not appear to be any data or theory that would suggest that college students would be forced to operate these processes any slower, in Wpm, as the material becomes more difficult from grade 2 to grade 14. The data are also scanty supporting the constancy of rate with higher difficulty levels for the model learning process (Carver, 1971b). The data are scanty again supporting the decline in rate with higher difficulty levels for the model memorizing process (Waters *et al.*, 1985). However, as the material becomes more difficult, it seems likely that the rate of a memorizing process

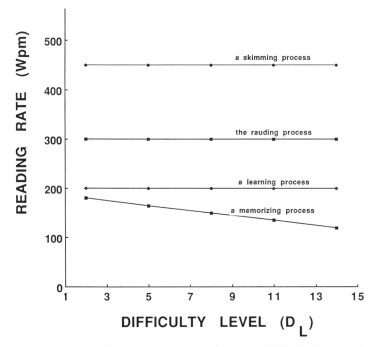

Figure 9.2 Theorized reading rate, in Wpm, as a function of difficulty level, D_L, for each of the five basic reading processes.

will decline because the sentences involve more infrequently used words and are expressed in increasingly complex grammatical forms that will require more rehearsal. The preceding ideas can be expressed as an interaction between passage difficulty and reading process in their effects upon reading rate, a process–difficulty interaction. The effect of passage difficulty upon reading rate for memorizing processes is expected to be different from the effects of difficulty upon reading rate for scanning, skimming, rauding, and learning processes.

A secondary factor influencing reading rate within a basic process is likely to be cognitive speed, C_s, as was mentioned earlier. It is theorized that individuals differ with respect to how fast they can think or process verbal information. Later, data will be presented from a Name Match task, sometimes called the Posner task, which seems to support the existence of this ability factor. So, after individuals have selected a particular reading process, then variations in rate are likely to be limited by individual differences in C_s. These individual differences can be measured using the Cognitive Speed Battery (Carver, 1988), which involves a version of the Name Match test, or Posner task, mentioned above. For example, it seems possible that about 25% of the variance between college students in reading rate can be accounted for by their cognitive speed when they are all engaged in the same reading process.

In summary, reading rate is primarily influenced by shifting up to scanning and skimming or shifting down to learning and memorizing in order to accomplish a particular goal. Rate within some of the five basic gears may be influenced by difficulty level. Rate within each of the five basic gears probably is influenced by individual differences in cognitive speed. It should be noted, however, that the factors that influence rate within each of the five basic processes are of secondary interest. Of primary interest are the factors that influence the rate at which the most important process operates, Gear 3, and those factors will be covered in the following section.

DETERMINANTS OF THE RAUDING PROCESS RATE

Introduction

What determines how fast individuals operate their rauding process? For example, if a group of college students are asked to read and understand the complete thoughts contained in the sentences of a relatively easy passage, what determines how fast they read it? The rauding process rate will be reviewed next, and then the four factors that affect this rate will be presented: apping, rauding rate, cognitive speed, and practice. The relationships among these factors influencing the rauding process rate are presented in Fig. 9.3. This figure should be referred to as the following explanatory sections are presented.

Rauding Process Rate

In Fig. 9.3, the rauding process rate is depicted by a circle at the far right side. This symbolizes the rate at which individuals operate their rauding process. Again, this is the rate at which individuals read when their goal is to understand the complete thoughts in the sentences of relatively easy passages. This rate could be measured experimentally by instructing individuals to comprehend the complete thought in each sentence of a passage, and then giving them test items containing a paraphrase and nonparaphrase of each sentence, as is done on the RELT (Carver, 1987b), a test mentioned earlier in this chapter.

Apping

The factor that primarily influences how fast individuals operate their rauding process is their *automatic pilot for prose*, called apping. Individ-

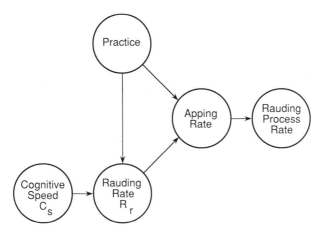

Figure 9.3 A graphic depiction of the theorized causal factors involved in determining how fast individuals operate their rauding process.

uals have rhythmic and habitual eye movements during ordinary reading, and this is called apping. Notice in Fig. 9.3 that the only factor depicted as directly influencing the rauding process rate is the apping rate; when individuals are operating their reading process under this automatic pilot, they are said to be apping.

When individuals read normally, it is being theorized that their eyes move in a habitual or natural manner that determines their reading rate. Therefore, apping rate can be measured experimentally by giving individuals relatively easy material, such as a popular novel, and asking them to read normally without giving them a test on what they have read. Apping rate has been found to be constant across levels of material difficulty (e.g., Carver, 1983), because individuals have been asked to read normally. It is being theorized that this apping rate determines the rauding process rate, ordinarily.

Later, the case will be made again that most individuals typically operate their rauding process at their rauding rate, R_r, which is the fastest rate at which this process can operate successfully. However, some individuals, maybe 20% of college students for example, do not typically read at their R_r. Instead of operating their rauding process at their rauding rate, as about 80% do, they typically read at the rate of a learning process. Thus, for this group of exceptional readers, R_r is *not* their typical reading rate. They have an automatic pilot for prose that is slower than their rauding rate. Again, for most individuals, such as 80%, their apping rate is exactly equal to their R_r so that their rauding rate, their apping rate, and their rauding process rate are all equal or the same.

But, the apping rate for the remaining 20% is slower than their rauding rate. For example, a test of rauding rate might estimate that a college student as an R_r of 250 Wpm but the individual may typically read at 200 Wpm due to an apping rate of 200 Wpm. This would mean that individuals like this are capable of successfully operating their rauding process at 250 Wpm on relatively easy materials but they do not do this, habitually.

The existence of apping will now be defended, rationally, and also by reference to other researchers. Apping is an automatic pilot type of process in the sense that the psychomotor aspects of the eye movements are so habitual that they operate with little or no manual control. The analogy to walking was made in an earlier chapter. When individuals walk they fall into a rhythm or pattern that requires little or no conscious control, and it is being theorized that a similar process operates with eye movements during apping. An individual learns to move the eyes ahead to the next words at just the right pace for each consecutive word to be perceived, lexically accessed, internally articulated, and sententially integrated for the most efficient understanding of the thoughts in the sentences. This coordination of the rate of eye movements with the optimal rate for understanding sentences does not proceed at different rates for different material but instead proceeds at a generally constant rate for different material.

The existence of rhythmic and habitual eye movements, such as apping, has been noted by many earlier researchers. Dearborn (1906) stated that ". . . one of the essentials of natural and rapid reading is that the reader's eye should at once be able to acquire a regular and uniform motor habit of reaction for each line" (p. 115), and ". . . the acquirement of a rhythmical sucession of movements is one of the means by which the fast reader attains his greater speed in reading" (p. 118). Huey (1908) reported the following observation: "The readers showed a strong rhythmic tendency. Each would fall into a reading pace that seemed natural to him, and then would read page-by-page in almost exactly the same time" (p. 175). Taylor (1965) reports that "generally speaking, as long as the reader is not reading material too far above or below his level, he will maintain a fairly characteristic pattern" (p. 196). Kolers (1972) says ". . . to our considerable surprise . . . the eye movements one learns for reading become deeply rooted" (p. 87), and then he summarized his research as follows:

> In sum, our finding was that the effect of learning to read in a particular direction leaves an indelible impression on a reader's visual scanning habits. The impress is so strong that it leads him to read nonsense in a familiar direc-

tion more rapidly than sense in an unfamiliar direction. Even when he is reading one word at a time, he proceeds more rapidly in the familiar direction. (p. 88)

Kolers also advocated that reading proceeds on a word for word basis as the following quotation indicates:

> . . . even the skilled reader has considerable difficulty forming a perception of more than one word at a time. Many students of reading believe that a reader does perceive several words at once, reading different parts of a line and particularly words near the one he is acquiring at a particular moment. Our experiments make it seem unlikely that such a strategy could be pursued profitably. (p. 86)

The idea that there is rhythm in eye movement has also received criticism. Sisson (1937) developed a "habit index" based upon the number of fixations per line, and he could find no statistically significant difference between his best and poorest readers on this index. Tinker (1946) devoted a section of review of eye movement research to this topic, and it was his opinion that the notion was ". . . not only a useless concept but a harmful one" (p. 98). Both Tinker and Sisson, who did his research in Tinker's laboratory, were concerned that this idea would contribute to eye movement training to improve reading ability when there was no solid evidence that such training would help.

O'Regan (1979) collected eye movement data which may be interpreted by some researchers as evidence against the rhythmic movements of the eyes. He investigated saccade lengths associated with the word "the" in an effort to adjudicate between what he called the "rhythmical scan" hypothesis and the "linguistic control" hypothesis. Under the rhythmical scan hypothesis, the fixation durations and the saccade sizes are considered as being approximately constant. Under the linguistic control hypothesis, the eye skips regions about which good predictions can be made but does not skip regions in the periphery where no confident hypotheses can be made. Apping would be possible under rhythmical scan but apping would not be possible under linguistic control.

The rhythmical scan hypothesis, as stated above, could not be correct during the operation of the rauding process because Carver (1983) has shown that putting an extra space between words has no effect upon typical reading rate. Thus, throwing the eyes a constant distance each saccade is not what readers typically do, otherwise it would take them longer to read material that contained an extra space between words. The data that O'Regan presented against the rhythmical scan hypothesis involved the measurement[1] of saccade lengths right before "the" and right before a three-letter verb. He said he got a "THE-skipping" result.

However, he admitted that both of the three-letter words were in fact skipped. On the average, the saccades that started in front of both words tended to land after them. The saccades that started in front of "the" tended to land one to two character spaces further than those that started in front of the three-letter verb. Therefore, O'Regan's data do not rule out a rhythmic movement of the eyes in the sense that it is an overlearned psychomotor habit where the eyes have learned to jump down a line just far enough so that each consecutive word has enough time to be lexically accessed, semantically encoded, and sententially integrated. It should also be noted that the conditions used by O'Regan were not entirely conducive to the rauding process. He used short sentences displayed one at a time in all upper case letters, under conditions wherein the rauding process may have occurred but could not be confirmed because no reading rate data were reported. These O'Regan data do not appear to provide sound data against apping.

Sisson (1939) appears to be one of the first to compare reading to walking. He said that "reading speed, like walking speed, may be habitually slow or fast," and that "both will usually lapse back into their customary condition when attention is directed elsewhere" (p. 212). Apping represents these habitual aspects of eye movements that Sisson considered as causal for rate. Apping is likely to be psychologically and physiologically most comfortable for individuals, in a manner similar to their normal walking pace; it is most comfortable because it requires little or no attention and it is almost effortless from a physical standpoint because it is an overlearned habit.

For those individuals who typically read relatively easy material, $A_L >$ D_L, apping rate will probably coincide with R_r. For some individuals, however, most of their reading involves relatively hard material, $A_L <$ D_L, so they are typically engaged in a learning process. Because the successful operation of a learning process proceeds at a slower rate than R_r, and because some individuals operate a learning process much more often than a rauding process, eye movement habits are likely to adjust to a learning process rate. For these individuals, their apping rate is slower than their rauding rate because they operate a learning process more often than a rauding process. For example, college students at an engineering school probably would have a rauding rate equal to English majors as measured by an objective test of rauding rate. However, the typical or ordinary reading rate, apping rate, of engineers would probably be lower than the English majors because the engineering students would do almost all of their reading in relatively hard materials while the English majors would spend some of their time reading novels that are relatively easy. Even though the English majors would also spend a great deal of time reading relatively hard materials, such as old English and Russian translations, they would probably have more variety and read enough relatively easy material to maintain their apping rate at their rauding rate. Stated in operational terms, mean scores on the Rate Level Test should be comparable for engineering majors and English majors but on a measure of typical or normal reading rate the English majors should have a higher mean.

Students who are below average readers in their grades are also likely candidates for having an apping rate that is below their rauding rate. The lower ability students are likely to be given textbooks that are above their ability level in difficulty, $A_L < D_L$. Therefore, in order for them to comprehend accurately, they will be forced to operate a learning process most of the time. They would probably be slow readers even if they were given easy materials most of the time because they are likely to have lower than average cognitive speed, C_s. However, their typical speed is likely to be even slower than their rauding rate because they have learned that apping at the slower rate of a learning process is helping them increase their accuracy of comprehension, A. These students are often denigrated by others because they have not learned to read faster when in fact they may have learned that slow reading is their only means of survival. For example, it is possible to interpret the poor reading college students in the I. H. Anderson (1937) research, reviewed in Chapter 5, as providing evidence for apping. They read everything between a mean of 153 wpm and 191 wpm whether it was relatively easy or relatively difficult, and it did not matter much if they were asked to read for detail or to read for general knowledge.

The existence of apping also explains a subjective phenomenon familiar to most readers. Occasionally while reading, individuals become distracted and suddenly become aware that their eyes have been moving across the line over the words but nothing has been registered in terms of awareness or comprehension for the last five or more words. This phenomenon can be explained by reference to the habitual characteristics of apping. The eyes are moving at the apping rate in accordance with the habitual eye movement characteristics of the rauding process but the cognitive components of the rauding process have become disengaged while the individual is thinking about something besides the words and the thoughts they represent. This phenomenon represents apping in its pure form, without either a rauding process or a learning process operating concomitantly, as they do 99.99% of the time.

One of the most important characteristics of apping is the forward, or left-to-right, movements of the eyes across the words on a line. Regressions are not part of apping but a momentary disruption of it that disrupts the constancy of rate. When the rauding process is proceeding successfully on each consecutive word there will be no regressions. Bayle (1942) conducted an excellent study of the nature and causes of regressions in reading, and her data and conclusions support apping in particular and rauding theory in general. She asked students to read passages that she had developed to elicit regressions. For example, she used a feminine pronoun when its antecedent was masculine. On the basis of her eye movement recordings, she noted that readers are forced to regress when the forward movement of the eyes has overreached the span of recognition, which would be a mechanical failure of apping. However, she concluded that for her skilled readers the most frequent patterns of regressions were due to a "... failure to recognize the meaning of a word within its context, failure to combine the meaning of a word with that of other words with which it appears, and failure to relate the meaning of a word to the conditions under which it appears" (p. 35). These failures listed by Bayle are failures of the rauding process and they result in regressions designed to make this process work successfully.

In summary, apping is an habitual eye movement process that ordinarily operates at the rauding rate because that is the rate at which most people are able to operate their rauding process successfully most of the time. However, those exceptional individuals who frequently read relatively hard materials have learned to move their eyes habitually at the slower rate of a learning process because that rate is most effective for them most of the time.

Rauding Rate

As noted earlier, the apping rate of individuals is ordinarily determined by their rauding rate, R_r. Before proceeding, let us review the concept of rauding rate.

When individuals are given relatively easy passages, $A_L > D_L$, so that they are capable of understanding the thoughts in all or almost all of the sentences, then the rauding rate is the fastest rate at which they can operate the rauding process and still be able to understand the complete thoughts in most of the sentences. Each individual has a certain fastest rate at which all the components of the rauding process can be successfully operated on relatively easy materials. Each individual has a certain minimum amount of time required to lexically access words, semantically encode them, and then integrate them into the complete thoughts represented by sentences, which in turn must fit into the context ordinarily afforded by prior sentences. This minimum amount of time required to operate these components successfully can also be expressed as a maximum rate, R_r, the rauding rate. This rauding rate, an attribute of the individual, is the upper limit for the rate at which the rauding process can successfully operate. If individuals have as their goal the understanding of the complete thoughts in the sentences of messages, and they ordinarily read relatively easy material, then it would be inefficient for them to operate their rauding process at a rate slower than their R_r. Since individuals ordinarily do not waste time, they are efficient and read at their rauding rate.

Since R_r is the optimal rate for most readers most of the time, it is not surprising that most individuals have developed the habitual eye movements of apping that proceed at the rauding rate. It is not likely to be an accident that the normal reading rate of college students, about 300 Wpm (see Carver, 1983), is approximately equal to the rate at which their efficiency of comprehension is a maximum, about 300 Wpm (see Carver, 1982).

If you want to predict how fast individuals typically operate their rauding process, that is, find out their apping rate, then some independent measure of the individual's rauding rate should be an excellent predictor. Indeed, the Rate Level Test (Carver, 1987a) purports to be an indicator of rauding rate. It measures how fast individuals can successfully semantically encode words in easy passages, and this test has been found to be an excellent predictor of the rate at which the rauding process typically operates, i.e., apping rate (Carver, 1986). The rate score on the Rate Level Test has been correlated with apping rate, an independent measure of how fast individuals operated their rauding process on an easy passage where time was surreptitiously recorded. When the correlation was corrected for attenuation due to the less than perfect reliabilities of the two measures, it was 0.98. This means that almost all of the reliable variance between individuals in the rate at which the rauding process typically operates can be accounted for by a measured attribute of the individual, called rauding rate, R_r.

Given that the apping rate is influenced by R_r, it then becomes important to delve more deeply into the factors that determine R_r. For example, why do some college students have a rauding rate of 350 Wpm and others have a rauding rate of 250 Wpm? As mentioned earlier, rauding rate is considered to be determined partially by cognitive speed, C_s, and this concept will be discussed next.

Cognitive Speed

During the execution of the rauding process, cognitive speed exerts its influence by setting a limit upon how fast the individual can operate basic verbal processes. Cognitive speed, C_s, is a fundamental attribute of the individual that is not subject to within-individual influence or educational influence. It is analogous to height. Students cannot take some kind of cognitive action and increase their height, nor their cognitive speed. Likewise, teachers cannot induce some kind of educational treatment and consequently increase the height of students, nor their cognitive speed. Height increases each year to maturity, and cognitive speed increases each year to maturity. The boys and girls who are tallest and shortest in the lower grades tend to be the same boys and girls who are tallest and shortest throughout the subsequent grades; the boys and girls who have the most and least cognitive speed in lower grades tend to be the same boys and girls who have the most and least cognitive speed throughout the subsequent grades.

As mentioned earlier, an indicant of cognitive speed can be obtained from the Cognitive Speed Battery (Carver, 1988) which uses a variant of the so-called Posner task (see Posner, Boies, Eichelman, & Taylor, 1969; Posner & Mitchell, 1967). This test presents examinees with pairs of upper and lower case letters, Aa, aB, bA, bB, Aa, Ab, Ba, Bb, to determine how fast the pair can be identified as containing the same or different letter names. The scores from the Cognitive Speed Battery can be used as an indicant of C_s. It should be noted that Cattell (1971) appears to be the first to use the term "cognitive speed."

Hunt, Frost, and Lunneborg (1973) discussed and researched the type of matching task used in the Cognitive Speed Battery, as an example of measuring individual differences in cognition and a new approach to intelligence. Later, Hunt (1978) reviewed prior research on this measure of information-processing capacity, and he argued that it represented a measure of a basic thinking rate involving a decoding function that is highly related to general verbal ability. Concomitantly, Spiegel and Bryant (1978) investigated other measures of information-processing speed, and they concluded that their results supported the existence of a general speed factor in intelligence.

Boles and Eveland (1983) presented data that called into question the idea that the pairs of letters in the Posner type of task must be named using a phonetic code. Whether or not a phonetic code is required to complete this task, it seems to represent a basic ability that is likely to influence rauding rate, R_r. Jacobowitz and Haupt (1984) found that scores on a Posner-type task correlated quite poorly with a measure of reading comprehension when a measure of listening comprehension had been partialled out. However, their measures of reading comprehension and listening comprehension were influenced to an unknown degree by rate so their data are not directly relevant to the theorized influence of cognitive speed upon rauding rate. Carver (1990a) correlated a cognitive speed measure, derived from the Cognitive Speed Battery, with three indicants of reading rate. When corrected for the unreliability of all the variables involved, the three correlations involved ranged from 0.28 to 0.62.

In summary, it appears that C_s has a sound theoretical basis, and the relevant research evidence also does not contradict the proposition that the C_s acts as a limiting influence on R_r.

Practice

It may be noted that there is an arrow drawn in Fig. 9.3 from the practice circle to the rauding rate circle depicting the idea that practice can affect rauding rate. Also in Fig. 9.3, it has been noted that practice is a factor that affects apping rate. These two causal effects of practice upon rauding rate and upon apping rate will be discussed in turn.

It is possible for an individual to have a very high cognitive speed and a low rauding rate. This possibility is illustrated most vividly by reference to adults who are reading in a second language. For example, Favreau and Segalowitz (1982) found that those bilinguals with slower reading rates in their second language also had slower reaction times for words in their second language. They suggested that these bilinguals may have had less practice in reading their second language. Their high R_r in their native language may reflect a high C_s. However, due to less practice (less time spent reading relatively easy material in the second language), their R_r for the second language is lower than for the first language. Practice in rauding thoughts in relatively easy materials, $A_L > D_L$, will build up the rauding rate of individuals to their capacity as set by their cognitive speed, and further rauding of such materials is probably needed to maintain their rauding rate at this level. Stated differently, reading a great many materials that are relatively easy, provides the practice needed to get the rauding rate up to a level that can be expected from the individual's cognitive speed and some practice is also needed to maintain it there.

Practice in rauding relatively easy materials also has the effect of developing an apping rate for individuals that is equal to their rauding rate. If individuals spend most of their reading time operating a learning process on relatively hard materials, then they are likely to develop an apping rate that is slower than their R_r. An implication of these theoretical ideas is that children who read a great many relatively easy books will be operating their rauding process at its highest level. Stated differently, these children will be reading as fast as they can raud. Children who spend almost all of their time operating a learning process on materials that are relatively hard for them, $A_L < D_L$, are likely to develop an apping rate that operates at a learning process rate rather than their rauding rate.

In summary, it appears that the effect of reading practice depends upon what type it is. Practice in the form of an exclusive operation of a learning process on relatively hard material will produce apping rates lower than rauding rates. Practice in the form of rauding relatively easy materials will maintain rauding rate at its maximum and will set the apping rate at the R_r.

CONCLUSIONS

The most important determinant of reading rate is the particular reading process operating, and that depends upon the goal of the reader. Ordinarily, the goal of the reader is to comprehend the complete thought in the sentences of a passage, so the rate at which the rauding process operates is the most important reading rate. Ordinarily, the rauding process operates at the R_r which is the fastest rate at which individuals can accurately comprehend relatively easy material.

It does not make sense to ask how fast individuals can read because individuals can read at various rates depending on which of the basic reading processes they are operating. It makes more sense to ask how fast individuals can raud. The answer to this question is their R_r which is the fastest rate at which they can successfully operate their rauding process. How fast individuals do raud (typically operate their rauding process) is determined by how fast they habitually read (their apping rate). Apping rate is determined by practice, and for most people it is equal to their rauding rate. So most people operate their rauding process at a rate that is equal to their apping rate and their rauding rate. However, some people read material that is relatively difficult for them almost all the time they spend reading and so have developed an apping rate that is equal to a learning process instead of the rauding process. They have set their "automatic pilot for prose" at a slower rate than their R_r. These people operate their rauding process at the rate of a learning process because that is their habitual rate. So, individuals who have extensive practice in reading relatively hard material will develop an habitual rate of reading that is lower than their rauding rate. Individuals who have extensive practice in reading relatively easy material will maintain their rauding rate at a level commensurate with their cognitive speed and they will also have an apping rate equal to their rauding rate.

As has been noted several times, R_L and A_L determine E_L and these three attributes of individuals comprise their rauding ability. So, rauding rate is a major aspect of rauding ability, and it is also the most important factor influencing how fast the rauding process ordinarily operates.

Part IV

Related Factors

Part IV contains nine chapters that deal with factors that may cause within-individual changes or between-individual differences in reading rate. Chapter 10 reviews research on flexibility, and conclusions are drawn with respect to whether readers are flexible or not. Chapter 11 reviews research on within-individual growth in reading rate during the years children spend in school. Chapter 12 contains a review of research on how rate is affected by the way words are recognized and then processed for comprehension. Chapter 13 reviews research on auding and how it relates to reading rate. Chapter 14 focuses on oral reading rate research and its relationship to silent reading rate. Chapter 15 reviews the effects of variations in the way textual materials are presented. Chapter 16 deals with the research on comprehension as a factor that is inextricably related to reading rate. Chapter 17, the last chapter in Part IV, presents the research evidence relevant to the effect of rapid reading training on reading rate.

These chapters in Part IV contain the bulk of the research that has been conducted on reading rate. Most of these chapters are organized in the same way: The topic will be introduced in the first section of the chapter, and then the relevant research will be reviewed. Finally, there will be a conclusions section and possibly an implications section.

10

FLEXIBILITY

INTRODUCTION

The traditional idea that reading rate should be flexible appears to be wrongheaded. Hoffman (1978) has expressed the traditional flexibility idea as follows: "It is practically a truism in our field that the good reader is the flexible reader, i.e., one who adjusts his rate to the difficulty of the material or the purpose for which he is reading" (p. 325). The part of this idea that good readers adjust their rate to the purpose for reading is misleading at best. The other half of the flexibility idea is that good readers adjust their rate to the difficulty of the material, and this is mostly wrong. The traditional ideas about difficulty flexibility and purpose flexibility need to be replaced by a new concept, called process flexibility. This idea focuses on shifting up or down out of third gear, the rauding process, in order to accomplish goals other than the typical one of comprehending the complete thoughts that the author intended to communicate. After the relevant research has been reviewed, this brief critique of flexibility will be revisited, justified, and refined.

There have been a number of articles published on the subject of flexibility that contain opinion, hypotheses, and theory about its nature, but no data. Existing opinions about flexibility will be reviewed first.

The quote by Hoffman given at the outset of this chapter reflects the conventional wisdom that good readers demonstrate purpose flexibility and difficulty flexibility (e.g., see Tinker, 1958). Some writers prefer to broaden the concept. For example, Weintrab (1967) has provided the following definition of flexibility: " . . . the ability to adjust one's rate and approach to reading with the purpose for reading, with the difficulty of material, and with one's background or knowledge of the particular subject matter" (p. 169). This idea that flexibility includes approach as well as rate and that it includes background knowledge as well as purpose and difficulty is shared by McDonald (1971) who prefers to use the term "versatility" to cover this wide range of factors. More recently, Hoffman (1979) has made this wide range of flexibility factors more explicit by advancing the following influential factors: purpose, difficulty level, structure and organization, coincidence of background and interest, instructional aids, social setting, and time constraints. Hoffman also discriminated among three strategies, scanning, skimming, and rauding, and concluded that "the earlier we begin to break the reading (rauding) habit, the easier will be the transition to the more advanced skills of proficient reading" (p. 329). Notice that Hoffman seems to consider the rauding process to be somewhat of a bad habit. This view appears to be in direct conflict with the data reviewed in the chapter on rauding (Chapter 7). The constant rate at which college students typically read materials from grade 1 to grade 14 in difficulty (about 300 Wpm) was also the same rate at which the efficiency of comprehension was the highest across the same range of difficulty levels (about 300 Wpm). The rate at which the rauding process operates appears to be the most efficient rate for accomplishing the typical goal of readers, i.e., to comprehend the complete thoughts in the sentences of passages.

The constancy of rate idea, which is a cornerstone of rauding theory, is also completely counter to the rate flexibility ideas of McCracken (1965). He argued for both external and internal flexibility of reading rate. He embraced the traditional ideas of purpose flexibility and difficulty flexibility but he contended that these ideas produced only external flexibility, i.e., what was called process flexibility earlier in this chapter. This shifting of gears from skimming to going "slowly when trying to gain total understanding" was not enough for McCracken because it implied a rigid rate once a person started reading. He argued that "flexibility of rate must be internal, a flexibility within the material being read, a flexibility within each paragraph, a flexibility within sentences" (p. 209). His main idea was that all reading should be " . . . a process of accelerating and decelerating, a process of stop and go according to the density of the ideas and reader's ability to understand the material" (p. 209). Perhaps McCracken has expressed best the polar opposite of the main idea of rauding theory, which is that the best readers have developed habitual eye movements that proceed at a constant rate because this rate is most efficient for them most of the time they read.

The opinion of one of the most prominent researchers in the field of reading, Miles Tinker, is also of interest. He published an article on reading in the *Journal of Experimental Psychology* in 1926, and his excellent research and theoretical opinions continued at least through 1969 with a review of eye movement research in the *National Reading Conference Yearbook*. Given this span of 43 years and over 70 publications in the field of reading, Tinker's opinions on flexibility are of special interest. In a review of eye movement research in the *Psychological Bulletin* in 1958, Tinker summarized some relevant research by Morse *et al.* (1968); this was the research reviewed in Chapter 5 which found that fifth and seventh graders did not vary their rate or eye movement patterns with the difficulty of the material. Tinker drew the following conclusions relevant to the Morse *et al.* data:

> This finding is indeed unfortunate. It indicates that the school children used as subjects had not been successfully taught to vary their pace according to the difficulty of the material, i.e., they were not flexible in adjusting reading procedure to difficulty of material. . . . When eye movements do not vary with the difficulty of the reading matter, pupils are immature readers. (p. 221)
>
> It is generally recognized that the mature reader is the versatile reader. He will change his pace (reflected in eye movements) to fit the purpose of reading and the difficulty of the material. . . . It is suggested that emphasis be placed upon helping the less flexible readers in reading improvement programs since they tend to do all their reading at about the same rate. (p. 223)

Later in a 1965 book, Tinker provides an additional relevant comment:

> There is no such thing as one speed of reading that is appropriate for various purposes and for all kinds of material. Appraisal of speed of reading must always be in some specific area, such as geography or literature. Speed of reading in one area bears little relation to speed in another if the reader adjusts his rate to the nature of the material as all good readers do. (p. 286)

Ideas similar to those of Tinker's from the 1950s and 1960s seem to have survived through the 1970s. For example, P. A. Miller (1978) reviewed research on reading flexibility, and she asserted that ". . . reading rate is not a unitary phenomenon, rather, it can vary at one point in predictable ways," and "an individual does *not* have a single base rate" (p. 73). Miller made no reference to the earlier contrary research results (Carver, 1971b, 1976; Coke, 1974; W. R. Dixon, 1951; G. R. Miller & Coleman, 1971; Seibert, 1943).

It would be a mistake, however, to suggest that views similar to those of Tinker and Miller, noted above, have been accepted without question. For example, Harris (1968) notes that few people have questioned ". . . the idea that an efficient reader should vary his rate of reading according to his purposes and the kinds of material he reads" while "research findings indicate, however, that most readers are rigid rather than flexible in their rate of reading" (p. 206). Also, McDonald (1971) questioned the research base for flexibility as follows:

> Rate flexibility rests on the fundamental assumption that readers can change their reading rate at will without also changing their purpose for reading and secondarily assumed that by telling a student to read faster that he would both do so and would read with better comprehension. Reading research, however, does not support these premises. (p. 169)

(Note: McDonald was one of the first to talk about shifting "reading gears.") Steinacher (1971) critiqued research on flexibility and drew the following conclusion: "It is my contention that instruction in reading flexibility is so weakly supported by available research that we cannot justify its being taught" (p. 145). Finally, Farr and Carey (1986) concluded that "There is actually little evidence that most students have any ability to adjust their reading rate to suit specific purposes" (p. 127).

The above review of opinion relevant to flexibility provides the background for the following review of relevant research.

RESEARCH

Walker (1933) conducted what appears to be the first study of the effect of difficulty and purpose upon reading rate, the first flexibility research. Walker was primarily interested in studying the eye movements of good readers. (Note: This research of Walker's was previously reviewed in connection with I. H. Anderson, 1937, in Chapter 5.) The subjects in this study were freshmen who scored in the highest decile on both a university entrance examination and a standardized reading test. These freshmen were given passages at three different levels of difficulty, "simple" elementary material, college level material and material from a scientific article of "extreme difficulty." The instructions and consequences were described as follows: "The requirement of comprehension, which was a moderate knowledge of the contents, was checked at the completion of reading by demanding three correct answers to four questions" (p. 100–101). The resulting three reading rates (converted from ems using Equation 2.8) were 292, 266, and 215 Wpm, respectively.

Given the above information, it would seem reasonable that Walker's subjects adopted the rauding process for the relatively easy material (292 Wpm) and a learning process for the extremely difficult material (215 Wpm). Since the college level material was approximately equal in difficulty to the ability of the readers ($A_L = D_L$), the process used was probably a mixture of rauding and learning depending upon how difficult the material was for the particular individual (266 Wpm).

Walker also had three passages that were approximately equal in difficulty, all at the college level. One of these three passages was read under instructions to obtain "a general idea of the content" (p. 109). One passage was read using the same instructions, noted earlier, when the effect of difficulty was being investigated. Another passage was read "for detailed knowledge of the content" (p. 109). The three resulting rates were 339, 266, and 197, respectively. Under the general idea purpose, the rate of 339 was somewhat higher than the rauding process rate of 292 Wpm for the relatively easy elementary school material. But, rate under the general idea purpose did not reach the model skimming rate of 450 Wpm (see Chapter 2), possibly because some of the individuals were still using their rauding process. Under the purpose of obtaining a moderate knowledge of these college level materials, as defined by answering three of four questions correctly, these above average freshmen read at 266 Wpm. This is slower than their estimated rauding rate but still faster than the model learning process. When instructed that their purpose should be to obtain detailed knowledge of this college level material, they adopted a learning process rate of 215 Wpm.

These data were interpreted by Walker (as well as subsequent researchers and practitioners) as indicating both purpose and difficulty flexibility. However, these same data can be alternatively interpreted as indicating process flexibility; individuals can be induced to shift up to a higher gear and down to lower gears when the goal requires it. Individuals can be induced to shift gears among their reading processes depending upon the instructions, the objective consequences, and the relative difficulty. But, it is at best misleading and at worst wrong to say that individuals should or do change their rates to match the difficulty of the material when there is strong evidence that rate stays constant when the material changes drastically in difficulty level (see research reviewed in Chapters 3, 5, 6, and 7).

With the large benefit of hindsight it seems best to interpret Walker's data as reflecting process flexibility, an updated version of purpose flexibility and difficulty flexibility that involves shifting gears from one process to another. When the instructions were to read for a detailed knowledge or the material became relatively difficult, these good readers shifted down to a learning process. When the instructions were to read for a general idea, these good readers shifted up to a skimming process. This kind of flexibility involves gear shifting from one reading process to another depending upon one's goal. If the rauding process is being used, then the difficulty of the material does not affect rate (e.g., see data presented in Fig. 7.1). If the material becomes relatively difficult, then individuals may shift down to a lower gear to accomplish their goal. Difficulty probably does not affect the rate at which the model scanning process or the model skimming process operate either, but that needs more research. Difficulty may affect most memorizing processes in the sense that reading rate probably slows as difficulty increases but that hypothesis needs more research also.

In summary, these data from Walker (1933) appear to have set the stage for flexibility research and practice for at least the following 50 years. That research is now being interpreted in a different way because good readers do not continually change their rate depending upon their purpose and the difficulty of the material. Instead, most readers do not change their rate most of the time, even when the difficulty of the material changes. This is because most readers operate their rauding process most of the time they read, and this process proceeds at a constant rate. As long as the material is relatively easy for them, individuals are likely to operate this process at a constant rate. If the material becomes relatively difficult for them, it is misleading to say that they demonstrate difficulty flexibility when they change their rate. Instead, it is better to say that they demonstrated process flexibility because they shifted gears to a different process that involved different components.

I. H. Anderson (1937) extended the above good reader research of Walker (1933), by using the same procedures and methods with poor readers. This study was reviewed extensively in Chapter 5, and the details of the method are exactly the same as that used by Walker described above. These college students, who were selected because they were in the bottom 25% on a standardized reading test, read the elementary primer selection at a learning process rate of 191 Wpm. For the college textbook material, they also read at a learning process rate of 188 Wpm. For the most difficult material (harder than a university textbook), they again read at a learning process rate of 175 Wpm. It appears that these poor readers have an apping rate around 190 Wpm which is most efficient for them most of the time. Even though they probably could have successfully operated a rauding process at a rate higher than 191 Wpm on the elementary primer, it was not their "normal" rate so they followed directions and used their apping rate. As noted in Chapter 9, these data of Anderson's seem to provide evidence for an apping rate for these exceptional readers that is separate from their rauding rate.

The poor readers of Anderson's study did not show the variability in rate that the good readers of Walker's did. Under the general purpose, the poor readers read at 174 Wpm, and under the complete and detailed knowledge purpose they read at 153 Wpm. It appears that the poor readers were incapable of shifting to a skimming process but their 153

Wpm rate for the most stringent purpose, suggests that they did shift into a lower gear than normal for them, i.e., using a memorizing process. So, these poor readers appear to have an apping rate that is based upon their learning process and they can shift down to a memorizing process but they showed no evidence of being able to shift up to a rate commensurate with a skimming process when asked to do so. Anderson summarized his findings as follows:

> The fact that good readers were more flexible in their eye-movements indicates that one aspect of their superior reading ability is the flexibility of their central processes in adjusting to increasingly difficult reading situations. (p. 32)
> . . . the purpose in reading is a more important determinant of eye movement behavior than the difficulty of reading material. (p. 33)

As noted earlier, the Walker and Anderson studies from about 50 years ago seem to have set the stage for many of the ideas about difficulty flexibility and purpose flexibility that are still current today. The good readers supposedly varied their rate with difficulty and purpose and the poor readers did not. Therefore, the inference was made that something was wrong with the poor readers because their rate remained relatively constant as the difficulty and purpose changed.

The Walker and Anderson results have been interpreted in an alternative way using the concept of process flexibility that is compatible with research that will be reviewed later. At the risk of being highly redundant, those interpretations will be reiterated for emphasis. Walker found purpose flexibility because the good readers could shift gears among three reading processes based upon the purpose directions given. He appeared to get difficulty flexibility in his good readers because his good readers shifted to a learning process in order to answer comprehension questions when the level of material difficulty was above their level of ability. Anderson's poor readers did not vary their rate with difficulty level because they were instructed to read normally. So, they used their slower apping rate with all material difficulty levels. The poor readers did not show purpose flexibility by adopting a skimming process under the directions to read for a general idea. Perhaps these poor readers did not know what this purpose meant, or they had not learned that the goal associated with this purpose could be accomplished more easily by a skimming process, or they were incapable of adopting a skimming process.

The flexibility research to be reviewed in the remainder of this chapter will be interpreted with respect to whether it supports (a) process flexibility, or (b) the purpose flexibility and difficulty flexibility that Walker found with good readers and Anderson did not find with poor readers.

W. R. Dixon (1951) investigated the reading rates and eye movements of university professors and graduate students (also see Morse *et al.*, 1968). (Note: This research has already been reviewed from a different perspective in Chapter 5.) Dixon noted that " . . . the concept of types of reading is based on reading rates which seem most appropriate for different kinds of material: a slow, careful rate for detailed and compact content of science materials; a rapid, skimming rate for the story type of content; and a relatively rapid rate for the extensive and expansive content of the social studies" (p. 117). At the outset, Dixon was convinced that " . . . reading performance is likely to vary from one type of material to another" (p. 124) but he wanted to know why. He commented: "We cannot say for sure whether these variations are due to differences in the difficulty of the material, whether they are due to the fact that different types of material require different types of reading, whether they are due to differences in the familiarity of the material or to what extent both types of reading and familiarity with the material may be factors in reading performance" (p. 124).

Dixon asked 48 professors and 48 graduate students in three departments, education, physics, and history, to read three passages at about the eighth grade level, one in each of the areas of education, physics, and history. So, it was probably the case that rauding accuracy level was at the college level or above, $A_L > 14$, and the difficulty level of the material was $D_L = 8$, so the material was relatively easy, $A_L > D_L$. These subjects read education material at an average rate of 300 Wpm, physics material at 300 Wpm, and history material at 317 Wpm. These data offer no support for the idea that good readers are flexible in that they change their rate with the nature of the reading material. When reading passages in their own field these subjects read at an average rate of 334 Wpm (as estimated from ems and explained in more detail in Chapter 2). When reading passages in the other two fields, they averaged 292 Wpm. Thus, these 96 excellent readers read about 12% slower when they were less familiar with the content area. Since both of these rates are reasonable rauding process rates, and since both rates are approximately equal, it seems prudent to interpret these results as indicating that there is little or no flexibility of rate relevant to the nature or familiarity of the relatively easy reading material.

In this research, Dixon asked his subjects to read normally and then gave them five relatively easy yes–no questions after each passage that were general in scope, " . . . to let the subject know that he was expected to read for meaning, but not enough to make him hyperconscious of the comprehension requirement" (p. 133). Thus, this research was designed to find out if good readers vary their rauding process rate across different subject matter areas when the difficulty of the material is constant at the eighth grade level ($D_L = 8$) and also below the accuracy level of the reader ($A_L > D_L$).

As noted earlier, Dixon's results can be interpreted as indicating that good readers are not flexible with respect to the nature or familiarity of the material when they are engaged in the rauding process. If purpose in reading is defined broadly enough to include reading different types of subject matter or reading more or less familiar materials, then there seems to be no purpose flexibility. The reason that there was no purpose flexibility was because all of these 96 subjects were probably using their rauding process for all of the material they were given. Reading rate did not vary because the particular reading process employed was constantly in Gear 3 whether the material was familiar or not. These data from Dixon indicate no purpose flexibility when purpose is defined broadly to include differing subject matter and familiarity.

Laycock (1955) studied the eye movements of flexible and inflexible readers. (Note: This study was reviewed earlier in Chapter 5.) He asked college students and graduate students (who were above average ability on standardized tests) to read one 2300-word passage at their normal reading rate and then he asked them to read a second 2300-word passage as fast as possible without missing important points (advanced rate). He also gave a "short quiz" after each selection and excluded anyone who did not score 75%. He did not describe the tests or report any test results; he did describe the reading passages as "very easy to understand." He calculated a flexibility score by subtracting the normal rate from the advanced rate, and then selected the 37 highest scores (flexible readers) and the 35 lowest scores (inflexible readers). Then, the subjects replicated the procedure using shorter passages (98 words) while their eye movements were tracked.

Due to regression to the mean, the flexibility scores should decrease for the flexible readers and increase for the inflexible readers. Indeed, this occurred. The flexible group had a mean flexibility score of 188.9 on the selection test and this score dropped slightly to 177.3 during the experiment. The corresponding scores for the inflexible group were 35.7 and 106.4, indicating a large gain for them. Although regression to the mean explains these changes, Laycock went to great lengths to try to explain the loss in flexibility for the flexible group and the gain in flexibility for the inflexible group.

The reading rates found by Laycock indicate that his flexible group increased their rate around 175 Wpm when asked to read faster than normal, while the inflexible group increased their rate about 100 Wpm under the same request. These data can be interpreted as indicating that college students are capable of shifting from their rauding process to a skimming process when asked to do so. Indeed, Laycock's data indicate that above average college students are quite capable of shifting from third gear (Flexibles read at 355.8 Wpm; Inflexibles read at 321.6 Wpm) to fourth gear (Flexibles read at 533.1 Wpm; Inflexibles read at 428.0 Wpm).

On the basis of these data, Laycock suggested that "tachistoscopic training in quick recognition, for instance, may help widen fixation span and improve reading accuracy and flexibility" (p. 319). He also thought that "simple passages take less time to read than difficult ones," (p. 312) and that the less flexible readers were not able to " . . . skip unimportant words" (p. 319). There appears to be no evidence to support these educational treatment ideas. As reviewed in Chapters 3, 5, and 7, the rauding process rate does not vary with changes in the difficulty of material. Nor should this rate vary since it has also been shown to be the most efficient for varying levels of difficulty (see Chapter 7). These data from Laycock are best interpreted as indicating support for process flexibility because these college students were able to shift up from their rauding process, around 300 Wpm, to a skimming process, around 450 Wpm (see Table 2.2).

Letson (1959) studied the separate effects of difficulty and purpose. He asked his 601 college freshmen to read four 2500-word passages and then answer questions based upon the material as far as they had read without looking back at the passage. To assess the effect of difficulty, one passage was "easy" and one "difficult" according to the Flesch Readability Formula, that is, about the sixth and eleventh grade level of difficulty (see Flesch, 1949). Notice that both passages were likely to be relatively easy for these college freshmen since it is likely that their rauding accuracy level was at $A_L = 13$. For both passages, the subjects were instructed "to read the selection as rapidly as possible and still understand it sufficiently to answer questions afterwards" (p. 238). To assess the effect of purpose, two passages of equal difficulty (level unreported) were administered with the following instructions: (a) "to be read as rapidly as possible for the story" and (b) "to be read for complete mastery of ideas and details" (p. 238).

Letson reported that the easy passage was read at a mean rate of 269 Wpm and the difficult one was read at 239 Wpm. This is a very small difference which disappears almost completely when these rates are appropriately controlled for word length. Applying the equations given in

Chapter 2, the easy passage was read at 246 Wpm and the difficult one was read at 234 Wpm, a trivial difference of 12 Wpm. No description of these freshmen was given but the estimated rauding rate of freshmen is 263 Wpm, from Table 2.1; therefore, it seems likely that most of these students were operating their rauding process on relatively easy material and that is why there was little or no difference in the two rates, 246 versus 234. Indeed, these data provide additional solid evidence for the constancy of rate across varying difficulty levels for the rauding process.

For Letson's two purpose conditions, the rate under the story purpose was 292 Wpm and the rate under the complete mastery purpose was 271 Wpm. This is also a trivial difference. However, it should be pointed out that the objective consequences were the same under both conditions, i.e., the same questions were used. Therefore, it seems possible that the consequences had more of an effect on the process adopted so that these instructions had little or no effect on gear shifting. Some of the students may have shifted from a rauding process under the story condition to a learning process under the complete mastery condition, and the change in rate for these few students may have accounted for the small rate difference, 292 versus 271 Wpm.

Letson's data may be interpreted as providing evidence *against* difficulty flexibility because these college students read the passage at grade 6 at almost exactly the same rate as the passage at grade 11. Also, these data of Letson's may be interpreted as evidence against purpose flexibility because the rates under the two different purpose instructions were almost the same, 292 versus 271 Wpm. The reason that there was little or no process flexibility was probably because the objective consequences were the same under both purpose conditions so the subjects used similar processes.

Nania and Moe (1962) gave "rate flexibility" training to 12 eighth graders who were called "able" and "superior." There was no control group. They defined rate flexibility as varying rate according to purpose, difficulty of material, and familiarity with the type of material to be read. They reported a median gain in rate from pre to post of 229 wpm. No comprehension scores were reported. One of their conclusions was that "pupils can learn to 'shift gears' as materials and purpose change" (p. 86). These data are compatible with the process flexibility concept.

Hill (1964) studied the flexibility of 54 advanced English majors who were well above average readers according to their scores on the Nelson–Denny Reading Test. Their mean reading rate was 376 wpm and this was the 83rd percentile rank using the Grade 16 norms; their mean scores on vocabulary and comprehension were also high, 72 and 74 percentile ranks, respectively. These students were given three different

1200-word passages to read, each with a different purpose. The three prereading directions were as follows: (a) "read this selection as a course assignment over which you are to be tested tomorrow" (Prepare for Exams), (b) "read this selection to identify its main ideas" (Identify Key Ideas), and (c) "read this selection to critically analyze the motives and attitudes of the author" (Analyze Author Motives). After reading a passage, 12 multiple-choice questions were given, untimed. The reading rates for the three groups were almost exactly equal, 176, 182, and 184 wpm, respectively. The percentages correct on the four items that measured comprehension of stated details were almost exactly equal, 59, 60, and 57, respectively; there was no indication that the direction to Prepare for Exam resulted in higher scores for stated details. The percentages correct on the four questions measuring comprehension of the main ideas were almost exactly equal, 49, 54, and 54, respectively; there was no indication that the direction to read to identify key ideas had any effect. The percentages correct on the four critical analysis items were almost exactly equal, 46, 45, and 42, respectively; the direction to Analyze Author Motives had no important effect on the scores on these critical analysis items. Hill noted that these instructions are " . . . frequent directions encountered by the student . . ." (p. 124).

These results from the Hill research outlined above may be interpreted as evidence for process flexibility and against purpose flexibility. When these good readers (rauding process rates around 375 wpm) were given passages to read in order to answer difficult questions, they adopted a learning process (about 180 wpm) so that they were able to answer about 50% correctly. Hill interpreted these results as indicating flexible reading; indeed, these good readers appear to have shifted from third gear to second gear, and for them this rate may even be indicative of shifting down to a memorizing process, i.e., first gear. But, it seems more reasonable to interpret these data as providing evidence against purpose flexibility because all three purposes produced almost exactly the same rates. Furthermore, there was no evidence that these good readers were able to concentrate on main ideas, for example, by skipping over unimportant words or sentences, and thereby increase their scores on these items while increasing their rate. Again it would be best to interpret these data as indicating that these good readers (a) showed process flexibility by shifting down from their rauding process, Gear 3, to a learning process, Gear 2, in order to answer difficult multiple-choice questions, (b) did not show purpose flexibility because three different purposes all produced the same rates, and (c) did not show purpose flexibility another way because each purpose failed to produce higher scores on those test items designed to measure the accomplishment of that purpose.

The above data collected by Hill will undoubtedly be interpreted by some as support for purpose flexibility since these good readers did shift down from a Nelson–Denny rate of 376 wpm to rates under 200 wpm when they had to answer difficult questions in this experiment. The problem in calling this "purpose flexibility" is a semantic one. For clarity, why interpret these data as supporting purpose flexibility when the three purpose conditions designed to elicit different rates and consequences did not do so? This is why it is misleading to say there is purpose flexibility; some purposes result in different rates and some do not. The only variations in purpose that seem to result in different rates are those that have been more accurately defined and described as process flexibility. Therefore, to facilitate communication it seems best to note that there is strong evidence for process flexibility whereas the evidence for purpose flexibility is misleading at best.

Kershner (1964) asked 420 adults to read four passages that varied in difficulty. The adults were described as ranging in age from 18 to 85 and varying in education from fourth grade to five years of graduate study. The subjects were obtained from 63 randomly selected blocks of a large city. They were given four separate passages to read. First, they were instructed to read the first two passages and judge which one of the pair was the more difficult to read. They were not told the fact that later they were going to be asked a comprehension question on what they had read during their reading of this first pair. Their reading of the second pair may be different from the first pair because it could be assumed that they expected to receive a comprehension question as well as to make the same judgment about the more difficult one. The time they spent reading was unobtrusively recorded so these adults were not aware that time or rate of reading was important.

Kershner reported that the time to read the second pair was "significantly" longer than the first pair. However, the median times for reading the first 2000 type spaces (333 Words) were almost exactly the same, i.e., 93 sec for the first pair and 104 sec for the second pair; this was 215 Wpm and 192 Wpm, respectively. Thus, expecting a comprehension question slowed the average rate by 11%, an effect size that is of questionable significance. Also, notice that the 215 Wpm rate is at the ninth grade level, from Table 2.1, and this would be a reasonable average rate for a random sample of adults to operate their rauding process.

Kershner also divided his passages into difficulty levels called hard, intermediate, and easy. He interpreted his data as indicating that reading rate was affected by the difficulty level. For example, he reported the mean reading times for the first pair of passages to be 113.5, 100.6, and 90.8 sec for the hard, intermediate, and easy passages, respectively; the corresponding rates would be 176, 199, and 220 Wpm. These data were subsequently referred to by Rothkopf and Coatney (1974) as evidence that greater readability resulted in faster "inspection speeds." Since these adults probably used their rauding process, it is important that this evidence of Kershner's be closely scrutinized. If these readers made important changes in their rauding process rate in response to changes in difficulty level, this would constitute evidence against rauding theory and for difficulty flexibility.

It is possible that Kershner's subjects shifted gears when they encountered the more difficult passages, but this is not likely since their task when reading the first pair of passages was to rate the difficulty of the material not to understand it. Therefore, it is unlikely that the typical adults in this study shifted out of their rauding process. However, the differences in rate associated with the differences in difficulty were not large, ranging from 220 to 176 Wpm which is a 20% drop. This 20% drop from easy to hard represents, for example, one passage taken from the magazine *True Confessions* and another taken from the *Annals of the American Academy of Political Science*. Only a 20% change in rate for a range of difficulty this large is not a major change.

More importantly, however, the 20% change found by Kershner was not even that large. Kershner committed what appears to be questionable design decision when he divided his 37 passages into the categories of hard, intermediate, and easy. He could have used a readability formula, but he did not. He could have used the ratings made by his own subjects but he did not. Instead, the "operational definition of readability used in the basic experiment employed the dual criteria of relative reading time and judged difficulty" (p. 26). Notice that the passages were divided into categories of hard, intermediate, and easy partly on the basis of how long it took to read them. Therefore, this criterion of difficulty was contaminated or confounded with rate. It is not surprising that the easy passages were read faster than the hard passages when the operational definition of "easy" and "hard" meant that "easy" is read faster than "hard." This method of dividing passages into easy and hard categories completely invalidates any attempt to use this evidence as indicating that individuals automatically adjust their rate to the difficulty level of the material. Instead, this evidence cannot be used against the constancy of the rauding process since there was only a 20% change in rate between easy and hard passages even though the easy passages were selected because they were read faster than the hard ones. Thus, Kershner's results not only provide no support for difficulty flexibility but instead can be interpreted as providing evidence against difficulty flexibility.

Kershner does deserve credit for pointing out "the dubious value of words per minute as a measure of reading speed" (p. 25) when there is no knowledge of the difficulty of the material. He noted that 2000 type spaces in one of his easy passages contained 396 words while this length contained only 298 words in one of his hard passages. By using 2000 type spaces to measure rate he was accomplishing the same kind of control for word length as using Wpm instead of wpm (see Chapter 2).

Boyd (1966) measured the reading rate of 241 New Zealand students who were asked to read under three purpose conditions, details, main ideas, and skimming. The reported age of these students made them comparable to twelfth graders in the United States. They were asked to read three articles that had been "rated within the easy readability range on the Fog Index" (p. 237). So, it can be assumed that the materials were relatively easy, $A_L > D_L$. Before reading, "a clearly stated purpose was given, upon which ten multiple-choice questions at the conclusion of the reading were based" (p. 237). The median rates for girls (G) and boys (B) were given as follows: details, G = 199 wpm, B = 193 wpm; main ideas, G = 219 wpm, B = 211 wpm; skimming, G = 238 wpm, B = 261 wpm. Notice that the rates for main ideas were approximately GE = 9 and 10 using Table 2.1, so it seems reasonable to assume that many of these students were employing their rauding process under this condition. Both boys and girls went about 9% slower when reading for details. When skimming, the girls went 9% faster and the boys went 24% faster. There is some evidence for gear shifting, or flexibility, but not much. However, it should be noted that the conditions of the experiment only manipulated the instructions. The objective consequences appeared to be the same under all three purpose conditions. Therefore, it does not appear reasonable to expect most students to shift from one reading process to another when the test conditions remained the same under all purpose conditions.

Otto, Barrett, and Harris (1968) investigated whether elementary school children could be trained to vary their rate. They trained 72 children, in grades 4, 5, and 6, to vary their rate under three purpose conditions, main idea, sequence, and specific fact. The training lasted for 30–45 minutes a day over a 7-day period. They reported that " . . . the children read most rapidly to find specific facts, they read less rapidly for main ideas, and they read most slowly for sequence" (p. 71). Unfortunately, they did not report any reading rates; they reported their results primarily in the form of nine ANOVA summary tables involving variability coefficients. Without any way to estimate actual rates, it is impossible to determine what reading processes these children may have been using and in fact exactly how much they did change their rates. This is not the only research on flexibility that suffers from this same lack of rate information (e.g., see Dee-Lucas, 1979; Shebilske & Reid, 1979).

Rankin (1970) studied what he called the internal flexibility of readers, the ability to change rates within an article by slowing down on the more difficult parts and speeding up on the less difficult parts. He asked 255 college students who were poor readers to underline the word they were reading every 15 sec when they heard the signal "mark." Then, he correlated the passage difficulty of 100 word segments, using a predetermined measure, with each subject's reading rate on the segment. A zero correlation would indicate no change in rate associated with difficulty. A negative correlation would indicate that the reader slowed down for the harder parts and speeded up for the easier parts, and the higher the negative correlation the more flexible that particular reader was. Rankin reported a mean correlation of -0.16 before a course in developmental reading was taken and a mean correlation of -0.27 at the end of a one-semester course. Since Rankin provided a frequency distribution of the posttest correlations, it was possible to determine that the median correlation at the end of the course was -0.21, hardly evidence of much change in rate associated with difficulty. Since the harder parts ordinarily contain longer words this correlation of -0.21 probably would have evaporated to zero if rate had been controlled for word length by being measured in Wpm instead of wpm. Rankin did not report any of the rates involved, only correlation coefficients, so the particular type of reading process used by the subjects could not be estimated with confidence.

About the most that can be discerned from the above research of Rankin's is that poor-reading college students showed little or no tendency to vary their rate when they were asked to "read as rapidly as you can and still understand what you read" (p. 35). Even a semester's course in developmental reading had little or no effect. If the subjects were operating their rauding process, it is understandable and laudable that they did not vary their rate. This study contained no data relevant to whether these students could shift gears from one type of reading process to another so nothing can be learned about process flexibility. It does seem reasonable to interpret these data as providing evidence against difficulty flexibility.

In 1972, Rankin and Kehle published additional analyses of the data described above. Further descriptive information was also reported. The 255 college freshmen scored below the 33rd percentile rank on a standardized reading comprehension test. The rate measures were taken on 2000-word passages that were described as "rather easy" for this group. The mean reading rates on the pretest and posttest were 256 and 293 wpm, respectively. After Rankin and Kehle had analyzed these data in different and creative ways that produced results which were unsatisfying to them, they made the following comments in their concluding summary section: (a) "the game is not worth the candle," (b) "one might question the whole concept of reading flexibility," and (c) " . . . a good deal of speculation and advocacy of the value of reading flexibility which has become a part of our conventional wisdom, should be curtailed until a substantial body of solid evidence is gathered to substantiate our claims" (p. 57). In summary, Rankin and Kehle found no evidence for difficulty flexibility.

For the above college students reading relatively easy material at rates of 256 and 293 wpm it is likely that they were operating their rauding process (see Tables 2.1 and 2.2). Therefore, with the benefit of hindsight based upon the previously reviewed research (Carver, 1971b, 1976, 1983; Coke, 1976; G. R. Miller & Coleman, 1971; Morse, 1951; Zuber & Wetzel, 1981), it is not surprising that Rankin found no flexibility associated with material difficulty. In fact, students read most efficiently when they do not change their rates because operating a rauding process at their rauding rate results in the highest efficiency of comprehension scores (Carver, 1982).

Kintsch and Keenan (1973) provided data which superficially seem to provide evidence against the constancy of reading rate. (Note: This research was reviewed earlier in Chapters 3 and 8 from a different perspective.) Using sentences which were all approximately the same length in words, Kintsch and Keenan varied the number of propositions from four to nine. They instructed their subjects that they should "work as fast as possible, keeping in mind that the important thing was how much they remembered not speed" (p. 261). They found that reading rate decreased as the number of propositions in the sentence increased. Thus, they found that rate varied as the number of words remained constant; this result is completely counter to rauding theory which would predict a constant rate as long as the number of standard words being read was constant. However, the average reading rates of the subjects in the research of Kintsch and Keenan varied from about 65 wpm for nine propositions to about 100 wpm for four propositions. For college students, it seems impossible to contend that these rates were representative of their normal or typical reading rate. As noted earlier, Taylor (1965) sampled over 1000 college students from all over the United States and found their average rate to be 280 wpm. Therefore, it appears that these results of Kintsch and Keenan's are relevant to first gear (a memorizing process) and are not relevant to third gear (the rauding process). This research by Kintsch and Keenan should *not* be interpreted as providing evidence to support the theory that individuals have difficulty flexibility when they operate their rauding process because these researchers were investigating a memorizing process. These data may be interpreted as evidence for process flexibility because these subjects appear to have shifted down to a memorizing process, Gear 1, when the objective consequences required it.

McConkie, Rayner, and Wilson (1973) gave seven different types of questions to subjects after they had read a passage (e.g., factual, recognition, higher order) and reported that their results "provided evidence that subjects can read for different types of information and . . . demonstrated the effectiveness of a method of manipulating this aspect of reading flexibility in the laboratory" (p. 5). (Note: This research was reviewed earlier in Chapter 3 from a different perspective.) A close scrutiny of their data reveals the following: (a) the mean reading rate for the seven types was 264 wpm; (b) of the seven types, the one read the fastest was called "number" and it was 16% faster than the grand mean; and (c) the type read the slowest was called "combined" and it was read 11% slower than the grand mean. Even if it were to be conceded that McConkie *et al.* succeeded in setting up a typical reading situation, this amount of flexibility is hardly of a sufficient size to provide evidence against the relative constancy of reading rate during the operation of the rauding process. Stated differently, these differences in rate among the seven types were statistically significant but a close look at effect size indicates that the amount of flexibility they found is relatively trivial (ranging from 234 to 306 wpm for the seven conditions). These data can be alternatively interpreted as indicating very little flexibility within students operating reading processes that are not drastically different from the rauding process.

Rothkopf and Coatney (1974) presented data which appeared to indicate that the difficulty level of the material encountered previously has an effect upon the rate at which subsequent material is read. (Note: These data were reviewed earlier in Chapter 3 from a different perspective.) Thus, their data seem to support Rothkopf's (1972) contention that individuals do tend to adapt their reading rate to the difficulty of the material, but their adaptation is a slow process so that there is carry over rate from one difficulty level to another. However, the subjects in this research probably were not using their rauding process.

Rothkopf and Coatney instructed their college student subjects to read "as rapidly as they could and still learn the essential elements of the content" (p. 680). These instructions to "learn the essential elements" coupled with the rest of the objective consequences of the experiment probably account for why the subjects read at a rate slower than normal. Rothkopf and Coatney presented their rates in syllables per minute, so it was possible to estimate Wpm using Equation 2.7. When this was done, it was determined that the reading rates in this research ranged from about 133 to 223 Wpm, a range that indicates that the more powerful first and second gears were being used (see Chapter 2). Thus, it appears that Rothkopf's generalizations about rate being affected by the difficulty level of material encountered previously must be restricted to a learning process and a memorizing process. The Rothkopf and Coatney data did not involve a rauding process and therefore cannot constitute evidence for difficulty flexibility during the execution of this process. These data may be interpreted as providing support for process flexibility because these college students obviously shifted down from their rauding process, Gear 3, to learning and memorizing processes, that operated around 130 to 220 wpm.

Samuels and Dahl (1975) investigated the effect of varying purposes on flexibility in 100 fourth graders and 84 college students. The fourth graders were given 500-word passages at the fourth grade level of difficulty, under both a detailed and a general purpose condition. Under the detailed purpose, students answered three detailed questions; under the general purpose, they answered three general questions. The directions given to these subjects are given below:

> The purpose of this study is to find out if people can adjust their reading speed according to the difficulty of the questions they will be asked. You will be given two reading tests. Each will be preceded by a practice test. The purpose of the practice test is to indicate to you the degree of difficulty of the test questions so that you can determine the speed at which you will read. You should read as quickly as you can but still be able to answer the questions which follow.

The success of this research depends upon the difficulty level of the questions administered, and an indication of difficulty comes from the percentage comprehension scores. For the fourth graders, Samuels and Dahl reported mean scores of 2.04 and 2.89 for the three detailed and three general questions, respectively; corrected for guessing and transformed into percentages, these two accuracy values became 52% and 94%, respectively. Therefore, it appears that the detailed questions were probably very difficult if these students could only score 52% even after they knew they were difficult and could shift to a lower gear to be more successful on this task. Also, the general questions must have been very easy if the mean score was 94% accuracy.

These fourth graders studied by Samuels and Dahl read at a rate of 286 wpm when reading to answer the very easy, general overview questions and they read at a rate of 188 wpm when reading to answer very difficult detailed questions. Adjusting for the difficulty level of the passages, these rates became 254 and 167 Wpm, respectively. From the data in Table 2.1, it can be determined that the average reading rate of the fourth graders is 158 Wpm. Since the fourth graders in this research were reading at 167 Wpm for the goal of answering detailed questions, they were probably executing their rauding process. Since they were reading 254 Wpm for the goal of answering the easy general questions, they were probably executing a skimming process.

These data suggest that these fourth graders were process flexible in that they were able to shift up to fourth gear when the questions were very easy; they could skim and still get almost all the answers correct, i.e., 94% accuracy. However, these fourth graders did not show much flexibility with respect to shifting into a lower gear, such as second gear, when the questions were very hard, 52% accuracy. Maybe these fourth graders needed to be given the two following instructions: (a) read as quickly as you can and still answer most of the easy questions correctly, and (b) read as slowly as you need to in order to answer most of the hard questions correctly. Under these modified instructions, maybe they would have shown they could also shift to a learning process that is slower than the rauding process but offers a better chance of answering most of the difficult questions correctly.

The college students in this research by Samuels and Dahl took part in a study almost exactly the same as the fourth graders, except they were given passages that were about 820 words in length that were at the twelfth grade level of difficulty. Their percentage comprehension scores were 71 and 86 for the detailed and general purposes, respectively. Their corresponding rates were 291 and 461 wpm, respectively. Given the 291 wpm rate and the corresponding 71% comprehension under the detailed purpose, it appears likely that the college students were able to engage their rauding process for the detailed questions and still do relatively well on them. The 461 wpm rate on the general questions and the corresponding 86% comprehension scores indicate that they probably engaged a skimming process and were successful in accomplishing the goal associated with this purpose. Those data provide evidence that college students are capable of shifting up to fourth gear when the goal can be accomplished by a skimming process.

The above two studies leave little doubt that when the goals of reading can be accomplished by faster rates and the subjects are made aware of this by explicit instructions and practice with the objective consequences, both fourth graders and college students can be induced to adopt a skimming process. Therefore, it seems reasonable to conclude that students at all levels can be induced to abandon their habitual rauding process operating at the apping rate and adopt a skimming process when they learn that their goals can be achieved this way. Yet this study leaves in doubt whether elementary students are equally capable of shifting down to a learning process in order to accomplish goals that require adding components in the reading process that require more time and effort.

At the conclusion of their report, Samuels and Dahl make the following comment: "the attempt of some researchers to find a *typical* reading rate would appear to be an ill-conceived notion in light of current conceptualizations regarding passage difficulty and purpose for reading" (p. 43). This comment is directly counter to the theory and research previously reviewed, and it therefore deserves careful consideration. There seems to be little doubt that college students will respond to different purposes with different rates as long as the goals associated with these purposes can be achieved by shifting away from the rauding process to other types of reading processes that are faster or slower. Thus, we can say that most college students are process flexible; they will abandon their more natural, comfortable, typical, and habitual apping rate when they learn that their reading goals can be better accomplished by a different reading process, one that operates either faster or slower. This kind of flexibility was already evident from the research reviewed earlier by Walker (1933), Laycock (1955), and Hill (1964).

Although there is a great deal of strong evidence for process flexibility, there is even stronger evidence against difficulty flexibility. Those researchers who have investigated flexibility within the rauding process by looking at changes in rate associated with varying levels of material difficulty have found little or no change (Letson, 1959; Rankin and Kehle, 1972). When reading rate is properly controlled for word length, there is very strong evidence that the rauding process operates at a constant rate across difficulty levels (see research reviewed in Chapters 3, 5, and 7). Therefore, there is also very strong evidence that most readers do have a *typical* rate, in spite of the protestation of Samuels and Dahl. Most readers do have a typical rate because apping is comfortable, fatigue resistant, and accomplishes the goals of reading in the most efficient manner most of the time. When Samuels and Dahl argued back in 1975 that *typical* reading rate was an ill-conceived notion, they could not have foreseen that typical reading rate would provide the foundation for most of the ideas in the present extensive review of reading rate research. In summary, this Samuels and Dahl research can be alternatively interpreted as evidence for process flexibility because the rates involved were very much in accordance with those predicted from the goals and objective consequences associated with the five basic reading processes (see Chapter 2).

In 1978, Rankin again tried out his version of a flexibility coefficient, the within-individual correlation between the difficulty level of the passage and the rate of reading the passage. Although this research article was lengthy, the description of methodology was skimpy. For example, there was no customary method section that described details about subjects or procedures, and there was no description of the directions that were given. However, we do know that the subjects were 44 sixth graders and the passages ranged in difficulty from 2.8 to 18 GE units. The measure of rate was not in wpm. Also, the time to read passages was combined with the time for answering the comprehension questions on the passages. The only results given were in the form of correlation coefficients. Remember, if an individual tends to speed up on the easy passages and slow down on the hard passages, then the individual will have a negative correlation, the higher this negative flexibility coefficient, the more flexible the reader. The average flexibility coefficient for the 44 subjects was -0.27.

This finding of Rankin's suggests that the typical sixth grader does not shift down to a learning process when it probably would pay off in terms of getting more questions answered correctly. However, it seems possible that some sixth grade students might shift down to second gear as the passages and questions became more difficult, up until the passages approached grade 18 in difficulty. At that point they might have reverted back to apping because there was little hope for success even if they used a learning or memorizing process. If this happened, then the flexibility coefficients, based upon a linear relationship, would incorrectly suggest that these students were not flexible.

Rankin also measured the total time to complete all the passages and the total comprehension score for all the passages. The correlation between the size of the flexibility coefficients and the total time to finish the test was negligible, -0.18. However, the correlation between these same flexibility coefficients and the total comprehension scores was -0.66. This means that the people who got the most questions right on the entire test tended to be the same people who slowed down on the more difficult passages. This is a satisfying finding because it indicates that those students who are willing and able to switch to a learning process or a memorizing process on the more difficult passages are the ones who do better on the test. So, these data of Rankin's suggest that (a) a typical sixth grader is not flexible in the sense of shifting down from Gear 3 to Gear 1 or 2 when a memorizing process or learning process is required to achieve the goal of answering test questions correctly, and (b) the sixth graders who have learned to be process flexible are the ones who answer the most questions correctly.

Shebilske and Fisher (1981) investigated flexibility of rate within a 2866-word passage by analyzing the eye movements of two adult college graduates without their being aware that their eye movements were being tracked. The passage was from a 10th grade biology textbook and neither subject was a biology major. It is likely that the material was relatively easy, $A_L > D_L$. They told their subjects to read " . . . as they would ordinarily read such a passage for a homework assignment" (p. 52). They also told them that " . . . they would be tested with detailed essay and multiple choice questions and that they would have an opportunity to reread the text before the test" (p. 52). On the basis of this information alone, it would be difficult to predict what type of reading process would be adopted. The text probably would be relatively easy for the subjects so it might be predicted that the rauding process would be adopted. Yet, the subjects were told that they would be given an essay test plus a multiple-choice test and these instructions might induce a memorizing process or a learning process. Then again, they were told they would get to read the passage again before taking the test so they might not have to adopt a learning process or a memorizing process on the first reading because they would have another chance to adopt those more demanding processes depending upon whether they were judged to be needed.

In their results, Shebilske and Fisher reported that the two subjects averaged 280 wpm on important idea units and 288 wpm on unimportant units during the first reading. These rates strongly suggest that the subjects used their rauding process on the first reading. Not only are 280 and 288 wpm well within the range of expected average rates for adult college graduates (see Table 2.1), but the trivial difference between important and unimportant idea units indicates that there was no rate change due to the nature of the material. These data suggest that the adults were operating their rauding process at their apping rate, without regard for whether the idea units were important or unimportant. On the second reading, the rate for the important idea units dropped to 229 wpm providing evidence for a shifting down to second gear for these parts in order to do well on the test that followed. On the unimportant idea units the rate shifted to 372 wpm suggesting that a skimming was often used for these parts, on the second reading. The most important aspect of their findings, however, was that they provided some objective evidence relevant to how the eyes actually move during a learning process, the second reading. They reported the following:

> It was not infrequent that readers finished a meaning unit before deciding to slow down and take another look at it. The verification process was also evident when they came to the last word in a unit (most likely an important unit) and then made a large regression, sometimes back to the first word. (p. 54)

These interpretations provide support for the components of the model learning process presented in Chapter 2.

Shebilske and Fisher also reported longer fixation durations and shorter interfixation distances for the important idea units. It seems likely that a learning process is slower for at least two reasons, more re-reading of phrases and sentences and a slightly longer time spent on each word. These data can be interpreted as supporting process flexibility because the subjects appeared to use a rauding process on the first reading and then on the second reading they shifted up to a skimming process on the unimportant parts and they shifted down to a learning process on the important parts.

DiStefano, Noe, and Valencia (1981) conducted perhaps the best study available of traditional flexibility. As noted at the outset of this chapter, flexibility has most often meant changing rates in response to different purposes and different passage difficulties and that is exactly what they investigated. They gave 170 eighth graders and 170 eleventh graders one 1471-word passage at the eighth grade level of difficulty and another 1305-word passage at the eleventh grade level of difficulty. The passages were presented under two purpose conditions: read for detail and read for overview. The following instructions were given:

> When you are reading, there are times when you read for overview and times when you read for detail. For example, when reading the morning newspaper before going to school, you may simply have a broad question in mind such as "What is this article about?" With this question in mind, you may read the article very quickly. This is reading for overview.
>
> On the other hand, there are times when you are studying for an important test, and you must read carefully and slowly. This is reading for detail. You are here today to help us find out if people can change their reading speed to answer overview questions and detail questions. You will be given a practice example followed by a real test. The practice example will show you the type of question you will have to answer in the real test. These questions will determine the speed at which you will have to read the real test that follows. (p. 603)

Notice that this study is very similar to the Samuels and Dahl (1975) research reviewed earlier except the present study varied passage difficulty in addition to purpose. Table 10.1 contains the results of this study. The data in Table 10.1 have been divided into the two purpose conditions, detail and overview. Under the reading for detail condition, it can be seen that the eighth graders read the two passages at almost the same rates (187 and 182 wpm), and the eleventh graders also read the two passages at almost the same rates (196 and 191 wpm). These rates probably represent the rauding process even though they are slightly lower than the 204 wpm average reading rate for the eighth graders and the 237 wpm average rate for the eleventh graders given in Table 2.1. Some of these students may have adopted a learning process given that the percentage comprehension scores under the reading for detail purpose ranged from 52 to 69%, and this may account for their rates being slightly below that typically associated with eighth and eleventh graders. Nonetheless, these data are well within the rates that would be expected for eighth and eleventh graders who were using their rauding process and not varying their apping rates across difficulty levels. Most importantly, these data may be reasonably interpreted as indicating that eighth graders and eleventh graders have no difficulty flexibility while they operate their rauding process.

The rates in Table 10.1 under the other purpose condition, reading for overview, were considerably higher for the eighth grade passages. Notice that the eighth grade passage had rates of 295 and 306 wpm with corresponding comprehension scores of 83 and 92%. These data strongly suggest that most of the eighth and eleventh graders were able to shift up to fourth gear and still answer almost all of the overview

Table 10.1

Reading Rate Means in Actual Words Per Minute and Percentage Comprehension for Two Grade Levels of Passage Difficulty and Two Grade Levels of Reader Ability When Reading under Two Different Purpose Conditions

Purpose	Grade	Rate (wpm)		Comprehension (%)	
		8th[a]	11th[a]	8th[a]	11th[a]
Reading for detail	8	187	182	57	52
	11	196	191	69	63
Reading for overview	8	295	220	83	52
	11	306	253	92	70

Note: These data were collected by DiStefano et al. (1981).
[a] 8th and 11th refer to passage difficulty.

questions on the eighth grade passage. However, the eleventh grade passage presents a different picture. Notice that the rates are much lower, 220 and 253 wpm, and so are the corresponding comprehension scores, 52 and 70%. Notice also that the effect of purpose on rate was very small for the eleventh grade passage; 182 versus 220 for eighth graders and 191 versus 253 for eleventh graders. The reason seems to be quite apparent. Whereas the subjects in the Samuels and Dahl research reviewed earlier were able to answer almost all of their general questions when shifting to a skimming process, it is quite evident that almost all of the overview questions in the present study could not have been answered correctly if the students had adopted a skimming process. The eighth graders could only answer 52% of the overview questions correctly on the eleventh grade passage. No wonder they did not read much faster under this purpose, 220 wpm, than they did under the detail purpose, 182 wpm.

Notice that DiStefano *et al.* have put these students in a situation where they seem to be expected to go fast under an overview purpose but the questions are so difficult for them that they cannot shift into a skimming process and still answer most of the questions correctly. These researchers interpreted their own data as follows: " . . . the interaction between purpose and difficulty determines the rate of reading and accompanying comprehension" (p. 605). Yet, it seems obvious that it is not the difficulty of the passage that made the subjects read the eleventh grade passage slower than the eighth grade passage when reading for overview. Instead, it is the difficulty of the questions that made them slow down. If the overview questions on the eleventh grade passage had been made easier, as Samuels and Dahl (1975) made their general questions easy even for fourth graders, then there is little doubt that these subjects would have adopted a skimming process. They could have accomplished their goal by dropping components and thereby reading faster.

These data from DiStefano *et al.* can be summarized as indicating that secondary students are quite capable of being process flexible and shifting to a skimming process when the questions that they are reading to answer are easy enough to answer correctly under this faster process. However, if the questions the researchers ask are *not* easy, they will not be flexible and shift gears because students are smarter than that; they seem to realize that the only justification for shifting up out of a rauding process is when the reading goal can thereupon be achieved by a shortcut sampling process such as skimming. These data therefore provide strong support for process flexibility. These data also provide additional support for the total absence of difficulty flexibility under the rauding process. This is another research study that supports the First Law of rauding theory, reviewed in Chapter 2, which holds that individuals tend to operate their rauding process at a constant rate.

The DiStefano *et al.* study has one glaring inadequacy: Reading rates were compared across difficulty levels without controlling for the longer word length associated with higher difficulty passages. Remember, from Chapter 3, the flurry of data collected in the early 1970s indicating the necessity of using this control, and it remains one of the most solid research findings available in the field of reading. Yet, this control was ignored about 10 years later in 1981, in one of the best available research studies on flexibility ever conducted. Such a methodological lapse should not be perpetuated. Therefore, Table 10.2 contains the same rate data as Table 10.1 except these wpm rates are now expressed as an estimated rate in Wpm using the formulas given in Chapter 2. Notice that under the reading for detail purpose, the rates for the eighth and eleventh grade passages became almost identical: 177 versus 179 Wpm for the eighth graders and 185 versus 188 Wpm for the eleventh graders. Otherwise, the pattern of results has not changed from that discussed earlier. The support for the First Law of rauding theory became even stronger when rate was expressed in Wpm.

Carver (1983) conducted a study of the flexibility of rate during the operation of the rauding process. (Note: These data were reviewed earlier in Chapter 7 from a different perspective.) Passages varying in difficulty level from grades 1 to 16 were read by 435 students varying from grade 4 through college. For each level of reading ability, reading rate was found to be approximately constant. College students typically changed their rate about 14% from one difficulty level to another but there was no general tendency to read easier passages faster than harder

Table 10.2

Reading Rate Means in Standard Length Words Per Minute (Wpm)
for Two Grade Levels of Passage Difficulty and Two Grade Levels
of Reader Ability under Two Different Purpose Conditions

		Passage difficulty	
Purpose	Grade	8th	11th
Reading for detail	8	177	179
	11	185	188
Reading for overview	8	279	216
	11	290	249

Note: These results represent a reanalysis of the rate data in Table 10.1, from DiStefano *et al.* (1981), using the equations in Chapter 2.

passages. For example, the college students read passages varying from grade 5 to grade 14 in difficulty at average rates that varied only from 310 to 290 Wpm. Also, there was no tendency for the better readers to have more difficulty flexibility than the poorer readers; for example, the readers at the fourth, fifth, and sixth grade levels of ability changed their rates 13.3%, on the average, between the first grade level and fourth grade level of difficulty while the readers at the college level of ability changed their rates 14.4%, on the average, among passages at the first, fourth, seventh, tenth, and thirteenth grade levels of difficulty. In summary, there was no evidence for difficulty flexibility when the conditions were appropriate for the readers in grades 4 through college to engage their rauding process on materials that ranged from grade 1 to grade 16 in difficulty.

Carver (1984b) investigated the effect of two different purpose conditions upon the accuracy of comprehension of passages presented at average rates varying from 62.5 to 100,000 Wpm. For the 102 college students involved, the accuracy of comprehension was measured four different ways: Understanding Judgments, Missing Verbs Test, Best Titles Test, and Sentence Halves Test. In one purpose condition, called Gist, one-half of the students were instructed " . . . to try to understand enough of the passage to answer correctly the questions on the Best Titles Test" (p. 209); they were paid a bonus on the basis of the number of these questions they answered correctly. In the other purpose condition, called Detail, the other one-half of the students were told " . . . to try to determine whether or not there was a verb missing in the passage" (p. 209); they were paid a bonus on the basis of how many questions they answered correctly on the Missing Verbs Test. All of the 102 students were administered all four measures but their bonus was primarily based upon the particular test associated with their purpose condition.

Average rate means that rate was under the control of these students. Time was controlled or constant. In this situation, Carver found that all four measurement techniques indicated that the effect of the purpose condition, Gist versus Detail, was so small and unreliable that it could be interpreted as being nonexistent. Carver interpreted his results relevant to purpose as follows:

> It appears that the individuals in the present experiment read the passages at their normal rate and in their normal fashion until the end of the time limit. It does not appear that different purposes during reading, at least given the range of purposes used in this research, had much effect upon what the individual did while reading. These data provide no support for those who would contend that purpose for reading has a large effect upon comprehension in relatively normal or typical reading situations. Those individuals who

were primarily trying to get the gist of the passage were no better able to accomplish this end than those individuals who were primarily reading each sentence to determine if a verb was missing. (p. 217)

These data and these interpretations reinforce the lack of support for purpose flexibility.

Nell (1988) studied the page by page variability of reading rate of 30 adults who were reading light fiction. These readers were called "ludic" readers, a label designating those individuals who read a great deal of light fiction for pleasure. These individuals read an average of about 16 books a month for pleasure. They were each asked to bring a book to the laboratory to read for pleasure, and the rate at which they read each page was measured over a period of 30 min. For each individual, Nell reported the mean laboratory reading rate in wpm, number of pages read in the laboratory, the highest and lowest page rates, and the "flexibility ratio" which was the highest page rate divided by the lowest page rate. Nell summarized these results as follows: "The mean flexibility ratio for the 30 subjects is 2.63, with a range of 1.46 to 7.79, indicative of a great deal of flexibility during natural reading" (p. 18).

On the surface, these data of Nell's appear to be strong evidence against the constancy of the rauding process, and against rauding theory. However, there are three major problems with interpreting these data this way. First, rauding theory purports to deal with most readers as they read most of the time. The mean reading rate for this group was 409 wpm, well above the average for college students. Furthermore, it seems reasonable that readers of light fiction would shift gears to a skimming process when, for example, the author was describing a scene that was of no interest to the reader. So these data may simply reflect that these readers periodically let comprehension suffer by skipping or skimming. Second, Nell reported that his measurements were subject to an error as large as 6.2 sec per page and this is especially troublesome when selecting the particular pages with the highest and lowest rates spread over 20–30 pages because these highest and lowest rates selected are most likely to involve this error. It is possible to estimate how serious this problem is by using Subject No. 220 who had a reported mean rate of 921 wpm over 62 pages for 30 min, which gives an average of 445 words per page. Suppose Subject No. 220 read a 445-word page at exactly 921 wpm but there was a 6.2 sec error, then the rate would vary from 759 to 1171 wpm, a nontrivial error that would be magnified on the pages that were shorter than average. Third, Nell did not report typical variability in rate but maximum variability in rate. It was possible to calculate the typical amount of variability, since Nell reported all the page rates for Subject No. 220 in his Figure 2. Reanalysis of his data was done by estimating rate from the graph presented and calculating how much each of the 62 rates changed from the mean rate, 921 wpm, in percent; the mean of the changes was 29%, not a drastic amount of typical variability considering that this individual represents one of the most variable individuals that could be found. Expressed differently, if all 62 pages had been exactly 445 words long, then the fastest page would have been read in 22 sec and the average page would have been read in 29 sec. If this same percentage change analysis is applied to the high and low rates of all 30 subjects, after adjusting for a 6.2 sec likely error, then the maximum change from each subject's average rate was only 32%, on the average. Also, the mean flexibility quotient dropped from 2.6 to 2.0 for the adjusted values; the median adjusted quotient was 1.8. These 30 ludic readers typically read their fastest page about twice as fast as their slowest page. (Note: It should also be pointed out that Subject No. 220 had a rate score that dropped from 921 wpm to 472 wpm when adjusted for comprehension; furthermore, this experimental passage was probably very easy since it was extracted from *The Caine Mutiny*.)

These data from Nell may be interpreted by some as providing evidence against the constancy of typical reading and supporting high flexibility in rate within material. However, this interpretation is subject to several qualifications. The subject with the highest flexibility quotient, 7.79, typically varied her rate from page to page only 29% from her mean rate. When interpreting this 29%, it should be remembered that Carver (1983) found that college students typically varied their rate about 14% from one difficulty level to another, i.e., rate is not absolutely constant. So, under the extremely favorable conditions for finding high flexibility, i.e., taking advantage of subject selection and measurement error, the subject with the highest flexibility scores only varied her rate 29% on the average. Furthermore, we cannot rule out the distinct possibility that this individual was shifting back and forth between rauding and skimming, i.e., between Gears 3 and 4.

CONCLUSIONS

Research reviewed in earlier chapters indicated that as long as college students and adults engage their rauding process they tend to read at a relatively constant rate around 300 Wpm even when the materials vary drastically in terms of difficulty level (Carver, 1976, 1983; Coke, 1976; G. R. Miller and Coleman, 1971; Zuber and Wetzel, 1981). There is also strong evidence that elementary and secondary students also operate this third gear of the basic reading processes at a relatively constant rate (Carver, 1983; Morse, 1951; Seibert, 1943). The research data that superficially seem to provide counter evidence (e.g., Kintsch and Keenan, 1973; Rothkopf and Coatney, 1974), in fact do not do so because these data involve reading processes that operate in first and second gear. Therefore, even before the flexibility research in this chapter was reviewed, there was strong evidence that difficulty flexibility did not exist while individuals are reading normally, naturally, typically, and ordinarily.

The research reviewed in this chapter that was explicitly designed to investigate the effect of difficulty on rate, further confirmed the fact that individuals do not have difficulty flexibility during the operation of their rauding process (Carver, 1983; DiStefano et al., 1981; Letson, 1959; Rankin, 1970; Rankin and Kehle, 1972; Shebilske and Fisher, 1981). It seems best to conclude that difficulty flexibility does not exist and should not exist because the rauding process operates most efficiently at a constant rate across difficulty levels.

Drawing the above conclusions relevant to difficulty flexibility was relatively straightforward. Drawing conclusions relevant to purpose flexibility is more complicated. When difficulty was held constant at the eighth grade level, Morse et al. (1968) found that college professors and graduate students did *not* vary their rate (a) between different subject matter areas, or (b) between familiar and unfamiliar material. Also, Hill (1964) found no evidence that college students who were good readers could successfully modify their rate or their reading process to better accomplish certain purposes such as "prepare for exams," "identify key ideas," and "analyze author motives." Also, Carver (1984b) found no important effects associated with two quite different purpose conditions: get the gist or find missing verbs. Yet, if the purpose conditions that were investigated required shifting gears up or down from third gear, then there was a great deal of evidence that college students could do this, starting with the research by Walker (1933) over 50 years ago.

Purpose flexibility depends upon what is meant by "purpose." For some purpose conditions there is flexibility and for others there is not. Therefore purpose flexibility is misleading. It seems best to abandon the concept of purpose flexibility because it is more confusing than illuminating. Instead, there is a great deal of empirical support for process flexibility, meaning the shifting of gears up or down from third gear to accomplish different goals more effectively, or to be successful on varying tasks (I. H. Anderson, 1937; DiStefano et al., 1981; Hill, 1964; Laycock, 1955; Samuels & Dahl, 1975; Shebilske & Fisher, 1981). The research with elementary students also suggests that they can shift up to a higher gear, such as a skimming process, but whether they can or will shift to a lower gear, such as a learning process, is in doubt (Samuels & Dahl, 1975). Yet, Carver (1987e) has argued that elementary students should not be given materials on which they cannot successfully operate their rauding process, at least until they reach the eighth grade level of rauding ability. So, it may be unnecessary for elementary students to have process flexibility and it may even be counterproductive to teach it to them.

Many of the older ideas about traditional flexibility can easily be integrated into rauding theory and process flexibility. The valid part of difficulty flexibility is that many individuals automatically shift down to a learning process when the material becomes relatively hard for them. The valid part of purpose flexibility is that many individuals do shift up or down to other reading processes when operating the rauding process is no longer the best way to accomplish their goal. Rauding theory supports the traditional idea of gear shifting that results in varying reading rates, but rauding theory primarily advocates a constancy of rate under the ubiquitous goal, or purpose, of understanding the complete thoughts in sentences, Gear 3. Rauding theory is consonant with reality in that a preponderance of research data indicate that individuals tend to operate their rauding process at a constant rate.

Traditional opinion and theory would suggest that educators must train individuals to change their rate each time difficulty changes or purpose changes. On the other hand, rauding theory holds that trying to train individuals to vary their rate during operation of their rauding process would be counterproductive. The data seem to indicate that individuals have their highest efficiency of comprehension when they operate their rauding process at their rauding rate (Carver, 1982). If traditional theory is correct, why is it that college students were not more efficient when they were forced to read easy material at faster rates?

In summary, it would seem best if rate flexibility based upon difficulty and purpose were no longer regarded as an ideal. This recommendation stems from the following: (a) even good-reading college students typically do not demonstrate difficulty flexibility, (b) difficulty flexibility during the operation of the rauding process would be counterproductive from the standpoint of efficient comprehension, and (c) purpose flexibility only exists for the best readers when purpose is narrowly confined to shifting gears to better accomplish certain goals. It appears that process flexibility is the only kind of flexibility which has empirical support and can be successfully defended as being desirable. Therefore, it appears that process flexibility is an ideal for those individuals who have learned to operate their rauding process at the eighth grade level of efficiency or higher. It is questionable whether readers below the eighth grade level of rauding ability are capable of shifting up and down to all five gears. It also seems questionable whether time should be spent teaching these students to shift out of third gear until they have learned to operate it at the eighth grade level of efficiency, a minimum standard for being literate.

Traditional flexibility of rate based upon difficulty and purpose has little or no empirical support, whereas the new concept of process flexibility appears to have the support of both theory and data.

⟦11⟧

GROWTH

INTRODUCTION

From grade 2 to college, the average rate that students read increases about 14 Wpm each year in school. Section I of this chapter will contain a review of the research that has measured reading rate across a range of grade levels, so that the growth of reading rate can be accurately described. Section II will look at the growth in rate for many different reading-related tasks, such as word recognition and oral reading rate, in an effort to find the cause or causes of growth in reading rate.

SECTION I

The growth of reading rate during the years between the beginning of school and college has been studied by several researchers. From a search of the literature,[1] the results presented in Fig. 11.1 represent the best data that could be located from the standpoint of the following: (a) adequate sample sizes, (b) adequate sampling techniques, (c) adequate range of grades represented, (d) rates adequately estimated in Wpm, and (e) adequate reliability of the data as indicated by the smooth curves produced.

The highest curve in Fig. 11.1 represents data collected in a study described by Carver (1983), and reviewed earlier in Chapters 3 and 10. The next highest curve represents data collected and reported by Taylor (1965), and presented earlier in Chapter 2. The short curve, which is third highest, represents data from the Nelson–Denny Reading Test. The lowest curve represents data collected by the National Assessment

---

1. Section I is primarily based on and taken from a recently published article (Carver, 1989b).

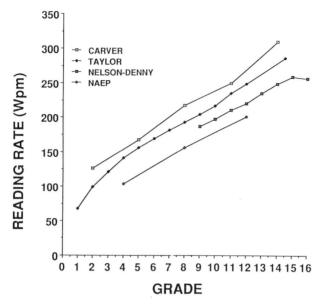

Figure 11.1 Reading rate, in standard length words per minute, Wpm, from grades 1 to 16, according to data reported in four different sources. (Fig. 1 from Carver, 1989b.)

of Education Progress (NAEP) (1972). It should be noted that all four sets of data indicate that reading rate in standard words per minute, Wpm, increases a constant amount each successive grade in school, about 10 to 20 Wpm; growth in reading rate each year prior to grade 6 is approximately the same as it is after grade 6.

The five data points for the Carver data in Fig. 11.1 represent the average reading rate of students at each of five measured levels of reading ability: Level 1, grades 1–3 in ability ($N = 34$); Level 2, 4–6 ($N = 85$); Level 3, 7–9 ($N = 72$); Level 4, 10–12 ($N = 146$); and Level 5, 13–15 ($N = 98$). These were median rates for reading passages at five levels of material difficulty.

As mentioned earlier, the Taylor data in Fig. 11.1 represent average rates of 12,143 readers from grades 1 through college. The Taylor values in Fig. 11.1 are the Wpm values that were presented in Table 2.1.

The eight Nelson–Denny data points in Fig. 11.1 represent an estimate of typical Wpm for each of grades 9–16. The data point for each grade was obtained from the test manual in the following manner: (a) finding an interpolated median of the words read in one minute from the norms given for that grade for each of the four forms of the test, A, B, C, D; (b) estimating the position of this median word on the reading passage from whence it was obtained, counting the characters in the passage up to that point, and then dividing by 6 to obtain standard length words per minute, Wpm; and (c) calculating the mean of these four medians.

The three data points representing the NAEP curve in Fig. 11.1, which is the lowest curve, were obtained from the 117 wpm, 173 wpm, and 195 wpm values given for a national sample of 9, 13, and 17 year olds respectively, when they were reading the first and easier of the two passages they were presented. The formulas given in Chapter 2 were used to convert the three wpm values into 104, 156, and 200 Wpm, which are the values plotted for grades 4, 8, and 12 in Fig. 11.1; the reported Spache formula difficulty of GE = 4 was used for the passage read by the 9 year olds; the reported Dale–Chall formula difficulty for GE = 5 was used for the 13 year olds; and the reported Dale–Chall formula difficulty of upper college, GE = 15, was used for the 17 year olds.

All four sets of data in Fig. 11.1 indicate an almost perfect linear relationship between reading rate and grade in school, from grade 2 through grade 12. Although the four curves are almost perfectly parallel, they reflect different absolute reading rates at each grade. The Carver curve is about 25 Wpm higher than the Taylor curve; the Taylor curve is about 25 Wpm higher than the Nelson–Denny curve; and the Nelson–Denny curve is about 20 Wpm higher than the NAEP curve.

The NAEP data has the disadvantage of representing only three grade levels. The Carver data has the disadvantage of not being a national sample; it is also based upon rates for students who were at a certain grade level of reading ability which therefore makes these values dependent upon the validity of the grade equivalents used to assign students to ability levels in the first place. The Nelson–Denny data only cover grades 9–16.

The Taylor data have the advantage of representing the rates for readers at each grade who demonstrated that they could read material rated at their own grade level of difficulty with ". . . at least 70% comprehension." The NAEP rates were representative of all those individuals at that age, many of whom no doubt could not comprehend at least 70% of the passage they were given. The Nelson–Denny data also included readers, no doubt, in each grade who could not comprehend 70% of the passage they were given, so the Nelson–Denny data probably also underestimate the rate of readers who could comprehend material at this grade level of difficulty.

A case can be made that the Taylor data are representative of the typical rates of students at a particular grade who can comprehend most of the complete thoughts in passages written at that same grade level of difficulty. Therefore, compared to the NAEP or Nelson–Denny data, the Taylor data may be said to be more representative of the rauding rates of readers in each grade who can comprehend material at that same grade level of difficulty.

The Taylor data in Table 2.1 have been converted into GE values which are represented in Table 11.1. For example, the reading rate of 141 Wpm for fourth graders in Table 2.1 was converted into a GE of 4.5 in Table 11.1 so that it represents the middle of GE = 4. After letting the Taylor values in Table 2.1 represent the middle of each GE score, the values in between were interpolated. Table 11.1 may be used to obtain grade equivalents for silent reading rates when they are given in standard words per minute, Wpm. As noted earlier in Chapter 2, the GE values for college and above, grades 13–18, are based upon the straight line formed by grade 12 and grade 14.5 (college) data points. The Taylor data can be used as a standard for establishing grade equivalents for rauding rate.

It will be helpful to compare the Taylor data to other data not represented in Fig. 11.1. Harris and Sipay (1985) have summarized the resulting rates from several standardized reading tests (exact sources not reported) by presenting the median rates of reading at each grade as

Table 11.1
Grade Equivalents for Rates in Standard Words per Minute, Wpm, Based Upon the Taylor (1965) Data

Rate in Wpm	Grade equivalent (GE)
0–81	1 (1.0–1.9)
82–108	2 (2.0–2.9)
109–130	3 (3.0–3.9)
131–147	4 (4.0–4.9)
148–161	5 (5.0–5.9)
162–174	6 (6.0–6.9)
175–185	7 (7.0–7.9)
186–197	8 (8.0–8.9)
198–209	9 (9.0–9.9)
210–224	10 (10.0–10.9)
225–240	11 (11.0–11.9)
241–256	12 (12.0–12.9)
257–274	13 (13.0–13.9)
275–292	14 (14.0–14.9)
293–310	15 (15.0–15.9)
311–328	16 (16.0–16.9)
329–346	17 (17.0–17.9)
347 and above	18 (18.0–18.9)

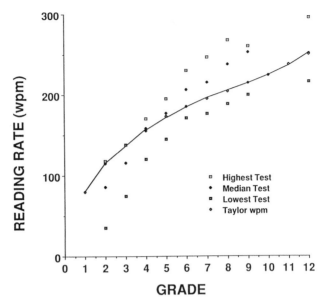

Figure 11.2 Median reading rate on the lowest, median, and highest tests sampled, in actual words per minute, wpm, from grades 2 to 12, according to data summarized by Harris and Sipay (1985); a curve representing comparable rates in wpm from Taylor (1965) is also given. (Fig. 2 from Carver, 1989b.)

reflected by the lowest, median, and highest tests. The values they reported in their Table 14.1 have been plotted in Fig. 11.2, along with the Taylor wpm values. Notice that the Harris and Sipay values are generally lower than the Taylor values in the lower grades and are generally higher in the upper grades. At grade 12, the Harris and Sipay median test value is almost exactly equal to the Taylor value. The most important aspect of these data, however, is that the Taylor values at each grade were always between the lowest and highest test values of Harris and Sipay. These summary data presented by Harris and Sipay replicate the general finding that rate increases in a roughly linear manner from grades 2 to 9. (Note: The curves would be more linear if these wpm values were transformed into Wpm values.) However, the rate of increase in Harris and Sipay data for grades 2–9 is higher than any of the data reported in Fig. 11.1. Furthermore, the Harris and Sipay data suggest that there is less of a gain in rate between grade 9 and grade 12. There seems to be no compelling reason, however, to accept these Harris and Sipay data as disconfirming the general findings from several sources presented in

Fig. 11.1; namely, that the increase in reading rate is approximately constant each year at least through grade 12.

The other data that will be presented come from Ballantine (1951); as mentioned earlier in Chapter 5 on eye movements, these data were also published later in a book (Morse *et al.*, 1968). Ballantine presented the rate of reading of students in grades 2, 4, 6, 8, 10, and 12 when rate was measured during the collection of eye movement data. He measured rate in ems per minute, a measure that controls for word length, as indicated earlier in Chapter 2; Equation 2.8 was used to convert these rates into Wpm. It should not go unnoticed that Morse *et al.* appear to be the first to suggest the use of a standard length word of six character spaces, as is used in Wpm.

Ballantine asked his 20 students in each grade to read a passage at the second grade level and also a graded passage that was at a grade level of difficulty equal to their grade in school. Figure 11.3 contains these results. There is one set of data points for the second grade passage that should have been relatively easy for almost all the students in grades 4–12. There is another set of data points for the grade level passage (for

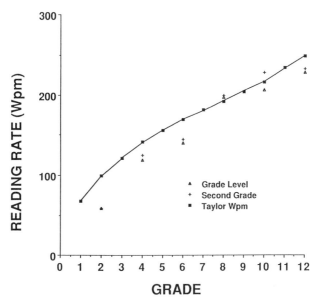

Figure 11.3 Reading rate on one passage at the second grade level and on another passage at grade level, for grades 2–12, according to Morse *et al.* (1968); a curve representing comparable rates in Wpm from Taylor (1965) is also given. (Fig. 3 from Carver, 1989b.)

the second graders, there was only one passage). The Taylor Wpm curve has also been plotted in this figure.

From Fig. 11.3, it should be noted first that there is a general increase in rate with grade in school, no matter which of the two passages is used. The curve is not smooth but this is likely due to sampling error since there were only 20 subjects in each grade represented. Second, it should be noted that from grades 4 to 12, the Ballatine data points are close to the Taylor curve thereby providing replication data. Third, it should not go unnoticed that in grades 4, 6, 8, and 12, the second grade passage was read at almost exactly the same rate as the grade level passage. The widest discrepancy was in grade 10 where the second grade passage, D_L = 2, was read 10% faster than the tenth grade passage, D_L = 10, still a very small difference in rate for the largest of the five comparisons. This is further replicative evidence for the constancy of rate across material difficulty, i.e., no difficulty flexibility, during the execution of a rauding process (see research reviewed in Chapters 3, 5, 7, and 10). For example, notice that the students in grade 12 read the GE = 2 passage at almost exactly the same rate as the GE = 12 passage.

Carver (1989b) has argued for using these Taylor (1965) data, presented earlier in Tables 2.1 and 11.1, when transforming reading rate into grade equivalent, GE, units. Now, a case will be made for using an alternative set of data for GE units. Carver (1987a) presented (a) an equation for rescaling raw scores on the Rate Level Test into GE units, and (b) an equation for rescaling raw scores on the Rate Level Test into Wpm units. These two equations have been transformed, algebraically, into the following equation:

$$R_L = 0.071399(\text{Wpm}) - 6.1119 \qquad (11.1)$$

Equation 11.1 can be used to rescale reading rate in standard words per minute, Wpm, into GE units that are symbolized as R_L and called rauding rate level. This equation can be expressed alternatively as

$$\text{Wpm} = 14.0(R_L) + 85.6 \qquad (11.2)$$

and compared with the Taylor data; see Fig. 11.4.

It can be noted in Fig. 11.4 that the curve based on the R_L measurement is slightly higher than the Taylor curve, from grade 3 through college. In grade 1, the R_L curve is considerably higher than the Taylor curve. From these data, it appears reasonable to regard growth in rauding rate (a) to be linear beyond grade 2, and (b) to be about 14 Wpm each year [the slope of Equation (11.2)]. Also, it appears reasonable to consider using R_L units whenever it is desirable to express rauding rate

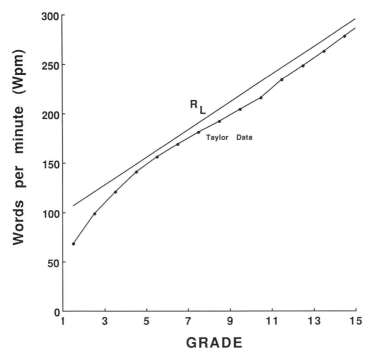

Figure 11.4 Rauding rate in Wpm for each grade in school for both the Taylor (1965) data and the R_L relationship expressed in Equation (11.2).

in GE units beyond $R_L = 2$. Appendix B contains a table that presents the corresponding Wpm and R_L values from grade 2.5 to 18.5.

The R_L units are actually based upon data collected for the Rauding Efficiency Level Test (Carver, 1987b) that was mentioned earlier in Chapter 9 and called the RELT. On this test, passages at difficulty levels 1–18 are presented at rates based upon the Taylor data. For example, a passage at grade 5 in difficulty level, $D_L = 5$, is presented at a fifth grade level rate, 156 Wpm. Paraphrase questions are administered after each passage, and the score on the RELT is the most difficult passage that can be passed with a 75% or higher score. During the practice for the test a passage at the second grade of difficulty is presented, and reading rate is timed. In effect, the R_L values given earlier are Wpm values on this surreptitiously timed apping rate measure that has been rescaled into GE scores on the RELT. However, these R_L scores are more than that. Individuals who have a R_L score of 5, for example, have a rauding rate that is equal to those people who score at the fifth grade level on the Accuracy Level Test, A_L = 5; see Carver (1987a, 1987c).

The advantages of using the R_L values are as follows: (a) they seem to be valid because they are close to the empirical data collected by Taylor, (b) they were derived from reading rates based upon very easy passages so they are likely to be more representative of rauding rates, (c) they were derived from GE units based partly upon Taylor data so they represent a refinement upon the Taylor data, (d) they represent a smoothing or averaging of slight irregularities in the linear growth depicted by the Taylor data, and (e) they provide theoretical and practical succinctness by summarizing growth of reading rate in one equation. Because of these advantages, these R_L data will be used henceforth in this review of research whenever it is desirable to express Wpm in GE units.

It can be concluded from these data presented in Section I that rauding rate, R_r, increases a constant amount each year in school, about 14 Wpm, for typical students beyond grade 2. The growth in rate between grades 1 and 6 appears to be quite similar to the growth in rate after grade 6, and there appears to be no change in growth around grade 6.

The above conclusion is mostly at odds with traditional and conventional wisdom based upon early eye movement research. Buswell (1922) investigated growth stages in silent reading by measuring the average number of fixations per line, the average duration of fixations, and the average number of regressions per line in each of grades 1–7 and 9–12. Similarly, Gilbert (1953) studied the same eye movement parameters in each of grades 1–10. Neither Buswell nor Gilbert reported reading rates, even though reading rate is composed of these parameters. Instead, both presented each of the above eye movement parameters on the vertical axis of a graph with the larger values at the bottom and the smaller values at the top so the resulting curves would go up as the grade level increased. By presenting these data this way, the curves increased rapidly in the lower grades, up to about grade 5, and then flattened out after grade 6 so there appeared to be little or no growth after about grade 6. On the basis of these curves, Buswell concluded that there was much greater growth in the first four grades and that what happened after grade 6 was quite different because of the small rise in the curves at grade 5 and thereafter. Gilbert contended similarly that "growth in directing the fine ocular coordination appears to be virtually completed by the time a pupil reaches the upper grades of elementary school" (p. 228), and that would be grade 6.

The traditional conclusions of Buswell and Gilbert would have found support in the data presented earlier in Fig. 11.1 if minutes per word (a time variable) had been presented on the vertical axis. Stated differently,

Words per minute (a rate variable) increases linearly with grade in school but minutes per word (a time variable) decreases curvilinearly with grade in school with the largest decreases in the early grades. There appears to be little doubt that Buswell and Gilbert would have found the same kind of linear relationship as represented by the straight lines in Fig. 11.1, if they had measured reading rate and plotted it on their vertical axis. If they had done this, it is not likely that they would have concluded that growth up to grade 6 was somehow different from growth after grade 6.

Growth in rate appears to be steady and approximately constant each year of school. Earlier researchers who purportedly found growth to be small after grade 6 based their conclusions upon variables that focused upon time instead of rate. The slowdown in growth at grade 6 can be more reasonably interpreted as an artifact and not real.

SECTION II

Introduction

Just as the growth in rauding rate is relatively constant for each successive school grade, so is the growth in rate for various reading-related tasks. Doehring (1976) gave 35 of these tasks to 150 children from kindergarten through grade 11. These data of Doehring's will be reanalyzed and reinterpreted in this section.

There are several reasons why these data deserve a lengthy reanalysis and review. First, Doehring's data seem to have been collected in a careful manner within a well-designed investigation of skills directly relevant to the factors that underlie reading rate. Second, Doehring focused on response time per item instead of a rate measure, such as items per unit of time, so he did not observe the lawful linear relationship between rate and grade in school, as was documented earlier in Section I of this chapter. Third, Doehring used the results of statistical significance testing associated with various analyses of variance (ANOVAs) to decide whether the differences he found were significant or important; using statistical significance testing this way is an example of what Carver (1987b) called a corrupt version of the scientific method. Since statistical significance depends on sample size, since Doehring had only 10 subjects per grade level after grade 2, and since it is questionable to investigate incremental changes in monotonic functions using analyses of variance (see Lindquist, 1953), the conclusions Doehring drew about where growth stopped are therefore highly questionable. Fourth, and finally, the most important reason for reanalyzing Doehring's data is that they seem to be providing important answers to a great many questions about how and why reading rate increases with each year in school, and these new answers are quite different from those of Doehring who concluded that there was growth up to about grades 5 and 6 but there were no consistent changes after grade 7. It is not surprising that Doehring found that growth stopped around grade 6, since his growth variables were not rate variables but were time variables similar to those of Buswell (1922) and Gilbert (1953), as discussed in the previous section.

These excellent data collected by Doehring will be reanalyzed in an effort to determine the cause or causes of growth in reading rate.

Purpose

Doehring stated that his main purpose ". . . was to estimate the relative course of acquisition of skills for processing the graphological features of letters, the orthographic regularities of letter combinations, the semantic features of words, and the semantic-syntactic constraints of word sequences" (p. 2). To accomplish this purpose, "graphological acquisition was estimated in terms of speed of response to letters relative to nonletter stimuli; orthographic acquisition in terms of speed of response to pronounceable nonsense syllables relative to syllables and single letters; and semantic-syntactic acquisition in terms of speed of response to meaningful discourse relative to nonmeaningful strings of words, syllables, and letters" (p. 5).

Subjects

Teachers were asked to select five boys and five girls in each of grades 3 through 11 who were typical according to certain behavior and academic criteria. In kindergarten through grade 2, there were ten subjects selected to represent each of the first and second halves of each grade, while the ten subjects in grades 3–11 were all selected from the first half of each grade.

Tasks

Doehring's 35 tasks were divided into four categories: visual matching, auditory matching, oral reading, and visual scanning. (Note: Some of the names Doehring used for his 35 tasks have been changed to facilitate communication.) Table 11.2 contains examples of the seven visual matching tasks. For example, the Numbers task involved a number, such as 8, appearing in a window of an apparatus. As fast as possible, the subject was supposed to push the one of the three other windows above it that contained a match for the target stimulus, e.g., 8, 1, or 6. Reaction time in increments of 0.1 sec was measured for each of these seven tasks:

Table 11.2
Doehring's (1976) Visual Matching Tasks and Examples

Task	Sample	Visual choices		
Numbers	8	8	1	6
Capital Letters	K	L	K	R
Capital and Lower Letters	D	p	b	d
Three-Letter Words	did	lid	did	dip
Four-Letter Words	long	lost	song	long
Three-Letter Nonsense Syllables	sig	sig	tig	sim
Three-Letter Strings	kzd	kzd	kzb	hzb

Table 11.3
Doehring's (1976) Auditory Matching Tasks and Examples

Task	Auditory sample	Visual choices		
Capital Letters	d	D	G	L
Three-Letter Words	set	met	set	sew
Four-Letter Words	find	mind	film	find
Two-Letter Syllables	pe	pe	pu	te
Three-Letter Syllables	cla	cra	cla	pla
Three-Letter Nonsense Syllables	pim	bim	pif	pim
Four-Letter Nonsense Syllables	sild	sild	rild	silp

Numbers, Capital Letters, Capital and Lower Letters, Three-Letter Words, Four-Letter Words, Three-Letter Nonsense Syllables, and Three-Letter Strings.

Table 11.3 contains examples of Doehring's auditory–visual matching tasks, hereafter called auditory matching tasks. For these tasks, the same apparatus was used as described above except that no target stimulus appeared in the window because it was given auditorily. For example, on the Four-Letter Nonsense Syllables task, the word "sild" was announced aloud to each of the subjects and their task was to push the window containing the letters "sild" (not "rild" or "silp") as fast as possible. Again, reaction time was measured on all of these auditory matching tasks.

Table 11.4 contains examples of the 11 oral reading tasks. For these tasks the subject had read aloud the stimuli presented as fast as possible. For example, for the Letters in Meaningful Discourse task, the subject was given "He must have a roof over his head" and was to say "H," "E," "M," "U," etc., as fast as possible. On these tasks, the subjects were in-

Table 11.4
Doehring's (1976) Oral Reading Tasks and Examples

Task	Examples
Color Naming[a]	(green) (blue) (grey) (black) (yellow)
Picture Naming[a]	(cat) (dog) (frog) (turtle) (duck)
Capital Letters	OL ESMP ZBJY H CVAO RFDX GNS KITU
Lower-case Letters	uj gybm vopq i asih xdns cft ekzr
Mixed Letters	SF Mzlh OndS p jXUI rEky bGt CvUA
Letters in Meaningful Discourse	He must have a roof over his head
Random Words	the ago over end made for year
Second Order Discourse	Lived by the sky by the trees
Seventh Order Discourse	On a rock and wiped his head to
Words in Meaningful Discourse	For some reason it always seems so
Nonsense Syllables	saro dalt rax vio feng pob jub

[a] Actual color patches and line drawings were used for color naming and picture naming.

Table 11.5
Doehring's (1976) Visual Scanning Tasks and Examples

Task	Examples
Rectangles	(rectangle) (rectangle) (rectangle)
Figures	(star) (cross) (circle) (crescent)
Numbers	1 8 9 4 2 7 6 4 3 5
Letters	v u s p f t s e s u c d
Two Letters	h g i b t d m e m t o b
Letter in Syllables	gevg finj hbjs pwzl vppi raie
Spaced Words	post tops stop spot sotp psot
Unpronounceable Nonsense Words	sfmb bfms sbmf fsbm fmbs
Pronounceable Nonsense Words	aprn apnr parn narp aprn rapn
Unspaced Words	t o p s s t o p s p o t s

structed to ". . . read or name as rapidly as possible without making errors, and to correct any errors that did occur" (p. 11). Response time was reported in seconds per syllable.

Table 11.5 contains examples of the ten visual scanning tests. These were paper and pencil tasks where the subject was supposed to underline all occurrences of the targeted response as fast as possible. For example, for the Two Letter task, the subject was supposed to underline all occurrences of "b" and "m." All the tasks were designed similarly in that ". . . the target item to be underlined occurred on the average of once per five items, with at least eight different nontarget items for each subtest" (p. 12). The only exception to the above was the first task listed in Table 11.5. On this Rectangles task, the subject underlined consecutive geometric rectangles as fast as possible as a measure of simple response speed. The time limits on each task, of either 30 or 60 sec, were set so that few if any subjects could finish. If a subject finished early then that time was used to calculate an average response time per item, the measure used in all these tasks.

Reanalysis of Data

Doehring (1976) presented tables containing mean error rates for each task as well as the mean response time per item for each task. Only his reported response times will be reanalyzed. For some of the tasks there were no data given for the first half of kindergarten, 0.0, the second half of kindergarten, 0.5, or the first half of first grade, 1.0, because these subjects were incapable of performing that particular task.

Doehring determined the median response time for each subject and then presented the mean of these medians for the ten subjects at each grade level. These data were presented by Doehring in four tables, one for each of his four types of tasks. For example, his results for the very first task, Numbers, are in parentheses right after the grade as follows: 0.0 (3.0), 0.5 (3.4), 1.0 (2.4), 1.5 (2.1), 2.0 (2.1), 2.5 (2.0), 3 (1.9), 4 (1.7), 5 (1.6), 6 (1.4), 7 (1.2), 8 (1.5), 9 (1.2), 10 (1.2), 11 (1.5). Notice that the response times generally decrease with each grade in school from about 3.0 sec in kindergarten, 0.0, to about 1.2 sec in both ninth grade, 9, and tenth grade, 10. Notice also that the response time for the eleventh graders, 1.5, was considerably higher than that of the ninth and tenth graders. Possibly the teachers did a good job of selecting typical or average reading students for each grade level except eleventh. The eleventh graders consistently responded more slowly than the ninth or tenth graders. This abnormality was dealt with in the following reanalyses by omitting the eleventh graders.

The first step in the reanalysis was to convert all of the mean response times to rates, on all 35 tasks for each of grades K through 10. For example, in the data given earlier, the third graders responded on the Numbers task in 1.9 sec per item, on the average. This was converted to a rate by inverting, i.e., $1/1.9 = 0.52$. So, 1.9 sec per item becomes a rate of 0.52 items per second. Since items per minute is easier to interpret (it is more similar to words per minute), all of these rates were multiplied by 60. For example, 0.52 items per sec on the Numbers task became 31.2 items per minute. Rate, in items per minute, was the basic unit in all of the subsequent reanalyses.

Results

Table 11.6 contains an overview of the reanalysis of the data from the visual matching tasks, corresponding to each of the tasks listed in Table 11.2. Least squares regression lines were fitted to the relationship between grade (from 0.0 to 10) and the corresponding mean rates for each task; the primary results of this analysis is summarized by a correlation coefficient, a standard error of estimate, the intercept for the regression line, and the slope of the regression line. For example, on the Numbers task, the correlation between the rates in items per minute (explained earlier) and the grade level (from 0.0 to 10) was 0.95; this extremely high correlation indicates that a straight line fits the data very well. The standard error of estimate (S.E.E.) was 3.4; this indicates that the rate at each grade can be predicted with an error of 3.4 items per minute, on the average. The intercept of 21.5 items per minute indicates that at the beginning of kindergarten, 0.0, it is being predicted that the rate of responding to Numbers is 21.5 items per minute. The slope of 3.1 indicates that for each additional year in school these subjects gain 3.1 items per minute on this task; this slope is the index of growth or acquisition that makes Doehring's data much easier to summarize and interpret.

Before starting the interpretation of these data in Table 11.6, it will be helpful to present some of the same data graphically. First, we will examine the nature of the relationship that Doehring studied by plotting his response times for Numbers for each grade in school. These data are presented in Fig. 11.5, along with the corresponding data for two other tasks, Capital Letters and Three-Letter Nonsense Syllables. Notice that the curves for the response times for each of the tasks in Fig. 11.5 tend to decrease from kindergarten, 0.0 and 0.5, to grade 6 and then flatten out to grade 10. The results from these three tasks are representative of the general pattern of results for all of Doehring's tasks.

Table 11.6

Results of the Correlational Analyses for Each of the Visual Matching Tasks[a]

Task	Correlation	S.E.E.	Intercept	Slope
Numbers	0.95	3.4	21.5	3.1
Capital Letters	0.95	3.3	21.1	2.8
Capital and Lower Letters	0.93	3.3	19.2	2.7
Three-Letter Words	0.97	2.1	19.4	2.9
Four-Letter Words	0.95	2.9	18.4	2.9
Three-Letter Nonsense Syllables	0.98	2.3	14.4	3.3
Three-Letter Strings	0.98	1.7	9.6	2.8

[a] These results represent a reanalysis of data collected by Doehring (1976).

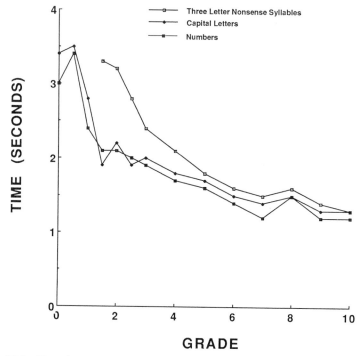

Figure 11.5   Time, in seconds, to choose the correct letter, number, or nonsense syllable in a visual matching task for grades 1–10. (Data from Doehring, 1976.)

In Fig. 11.5, it may be noted that the most difficult of these three tasks was Three-Letter Nonsense Syllables because it took longer to respond on this task at each grade level; it had the highest curve. The easiest task was Numbers because it had the lowest response times at each grade level; it had the lowest curve. Notice also that the Number task and the Capital Letters task were almost identical tasks because their two curves were almost coincidental at each grade.

The data for time, in seconds, from Fig. 11.5 have been replotted in Fig. 11.6 as rate, in items per minute; the Capital Letters data have been omitted to prevent clutter on the figure. So, Fig. 11.6 contains the rate data for Numbers and Three-Letter Nonsense Syllables. Notice that the points plotted for each task are very close to the straight line that has been plotted. The degree to which these data in Fig. 11.6 fit a straight line, for each task, is measured by the correlation coefficient presented in Table 11.5. For example, the Numbers data are represented by the upper line in Fig. 11.5, and the degree to which the points fall along a

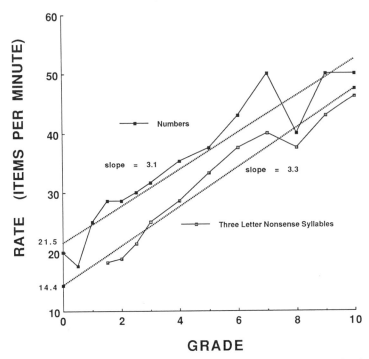

Figure 11.6 Rate of choosing the correct number and nonsense syllable in a visual matching task for grades 1–10; these data represent a reanalysis of the same data presented earlier in Fig. 11.5. (Original data from Doehring, 1976.)

straight line is represented by the 0.95 correlation coefficient presented in Table 11.6. The intercept and slope of this straight line are presented in Table 11.6 as 21.5 and 3.1, respectively, and these values are also presented on Fig. 11.5 itself. Looking again at Table 11.6, it can be seen that the Three-Letter Nonsense Syllables task comes very close to forming a straight line because its correlation coefficient is 0.98. This phenomenon can be visualized graphically from the dashed straight line in Fig. 11.6. Again the most phenomenal aspect of the statistics in Table 11.6 is the fact that the data from each of these seven tasks fit a straight line extremely well; the lowest correlation was still very high at 0.93 for the Capital and Lower Letters task.

Given the exceptionally lawful nature of this linear relationship between rate of responding on these tasks and grade in school, it is relatively easy to interpret these data. Notice that the slopes of the seven relationships presented in Table 11.6 are almost all exactly the same, ranging only from 2.6 to 3.1, while the intercepts vary considerably from

9.6 to 21.5. This means that at the beginning of school the rate of responding to Three-Letter Nonsense Syllables, 9.6, is a great deal slower than the rate of responding to Numbers, 21.5, but thereafter the gain in rate each year is about 3 items per minute on all seven of the tasks (2.7 to 3.3). So the rate of growth or acquisition for all seven visual tasks was almost exactly the same, whether the task involved numbers, letters, words, pronounceable nonsense syllables, or three-letter strings that were not pronounceable.

Doehring's stated purpose was to study the relative course of acquisition on the various tasks so as to be able to make inferences about graphological, orthographic, lexical, and semantic-syntactic acquisition by comparing 'the acquisition curves in the various tasks. *The most astounding result of this reanalysis is that the growth in rate on all of the tasks is almost exactly the same, and any differences in rate of growth are likely due to measurement error.* Doehring interpreted these same data, *expressed in response time,* as indicating that the response time decreased consistently until grade 6 for all these visual matching tasks. When *expressed in rate* instead of time, it is clear that rate of responding increases about 3 items per year from kindergarten through grade 10 and there is no evidence that grade 6 was a stopping point or limit for further acquisition. These data replicate the growth data for reading rate presented in Section I because all of these data indicate that the growth in rate is approximately the same each year in school, a linear relationship between rate and grade in school.

There are wide differences in response rate for each task that are inherent in the task, as indicated by the intercepts in Table 11.6. These differences are manifest in kindergarten, and then continue throughout the grades. However, since the rate of gain each year is constant on all of the tasks, as indicated by the slopes, it seems very likely that the same factors is accounting for the growth each year. The most likely candidate for the cause of this gain is a maturational gain in three-choice reaction time. Wickens (1974) reviewed reaction time research from a developmental perspective and concluded that choice reaction time was a function of age or maturation. Each successive year in school students react faster to stimuli of all kinds in choice reaction time situations, so this factor seems to best explain the growth in rate on all of these tasks.

If there was a learning or acquisition factor at work, then there should be differences in the rate of growth (slopes) for these tasks. For example, if practice in reading words resulted in perceptual learning for the shape of words, then the slope of the word tasks should have been higher than the slopes for the nonsense syllable task and the letterstrings task. The easy words used in these tasks are encountered many thousands of times in print but the nonsense syllables and the three-letter strings may never have been encountered before. So, the slope for the Three-Letter Words (2.9) should have been higher than the slope for Three-Letter Nonsense Syllables (2.9) if practice had any effect on the acquisition of rate. Instead, the slopes were exactly equal indicating that extra practice or experience with meaningful words does not increase the rate at which they can be recognized.

Table 11.7 contains data for the auditory matching tasks that are similar to the data in Table 11.6 for the visual matching tasks. Notice that a straight line fits these data from these tasks just as well as the visual matching data discussed above; the correlations in Table 11.7 ranged from 0.93 to 0.99. Notice also that the standard errors, S.E.E., were relatively small, ranging from 1.5 to 3.1. The intercepts ranged from 16.1 for the most difficult task, Four-Letter Nonsense Syllables, to 27.6 for the easiest task, Capital Letters. Again, the slopes for all seven tasks were almost exactly the same, ranging only from 2.6 to 3.0, or about 3 items per minute during each year.

To make comparisons between the visual matching tasks and the auditory matching task, the values for corresponding tasks can be compared. The only difference between the Capital Letters task from Table 11.6 and the Capital Letters task from Table 11.7 is that the target letters were presented visually in the first task and auditorily in the second. For these two tasks notice that the correlations were equal, 0.95 and 0.95, their standard errors differed very little, 3.3 versus 2.9, their intercepts differed the most, indicating that the visual stimulus could not be reacted to as fast as the auditory stimulus, 21.1 versus 27.6, and their slopes were almost identical, 2.8 versus 2.6.

To facilitate comparisons between the similar visual and auditory

Table 11.7
Results of the Correlational Analyses for Each of the Auditory Matching Tasks[a]

Task	Correlation	S.E.E.	Intercept	Slope
Capital Letters	0.95	2.9	27.6	2.6
Three-Letter Words	0.96	2.4	22.7	2.7
Four-Letter Words	0.93	3.1	22.6	2.6
Two-Letter Syllables	0.97	2.3	18.2	2.9
Three-Letter Syllables	0.98	1.8	18.2	3.0
Three-Letter Nonsense Syllables	0.97	2.3	18.1	2.7
Four-Letter Nonsense Syllables	0.99	1.5	16.1	2.9

[a] These results represent a reanalysis of data collected by Doehring (1976).

Table 11.8
A Comparison of the Intercepts and Slopes for Four Pairs
of Corresponding Visual and Auditory Tasks[a]

Task	Intercepts		Slopes	
	Visual	Auditory	Visual	Auditory
Capital Letters	21.1	27.6	2.8	2.6
Three-Letter Words	19.4	22.7	2.9	2.7
Four-Letter Words	18.4	22.6	2.9	2.6
Three-Letter Nonsense Syllables	14.4	18.1	3.3	2.7

[a] These results represent a reanalysis of data collected by Doehring (1976).

tasks, Table 11.8 contains the intercepts and slopes for the four tasks that correspond: Capital Letters, Three-Letter Words, Four-Letter Words, and Three-Letter Nonsense Syllables. Notice that the intercepts of the auditory tasks were consistently 4 to 5 items per minute higher than the visual tasks, indicating that the auditory task could be responded to slightly faster no matter what the grade level. This reflects a constant reaction time advantage for the auditory presentation that is not of theoretical interest here. (Note: This difference is probably due to the fact that the individuals could be looking at the three choices during the auditory task whereas they had to look at the target word before looking at the three choices in the visual task.)

In Table 11.8, the slopes of the pairs of visual and auditory tasks in each of the four comparisons were almost exactly the same, indicating that the gain each year in speed of responding was the same whether the task was visual or auditory. Furthermore, the slopes for all eight tasks in Table 11.8 are all very similar, i.e., about 3 items per minute, indicating that the gain in speed of responding each year has nothing to do with the nature of the stimulus, whether it is auditory or visual, whether it is letters, words, or nonsense syllables. Again, these results suggest that the same factor is likely to be causing the gain for all of these tasks, the most likely candidate being gain in three-choice reaction time which is possibly related more to cognitive speed, C_s, than simple reaction time. (Note: Cognitive speed, C_s, was described and discussed in Chapter 9.)

The implication of these data in Tables 11.6, 11.7, and 11.8, plus Fig. 11.5 and 11.6, is that each individual has a limit to how fast a verbal symbol can be recognized and once this limit is reached then further practice or experience with words has absolutely no effect upon how fast they can be recognized. Eighth graders, for example, have had thousands of experiences with reading and hearing familiar words during a year but no experience at all with nonsense syllables, yet the eighth graders gained just as much during a year in their rate of reacting to nonsense syllables as they gained in their rate of reacting to familiar words. The constant gain in rate of recognizing words is likely to be due to a maturational gain in cognitive speed that has nothing to do with the nature of the stimulus but has a great deal to do with age. Therefore, it seems reasonable to hypothesize that the yearly gains of about 14 Wpm in rauding rate, noted earlier in Section I of this chapter, are not due to perceptual learning resulting from practice in recognizing familiar words. Instead, these yearly gains in rate of 14 Wpm are more likely due to maturation instead of education or experience.

Table 11.9 contains the reanalyzed data for the oral reading tasks. For these data, the original correlations ranged from 0.71 to 0.97. The two tasks with correlations below 0.90 were the Seventh Order Discourse task, 0.86, and the Nonsense Syllables task, 0.71. The correlation for the Nonsense Syllables task happened to be severely affected by an aberrant data point for the tenth graders; when this point was removed the correlation jumped to 0.91, the standard error, S.E.E., dropped to 9.5, the intercept became 15.1, and the slope became 7.3. For the Seventh Order Discourse task, it may be noted that it not only had a low correlation, 0.86, but its standard error, 39.5, was about twice as large as the slope, 21.5. For most of the oral reading tasks, as well as the visual matching and auditory matching tasks discussed earlier, the standard error was usually slightly below or slightly above the slope, indicating that the re-

Table 11.9
Results of the Correlational Analysis for the Oral Reading Tasks[a]

Task	Correlation	S.E.E.	Intercept	Slope
Color Naming	0.96	9.2	39.5	9.7
Picture Naming	0.97	5.8	44.7	6.8
Capital Letters	0.96	14.1	38.2	14.7
Lower Case Letters	0.95	15.4	27.9	14.1
Mixed Letters	0.95	15.3	35.1	13.9
Letters in Meaningful Discourse	0.96	16.2	43.9	17.5
Random Words	0.94	17.8	24.2	15.2
Second Order Discourse	0.93	29.4	26.9	23.2
Seventh Order Discourse	0.86	39.5	26.5	21.5
Words in Meaningful Discourse	0.91	42.0	41.2	29.4
Nonsense Syllables	0.71	57.8	−26.6	18.8
Nonsense Syllables (Without grade 10)	0.91	9.5	15.1	7.3

[a] These results represent a reanalysis of data collected by Doehring (1976).

liability of the predictions made from the regression line were about equal to the gain in rate each year. Stated differently, for almost all the 25 tasks reanalyzed so far, the error associated with predictions made from a perfectly linear relationship was about one GE unit. However, in Table 11.9 it can be noted that the exceptions were the Second Order Discourse task, the Seventh Order Discourse task, and the Words in Meaningful Discourse task; all three had standard errors considerably larger than their slopes but not twice as large as slopes, thus indicating an error less than two GE units.

To facilitate the interpretation of these oral reading data, an additional data reduction step was taken: the reliability of the data was increased by combining tasks that seemed to provide nearly identical results. Considering the tasks in the order they are listed in Table 11.9, the data for the Color Naming and Picture Naming tasks were combined because their intercepts and slopes were very similar. This means that naming colors and naming pictures as fast as possible are equally slow in kindergarten and the gain in speed each year is almost exactly the same so their intercepts were averaged and their slopes were averaged to form a new combined task called Color-Picture Naming. This same process was applied as follows: (a) Capital Letters, Lower Case Letters, Mixed Letters, and Letters in Meaningful Discourse were averaged to form the new combined task called Letters, and (b) Second Order Discourse and Seventh Order Discourse were averaged to form Approximate Discourse.

The remaining three tasks in Table 11.9 were not enough alike to justify combining them. The intercepts and slopes for the latter three original oral reading tasks and the three new combined tasks were used to plot the straight lines in Fig. 11.7. These lines summarize the acquisition of oral reading rates for these tasks.

From these linear relationships in Fig. 11.7, it is evident that the nonsense syllables were read orally the slowest in all grades. Students in kindergarten and first grade were able to read colors and pictures slightly faster than letters, but by second grade (and beyond) letters were consistently read faster. Notice also that letters were read slightly faster than random words at each grade; yet, the slopes were identical indicating that the gain each year in oral reading rate for letters was exactly the same as the gain in oral reading rate for randomly ordered words. Words that approximate meaningful discourse were read slower than meaningful discourse. Words in meaningful discourse were read the fastest of all the oral reading tasks.

One of the most interesting aspects of these data in Fig. 11.7 is that all four of the tasks that involve naming words, i.e., Words in Meaningful Discourse, Approximate Discourse, Random Words, and Nonsense Syl-

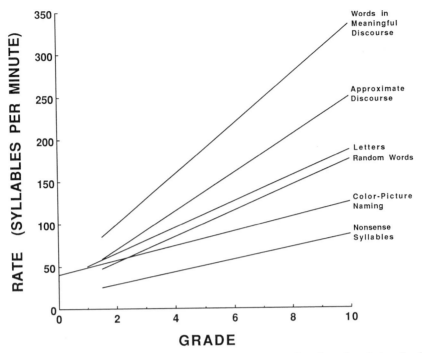

Figure 11.7 Rate of responding in syllables per minute, as a function of grade in school for various visual matching tasks when the relationship is represented by the best fitting straight line. (Reanalysis of data collected by Doehring, 1976.)

lables, converge at approximately the same point. That point is between grade -1 and grade -2 when rate is extrapolated back to zero syllables per minute. This may be interpreted as indicating that for these children the rate of orally reading words starts at zero around 3–4 years of age and increases steadily each year thereafter. The gain in this rate each year (the slope) varies considerably depending upon the kind of words and their context. The yearly gain in rate for nonsense syllables is only about 7 syllables per minute (slope = 7.3), but the corresponding gain in rate for words in meaningful discourse is about 29 syllables per minute (slope = 29.3), which is four times as large.

Before proceeding any further with this discussion, it will be convenient to transform syllables per minute into standard length words per minute using the conversion factor established earlier in Chapter 2, i.e., 1.66 syllables per one standard length word. With this conversion, the yearly gain in maximum oral reading rate, in Wpm, for these four word tasks are as follows: Nonsense Syllables, 4.4 Wpm; Random Words,

9.2 Wpm; Approximate Discourse, 13.4 Wpm; and Words in Meaningful Discourse, 17.7 Wpm. Notice that by extrapolation, average students have a maximum oral reading rate of 0 Wpm when they are about 3-1/2 years of age and then they increase this rate about 18 Wpm each year until the twelfth grade where they are reading orally at 237 Wpm.

The gain in rate for Nonsense Syllables of 4.4 Wpm probably reflects a yearly gain in simple or choice reaction time. The gain in acquisition from 4.4 Wpm for Nonsense Syllables to 9.2 Wpm for Random Words probably reflects an extra yearly gain in cognitive speed that becomes involved when the task requires decoding overly learned, printed verbal symbols. The gain from 9.2 for Random Words to 17.6 Wpm for Meaningful Discourse possibly reflects an extra yearly gain in articulation speed that becomes involved when words can be chunked in memory based upon their meaningful associations. For example, the eye–voice span (see Geyer, 1968) would be expected to increase as the approximation to meaningful discourse increased, thus indicating that more words can be stored when the discourse approaches full meaningfulness, and allowing the rate of articulation to increase. When 100% meaningful discourse is reached, the rate of oral reading is at its maximum because at this point it is only limited by the maximum articulation rate of the individual. For example, the memory load for articulating the letters of the alphabet in order is not a bottleneck in slowing articulation rate so naming letters can proceed as fast as possible under this condition. However, when the letters are in random order, then the naming rate is slowed because there is a load on memory for storing the letters ahead of time so they can be read out of memory as quickly as possible. Similarly, rate of reading meaningful discourse can proceed at its fastest possible rate when there is little load on memory under the conditions where the upcoming five to eight words can be easily remembered and read out of memory. However, for randomly ordered words there is no meaningful association between the words to allow more than two to four to be stored ahead of the word that is being produced.

Since these maximum oral reading rates in Doehring's research involved easy words, it seems doubtful that the context had any influence upon the speed at which they can be recognized. In fact, if contextual redundancy has an effect upon word recognition speeds during oral reading, then Coke (1974) should have found that oral reading rate became faster as the difficulty level of the material becomes easier, but she did not find this (see Chapter 3). Instead, she found that maximum oral reading rates were constant across widely different degrees of contextual redundancy, as reflected by measures of readability.

These data of Doehring's on maximum oral reading rates can be interpreted as indicating that an individual's rate of reading randomly ordered words improves each year due to two maturational factors related to simple or choice reaction time and cognitive speed. It may also be noted that meaningful discourse can be read aloud about twice as fast as randomly ordered words probably because there is no load on memory that prevents the words from being articulated aloud at the maximum possible articulation rate.

Before going on with this reanalysis of Doehring's four sets of data, it will be informative to compare the maximum oral reading rates for words in meaningful discourse with the Taylor rates presented earlier in this chapter. Figure 11.8 contains these data. The Taylor silent reading data come from Table 2.1 except the Wpm values at each grade have been plotted at the center of each grade, e.g., grade 3 is plotted at 3.5. The Doehring data come from a smoothing of the Wpm rates in grades 1.5 to 10; the mean of three adjacent points was used. For example, the rate plotted at grade 2.0 was the mean of the three rates at 1.5, 2.0, and 2.5. In this curve-smoothing process, the two end data points are lost,

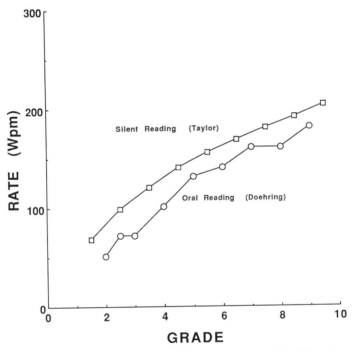

Figure 11.8 Reading rate, in Wpm, as a function of grade in school for silent reading (from Taylor, 1965) and for oral reading (from Doehring, 1976).

i.e., 1.5 and 10. Notice that the silent reading rates of Taylor's are around 25 Wpm faster than these maximum oral reading rates of Doehring's. Rauding rate might be accurately estimated by obtaining maximum oral reading rate and then adding around 25 Wpm, assuming both of the samples represent the same population. Or, Doehring may have found rates 25 Wpm faster if he had allowed his students to read the passage first, silently, before asking them to read orally. Or, the 25 Wpm difference between these two curves may simply represent the fact that the Doehring subjects were selected because they were typical for that grade level whereas the Taylor data represents an above average group for each grade since they had to be able to comprehend 70% of the passage they read at that grade level.

The relatively close correspondence between these silent and oral rates in Fig. 11.8 is consistent with the theory that silent reading is paced by an internal articulation of syllables per minute which is similar to maximum oral reading (Carver, 1977). This close correspondence exists even though maximum oral reading does not require a concern for understanding or comprehending the thoughts in the sentences. Recently, Carver (1989a) has found that there is a high relationship between maximum oral reading rate and rauding rate—the two rates seem to be almost exactly the same within individuals between grades 2 and 12.

The task that is parallel to maximum oral reading would be maximum silent reading where subjects would be asked to read silently as fast as they could just like they did orally. This rate would produce curves higher than the Taylor data in Fig. 11.5 because the extra time consuming component of sentence integrating would probably be eliminated. Maximum oral reading also does not require sentence integrating so it can proceed faster than typical oral reading which would ordinarily involve sentence integrating. For college students, maximum oral reading rate may be slower than the rate at which the rauding process operates because of the time required to make sure the word is articulated clearly at a high enough sound level so it can be perceived by others besides the reader.

The data from the fourth type of tasks used by Doehring, the scanning tasks, are presented in Table 11.10. A straight line fits very well the growth in speed on these paper and pencil tasks; the lowest of the ten correlations was 0.94 and the other nine ranged only from 0.97 to 0.99. The first task, Rectangles, had the highest intercept and the highest slope; it was a measure of simple response speed or reaction time. It should not be surprising that this task was the fastest since all the subject had to do was underline consecutive rectangles as fast as possible. However, the fact that this task also had the highest slope indicates that the

Table 11.10
Results of the Correlational Analysis for the Scanning Tasks[a]

Task	Correlation	S.E.E.	Intercept	Slope
Rectangles	0.98	7.3	46.7	9.8
Figures	0.99	3.8	20.4	6.6
Numbers	0.99	2.6	13.5	6.3
Letters	0.99	3.8	14.3	6.4
Two Letters	0.99	1.9	9.9	3.8
One Letter in Syllable	0.98	1.7	4.2	2.3
Words	0.97	1.5	4.5	2.0
Unpronounceable Nonsense Syllables	0.99	0.9	1.9	2.3
Pronounceable Nonsense Syllables	0.94	1.9	2.1	1.6
Unspaced Words	0.99	0.5	1.5	1.2

[a] These results represent a reanalysis of data collected by Doehring (1976).

psychomotor skill of underlining greatly increases each year. Slower than the Rectangle task were Figures, Numbers, and Letters, all of which had approximately equal slopes and intercepts. Next was the Two Letters task; it required the subject to keep two letters, b and m, in memory while scanning for either one. This task was slower than scanning for only one target, whether it was a figure, number, or letter.

All the remaining tasks in Table 11.10 involved scanning four-letter strings and they were all slower. Crossing out each e in four-letter syllables, called the One Letter in Syllable task, was almost exactly equal to crossing out words; the intercepts were 4.2 and 4.5, respectively, and the slopes were 2.3 and 2.0, respectively. Notice that the four-letter word in the Words task was not scanned as fast as a single letter, as might have been predicted given that a single word was recognized about the same rate as a single letter in the visual matching task. There are several differences in these two types of scanning tasks, however. First, the subjects might have taken longer to draw a longer line under a four-letter word compared to a single letter, whereas movement time was exactly the same for the two tasks involving visual matching. Second, in visual scanning the target words and letters are embedded within adjacent words and letters. Third, the target probably has to be continually rehearsed so that it does not drop from memory so it might take less cognitive processing time to keep a single letter in immediate memory as compared to a single word.

The pair of nonsense syllable tasks were approximately equal and if their slopes and intercepts are averaged to give 2.0 and 2.0, respectively, it can be seen that they are slower than crossing out words but their averaged slopes, 2.0, is exactly equal to the Word task. This means that the gain each year for nonsense syllables is no greater than the gain each year for words, a finding that is consistent with the visual and auditory matching tasks discussed earlier.

Finally, the slowest task was Unspaced Words. It had the lowest intercept, 1.5, and the lowest slope, 1.2, indicating that it was the slowest in grade 1 and also showed the least gain each year thereafter. Growth on this task was also the most reliably predicted from linear regression: the standard error, S.E.E., was only 0.5, and that is less than half of the yearly gain. All the tasks but one had standard errors lower than the slope, indicating a reliability of less than one GE unit.

Of the four types of tasks studied by Doehring, these visual scanning ones seem to provide the least useful information relative to reading rate. They do confirm beyond a reasonable doubt that gains in rate on reading-related tasks increase linearly each grade, or year in school. They do show that there is no difference in acquisition, or yearly growth, between scanning for numbers, letters, or figures. They do show that there are no important differences in acquisition, or yearly growth, in scanning for words, unpronounceable nonsense syllables, or pronounceable nonsense syllables.

Caveats

Some facts should be reviewed regarding Doehring's data, so as to put the subsequent conclusions in context. The grade 11 data were omitted from the preceding analysis. Including it would certainly have lowered the degree to which a straight line would fit these data, i.e., decreased the degree to which the evidence supported a linear relationship. Also, Doehring reported his data to the nearest 0.1 of a second because this was as accurate as his recording devices could measure an individual's response. For some tasks, the mean response times reported by Doehring were exactly the same across some of the higher grades, e.g., for maximum oral reading rate of words in meaningful discourse the means for grades 7 to 11 were all exactly the same, 0.2. At the higher grades the gain in response time would sometimes have to be less than 0.1 of a second under a linear hypothesis so Doehring's data were not measured as accurately as preferred on the basis of hindsight. The smoothing of curves and fitting of straight lines used in the reanalysis are data reduction devices designed to increase the reliability of the data by averaging over many points.

The strategy designed to overcome this error of measurement problem noted above can be illustrated by presenting Taylor's (1965) data in seconds per word, the same units as Doehring used. These data are pre-

Table 11.11

Taylor's (1965) Rate Data Presented in Wpm,
Seconds per Word, and Words per Minute

Grade	Wpm	Seconds per Word	Words per minute
1	68	0.9	66.6
2	99	0.6	100.0
3	121	0.5	120.0
4	141	0.4	150.0
5	156	0.4	150.0
6	169	0.3	200.0
7	181	0.3	200.0
8	192	0.3	200.0
9	204	0.3	200.0
10	216	0.3	200.0
11	234	0.3	200.0
12	248	0.2	300.0

sented in Table 11.11. Taylor's data, in seconds per word, were rounded to the nearest 0.1 of a second to provide a measure of accuracy similar to Doehring's data. Then, these values were converted back to words per minute in the last column of Table 11.11, to provide data similar to the reanalysis of Doehring's data. Notice that rate in Wpm was measured accurately enough that a yearly gain in rate of 11–18 Wpm is evident between grade 6 and grade 11, in the column headed "Wpm." However, when these data are measured to the nearest 0.1 of a second per word, notice that there is no gain in rate between grade 6 and grade 11, in the last column headed "Words per minute." Still, if a straight line is fitted to the relationship between the grade variable and the Words per minute variable in the last column, as was done with the Doehring data presented in Tables 11.6, 11.7, 11.8, 11.9, and 11.10, then the correlation was 0.91, the standard error of estimate was 23.7, the intercept was 58.4, and the slope was 15.4. Notice that these relatively inaccurate data in the last column of Table 11.11, which showed no improvement from grade 6 to grade 11, have been averaged over all grades to show a yearly gain in rate of 15.4 which is very close to the actual gains of 11–18 each year between grade 6 and grade 11. The point of these calculations is to show that this kind of reanalysis can be used on data that were not measured with high accuracy to produce a relatively accurate estimate of average yearly gains.

Given the fact that the grade 11 data were omitted in the reanalysis of Doehring's data, and given the fact that the accuracy of the data at the higher grades was less than desirable to test the linear growth hypothesis, it is possible to question the definitiveness of this reanalysis. However, using the rate data in the reanalysis showed no consistent evidence for a break point in growth around grades 5 to 7 and it consistently paralleled the reading rate data in Section I. Therefore, it seems reasonable to make inferences about the growth being linear in general.

In any event, it should not go unnoticed or unsaid that these data collected by Doehring represent a monumental contribution to our empirical knowledge about growth in reading-related tasks.

Conclusions

This reanalysis of Doehring's data indicates that the rate of performing all 35 of his tasks improves approximately a constant amount each year from kindergarten through tenth grade, at least. This constant rate of improvement can be empirically summarized by noting that 33 of the 35 correlation coefficients (which measure the degree to which the rate of growth is constant) were above 0.90, and 27 of 35 were 0.95 or higher. This constant increase in the rate of performing reading-related tasks is exactly the same kind of result noted earlier for growth in reading rate in words per minute. The growth rates for the visual and auditory matching tasks which involved rapid word recognition were all almost exactly the same, whether the task involved numbers, letters, words, or nonsense syllables. Therefore, it appears that growth in the speed of recognizing familiar words cannot be attributed to practice or experience with these words. Instead, growth in the rate of lexically accessing familiar words is probably caused solely by maturational increases in choice reaction time or cognitive speed.

The data from the oral reading tasks were also interpreted as providing support for the hypothesis that growth is caused partly by growth in choice reaction time and partly by a cognitive speed factor that involves decoding linguistic symbols. The growth in the rate of reading meaningful discourse orally as fast as possible coincides closely with the rate of growth in reading silently. Although these two processes involve important differences, such as no comprehension being required in the oral task and no audible decoding required in silent reading, they seem to involve enough similarities to result in common yearly growth rates, i.e., about 17 Wpm for oral and about 14 Wpm for silent.

IMPLICATIONS

The research reviewed in this chapter seems to indicate quite clearly that yearly growth in rauding rate is constant for typical students. This constant growth may be due to maturational increases in decoding and manipulating linguistic symbols, called cognitive speed.

It is somewhat surprising that there were no data that would suggest that these gains in rate were due to practice in reading. On the other hand, if practice had a major impact on rauding rate, then rauding rate should keep improving each year even during adulthood for those many adults who spend at least an hour a day engaged in reading. Yet, there is no evidence to suggest that this happens. Practice beyond that minimally required to maintain rauding rates up to their maximum probably cannot increase an individual's rauding rate. So, spending an hour each day over a year's time engaged in practice of the process of rauding, using relatively easy material such as light fiction, should not have any important effect upon rauding rate for most individuals except to maintain this rate at its maximum set by their own cognitive speed, C_s. Such practice is likely to have an effect only for someone who has not done enough regular reading of relatively easy material to maintain rauding rate up to its maximum. This kind of practice may also help those individuals who have previously been operating a learning process most of the time; it may help them increase their apping rate up to their rauding rate which is limited by their cognitive speed.

12

WORD RECOGNITION AND
COGNITIVE SPEED

INTRODUCTION

The words in sentences must first be recognized, i.e., lexically accessed, so their meaning in the context of a sentence can be used to formulate the complete thought the author intended to communicate. Therefore, the speed at which words can be recognized has the potential for limiting the rate at which all subsequent processes operate. Individual differences in the speed of word recognition are likely to be limited by how fast an individual can think about words, i.e., their cognitive speed, C_s. This chapter will focus upon the role of word recognition speed and cognitive speed, two factors that influence the rate at which the rauding process can be executed.

Gough (1984) has presented an excellent critique of the research on word recognition. He opens with the statement, "Word recognition is the foundation of the reading process" (p. 225). Of course, this statement could be edited so as to be more theoretically satisfying; it would be better to say that word recognition is the foundation of *all* reading processes, instead of *the* reading process (see Chapter 2). Gough reviews the role of letters versus words, word length, silent speech, frequency, and then he tackles the effects of context. The common finding in this latter area of research is that providing an individual with appropriate sentential context will speed up word recognition (Tulving & Gold, 1963). However, Gough points out that the research on the effects of context upon the speed of word recognition is seldom done in a manner that is likely to generalize to ordinary reading. He says that "it remains an open (and important) question whether the average context has any effect at all on the average word read by the skilled reader in good light" (p. 245).

There does seem to be a partial answer to the question about context that Gough decided was unanswered. Context provides redundancy and thereby reduces the number of choices if a person is guessing succeeding words in prose passages. Carver (1976) has shown that two separate measures of redundancy decrease as the readability of material decreases from grade level 2 through grade level 14. Since contextual constraint is lessened as the difficulty of the material increases, this would seem to mean that reading rate should slow down because the words cannot be recognized as fast when each succeeding word is less likely to be correctly predicted. Yet, reading rate does not decrease as redundancy decreases, as the data reviewed in earlier chapters on rate and difficulty level have indicated (Ballantine, 1951; Carver, 1971b, 1976, 1983; Coke, 1976; DiStefano *et al.*, 1981; Letson, 1959; G. R. Miller & Coleman, 1971; Morse, 1951; Zuber & Wetzel, 1981). In short, the rauding process tends to operate at a constant rate even though it would be predicted from word recognition research that rate would decrease as the difficulty of the material increases due to the lack of contextual constraint. Variability in the contextual constraint of ordinary prose seems to have no effect upon the rate at which words are recognized during typical reading, otherwise rate should decrease as the redundancy of the material decreases. The answer to Gough's question seems to be that the amount of context has no effect at all on the rate that words are recognized by skilled readers during the operation of the rauding process.

This failure of a basic law of word recognition research to generalize to the rate at which the rauding process operates should temper any attempts to generalize about the rauding process from research that does not involve the rauding process. Indeed, it seems safe to ignore much of the research on word recognition and context effects because of its questionable relevance to the rate at which the rauding process operates. Of special interest in this chapter will be those studies which appear to instruct us about the word recognition factors that do affect rauding rate. Individual differences in word recognition speed seem likely to be heavily influenced by cognitive speed, C_s, and the research relevant to both of these factors will be focused upon in this chapter.

RESEARCH

DuBois (1932) found evidence for a speed factor in mental tests. His speed tests involved arithmetic computations, analogies, following verbal directions, mental arithmetic, and finding synonyms of easy words. All of these tasks involved a substantial amount of reading and thinking. This speed factor found by DuBois probably best represents a combination of rauding rate and cognitive speed, C_s. Individual differences on these mental tests no doubt were influenced by individual differences in speed of word recognition as well as individual differences in the more general ability called cognitive speed. So, it is fitting to begin this review of research on word recognition and cognitive speed with this pivotal research by DuBois completed over 50 years ago.

Traxler (1934) investigated a processing determinant of slow reading, which he called "speed of association of ideas." He said that some psychologists believe that this was a causal factor since "slow thinkers tend to be slower readers" (p. 357). One of his measures of the speed of association, or thinking speed, involved the presentation of words by a tachistoscope and then the measurement of the latency of a free association response. Reading rate for most groups was measured by having individuals read "continuous material" and measuring words read per second. For 57 seventh grade students, the correlation between the speed of association and rate of reading was 0.53, and for 27 university freshmen the correlation was 0.49. Using Cohen's (1977) criteria for effect size ($r = 0.10, 0.30$, and 0.50 for small, medium, and large, respectively), these correlations of 0.53 and 0.49 were large in effect. Their size seems to justify the following conclusion drawn by Traxler: "There is ground for thinking that slow association rate may be so closely related to the retarded reading rate of some slow readers that the teacher should not utilize the usual methods to get them to read more rapidly" (p. 365). This study by Traxler, over 50 years ago, appears to be the first investigation of the distinct possibility that reading rate may be limited or influenced by a more general ability to process verbal information quickly, i.e., thinking rate or cognitive speed.

Bear and Odbert (1940) attempted to replicate the above findings of Traxler (1934). They measured speed of association in a manner similar to Traxler and reading rate was measured using the Iowa Silent Reading Test. However, the subjects they tested were quite different from Traxler's; they were freshmen who had enrolled in a one-half semester course in "corrective reading and study methods." These researchers noted that their subjects were more "homogeneous." Indeed, from the data reported, it should be noted that Traxler's subjects had a mean of 275 wpm, SD = 61, while the subjects in Bear and Odbert's research had a mean around 240, and an SD around 30. The variance in reading rate of the Bear and Odbert subjects was only about one-fourth as large as Traxler's subjects. With this drastically reduced variance, it should not be surprising to find that they found much smaller correlations than Traxler. For the 47 subjects in one group, they found a correlation of 0.29 between their speed of association measure and rate on the Iowa test. In their second group of 38, they reported a 0.19 correlation coefficient. Given the drastic reduction in range for their homogeneous groups, it is still reasonable to interpret their data as providing support for the hypothesized large effect of speed of thinking upon reading rate.

It should also be noted that Bear and Odbert found no correlation between the speed of association measure and gain in reading rate during a course that was partially devoted to improving reading rate. They interpreted this finding as evidence against Traxler's conclusion that speed of association (a) somehow limited rate, and (b) should be instructive for teachers who try to help students improve their rate. However, in Bear and Odbert's research, rate was not measured in a way that discouraged students from shifting gears to a skimming process during their rapid reading training. So, these data cannot be validly interpreted as evidence against Traxler's suggestion that teachers should not try to get slow thinkers to increase their reading rates.

Stroud (1945) acknowledged that "thinking-time, as measured by speed of association, had been found to bear a positive relationship to reading rate" (p. 488). He then went on to announce his intention to investigate further the influence of "perception-time" as a factor influencing reading rate. He wanted to build upon earlier research, such as had been conducted by Gates (1926). For a measure of rate, he used the Chapman–Cook Speed of Reading Test; it is similar to the Tinker Speed of Reading Test (see Carver, 1971c) which requires that anomalous words at the end of sentences be marked out with a pencil as fast as possible during the time allotted. For measuring the speed of perception, he used items similar to the following sample from the Letter Selection Test:

stuvw: sfuvn struw stuvw efuvw

The examinee was asked to cross out with a pencil mark the answer on the right that corresponded to the item stem on the left. Besides the Letter Selection Test, there were similar tests called Word Selection, Digit Selection, Paired Digits, Paired Letters, and Paired Drawings, all of which involved the number correctly marked during a two-minute time limit. The battery of tests was given to 570 pupils in grades 4, 5, and 6 who were selected "to give a representative cross section of the pupils in a city of 60,000 inhabitants" (p. 492). The results were presented by averaging the correlations across the three grades. The test that correlated the highest with reading rate was Word Selection, $r = 0.51$, a large effect size correlation, using the Cohen (1977) criteria noted earlier (also see Carver, 1984a). One problem with those correlations, however, is that both the reading rate measure and the perceptual speed measure include how fast individuals can use a pencil to mark out items. Thus, the correlations will be inflated somewhat. Nonetheless, it appears that Stroud's research results leave little doubt that the speed at which individuals can recognize words and match them to target words is importantly related to reading rate, and may be an important factor determining reading rate.

Toward the end of Stroud's report of his research, he notes that about 200 university freshmen were randomly selected for special training in reading to see if the scores on the tests of perceptual speed could predict the gain in reading rate as a result of taking this training. He noted that the gains in rate were "rather substantial" but "preliminary calculations" indicated that the correlations between the gain in reading rate and the speed of perception tests were "negligible." However, Stroud did not say that the Chapman–Cook test was used to measure rate so it must be assumed that it was not, an unfortunate occurrence. If the Chapman–Cook had been used to measure gain in reading rate it is doubtful if the gains would have been "substantial" because this type of test does not allow any gear shifting to a skimming process. So, it seems likely that gains in reading rate were probably measured by having students simply read a passage for a certain length of time and then counting the words they covered. Therefore, these gains in reading rate probably are not valid for reflecting gains in the rate at which the rauding process operated. Since the gains in reading rate were interpreted at that time as valid or legitimate, these secondary findings were probably interpreted by many as undercutting the theory that reading rate was in part determined by these more basic rates associated with thinking speed. Nevertheless, it should not go unnoticed that two measures of a basic rate of thinking speed, one by word associations and the other by matching words, had large relationships with reading rate.

Buswell (1951) tested the hypothesis that "rate of silent reading varies directly with rate of thinking" (p. 339). He noted that if this hypothesis is correct, then "the school should accept as satisfactory a slow rate of reading provided it is commensurate with the students' rate of thinking" (p. 339). He found a 0.50 correlation between his "rate of comprehension measure" and a combined "rate of thinking" measure that involved a vocabulary test, the "Science Research Associates Nonverbal," and a listening test. Buswell's measures of rate of thinking were hardly tapping a basic thinking rate but instead were highly contaminated by the same factors involved in his reading rate measure. Buswell went on to interpret his data as providing support for his idea that subvocalization was a primary cause of slow reading (an idea that was regarded as erroneous in Chapter 4).

The above research published by Buswell marks the end of an era where theory and the research were generally supportive of the idea that reading rate was limited or influenced by a more basic thinking rate. These ideas seem to have been disregarded by later researchers. The practical importance of these ideas was in predicting who could gain the most in reading rate, and the data suggested that such gain could not be predicted. At that time, no one questioned the validity of these gains in reading rate as a criterion variable, so the idea of a basic thinking rate that limits reading rate appears to have died out because empirical support was seemingly lacking.

Samuels (1969) conducted a classical word recognition study, and then he appears to be the first to use the results to generalize about reading rate. It was a classical study in the sense that a word was presented by a tachistoscope with latency of response (giving the name of the word) measured in milliseconds. Quoted below is Samuels' interpretation of his results.

> The same processes which influenced speed of word recognition in this study can explain how reading speed is influenced in reading meaningful connected prose. Various cues, for example, from context as well as from synergistic word associations, help the reader anticipate what the following words will be. If the reader's partial perceptions match the words he anticipates, he can read rapidly, never having to discriminate all the letters. (p. 99)

The problem with this theoretical interpretation, from the vantage point of hindsight, is that twelfth graders ought to read second grade level material faster than they read twelfth grade level material, but they do not (as was noted in Fig. 11.3 of the previous chapter). Indeed, more and better context does not speed up word recognition when the rauding process is operating, otherwise a host of researchers would not have found that reading rate is constant across a wide range of material difficulty ranging from grade level 2 to grade level 14 (as noted at the outset of this chapter). However, in fairness to Samuels, it should be pointed out that most reading researchers have failed to consider this empirical fact when they have theorized about reading in general and reading rate in particular.

Katz and Wicklund (1971, 1972) conducted a pair of studies on word recognition during scanning. They found that good reading fifth graders could recognize words faster than poor reading fifth graders. However, they found no differences between good and poor readers with respect to how fast they could recognize letters, whether working with second graders or sixth graders. These data can be explained by a speed of thinking factor that is more associated with the symbol manipulation. Scanning for letters does not require any symbol manipulation. So, this task may be more akin to simple reaction time and less akin to the basic thinking processes that limit or influence reading rate. The Katz and Wicklund research also contained an anomalous result whereby they found no difference between good and poor readers with respect to adding an additional word to their scanning list; if cognitive speed is a causal factor then the extra word should have taken the poor readers more time than the good ones. Some of their data collection was designed to explain this anomaly, but they did not succeed. This would constitute cause for alarm or caution were it not for the fact that their anomaly was not replicated in a somewhat similar study by Hogaboam and Perfetti (1978), which will be reviewed later.

M. D. Jackson and McClelland (1975) investigated the sensory and cognitive determinants of reading speed. At the outset, they noted that "the term 'reading' has been used to refer to a number of different processes," and that they were more interested in the kind of reading that results in an "... adequate understanding of the material read ..." (p. 265). It should not go unnoticed that Jackson and McClelland were arguing over 10 years ago for a primary thesis of this book. Namely, there are many different reading processes and it is important to know exactly which one is being investigated in a research study. It appears that Jackson and McClelland were interested in the rauding process, not a skimming process for example. They used a tachistoscope to study how much information can be perceived during a 200 msec fixation duration for "fast readers" and "average readers." Average readers were college students who read a 4286-word passage between 200 and 300 wpm with a 70% or higher score on their comprehension text. Fast readers were graduate students and undergraduates who purportedly read the passage between 451 and 855 wpm with a 70% or higher score.

One of the tachistoscopic tasks used by Jackson and McClelland was for a subject to report two letters presented, one presented on the left and another presented on the right, separated by 11 to 31 character spaces. On this task, there was no difference between the fast and average readers. On the other tasks, such as perceiving all the words in five-word sentences, the fast readers were better than the average readers; on this task the fast readers got 39% of the sentences correct while the average readers only got 16% correct. They interpreted these results as follows: "the breadth of field from which the reader can utilize visual information was approximately the same for the fast-reader group and the slow-reader group," but the "faster readers are able to pick up more information from each fixation" (p. 572). They concluded that "greater efficiency of encoding of visual information could free limited processing resources to deal with the conceptual content of what is read and to guide eye movements to a useful place to begin the cycle anew" (p. 573). These results suggest that the rate of reading does not seem to have anything to do with superior sensory processes associated with keen eyes or vision.

Another of the tasks used by Jackson and McClelland involved pairs of sentences which had exactly the same five words except one letter in one word was different and thereby changed the meaning of the word and the meaning of the two sentences. Fast readers got 8% more of these sentences correct, thus suggesting that the fast readers ". . . must be picking up more information about the critical letter than are the slow readers," so they eliminated the hypothesis that ". . . faster reading is solely due to an ability to guess missing information in the sentence based on contextual cues and knowledge of the language" (p. 572).

These data can be interpreted as indicating that some people think faster than other people and are thereby able to process exactly the same visually perceived information faster through the components of lexical access, semantic encoding, and, when required, sentence integration. Possibly, the point could be made clearer by saying that the fast readers would also likely perform better on similar tasks presented auditorily because of their superior cognitive speed, not because of any superior sensory skill associated with vision or hearing.

Perfetti and Hogaboam (1975) conducted a classical word recognition study with high and low comprehending elementary students, namely, third graders and fifth graders. The results for their third graders are presented in Fig. 12.1. On the left side of the figure are the results presented with mean vocalization latency (time to pronounce the word) as the dependent variable. On the right side of the figure is the same data after they have been reanalyzed using rate of word vocalization as the dependent variable, in Wpm. Notice that on the left side of Fig. 12.1, the difference between the high and low comprehension groups (good and poor readers) is small for high frequency words but large for nonwords, with low frequency words in between. Perfetti and Hogaboam interpret these data as indicating that "the superiority of the skilled reader is greater for pseudowords and low frequency real words than for highly familiar words" (p. 467). However, when these same data are presented in terms of rate instead of time, on the right of Fig. 12.1, it can be seen that the differences in rate between the good and poor readers (high and low comprehension groups) is almost exactly the same for all three types of words, high frequency (16.5), low frequency (20.0), and nonwords (15.5) with the difference for high frequency being slightly larger than the difference for nonwords. Stated differently, Perfetti and Hogaboam used the time variable as their dependent variable, and they found an

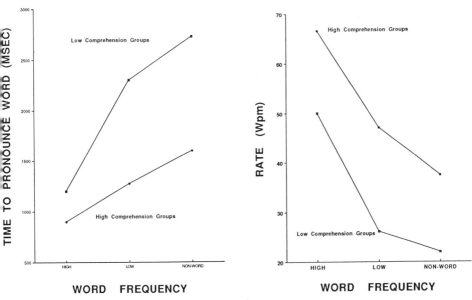

Figure 12.1 Time required to begin to pronounce a word as a function of word frequency for low and high comprehension groups. The data on the left side of the figure have been reanalyzed and presented on the right side in terms of rate, in Wpm. Original data from Perfetti and Hogaboam, (1975).

interaction between the word frequency factor (high, low, nonword) and the group factor (low and high comprehension), but the same data can be analyzed by converting their time variable into a rate variable and then the interaction evaporates completely.

These data of Perfetti and Hogaboam are readily explained by a cognitive speed factor, C_s. Faster thinkers have a faster rate of cycling through the steps involved in recognizing words so that they recognize them a constant amount faster, no matter whether they are easy words (high frequency), hard words (low frequency), or even nonwords that can be orally produced. The above interpretation is not in conflict with their interpretation that "we are dealing with a basic 'low-level' skill difference, not dependent on knowledge of meanings" (p. 467). However, by presenting the data in terms of rate, it is easy to see how a basic low-level skill can easily explain the differences between the good and poor readers for all three of the word types. If the difference between the groups was due to practice or experience with the words, then the rate differences between these two groups should have been smaller for the nonwords, but it was not.

The above data provide additional support for the idea presented in Chapter 9 that one of the main factors influencing reading rate is a basic thinking rate such as cognitive speed, C_s. This factor can explain the differences in the speed at which words are recognized and this factor can explain why some individuals have faster rauding rates. Fast readers are able to recognize words faster because they have a faster cognitive speed that allows them to complete the processes involved in word recognition faster.

Mitchell and Green (1978) investigated whether readers predict the structure of material before reading it, and whether such predictions affect reading rate. They presented three words at a time on the screen and the subjects pushed a button to signal that they were through reading so that the next three words would be presented. After describing four separate experiments, they concluded that reading rate (a) "is modulated by the frequency of the words and by the number of characters in the display," and (b) is "largely determined by the speed with which a reader can access the meaning of words and construct a representation of the text rather than by the speed with which they can test successive predictions about it" (p. 609). These data again indicate that rauding rate does not increase as the redundancy or predictability of the words in passages increases. Also, cognitive speed could easily be the factor that Mitchell and Green speak of when they talk about the "speed with which a reader can access the meaning of words. . . ." (p. 609).

Ellis and Miles (1978) investigated "visual information processing as a determinant of reading speed." They correlated reading rate (combined from a number of measures that seemed to involve mostly the rauding process) with the threshold time taken to report correctly five digits (presented tachistoscopically). They also had subjects scan randomly generated letters to find instances of "tg" as quickly as they could. The combined measure of individual differences in rauding rate (a) correlated 0.48 with the time to process the five digits, and (b) correlated 0.49 with rate of finding the tg's. Their results suggest that speed of information processing is a factor limiting the rate at which the rauding process can operate. Again, their data may be interpreted as supporting the influence of cognitive speed upon rauding rate.

In another study, Hogaboam and Perfetti (1978) reported upon three experiments that studied how fast elementary school children could begin to say one- and two-syllable words and pseudo words. In Experiment I, they found that the latencies were higher for pseudo words, but more importantly, they found that the cost of the second syllable, i.e., two-syllable latency minus one-syllable latency, was about 300 msec for the skilled readers but around 800 or more msec for the less-skilled readers.

This difference can be readily explained as a difference in cognitive speed. In Experiment II, they found that practice in seeing and saying pseudo words decreased the response time but that it helped the skilled as much as the less skilled, so the individual differences prior to training remained after training. Again, it would seem that individual differences in cognitive speed prevents practice from eliminating individual differences in the operation of lexical access time. In Experiment III, they manipulated the frequency of exposure to pseudo words and found that both groups became faster with exposure but the less-skilled readers improved much more with practice. Furthermore, the curve for the less skilled also asymptoted at a latency that was more than 1000 msec higher than the skilled. Again, this difference in asymptote between the skilled and less-skilled curves can be explained by a difference in cognitive speed.

These data of Hogaboam and Perfetti suggest that students can learn to name new words and thereby process them faster by engaging in practice. However, with practice they reach a certain limit of lexical access speed that varies between individuals, and this factor seems to be cognitive speed, C_s.

Kail and Marshall (1978) investigated differences between skilled and less-skilled readers in the rate at which they scan memory. Children in grades 3 and 4 participated in a series of four experiments involving how fast they answered questions following the presentation of sentences. They found that the skilled readers answered questions approximately 600 msec faster, even when reading rate was statistically controlled. They interpreted their results as indicating that skilled readers search memory for information faster. They contended that this difference would affect the comprehension process during ordinary reading. Indeed, these data may be readily interpreted as another example of individual differences in cognitive speed. The same thinking rate difference that explains the earlier word recognition data would also explain these data. However, Kail and Marshall argue that this alternative seems unlikely since Katz and Wicklund (1971, 1972) ". . . have shown that skilled and less-skilled readers search visual displays of letters or words at approximately the same rate" (p. 814). Kail and Marshall are referring to the anomalous result of the Katz and Wicklund research that was reviewed earlier in this chapter. However, that research finding was not replicated by Hogaboam and Perfetti (1978) who found that the second syllable in a word cost the less-skilled readers more in recognition time. Furthermore, the finding that the time needed to start naming a word increases with the number of syllables has been replicated (Eriksen, Pollack, & Montague, 1970; Spoehr & Smith, 1973). Also, Katz and Wicklund reported that they threw away one-third of their data that would have been directly relevant to this issue, so it does not seem reasonable to use this single empirical finding to rule out the idea that less-skilled readers suffer from a basic processing deficit that affects the rate at which verbal material can be searched.

In yet another study, West and Stanovich (1978) measured latencies of word responses after giving either congruous context, incongruous context, or a no context control condition. For example, the word "cat" would be preceded by "the dog ran after the" (congruous) or "the girl sat on the" (incongruous). For fourth graders, sixth graders, and college students, the congruous context improved speed of word recognition by about 7–9%. Also, the incongruous context slowed word recognition by about the same amount for the fourth graders (7%) and sixth graders (6%) but had no effect on the college students. In another task that was exactly the same except the words were in color and the students had to name the colors, the context had no effect upon the college students but both the congruous and incongruous context slowed the responses of the fourth graders and sixth graders by 8–14%. They interpreted their results as evidence that the younger and poorer readers were strongly influenced by context as they recognized words, but for the older and better readers the word recognition process operates so rapidly that the influence of context was mitigated or eliminated.

The above data seem to indicate that context can speed up word recognition but it seems to help poor readers more than good readers because good readers recognize words so quickly that context seems to have little affect. West and Stanovich do caution, however, that context may help adults when they read more difficult material. Translated, it appears that contextual cues do *not* speed up the normal operation of the rauding process because it is operating at maximum speed already, under conditions of maximum context, whether for better readers or poor readers. In 1981, Stanovich and West replicated these 1978 findings and extended them; they found that adult readers were influenced by context when the words were more slowly recognized. Thus, under typical reading conditions where the rauding process is operating on relatively easy material, processing is generally being executed at maximum speed and variations in contextual constraint appear to have no effect upon rate.

M. D. Jackson and McClelland (1979) advanced the line of research they started with their 1975 study, reviewed earlier. Again, they studied what faster readers and average readers get out of one eye fixation while reading, using a tachistoscope. They used "effective reading speed," as their criterion measure (percentage comprehension score multiplied by wpm). In this research, their fast readers were the top 12 out of 48 college students who met their criteria on the selection tests; their average readers were the bottom 12. This time Jackson and McClelland used two reading measures for selection. The first one was the same as was used in 1975, giving ten short answers to a 4286-word article written by Isaac Asimov on the subject of asteroids. The second test was always given after the first was completed and it consisted of ten paragraphs (317 words average length) with three questions given afterwards. The paragraphs were taken from " . . . a number of scholastic aptitude test preparation books and covered a variety of topics" (p. 156). Quoted below is their description of what they told their subjects:

> Instructions were the same for both reading tests. Subjects were told that the purpose of the reading test was to obtain an estimate of their actual reading speed. Subjects were instructed to read each passage as fast as possible, consistent with good comprehension, and were warned that afterwards they would be given a comprehension test. Subjects were instructed to write a brief answer to each comprehension question. (p. 156)

These instructions sound conducive to the rauding process, especially for the Fast group. For this group, their rauding accuracy level, A_L, is very likely to be higher than the difficulty level, D_L, of the material, thus making the material relatively easy for them. Also, while they were reading on the first test they would have no idea what the task demands for comprehension would be like so they would have little or no reason not to use their rauding process. The selection of the average readers from the bottom 12 (of freshmen and sophomores) leaves some doubt about the relative difficulty of the material for this group, A_L compared to D_L, so their instruction about "good comprehension" leaves it questionable as to whether the average readers would adopt a rauding process or a learning process.

On the second test three conditions had changed. First, the difficulty of the passages was likely to be higher, e.g., $D_L = 14$, because they were taken from SAT preparation books. Second, the subjects were administered the tests after each of the ten paragraphs. Third, there was one question per each 106 words whereas there was only one question per each 417 words on the first test, thus putting much more accent on the comprehension criterion for the second test. It seems very likely that on the second test most of the members of both groups would be using a learning process.

The above expectations about processes were mostly confirmed from the rate and comprehension data reported. On the first article, fast readers averaged 396.4 wpm and average readers averaged 216.1 wpm. The difficulty level of the first article appears to be about $D_L = 10.6$ from

Equation 2.1 using a random sample of lines from the article to calculate character spaces per word, cpw = 5.8. With this estimate of cpw, the above rates for the fast readers was 383 Wpm from Equation 2.6. It is likely that the fast readers were using a rauding process at 383 Wpm since they were selected because they were above average (college readers average about 260–300 Wpm). The mean comprehension score for these fast readers was 70.8% which suggests that the questions were not superficial. Given that the second set of passages were likely to be relatively difficult, it is not at all surprising that they shifted to a learning process at 290.4 wpm, or about 293 Wpm, on the second test. By operating a learning process, they were able to keep their percentage comprehension scores at a comparable level, 71.8%.

Average readers read the first test passage at 216 wpm, which is an estimated 209 Wpm, with a 45% comprehension score. Given this comprehension score and given this rate, it is misleading to call this group average readers. They could not operate a rauding process at 260–300 Wpm and show evidence that they comprehended about 75% of tenth grade level material, as did the fast readers. Therefore, they cannot be considered as average reading college students. They were "poor" reading college students but *possibly* average for their age group. The main point, however, is that it is questionable whether they were operating their rauding process. On the second test, their average rate dropped to 169.3 wpm which is about 171 Wpm, and their comprehension score was slightly higher at 59.1%. Thus, there is little or no doubt that most of the average readers were operating a learning process on the second test.

As explained earlier, Jackson and McClelland calculated on "effective reading speed" for each test and these two measures were the twin criteria for investigating what happens during a single eye fixation, as will be reviewed later. Effective reading speed was the product of an indicant of accuracy, A, and a correlate of rate, R. From Chapter 2, it may be remembered that efficiency of comprehension, E, was defined as the product of A and R. At the moment, it needs to be emphasized that the first measure used by Jackson and McClelland was a correlate of efficiency, E, during the execution of the rauding process for most of their 24 subjects. The second measure was also a correlate of efficiency, E, determined from the execution of a learning process. Thus, these measures will be renamed to reflect more accurately what they seem to be measuring: $A1$, $R1$, and $E1$ from the first test and $A2$, $R2$, and $E2$ from the second test.

In their first table of results, Jackson and McClelland report the correlations among several of their measures. $E1$ correlated 0.79 with $E2$. Each of these two measures correlated higher with SCAT Verbal than

SCAT Quantitative. Each correlated highly with a Listening test, 0.67 for $E1$ and 0.59 for $E2$. The Listening test consisted of a set of paragraphs and questions that were comparable to those used on the second test; the passages were presented auditorily at 200 wpm. Notice that the Listening test was presented at a rate that was much slower than the rate the comparable passages were read by the fast readers (290.4 wpm) and a little faster than the rate they were read by the average readers (169.3 wpm). Thus, R has been held constant for both groups so that the only thing varying with the Listening test is accuracy, A. This means that the Listening test, which is an indicant of A, should correlate higher with other indicants of A as compared to indicants of R. Indeed, this result was as expected. The Listening indicant of A correlated 0.65 with $A1$ and 0.36 with $R1$; it correlated 0.55 with $A2$ and 0.47 with $R2$.

In this 1979 research, M. D. Jackson and McClelland were able to replicate their 1975 findings under conditions that extended technical controls. Again, they found no important differences between the fast and average readers on their sensory tasks. The fast readers could not identify a single letter separated on a line any further apart than the average readers. Again, the fast readers did not seem to be any keener in eyesight, either by how fast they could perceive letters during a single fixation or by the width of the visual span during a single fixation. Jackson and McClelland used a number of other tasks, the most important of which was a variant of the Posner task (Posner *et al.,* 1969), described in Chapter 9 as the technique used to test for cognitive speed. As noted earlier, this task measures how fast subjects can correctly respond "same" or "different" to whether pairs of letters have the same name when they vary between upper and lower case, e.g., "Aa" are same and "bA" are different. This task is obviously a speed of processing variable that would likely be more related to indicants of R than indicants of A. However, Jackson and McClelland did not report how scores on this task correlated with the indicants of A and R on the two reading tests. So, Name Matching is a correlate of rate, R, but it is more specifically a correlate of cognitive speed, C_s.

Out of 14 predictor variables in this Jackson and McClelland research, the highest correlate of $E1$ was the Listening test indicant of A, 0.75, the second highest correlate was SCAT Verbal, 0.56, and the third highest was Name Matching, 0.45. SCAT Verbal is a timed test that is likely to be loaded both as a correlate of A and a correlate of R, so it is not surprising that (a) SCAT Verbal correlated 0.47 and 0.41 with $A1$ and $R1$, respectively and (b) SCAT Verbal correlated 0.55 and 0.44 with $A2$ and $R2$, respectively. Thus, SCAT Verbal correlated highly with these correlates of A and R because it is an efficiency measure involving A and R.

Jackson and McClelland did a stepwise regression analysis and found that the two primary predictors of $E1$ were the Listening test and the Name Matching test, $R = 0.71$. For $E2$ the two primary predictors were exactly the same, $R = 0.69$. Given the amount of unreliability that could be expected in all three of the measures involved in these correlations, it is impressive that these two variables could account for this much of the variance. Jackson and McClelland also focused a great deal of discussion and supplementary analyses upon these two tasks. Yet, from the perspective of hindsight, it is not surprising that these two reading efficiency measures, $E1$ and $E2$, would correlate highly with a correlate of A (Listening) and a correlate of R (Name Matching) since $E1$ and $E2$ are composed of A and R (see Law II of rauding theory in Chapter 2). Furthermore, it is not surprising that other variables that were measuring portions of A or portions of R would drop out because they were contributing less unique variance.

Since Jackson and McClelland found the Name Matching test to be such an important factor in predicting efficiency ($E1$ and $E2$), they devoted a great deal of discussion to analyzing what it measures. They hypothesized that it represented "speed of processing visual information," and they discounted that it was measuring a general memory factor because it correlated so poorly with the Listening test ($r = 0.17$). Again, it is not surprising on the basis of hindsight, that the Name Matching test, a correlate of C_s, would correlate poorly with their Listening test, a correlate of A; there is no *a priori* theoretical reason to expect a nonrate measure such as a correlate of accuracy, A, to be related to a rate measure such as a correlate of cognitive speed, C_s. Suppose the Name Matching test also would not correlate with the rate at which the individuals chose to listen, using a time-compressed speech machine that allows subjects to vary listening rate just as rate is varied during reading. Then, there would be grounds for ruling out a general processing factor that was specific to vision. Their reasoning, however, led them to design a second experiment to investigate further what the Name Matching test was measuring. In addition to the Name Matching test, they gave subjects a pattern matching test that involved no letters or words, but only dot patterns. Again, they found differences between Fast and Average readers on the Name Matching test but no differences between the two groups on the Dot Pattern test, even though the latter test had longer reaction times and therefore involved more processing. They interpreted these results as indicating that ". . . the fast reader advantage in the name-match task is due specifically to more efficient access to letter-code information in memory (p. 177)."

From these Jackson and McClelland results, it seems reasonable to conclude that this Name Matching task measures a primary ability, C_s, that is a cause of individual differences in rauding rate, R_r. Since R_r also is likely to be a major factor influencing R during a learning process, it seems easy to see how this ability to perform the Jackson and McClelland task affects both $E1$ and $E2$. It is easy to see because any E-type measure involves R, and C_s limits R, theoretically. Jackson and McClelland lean toward an interpretation that the Name Matching task is measuring an ability more associated with the visual process during reading. However, it seems more likely that the Name Matching task is measuring a general ability that is limiting the rate at which the rauding process can successfully operate during both reading and auding, or listening.

The general ability measured by the Name Matching task has been referred to as reflecting cognitive speed, C_s. The Name Matching test seems to measure individual differences in the speed at which individuals can lexically access the names of verbal symbols, whether visually or auditorily presented, and make comparisons between them. Empirical data are needed to determine whether in fact the Name Matching test taps more than visual information-processing speeds, as it is being theorized here. Jackson and McClelland go on to suggest that this Name Matching ability is a product of practice (as well as a cause of reading ability) but one which is probably not readily amenable to training. At this point, it seems equally reasonable to add that cognitive speed probably is so closely associated with inherent brain structures that it can be expected to increase with age due to maturation but that this ability is probably already overlearned and quite resistant to further training (see Chapter 9). For example, a great deal of practice on name matching with pairs of aB and Ab may increase speed on pairs of aB and Ab but not speed on pairs of E and f. At this point, cognitive speed as measured by the Name Matching test appears to represent a basic mental ability that limits rauding rate, R_r, and thereby crucially influences all reading processes.

The M. D. Jackson and McClelland research (1975, 1979) leaves little doubt that the reason why some people have faster rauding rates, R_r, than others is *not* because they have lower thresholds for identifying single letters or because they can see letters in a wider span of vision. Instead, it appears that the faster rauders are faster at processing the verbal information contained in each fixation during rauding. It appears that the lexical access component of rauding limits the rate at which the subsequent components of the rauding process can operate. However, as long as the rauding process is operating on relatively easy material, $A_L > D_L$, then the semantic encoding should proceed just as fast as individuals can process verbal information, i.e., as limited by cognitive speed.

Also, there *may* be important individual differences in the sentence-integrating component, but again as long as the material is relatively easy and the rauding process is operating, all of the components should be operating successfully, and just as fast as the organism can process verbal information. So, it seems that rauding process rate, R_r, should be primarily limited by cognitive speed. Stated differently, a measure of cognitive speed, C_s, should account for an important part of the variance in a measure of rauding rate, R_r.

Mason (1980) carried on the sensory aspect of the Jackson and McClelland research by determining the accuracy of letter recognition of highly skilled and less skilled college students under various durations. She also found that the highly skilled were no different from the less skilled on letter identification. However, when she varied the location of the letter to be identified she found that the highly skilled were able to identify these letters more accurately at the exposure durations she used (from 20 to 130 msec). She argued that these data implicate sensory differences. This is a reasonable interpretation. However, it puts a focus on sensory differences that is counter to most other theory and research so it seems best to await future data and theory to adjudicate this anomaly. Furthermore, Underwood and Zola (1986) studied the span of letter recognition for good and poor reading fifth graders and they found "no evidence to suggest that skilled readers utilize letter information from a wider range of text than do less able readers" (p. 6). Thus, the weight of the evidence is against sensory advantages explaining the superiority of the better readers.

M. D. Jackson (1980) further investigated the hypothesis that better readers are faster at accessing the names of characters, as in the letter name-matching task. He wanted to determine if the higher performance of better readers was due to practice with the symbols and their names. He selected college students who were high and low on an efficiency of reading task. Both the skilled group and the less-skilled group were given practice on novel characters and their nonsense syllable names. There was no difference between the two groups when the task was simply to react to the stimuli without having to decide if they had the same or different names. However, when the task involved naming the novel stimuli, then there was about a 100 msec mean difference between the two groups. He concluded that (a) "faster access to letter identity codes allows better readers to recognize more letters and words from the visual pattern of text in a given amount of time," and (b) "the memory access speed advantage possessed by better readers is not solely a characteristic of the letter recognition process but reflects a more general speed advantage for accessing the memory codes of any visual pattern having a learned abstract representation" (p. 693). This general ability that Jackson has isolated appears to be the same factor that has repeatedly been called cognitive speed, C_s.

Boles and Eveland (1983) investigated whether the letter name match task involved a visual memory code versus a phonetic or name code. After a series of five experiments with college students, they concluded that this task involves a visual memory code and does not involve phonetic representations of letter names. Whatever kind of coding this task involves, it still seems to reflect a factor called cognitive speed.

Sanocki *et al.* (1985) studied the effect of context upon word identification within sentences. Illegal words (such as "lontards" and "nured") were placed inside of sentences (such as, "Many residents ate the cold lontards.") and sets of scrambled words (such as "The by nured sun was Mary."). Some sentences and scrambled word sets did not have illegal words, so the task for the college students was to determine as quickly as possible which sentence, or scrambled words, contained an illegal word. They summarized the facilitative effect of having sentence context upon word recognition speed, in their three experiments, as follows: "In the present experiments, we found robust facilitation effects, ranging up to 70 msec per word, averaged across all types of words in sentences" (p. 154). It was pointed out at the beginning of this chapter that variability in contextual constraint appears to have no effect upon the rate at which the rauding process operates because all the words are recognized at their fastest possible rate. These findings of Sanocki *et al.* seem to support this interpretation because the words could be recognized faster when they were in the context of sentences and at their fastest recognition rate.

CONCLUSIONS

Word recognition can easily become a bottleneck and slow down an individual's reading rate, no matter what gear is being used; this is readily apparent when trying to raud poor handwriting. In normal reading situations, however, as long as the material is relatively easy for the reader, lexical accessing probably proceeds at a relatively constant rate in Wpm across a wide range of material redundancies or difficulty levels. This idea was alluded to earlier in Fig. 9.2 by showing the constancy of a scanning process across a wide range of material difficulty. Context can facilitate the rate that words can be identified, but there appears to be a limit to this facilitation. This limit is reached when known words are presented under standard viewing conditions, i.e., about 100 msec per standard length word for typical college students. Having to determine the meaning of these words within a sentence, i.e., semantically encode them, slows a reading process about 33 msec so that a typical college student requires about 133 msec per standard length word. Having to integrate the meaning of the word into the meaning of the sentence within the context of the passage slows this process another 67 msec so that a typical college student can do this at a rate of about 200 msec per standard length word. When individuals are given words that are known and overlearned so that they cannot improve the speed at which they can be identified by practicing on them, there are still wide individual differences with respect to how fast these words can be rauded. These individual differences are influenced by a more general factor, called cognitive speed, the rate at which the meaning of verbal symbols can be accessed. Therefore, it would appear that cognitive speed would account for a large part of the individual differences in the rate of lexical accessing, or word recognition, because speed of lexical accessing is limited by this more general factor of cognitive speed, C_s.

In summary, speed of word recognition, or lexical accessing, probably accounts for at least half of the time required for individuals to process words during the rauding process. Thus, it should be no surprise that word recognition speed has a major effect upon the speed at which the rauding process operates. However, classical research on speed of word recognition has focused upon the major effects of contextual constraint, even though this factor appears to be of no differential consequence during typical reading because the context is at a maximum for all the words in the sentences of the material.

Evidently, the rauding process ordinarily operates at its fastest possible rate, which is limited primarily by an individual's cognitive speed. There are no important variations within individuals in word recognition speed during typical reading, even when the material varies greatly in difficulty level or redundancy, because each word is being recognized and processed at its fastest possible limit set by its length, maximum context, and the cognitive speed of the individual. Individuals who have the fastest word recognition rates tend to raud the fastest because both word recognition rate in particular and rauding rate in general are limited by individual differences in cognitive speed, C_s.

13

AUDING

INTRODUCTION

What is the relationship between reading rate and the rate at which an individual can listen to sentences and comprehend them, called auding? Or, what is the relationship between rauding rate during auding and rauding rate during reading? Up to this point, the term rauding rate primarily has been used in the visual sense. Now, we will look at the auditory side of rauding and see how it relates to the visual side.

T. G. Sticht is mainly responsible for theorizing and researching the relationship between auding and reading. He and his colleagues (Sticht, Beck, Hauke, Kleiman, & James, 1974) have advanced a developmental model which they summarized as follows:

> ... the person comes into the world with certain basic adaptive processes which [s]he uses to build a cognitive content and to acquire language competency. The bulk of this competency is verbal language competency, acquired and expressed by auding and speaking, respectively. In learning to read, the child uses the same cognitive context and languaging competencies used earlier in auding, plus the additional competencies involved in decoding print-to-language. (p. 114)

From their model, above, four hypotheses were developed and investigated by reviewing the relevant research literature. Their hypothesis that deals directly with rate is: "Rate of languaging and conceptualizing should produce comparable optimal rates of auding and reading when the latter skill is developed beyond the learning-to-decode stage" (p. 115). After reviewing the evidence relevant to this hypothesis Sticht *et al.* concluded that the "... maximal rate of silent reading with accurate retention corresponds closely to maximal rates of speaking and auding, with 250–300 words per minute representing a best rough estimate of the

optimal rates for these processes" (p. 115). The above conclusion pro-
vokes an answer to the question posed at the outset of this chapter: rauding rate during reading and rauding rate during auding are exactly the
same. After the relevant research evidence has been reviewed later, the
validity of this answer will be reevaluated. It should be noted that Sticht
and James (1984) have provided an updated review of the research literature relevant to listening and reading; this review contained one page
devoted to auding rate and reading rate with no changes in the conclusions that were drawn in 1974, as quoted earlier.

Before starting the review of relevant research, some additional background will be given. One of the studies to be reviewed used the Nelson–Denny Reading Test to measure the effectiveness of listening experiences upon reading rate and comprehension. Since this test seems to
be the most popular one used in college development reading classes, it
will be helpful to describe and critique it prior to reporting the research
which used it; use of this test involves artifacts that need to be discussed.
So, the section immediately following will be devoted to the so-called
Nelson–Denny Artifacts. Then, relevant research will be reviewed. Finally, a section will be devoted to conclusions and implications.

THE NELSON–DENNY ARTIFACTS

The Nelson–Denny Reading Test, Forms A, B, C, D, E, and F, is used
with ninth graders through college and adults. It provides three scores,
Rate, Comprehension, and Vocabulary. The Nelson–Denny Artifacts involve the Rate and Comprehension measures, so these two scores will be
described in some detail. The Rate score is obtained while the examinee
is reading the first passage on the test, about 600 words long. The examiner announces "mark" exactly one minute after the comprehension
test has begun and the examinees circle the number at the end of the
line they were reading at the moment. This number is a count of the
number of words read during one minute and is the student's Rate score
in words per minute, wpm. The student then continues reading the passage and answering the eight multiple-choice (MC) questions after that
first passage. These eight MC questions plus four MC questions after
each of the remaining seven passages give a total of 36 MC questions.
The test was designed to reflect individual differences in reading ability,
that is, how well someone reads in comparison to other individuals; it
was designed to be a psychometric test. It was not designed to be used to
measure gain, improvement, or progress in reading ability; it was not
designed to be an edumetric test (see Carver, 1974).

The first Nelson–Denny Artifact refers to the large gain in the Rate score that is ordinarily made by students when this test is employed to evaluate the effect of some treatment, even when there is no gain in the rate at which the rauding process operates. The gain in the Rate score from the pretest to the posttest is an artifact due to the idiosyncrasies of this psychometric test that was not designed to measure rate gain. Since there is no measure of comprehension to accompany the first minute of reading, it is possible and likely that students can be induced by a prior treatment or training procedure to shift up and use a skimming process with a higher than ordinary rate during this first 60 sec of the posttest. However, the examinees quickly learn after encountering the first eight MC questions that this high rate does not allow them to do well on the comprehension questions. Therefore, they are likely to go back and read the passage again using their rauding process or a learning process. At least, they will not use a skimming process on the subsequent passages. So, the first Nelson–Denny Artifact almost guarantees that the researcher who administers some type of rate training will find that the treatment group has increased its Rate score from pretest to posttest without any drop in the Comprehension score.

The second Nelson–Denny Artifact refers to a quirk in the scoring of the test. It is possible to improve one's Comprehension score by simply going faster on the entire test (see Davis, 1962). This is because there is no correction for guessing. For example, suppose a student is given the Nelson–Denny before and after a treatment designed to improve reading rate. On the pretest, this student has a Rate score of 200 wpm and a Comprehension score of 20; the student read the first four passages very carefully and answered all the questions correctly. On the posttest, the student has a Rate score of 400 wpm, finishes all eight passages and 36 questions, and answers 24 of the 36 questions correctly. This student has doubled her reading rate and improved her comprehension score from 55% to 67%, quite an impressive improvement, seemingly. However, if a correction for guessing had been applied to the scores on the passages that had been read, the percentage comprehension on the pretest would have been 100% and the percentage comprehension on the posttest would have been 61%, a large loss in an indicant of the accuracy of comprehension, A, which accompanied the increase in rate.

The Nelson–Denny test was *not* designed to measure gain or loss in rate or comprehension and it should *never* be used for these purposes. Whenever it is inappropriately used in this manner, beware of these two Nelson–Denny Artifacts.

RESEARCH

Jester and Travers (1966) gave college students passages for auding and reading at rates of 150, 200, 250, 300, and 350 wpm. On the multiple-choice tests they administered, the auding scores were 14.7, 14.2, 7.3, 4.9, and 5.2, respectively, and the comparable reading scores were approximately equal to the corresponding auding scores, 15.5, 10.8, 9.1, 10.1, and 5.9. At 200 wpm, the auding score was higher than the reading score (14.2 versus 10.8) and at 300 wpm, auding was lower than reading (4.9 versus 10.1). These data are somewhat inconclusive with respect to whether comprehension during auding is higher or lower than reading. The most reasonable interpretation of these data is that the accuracy of comprehension at equal auding rates and reading rates are roughly comparable, and that the differences found are primarily measurement error.

Jester and Travers also analyzed their data in terms of efficiency at each rate; they multiplied the accuracy of comprehension by the rate. The highest efficiency score for auding was at 200 wpm, and the highest efficiency score for reading was at 300 wpm. These data suggest that the rauding process operates most efficiently during reading at around 300 wpm but it operates most efficiently during auding at around 200 wpm. However, there was no practice with compressed speech so the optimal rate during auding could increase when individuals are given more experience with this novel way of increasing speech rate.

Foulke and Sticht (1966) asked 100 college students to give their preferred rate for listening to a selection that was at the eighth grade level of difficulty. The mean of the preferred rates was 207 wpm. They concluded that "... it is likely that with experience in listening to accelerated speech, even faster word rates would be preferred ..." (p. 401).

Foulke (1968) investigated the functional relationship between speech rate and comprehension by administering a 2925-word listening passage and a 50-item multiple-choice test to groups of 30 subjects each. The passages were presented to each group at rates ranging from 125 to 400 wpm, in 25 wpm increments. No measure of the difficulty level of the passages was reported but it was stated that it was "appropriate in interest and difficulty for a college population" (p. 200). From his results Foulke concluded that "... listening comprehension is little affected by increasing word rate until a word rate in the neighborhood of 250 or 300 wpm is reached, but substantially affected thereafter" (p. 205). This conclusion is somewhat at variance with the 200 wpm optimal rate reported by Jester and Travers (1966), and it is also at variance with the preferred rate of 207 wpm found by Foulke and Sticht (1966). The lower values around 200 wpm could be due to a lack of experience with time-compressed speech whereas the higher values at 250–300 wpm could be due to the practice afforded by a lengthy 2925-word passage. This optimal rate of Foulke's for auding is more comparable to Jester and Traver's 300 wpm rate for reading. Later, Foulke and Sticht (1969) reviewed the research on time-compressed speech and concluded that ". . . listening comprehension declines at a slow rate as word rate is increased, until a rate of approximately 275 wpm is reached, and at a faster rate thereafter" (p. 60).

Thames and Rossiter (1972) investigated whether the use of compressed speech as a pacing device would increase reading rate and listening ability. With the benefit of hindsight, it is now evident that the research question was ambiguous. Did these researchers want to determine if individuals could be induced to shift to a higher gear, such as skimming, or did they want to find out if rauding rate, R_r, could be increased by this treatment? In their research, two groups of high school students ($N = 46$) were randomly assigned to either a reading condition or a reading plus auding condition. The control group simply read the ten English assignments (stories) each day for 20–30 min. In the experimental group, the subjects were paced in their reading by listening to the same stories at rates that started at 150 wpm on the first day and increased steadily in 50 wpm increments to 250 wpm on the last day. Form A of the Nelson–Denny Reading Test was given before the treatment and Form B afterwards. The Brown–Carlsen Listening Test was also given pre and post. The Rate score on the Nelson–Denny improved from 225 to 294 wpm for the experimental group but declined from 247 and 214 for the control group. No change was reported for the Comprehension scores on the Nelson–Denny or for the Brown–Carlsen. The Nelson–Denny was also given nine months later to 38 of the 46 subjects; those in the experimental group had Rate scores 25 wpm faster on the average than those in the control group, 304 versus 279. Thames and Rossiter concluded that: "reading practice with accompanying compressed speech as a pacer resulted in a significantly greater increase in reading rate without an accompanying loss in comprehension . . ." and ". . . using compressed speech as a pacer can be effective in increasing rate" (p. 40).

Another way to interpret the above data of Thames and Rossiter is to say that this is a good example of a Nelson–Denny Artifact. By getting these subjects to read fast, 350 wpm, on their stories when paced by compressed speech, Thames and Rossiter were inducing a skimming process which their subjects used during the first minute on the Nelson–Denny. However, it is safe to assume that comprehension did drop during that one minute, but it was not noticeable because these subjects were able to switch back to a lower gear before answering the questions. If, in fact, this treatment induced the subjects to operate their rauding process faster with no loss in the accuracy of comprehension, then they should have been able to answer more comprehension questions correctly during the time limit for the test. However, the comprehension scores did not increase on either the reading or the auding tests. This finding reinforces the theory that rauding rate is not readily amenable to improvement, especially by a few hours of listening to compressed speech.

Carver (1973a) investigated the effect of varying rates during both auding and reading. Ten prose passages, each around 325 words in length and at the college level of difficulty (D_L = 13.3), were presented visually (N = 54) and auditorily (N = 54) to college students. The passages were presented at rates varying between 75 and 450 Wpm. Degree of understanding of each prose passage, in terms of percentage of sentences understood, was subjectively rated by each subject after the passage had been presented and before taking one of three types of objective tests, chunked, 20% cloze, and revised cloze.

The results of this research indicated that the most reliable and sensitive measure of the effect of rate changes was the percentage of understanding ratings, rather than the two objective measures which tended to provide replicative evidence of the understanding ratings. Later, Carver (1973b) interpreted these Carver (1973a) data as indicating a threshold value around 150 wpm rather than the 250–300 wpm value found by Foulke (1968). However, some years later, Carver (1977) reanalyzed these same data using the insights and concepts afforded by rauding theory. He recanted on the 150 wpm interpretations. When the data were analyzed in terms of efficiency, E, at each rate, it became obvious that the optimal rate was around 250 Wpm for the auding rates. Also, the highest efficiency for reading was also around 250–300 Wpm. So, these data of Carver's (1973a) appear to be reasonably interpreted as supporting the 250–300 optimal auding rate suggested by Foulke (1968), and they also support the 300 Wpm optimal rate for reading suggested by Jester and Travers (1966).

Neville (1975) studied the use of time-compressed speech to pace reading rate. A total of 136 second graders was given passages at three rates, 86, 108, and 143 wpm. One group simply listened to the tape-recorded versions of the passages while another comparable group was paced in their reading by listening to the same tapes. After each passage, there were ". . . eight literal comprehension questions to be answered by the subject in his own words" (p. 37). These above three rates can be converted to times, in msec/Word, so that the effect of spending more time can be observed. For the group that was paced by listening while reading, comprehension test scores increased in a straight line as more time was given (rate decreased), 46%, 55%, and 62%. The group that simply listened scored lower at the corresponding times, 38%, 42%, and 38%. It was not clear why this latter group should score so low, relatively, under the condition where they were given the most time; they scored 38% at the slowest rate. Possibly, the slowing down of the speech rate to 68 wpm hampered the intelligibility of the speech. The reading group scored highest at this slowest rate, 62%, probably because they could read the material while being paced by the listening.

This research indicates that auding rate can be used to influence or pace the reading rate of small children. If these students had simply been listening, instead of reading along at the pace of the auditory presentation, then they would not have scored higher under the reading while listening condition, i.e., differences of 8%, 13%, and 24%, respectively. Since there was no reading-only condition, it is not clear if auditory pacing of reading results in higher comprehension than reading alone. Yet, these data do indicate that if higher comprehension is desired, then reading rate can be *slowed* via the pacing so that the slower rate results in higher comprehension.

DeHaan (1977) investigated threshold auding rate. This research was a more sophisticated replication of the Foulke and Sticht (1966) research reviewed earlier where 207 wpm was found to be the preferred auding rate. The subjects were 32 military personnel who had high aptitude test scores (at least 110 on the Armed Forces Qualification Test). They were given passages from a relatively easy book, and asked to adjust the rate up and down until they found the preferred rate for understanding. These subjects would be comparable in ability to college students, and their mean threshold rate was 266 wpm. These results are higher than the 207 wpm found by Foulke and Sticht (1966) and are more in keeping with the 250 to 300 wpm optimal rate suggested by Foulke (1968) and Carver (1977).

Hausfeld (1981) studied comprehension during comparable reading and listening conditions to see if there were any differences. Prose passages at about the eighth grade level (easy) and about the fourteenth grade level (hard) were given to 30 college students at three rates, 180, 290, and 380 wpm. Under the reading condition, reading was paced by a machine that moved a window down a page at the desired rate. Listening rates were obtained using time-compressed speech. There were five questions on each passage, and subjects were also asked to rate their comprehension on a scale from 1 to 5. For the hard passages, the comprehension scores for reading and listening were almost identical at all three rates. For the easy passages, there was more variability but no consistent difference in favor of either reading or listening. As for the ratings results, listening was rated higher than reading at 180 and 290 wpm but lower at 380 wpm. Hausfeld concluded that "no difference between reading and listening emerged for normal or speeded presentation in either level or quality of comprehension" (p. 317). These data suggest that the accuracy of comprehension that accompanies a particular reading rate will also accompany a similar auding rate.

Carver (1982) investigated the relationship between the optimal rate of reading and the optimal rate of auding. (Note: This research was reviewed earlier in Chapter 7 from a different perspective.) A total of 108 college students was administered three different measures after they had read or listened to 100-word passages. The passages were presented at rates varying from 83 to 500 Wpm, and they were at four grade levels of difficulty, 5, 8, 11, and 14. All three measures of comprehension, multiple-choice, a version of cloze, and understanding judgments, tended to give the same pattern of results from both reading and auding (see Fig. 7.2). Accuracy of comprehension decreased as rate increased. However, the efficiency of comprehension (accuracy times rate) increased initially as rate increased, then efficiency peaked and started to decline as rate continued to increase (see Fig. 7.3). For reading material at grade level 5, the optimal rate was around 300 Wpm. For reading at each of the other grade levels of difficulty, 8, 11, and 14, the optimal rate was also about 300 Wpm. For auding material at grade level 5, the optimal rate was around 300 Wpm. For auding at each of the other grade levels of difficulty, 8, 11, and 14, the optimal rate was also about 300 Wpm. Notice that this means that at each level of material difficulty, 5, 8, 11, and 14, the rate at which college students could comprehend the most per the time given, was the same whether they were reading or auding, about 300 Wpm in each mode at each difficulty level. It seems reasonable to interpret these data as indicating that 300 Wpm was the average rauding rate for these individuals, whether they were auding or reading.

CONCLUSIONS

From the research on auding that has been conducted relevant to reading rate, it appears that there is little or no difference between the execution of the rauding process during reading and the execution of the rauding process during auding. The rauding process seems to operate equally well during auding and reading, at least as long as the materials are relatively easy, $A_L > D_L$, and the rates are comparable. When reading rates and auding rates are manipulated to the same levels above and below the rauding rate, then the accuracy of comprehension is approximately equal for these two modes. During reading, the optimal rate for college students seems to be around 250–300 Wpm (Carver, 1982; Jester & Travers, 1966). During auding, the optimal rate for college students also appears to be around 250–300 Wpm (Carver, 1977, 1982; deHaan, 1977; Foulke, 1968) whenever the auding is preceded by practice to eliminate the negative novelty effect.

Knowledge of the Nelson–Denny Artifacts, which involve gains in the Rate and Comprehension scores, should help eliminate erroneous interpretations of research results involving this test. A pretest to posttest gain in the Rate score on this test does not mean that rauding rate, R_r, has improved. Similarly, failure to find a loss in the Comprehension score does *not* necessarily mean that the accuracy of comprehension accompanying the rauding process has remained the same. Any research involving the Nelson–Denny Reading Test, whether involving auding or reading, should avoid misinterpretations based upon the Nelson–Denny Artifacts.

In their review of time-compressed speech research, Foulke and Sticht (1969) concluded that "the understanding of spoken language implies the continuous registration, encoding, and storage of speech information, and these operations require time" (p. 60). Finding threshold and optimal rates for both auding and reading around 250–300 Wpm for college students strongly suggests that the same processes are involved in both and the same limiting factors are involved in both. The research on auding rate reviewed in this chapter has provided support for rauding theory; it holds that the rauding process operates most efficiently at the rauding rate, which is at threshold and optimal. Individuals appear to have a maximum rate of comprehending relatively easy material (rauding rate) and that they ordinarily operate their rauding process at this rate because it is optimal and at threshold. The auding research reviewed in this chapter has indicated that the rauding process also operates optimally at the rauding rate during auding. Thus, there is support for Law III of rauding theory (see Chapter 2), both from the standpoint of reading and auding.

Reading rate can be effectively manipulated using auditory pacing. This means that the accuracy of comprehension, A, can also be manipulated by slowing the rate to levels below the rauding rate. Furthermore, for younger children, auditory pacing of reading probably results in higher comprehension than either mode presented separately. Auditory pacing may offer a technique whereby students can be induced to operate a learning process, i.e., shift to a lower gear in order to increase the accuracy of passage comprehension.

It seems clear that reading and auding have basic similarities even though there are certain differences (e.g., see Kavanagh & Mattingly, 1972). Rauding theory focuses upon the idea that the rauding process involves the same basic cognitive components whether the stimulus input is written or spoken words. This idea is not new. Larsen and Feder (1940) argued that their research ". . . supports the conclusions of previous studies that comprehension is largely a centrally-determined function operating independently of the mode of presentation of the material" (p. 251). Goodman (1966) said that "the process of reading comprehension differs from the process of listening comprehension only in the form of perceptual input" (p. 168). Smiley *et al.* (1977) said that their research findings were ". . . consistent with the notion that comprehension of heard or read material involves the same process" (p. 386).

Not all opinions have been favorable toward the idea that the auding and reading processes are the same. Danks wrote a commentary in 1974, which was published in 1980, that considered the merits of a unitary process for auding and reading versus separate comprehension processes for these two modes. At that time, Danks thought the evidence was inconclusive for choosing between these two positions. His analysis makes it imperative to point out that the similarities between auding and reading focused upon in this chapter are primarily based upon the communalities between (a) an individual who is rauding a printed prose passage, and (b) a comparable individual who is rauding an oral rendition of the same printed prose passage. In this later situation, there seems to be no doubt that reading and auding involve the same comprehension process, given the research that has been conducted since 1974.

From a theoretical standpoint, it appears that individuals have a certain maximum rate at which they can comprehend sentences efficiently during auding. This maximum rate is limited by the individual's cognitive speed, C_s, which in turn limits how fast individuals can identify words, which in turn limits how fast words can be semantically encoded and sententially integrated into the complete thoughts represented by sentences in passages. From extensive oral language experiences, individuals are able to operate this process at its maximum rate. Ordinarily, individuals are only slowed by new words, unintelligible words, or incomprehensible thoughts. For beginning readers, the initial problem is learning to decode the printed symbols so that the meaning inherent in its spoken form can be unlocked, and then the word must be practiced until the printed words can be processed as fast as the spoken words. Beyond the stage of beginning reading, words will be encountered that are not known auditorily so an additional step is required in the process. As for rate, however, the requirements are the same whether auding or reading. A new word must be encountered enough times so that its meaning within a sentence can be processed at its maximum rate which is the rauding rate for that individual.

From the meta-analyses of Sticht *et al.* (1974), it seems that the reading ability of typical students catches up to their auding ability in grades 7–8. This interpretation was supported in another way by additional data presented by Sticht and James (1984); adult men reading at grade level 7 and below had reading abilities below their auding abilities but those at grade level 8 and above had reading abilities equal to their auding abilities. The above research results would imply that rauding rate during reading may lag below rauding rate during auding until individuals have had the amount of practice in recognizing printed words that is needed to reach the eighth grade level of rauding ability. However, research is needed to investigate the following hypotheses: (a) individuals who cannot raud as fast during reading as they can during auding could probably profit from additional practice in reading relatively easy materials, and (b) individuals who can raud as fast during reading as they can during auding probably cannot increase their rauding rate during reading, or auding, by participating in a special treatment.

If rauding rate, R_r, is eventually considered to be just as important to monitor and maintain as the accuracy of comprehension, then it will become important to acknowledge that we know very little about how to maintain and improve this rate. We need to know (a) how much material a student should raud each week, (b) the optimal level of material difficulty for rauding, and (c) whether reading and auding the material are equally effective.

The above unknowns, however, should not detract from what we now know about auding and reading rates. Prose passages presented by auding and reading at the same rates result in equal accuracy of comprehension, A, at least between about 150 and 500 Wpm. It appears that the rauding process operates equally well in the two modes as long as rate, R, is comparable. Furthermore, the rauding rate of college students seems to be about 300 Wpm, whether they are reading or auding, and this rate also seems to be their most efficient rate of comprehension whether reading or auding.

ORAL READING

INTRODUCTION

Oral reading rate probably has a very lawful relationship to rauding rate, R_r. Maximum oral reading rate (MORR), the fastest rate at which an individual can correctly pronounce all the words in a passage, was shown in Chapter 11 to have the same yearly growth as rauding rate (see Fig. 11.7). Therefore, it may be possible to measure MORR and use it to estimate R_r quite accurately. Using the Taylor (1965) data to estimate R_r and using the Doehring (1976) data to estimate MORR suggested that

$$R_r = \text{MORR} + 25 \text{ Wpm} \tag{14.1}$$

However, Equation (14.1) is only an hypothesis because it was based upon two different samples that are not likely to represent the same population with respect to rauding rate. Also, the above relationship is for group means and may not hold for individual differences within each grade. Much more research is needed to confirm, deny, or refine the linear relationship hypothesized in this equation. Nevertheless, it illustrates the potential close relationship between rauding rate and oral reading rate.

Beside MORR, there are at least two other oral reading rates that can be theoretically discriminated. First, consider the rate at which an individual reads aloud for others to comprehend and/or be entertained; this can be called a performance oral reading rate (PORR). It is assumed that PORR would always be lower than MORR: PORR < MORR. PORR is likely to vary drastically within individuals from one situation to another because it must be tailored to the target audience. Therefore, PORR is of little theoretical interest here. Second, consider the rate at which an individual reads aloud while attempting to comprehend; this can be called a rauding oral reading rate (RORR). It is assumed that RORR would also be less than MORR: RORR < MORR.

When research is conducted on oral reading rate, it is not always clear whether the individuals are reading aloud at their MORR, PORR, RORR, or some combination. In many research situations it seems likely that the subjects often try to satisfy both the performance and rauding aspects by a compromise between PORR and RORR. This means that it seems likely that if adults are given a passage that is not easy for them to understand, then they may go a little slower than PORR in order to comprehend better and they may go a little faster than an ideal RORR so that they meet a perceived social goal of sounding acceptable to those listening. Therefore, unless the instructions and task demands are carefully designed to produce either PORR or RORR, invalid rates for either will probably result. On the other hand, giving individuals relatively easy passages, $A_L > D_L$, and requesting that they read aloud as fast as possible should produce rates that are highly reliable and valid for MORR.

For relatively easy material, it is assumed that an individual will have only one MORR and RORR. However, PORR is likely to vary considerably depending upon the audience or task, as noted above. It is assumed that there are causal relationships among R_r, MORR, and RORR. If an individual's R_r increases during the year, then it is assumed that RORR must also have increased during the year; the factors that influence rauding rate during silent reading are assumed to be many of the same factors that influence the rauding rate during oral reading. It is also assumed that the primary factors that influence R_r during silent reading are the same ones that influence how fast an individual can recognize and pronounce the words during maximum oral reading, MORR.

It is possible to consider R_r as causing RORR and MORR and it is also possible to consider RORR and MORR causing R_r. It may be reasonable to consider oral reading rate as a causal factor for R_r in the early years of learning to read, but it is clear that eventually R_r must be considered as causing RORR and probably causing MORR.

There has been a great deal of research conducted that has involved oral reading, most of which has been little concerned with rate and even less concerned with silent reading rate. The following review of the research literature will be focused upon those oral reading studies that have direct implications for oral reading rate and its relationship to silent reading rate during the operation of the rauding process.

RESEARCH

Huey (1908) reported silent and oral reading rates for 20 "post-graduate students." This group read silently at an average rate of 5.25 words per second, 321 wpm, when the reading was by the reader's "own method."

Huey also reports that: "reading aloud was 66 per cent slower than reading silently, at the normal rate, and 56 per cent slower at the maximal rate . . ." (p. 120). The above values convert into 109 and 141 wpm, respectively, if Huey's language is translated at face value. However, it seems more likely that he based these percentages on time instead of wpm, so a more likely estimate of MORR would be 206 wpm. It is not known whether the individuals were allowed to read the material silently, once, prior to reading it orally. In any event, Huey's data establishes an average silent reading rate for college graduates of around 300 wpm and a corresponding MORR that was considerably slower, around 200 wpm.

Mead (1915) conducted what appears to be the first extensive comparison between RORR and silent reading involving 112 sixth graders in five different classes. He was replicating a smaller study by Pintner (1913) involving 23 fourth graders. Averaging over the five classes in Mead's research, these students read aloud for comprehension about 15% slower than they read silently (rate was given in lines read), and comprehension scores were higher for silent reading. One purpose of this early research was to provide data relevant to the practice of teaching oral reading to the exclusion of silent reading. Mead (1917) presented more extensive data from 340 students in grades 3–10 which tended to replicate the earlier research that rate was a little faster (17%) and comprehension was a little higher for silent reading. These RORR data were probably influenced somewhat by performance factors, as is the case for almost all RORR research unless there is some instruction to the subjects to disregard the performance aspect and concentrate solely on comprehension.

Swanson (1937) studied college freshmen and reported the mean oral reading rate for 70 poor silent readers to be 145 wpm while the corresponding rate for 10 good silent readers was 178 wpm. These rates represent a combination of RORR and PORR because the subjects were given a comprehension test after they had been asked "to read the material once so that the meaning would be clear to himself as well as to a listener" (p. 38). Unfortunately, this is an example of research that tells us little or nothing about RORR because it is contaminated by PORR.

I. H. Anderson and Swanson (1937) studied the eye movements of 124 college freshmen while reading. The subjects were asked to read "two short selections of moderate difficulty" (p. 62), one orally and one silently. They were instructed to "read to understand, not to interpret the material," and "the requirement of comprehension was a moderate knowledge of the reading material, measured by a correct response to three out of four true–false statements on the content" (p. 62). These instructions should have produced a valid measure of RORR. The subjects were divided into three groups: poor readers, unselected readers, and good readers. The results were as follows: (a) the poor readers read silently at 166 Wpm and orally at 123 Wpm, (b) the unselected readers read silently at 204 Wpm and orally at 143 Wpm, and (c) the good readers read silently at 253 Wpm and orally at 159 Wpm. (Note: These rates were converted from ems using Equation 2.8.) When the task demands were constant across these silent and oral conditions, RORR was slower in the three groups by 26%, 30%, and 37%, respectively. When the individual differences in rate for silent and oral were correlated for each of the three groups, the correlations were 0.78, 0.68, and 0.64, respectively. Correlations about equal in size were found for mean duration of fixation, mean size of fixation, and mean regression per line.

Anderson and Swanson concluded that their results supported "the contention that there are common elements in silent and oral reading" (p. 69). Another way of interpreting their results is to note that the instructions, task, and silent rate of 204 Wpm for the unselected group point toward a learning process, so the "moderate difficulty" reported probably means that these college freshmen shifted down from third gear to second gear. The operation of their learning process, Gear 2, while reading aloud seemed to require extra attention which slowed this process around 25–35% for poor, average, and good college readers alike so that the correlation between individual differences in these oral and silent rates was high. Unfortunately, this is another example of research that is not directly relevant to the rauding process, Gear 3, the focus of the present review.

Landauer (1962) published the results of a little study that is of considerable interest, in spite of the fact that the report is only one page long. Four adults practiced speaking aloud (oral) and thinking to themselves (silent) using numbers, the alphabet, and the American pledge of allegiance while "attempting to go as fast as possible without skipping" (p. 646). Under both the oral and silent conditions the times for the various tasks were almost exactly the same. Landauer concluded that "it seems that one does not think words and numbers appreciably faster than one can say them aloud, suggesting that the two behaviors may involve much the same processes" (p. 646).

These data of Landauer suggest that MORR may be an overt indication of rauding rate, R_r. If R_r turns out to be higher than MORR for some people, then it could be an artifact of the measurement conditions; it is possible that allowing the passage to be read silently once before reading orally would result in MORR being equal to R_r. If so, this would constitute evidence for the hypothesis that R_r is in fact a maximum rate of comprehension with the limiting factor being how fast the words can be internally articulated during silent speech (see Carver, 1977).

Morton (1964) investigated MORR for 32 male subjects who were "senior and student members of the university." (Note: This probably means approximately the same as undergraduates and graduate students in the United States.) Morton used MORR for 200-word passages to investigate "statistical approximations to English." He reported rates in milliseconds per letter space; these values can be directly transformed into Wpm (see Chapter 2). He found that zero approximation to English, i.e., randomly ordered words, were read at a MORR of 124 Wpm, the slowest rate. The corresponding value for normal English text, the fastest rate, was 216 Wpm. He also included the following statistical approximations to English: First, Second, Third, Fourth, Fifth, Sixth, and Eighth (he did not include Seventh); the corresponding rates were 157, 181, 195, 203, 203, 208, and 206, indicating that MORR generally increases with the redundancy of the passages.

The above 216 Wpm MORR for normal text found by Morton is similar to the rate found by Huey, 206 wpm. Huey did not describe the nature of the materials or the exact instructions given to his subjects. Morton's normal text came from a book entitled *Economics of Everyday Life*, and he instructed them to read "as quickly as possible, minimizing errors," "without trying to give them any meaning," and "without regard to punctuation or meaning" (p. 342). These are ideal instructions for measuring MORR.

The most outstanding aspect of Morton's data is his finding that MORR generally increases with each increase in the redundancy of the material being read. Superficially, this might suggest to some that R_r would also increase with increases in the redundancy of textual materials. However, rauding rate has no meaning outside the context of comprehending the complete thoughts in sentences, and statistical approximations to English do not involve sentences, so redundancy of this type is not relevant to rauding rate. Furthermore, the data reviewed in Chapters 3, 5, 7, 10, and 11 have already indicated that the rauding rate of college students does not increase with the redundancy of normal text, when it varies in difficulty from beginning reading material to college level material.

The inconsistency between the two above findings relevant to redundancy and rate, from oral rate and silent rate, is more apparent than real. Redundancy improves the speed at which MORR operates up until the individual's rauding rate, R_L, is reached for relatively easy material, $A_L > D_L$. From this point on, decreasing the redundancy of passages by increasing D_L has no effect upon R_r and has no effect upon MORR. The large amount of data reviewed in earlier chapters leave no doubt about redundancy having no effect upon R_r. And, the 1974 research by Coke (reviewed earlier in Chapter 3) leaves little doubt about the redundancy of relatively easy passages, $A_L > D_L$, having no effect on MORR.

Poulton and Brown (1967) reported upon a study that demonstrated that oral reading rate depends upon whether it (a) is a performance for an audience, PORR, (b) involves attending to the accuracy of comprehension, RORR, or (c) is done at maximum speed without regard for comprehension, MORR. Three groups of housewives, eight per group were asked (a) "to read aloud with expression," (b) "to read aloud as quickly as possible" while still comprehending, and (c) "to read aloud so quickly that punctuation, expressions, and meaning were neglected" (p. 220). These instructions should produce valid measures of PORR, RORR, and MORR, respectively. The three resulting rates for the 450-word passages used were 166, 227, and 245 wpm, respectively. These data confirm the theoretical expectations, presented at the beginning of this chapter, that PORR < MORR and RORR < MORR. Furthermore, the MORR rate of 245 wpm for these "housewives" is probably not far from their rauding rate, R_r.

Kolers and Lewis (1972) reported upon the reading skill of their college student subjects. They indicated that this group "read a single page of connected discourse aloud as rapidly and as accurately as they could" and individual differences in their "speed varied from 155 to 284 words per min." (p. 115). These data are in keeping with the mean MORR values reported earlier for adults and college students, namely, 206 wpm from Huey (1908), 216 Wpm from Morton (1964), and 245 Wpm from Poulton and Brown (1967).

Bouma and deVoogd (1974) reported upon MORR for seven adult Dutch subjects, ages 25–40, who were members of a research institute. They had a mean MORR of 240 Wpm, with a range of 180 to 280 Wpm (converted from letter spaces per second; see Chapter 2). This range seems to be very close to what Kolers and Lewis (1972) reported for their college students (155 to 284 wpm).

Coke (1974) gave 20 college students passages to read aloud, and she ". . . emphasized the need to read rapidly without sacrificing intelligibility" (p. 406). (Note: These are the data that were mentioned earlier in this chapter; this research was reviewed earlier in Chapter 3 from a different perspective.) Coke presented a scatterplot of syllables read per minute as a function of the difficulty of the passages being read. From these data, it can be estimated that MORR was 310 syllables per minute, or 187 Wpm, no matter what the difficulty or redundancy of the passage. This 187 Wpm MORR value for Coke's college students compares

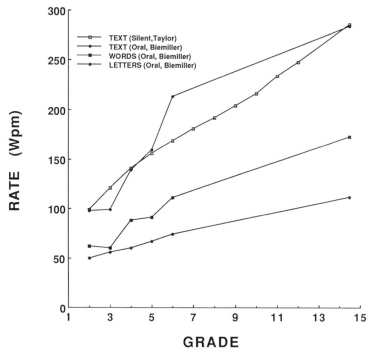

Figure 14.1 Reading rate, in Wpm, as a function of grade in school for the oral reading of text, words, and letters (from Biemiller, 1977) plus silent reading (from Taylor, 1965).

favorably with Huey's 206 wpm and Morton's 216 Wpm value but is lower than Bouma and deVoogd's 240 Wpm and Poulton and Brown's 245 Wpm.

Doehring (1976) collected MORR data from students in each of grades 1 through 10. (Note: These data were reviewed in considerable detail in Chapter 11 and presented in Fig. 11.7.) These are the same data that prompted the hypothesis presented at the outset of this chapter, namely, that rauding rate is about 25 Wpm faster than MORR.

Biemiller (1977) investigated the development of MORR. He studied second graders through sixth graders in a laboratory school over a period of seven years, plus college students. He gave letters, random words, and normal first grade text to about 20 students in each grade. He reported his results in mean seconds per letter, or word. Figure 14.1 contains a plot of his results, when the random word and normal text rates were converted to Wpm using the equations in Chapter 2. Since letters are all one syllable, except for "W", their rates were considered as seconds per syllable and this was converted to Wpm using Equation 2.7. In Fig. 14.1, Taylor's rates (described in Chapter 2) have also been presented. Rate generally increases a constant amount each year, similar to the data of Doehring presented in Chapter 11. The primary differences between the Biemiller data and the Doehring data is that Biemiller's subjects had a MORR for normal text that closely coincides with Taylor's silent reading rate data, except at grade 6. Thus, it seems important that both rauding rate data and MORR data be collected on the same subjects so that the relationship between R_r and MORR can be more validly determined. It would seem that growth in MORR would probably parallel growth in R_r, at least until highly skilled readers are considered. College students and graduate students may have a MORR on relatively easy material that is less than R_r, as Huey's (1908) data would suggest.

Allington (1978) asked fourth graders to read aloud a second grade basal story, 12 were good readers, GE = 4.9, and 12 were poor readers, GE = 2.8. He also asked them to read aloud the same words in random order. He did not report whether he asked them to read at their fastest rate or not. Therefore, these results cannot be interpreted with respect to PORR, RORR, or MORR.

Juel and Holmes (1981) asked second and fifth grade students to read sentences orally and silently. They gave them a four-choice picture test after each sentence to determine if in fact the sentence had been rauded. From their results they concluded that oral and silent reading represent the same processes, and that "... there is no indication that readers of differing abilities are accessing meaning in a qualitatively different fashion in oral than in silent reading" (p. 565). In one of their data analyses, they presented mean reading times, in seconds, for the 24 good and 24 poor readers that they studied under both oral and silent reading. Converted to estimated wpm, the good readers read the sentences orally at about 90 wpm and they read the sentences silently at the same rate, about 90 wpm. This result suggests that good readers in elementary school may have a RORR that is equal to their rauding rate during silent reading, RORR = R_r. This relationship seems plausible. However, this hypothesized direct connection between RORR and R_r may only hold for reading short sentences (five words in length) as long as saying the words aloud and internally at the same rate is the best strategy for remembering the sentence long enough to do well on the subsequent test on each sentence. It seems more likely that good reading sixth graders, for example, will be able to execute their rauding process faster when it is not encumbered with the additional requirement of having to enunciate each word out loud. Yet, it does seem plausible that silent reading is simply reading out loud to oneself for lower level elementary students so that the two processes are identical in every way including rate.

Compared to these good readers, the poor readers read more slowly in the Juel and Holmes study. They read silently at about 60 wpm, and they read orally even more slowly, about 40 wpm. Yet, this 20 wpm difference may be entirely explained by the fact that it takes longer to try to pronounce aloud unknown words. Poor reading second and fifth graders could be expected to stumble when trying to pronounce some of the words Juel and Holmes gave as examples: crown, pearl, glamour, envy, muffin, patient, and disease. Therefore, these data for the poor readers should not be taken as indicating that RORR is less than R_r because this comparison should not be made unless the material being read is relatively easy.

Burge (1983) gave two forms of an informal reading inventory (IRI) to 18 fourth graders who had a 2.9 GE score on a standardized reading achievement test. The second, third, and fourth grade level passages were read orally on one form of the IRI and were read silently on the other form. The mean of the three oral reading rates ranged from 87 to 93 wpm, and the corresponding rates for silent reading were slightly higher, ranging from 98 to 103. The oral reading rates averaged about 10% slower than the silent reading rates. Thus, for these poor reading elementary students their R_r appears to be only slightly higher than RORR. It would seem likely that for these students, MORR would equal R_r but MORR was not measured.

Burge's most important finding was that comprehension during oral reading was relatively constant for the second, third, and fourth grade passages, 73.1, 77.3, and 70.4, respectively, while comprehension declined with increasing grade level for silent reading, 67.3, 55.0, and 37.0, respectively. He speculates about why this happened but he did not mention one highly probable cause. These poor readers were greatly aided by the highest level of subvocalization, which is vocalization or reading aloud. For them, subvocalizing these relatively hard passages, $A_L < D_L$, during silent reading is not as effective as vocalizing them. This would be similar to good reading adults who also resort to reading difficult material aloud when they have trouble understanding.

Backman, Lundberg, Nilsson, and Ohlsson (1984) gave passages to 144 seventh and eighth graders, both good and poor, and instructed them to read ". . . aloud as fast as possible, and then immediately to produce a written recall of the whole text as accurately as possible during seven minutes" (p. 117). There were two passages, each of which was revised so that there was an easy and difficult version. These instructions and objective consequences were likely to induce a learning process, or even a memorizing process for the difficult version. Indeed, the mean rates reported for the difficult versions ranged from 79 to 138 wpm for the poor readers and from 97 to 168 for the good readers; the rauding rates in wpm for average readers estimated from the Taylor data in Table 2.1 are considerably higher at 195 and 204 wpm. The mean rates for the easy version ranged from 87 to 163 for the poor readers, and 110 to 205 for the good readers. These students probably shifted gears to a learning process but it is questionable to infer this from these rates since they represent reading aloud not silent reading, i.e., they were for RORR.

Backman *et al.* interpreted their data as providing evidence against the constancy of rate. They stated: "The demonstrated variations in reading speed makes Carver's (1983) statement of a constant reading speed independent of degree of difficulty somewhat dubious" (p. 123). There are several problems with this interpretation of Carver's (1983) assertions about rate constancy. First, the constancy reflected in Law I of rauding theory (Carver, 1981) was not intended to be generalized to reading aloud for comprehension, RORR. Second, the constancy was intended to apply to typical reading, not reading so as to be able to produce a written recall of whole text varying from relatively easy to relatively hard. Third, the constancy of rate is only evident across difficulty levels when rate is controlled for word length, yet Backman *et al.* measured rate in wpm not Wpm. What is "dubious" in this situation is the attempt to depreciate the lawfulness of rate constancy when the research involved none of the following prerequisite conditions: (a) instructions and objective consequences designed to elicit typical silent reading, (b) relatively easy material, and (c) rate measured in a manner that controls for word length.

N. E. Jackson and Biemiller (1985) asked second graders, third graders, and precocious kindergartners to read aloud a 100-word primer level text as fast as they could. This appears to be an excellent measure of MORR on relatively easy material. They sampled their second graders ($N = 66$) and third graders ($N = 62$) across 17 schools in a way that was designed to be representative of urban, small city, small towns, and rural areas. MORR rates were 107 wpm (second graders) and 143 wpm (third graders), and these rates were very close to their rauding rates in wpm as would be expected from the Taylor data given in Table 2.1, 115 wpm and 138 wpm, respectively. The precocious group read at 125 wpm which is about half way between second and third grades. These data suggest that MORR = R_r.

Salasoo (1986) gave 12 passages to 16 college students and asked them to read them silently and orally. From the methodology given it appeared as though this research would involve a comparison between RORR and R_r. Indeed, Salasoo reported that the students took longer to read aloud than silently. Unfortunately, it was impossible to determine the reading rates in wpm or Wpm.

Breznitz (1987) gave 60 first graders the items on a reading test under two oral reading conditions, self-paced and fast-paced. The fast-paced condition was set at 20% faster than the individual's self-paced condition. The self-paced condition was RORR and the fast-paced condition asked for comprehension under a rate that was probably closer to MORR. Breznitz found that the students averaged fewer oral errors and fewer comprehension errors under the fast-paced condition. She interpreted her results, over all four experiments, as follows: "If teachers wish to increase student's comprehension and reading accuracy, they should encourage their students to read orally at their maximum normal reading rates" (p. 242). Unfortunately, Breznitz did not report any of her data in a manner that allowed rate to be determined in wpm or Wpm. Furthermore, it is not clear if Breznitz is advocating RORR or MORR when she recommends maximum "normal" reading rates. It seems best to await replication of these data under conditions wherein rate in wpm or Wpm is reported and RORR or MORR is explicated, before spending a great deal of effort trying to understand why she obtained this theoretically unorthodox result suggesting that first graders comprehend more if they are induced to read faster.

Carver (1989a) studied the relationships among MORR, silent rate, and rauding rate, R_r. Students in grades 2–12 were given: (a) a passage to read silently prior to reading it out loud, (b) the same passage to read out loud as fast as possible, and (c) the Rate Level Test as a measure of R_r. For the 44 students with no missing data, the correlation between MORR and silent rate was 0.79, and the correlation between MORR and R_r was 0.81. The means for the three variables were almost exactly the same, ranging from 143 to 159 Wpm. The median of the absolute differences (a) between MORR and silent rate was 19 Wpm, (b) between MORR and R_r was 21 Wpm, and (c) between silent rate and R_r was 28 Wpm. It appears that MORR is very closely related to silent rate and R_r. A factor analysis of the partial correlations among the three variables, controlled for age, produced one factor; the variable with the highest loading was MORR. These data suggest that MORR is measuring best whatever was being measured by silent rate, MORR and R_r. If silent rate is taken as an indicant of apping rate, then these data suggest that apping rate is almost exactly the same as rauding rate, R_r (as was theorized in Chapter 9), and that MORR is more closely related to these two rates than they are related to each other. Thus, MORR seems to be an excellent predictor of silent reading rate, or apping rate, and it is also an excellent predictor of the fastest rate at which the rauding process can operate successfully, i.e., R_r.

CONCLUSIONS

With respect to the relationship between oral reading rate and silent reading rate, the existing data are lawful enough to be enticing but not yet completely definitive. It seems highly likely that there are reliable and lawful relationships between an individual's rauding rate, R_r, and the rate at which the individual reads orally, especially oral reading rate during rauding, RORR, and maximum oral reading rate, MORR. However, most of the research on oral reading has involved a version of RORR that is contaminated to an unknown extent by performance, i.e., a combination of RORR and PORR. The research on MORR should be much more reliable because it is likely to be less susceptible to variations in instructions and task demands. Existing data suggest that MORR for adults and college students is around 200–250 Wpm, which seems to be close to their R_r, but somewhat lower. Existing data also suggest that MORR and R_r are equal for students in elementary and secondary school.

It would appear that oral reading is ripe with potential for making strong inferences about rauding rate, the most important reading rate of all. It seems likely that R_r causes MORR so that MORR could be measured and used as an indicator of R_r. MORR offers an objective indicator of R_r, which is a theoretical construct involving internal attributes not easily amenable to direct measurement. Students can be given relatively easy passages to read as fast as they can with no comprehension requirement; the rate at which they do this, measured in Wpm, would seem to provide an indicant of their rauding rate. There appears to be great potential offered by further research on the relationship between MORR and rauding rate.

15

TEXTUAL PRESENTATION

INTRODUCTION

Reading rate is substantially affected by the form of the printed symbols. For example, reading rate is slowed when reading at night with weak batteries in a flashlight, when reading fuzzy xerox copy, and when reading poor handwriting. Under adverse stimulus conditions, the rauding process continues to operate, often just as successfully as under optimal presentation conditions, but at a rate slower than the rauding rate, R_r.

In this chapter, research on various textual presentation conditions will be reviewed. Not reviewed, however, will be the vast amount of research relevant to printing; this is research that has varied type face, line width, and brightness contrast between print and paper. After giving 66,062 reading tests to 33,031 subjects over a period of 12 years, Patterson and Tinker (1940) were able to provide guidelines for printing any material. Tinker's book, entitled *Legibility of Print* (1963), has been referred to in journalism (Bostian, 1976) as "the bible of legibility research" (p. 328). The following review will concentrate on research that reflects the degree to which reading rate can be affected by the nature of variations in the text, exclusive of the traditional printing choices associated with type face, line width, ink, and paper.

It will be helpful to conceive of a standard presentation, such as a typewritten text using the American Psychological Association (APA) style manual standards. This APA standard requires upper and lower case using 10 or 12 spaces per inch (pica or elite) with a line width of 5-1/2 in and a maximum of 25 lines per page without right-justified margins. From this point on, this normal typewritten copy for manuscripts, which is familiar to most researchers, will be referred to as the standard for comparison purposes. It is assumed that most of the research that has been reviewed so far has used either the standard or some other printed version that is comparable or equivalent.

RESEARCH

Tinker and Patterson (1928) found that reading all capitals (upper case) was about 12% slower than the standard format that contains both upper and lower case letters. Thus, it appears that using all upper case text slows reading rate about 12% below the standard text. However, their research was based upon how fast they completed items on a reading test so the 12% result may not generalize to Wpm for a normally operating rauding process.

North and Jenkins (1951) investigated the effect of grouping words on a page into what they called "thought units." They put extra spaces between phrases that were three and four words long within a sentence. Their subjects read for 2 min, and the spaced unit text was read about 11% faster than the standard, 247 wpm versus 222 wpm; the accuracy scores on the comprehension test were about equal, 87% versus 85%. However, the 222 wpm rate for the university freshmen is a bit too low to be sure that these subjects were operating their rauding process. This rate is about average for students in grade 10 (see Table 2.1). It is more likely that they were using a learning process, Gear 2, and it seems possible that separating the sentences into thought units would help them answer the questions. There was about 1 question every 50 words but the nature of this "objective test" was not described. This research does not provide support for the hypothesis that chunking sentences into meaningful phrases increases rauding rate because it seemed to involve a learning process.

Klare, Nichols, and Shuford (1957) used a spacing technique similar to that of North and Jenkins, described above, but they could not replicate the North and Jenkins results. They used a 1206-word technical passage dealing with an aircraft engine, and their 533 subjects were military airmen. Subjects read the standard at 161 wpm, and the spaced unit text was read more slowly at 156 wpm. The ability level of these subjects was not measured, but given the fact that they had to answer a multiple-choice question over every 24 words of text, on the average, it would seem that these low rates probably reflect a learning process rather than the rauding process. Thus, this research does not even provide replicative support for the earlier hypothesis that separating sentences into thought units increases the rate at which a learning process can successfully operate.

Coleman and Kim (1961) investigated several different ways of presenting words on a page in an effort to improve upon the conventional
or standard format. Altogether, there were eight separate experiments
involving a total of 267 college students. To investigate the effect of spacing between meaningful groups of words within sentences they used
1500-word passages selected from Woodworth's (1938) *Experimental Psychology;* a 25-item test was administered after each reading. There were
three spaced formats: space between clauses, space between grammatical
units, and space between phrases. No information was given about how
these college students were instructed to read. However, the standard
format was read the fastest at 260 wpm, which is the expected rauding
rate of college freshmen (see Table 2.1). So, it would be reasonable to
infer that they were inducing the rauding process in spite of the difficulty of the material and the extensiveness or density of the testing (1
test item for each 60 words). All three of the spaced formats were read
at 261 wpm, and the mean comprehension scores for all four conditions
ranged only from 13.2 to 14.0. These results were not supportive of the
hypothesis that setting off meaningful units within a sentence would improve rate or the accuracy of comprehension during a rauding process.
Coleman and Kim also investigated several vertical formats, such as a
short phrase on each line. Again, no information was given about instructions but the standard format was still read the fastest, 260 wpm.
So, it appears reasonable to assume from the 260 wpm rate for the standard that the students were using their rauding process, and the vertical
format was detrimental to the rate at which the rauding process operated. Coleman and Kim also conducted some of their experiments using
a tachistoscope. They reported that in these experiments the vertical formats were superior to the standard format. However, in a series of three
subsequent experiments using the most promising vertical format that
involved one word per line, Coleman and Hahn (1966) concluded that:
"Coleman and Kim's (1961) finding that vertical typography might be
superior to conventional was not replicated in three studies that used
several samples of *S*s, several samples of reading material, several methods of presentation and several measures of reading efficiency" (p. 436).
So, this research does not support the idea that a format setting off
meaningful units will speed up an individual's rauding rate.

F. Smith (1969) investigated the effect of disrupting standard text by
using various letter combinations. He used a 150-word passage typed in
six different styles and given to six groups of 15 different adults. They
were asked to read aloud at their "normal reading speed," and there
were no "special instructions with respect to reading speed" (p. 261). No
description of the difficulty of the text was given so it will be assumed

that it was relatively easy, $A_L > D_L$. The "normal reading speed" instruction would probably induce a Performance Oral Reading Rate, i.e., PORR, as defined in Chapter 14. The standard text was read at 170 wpm and the upper case text was read at 169 wpm, essentially equal rates and seemingly contrary to the findings of Tinker and Patterson (1928), noted earlier. However, it seems reasonable that the slow reading rate associated with reading aloud under PORR or RORR conditions may allow the capitals to be recognized 13% more slowly without affecting PORR. This is because this process may have a speed limit that is associated with how fast the words can be pronounced for a good oral rendition. By analogy, suppose I am a 90 Wpm typist but I have to slow to 50 Wpm when typing from one of those devices where people read words as they appear, move across a screen, and then disappear. My typing would be limited by the rate of the input stimulus, not my own rate. The material could be presented in handwritten form without noticing any effects because I could still keep up with the 50 Wpm rate. However, if you asked me to go at my maximum rate, you could probably detect a difference between the handwritten and typewritten textual stimulus upon my rate. Similarly, this research of Smith's which used PORR as a criterion may completely explain why he got no difference between the standard and upper case.

In two of the other textual presentations used by Smith, the letters in the words were switched between upper and lower case (but the ascenders of lowercase letters were readily discriminable). These two conditions were read at the same rate as the standard, 171 and 169 wpm. Thus, four of the six conditions varied only from 169 to 171 wpm. In the remaining two conditions, the ascenders of lower case were not discriminable and rate was slowed to 155 and 135 wpm. Smith interpreted these results as indicating that they did not support ". . . a traditional theory of reading that the total configuration of a word is the dominant cue for word identification" (p. 261). Yet it seems unlikely that Smith would have found his fastest four conditions varying only 2 Wpm if he had used MORR as his measure, or some measure of R_r. Thus, it appears likely that Smith's finding that three unusual combinations of upper and lower case were read just as fast as the standard was probably due to his inducing a reading process other than the rauding process. If he had chosen an experimental procedure designed to induce the rauding process, instead of a "normal" oral rate, it seems likely that he would not have found that all upper case text was read as fast as the standard.

Poulton (1969) compared all capitals with the standard format. Adults were given 90 sec to read 450-word passages of unknown difficulty; they were given "10 open-end questions on each passage to test for comprehension" (p. 245). There were 60 good readers and 66 poor readers; they were compared on three different passages and tests, one-half of each group was given all capitals and one-half was given the standard format. It is not known what instructions were given but the rate required to finish the passages was 300 wpm so it seems reasonable to assume that the rauding process was used. In this study where time was held constant, the number of questions answered correctly is an indicator of efficiency. For the good readers, there was no consistent advantage for the standard format. However, for the poor readers there was a consistent advantage; the advantages for the three tests were 11%, 12%, and 26%. Thus, the original 12% advantage of the standard format over the all-capitals format reported in 1928 by Tinker and Patterson was replicated for poor reading adults but not good reading adults.

Carver (1970) studied the effect of chunking (grouping) words into meaningful phrases using extra spaces between chunks. In a series of three different experiments, he gave college students passages from the Nelson–Denny Reading Test typed in various chunked formats. In Experiment 3, he paid 70 subjects bonuses for correct answers while taking the Nelson–Denny test using a machine that allowed a maximum of 6 min for reading passages but unlimited time for answering questions. There were three textual presentations, chunked, newspaper, and no capitalization. In the chunked condition, there was one chunk per line, as in the example which follows:

> The night was cloudy,
> and a drizzling rain,
> which fell without intermission,
> added to the obscurity.

In the newspaper condition, the same material was presented in a newspaper column format with a justified right margin. In the no-capitalization format, all the punctuation was removed, including all capitalization of words, all commas, and all periods. In this latter format, there were no typographical cues marking the beginning or endings of sentences.

Carver found that the chunked format was not read any faster than the newspaper format, 291 and 292 wpm, respectively. The percentage of comprehension questions answered correctly using the chunked format was slightly lower than for the newspaper format, about 70 and 74%, respectively. The above rates of reading for college students were around 300 Wpm so the rauding process was probably used (see Tables 2.1 and 2.2). Therefore, these data suggest that spatially grouping words into meaningful phrase units within a sentence does not increase the rauding rate over that for the standard text. However, when the spatial cues for grouping words into sentences were removed, reading rate dropped 14% and comprehension scores were 20% lower, compared to the newspaper format. If a newspaper format is assumed to be roughly equivalent to the standard, then it seems that the spatial cues for grouping words into sentences are very helpful, since rauding rate dropped 14% and comprehension dropped 20% when these cues were removed. However, the attempt to add cues for the meaningful grouping of words within a sentence had no positive effect upon the rate at which the rauding process operated.

Gregory and Poulton (1970) investigated the effect of a right-justified margin. They gave a constant amount of time to read so that the number of comprehension questions that were answered correctly became an indicator of reading rate; the comprehension questions were evenly spaced across the passage. The time limits were chosen so that most of their adult subjects would get through about half of a passage and thereby answer about 50% of the questions correctly. On the basis of a selection test, the subjects were grouped into five levels of ability, A, B, C, D, and E. The best readers, groups A and B, showed no consistent tendency to be hurt or helped by the right justification. However, group C showed about a 10% decrement for the right justification. For groups D and E, Gregory and Poulton widened the average line width from the 4.5 inch used in groups A, B, and C to 11.8 inch. With this line width, they found no disadvantage of the right justification for the poorer readers. They concluded that with shorter line width, the right-justified margin sometimes produces spacing that is disruptive to the poorer reading adults.

Ehri and Wilce (1974) investigated the effect of spatial cues that involved the use of three different sizes of words. They gave four different textual presentations to 40 third graders and 40 fourth graders, with 10 students per format. Their standard format was regular print in medium size. For their "intoned" format, the size of the word varied with the ". . . levels of pitch and stress which might be assigned by a person reading the story aloud" (p. 170). In the "form class" format, noun phrases and pronouns were printed in the largest size, relative pronouns in the smallest size, and all the other words were printed in the medium size. For the "random form" format, the three word sizes were randomly assigned to the words. Their subjects were tested individually. They were given a practice passage first. After each page of the practice, ". . . the experimenter presented comprehension questions to the child to insure that they paid attention to the story's meaning" (p. 170). Before the experimental passage was administered "the child was to read this story to himself, and he was warned that afterwards he would be asked some questions about it" (p. 271). The children were all above the 50th percentile rank on a standardized reading test.

Ehri and Wilce gave examples of the different formats using a 63-word excerpt from the 510-word passage, and this example was used to calculate cpw so that the mean time results they reported could be translated into Wpm using the equations in Chapter 2. The average reading rates for all 40 third graders and all 40 fourth graders were 127 Wpm and 152 Wpm, respectively. These two rates are very close to the rauding rates expected of third and fourth graders (135 and 149 Wpm, respectively, from Appendix B). For the third graders, the standard format group read the slowest, 112 Wpm. However, on the 21 short-answer questions given after reading, this standard group had the highest score. The intoned group of third graders had the fastest rate, 157 Wpm. For the fourth graders, the standard format was again read the slowest, 144 Wpm. The intoned format was read faster at 167 Wpm. But, the fastest rate was for the random format, and it also had the highest comprehension score means. Ehri and Wilce interpreted these results as being in accordance with their hypothesis that third graders are more affected by the relationship between speech and reading and that was why third graders read the intoned format the fastest but fourth graders did not.

There is another way to interpret the above data that seems more plausible. The differences among the reading rates were probably due to sampling errors associated with a small sample size, $N = 10$, and large variability. The standard deviations were not reported so it is impossible to calculate the standard errors associated with these means. This latter hypothesis explains why the random format was read at a rate that was 25 Wpm (16%) faster than the standard format. Assuming the validity of the sampling error hypothesis, the rates and comprehension scores were averaged across the two grades to provide more reliable means. In this situation, their standard format was still read the slowest, 128 Wpm, and the intoned format was still read the fastest, 156 Wpm. However, the random format was read at 150 Wpm, only 4% slower than the intoned. The comprehension means were trivially different except the form class format was lower than the others. It does not seem reasonable to consider these data as providing evidence that changing the size of words to reflect their pitch and stress when read aloud will increase reading rate 40% in third graders but have little or no effect on fourth graders. Instead, it seems more reasonable to interpret these data as too unreliable to be interpreted as support for an hypothesis that the rauding rate of third graders and below can be increased using this type of print that is intoned by word size.

Bassin and Martin (1976) investigated the effect of three schemes of deleting words from prose, hypothesizing that ". . . there is some word redundancy which serves to make a sentence grammatically correct but does not contribute substantially to the understanding of the sentence" (p. 649). In essence, they were hypothesizing that a considerable number of words can be deleted from the sentences of published material with no loss in their comprehension. A 2217-word passage at the college level of difficulty was presented after deleting 10, 30, or 50% of the words by frequency, grammatical, and subjective methods. Under the frequency method, each word in the passage was ranked according to the number of times it was used in the passage, and then the words ranked at the top were deleted first (such as the, of, and a). Under the grammatical method, the least important grammatical categories were deleted first, in order of prepositions, articles, adverbs, conjunctions, pronouns, adjectives, verbs, and nouns. For example, in the 50% category of reduction, all of the words in the first five categories were eliminated, leaving 50% of the adjectives, 100% of the verbs, and 100% of the nouns. Under the subjective method, 10 college students rank-ordered the words in each sentence in terms of ". . . each word's contribution in conveying the intended meaning of the sentence" (p. 650). Then, the words were put into three levels within a sentence and the reduction scheme eliminated words starting with the least important levels.

After Bassin and Martin had determined which words should be eliminated, the passages were retyped without leaving any clues as to where a word had been deleted. Three levels of reduction, 10%, 30%, and 50%, for three methods of reduction, frequency, grammatical, and subjective, gave nine different passage types. These were administered to each of nine different groups of college students ranging in size from 18 to 22. The tenth group was administered the passage in its original form. A 32-item, four-alternative, multiple-choice test was administered afterwards. Subjects were told that ". . . some of the passages had words deleted from them but that they were to read at their normal reading rate," and that they should *not* ". . . reread any portion of the passage and to record the elapsed time when they finished reading the passage" (p. 650). These instructions sound as if they should have induced the rauding process. However, the objective consequences evidently were not consonant with the instructions because the low scores on the test (17% to 46%) plus the low reading rates (103 to 208 wpm) leave little doubt that these college students were mostly engaged in a learning process or even a recalling process (see Table 2.2). So, Bassin and Martin did not appear to study the effect of these redundancy deletion schemes upon the rauding process, as their instructions seemed to suggest that they wanted to do.

For each of the 10 groups, Bassin and Martin provided the mean and SD for the number of multiple-choice questions answered correctly, reading rate in wpm, and reading time in minutes. For example, the 50% frequency reduction group had a mean of 13.81 items answered correctly, a mean rate of 109.18 wpm, and a mean reading time of 11.00 min. Reading rate for the reduced passages was based upon the time taken for the total words remaining in the passage, i.e., only about 1108 for the 50% reduction. An eleventh group was administered the 32-item test without first reading the passage and they answered a mean of 10.00 items correctly. This 10.00 bottom for the test (instead of the usual chance bottom of one-fourth of 32, or 8.00), was used to develop a correction for guessing formula to convert all of the test scores into an accuracy of comprehension percentage. For example, the 13.81 score given above, was recalculated by Bassin and Martin into a 17% comprehension score.

Bassin and Martin found that under the original passage condition, i.e., no words were deleted, there was a 46% comprehension score, a 208 wpm rate, and a reading time of 11.35 min. All of the nine reduction conditions resulted in rates lower than this standard, ranging from 103 to 188 wpm; they also resulted in lower accuracy of comprehension, ranging from 17% to 45%. In general, the more words cut out of a passage, the lower the accuracy of comprehension. The subjective reduction was clearly the superior of the three reduction schemes, and the 10% condition was the superior of the three levels of reduction. Under this 10% condition, comprehension was 1% less than the standard (45%) and the total time taken was also 1% higher (11.50 min). So, the best of nine redundancy schemes was still inferior to reading the passage in its original unreduced form. For all three reduction schemes, the 30% and 50% reduction had lower comprehension scores and higher total reading times, leaving little doubt as to their inferiority.

From the data reviewed above, it seems safe to conclude that deleting words from sentences is harmful to the successful operation of a learning process, Gear 2, and that more words deleted will be more harmful. Deleting only words that are judged to be least harmful is likely to have little effect if this involves only about 10% of the total words. Yet, there would seem to be no good reason to do this except to make the point that subjects are able to answer almost the same number of multiple-choice questions after executing a learning process. The more important theoretical point to be made is that ordinarily there are few if any unnecessary words in the sentences of edited published materials, and deleting any of these words without rewriting will have an adverse effect upon the time required to understand the sentences. The rauding process ordinarily needs to operate on every word in a sentence in order to operate successfully at its typically high rate. The 10% subjective reduction in the present study appeared to have a small adverse effect upon a learning process (operating in the more powerful second gear) but this adverse effect would likely grow in size under the execution of the rauding process (operating in the less powerful but faster and more typical third gear).

The above interpretations of these data are at odds with the interpretations of Bassin and Martin. They concluded that "the objective reduction methods yielded promising results at lower reduction levels for future mechanical abridgement of prose" (p. 649). This conclusion was based upon their interpretation that ". . . regardless of the method of reduction, comprehension as measured by the multiple-choice test was not significantly impaired at 10% and 30% reduction levels when compared to performance of these subjects reading the original version" (p. 652). Notice the words "not significantly impaired." This means that they conducted a test of statistical significance and found no statistically significant difference so they concluded that the difference was not important. There are several problems with this interpretation and their earlier conclusion that follows from it. First, it is an example of the corrupt form of the scientific method that Carver (1978b) warned about; important differences will not be statistically significant when the sample size is low in relationship to the variability involved, and unimportant differences will be statistically significant if the sample size is large in relationship to the variability involved. Second, it is an example of a common pitfall involving the testing of statistical significance between points on a functional relationship (see Lindquist, 1953); in any functional relationship, such as this one where comprehension scores decline with each higher percentage of words deleted, any pair of differences along the curve will be found to be statistically nonsignificant if the distance between the points on the horizontal axis is made small enough. Third, concluding there is no difference from a failure to find a statistically significant difference is ordinarily considered wrong even by those who endorse statistical significance testing.

It should be noted that this Bassin and Martin (1976) research was a follow up to an earlier and smaller study by C. J. Martin and Herndon

(1972) who compared an original passage condition to a 10% and 30% deletion scheme. The original passage was read at 217 wpm so this research also involved a learning process. Even the 10% deletion was detrimental: reading time increased 39%, reading rate decreased 20%, and the number of comprehension questions answered correctly dropped 10%. However, because of a failure to find statistically significant differences, it was concluded that "The results demonstrated that it was possible to randomly delete 10% of the words from the experimental passage without significantly decreasing comprehension . . ." (p. 33).

Given the above evidence and argument, it seems reasonable to conclude what we should have known all along. All of these words that authors struggle over when writing sentences, and editors struggle over when reading them, are in fact needed when operating a learning process, Gear 2. They are needed even more for the rauding process, Gear 3, to operate successfully at the rauding rate, which is faster than a learning process. Those who have urged readers to skip over redundant and unnecessary words, or even eliminate them, have formulated this advice from theoretical ideas that have not had the backing of solid empirical evidence relevant to typical reading.

Patberg and Yonas (1978) studied the perceptual span of 32 good and poor reading eighth graders, and 32 skilled reading adults. They compared a standard text with a wide-spaced text where 13 character spaces had been inserted between words. For each condition (standard and wide-spaced), they used four 312-word passages, two at the 5–6 grade level of difficulty and two at 11–12. After subjects read a passage, Patberg and Yonas administered ten multiple-choice questions with four alternative answers. They instructed their subjects to "read the passages as quickly as you can, but also carefully, so you will be able to answer questions about the passage" (p. 548). They gave their subjects two practice passages and tests to familiarize them with the two modes of presentation and with the type of questions. These directions and this task are ambiguous with respect to predicting whether a learning process or the rauding process would be induced. The reading rates that resulted were also ambiguous. The skilled adults, graduate students, read the standard text formats at 262 and 249 Wpm, for the easy and difficult passages, respectively. These rates suggest that some of these adults were using their rauding process and others were using a learning process (see Tables 2.1 and 2.2).

The results of Patberg and Yonas were presented as mean reading times in seconds and mean number of items correct. These data have been converted into estimated Wpm and percentage accuracy of comprehension to aid interpretation later. For the eighth grade good readers and the adult good readers, the wide-spaced text slowed their reading rate 22–24% for both the easy and hard passages; comprehension remained relatively constant (within 2–5% of the standard). This result again reflects the tendency of readers to slow a reading process when the stimulus is not standard, but to keep the accuracy of the process at the same level.

In this research, the wide spacing between words, 13 characters of blank space between words, had a dramatic slowing effect upon the process for these two groups of good readers (22–24% decrement). For the poor reading eighth graders, however, the wide spread words *improved* their rate 7% for the easy passages and 12% for the hard passages while improving their comprehension scores 13% and 11%, respectively. The standard text obviously was not the optimal text for these poor readers. It appears that some form of wide-spaced words helps poor readers, although it is not clear from this particular research exactly what population this sample of poor readers represents.

Patberg and Yonas interpreted the above results as yielding support for their hypothesis that ". . . as reading skill improves, the perceptual span increases beyond a single word" (p. 550). But they also recognized two alternative hypotheses. First, it could be that the ability of the skilled readers to recode words into memory in phrases is disrupted by the widely spaced words. Second, they reported a personal communication from M. Posner who hypothesized that the skilled readers might be disrupted more ". . . by any change in the task requiring a modification of well-practiced techniques" (p. 551). This second hypothesis is very much in accordance with the apping hypothesis introduced earlier in Chapter 9. If skilled readers have an automatic pilot type of rauding process where the eyes habitually move down the standard line at a distance and rate commensurate with the internal articulation of the words being recognized, then spreading the words this far apart could greatly hamper these habitual eye movements. There seems to be no doubt that putting 13 spaces in front of and behind such words as *the, of, and,* would eliminate their perception during a fixation upon other adjacent words, thereby increasing reading time. However, this perceptual span effect may account for only a small part of the 22–24% decrement in rauding rate. The apping hypothesis seems more potent, as Posner seems to be suggesting.

Patberg and Yonas also point out that there was no evidence that the size of the perceptual span becomes larger for easier materials and shorter for harder materials because the wider spacing had almost exactly the same effect for easy materials as it did for hard. Instead, they contended that the perceptual span was more likely to be a stable characteristic of a reader that only changes ". . . with the gradual increase in reading skill rather than under the influence of variations in the difficulty of the text being read" (p. 551). This interpretation is quite compatible with the lack of empirical support for difficulty flexibility, pointed out in Chapter 10. Indeed, their data provide support for the constancy of rauding rate across material difficulty; the difference in rates for the 5–6 and 11–12 grade materials was only 5–6% for the two groups of skilled readers (262–249 Wpm for the adults and 200–188 Wpm for the good reading eighth grade readers). Patberg and Yonas conclude their report by noting that their data provide ". . . no support for F. Smith's (1971) contention that decreasing speed by reading one word at a time overloads short term memory and impairs comprehension" because the widely spaced words ". . . produced no change in the comprehension of high-ability readers and it improved the comprehension of low-ability readers" (p. 551).

In summary, the Patberg and Yonas research can be interpreted as providing evidence that textual presentations using widely spaced words (a) slows the rauding process rate more than 20% for good readers, and (b) speeds up the rate and increases the accuracy of the rauding process for poor readers. Left in doubt, at this point, are the boundaries for describing the two populations to be included in "good readers" and "poor readers." It seems likely that the normal spacing of a standard text allows the rauding rate to be optimal for good readers but it is not clear whether this is solely due to the advantages afforded by more information being included within the perceptional span, or whether it has more to do with the habitual eye movements, called apping.

Frase and Schwartz (1979) investigated the effect of spatial cues and concluded that their "meaningful segmentation plus indentation" resulted in 14–18% faster rates than the standard format. Their format was very similar to the chunked format used by Carver (1970), and illustrated earlier in this chapter. However, their task involved searching a technical passage for the answer to a true/false question. For example, in their first experiment they gave their subjects, who were college graduates, a 279-word passage on equipment components, and the mean time they reported for the standard format was 27.71 sec which is 604 wpm. Thus, it is readily apparent from this very high rate that the reading process being employed was not the rauding process. It seems easy to concede that scanning a technical manual for target information and then deciding whether the prequestion is true or false could be facilitated 14–18% by this chunking format. However, this does not mean that it will increase the rate the passage can be rauded. Furthermore,

Hartley (1980) designed a replication study of Frase and Schwartz but could not replicate the superiority of their spatial cueing technique.

In 1980, Matthews, Coon, and Rosenthal used standard text plus the same text with 20 spaces between words, syllables, or letters. They asked students in each of grades 1–6 to read aloud all of these four textual presentations. The instructions given to these students were not reported so it is impossible to know whether the rates reported were MORR, PORR, or RORR, as defined in Chapter 14. It was possible to estimate Wpm because the passages used were at grade level for the students in that grade. Amazingly, the fifth and sixth graders read the standard text slower (102 and 92 Wpm, respectively) than the second graders (112 Wpm). According to the grade equivalents presented in Appendix B of this book, these fifth and sixth graders were reading aloud at the silent rauding rate of first graders. Since it is impossible even to estimate the process used and since the rates obtained do not consistently increase with grade level, it seems questionable to try to make any generalizations from these data about textual presentation.

Potter, Kroll, and Harris (1980) used Forster's (1970) rapid serial visual presentation (RSVP) to study rate and comprehension. This technique involves the presentation of textual material one word at a time, or a few words at a time, in the same position on a screen; the eyes remain fixated in the same position while the words change rapidly in the serial order of the text. The passages were relatively easy for the subjects and they were told that "they would do better if they just attempted to understand the paragraph rather than trying to 'memorize' it during presentation" (p. 403). Afterwards they were asked to write down everything they could remember and the recalls were scored in idea units. Three rates of presentation were used, 240 wpm, 480 wpm, and 720 wpm. Although the task required verbatim recall, the subjects had no control over the rate and it does seem likely that they would be attempting to operate their rauding process as directed. They also compared RSVP to the following: (a) reading a standard format for equivalent lengths of time, and (b) listening to tape recorded versions of the passages at the 240 wpm rate. The total number of idea units recalled under the 240 wpm condition was almost exactly the same under the RSVP and the standard format, as well as the listening condition. After this series of three experiments, Potter et al. concluded that (a) "the similarity in recall for all three modes suggests that a major determinant of memory is the processing that occurs at a level beyond modality-specific language mechanisms" (p. 413), (b) a very important determinant of reading rate is the time needed to stabilize the material in memory, and

(c) "the processing of each sentence is influenced by the higher-order structure already developed, so that the sentence is incorporated directly ·into the growing text structure as it is processed, not afterward" (p. 401), and (d) "the semantic and syntactic processing take place word by word and phrase by phrase following closely on the heels of presentation as the sentence permits" (p. 414).

These results suggest that the presentation of passages using the RSVP technique is just as good but no better than the standard format, i.e., RSVP does not increase the rate of rauding. These results and interpretations provide support for the ideas of rauding theory that (a) reading and auding involve a similar rauding process and (b) the major factor limiting rauding rate is the cognitive speed of the individual because a certain amount of time is required for each consecutive word of a sentence to be integrated into the complete thought.

A. J. Campbell, Marchetti, and Mewhort (1981) studied the effect of right justification using two types: extra space between words or extra space within words. They gave college students a passage from a children's encyclopedia that contained 442 standard length words. They administered a ten-question comprehension test afterwards that was not described in any detail. They told their subjects that they were interested in "how quickly and accurately" the subjects could read the text. The description of the instructions and objective consequences were too ambiguous to predict the most likely process that the subjects used. However, the mean reading rates varied from 160 to 209 Wpm and the percentage comprehension scores varied from 71 to 81 so it appears that a learning process was used (see Table 2.2).

The Campbell et al. results were presented for five groups that varied in size from 25 to 33. One group read the standard text at 160 Wpm with a 78% comprehension score. The other four groups were divided into Experiment 1 and Experiment 2, with each of the two forms of right justification being presented in each experiment. All four of the right justification groups read faster than the standard text group. However, the two groups that read the fastest, 209 and 180 Wpm, also had the lowest comprehension scores, 76 and 71%. In order to better compare the five groups, their data were reanalyzed using an effective reading rate score. It was calculated by multiplying the percentage comprehension score (expressed as a proportion) by the rate in Wpm; this effective reading rate score has been used by M. D. Jackson and McClelland (1979) and is a correlate of E, efficiency of comprehension. These efficiency indices were all approximately equal for the following three groups: the standard text, 125 Wpm; extra space between words in Experiment 1, 127 Wpm; and extra space between words in Experiment 2,

133 Wpm. The two groups that received the extra spacing within words were more efficient, 159 Wpm in Experiment 1 and 144 Wpm in Experiment 2. These data suggest that the extra space within words can be read about 20% more effectively than either standard text or the regular method for producing right-justified margins. Right justification usually involves leaving the spacing between the letters within words exactly the same but adding extra space between words. This new method of right justification leaves one space between words but adds microspacing between the letters within words.

It is not clear why extra spaces between letters, within words, would increase the efficiency of the learning process around 20%, compared to the standard or the regular method of producing right-justified margins. Campbell *et al.* gave examples of all three forms of the text they used and the difference between the two forms of right justification is not apparent upon first glance. How a difference that is so unapparent could have such a pronounced effect is a small mystery. Campbell *et al.* suggested that the eye movement control mechanism may base its prediction about where to shift the fixation point on the spatial predictability of successive words, so the slower rate of the regular method can be explained by the erratic movements it requires due to the variable space between words. This kind of an explanation would seem to give support to the existence of apping, the habitual eye movements discussed in Chapter 9. However, in order for this kind of explanation to make sense, the regular justification would have to be less efficient than the standard, and it was not.

The above data point toward two drastically different interpretations. Taken at face value, they suggest that the efficiency of learning processes can be greatly improved, by around 20%, simply by switching from a standard text to a right-justified text that adds space between the letters of words, instead of space between the words as does the regular method of right justification. Furthermore, acceptance of the reality of this improvement puts a tremendous load upon theoreticians and experimentalists to explain why such a seemingly small spatial change should have such a large impact. The second interpretation is that these data are externally invalid for some unknown reason and cannot be replicated. It seems prudent to accept the latter interpretation until forced to do otherwise by subsequent data and theory.

Kolers, Duchnicky, and Ferguson (1981) used eye movements and total reading time to study various textual presentations on a cathode ray tube (CRT) screen. They asked 20 college students to read 300-word passages that seemed to be around college level in difficulty as judged from the examples given; the following excerpted sentence reflects their difficulty level: "It is not possible to lay psychological phenomena end to end or put them in a scale pan—to add them in the familiar sense that lengths or weights can be added—whence it is necessary to invent new procedures that differ from, but are logically equivalent to, the operations of physical measurement" (p. 520). After each of the 20 passages had been read, 20 questions were presented and subjects had to tap a key answering yes or no as to whether the question was answerable from the information in the passage. No information was given about the instructions given to the subjects so it can be assumed that the objective consequences forced a choice among reading processes. The subjects correctly answered 88% of the questions; 50% would be chance. From the difficulty level of the material and the nature of the task it would be reasonable to predict that a learning process would be used, and this prediction was confirmed by the 204 wpm overall reading rate, the average wpm rate of students in grade 8 (see Table 2.1).

Kolers *et al.* found a trivial difference between single spacing (202 wpm) and double spacing (206 wpm). They found a larger and more important difference between an 80-character line (221 wpm) and a 40-character line (189 wpm). Their main purpose was to study the scrolling of the page, and they concluded that "the data suggest that people read a static page more efficiently than a page scrolled at their preferred rate" (p. 525). It should not be generalized from these results that rate of rauding can be increased by an 80-character line or that single spacing has no detrimental effect on rauding rate, because this research involved a learning process, Gear 2, not the rauding process, Gear 3.

Juola, Ward, and McNamara (1982) extended Forster's (1970) RSVP technique to the study of reading for comprehension. As noted earlier, this technique involves presentation of textual material either one word at a time, or a few words at a time, in the same position on a screen so that the eyes remain fixated in the same position while the words change rapidly in the serial order of the text. In one of their studies, they used the McCall–Crabbs passages (D_L = 7–8) and in the other they used Nelson–Denny passages (D_L = 9–10). All passages were presented via a computer terminal. In the standard text, a full page of text appeared on the screen for varying lengths of time. In the RSVP condition, the words were presented under two different duration conditions, 200 or 300 msec, and three different window size conditions, 5, 10, or 15 character spaces, on the average, yielding a total of six separate average rates for both the McCall–Crabbs and the Nelson–Denny passages. After the passage had been presented, four multiple-choice questions were presented, each with four alternatives. Subjects were given practice passages and test items under the various conditions. Under the standard text presentation, the passages were preceded with the following instructions: (a) "read normally" when the rate required to finish the passage was 201–205 Wpm, (b) "read rapidly" when the rate was 308–314 Wpm, and (c) "read very rapidly" when the rate was 658–676 Wpm. (Note: Wpm was estimated using difficulty levels and the equations in Chapter 2.) These instructions and objective consequences would seem to involve (a) a learning process under the read normally condition, (b) the rauding process under the read rapidly condition, and (c) a scanning process under the read very rapidly condition. However, it is possible and even likely that the subjects would try to operate their rauding process at all three rates because it might produce the most successful results on the comprehension tests.

In general, the results obtained by Juola *et al.* indicated that the RSVP textual presentation was comparable to the standard. For the McCall–Crabbs passages and tests, the 10-character window and 300 msec duration produced a rate of 335 Wpm and an accuracy of comprehension score of 40%; this was slightly better than the standard condition rate of 314 Wpm and 37%. The corresponding values for the Nelson–Denny were 318 Wpm with 53% accuracy of comprehension for RSVP, and 308 Wpm with 63% for the standard. So, under rates comparable to the rauding process, RSVP was a little better than the standard for the McCall–Crabbs and a little worse than the standard for the Nelson–Denny. Under the rates comparable to a learning process and using the McCall–Crabbs passages, the RSVP yielded 37% accuracy of comprehension at 205 Wpm and the standard yielded 44% at 205 Wpm. Using the Nelson–Denny passages, the RSVP yielded 74% accuracy of comprehension at 201 Wpm and the standard yielded 73% at 201 Wpm. Again, the differences between RSVP and the standard appear to be trivial for a learning process rate. Under rates comparable to a scanning process and using the McCall–Crabbs passages, the RSVP yielded 23% accuracy of comprehension at 676 Wpm and the standard yielded 29% at 658 Wpm. With the Nelson–Denny passages, the RSVP yielded 34% accuracy of comprehension at 658 Wpm and the standard yielded 29% at 658 Wpm. Again, these differences between the RSVP and the standard for a scanning process rate seem to be trivial.

These Juola *et al.* data were reanalyzed by plotting them on a graph with msec per standard length word on the horizontal axis. Percentage comprehension increased in a linear fashion as time per word increased, up until the rauding rate is reached, around 200 msec/Word. Then, accuracy of comprehension leveled off, just as would be predicted from rauding theory (see Chapter 2) except the function was more erratic at the fastest rates, possibly indicating unreliability of the McCall–Crabbs passage as the scores approach chance levels on the tests. But, there was no consistent superiority of either the standard or the RSVP.

The comparability of RSVP to the standard presentation of text, has practical implications for computerized displays of sentential information. These results also have major theoretical implications. For example, some eye movement researchers, such as Just and Carpenter (1980), have assumed that individuals automatically vary their fixation durations and locations in a way that gives clues about cognitive processing based on the varying importance or function of the words within a sentence. Yet, the data reviewed above indicate that a fixed amount of time spent on each word has little or no effect upon the success of the rauding process. Stated differently, these data from the use of the RSVP technique suggest that during the execution of the rauding process, readers do not need to weight some words or some sentences higher than others in of spending more time on the more important units. These data give no support to those researchers dealing with the structure of text who have theorized that ordinary reading somehow involves (or should involve) more attention or processing on higher order words or sentences. Instead, these data support the tenets of rauding theory which hold that individuals read on mostly a word for word basis that involves a constant rate in letters, syllables, or standard length words per minute. *Forcing individuals to read word for word with no eye movements had no detrimental effect, which suggests that individuals have learned to move their eyes, habitually, in a manner that makes the rauding process operate at maximum efficiency of comprehension, as is contended in rauding theory.*

It seems that this RSVP technique, discussed above, could be used to determine whether the rauding process during reading is mainly driven visually by character spaces or subvocally by syllables. If a word is presented on the screen at the rauding rate of individuals in terms of character spaces per second, and this produces higher comprehension than presenting the words at their rauding rate in terms of syllables per second, then this would suggest that eye movements during the rauding process were probably being visually driven rather than by rate of silent speech.

Foster and Bruce (1982) studied the difference between words in lower case versus upper case as text is presented on television screens. A screen full of randomly ordered words was presented to 40 students of "above-average competence," and their task was to read aloud the words as fast as possible, i.e., a random word version of MORR was the measure used (see Chapter 14). There were six different passages read by each subject, 20 for the lower case and 20 for upper case. The first passage was read more slowly than the subsequent five in each group, 131 and

130 Wpm for the lower and upper case, respectively. (Note: An example of one of the experimental passages containing 105 Words was presented, and this word count was used to estimate all of the Wpm values.) The remaining five passages were all read at almost exactly the same rate in each of the two conditions: lower: M = 143 Wpm, SD = 1.7; upper M = 139 Wpm, SD = 1.9. In summary, the upper case was read about 3% more slowly than the lower case when the measure was MORR for skilled readers reading randomly ordered words. This finding of no decrement for upper case is not consistent with research reviewed earlier. However, the measure was MORR for randomly ordered words and this measure may or may not be generalizable to the rauding process.

Muter, Latremouille, Treurniet, and Beam (1982) compared reading a book with reading the same material on a television screen when reading for a two hour duration. The textual material was 47 short stories all written by the same author and published in a single volume. Half of the 32 subjects read this material in its original printed form in the book and the other half read the material on a television (TV) screen. Under the TV condition, subjects initiated requests for new pages by pressing a key on a hand-held key pad. The subjects were told that their comprehension and reading rate would be measured but that they should try to read the stories as they would if they were reading them for pleasure; these instructions should induce the rauding process. They were not allowed to turn back to a previous page. The subjects were 32 people who had responded to advertisements posted on a college campus, but it was not clear if they were all college students. The advertisement stated that subjects had to be able to read English but the researchers noted that English was not the first language of some subjects.

The subjects in the standard book condition read during the first hour at 211 wpm and they increased their rate 10% during the second hour, 233 wpm. Given the description of the subjects, it seems possible that these low rates may have been indicative of the rauding process being used instead of a learning process. The subjects in the TV condition read the first hour at 150 wpm and they increased their rate 11% during the second hour, 167 wpm. The most outstanding aspect of these results is the much slower rate of reading from the television screen, 29% slower the first hour and 28% slower the second hour. It is quite possible that this difference was due to sampling error; more of the subjects who spoke English as a second language may have been in the TV condition and thereby lowered the rate. Muter et al. only presented the results of the eight comprehension questions covering eight stories that everyone read; the TV group scored 9% higher the first hour but there was no difference between the two groups for the second hour; self-reported measures of dizziness, headache, nausea, fatigue, and eye strain revealed no important differences between the two groups.

In summary, reading from a television screen was 28% slower than reading from a book but this was a between subjects comparison that could evaporate when subjects are used as their own controls. Rather than concluding from the Muter *et al.* research that reading from a video screen is 28% slower and then trying to figure out why, it would seem prudent to determine first whether this is a replicable result.

Carver (1983) investigated the effect of putting one extra space between words and sentences during the operation of the rauding process. (Note: This same research study was reviewed earlier in Chapter 7 from a different perspective.) Passages varying in difficulty level from $D_L = 1$ to $D_L = 16$ were given to 435 students in grade 4 through college. Each passage was presented (a) in a standard format and (b) in an extra space format which had two spaces between words and three spaces between sentences. The students were told that (a) the purpose was to get an idea about their normal reading rate, (b) there would be no test on what they read, and (c) the material should be read at the rate they normally read. These instructions were designed to induce the rauding process and the average of around 300 Wpm for college students was strong evidence that they typically read the material at their rauding rate (see Appendix B and Table 2.2).

The results of the above research by Carver left no doubt that most readers are not affected by the extra space between words because they read the extra spaced text at the same rate they read the standard. However, those students at the lowest level of ability read the extra spaced text at a faster rate.

In the above research by Carver, reading ability was measured by a standardized test that provided estimates of rauding ability, and the data were analyzed by grouping students into five GE levels: 1–3, 4–6, 7–9, 10–12, and 13–15. Only the readers from grade levels 1 to 3 in ability were affected by the extra spacing; they read the extra spaced text at a rate about 30% *faster* than the standard text. Therefore, the research by Patberg and Yonas (1978), reviewed earlier, has been replicated. They found that 13 extra spaces between words hindered the good readers but facilitated the poor readers, but it was not clear how to describe the population of good and poor readers. These data collected by Carver suggest that individuals at grade levels 1–3 in rauding ability tend to read faster if extra spaces are put between words, whereas individuals at higher levels of ability are not helped. At some point, between 2 and 13 spaces between words, the rauding rate of individuals above the third grade level of ability is slowed by the extra spaces between words. In contrast, the low ability readers experienced a 30% increase in their rate of operating the rauding process compared to the standard; this result suggests that students at the beginning levels of reading ability should be given nonstandard spaced text whenever possible. This result also suggests that the beginning level readers can recognize words much faster when they are made more discriminable by extra blank space on each side. Finally, these data suggest that the higher ability readers (above grade three in rauding ability) have overlearned the habit of moving their eyes down a line without regard for one or two spaces between the lines; stated differently, their apping is not affected by placing an extra space between words (apping was described in Chapter 9).

Apping would also seem to account for why the variable extra blank space between words in right-justified text has little or no effect. However, there is a limit to how far the eye movements of higher ability readers can automatically adjust to extra space between words during apping, and the 13 spaces investigated by Patberg and Yonas (1978) obviously exceeded that limit. As the extra space is increased between 2 and 13 spaces, at some point attention must be directed to moving the eye a distance further than it is habitually programmed to move automatically without attention. By analogy, we can increase our walking speed slightly to accommodate the gate of a faster walking friend without affecting the quality of our conversation, but there is a limit to this increase. When this limit is exceeded, we must consciously attend to our walking and the quality of our conversation suffers. The attention required to move the eyes a distance greater than that which ordinarily accompanies apping will distract from the attention to the rauding process so that the process must be slowed in order to keep its success rate at the same high level.

Henney (1983) investigated the effect of upper case versus lower case, on a computer screen. Using each of these two formats, she administered a reading rate test to sixth graders and college students. The test contains a series of one or two sentences on a topic with one word toward the end that does not fit the intended meaning in each item. The task is to locate the anomalous word in each item as fast as possible. The task requires the operation of a rauding process in a limited sense, i.e., one or two sentence passages. The scores could not be converted into wpm or Wpm. For the sixth graders, there was no important or consistent difference that favored either format. For the college students, the upper case was consistently read about 3–7% slower but the upper case was also read about 1–4% more accurately in terms of percentage of correct items. It would not be prudent to conclude that the upper case was inferior to the lower case since the lower rate was accompanied by a higher accuracy. Thus, these data suggest that the rate of operating the rauding process on text presented by a computer terminal is not detrimentally affected by all the words being in upper case. This result is counter to the small detrimental effect of all capitals found by earlier researchers. The reason for this inconsistent result is not clear except that it is quite possible that the slowing effect of upper case text is small, such as 3–5%, and varies somewhat with the nature of the task so that its effect is near zero in some situations and around 10% in others.

Gould and Grischkowsky (1984) compared the rate of proof-reading on a computer terminal versus standard hardcopy text. They asked 24 clerk typists to check for spelling errors during two 6-hour working days. There was a word randomly selected and deliberately misspelled about every 150 words. When working with the computer terminal, the subjects missed 3% more of these spelling errors compared to the standard hardcopy, 33% versus 30% error rate. Furthermore, proof-reading on the computer terminal was accomplished 22% more slowly, 159 versus 205 wpm. The difference could not be accounted for by the difference in time required to identify a misspelled word in the two lists. It was not clear what slowed the proof-reading rate but the size of the decrement associated with reading from a screen was consistent with the research reviewed earlier by Muter *et al.* (1982).

Kruk and Muter (1984) investigated some of the possible reasons why reading from a television screen was found to be slower. They used similar methods and replicated the earlier findings by Muter *et al.* (1982) that reading from a television screen was about 28% slower than reading from a book. This time Kruk and Muter found 24% slower reading on the television screen. They explored several possible causes for this decrement. The extra time required to fill the television screen was not the cause. Varying the contrast ratio of the video images and varying the distance between the screen and the readers also had no effect. They also investigated the effect of spacing on the printed page and spacing on the television screen. They reported that book spacing of 39 characters per line and 20 lines per page was read 9.5% slower than 60 characters per line and 40 lines per page, 214 versus 237 wpm, respectively. However, they failed to note that this difference was completely explained by the higher accuracy of comprehension under the slower rate, 48% versus 42%. Therefore, their manipulation of spacing in the book cannot account for any of the 24% difference they found between the book and the television screen. When they compared single spacing versus double spacing on the television screen, they found that double spacing was read about 12% faster than single spacing, 245 versus 219 wpm, respectively. These investigators noted that the results of Kolers *et al.*

(1981) suggested that single spacing was a negligible problem. Kruk and Muter then suggested that "perhaps single spacing should be particularly avoided with computer displays in which the space between lines is small relative to the height of the characters" (p. 345).

Granaas, McKay, Laham, Hurt, and Juola (1984) investigated the effect of a moving text, such as the Times Square moving news display where the text moves from right to left on a single line. They compared the standard text in the form of a single page to a moving text which jumped seven character spaces to the left. They had two rate conditions: at 300 wpm the pause durations between jumps was 258 msec and at 500 wpm the pause duration was 155 msec. They used 48 passages at two different difficulty levels: about the sixth to eighth grade level for passages taken from McCall–Crabbs test which they called intermediate, and Nelson–Denny Reading Test passages which they called secondary. Each passage had four multiple-choice questions. They reported that a control group of college students answered 37% of the intermediate questions correctly without reading the passages, and the corresponding value for the secondary questions was 35%. The task for the 20 college students in the experiment was to comprehend the passages as well as they could during the time allowed so that they could score as highly as possible on the indicants of A, accuracy of comprehension.

In general, Granaas et al. found the moving text to be inferior to the standard. At 300 wpm, a likely rauding rate for these college students, the comprehension score was lower for the moving text: 65 versus 75% for the intermediate passages, and 53 versus 59% for the secondary passages. At 500 wpm, a skimming rate, the corresponding scores were 50 versus 58% and 52 versus 54%. These data indicate that a moving text is inferior to the standard; when rate of comprehension, R, is held constant at the rauding rate of 300 wpm, accuracy of comprehension, A, is lower for the moving text.

Belmore (1985) compared a standard text to text presented on a computer monitor. The eight passages (mean length = 187 words) and their comprehension questions were taken from standardized reading tests. The 20 college students involved were instructed to ". . . read each passage through once at their normal speed, and were to read for meaning in anticipation of a comprehension test" (p. 13). The objective consequences must have induced the subjects to use a memorizing process (see Table 2.2) because the mean rate for the standard text was 134 wpm and the mean rate for the computer text was 119 wpm, 11% slower. No conclusions about effects relevant to the rauding process, Gear 3, are warranted.

Jandreau, Muncer, and Bever (1986) investigated the effect of putting extra blank space between phrases within sentences. They used the Chapman–Cook Speed of Reading Test which involves marking out the anomalous word at the end of sentences. They found that community college students were able to answer more of the items in 2.5 min when the text was phrase spaced, 16% faster in Experiment 1 and 20% faster in Experiment 2. Since the items on this test are relatively easy for college students, these data definitely suggest that the rauding process can be speeded by a technique that helps readers identify phrases within sentences. However, there was a possible artifact in this research. The normal spacing that provided the control may not have represented the standard. Both the normal and spaced versions were typed by a dot matrix printer that used proportional spacing. The size of the letters varied from 6 to 18 dot spaces with 150 dot spaces per inch. Proportionally spaced text created by dot matrix printers are not necessarily easy to read. It seems prudent that judgment be suspended on these results until (a) the 16% advantage is replicated when compared to a condition that is more readily accepted as the standard, and (b) the results can be replicated under passage reading conditions that are more readily accepted as representing the rauding process.

Cushman (1986) compared the rate of reading from microfiche and video display terminals with that of reading from printed paper copy, the standard. The 76 subjects were adult employees of Eastman Kodak company. They read material at about the ninth grade level of difficulty (Flesch scores from 57 to 60) for 80 min. The instructions given to the subjects were not reported. However, they did know they would be given a comprehension test because part of the design was repeated measures so that 16 of the subjects read under five different viewing conditions. The nature of the comprehension tests was not described. Therefore, it is difficult to predict whether a learning process, Gear 2, or the rauding process, Gear 3, would be used. The reading rates varied from a low of 199 wpm to a high of 218 wpm for the standard. This standard rate converts into 208 Wpm [Equations (2.2) and (2.6)], which in turn converts into a rauding rate level, R_L, of 8.7 [Equation (11.1)]. It is possible that these adults operated their rauding process at 208 Wpm which is equivalent to the eighth grade level. However, it seems more likely that the tests induced these subjects into a learning process, Gear 2. The comprehension scores were approximately the same for all conditions, 76–80%. However, there was a negative correlation between rate and the accuracy of comprehension; the faster rates tended to be associated with the lower comprehension scores. It seems best to conclude that reading from microfiche and video display was not less efficient than reading the standard when the reading process was a learning process. Two aspects of these Cushman data should be noted: (a) they do not replicate the detrimental effect associated with reading from computer terminals which are video displays, and (b) they need to be replicated under conditions wherein we can be confident that the rauding process was operating because it is the process likely to be used most often when viewing text from microfiche and video displays.

Trollip and Sales (1986) compared the standard to text with the right margin justified. There were two experiments. In Experiment 1, 46 undergraduate and graduate students read a 14.5-page article on the history of pepper from the *Smithsonian* magazine. This would likely have been relatively easy for them. About one-half of the students were given the text in a right-justified format and the other half received the same text with the same number of words on each line but only one space after each word. It was reported that "At the beginning of each session, the experimenter explained the procedures for the study" (p. 161). After reading, the students were asked to complete 15 "fill-in-the-blank questions covering factual information contained in the passage" (p. 161). It was not clear whether these students had a good idea of the difficulty or easiness of the task before they read. Since they had no practice, it seems possible that the rauding process was used. And, the length of the passage was not described in enough detail to estimate accurately the rate in wpm or Wpm. However, this article has been included because the experiment probably involved the rauding process and the results are likely to be relevant to apping.

In the above research, Trollip and Sales found that the right-justified text was read 13% slower than the standard. Furthermore, a similar deficit was found, 10%, in a second experiment where another group of students were given 15 multiple-choice questions afterwards. It is possible that these data are only representative of a learning process. It also seems possible that the extra spaces inserted between words for a right-justified text were slightly disruptive for habitual eye movements, called apping. It seems important to determine whether this result can be replicated under conditions especially designed to induce the rauding process, Gear 3.

Gould *et al.* (1987) studied why reading is slower from CRT displays compared to paper. They reported upon the results of ten experiments wherein the dependent variable was almost exclusively wpm for proofreading. Experiment 3 was the only one that involved reading for comprehension. In Experiment 3, there were nine research professionals and clerical people who were told to read newspaper articles and magazines for the purpose of "briefly summarizing them afterwards into a tape recorder" (p. 278), even though "these summaries were not ana-lyzed" (p. 278).

These relatively easy materials, these instructions, and these objective consequences were likely to induce the rauding process. Indeed, the rate for reading the paper text, which was the standard, was 283 wpm thus verifying the high likelihood that the research involved the rauding process. The CRT rate was 15% slower at 240 wpm. Another nine indi-viduals proof-read the same materials, 206 wpm for the standard and 184 wpm for the CRT.

Gould *et al.* summarized the results relevant to why reading is slower on CRT displays as follows:

> Results show that no one variable studied (e.g., experience in using CRT dis-plays; character size, font, or polarity) explains it. The tentative conclusion is that the difference is due to a combination of variables, probably centering on the image quality of the characters themselves. (p. 269)

The above research was immediately followed by six more proof-reading studies published by Gould, Alfaro, Finn, Haupt, and Minuto (1987). In this research, they displayed text on CRT screens that were similar to printed text in font, resolution, and contrast. Under these conditions wherein the CRT condition presents an image similar to the standard, proof-reading was just as fast and just as accurate.

It appears that the rauding process is definitely slowed when reading from computer terminals that are typical for this time period. Most of the relevant research has been conducted on proof-reading. However, it appears that the deficits involved are associated with the character per-ception so that word recognition, or lexical access, is detrimentally af-fected during both proof-reading and the rauding process. As computer terminals approach paper in terms of equivalent stimuli, then it is ex-pected that rauding from a computer terminal will be just as fast and accurate as rauding during auding or rauding from printed text.

Reinking (1988) administered three versions of computer-mediated text, plus a comparable standard printed text, to 33 fifth and sixth grade students. In all four versions, six multiple-choice questions were pre-sented after a passage had been read. In one computer version, the reader was given the option of selecting supplementary aids that were designed to help comprehension (option-aids). The supplementary aids consisted of (a) another version of the same passage that was written to be easier, (b) the definitions of difficult words in the passage, (c) impor-tant background information, and (d) a statement expressing the main idea of the passage. These aids were not available in a second computer version (no-aids), and they were mandatory in the third computer version (mandatory-aids). There was no report of the instructions given to the subjects that might affect what reading process they used. However, each subject received all four versions and was practiced in the task of reading the short paragraph in order to answer the six questions afterwards, so the objective consequences probably were much more important than the instructions. The difficulty level, D_L, of the four passages ranged from 5.7 to 11.2 with a mean GE of 8.1. The readers were divided into good and poor groups based upon whether they scored above or below the 50th percentile on the California Achievement Tests. So, asking these fifth and sixth graders to read passages at approximately the eighth grade level of difficulty (8.1) probably meant that the material was relatively hard for both the poor reader group and the good reader group. Given that the task required answering a question on every 25 words, approximately, and given that the passages were relatively hard, it would be predicted that these students would adopt a learning process.

Reading times for the passages were reported by Reinking, but reading rates could not be accurately estimated because the length of the passages were given as "140–180 words." However, if it is assumed that the passages were approximately 160 words in length, then the mean reading rates varied from a low of 28 Wpm to a high of 98 Wpm (using equations in Chapter 2). These rates were much too slow to represent the rauding process for these students (see Appendix B), so it is likely that a learning process was used as predicted.

Reinking reported eight means on the comprehension test items, one mean for each of the four versions in each of the two groups, good and poor readers. The highest mean out of the eight was 3.92 for the good readers under the mandatory-aids version. These means can be corrected for guessing and converted to percentages. The above 3.92 value became 54%, representing the highest accuracy of comprehension estimate out of the eight reported. It should also be noted that the rate that accompanied this 54% accuracy of comprehension was 31 Wpm, the slowest rate of all four reported for the good readers. The highest accuracy percentage for the poor readers was also on the mandatory-aids version, 37%. The lowest estimate of the accuracy of comprehension, A, was 2% for the poor readers when they were given the no-aids version.

For the eight pairs of means reflecting both the accuracy of comprehension, A, in percent, and the rate of comprehension, R, in Wpm, there was a -0.62 correlation. This relatively large correlation indicates that those versions with the highest estimates of comprehension accuracy tended to have the slowest reading rates. These data were reanalyzed by calculating the same correlate of efficiency used by M. D. Jackson and McClelland (1979). This measure of "effective reading speed" was cal-

culated by multiplying the estimates of comprehension accuracy in pro-
portions, e.g., 0.54, by the Wpm estimates of rate, e.g., 31, to give a
correlate of efficiency, e.g., 17 Wpm. This efficiency correlate of 17 for
the mandatory-aids version, as read by the good readers, was approximately equal to the standard version, 16. The version with the highest
efficiency correlate for these good readers was option-aids, 31. For the
poor readers, their efficiency correlate under the mandatory-aids version
was 10, and it was also approximately equal to the standard version, 11.
The highest efficiency correlate for these poor readers also occurred
when reading the option-aids version, 14. Thus, the pattern of results
for the four versions was the same whether the readers were good or
poor: the estimate of the accuracy of comprehension, A, was highest
under the mandatory-aids version and the estimate of the efficiency of
comprehension, E, was highest under the option-aids version.

These reanalyzed data would suggest that presenting passages using
a computer version that required individuals to use mandatory-aids
(read an easier less technical version, read the definitions of difficult
words and phrases, read important background information, and to read
the main idea) does increase A during a learning process. However, the
corresponding E will be comparable to a standard printed version that
does not have these supplementary aids. But, if the supplementary aids
on the computer are made optional at the request of the reader, then E
will be the highest of all versions, for both the good readers and the poor
readers.

It should not go unnoticed that whatever has been learned from
Reinking's research about increasing A (by requiring supplementary
comprehension aids using a computer), or increasing E (by making such
aids optional), it will not necessarily generalize to the rauding process
because a learning process was operating. Furthermore, it is questionable whether it would be a good instructional practice for reading educators to give passages to poor reading fifth and sixth graders that are
relatively hard for them (see Carver, 1987e), and result in very low estimates of A (below 40%) even when R is also very low (below 100 Wpm).
This might be considered poor instruction even though certain versions
of these computer-mediated aids to comprehension resulted in higher
estimates of accuracy and efficiency of comprehension than the standard
printed version.

CONCLUSIONS

The research reviewed in this chapter on textual presentation indicates
that the standard text is optimal for readers above grade level three in

ability, $A_L > 3$. However, the stimulus conditions under which passages are presented can have a large detrimental effect upon reading rate. Compared to a standard text, the loss in rate may approach 20–30% under conditions wherein small or trivial differences might have been anticipated.

Rapidly presenting passages one word at a time in the center of a computer screen resulted in no loss in indicants of the accuracy of comprehension, A, at rates ranging from about 200 to 600 Wpm. These findings suggest that word grouping is not a major factor influencing the accuracy or rate at which the rauding process operates. The research reviewed was not at all encouraging for those who hypothesized that the rauding process could be speeded up without loss in the accuracy of comprehension by use of new and different word spacing schemes, based upon grouping into meaningful phrases or units. Improving upon the standard text would seem to be limited to 1–5% increments at best. On the other hand, departures from the standard text can easily produce large decrements in reading rate, as was found in the wide spacing between words and the spacings associated with text presented on television screens and computer screens.

The standard text itself appears to produce large decrements in rate for individuals at the beginning reader level, probably because they have not yet developed the overlearned eye movement habit called apping. These students could read a text with one extra space between words and sentences about 30% faster while the more skilled readers were unaffected by this spacing. Therefore, it appears that text with an extra space between words and sentences should be adopted when beginning level readers are likely to be involved and a rate decrement is of consequence.

As for research work using text read from computers and television screens, it would seem best to use an extra space between words and double spacing between lines whenever a decrement in rate is of major consequence. This extra space probably will not affect the better readers but it will help the poorer readers operate their rauding process closer to their rauding rate.

The results reviewed in this chapter have important theoretical implications. Using the RSVP technique of presenting words one at a time, so that no eye movements are required, seems to have little or no detrimental effect upon the rauding process. Therefore, it appears that the psychomotor habit of apping has evolved after many hours of practice and experience so that reading can take place with eye movements at a level of efficiency that matches auding and RSVP. Notice that we humans have learned to scoop up the information from each consecutive word in the sentences of textual material in a manner that matches the high efficiency of two other rauding processes that involve no eye movements, auding and RSVP. This makes apping a rather remarkable feat. Students beyond the third grade level of rauding ability, $A_L > 3$, have learned a psychomotor eye movement habit that can be carried out on a wide variety of text spacings that allows each consecutive word of relatively easy text to be processed just as successfully as when no eye movements are required. It appears that a standard text can be rauded by college students most efficiently at a rate around 300 Wpm, whether it is presented in its normal printed format that requires eye movements or by the two techniques that do not require eye movements, RSVP and auding. Apping helps the rauding process work at its maximum efficiency on standard text.

The standard format appears to be the best way to present text for operating the rauding process because apping has evolved in a manner that allows the process to operate just as efficiently as when no eye movements are required.

COMPREHENSION

INTRODUCTION

Those individuals who operate their rauding process the fastest also tend to have the highest accuracy of comprehension; when reading rate is increased, an individual's accuracy of comprehension decreases. Using more technical terminology, the between-individual correlation between rauding rate level, R_L, and rauding accuracy level, A_L, is positive, but the within-individual correlation between rate of comprehension, R, and accuracy of comprehension, A, is negative. This means that (a) those individuals who tend to read the fastest also tend to comprehend the most, a positive between-individual relationship, and (b) when individuals increase their rate then their accuracy of comprehension decreases, a negative within-individual relationship. The failure to discriminate between these two fundamentally different correlations, one negative and one positive, has been a major factor contributing to the confusion surrounding the relationship between comprehension and reading rate. Just because Mary reads faster than Joe and also comprehends more than Joe, does not mean that Joe will comprehend more if he is induced to read faster; in fact, Joe will tend to comprehend less as he increases his rate.

Perhaps it will be helpful to review the rauding theory constructs from Chapter 2 that are directly relevant to making sense out of the rate and comprehension relationship. The accuracy of comprehension, A, refers to the proportion or percentage of a particular passage that has been comprehended by an individual, such as Mary. For example, if there are 10 Sentences in a passage and 8 are comprehended by Mary then $A = 0.80$ or 80%. If the 10 Sentences were presented in 2 min, then the rate of comprehension, R, would be 5 Sentences per minute. Since $E = AR$, then Mary's efficiency of comprehension, E, would be $(0.80)(5) = 4$ Sentences per minute. Suppose Mary has a rauding accuracy level of 8, a rauding rate level of 6, and a rauding efficiency level of 7 (A_L = 9; R_L = 6; E_L = 7). This particular rauding accuracy level, A_L = 8, indicates an ability to read passages at the eighth grade level of difficulty, D_L = 8, with an accuracy of comprehension greater than 75%, A > 0.75, when these eighth grade passages are read at the individual's own rauding rate, R_r. This rauding rate level, R_L = 6, indicates a rauding rate, R_r, equal to the average rauding rate of individuals at A_L = 6. This particular rauding efficiency level, E_L = 7, indicates an ability to read passages at D_L = 7 with an accuracy of comprehension of 75%, A = 0.75, while reading them at a rate equal to the average rauding rate, R_r, of individuals at A_L = 7. Suppose Mary has been administered a relatively easy passage that was 300 Words long, took 2 min to read it, and then answered three of five comprehension questions correctly. In this situation, rate would be reported as 150 Wpm, or 9 Spm, and this would be another estimate of rauding rate, R_r. Accuracy of comprehension would be reported as 0.60, and this would be an estimate of rauding accuracy, A_r. Rauding efficiency, E_r, would be (9)(0.60) = 5.4 Sentences per minute.

When the constructs of A, R, E, A_r, R_r, E_r, A_L, R_L, and E_L, are estimated for a group of people, then the indicants of A, A_r, and A_L will be highly correlated, the indicants of R, R_r, and R_L will be highly correlated, and the indicants of E, E_r, and E_L will be highly correlated. Also, the efficiency estimates will ordinarily be highly correlated with the rate estimates and the efficiency estimates will also be highly correlated with the accuracy estimates because the efficiency estimates are composed of both accuracy and rate.

The constructs illustrated in the foregoing examples will be needed to sort out the confusions in the rate and comprehension research. Rate is often an ambiguous concept because it could refer to any of the constructs of R, R_r, or R_L. Comprehension is often an ambiguous concept because it could refer to any of the constructs that involve accuracy, such as A, E, A_r, E_r, A_L, or E_L. Furthermore, in research studies we are often dealing with correlates of the above constructs and it is often difficult to determine which construct is relevant since the constructs are interrelated. It will be impossible to make sense out of the relationship between rate and comprehension without a firm grasp of the differences among A, R, E, A_r, R_r, E_r, A_L, R_L, and E_L.

In this chapter, an attempt will be made to clear up most of the confusions and contradictions associated with the relationship between rate and comprehension in reading. Before reviewing the relevant research, a section will be devoted to a lengthy review of some of these confusions and their sources.

CONFUSIONS

Eurich (1930) published an article, entitled "The relation of speed of reading to comprehension," and it appears to be the first devoted specifically to the topic of this chapter. He reviewed several earlier studies that correlated measures of reading rate with comprehension; the average correlation coefficient in those studies was 0.31. Two years later, Tinker (1932) published an article in the same journal, *School and Society*, with exactly the same title. Tinker presented a series of correlations ranging from 0.46 to 0.86 which he used to support his generalization that the correlation is high when the subject matter is similar, but low when the subject matter is different. Later, Tinker (1939) presented more correlations among various measures on reading tests to reinforce his generalizations that "as the content of the second test differs more and more from the first or the technique of measurement in the second diverges from that in the first, the intercorrelation becomes lower" (p. 81). He also reported a series of correlations, 0.83, 0.69, 0.62, 0.59, 0.42, and 0.42, as evidence for his generalization that "as the materials become harder, the correlation is lowered."

Not long after Tinker's data and interpretations were published, I. H. Anderson (1937) discussed the subject of rate versus comprehension in reading, after presenting his eye movement research data. (Note: this research was reviewed earlier in Chapter 5.) He argued that it was superficial and arbitrary to regard rate and comprehension as if they were independent because rate is the necessary outcome of time consuming comprehension functions. He goes on to criticize Pressey (1928), Ring and Bentley (1930), Gray (1922), Moore and McLaughlin (1934), and Robinson (1933) for designing ". . . exercises for 'pacing' eye-movements in order to increase the span of visual apprehension in poor readers" (p. 30). He said that the above writers implied that ". . . eye-movements are important causal factors in reading and that training of eye-movements will improve reading proficiency" (p. 30). Anderson was convinced from the data available that eye movements did not "govern" ability. He thought that ". . . the intimate relationship between eye-movements (rate) and comprehension often has been overlooked" and that "attempts to improve reading ability by training eye-movements violate laws governing the direction of the relationship between eye-movement behavior and the conscious processes involved" (p. 31).

The above research and opinion in the 1930s relevant to rate and comprehension was rounded out by the following cogent comments by Sisson (1939):

By what techniques, then, can we increase speed of reading with no serious loss to comprehension? Since we have said before, speed or rate is the temporal dimension of comprehension, the way to increased speed would seem to lie in lessening the demands upon comprehension. (p. 211)

Notice that Sisson is giving a law in 1939 that seems to be equally valid about 50 years later: if you want to go faster, then try to comprehend less (see also Just & Carpenter, 1987). Sisson was also convinced that the important role of intelligence should not be overlooked. He commented as follows:

Reading comprehension, then, is partly a function of the intelligence of the reader, and we should expect readers of equal intelligence, reading at the same rate, to be equal in comprehension. Conversely, readers of equal intelligence, reading with the same degree of comprehension would be expected to do it in the same time. (p. 207)

From the outline given above, it is now obvious that a number of researchers were very interested in how reading rate, R, was related to comprehension, A, during reading. However, the important distinction between a within-individual relationship involving A and R and a between-individual relationship between A_L and R_L had not been recognized. I. H. Anderson (1937) was concentrating his attention upon the within-individual relationships, factors that influence the intimate relationship between rate of comprehension, R, and accuracy of comprehension, A, within an individual. He was convinced that it was the comprehending functions that were causing rate changes. For example, when the materials get more difficult for an individual to understand, then the lack of comprehension would be the cause for the eyes to slow down and regress in an effort to achieve a higher accuracy of comprehension; therefore, R would decline in response to the demand for higher A. Sisson (1939) was also keenly aware of the importance of these within-individual relationships when he wisely noted that the way to increase your rate of comprehension was to demand less accuracy of comprehension. But, Sisson also opened the door to between-individual factors when he noted the influence of intelligence. This between-individual type of relationship also had captured the attention of Eurich (1930) and Tinker (1932, 1939). They were studying how individual differences in reading rate, R_L, were related to individual differences in the ability to comprehend, A_L. Both Eurich and Tinker were interested in the correlation between a measure of reading rate and a measure of comprehension for a group of individuals, i.e., a between-subject relationship. The failure to discriminate between these two types of relationships, or correlations, has caused numerous confusions and ill-advised practices through the years. Many students have had to endure hours of wasted effort engaged in rate training activities that were supposed to make them better readers (see Chapter 18), an indirect consequence of the failure to discriminate between within-individual relationships and be-tween-individual relationships found in research.

In the 1940s, there was much more research conducted and much more opinion generated. This era was ushered in by a dispute between Robinson (1940) and Tinker (1940). Their source of disagreement was mainly a failure to discriminate between within-individual and between-individual correlations. So, the ill effects of this failure to discriminate between these two fundamentally different relationships became more acute.

Stroud (1942) noted that the prior 25 years of research had produced an average correlation of "about 0.40" between reading rate and com-prehension. Stroud then struggled with the conceptual issues. He said "the question at issue is whether those who read at a rapid rate under-stand more, learn more, get more out of reading, than do those who read at a slow or moderate rate" (p. 175). This is the between-subject relation-ship, such as between A_L and R_L. However, three sentences later, he tackles the within-subject relationship between R and A by saying "what we really wish to know is the relationship between the speed at which a person reads and what he gets out of a reading—what he learns" (p. 175). He gave no hint that he was aware of the important distinction between these two types of relationships—A_L related to R_L versus A re-lated to R.

The following year, Stroud and Henderson (1943) published their re-search that was supposedly designed to investigate what Stroud (1942) "really wished to know" about the within-individual relationship between rate and comprehension (A related to R). Unfortunately, Stroud and Henderson used a between-individual correlational design and therefore failed to study what they seemingly wanted to know. If they were in fact interested in the within-individual relationship, then they should have forced subjects to read material at different rates and then determined how much they comprehended at each rate. This would be an experi-ment where (a) rate of comprehension, R, was a manipulated indepen-dent variable, (b) accuracy of comprehension, A, would be the depen-dent variable, and (c) the within-individual relationship would be revealed. However, they did not do this. Instead, they studied between-individual relationships involving correlates of rauding ability.

Stroud and Henderson seem to be the first researchers to find a zero between-individual correlation between measures of rate and comprehension. Over three separate studies involving fifth graders through graduate students, rate was measured by how long it took students to read a passage (a correlate of R_L) and comprehension was measured by a multiple-choice test given after reading (a correlate of A_L). They found that ". . . rate and quality are virtually unrelated" (p. 205). This was interpreted by them to mean that their research gave ". . . no support to the claim that pupils who read at a rapid rate learn more per reading than those who read at a slow rate," and "neither was there any evidence that they learned less, which still makes fast reading altogether desirable" (p. 201). Here we have what appears to be the first hint as to how these between-individual results involving correlates of A_L and R_L are going to be misinterpreted. Notice that Stroud and Henderson supposedly intended to find out what happens to comprehension of a passage if an individual read it slower compared to reading it faster. Instead of investigating this cause and effect relationship by varying the rate, R, for individuals and observing what happens to within-individual changes in the accuracy of comprehension, A, they looked at the between-individual correlation between a correlate of R_L and a correlate of A_L—and reported a zero correlation. Therefore, on the basis of this zero correlation they are suggesting that fast reading is still "altogether desirable." Even if the faster readers are not necessarily the poorer comprehenders and the better comprehenders are not necessarily the slower readers, this still does not have anything to do with "the relationship between the speed at which a person reads and what he gets out of reading." Stated differently, the correlation between individual differences in R_L and A_L has nothing to do with the causative influence of increasing R upon A within an individual. In fact, it is quite possible for there to be a high positive correlation (as found by Tinker, 1939) indicating that the fastest readers are the best comprehenders, and at the same time, it is also quite possible for there to be a high negative correlation indicating that when individuals read faster they comprehend less. From this point on, dating from this study by Stroud and Henderson (1943), the research, opinion, and instructional practices related to comprehension have suffered from gross misinterpretation.

Blommers and Lindquist (1944) published a 25-page research article in the *Journal of Educational Psychology* entitled "Rate of comprehension of reading: Its measurement and its relation to comprehension." Early in their article, they comment that ". . . it is quite apparent that the rate at which an individual reads an easy passage may differ considerably from that at which he reads a difficult passage of the same length," and they found that their results gave some support to this. They concluded that "good comprehenders adjust their rate of reading by slowing down as the material increases in difficulty, where as poor comprehenders apparently read easy and difficult materials at the same rate" (p. 472). They also commented that their results were contrary to Tinker's (1939) who found that the relationship between rate and comprehension decreased as the materials became more difficult; they found a 0.29 correlation between rate and comprehension for easy materials and a 0.31 correlation for difficult materials.

With the benefit of hindsight, the apparent inconsistencies noted above are readily explained. The rate of operating the rauding process is constant at the apping rate across material of varying levels of difficulty as long as the level of difficulty is below the individual's level of ability (when $A_L > D_L$, R is constant at R_r). Rate of rauding may even stay constant when the materials become relatively hard, $A_L < D_L$, but many individuals will automatically switch from their rauding process to a learning process that is slower. It is possible that poorer readers are not process flexible in the sense that they are more resistant or least able to switch from their rauding process to a slower learning process. Or, they habitually operate their rauding process at a learning process rate no matter whether the materials are relatively easy or relatively hard. The poorer readers may have an apping rate that has evolved from high usage of a learning process so they read almost all of the material they encounter at the same slow rate of a learning process because this is an effective strategy for them to keep their accuracy of comprehension, A, at a high level.

Blommers and Lindquist (1944) stressed the fact that they found a correlation of about 0.30 between rate and comprehension. Tinker (1945) reported more correlations involving various measures on the Iowa Silent Reading Test, and he stressed that these correlations varied from 0.23 to 0.95 depending upon how rate and comprehension were measured. His comprehension measures were correlates of both rauding efficiency level, E_L (which includes rate), and rauding accuracy level, A_L. (Note: Tinker's rate measures were actually time measures so his correlations were reported as being negative, but they are in fact positive when converted into a measure of rate.) Tinker concluded that ". . . the fast reader tends to comprehend better" (p. 227) but he tempered this with the following explanation:

There are many reading skills which are somewhat independent of each other. The relationship between rate and comprehension need not be the same in any two reading situations if there are differences in textual content, nature of response required from reader, purpose for which the material is read, and difficulty. Furthermore, the conclusions in any study probably can be applied only to the reading of groups like the one measured. (p. 226)

Tinker seems to be saying that we should be prepared to find any size correlation between rate and comprehension, depending upon innumerable situational variables but he is still contending that there is a "significant relation between rate and comprehension in reading" because "the fast reader tends to comprehend better" in spite of all these different sized correlations that depend upon the situation.

The above conclusions of Tinker's may appear to be internally inconsistent but they can be interpreted as prophetically on the mark. When investigators measure rate in various ways (words of text read in one minute, number attempted score on a reading rate test, etc.), when they vary the difficulty of the materials (from $D_L = 1$ to $D_L = 18$), when they do not control for the type of reading process (from memorizing to scanning), and when comprehension is measured in a variety of ways (from total multiple-choice questions correct to number of verbatim words recalled), it is reasonable to expect great variety in the size of the correlation between these measures of rate and comprehension. The variability in the size of the correlation coefficient is also dependent upon statistical parameters that have little or nothing to do with the substantive relationships, such as amount of variability in the sample and the psychometric reliability of the measures; these latter problems can be partially overcome by reporting standard errors of estimates and corrections for attenuation.

Given all of the above reasons for finding erratic correlation coefficients, it still seems likely that in almost any group of readers such as college students, there will be a between-individual correlation coefficient of 0.50 or higher when a correlate of rauding rate level, R_L, is related to a correlate of rauding efficiency level, E_L. This sized correlation will exist most of the time because efficiency is partly composed of rate; the two measures must be related because one is included in the other. When a correlate of R_L is related to a correlate of rauding accuracy level, A_L, then the correlation between "rate" and "comprehension" will tend to be lower but still positive because those individuals who tend to have the highest accuracy levels also tend to have the highest rate levels. So, it is not surprising that Tinker seems to be confident that rate and comprehension are related this way. Nonetheless, there is still no evidence that any of these early researchers recognized the crucial distinction between within-individual relationships involving A and R and the between-individual relationships involving A_L and R_L, let alone the confusions that result when "comprehension" is measured by a test that reflects E or E_L instead of A or A_L.

Buswell (1947) appears to be the first to misinterpret the near-zero and positive correlations found between rate and comprehension for the between-subject relationships. He advised:

> There has long been a popular notion that, when comprehension in reading is low, the reader should be advised to read more slowly. The scientific evidence does not justify this advice. In fact, many slow readers have low comprehension because their rate of thinking is more rapid than their reading rate and, consequently, their minds wander. (p. 194)

Buswell gives no direct indication of the source of this "scientific evidence" he is referring to. However, there can be little doubt that he means the positive or near-zero between-individual correlations found a few years earlier by Stroud and Henderson (1943) and Blommers and Lindquist (1944). Yet, he takes the big leap and infers that if the correlation found between these measures of rate and comprehension is not negative, then this means that increasing your reading rate will not necessarily lower your comprehension and it could well improve it, as he contends. It cannot be emphasized too strongly that there had been no research prior to these 1947 remarks of Buswell's that supported his contentions. If, in fact, there had been some research indicating that prodding slow readers to read faster in fact resulted in higher comprehension scores when they read faster, then Buswell would have had the scientific evidence he claimed he had. Not only was there a complete lack of factual evidence supporting the contention that slow readers will comprehend more if they read faster, there was also no evidence reported to support the hypothesis that the reason why they could increase their comprehension this way was because their minds would "wander" less.

In spite of the complete lack of any scientific evidence relevant to Buswell's claims, the seed was sown for a great deal of subsequent nonsense to be perpetuated in the field of reading. After noting that the between-subject correlation found between rate and comprehension was zero or positive (not negative), this has been erroneously interpreted as suggesting that readers can be induced to go faster without losing comprehension and possibly comprehending more. Again, there has been no recognition of the fact that the relationship found in all this prior research on between-individual differences involving correlates of R_L, A_L, and E_L, has absolutely no connection with the relationship between rate of comprehension, R, and accuracy of comprehension, A, within individuals.

And, it is research on the within-subject relationship between A and R that was crucially lacking.

At the end of the 1940s, Carlson (1949) conducted a study entitled "The relationship between speed and accuracy of comprehension." However, his results are impossible to interpret meaningfully for the following reasons: (a) no reading rates or reading times were reported, and (b) he divided his sample into three levels of intelligence and two levels of rate and then compared their comprehension scores by a t-ratio leaving no trace of any measure of effect size. For his total sample, he did report twelve correlations between rate and comprehension ranging from -0.29 to $+0.29$ for various levels of difficulty and various purpose conditions. This study only perpetuated the basic confusions.

Shores and Husbands (1950) started off the decade of the 50s with an investigation of the between-individual relationship between rate and comprehension in a studying situation. There were over 80 students in grades 4–6 who were given a 700-word passage on biological science material, and then they were given 20 multiple-choice questions. Five of the 20 questions were factual, 14 required "the use of facts in the making of simple and more complex inferences" (p. 55), and the last question required a solution to the original problem given in the purpose for reading. The original purpose given to all subjects was as follows: "What is the best way for the farmer to keep grub worms from harming his crops?" (p. 54). From this description, it would seem best if the subjects used a variety of reading processes to accomplish this purpose, i.e., scanning and skimming to find the best relevant sentences in the passage, rauding to understand the sentences, and learning the ideas contained in the difficult sentences. Shores and Husbands found a low negative correlation of -0.13 between the time taken to read the passage once, and the score on the 20-item test. This correlation was contaminated by the fact that the students were allowed to go back and reread the material while they were taking the test. These results, and those of a replication study by Shores (1961), are not directly relevant to any particular one of the five basic reading processes. The main reason for reviewing this research was to help make the point that results from studying situations such as these have no external validity for generalizing to the rauding process or any particular basic reading process.

Preston and Botel (1951) found a 0.21 between-subject correlation between rate and untimed comprehension scores, i.e., correlates of R_L and A_L. From this date on, these between-subject studies were grinding to a halt.

Letson (1958) tried to design his research to overcome some of the problems inherent in the earlier research; this appears to be the final study in this series that started with Eurich (1930). Letson wanted to find out the between-individual correlation between rate and comprehension using two levels of material difficulty and two different purposes for reading. He found that if comprehension was measured by simply the number correct on the comprehension test (a correlate of rauding efficiency level, E_L) then the relationship with rate (a correlate of R_L) was high and positive (the four correlations ranged from 0.46 to 0.80). But, if comprehension was measured as the percent correct (a correlate of accuracy level, A_L) then the relationship with rate (a correlate of R_L) was low and slightly negative (the four correlations ranged from -0.10 to -0.13). He also reported that the correlation dropped from 0.77 on the easy material to 0.46 on the difficult material for the number correct measure (a correlate of E_L) as Tinker earlier had contended. But, when the percent correct measure was used (a correlate of A_L), the correlation was -0.10 for both the easy and difficult materials. The correlations did not vary across the purpose conditions. Evidently, this investigation of Letson's must have settled the issue to the satisfaction of most of the researchers at that time; his study appears to have closed the era. When comprehension is measured using a correlate of A_L, i.e., percent correct, the correlation with a correlate of rauding rate level, R_L, was low and near zero, -0.10 to -0.13, no matter what the level of difficulty and no matter what the purpose. The high correlations of 0.80 between a correlate of rauding rate level, R_L and a correlate of rauding efficiency level, E_L, is to be expected because efficiency measures are a composite of rate and accuracy measures. It should not go unnoticed that Letson's research probably involved some subjects engaged in their rauding process and some subjects engaged in a learning process; there was no attempt to control for the type of reading process used by the subjects.

Since Letson, there have been two reviews published. One by Rankin (1962) in which he concludes that ". . . it appears that the confounding of rate and comprehension on measurements is, at least in part, responsible for some of the earlier findings that fast readers are good readers" (p. 4). Translated, this means that where comprehension is actually an efficiency measure instead of an accuracy measure, it is not surprising that a high correlation has been found with rate. Rankin covered the prior research in an admirable manner but without noting the distinction between the within-subject and between-subject relationship. Another brief review was conducted in 1969 by Leeds. Also, in this decade of the 1960s, credit must be given to Davis (1962) who warned that (a) measuring reading rate during skimming was not the same as ordinary reading, and (b) under ordinary purposes the *positive* correlation between rate and comprehension for individuals ". . . does not contradict the finding that there is a *negative* relationship between rate of reading and extent of comprehension if other factors are held constant" (p. 34). A careful reading of this article by Davis suggests that he was aware of most of the problems involved in investigating the relationship between rate and comprehension.

The preceding introduction to confusions about rate and comprehension has been lengthy, as promised at the outset. None of the above mentioned research on the relationship between rate and comprehension has been relevant to what happens to the accuracy of comprehension, A, for individuals when the rate of comprehension, R, increases or decreases. However, it seemed prudent to take note of this prior research so that future researchers and practitioners would not continue to make the mistake of drawing inferences about the effect of within-individual rate changes from these earlier between-subject correlations.

Before the relevant research is reviewed it will be helpful to review once again the constructs of rauding theory by applying them to a reading comprehension test such as the Comprehension section of the Nelson–Denny Reading Test. This test allows 15 min for reading passages and answering up to a total of 36 questions, as described earlier in Chapter 13. The number of items attempted on the test is a correlate of the individual's rauding rate level, R_L. The proportion, or percentage, of these items that were answered correctly is a correlate of rauding accuracy level, A_L. The number of questions answered correctly (percent correct, A, multiplied by the number attempted, R) is a correlate of rauding efficiency level, E_L. The values of E_L, A_L, and R_L and their correlates all reflect upon an individual's rauding ability.

The between-individual relationships involving R_L, A_L, and E_L (or their correlates) are likely to be positive relationships. However, when a particular individual (at any rauding ability level) is forced to read passages (of equal difficulty) at increasingly higher rates, then the accuracy of comprehension, A, will go down as the rate of comprehension, R, goes up. Therefore, within-individual relationships between A and R are likely to be negative.

One of the major stumbling blocks that has prevented clearing up these confusions regarding rate and comprehension is that the concepts of rate and comprehension are themselves inadequate, as has been argued several times earlier in this chapter. When the focus is upon a passage (a) rate can be replaced by the rate of comprehension, R, and (b) comprehension can be replaced by the accuracy of comprehension, A, so that it is not confused with the efficiency of comprehension, E, which is a composite of A and R. When the focus is upon the ability of the individual (a) rate can be replaced by rauding rate level, R_L, and

(b) comprehension can be replaced by rauding accuracy level, A_L, so that it is not confused with rauding efficiency level, E_L, which is a composite of A_L and R_L.

This concludes the background explaining the confusions relevant to the theory and research surrounding the earlier concepts of rate and comprehension. The following review of research will be focused upon the effect of rate, R, upon comprehension, A.

RESEARCH

Greene (1931) contributed the earliest known article in the literature relevant to the within-individual relationship between rate and comprehension in reading, even though it was not presented or interpreted as an investigation of the relationship between rate and comprehension. Six groups of college students ($N = 541$) were administered various treatments involving the rate and duration of reading. On the basis of his results, Greene stated that, on the average, the process of one slow reading seems to be just as effective and no more effective than two fast readings. He further states that the total amount of time spent is the important variable. Thus, as early as 1931, there is the suggestion that the time spent reading the materials is one of the most important variables affecting the comprehension and retention of what was read. Since the time spent on a passage is a correlate of the inverse of rate, i.e., $1/R$, it can be seen that Greene was talking about the effect of $1/R$ upon A.

Poulton (1958) further advanced the idea that the time spent reading is the crucial variable determining the accuracy of comprehension. He gave 192 British navy enlistees (most of whom were high school dropouts) sentences to read at 37, 73, 146, and 293 wpm plus a no-text control condition, to be called infinity (∞) wpm. There were three different types of comprehension measures immediately following the presentation of the sentences: Two Key Words, Meaning, and Recognition. The Two Key Words measure was the percentage of the pairs of key words in the statements that were literally recalled under a cued response procedure. The Meaning measure was the percentage of statements that were recalled to a criterion of proving "correct substance." The Recognition measure was the percentage of statements that could be correctly recognized when included with other statements that had not been presented for reading.

The resulting data that Poulton presented in his tables have been reanalyzed by Carver (1990c). Figure 16.1 contains a plot of Poulton's data when proportion correct is presented as a function of the time allowed for reading, in minutes per sentence. Notice that proportion cor-

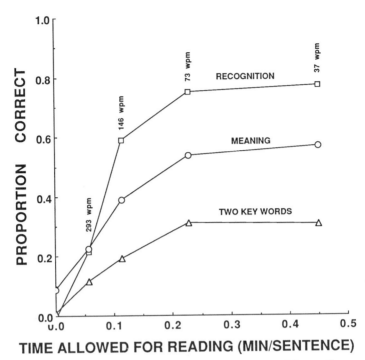

Figure 16.1 Proportion correct as a function of the time allowed for reading a passage, in minutes per sentence, for three different measurement techniques. (Original data from Poulton, 1958.)

rect increases in a linear fashion, initially, for all three measures, and then starts to level off after about 150 wpm, or about one-fifth of a minute per sentence (0.20 min/sentence). Also, notice that the most difficult measure was the Two Key Words since a mean score of only about 0.30 (or 30%) was achieved at the very slow rate of 37 wpm, or about 0.45 minutes per sentence. Recognition was the easiest measure since a mean score of about 0.80 (or 80%) was achieved at around 37–73 wpm.

These data in Fig. 16.1 have been rescaled to provide estimates of the accuracy of comprehension, *A*, using the Rauding Rescaling Procedure (Carver, 1985a). This rescaling purports to provide absolute instead of relative estimates of comprehension accuracy. The results have been presented in Fig. 16.2. In this figure notice that all three measures start with zero accuracy when zero time is allowed for reading, and then increase linearly to around 60 to 75% accuracy. Then, accuracy levels off so that further increases in time, $1/R$, result in diminishing returns with respect to accuracy, *A*. Look at Fig. 16.2 and note the point where the straight line ends and the curvilinear line begins; this is theorized to be the rauding rate, R_r. For these three curves, rauding rate varied only 123 to 130 wpm when converted from min/sentence to wpm. This estimate of rauding rate corresponded closely to Poulton's report that these individuals were reading around 146 wpm. Using Table 2.1 it can be determined that these individuals were reading at a rate around the fourth grade level, $R_L = 4$. This result seems entirely reasonable given that Poulton reported that "most had left school at about 15, and had been apprentices or had taken miscellaneous jobs before joining the navy" (p. 234).

These data of Poulton's and the subsequent reanalysis by Carver support the laws and equations presented in Chapter 2. The accuracy of comprehending sentences increases linearly with the amount of time allowed for reading, up until enough time has been allowed for the rauding process to reach the end of the passages. At that point, the accuracy

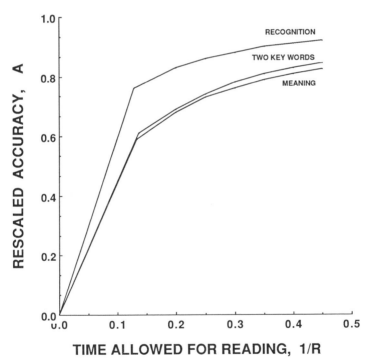

Figure 16.2 Rescaled accuracy of comprehension, A, as a function of the time allowed for reading, $1/R$, in minutes per sentence; a reanalysis of the data presented earlier in Fig. 16.1. (Original data from Poulton, 1958.)

of comprehension has reached its point of diminishing returns where it increases less with each additional amount of time spent. Since rate, R, varies inversely with time allowed for reading, this means that the accuracy of comprehension, A, increases as the rate of comprehension, R, decreases, a negative relationship between A and R. Therefore, these 1958 data of Poulton's appear to be the first available for tracing the functional relationship between A and $1/R$, and establishing the relationship between A and R as negative.

Jester and Travers (1966) induced college students to read at rates that varied from 150 to 350 wpm in 50-word increments. (Note: This research was reviewed earlier in Chapter 13 from a different perspective.) They presented passages from the Davis Reading Test that varied in length from 17 to 390 words; they also used the multiple-choice questions from the Davis test. Rate was manipulated by presenting one or two sentences at a time via a slide projector. For each of the five rates they used, there were 12 subjects. The mean scores they reported for each rate varied from a high of 15.5 at the slowest rate of 150 wpm to a low of 5.9 at the fastest rate of 350 wpm. The correlation can be calculated between these five pairs of R and A means, and it turned out to be -0.90. So, these data provide strong support for the hypothesis that the within-subject relationship between rate of comprehension, R, and accuracy of comprehension, A, is high and negative. This means that the faster that individuals read the less they comprehend, or the slower that individuals read the more they comprehend. Notice that this finding is directly relevant to what Stroud (1942) appeared to want to know but did not design his subsequent research to find out (Stroud and Henderson, 1943). Notice also that this finding is completely counter to Buswell's (1947) contention that students who want to improve their comprehension should speed up their reading.

Carver (1973a) presented passages to college students for varying lengths of time that provided average reading rates between 75 and 450 Wpm. (Note: This research was reviewed earlier in Chapter 13 from a different perspective.) Three different objective measures of comprehension were used: chunked, 20% cloze, and revised-cloze. Subjects were also asked to rate the percentage of each passage that they thought they had understood, no matter which one of the three types of objective tests they were given. For the understanding ratings and all three types of objective tests, as rate of comprehension, R, increased from 75 to 450 Wpm, the group means for accuracy of comprehension, A, decreased. The subjects reported that they understood around 80% of these passages at 75 Wpm and percentage understanding declined as rate increased until it was around 40% at 450 Wpm. Accuracy of comprehension, A, *decreased* as rate of comprehension, R, increased. Again, this is contrary to Buswell's contention that accuracy of comprehension would *increase* as individuals increase their rate.

The data that Carver presented in his Fig. 3, indicating mean percentage comprehension scores for the three groups at each of nine rates, were reanalyzed by (a) calculating the mean percentage scores for the three groups at each rate, and (b) calculating the correlation between the nine pairs of rate and percentage comprehension scores. Instead of there being no correlation between rate and comprehension as Stroud and Henderson (1943) suggested, and instead of a positive correlation between rate and comprehension as Tinker (1945) suggested, this correlation between measures reflecting rate of comprehension, R, and accuracy of comprehension, A, was nearly perfectly negative (-0.98), replicating the highly negative correlation of -0.90 found earlier for the Jester and Travers' (1966) data. Again, the difference between the latter negative correlations and the earlier positive or zero correlations is that the latter involved within-subject relationships reflecting R and A, and the former involved between-subject relationships reflecting R_L, A_L, and E_L. If you want to know what will happen to the accuracy of comprehension, A, when individuals increase their reading rate, R, then it is the latter findings that are relevant, not the earlier ones.

Keesey (1973) studied memory for prose material and rate of presentation. He measured normal reading rate in a no-test situation that was vaguely described; the mean rates of four different groups ranged from 315 to 370 wpm, i.e., reasonable rates for the rauding process of college students (see Tables 2.1 and 2.2). Then, a retention test was given at the normal rate for each subject plus three rates that were 50, 100, and 200 wpm faster. Scores on the retention test declined steadily as rate increased, suggesting that the normal rate was optimal, as would be predicted from rauding theory (Carver, 1981). Scores on a cloze test did not decline but a cloze test is relatively insensitive to changes, or group differences, in comprehension (see Carver, 1973a). Keesey also suggested that the optimal rate was at 480 wpm but this was based upon a second data analysis that did not control for individual differences across conditions.

In 1982, Carver replicated the general design of his 1973 research while expanding upon it in several ways. (Note: This research was reviewed earlier in Chapter 7 from a different perspective.) It may be remembered from earlier reviews that (a) Jester and Travers (1966) investigated the effect of five different rates (between 150 and 350 wpm) upon the accuracy of comprehension, A, and found evidence that A decreased as R increased, and (b) Carver (1973a) investigated the effect of ten different average rates (between 75 and 450 Wpm) upon the accuracy of comprehension, A, and found similar evidence that A decreased as R increased. In this later 1982 research of Carver's, the relationship between A and R was investigated by manipulating the reading rate of college students by using motion picture film (between 83 Wpm to 500 Wpm). The film was made using a two-line window that moved down the passage one line at a time at the prescribed rate. The same ten reading rates were used to present passages at four different grade levels of material difficulty: fifth, eighth, eleventh, and fourteenth. There were two different types of objective tests, reading storage tests and paraphrase tests, plus understanding ratings. The results replicated the earlier findings. As rate increased from 83 Wpm to 500 Wpm, indicants of the accuracy of comprehension, A, decreased for all three indicators of comprehension and at all four levels of material difficulty (see Fig. 7.2). Again, a high and negative within-individual relationship was found between rate and comprehension, indicating that the accuracy of comprehension, A, declines as the rate of comprehension, R, increases.

Juola, Ward, and McNamara (1982) investigated the effect of various presentation rates upon comprehension. (Note: This study was reviewed earlier in Chapter 15 from a different perspective.) Forty-eight college students were presented 200-word passages at rates varying between 200 and 700 wpm. Comprehension was measured by multiple-choice questions. The primary purpose was to compare the effects of three different presentation conditions: 200 msec per word, 300 msec per word, and a full page. No matter which presentation condition was used, the comprehension decreased as rate increased. This was another replication of the earlier findings of a high and negative relationship between rate of comprehension, R, and accuracy of comprehension, A.

In another study, Masson (1982) investigated several skimming rates to see if subjects were able to be selective in the type of information they attend to when time is limited. (Note: This study was also reviewed earlier in Chapter 6.) Masson reported results from four separate experiments. In each experiment, Masson administered the test items to a group of college student subjects who did not get to see the passages. In Experiment 1, accuracy of comprehension scores declined as rate of comprehension increased from 232 to 382 wpm for three different types of questions, inference, macrostatement, and microstatement, and two different types of passages, narratives and newspaper stories. In Experiment 2, accuracy of comprehension scores declined as rate of comprehension increased, 225, 375, and 600 wpm, for each of the same three types of questions and for both narrative and newspaper messages. In

Experiment 3, accuracy of comprehension scores declined as rate of comprehension increased, 225, 375, and 600 wpm, for relevant questions, irrelevant questions, macrostatements and microstatements. In Experiment 4, accuracy of comprehension scores declined as rate of comprehension increased, 225, 375, and 600 wpm, for both important and unimportant questions. These data of Masson's provide further replication for the high and negative within-individual relationship between the rate of comprehension, R, and the accuracy of comprehension, A.

Carver (1984b) investigated further the relationship between rate and comprehension using rates that varied between 62.5 and 100,000 Wpm. (Note: This research was reviewed earlier in Chapter 10 from a different perspective.) A total of 102 college students were given 100-word passages for lengths of time that varied from about 98 sec (for the average rate of 62.5 Wpm) to 1/18 of a second (for the average rate of about 100,000 Wpm). There were four different methods used to reflect accuracy of comprehension: understanding judgments, missing verbs, best titles, and sentence halves. There were also two purpose conditions: to get the gist and to detect the missing verbs. Accuracy of comprehension scores declined as rate of comprehension increased under both purpose conditions for each of the four measures of accuracy. However, there was evidence that the accuracy of comprehension, A, was zero at average rates, R, above 1000 Wpm. So, the above relationship of A declining with R increasing does not hold after average rates of 1000 Wpm are reached because A cannot decline below 0.

If individuals are induced to read faster they will lose accuracy of comprehension, and if they are induced to read more slowly they will gain accuracy of comprehension, at least under ordinary reading conditions wherein rates vary between about 100 and 1000 Wpm. The nature of this relationship is approximately linear in that each increment in R produces a similar decrement in A. However, this relationship is only *approximately* linear. The remainder of this section will contain a drastically different approach to the data that were reviewed earlier. Instead of focusing upon rate, R, the focus will be upon time, designated as $1/R$. Earlier it was noted that both Greene (1931) and Poulton (1958) contended that time was more important than rate when studying the accuracy of comprehension. This idea was also elaborated by Carver (1971d), and now it will be elaborated again using empirical data.

Carver (1977) reanalyzed the Carver data (1973a) (reviewed earlier) in terms of time per unit, $1/R$, instead of units per time (Words per minute). Instead of concentrating upon the decrease in the accuracy of comprehension, A, as the rate of comprehension, R, increased, he focused

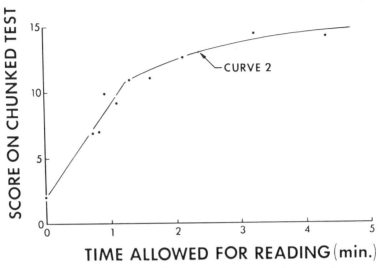

Figure 16.3 Score on the Chunked Test, corrected for guessing, as a function of the average time allowed for the reading of a passage, in minutes, together with a curve representing theoretical predictions (called Curve 2). (Fig. 11 from Carver, 1977.)

upon the increase in A as more time was allowed for reading, i.e., $1/R$ increased. Intuitively, this focus upon reading time should make a great deal of sense. Individuals should be able to increase their accuracy of comprehension of a passage as they are given more time to read it. Figure 16.3, taken from Carver (1977), illustrates that allowing more time for reading passages from the Nelson–Denny Reading Test (approximately 325 words in length), from 0 min to a little over 4 min, resulted in higher scores on the chunked test of comprehension, from about 2 to about 14. The curve fit to the data points in Fig. 16.3 is a straight line between 0 and about 1.25 min, and at 1.25 min the curve starts to taper off into a curvilinear function. This function illustrates the tenet of rauding theory which holds that initially the accuracy of comprehension, A, increases linearly as the time allowed for reading a passage, $1/R$, increases (see Chapter 2). However, this linear relationship only holds until the time needed for the individual to finish reading the passage at the rauding rate is reached, in this case about 1.25 min, or about 270 Wpm. Allowing more than about 1.25 min resulted in diminishing returns with respect to comprehension; after 1.25 min each additional minute spent on reading resulted in less of an increase in the accuracy of comprehension as compared to each minute before 1.25 min.

It was these data from Carver and this theoretical framework that moved the study of the rate–comprehension relationship into the realm of precise mathematical equations (see Carver, 1977). No longer would it be enough to study the within-individual relationship between A and R. Instead of investigating the effect of R in Wpm, it became possible and desirable to investigate the effect of time allowed for reading, in minutes per Sentence or in msec per Word, i.e., $1/R$. Instead of measuring comprehension by any method that seemed handy, it became desirable to discriminate among methods that provided reasonable indicators of the accuracy of comprehension, A, and other methods that were not reasonable estimates of A. Furthermore, it became possible to use the breakpoint between the initial straight line function and the subsequent curvilinear function to estimate rauding rate, R_r (see Carver, 1985a). The general equation relating A to $1/R$ for the initial straight line function in Fig. 16.3 was given in Chapter 2 as Equation 2.11. The general equation for the curvilinear function in Fig. 16.3 was given in Chapter 2 as Equation 2.12.

Before proceeding any further, it should be noted that Equations 2.11 and 2.12 were designed to hold when individuals are reading at a rate of their own choosing so that R is an average rate at which the passage is covered, and time is the variable being manipulated (see Carver, 1981). If rate of comprehension, R, is manipulated by using motion picture film, or the RSVP technique described in Chapter 15, then these equations were not designed to express this relationship. Out of the studies reviewed earlier, there were two that manipulated time instead of rate, and they will be reviewed now from this new perspective.

In the experiments by Masson (1982), the subjects were allowed to read at a rate of their own choosing while time was manipulated to produce average rates, R. Masson's Experiment 1 will not be analyzed because at least three data points are needed to provide a test for a linear relationship and his design provided only two. The results of Masson's Experiment 2 have been presented in Figs. 16.4, 16.5, and 16.6. The indicants of the accuracy of comprehension, A, were obtained by subtracting the reported proportion of false alarms (incorrect responses) from the reported proportion of hits (correct responses) to give an indicant of the accuracy of comprehension, A, when corrected for guessing. Those treatment conditions involving times less than 200 msec/word were assumed to provide less time than that required to finish reading the passage once at the rauding rate (see Table 2.2), so a straight line was fitted to these data as a test of the straight line relationship represented by Equation 2.11.

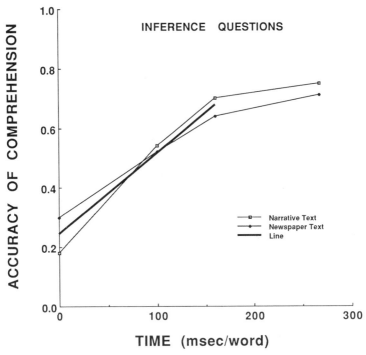

Figure 16.4 Accuracy of comprehension as a function of the time allowed for reading, in milliseconds per word, when inference questions were used to measure comprehension on a narrative text and a newspaper text. The dark line is the regression line that was fitted to the first six data points. (Original data from Masson, 1982.)

In Fig. 16.4, the straight line relationship has been assumed between 0 and 160 msec/word, and the regression line has been plotted for the best fit to the six relevant points for these inference questions, $r = 0.92$. A similar straight line has been plotted for the macro questions in Fig. 16.5, $r = 0.99$, and the micro questions in Fig. 16.6, $r = 0.99$. These data provide strong support for the linear relationship between $1/R$ and A that has been theorized (Carver, 1977, 1981) and expressed in Equation 2.11 because these correlations ranged from 0.92 to 0.99 thereby indicating that a straight line fits these data exceptionally well.

In Masson's Experiment 3, there were four types of questions but there were no control data for the relevant and irrelevant questions, leaving only two data points at times below 200 msec/word. For the macro statement questions and the micro statement questions that remained, a mean was obtained for the two values at each rate. The degree to which a straight line fits the three relevant data points was once again quantified by calculating the correlation, and $r = 0.94$, again, strong support for the theorized linear relationship.

In Masson's Experiment 4, the same rates were used but the method of measuring comprehension was changed from the use of questions to the proportion of propositions recalled. For this experiment, there was no control condition but it is reasonable to assume that this measure of the accuracy of comprehension would be zero at 0 msec/word ($A = 0$ when $1/R = 0$). For the three data points below 200 msec/word, the correlation for unimportant propositions was 1.00, and the correlation for the important propositions was also 1.00. These data from Experiment 4 provide perfect support for the theory that comprehension increases linearly with increases in msec/word allowed for reading, as long as the time allowed to read is less than the time required to read the passage once at the rauding rate.

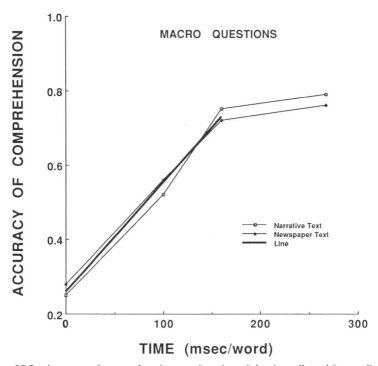

Figure 16.5 Accuracy of comprehension as a function of the time allowed for reading, in milliseconds per word, for macro questions on a narrative text and a newspaper text. The dark line is the regression line that was fitted to the first six data points. (Original data from Masson, 1982.)

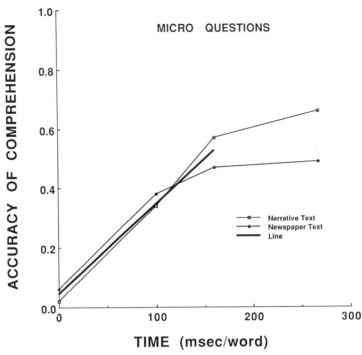

Figure 16.6 Accuracy of comprehension as a function of the time allowed for reading, in milliseconds per word for micro questions on a narrative text and a newspaper text. The dark line is the regression line that was fitted to the first six data points. (Original data from Masson, 1982.)

The final study that manipulated time instead of rate was the research of Carver (1984b), reviewed earlier, which varied rate from 62.5 to 100,000 Wpm. Figure 2 from that research has been reproduced and presented herein as Fig. 16.7. It illustrates very well the nature of the relationship when comprehension is measured by the use of four different methods. *It should be emphasized that the curve fit to the data in Fig. 16.7 was not empirically derived from these data points but was predicted from independent measures of the ability of the subjects and the difficulty of the materials.* The close fit of the theoretical predictions to the empirical data points further supports the nature of the theoretically derived relationship between the time allowed for reading a passage and the degree to which the passage is comprehended.

These data in Fig. 16.7 have been further analyzed by Carver (1985a). As noted earlier, Carver has developed a method for rescaling these

kinds of data to produce estimated absolute amounts of passage comprehension in percentages. He found that the correlations between his rescaled curves fit to these data, and the actual data points ranged from
0.98 to 1.00. He concluded that his rescaling technique provides a
method for measuring the accuracy of comprehension, A, on a ratio
measurement scale with absolute units rather than the relative units now
being used.

In summary, the relationship between the time allowed to read a passage, $1/R$, and the accuracy of comprehension, A, appears to be a rather
precise function that is initially linear but changes to curvilinear at the

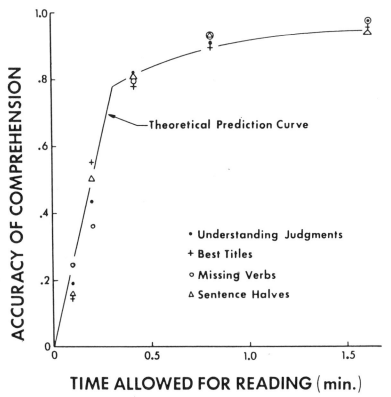

TIME ALLOWED FOR READING (min.)

Figure 16.7 Accuracy of comprehension as a function of the time allowed for reading, in
minutes, for four different measures of comprehension. Also presented is the independently derived and theoretically predicted relationship between accuracy of comprehension, A, and time, $1/R$. This theoretical curve was derived for this group of individuals who
have an estimated ability level at GE = 13.5, and were reading passages with an estimated
difficulty level at GE = 10. (Fig. 2 from Carver, 1984b.)

point where individuals are allowed enough time to finish the passage once while operating their rauding process (Carver, 1977, 1981, 1985a). The relationship between comprehension and rate is a rather precise relationship when taken to mean the relationship between A and R, and can be expressed quite succinctly by the equations given in Chapter 2.

Now that the interrelationships among A, R, and E have been explicated, it seems fitting to end this review of research on the relationship between rate and comprehension by revisiting the research on the relationships among A_L, R_L, and E_L which contributed to the early confusions. Standardized tests now exist that provide highly valid indicants of A_L, R_L, and E_L. The Accuracy Level Test (Carver, 1987c) and the Rate Level Test (Carver, 1987a) provide indicants of A_L and R_L, respectively, and the average of these two measures provides an indicant of E_L. Recently, it has been reported (Carver, 1990d) that the correlation between rauding accuracy level, A_L, and rauding rate level, R_L, was (a) 0.67 for 102 seventh and eighth graders, and (b) 0.16 for 64 college students. For these same two groups of students, the correlations (a) between rauding accuracy level, A_L, and rauding efficiency level, E_L, were 0.85 and 0.56, respectively, and (b) between rauding rate level, R_L, and rauding efficiency level, E_L, were 0.89 and 0.56, respectively. Notice that if reading comprehension means efficiency level, then the correlation between these measures of rate and comprehension is high, 0.56 to 0.89, but if reading comprehension means accuracy level, then the correlation between these measures of rate and comprehension is high for junior high students, 0.67, but low for college students, 0.16. Thus, it appears that indicants of A_L and E_L will consistently correlate highly because E_L includes A_L. However, indicants of A_L and R_L are highly related in the lower grades and become less related as the grade level of the students approaches the college level.

CONCLUSIONS

The research reviewed in this chapter clears up a number of confusions. There appears to be an extremely lawful relationship between the rate of comprehension, R, and the accuracy of comprehension, A. As the rate of comprehension increases the accuracy of comprehension decreases, or stated more precisely, as R increases A decreases. However, the relationship can be expressed even more precisely by mathematical formulas when minutes per word (or some other time measure) is used instead of words per minute. As the time allowed to read a passage increases from 0 min, the accuracy of comprehension, A, increases in proportion to the amount of time allowed. This linear function has been given in Equation

2.11; it holds up until the individuals have had time to finish executing their rauding process on the passage. From this point on, the relationship is curvilinear according to Equation 2.12.

Given the large amount of empirical support for the above theoretical relationships, it is wrong to suggest that individuals can improve their comprehension when they read if they will simply increase their rate. It may be that unique circumstances exist where individuals can increase their accuracy of comprehension by going faster. Yet, existing data and theory would point toward advising individuals to slow down and spend additional time reading if they want to increase their accuracy of comprehension on the passage. If you want to increase your comprehension, A, then decrease your rate, R.

As for the early research on rate and comprehension, it was not relevant to the within-individual relationship between R and A that many of those early researchers seemed to be interested in exploring. Those studies in the 1940s and 1950s actually investigated between-individual relationships among correlates of A_L, R_L, and E_L; they found their correlations to range from slightly negative and zero to highly positive. From these near-zero correlations involving between-individual relationships, an erroneous conclusion was drawn that the within-individual relationship between accuracy, A, and rate, R, was also zero. There appears to be no direct evidence that those early researchers recognized this logical fallacy, even though the end of the era of between-individual correlations (Letson, 1958) almost perfectly coincided with the beginning of the era of within-individual theorizing and data collection (Jester & Travers, 1966; Poulton, 1958). Perhaps the idea was intuitively understood but not articulated well enough (see Davis, 1962).

Summarized below are the reasons for prior confusions regarding the relationship between rate and comprehension:

1. There has not been a common definition of "comprehension" and how it should be measured. This word sometimes meant the number of multiple-choice questions on a passage that were correctly answered during a limited amount of time, and sometimes it meant the proportion correct; the former is often a reasonable indicator of the efficiency of comprehension, E, and the latter is often a reasonable indicator of the accuracy of comprehension, A. The confusions associated with the relationship between rate and comprehension existed because comprehension sometimes meant A and comprehension sometimes meant E; the relationship between R and A is quite different from the relationship between R and E. Also, the relationship between rate and comprehension was some-

times investigated using measures of individual differences in ability, such as correlates of R_L, A_L, and E_L. Again, the relationship between R_L and E_L is quite different from the relationship between R_L and A_L.

2. There has not been a common definition of "rate," and how it should be measured. This word sometimes meant the number of items *attempted* on a test, such as the Chapman–Cook or the Tinker Speed of Reading Test, and other times it meant the number *correct* on one of these tests. In other cases, it meant the number of words read during a certain length of time, such as on the Nelson–Denny Reading Test. Indicants of rauding rate R_r, from such tests may not correlate highly with words read per minute because some people will adopt a skimming process, Gear 4, or a learning process, Gear 2, and have an inordinately high or low rate compared to those who have executed the rauding process, Gear 3. Unless reading rate is refined by association with a certain reading process, such as the rauding process, and then refined by association with a certain construct, such as R, R_r, or R_L, there will continue to be confusions that are inherent to using such a broad concept as "reading rate."

3. Using the same words to mean separate things has contributed monumentally to the confusions, as described above, but these problems do not compare to the failure to keep between-individual correlations separate from within-individual correlations. Within the same individual, R and A are highly negatively correlated. However, between individuals, R_L and A_L are generally positively correlated.

4. When rate is measured on relatively hard materials, some individuals continue to operate their rauding process without a high degree of success and other individuals demonstrate process flexibility by shifting gears to a learning process with its lower rate. This is likely to make rate measurements on relatively hard materials inconsistent because all of the individuals are not using the same reading process.

Now that many of the confusions about the relationship between rate and comprehension have been eliminated, and the within-individual relationships have been explicated, it seems appropriate to return once again to the early research of the 1930s and 1940s. With the benefit of hindsight, it now seems evident that it is too simplistic to ask about the relationship between reading rate and reading comprehension because (a) individuals have many different possible reading rates depending upon what reading process they execute, and (b) rate and comprehension during the rauding process need to be defined more precisely in terms of A, R, E, A_r, R_r, E_r, A_L, R_L, and E_L. However, it is appropriate to ask about the relationship between rauding rate level, R_L, and rauding accuracy level, A_L. Students in a particular grade in school who raud faster tend to be able to raud more difficult materials; this relationship between R_L and A_L is high, above 0.50 toward the beginning grades of school. The relationship declines in strength as the grade increases so that it is likely to be below 0.50 for college students. Also, it is appropriate to ask: How does the accuracy of comprehension, A, relate to the rate of comprehension, R? This question is answered quite precisely by the equations given in Chapter 2 which indicate that A depends not only on R but also upon R_r, A_L, and D_L.

In summary, the faster an individual reads material the lower will be that individual's accuracy of comprehension; there is a high *negative correlation* between R and A within individuals as they read passages. However, those individuals who have the highest rauding rate level within a group will tend to be the ones who can accurately comprehend the most difficult material; there tends to be a *positive correlation* between the two primary measures of rauding ability, R_L and A_L.

17

AUTOMATICITY AND PRACTICE

INTRODUCTION

This chapter will contain a review of some of the theory and research associated with automatic information processing in reading, focusing upon the implications for the effect of practice upon rauding rate. First, the theory will be outlined, and then relevant research will be reviewed.

AUTOMATICITY THEORY

LaBerge and Samuels (1974) presented the theoretical ideas which are commonly referred to as automaticity theory. Their ideas are directly relevant to reading rate and how it can be increased because they contend that practice in recognizing a word will decrease the time it takes to recognize it. They were concerned with the perceptual learning associated with the recognition rate of letters and words.

LaBerge and Samuels presented data from 16 college-age subjects whose responses to familiar and unfamiliar letters were measured over 5 days of practice. The response times decreased with practice for the unfamiliar letters but stayed constant for the familiar letters, suggesting that perceptual learning was taking place for the unfamiliar letters, i.e., the unfamiliar letters were recognized faster with practice. In another study, using familiar and unfamiliar letters, the subjects were given another task to perform so that attention could be strictly controlled at the moment the letter appeared. The results of this study indicated that response latency to the unfamiliar letters decreased as expected over 18 days of practice but the unfamiliar letters were still responded to about 300 msec more slowly than the familiar letters. They interpreted these data as indicating that the unfamiliar letters were still requiring additional attention not required by the familiar letters, and that it would take many more days of practice before unfamiliar letters could be named as automatically and fast as familiar letters. The implication of these data for reading, according to LaBerge and Samuels, is that using an extra 300 msec, for example, just to decode a letter or word, will detract from or impede comprehension because attention capacity is limited. So, unless words are practiced to automaticity, the extra time taken for recognition will detract from comprehension.

There is little doubt that encountering a word that does not make sense will force a focus of attention upon that word. The rauding process may be completely disrupted and a regression to the beginning of the sentence may be required. However, LaBerge and Samuels claim that "the important growth of automaticity takes place after the subject has achieved accuracy" (p. 317). Therefore, the type of attention disruption associated with encountering *unknown* words is not addressed by these theoretical ideas.

The part of automaticity theory that is most relevant to reading rate is the idea that extensive practice in perceiving words is likely to increase perceptual or decoding rate. Since LaBerge and Samuels reported large differences in the reaction to familiar and unfamiliar letters, even after 18 days of training on the unfamiliar letters, it seems prudent to predict that measurable gains in rauding rate due to gains in perceptual recognition rate may require many practice trials. Indeed, it is interesting to speculate about how much of the yearly gain in rate of about 14 Wpm shown by a typical student in Chapter 11 is due to maturation in cognitive speed and how much is due to perceptual learning resulting from practice. Or, how many hours would a fourth grade student have to spend practicing the rapid recognition of second grade words in order to be able to gain 14 Wpm in how fast they could be read?

Automaticity theory has forced a focus upon the role of repetition as a primary factor that causes improvement in reading rate. Practice in decoding known words supposedly should result in their being read more rapidly and with little attention because they will be perceived more rapidly while attention is being directed toward understanding the complete thought represented by all the words in the sentence.

The research to be reviewed later can be more easily and systematically interpreted by first introducing a theoretical learning curve that reflects rauding rate for increasing amounts of practice on a word. Figure 17.1 contains a sketch of such a learning curve for a good reader and also for a poor reader. The curve is based upon the ideas of Ehri and Wilce (1979) who (a) emphasized the importance of discriminating between automaticity and speed, and (b) contended that the ability to recognize words has three aspects: accuracy, automaticity, and speed.

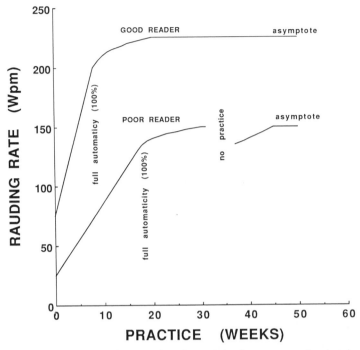

PRACTICE (WEEKS)

Figure 17.1 Learning curves for a good reader and also for a poor reader that depict the theoretical relationship between the rauding rate of a word and the amount of practice on the word, expressed in weeks of intermittent exposure after the word has first been accurately recognized.

This figure represents the effect of practice on speed, or rate, after a word can be accurately recognized or identified. Rauding rate is presented as a function of practice, yet, it is unorthodox to talk about the rauding rate for a particular word because rauding rate refers to comprehending sentences in passages. It will be helpful to conceptualize a certain amount of time in msec required to recognize or identify a Word during the operation of the rauding process, then that time per Word can be inverted so it is expressed in Words per minute instead of msec per Word. One advantage of plotting rate in Wpm instead of time in msec is that the point where rapid gains due to practice (the straight line part of the curve ends) and the diminishing returns begin (the flat curvilinear part begins) is readily apparent in Wpm whereas it would not be if msec per Word were plotted. This transition point on the learning curve is hypothesized as representing the point where partial automaticity ends and full automaticity begins. That is, up until this transition point, attention is directed toward recognizing the word whereas after this point, the word is recognized without any attention directed to lexical access. Therefore, between the time the word is first accurately recognized and the time where extra attention is no longer needed for recognizing the word, gains in rate due to practice are steady and relatively large because automaticity is gradually being achieved. We say that the word has reached automaticity when it is recognized automatically without any direct attention, and that point is hypothesized as being at the same time as when each unit of additional practice results in diminishing returns in rate. After the point of full automaticity is reached, then further gains in rauding rate will occur with further practice but the gain will be smaller per unit of practice. There is likely to be an asymptote on the curve that reflects the limitations of the individual's cognitive speed; this asymptote depicts a ceiling effect, as has been suggested by Raduege and Schwantes (1987) as limiting word recognition speed. The vertical distance between the two curves in Fig. 17.1 reflects the difference between the cognitive speed of good and poor readers. Notice that the good reader curve reaches full automaticity faster, i.e., with fewer weeks of practice, and also asymptotes at a higher rate.

Also notice in Fig. 17.1 that after automaticity is reached a gap is depicted in the poor reader curve. This reflects a possible lack of practice in rauding that particular word for a few weeks. When this lack of practice occurs for a word that has already reached automaticity, then the next encounter of the word will result in a lower rate compared to the immediately previous encounter. However, if practice is resumed then it does not take long for rate to increase to where it was before the lack of practice occurred.

The no-practice gap in the learning curve in Fig. 17.1 helps explain why it is necessary to continue to raud words that have already been automatized, whether poor readers or good readers. Failure to practice these words will result in lower rauding rates. Practice beyond automaticity helps reach the maximum or asymptotic rate and practice also helps maintain this rate once it has been attained.

Limited support for the nature of the theoretical learning curves depicted in Fig. 17.1 comes from the data of Hogaboam and Perfetti (1978). They gave skilled and less-skilled third graders varying amounts of practice in learning to pronounce pseudo words (CVCVCs). They used both listening and reading conditions. The results of the reading condition are presented in Fig. 17.2. Notice that as the number of practice trials increases from 0 to 6 for the less-skilled readers, the time required to begin to pronounce the word (latency) decreases rapidly, but from trials 6 to 18 there is very little decrease evident. For the skilled readers, there is a decrease in time from 0 to 3 practice trials, but from 3 to 18 there was no evidence of any further decrease. These results have been converted into Wpm by dividing 60 sec by the time in seconds per word. Figure 17.3 contains the same data as in Fig. 17.2 except rate in Wpm is on the vertical axis. A hand-drawn theoretical curve has been fitted to both sets of data to show the close fit between the shape of the theoretical learning curves presented in Fig. 17.1 and the data collected by Hogaboam and Perfetti. There seems to be some empirical support for the shape of this theoretical learning curve.

One outgrowth of automaticity theory is the idea of repeated readings; in 1979 Samuels talked about the efficacy of repeatedly reading the same passage over and over. A number of researchers have discussed automaticity, practice, and repeated reading (e.g., Allington, 1983; Lopardo & Sadow, 1982; Moyer, 1982; Samuels, 1985; Schreiber, 1980), and there are anecdotal accounts of the efficacy of treatments based upon these ideas (e.g., J. W. Cunningham, 1979; Lauritzen, 1982). Oth-

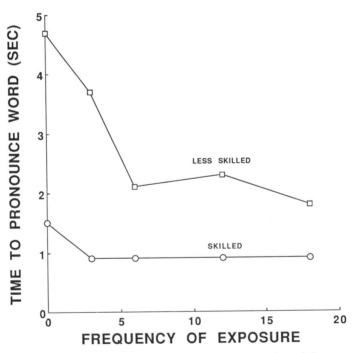

Figure 17.2 Time required to begin to pronounce a presented word, in seconds, as a function of the frequency of exposure, i.e., practice trials, for both a skilled group and a less skilled group. (Data from Hogaboam and Perfetti, 1978.)

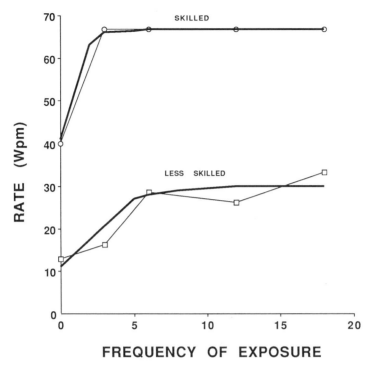

Figure 17.3 Rate, in Wpm, for recognizing a word as a function of frequency of exposure, or practice, for a group of skilled readers and a group of less skilled readers; a reanalysis of the data presented in Fig. 17.2. (Original data from Hogaboam and Perfetti, 1978.)

ers have presented data deemed not relevant enough to deserve a full review.

With this background, research will be reviewed that is relevant to automaticity and practice.

RESEARCH

Fleisher, Jenkins, and Pany (1979) gave poor reading fourth and fifth graders practice in recognizing isolated words. Passages were selected at the sixth and seventh grade levels of difficulty, and then the words in these passages were randomly ordered so that all of the words in the passage were included in a word list. After a great deal of practice in recognizing the words on the word list, posttests were given to the trained group and also to a control group of poor readers and control group of good readers. Their results clearly indicated that giving the poor readers practice in recognizing the words resulted in their being recognized in isolation just as fast as the good readers. Also, this increase in rate of recognition transfered to reading the words in context because the trained group read about 20–30 wpm faster than the untrained group. But, the trained poor readers still read over 35 wpm slower than the good readers. Most importantly, the trained poor readers could not comprehend what they read any better than the untrained poor readers.

The results of this research by Fleisher *et al.* will be interpreted by some as providing strong evidence against one of the main aspects of automaticity theory. That is, being able to recognize the words in a passage faster had no effect upon how accurately the passage was comprehended. However, there was no direct evidence that the poor readers had reached automaticity for recognizing the words in context, a crucial tenet of automaticity theory, even though the trained poor readers had reached a rate of recognition of the isolated words that was comparable to the good readers. More importantly, however, the poor readers tested out at a second grade level of reading ability and they were given passages at the seventh grade level of difficulty. With these estimates of $A_L = 2$ and $D_L = 7$, it is evident that these passages were relatively hard, $A_L < D_L$. With the advantage of hindsight, it should come as no surprise that practice in quickly pronouncing randomly ordered words taken from passages at the sixth and seventh grade level would not make these passages more comprehensible to fourth and fifth graders who were reading at the second grade level. It is the lack of knowledge of what the words mean, not their speed of correct pronunciation, that is mainly responsible for the uncomprehensibility of a sixth or seventh grade passage for a reader at the second grade level of ability. One implication of these data, then, is that helping poor readers recognize words faster in relatively hard passages is not a sufficient condition for improving their rauding accuracy, A_r.

The above research of Fleisher *et al.* has stimulated the following question: If these researchers had used passages at the second grade level, instead of the sixth and seventh grade level, would their trained poor readers have comprehended these second grade level passages any better? We do not know the answer to this question, but it seems reasonable to assume that the answer is no. Giving fourth and fifth graders, reading at the second grade level, a great deal of practice in recognizing second grade level words would probably not help them increase their A_r for second grade level passages. There are two reasons for this expectation. First, the words in the second grade level passages are probably already automatized so that additional practice may result in faster rates but have no or little effect upon automaticity. Second, if the individual can already comprehend the material relatively well, there is no evidence that increasing rate, R, will improve accuracy, A; such evidence would be counter to the data and theory presented in Chapter 16.

The focus of the present review of research is upon rauding rate, R_r, and a passage must contain words that can be accurately recognized in order for rauding rate to have any meaning. Therefore, it is a reasonable assumption that the words in passages which are relatively easy to raud have already reached full automaticity. Since passages at a difficulty level, D_L, below an individual's accuracy level, A_L, are likely to be automatized, practice in word recognition rate at this level is not likely to affect the accuracy of comprehension at all. And, such practice is likely to produce little gain in rauding rate after automaticity has been reached, unless asymptote has not been approached or there has been little or no practice in recent weeks. The importance of the Fleisher *et al.* research seems to be that we now know beyond a reasonable doubt that teaching children to decode faster the words contained in relatively hard passages will not help them increase A_r because this training has no effect upon the semantic encoding and sentence integrating components of the rauding process. Yet, these Fleisher *et al.* data are not directly relevant to whether such practice affects R_r because relatively easy passages were not involved.

Snowling and Frith (1981) gave seven year olds normal and distorted passages to read aloud. They measured the time taken to read these passages, which were 26 words long. There were three types of distortions: phonologically similar (e.g., tuk for took), visually similar (e.g., tho for the), and multiple script (e.g., hEr for her). The normal text was read by the good reading group at 134 wpm and was read by the poor reading group at 33 wpm. The multiple script was read the fastest of the three distortions but it was still read 44% slower than the normal text in each group, 93 wpm and 23 wpm, respectively. The phonologically similar passage was read the slowest in each group, 50 wpm and 19 wpm, with the visually similar text read somewhat faster than the phonologically similar, 62 and 23 wpm respectively. These researchers contended that the results imply that children do not memorize the shape of words or the sounds of words and then learn to read faster by recognizing the shape or sound faster; this is because the symbols that were similar in shape or sound were read at a slower rate than both the normal text and the multiple text. In contrast to their interpretation, it should be noted that all three distortions were read at least 44% slower than the normal text; therefore, there must be some perceptual learning associated with the normal shape of words. So, it seems reasonable to retain the idea that learning to read faster is partly associated with perceptual learning that involves recognizing the visual shape of a word faster each time it is encountered, up until the maximum or asymptote rate is reached.

Stanovich, Cunningham, and West (1981) studied automaticity in first graders by using the Stroop task. Words were presented in colors and the task was to name the color as fast as possible; automaticity was measured by the increase in time taken to name the color of a word versus nonwords due to the automatic attention paid to recognizing the word. They studied first graders because other research (Guttentag & Haith, 1978; West & Stanovich, 1979) ". . . strongly suggested that it is during the first grade that the most marked changes occur" (p. 60). Their research was developmental in that they tested the same students at the beginning, middle, and end of their first grade year.

Stanovich *et al.* measured developmental changes during the year, involving letters, high-frequency words, and low-frequency words. There was automaticity for letters at the beginning of the year but not for words. By the end of the year there was automaticity for words also. There was consistently more automaticity for high-frequency words than for low-frequency words. These results are all in accordance with the idea that there is no automaticity (0%) before the word is recognized with 100% accuracy. When the word is learned, i.e., 100% accuracy is reached, then further practice results in less attention to the word. As attention decreases with further practice, we say that automaticity increases. So, automaticity increases from 0% (at 100% accuracy) to 100% when the point is reached of diminishing returns with practice (see Fig. 17.1). Stanovich also tested some second graders on the same words and found no further increases in automaticity. Also, the first graders were divided into skilled and less skilled and the differences between these two groups were in accordance with predictions made from automaticity theory. Individual differences in automaticity for the words were correlated with measures of reading ability and most of these were medium to large in effect size, 0.30 to 0.50, when there was evidence that automaticity existed. However, these researchers deprecated the size of these correlations, and they did not consider the fact that the correlations were severely attenuated due to the notoriously low reliabilities associated with difference scores and ratio scores.

The above results were interpreted by Stanovich *et al.* as implicating the first grade as the critical period for the development of automaticity. They also concluded that:

> An important implication of the research reported here is that word recognition speed continues to increase even after recognition has become automa-

tized. Thus, it is crucial that the distinction between speed and automaticity be made by reading theorists. (p. 72)

The above implications are in accordance with the theoretical learning curve presented in Fig. 17.1. Also, the reason why first grade is so important is probably because that is the period when almost all the words encountered are at some level that is below the maximum rate, and a very high proportion of those encountered are at some level of automaticity between 0 and 100%. Beyond first grade, most of the words encountered by a typical student are likely to be automatically recognized.

In another study, Carver and Hoffman (1981) studied the effect of practice via the repeated silent reading of passages. A computer was used to administer 50–70 hours of practice to ninth and tenth graders reading at about the fifth grade level. Each student was presented 160 passages, about 100 words in length, that ranged from grade level 2 up to grade level 9 in difficulty. Every fifth word in a passage was presented with an alternative wrong word selected from the passage, and the student was supposed to select the original word that belonged in the passage by pressing one of two keys. Each passage was presented first as a test, with the student instructed to select the correct answers to the approximately 20 items as quickly as possible. Then, the passage was repeatedly administered until all 20 of the items were correctly answered. After 100% accuracy, the passage was administered again as a posttest under the same test conditions as the pretest. On a paper and pencil test that was similar in nature to the experimental task, there was a gain from the fifth grade level to the eighth grade level. However, this gain of three grade equivalents was not obtained on the various sections of the Gates MacGinitie Reading Test; the gains were very small. Thus, this large effect size due to the treatment seemed to be specific to a type of test that was exactly similar to the experimental task.

The above data indicate that giving poor reading high school students a great deal of reading practice involving decoding words and determining semantic meaning within the context of a sentence does not necessarily result in a large effect upon reading level, A_L, as measured by a typical standardized reading test. On the other hand, there was a 15% gain due to practice in a Rate of Good Reading measure used by these researchers. It is possible that this gain reflects a gain in rauding rate of 15% that would not be inconsequential. For example, if the rauding rate of these students was also at the fifth grade level (5.5), then it would be 163 Wpm, according to Appendix B, and a 15% gain would result in a rate of 187 Wpm which is the seventh grade level (7.2). Therefore, the Carver and Hoffman research on repeated reading practice leaves open the possibility that poor readers can improve their rauding rate level, R_L, by practicing a task that requires lexical access and semantic encoding of the words in passages. However, these poor readers probably have slower cognitive speeds and may not be able to achieve decoding rates that approach those of good readers. Still, the poor readers may not read enough to keep their recognition rates up to their own maximums, and this type of repeated-reading practice may result in this type of benefit.

Ehri and Wilce (1983) gave first, second, and fourth graders 6 and 18 trials of practice on pronounceable nonsense syllables (CVCs), and then measured their pre and post reaction times to these pseudo words; this research followed up some of their earlier work in this area (Ehri and Wilce, 1979). Besides these CVCs there were three-letter, high-frequency words, e.g., "cat" and "eat," and also digits. And, there were skilled and less-skilled groups in each grade. Practice resulted in lower reaction times to the CVCs. Practice also resulted in about 400 msec lower reaction times to the high-frequency words for the less-skilled readers but not for the skilled readers. Practice did not result in a lower reaction time for digits.

The above results can be interpreted as providing more support for the theoretical learning curves presented in Fig. 17.1. The CVCs did show gain due to practice because none of these words had been practiced before so they could not have reached asymptote, or maximum rate. There were no gains associated with practice on the high-frequency words for the skilled readers because they had already reached asymptote, but there were gains for the less-skilled readers because they had not practiced enough to reach asymptote. The digits were highly practiced and were at asymptote for both groups, and that is why there was no improvement in digit-recognition speed due to practice in either the skilled or less-skilled groups.

Ehri and Wilce interpreted their own results as providing support for a concept that they call "unitized" speed. They have conceived of a maximum rate for each word that is constant for all words. For each word as a unit, no matter how long the word in letters, they are theorizing that with practice each word can reach the same maximum rate. This theoretical idea of theirs may be credible for the laboratory where rate is measured in terms of reaction times to individual words. However, it is an idea that would not likely generalize to the rate at which the rauding process operates. If the rauding rate of long words was exactly the same as short words, then college students should raud 100 actual words in fifth grade level passages at the same rate in wpm as 100 actual words of eleventh grade level passages, but they do not. Carver (1983) found that college students read fifth grade level material faster than eleventh grade level material when rate is measured in actual words, wpm, instead of standard length words, Wpm. Thus, the unitized idea does not seem promising for generalizing about rauding rate. Instead, it seems more likely that the maximum rauding rate for a word varies with the length of the word in letters, or syllables, because fifth grade level material with shorter words is read at the same rate as eleventh grade level material with longer words when rate is measured in Wpm and the reader is likely to have reached asymptote for all the words.

Ehri and Wilce's research lends further credence to their idea that practice in decoding a word passes through the following phases:

> In Phase 1, unfamiliar words become familiar and recognized *accurately* by readers directing their attention to component letters as they map sounds. During Phase 2, as a result of more practice, familiar words come to be recognized *automatically* as wholes without attention and without deliberate processing of component letter–sound relations. In Phase 3 the speed of processing familiar words increases to a maximum as the components involved in stimulus recognition and response production become consolidated or "unitized" in memory. (p. 3)

Their summary, above, is being questioned only with respect to the generality of the whole word or unitized concept. As noted above, it seems impossible for there to be a constant maximum rauding rate that is the same rate for each actual word. Instead, the maximum rauding rate probably varies across words for each individual depending upon the length of the word. Also, the maximum rate probably varies across individuals depending upon their cognitive speed, and this explains why the skilled readers reacted faster than the less skilled readers under every condition tested, including the highly overlearned digits. Finally, their research suggests that practice in decoding a known word results in a faster rauding rate as long as the word has not been encountered so many times that it has reached asymptote. In general, the three phases advanced by Ehri and Wilce are in accordance with the theoretical curves presented in Fig. 17.1.

Favreau and Segalowitz (1983) measured reaction times to English words and French words when presented to 60 bilingual readers, with English as the first language for 30 of these readers and with French as the first language for the other 30. Within each group of 30, 15 were reading at approximately the same rate in both languages (about 275 wpm) and 15 were reading slower in their second languages (318 versus 234 wpm). They reported that ". . . reduced automatic processing by the unequal-reading-rate subjects in their second language compared with that in their first is of special interest because these bilinguals possess fluent and native-like language skills under normal conditions of listening, reading, and speaking" (p. 571). Notice that Favreau and Segalowitz did not make any distinction between automaticity and rate. Since they did not study automaticity in any more direct way than reaction time to words, it seems prudent to interpret their results with respect to rate, rather than automaticity. This means that it is highly likely that all 60 of their subjects had reached automaticity for all of their experimental words, e.g., bird, carrot, and potato, and that the reason why their slower reading language groups reacted slower to the second language was because they had not yet practiced them enough to reach asymptote. Indeed, these researchers hypothesized that a lack of practice may explain their results, and they did find that ". . . the equal-reading-rate bilinguals had been schooled longer in their second language than had the unequal-reading-rate bilinguals . . ." (p. 571). Given that the unequal group read their second language at a mean rate of 234 wpm, it seems unlikely that they had not reached full automaticity for the high-frequency words used in the experiment. Yet, it is quite reasonable to accept the idea that they had not yet practiced them enough to reach the same asymptote as high-frequency words in their first language. Thus, these data also may be interpreted as providing empirical data in accordance with the theoretical learning curves presented in Fig. 17.1, especially the part of the curve between full automaticity and asymptote.

Rashotte and Torgesen (1985) asked 12 "learning disabled" children to take part in two types of repeated reading training and one control condition. (Note: These data were from a category excluded from the review, as stated in Chapter 1; these data were included because of the paucity of research on the effect of practice.) In both types of repeated reading, the same passage was read aloud four times on each of seven days. In one of the two repeated reading conditions the seven 100-word passages were specially selected so that they had three times as many overlapping or common words as the other repeated reading condition. These two types of repeated readings were compared to a control condition wherein 28 different, unrelated, and nonoverlapping stories were read, 4 per day for 7 days. Under each condition, all of the students read four passages for about 15 min a day, for 7 days. Since all students took part in all three conditions, in different orders, the entire experiment took 21 days. The students were all reading at grade level 3 or higher and all the passages used in the experiment were at grade level 2 difficulty, so the materials were relatively easy, $A_L > D_L$.

Rashotte and Torgesen reported that these students read an average of 49.7 wpm on the pretest and with only 6.45% word errors. Reading the same passages four times in one day resulted in mean gains from the first to the last reading of about 35 wpm for the two repeated-reading conditions. Unfortunately, there were no data presented that indicated how much gain there was orally in reading rate under each condition from the first passage read on Session 1 to the first passage read on Session 7. Instead, the rate of gain was presented in terms of the slope across all seven conditions, after being controlled for variations in intercept. Statistically, this is all very proper and logical. However, some people will have trouble judging the size of the effects from the slopes presented. The most gain occurred when the seven passages being read had approximately 60 words in common; the slope was 1.1. This means that there was a gain in reading rate of about 1 wpm each 15 min session. If this rate of gain continued each day for an entire school year, it would represent a *gain* of 150 wpm. This would be a tremendous gain but it would not be meaningful because these gains would be very specific to the same 60 words. Much more relevant is the gain associated with passages that had few overlapping words, 20 or less, because these passages represent a more normal repeated-readings situation; the passages are more representative of the population of passages at the second grade level and inform us better about the transfer effects for repeated-reading training. Under this condition the slope was 0.20 indicating that there would be gain of 1 wpm every 5 days; extrapolating to a year in school with 150 days, this gain would be 30 wpm instead of the 150 wpm extrapolated value for the overlapping passage condition. Yet, the slope of the low overlapping condition, 0.20, needs to be compared to the slope of the control condition, 0.37, indicating a rate of gain for the control condition almost twice as large as the latter repeated-reading condition. Again, extrapolating over a year's time, this would represent a gain in oral reading rate of 56 wpm for the control condition. So, when extrapolated over a year's time, the more normal repeated-reading condition resulted in the least gain, about 30 wpm, considerably less than the gain of 56 wpm from simply spending the same time reading new passages. Again, the highest gain of all resulted from the repeated-reading condition that involved passages that were especially selected because they had 60% overlapping words, about 150 wpm, but this result could only be generalized to a limited number of words and is not representative of normal repeated-reading training.

These data of Rashotte and Torgesen suggest that the gain in rate due to repeated readings is very specifically tied to the number of practice trials associated with each encountered word. Therefore, any gains due to repeated readings are specifically associated with the particular words involved. Reading different passages once produced more gain in rate than repeatedly reading the same passage.

Herman (1985) gave repeated-reading practice to eight students in grades 4–6 who were selected from a class of 42 remedial readers who read aloud exceptionally slowly, 35–50 wpm. The practice averaged 21 treatment days spread over a 3-month period. The practice involved stories at instructional level which were repeatedly read until a rate of 85 wpm was reached. The pre to post gain in rate of reading aloud was from a mean of 47 to 70 wpm. This gain appears to be substantial, and probably reflects a substantial gain in rauding rate. However, several caveats are in order. First, there was no control group. Second, these readers were exceptionally poor readers. Third, it was not perfectly clear whether or not the selection test was also the pretest; if it was, the results may be due entirely to regression to the mean.

O'Shea, Sindelar, and O'Shea (1985) compared two purpose conditions while students were engaged in repeated readings. The stories used were at the fourth grade level and the third grade students were selected so that these passages were at their instructional level. The 30 students were divided randomly into two treatment groups: one was instructed to read aloud as quickly and correctly as possible (the rate group) and the other was instructed to read aloud to try to remember as much of the story as they could (the comprehension group). There were three experimental stories, and each student read each one under three repeated-reading conditions: once, three times, and seven times. When the story had been read the specified number of times, both groups knew that they would be asked to retell as much of the story as they could.

Using the nomenclature from Chapter 14, the rate group was engaged in a mixture of MORR (Maximum Oral Reading Rate) and RORR (Rauding Oral Reading Rate) because they were asked to read as fast as possible but they knew they would have to retell the story later. It is not surprising, therefore, that their mean rate prior to repeated readings (the once condition) was 117 wpm, considerably lower than the 158 wpm rate given for fourth graders in Table 2.1. The comprehension group was engaged purely in RORR and they read even more slowly at 101 wpm. As might be expected, the rate group had consistently higher rate scores under all three repeated measures conditions, and the comprehension group had consistently higher comprehension scores under all three of these conditions. Both groups had increased their rate and comprehension scores at the end of three repeated readings, and there was another increase in these two measures at the end of seven repeated readings. These data verify that repeatedly reading the same passage results in higher reading rates, and also higher accuracy of comprehension scores (see Carver, 1985a). However, these data do not indicate how much, if any, this repeated-reading practice improves, or helps maintain, rauding rate, R_r, because there was no measure of possible transfer effects at the end of the treatment.

CONCLUSIONS

This chapter on automaticity and practice has presented research that leaves little doubt that the recognition of words involve three phases. The first phase involves learning to decode accurately, and has nothing directly to do with rauding rate. The second phase involves practice in decoding the word (a) with a resulting decrease in the time required to perceive the shape of the word, and (b) with a resulting decrease in the attention needed to recognize the word. After the word is recognized with little or no attention in the second phase, i.e., it has been automatized, then the third phase has been reached wherein further practice results in further reductions in the time required to recognize the word until an asymptote is reached. This asymptote, or maximum rate, definitely varies between individuals with more highly skilled readers having a higher rate than less highly skilled readers. The above phases seem to apply especially well to beginning readers who already know the contextual meaning of the words they are learning since they are within their auditory vocabulary.

A theoretical learning curve was presented earlier in Fig. 17.1 that is more specific about the nature of the three phases, noted above. This learning curve contains the hypothesis that automaticity is directly associated with the initial part of the curve where automaticity increases from 0% to 100% as the rate of recognizing the word increases linearly. When full automaticity is reached, 100%, it is hypothesized that further practice results in diminishing returns with respect to further increases in rate. Then, it is hypothesized that an asymptote is reached for each word for each individual. This maximum rate varies within individuals between words depending upon word length, and varies between individuals depending upon their cognitive speed, C_s. Furthermore, it is theorized that a lack of practice for a word results in a lowering of its rauding rate. The preceding theoretical ideas (a) explain the reaction times of skilled and less skilled readers due to varying amounts of practice (Hogaboom & Perfetti, 1978); (b) explain why good readers read normal text faster than poor readers, and distorted text is read slower than normal text (Snowling & Frith, 1981); (c) explain why automaticity does not exist before a word is learned, increases as it is learned, and no longer increases after it is highly practiced (Stanovich et al., 1981); (d) explains why further practice on words that have already been highly practiced results in no further gains in rate for skilled readers but does result in further gains for less-skilled readers (Ehri & Wilce, 1983); and (e) explains why repeatedly reading the same passage will only result in a higher rate for other passages when most of the words are the same (Rashotte & Torgesen, 1985).

The method of repeated readings is one way of practicing words that have not reached asymptote, i.e., to read the same passage more than once results in a faster reading rate for the same words. However, it is clear that simply being able to recognize the words in a new passage faster does not guarantee that the passage will be comprehended any better (higher accuracy, A), especially when the passage is relatively difficult (Fleisher et al., 1979). Repeated-reading training is not likely to increase rauding rate because rauding rate is only meaningful when the material is relatively easy, $A_L > D_L$, and therefore is likely to already be at asymptote. On the basis of hindsight, it seems clear that the method of repeated readings will only increase rauding rate when the passages contain words that have been practiced to automaticity but have not yet reached asymptote.

The method of repeated readings is probably most effective in a situation that is not directly relevant to rauding rate and not directly relevant to automaticity theory. Repeatedly reading a passage is probably only effective when many of the words in the passage (e.g., 10% or more) have not yet been learned to 100% accuracy, even though the meaning of the words are known auditorily. This situation probably only occurs when the individual is at the first grade level of rauding ability. Once the second grade level of ability is reached, repeatedly reading first and second grade level passages will not help much because these words are already up to automaticity. Repeatedly reading third grade level passages may be helpful since the unknown words are probably known auditorily; however, there will be so many known words in relationship to unknown words, that reading the same passages four times is not as effective as reading four new passages once. Indeed, the data that have been reviewed seem to support the following neo-automaticity theory: the best way to increase rauding rate would be to spend a great deal of time rauding relatively easy passages so as to keep all of these known words up to asymptote. The only place that repeated reading is likely to be especially helpful is for students at the first grade level of rauding ability wherein almost every passage they encounter has many visually unknown words but 100% of the words are known auditorily. In this situation, the method of repeated readings will help get the unknown words up to 100% accuracy, and at the same time will provide practice on many visually known words that are not yet up to full automaticity.

Extensive practice in recognizing known words in relatively easy material is likely to have no effect on rauding rate because there can be no improvement beyond asymptote, and this maximum rate can probably be maintained without the extensive practice associated with repeated readings. However, as readers progress up the scale of rauding accuracy level, A_L, they will always be encountering unknown words when the materials are at a matched level of difficulty, $A_L = D_L$, or are relatively difficult, $A_L < D_L$. Therefore, these unknown words will all have to pass through the automaticity phase where they must be practiced enough to reach full automaticity. Even though rauding rate inherently involves full automaticity, the attempt to operate the rauding process at the rauding rate will often fail when the material being read is at matched level, $A_L = D_L$, or relatively hard, $A_L < D_L$. Therefore, improvement in rauding ability involves practice in reading materials at $A_L = D_L$ so that the rauding process can eventually operate at the rauding rate on these materials. So, automaticity is continually involved in rauding ability because it is an inherent part of R_L and it is directly involved in improving A_L.

Probably the most helpful consequence of automaticity theory is that it has stimulated research on rate and practice. These two factors have been neglected by almost all researchers in recent years, except for those who have been interested in testing automaticity theory and related hypotheses. Since practice in the execution of the rauding process on relatively easy material is probably the only way that individuals can maintain their rauding rate at the maximum set by cognitive speed, and since practice in decoding new words at matched level, $A_L = D_L$, is probably the most important way to improve A_L, it follows that practice in rauding deserves a great deal more research. The potency of rauding practice as the primacy cause of improvement in rauding ability needs to be empirically determined.

RAPID READING TRAINING

INTRODUCTION

Rapid reading training (RRT) is effective in getting students to read faster because it is not too difficult to induce students to shift up from their rauding process to a skimming process that proceeds at a faster rate. Students can be trained to increase their reading rate to two to three times normal with only a few minutes or a few hours of instruction (e.g., see Raygor, Wark, & Warren, 1966; Tirrell, Mount, & Scott, 1977). It is not particularly difficult to get students to read faster when they are given questions after reading that are easy to answer even at the faster skimming rates. However, there is no evidence that the rauding rate, R_r, of individuals can be improved by such training. Research data do exist suggesting that reading rate can be increased by 50% or more without any loss of comprehension; however, those data are not valid for drawing sound conclusions, as will be discussed later.

This chapter will review the research that has been conducted on rapid reading training. However, this subject has generated much more opinion than research. For example, Evelyn Wood (1960) claimed to have discovered a "breakthrough" in reading, relevant to her commercially available speed reading course, and Spache (1962) among others, has questioned that breakthrough. The pro opinions (e.g., Combs, 1966; Hellebust, 1973) and the con opinions (e.g., Ekwall, 1969; Graham, 1975) will not be reviewed, and neither will the various books, video cassettes, and audio cassettes that tell you how to speed read (e.g., see N. B. Smith, 1957). Furthermore, there have been numerous review articles in this area and they will not be treated (e.g., Berger, 1966; Carver, 1987d; Poulton, 1961).

As noted above, the subject of speed reading and rapid reading does not suffer from a lack of firm opinion, representing wide disagreements. Ordinarily, research is counted upon to reduce the confusions that fuel conflicting opinions. Unfortunately, most of the research on rapid reading training has added to the confusion instead of lessening it. This is because of many methodological pitfalls that have not been avoided in prior research. In short, most of the research has not met minimum research standards. D. T. Campbell and Stanley (1963) have classified research designs into pre-experimental and experimental; pre-experimental designs lack the appropriate controls for internal and external validity. Probably more than half of the RRT research that has been conducted is readily classified as pre-experimental. Even the experimental research has failed to avoid pitfalls. Before reviewing the relevant research, an entire section will be devoted to explicating known methodological pitfalls.

METHODOLOGICAL PITFALLS

Rate-Measurement Pitfall

Any measure of rate that counts the number of words read in a certain length of time but fails to estimate the degree to which the words have been comprehended should not be used to determine the effectiveness of rapid reading training. For example, the Nelson–Denny Reading Test measures reading rate by counting the number of words read during the first minute of reading a 600-word passage. (Note: Some of the limitations of the Nelson–Denny Reading Test were discussed at length in Chapter 13.) This measure of rate includes no estimate of the percentage of comprehension that accompanied the words read during that one minute. A typical college student will have a reading rate score of about 250–275 wpm when the Nelson–Denny is given before training—as a pretest. Since training ordinarily consists of getting students to use a skimming process, they will ordinarily read much faster during the one minute that rate is measured at the beginning of the posttest. They may skim 500 words during this one minute on the posttest, but there is no accompanying estimate or measure of what percentage of the ideas or sentences were comprehended. It is a pitfall to use a measure such as this to evaluate improvement in rauding rate. This pitfall will be called the Rate-Measurement Pitfall. Other tests, such as the Diagnostic Reading Tests, suffer from the same limitations as the Nelson–Denny when they are used to evaluate training or instruction in reading. However, the pitfall occurs most often with the Nelson–Denny Rate score because it has been used more than any other test to evaluate reading improvement courses (Sweiger, 1972). The nature of this pitfall has been aptly stated by Morton (1959), as follows:

> Use of a rate of reading measure, without reference to the individual's comprehension level in the same passage, a measure used by many investigators, would seem totally unsatisfactory, since, at its crudest, one has only to instruct the student to read at twice his normal speed to double his rate of reading. (p. 226)

Examples of studies that have failed to avoid the Rate-Measure Pitfall are Carpenter and Jones (1975); Collins (1979); Cosper and Mills (1953); Rankin (1963); Swalm and Kling (1973).

Comprehension-Measurement Pitfalls

There are two pitfalls to avoid when measuring comprehension, and they will be discussed in turn. The first and most important pitfall associated with comprehension measurement is the use of questions that are easy to answer without rauding the materials. It is quite simple to write multiple-choice questions on a passage that are not sensitive to changes in comprehension. For example, look at the item below that was taken from an actual test used in an unpublished research study designed to investigate speed reading training.

Which one of the following least represents a folk society?

1. A group of people of similar ethnic backgrounds living close together in a city.
2. A group of survivors from a ship who land on a desert island.
3. The Aborigine of Australia.
4. The Pueblo Indians of the Southwestern United States.

Notice that it is not too difficult to figure out the most likely answer to this item without even reading the passage. The item is not passage dependent (see Tuinman, 1973). Therefore, items like these will produce mean scores around 75% when the passage has been read at a rate of 250–300 Wpm and these kinds of items will also produce mean scores around 75% when the rate is 450–500 Wpm. The item is relatively insensitive to the drop in the accuracy of comprehension, A, due to a switch from the rauding process to a skimming process. Therefore, the items might be called skimming items because 70% or more can still be answered correctly after the execution of a skimming process. This first pitfall associated with comprehension measurement will be called the Skimming-Items Pitfall. Laffitte (1964) apparently was aware of this pitfall when he suggested that "a student can learn to skim material on reading tests and still perform relatively well on comprehension questions which query them on material found in a few major portions of selections" (p. 165).

Research on the effects of RRT can attempt to avoid the Skimming-Items Pitfall by collecting data on the items themselves. One technique that has been used is to administer the items to a comparable control group without administering the experimental treatment. Scores made under this no-passage-control condition provide an estimate of zero comprehension. For example, Carver (1972a) used a no-passage-control condition to help measure the sensitivity of the test items used to evaluate a speed reading course taught using the Evelyn Wood Reading Dynamics method. The no-passage-control group correctly answered 51% of the items on a fiction passage and correctly answered 57% of the items on a nonfiction passage. Therefore, a 51% score on the fiction test can be interpreted as 0% accuracy of comprehension and a 57% score on the nonfiction test can also be interpreted as 0% accuracy of comprehension. The corresponding scores made by the speed reading trainees in that research look quite respectable at 68% for fiction and 68% for nonfiction, until it is noted that 51% and 57% represent 0% accuracy of comprehension.

This no-passage-control condition has also been applied to the Nelson–Denny Reading Test. Carver (1971e) reported that 60 college students taking both the Form A and Form B test questions without reading the passages averaged 40% on the tests. From these results, raw scores of 14.4 correct responses out of the 36 items on this test, 40%, could be interpreted to mean that none of the complete thoughts in the passages was comprehended. Put another way, none of the information used to respond correctly to the questions came from reading the passages. Poulton (1961) reported that he was able to answer 63% of the 120 questions on the passages used for one rapid reading program without ever reading the passages themselves.

Sometimes, standardized tests like the Nelson–Denny are not used; instead, specially developed passages and test items are used. The time to read each passage is used to calculate wpm and then the comprehension items are administered untimed. One of the best ways to avoid the Skimming-Items Pitfall under these test conditions would be to administer the passages and the comprehension test items to a comparable control group under the same time conditions as the speed reading trainees. For example, suppose the speed reading trainees read the 300-word test passages at an average rate of 600 wpm and scored 75%. A comparable control group could be given the test passages to read for 30 sec, which is an average rate of 600 wpm. Then, if this control group scored lower than 75% under this condition such as 25% to 50% we would be in a better position to surmise that the speed reading training was likely to have improved the reading ability of the experimental group. On the other hand, if this control group scored close to 75% we could surmise that the test consisted of skimming items, and that speed reading training was not effective.

In summary, the two techniques advanced for avoiding the Skimming-Items Pitfall were the use of a no-passage-control group and a skimming control group. Without some evidence that the Skimming-Items Pitfall has been avoided in research, it would seem to be reasonable to assume that the research findings were not valid. Examples of research that failed to avoid this pitfall are Brown and McDowell (1979); Mullins and Mowry (1953); Tuckey (1960).

The second pitfall associated with comprehension measurement involves the failure to estimate properly the percentage comprehension associated with the material that was read. For example, suppose the Nelson–Denny Reading Test is used as a pretest and as a posttest for a group of college students who have taken an 8-week course in rapid reading training. This test has eight items on the first passage, and four on the remaining seven passages for a total of 36 items. Consider a typical sophomore who has time to finish the first six passages and answers 24 out of these 28 items correctly. The best available measure of comprehension in this situation would be to correct for guessing using a standard correction for guessing formula such as

$$C = R - [W/(A - 1)] \qquad (18.1)$$

where C is the corrected for guessing score, R is the number right, or number of correct items, A is the number of possible alternatives to each item, and W is the number of wrong items. The Nelson–Denny has five alternatives for each answer so the score of 24 correct, in the example above, would be corrected as follows:

$$C = 24 - 4/4 = 23$$

In this example, the best available indicant of the accuracy of comprehension would be 23/28 which is 82%, or $A = 0.82$. On the posttest, suppose this individual had been successfully induced to operate a skimming process that operated about 50% faster so she finished the entire test and again answered 24 correctly. This time, however, it was 24 correct and 12 wrong out of 36. The corrected score would be:

$$C = 24 - 12/4 = 21$$

The best available indicant of the accuracy of comprehension would be 21/36 which is 58%, or $A = 0.58$. In this latter situation, the individual has actually read the passages about 50% faster but the best available estimate of the accuracy of comprehension indicates that A dropped from 82% on the pretest to 58% on the posttest. The pitfall here involves the failure to calculate the best available estimates of the accuracy of comprehension, noted above. The Nelson–Denny uses the number correct score and does not correct for guessing. Therefore, in this situation the individual's comprehension score would be reported as 24 on the pretest and 24 on the posttest, and interpreted as no loss in comprehension. Instead, the best available estimates would indicate a 24% drop from the pretest to the posttest in the accuracy of comprehension.

This second pitfall associated with measuring comprehension, described above, will be called the Percent-Comprehension Pitfall. There is seldom a good excuse for estimating comprehension in a manner that fails to use the standard formula to correct for guessing because guessing is ordinarily what is involved when individuals answer well-written, multiple-choice questions on a passage they have just finished skimming. Therefore, investigations of the effects of speed reading training that do not properly estimate the degree of comprehension of the material that was read by using a correction for guessing formula have succumbed to the Percent-Comprehension Pitfall; the results are therefore relatively invalid with respect to generalizations about the accuracy of comprehension. An example of a study that failed to avoid this pitfall was conducted by Averill and Mueller (1928).

In summary, the two pitfalls associated with comprehension measurement are the Skimming-Items Pitfall and the Percent-Comprehension Pitfall. When RRT is being evaluated, items that purport to measure the accuracy of comprehension must be sensitive to drops in the accuracy of comprehension, i.e., the Skimming-Items Pitfall must be avoided. Furthermore, percentage comprehension must be measured on material that was covered using a correction for guessing formula, i.e., the Percent-Comprehension Pitfall must be avoided.

Efficiency-Index Pitfall

This pitfall involves the failure to recognize that the comprehension score on a test such as the Nelson–Denny is a relatively valid correlate of rauding efficiency level, E_L. Remember the example earlier where an individual correctly answered 24 of 28 items on the pretest and 24 of 36 items on the posttest. The corrected scores of 23 and 21, respectively, would validly reflect individual differences in rauding efficiency level. In this example, the individual's index of rauding efficiency level would have declined (from 23 to 21) as a result of taking a course in rapid reading. In this example, the effect of spending 8 weeks taking a course in reading improvement would have resulted in a loss in reading ability as indexed by this test because less was being comprehended in a fixed amount of time.

As discussed above, the best available index of efficiency of comprehension on the Nelson–Denny test would be the corrected for guessing score on the test; but this score is not ordinarily calculated, only the number correct is reported. It should be noted, however, that the number correct is usually not very different from the corrected for guessing scores; in the example above, the two uncorrected scores were 24 and 24 while their corresponding corrected scores changed only to 23 and 21, and this is probably an extreme example because most individuals will finish more than six of the eight passages on the pretest. Therefore, the Comprehension score on the Nelson–Denny provides a valid rough correlate of individual differences in rauding efficiency level, E_L. Since a group given RRT is likely to answer more items on the posttest, equal pretest and posttest scores would mean that efficiency has actually decreased because the correction for guessing score on the posttest is likely to be lower than the pretest in these situations.

Earlier, in Chapter 9, it was noted that there is research evidence supporting the theoretical assertion that the Nelson–Denny Comprehension score is a correlate of efficiency, i.e., E_L. Carver (1990d) factor analyzed the three scores on the Nelson–Denny test (Rate, Comprehension, and Vocabulary) and found that the Comprehension score was measuring an efficiency factor. Notice that reading comprehension on the Nelson–Denny does not mean the accuracy of comprehension, as might be expected; instead, reading comprehension is actually an indicant of rauding efficiency level, E_L, which includes both rauding rate level, R_L, and rauding accuracy level, A_L.

It is a pitfall when the Rate score on the Nelson–Denny increases pre to post and then the lack of a drop in the comprehension score is misinterpreted as indicating that rate can be increased with no loss in comprehension. Instead, the invalid Rate score on the Nelson–Denny should be disregarded because of the Rate-Measurement Pitfall and the Comprehension score should be interpreted as providing a roughly valid correlate of E_L. If there is no pre to post change in the Comprehension score on the Nelson–Denny, then that means that the RRT was ineffective because reading faster did not result in any more comprehension questions being answered correctly during the time allowed, i.e., the individual's rauding efficiency level did not improve. Stated differently, the

Comprehension score on the Nelson–Denny does not reflect accuracy but does reflect reading efficiency.

It is somewhat surprising that there was no indication in the research literature that this pitfall has been previously recognized. If RRT does result in passages being read two to three times faster with no loss in comprehension, why would the RRT trainee not finish more passages on the posttest and thereupon answer more items correctly? If, in fact, there was an increase in the rate but no loss in the accuracy of comprehension after RRT, then an increase in the Comprehension score would constitute evidence for an increase in efficiency. When there is no change in the Comprehension score on the Nelson–Denny, this means (a) no change in efficiency not accuracy, and (b) probably a drop in accuracy since rate is likely to have increased.

This failure to use the comprehension score on tests similar to the Nelson–Denny as an index of efficiency level when evaluating the effects of RRT has been called the Efficiency-Index Pitfall. Those research studies that found rapid reading trainees to have increased their Rate score on the Nelson–Denny, for example, but showed no loss in the Comprehension score have been misinterpreted as providing support for RRT. Instead, all of these studies that succumbed to the Efficiency-Index Pitfall must be reinterpreted as providing evidence against the helpfulness of RRT because it did not result in any increase in reading efficiency as reflected by a correlate of E_L.

All of the following are studies that failed to note that their comprehension scores did not provide support for the efficacy of RRT because they reflected no improvement in reading efficiency: Averill and Mueller (1928); Brandt (1975); Collins (1979); Cosper and Mills (1953); Labmeier and Vockell (1973); Laffitte (1964); Rankin (1963).

No-Control-Group Pitfall

There are a number of problems associated with the failure to have a comparable control group when evaluating RRT. All of these pre-experimental designs suffer from the known threats to internal validity that have been explicated by D. T. Campbell and Stanley (1963), as was noted earlier. There is the testing effect whereby the rapid reading trainees improve their scores from pre to post simply because they had practice with the tests, not because of the treatment. For example, Labmeier and Vockell (1973) found a pre to post comprehension gain on the Nelson–Denny of 18.2 to 20.0 questions answered correctly. However, this gain of about 2 more questions answered correctly could easily have resulted from practice in taking the test, a difference between Form A and Form B, or even guessing due to answering more items (the Percent-

Comprehension Pitfall). A control group would help eliminate some of these threats to internal validity. There is also the problem of dropouts: those students who are least motivated and benefit the least from the instruction are more likely to drop out before post-testing thereby inflating the group means in an artifactual manner. Any research that does not include a control group should not be seriously considered as providing evidence for the efficacy of RRT.

The problems associated with having no control group in reading research were discussed by McDonald (1963). He was most concerned with "placebo" responses. He said:

> In fact, placebo responses may account for 60 to 80% of all outcomes of programs which are taught by highly enthusiastic instructors who have thrown off the "fetters" of "old-fashioned statistical and experimental methods," and who rely principally on non-standardized methods of evaluation. Almost every review of research cites one or more reports of "gains" produced by the simple device of urging the students to read faster or by the somewhat more sophisticated method of using daily rate tests without comprehension checks. (p. 225)

Studies that have been published but did not avoid the No-Control-Group Pitfall are as follows: Averill and Mueller (1928); Bain (1971); Brim (1968); Carpenter and Jones (1975); Cosper and Mills (1953); Flynn (1977); Goldstein and Justman (1942); Labmeier and Vockell (1973); Mann (1957); McCracken (1960); Mullins and Mowry (1953); Remmers and Stalnaker (1928); Ruppel (1979); Schale (1972); Schmidt (1972); Simpson (1940); H. P. Smith and Tate (1953); Thompson and Whitehill (1970); Tuckey (1960).

Test-Treatment Pitfall

In some research situations, the rapid reading training involves answering questions on passages that are just like the questions and passages given pre and post to evaluate the training. In this situation, the gain is quite specific to the treatment and thereby has no external validity. The trainees may learn from feedback during each class about how to read the passages faster and still be able to answer the kinds of questions on the tests, especially when the questions are more associated with the beginning, ending, facts, overview, etc. Besides learning how to spend their time on the passages more effectively, the trainees may also learn certain skills that help them answer the test questions themselves. It is difficult for an item writer to make all distractors equally difficult and there are likely to be stylistic factors that trainees could learn that a control group would not be able to learn. Therefore, even research studies which have avoided all of the above mentioned pitfalls may succumb to this one. In these situations the pitfall can be avoided by including pre and post measures that are dissimilar to those involved during RRT, thereby reducing the threat to external validity posed by this pitfall.

Two research studies that illustrate the failure to avoid the Test-Treatment Pitfall are Goldstein and Justman (1942); and McCracken (1960).

Statistical Significance Pitfall

Too often it is not recognized that (a) a statistically significant difference can be a small and trivial difference when the sample size is large, and (b) a statistically *not* significant difference can be a large and important difference when the sample size is small. It is best if the statistical significance of the results is completely disregarded because the use of statistical significance to make decisions in research involves a corrupt form of the scientific method (Carver, 1976). However, it is not a pitfall to report the results of tests of statistical significance because these data can be safely disregarded by any reader without any negative consequences. The pitfall is to report only the p values and other results directly associated with the tests of statistical significance without giving any of the data from the study which allow an evaluation of effect size (see Carver, 1984a) and sampling error. For example, some studies of the effects of RRT have not reported means or standard deviations of the rate scores or the comprehension scores—only p values, t-values, F-values, df values, etc. have been reported. When this information about statistical significance is justifiably disregarded because it tells us nothing about whether the size of the differences obtained are small, medium, or large, or whether they are reliable or unreliable, then there is nothing left to evaluate the effect of the training.

Several studies have succumbed to this Statistical Significance Pitfall, such as the following: Berger (1968a); Collins (1979); Francis, Collins, and Cassell (1973); Hansen (1977); Moss (1980); Sailor and Ball (1975).

No-Test-Description Pitfall

The failure to describe the items or techniques used to measure comprehension is a serious pitfall. There needs to be a description of the item type, such as multiple-choice or true–false, how many items there were, how the comprehension score was obtained, etc. This kind of information is basic to any study and the failure to provide it is a sure sign that the research can be safely disregarded when evaluating the effects of RRT.

The following studies illustrate the failure to avoid this No-Test-Description Pitfall: Brown (1976); Francis *et al.* (1973); Himelstein and Greenberg (1974); Lewis (1949); Moss (1980); Remmers and Stalnaker (1928); Schale (1972).

No-Comprehension-Measure Pitfall

This last pitfall is perhaps the most serious one of all. It is the failure to include any measure of comprehension when using silent reading to evaluate the effects of RRT. Three studies that failed to avoid the No-Comprehension-Measure Pitfall were as follows: Lauer (1936); Thompson and Whitehill (1970); Tirrell *et al.* (1977).

RESEARCH

In 1920, Stone and Colvin published what appears to be the first study of RRT. However, this research will not be reviewed in any detail because the treatment was only sketchily described. Two years later Stone (1922) published a much more descriptive report and it appears to be the first thorough study of the effects of RRT. At the outset, it is interesting to note that among the motives for improvement listed by Stone was "the large amount of silent reading demanded by the life of today" (p. 10), a reason still being given over 60 years later for inducing students to take a course in rapid reading.

Stone's treatment consisted of extensive practice. Students were expected to use their "required reading" for practice, such as their textbooks for an educational psychology class. They were asked (a) to refrain from "lip movement and inner articulation," (b) to concentrate on reading faster while still trying to comprehend, (c) to concentrate effectively, (d) to make long, well controlled eye movements, and (e) to "perceive meanings at a glance." He reported that students were encouraged and helped to remove their own hinderances to faster reading and that the most difficult hinderance to remove was inner articulation. It should not go unnoticed that these fundamentals of RRT are almost exactly the same as present day techniques for RRT (see Bergquist, 1984).

Stone reported average gains in rate on a test, called the Monroe III and Stone Extensions, to be from 36% to 108% in four classes that ranged in size from 31 to 39 students. A control group that did not take the test had a rate gain of 32%. The gain in average comprehension scores on this same test ranged from 36% to 74% for these same four classes while the control group gained 21%. On the surface, these data appear to provide strong support for RRT but I was not able to obtain enough descriptive information to evaluate this test properly. The *Sixth Mental Measurement Yearbook* by Buros (1965) contains two reviews which were in strong agreement that the Monroe test was not good enough for anyone to use. The Stone Extensions were never described. Stone (1922) concluded that (a) "the typical college student may readily increase his rate of silent reading ability 50% to 100%," (b) "the limits of silent reading ability are not known and probably have not been reached," and (c) "marked improvement may be secured by approaching improvement through emphasis on increased rate—increased rate with increased comprehension" (p. 22). As noted earlier, this study seems to provide strong support for RRT. Yet, it is probably best if this study is not interpreted with respect to whether RRT improves rauding rate, R_r, at least until enough descriptive information is obtained about the test that was used to determine whether Stone avoided known pitfalls.

O'Brien (1926) reported upon the most extensive study of RRT ever conducted. He measured the reading rate of 848 students in 20 schools scattered across Illinois. It involved grades 3–8, and required 289 pages to report. He created equally matched pairs in each of the classrooms. One of each pair matched on reading rate was given 8 weeks of daily instruction (30 min/day) in RRT (experimental group, $N = 424$) while the other one of each pair was not given the instruction (control group, $N = 424$). RRT for O'Brien, as well as for most of his subsequent counterparts such as Bergquist (1984), noted earlier, consisted in admonitions to go fast, not subvocalize, and not regress, with most of the training sessions devoted to practice in reading rapidly. O'Brien reported a 31% increase in reading rate (a gain of 46 words per minute) for the experimental group as compared to the control group. He also reported that the experimental group was 1.6% more accurate in answering the questions correctly on the *Courtis Silent Reading Test*. O'Brien (1926) himself pointed out that this test has a major weakness; he said, "At the time the score for rate of reading is determined, there is no measure taken of the comprehension that accompanied such reading" (p. 167). Thus, O'Brien was aware of the Rate-Measurement Pitfall. Therefore, it is quite likely that the students who received the RRT slowed down immediately after their rate was measured so they could answer the questions more accurately. One indication of whether or not the Rate-Measurement Pitfall was important would come from the number of questions they attempted and also from the total number of questions they answered correctly, compared to the control group. As a secondary analysis, O'Brien did look at the total number of questions answered correctly by 247 randomly selected members of the experimental group, but it is a mystery as to why he never reported any corresponding results for the control

group. Since the author devoted three pages to a lecture on the importance of "individual control" as reflected in matched pairs, it is strange
to say the least that the results of the control group for the most important measure in the entire study were omitted—especially in a 289-page
report.

In summary, O'Brien conducted an exquisite study of rapid reading
training from the standpoint of experimental design, with his large
sample sizes and his detailed attention to the control groups. But, from
a 1980s perspective, his measures of the accuracy and rate of comprehension were inadequate and his analyses of the data were inconsistent
and flawed. Unfortunately, it is impossible to ascertain whether his results support RRT or not.

Averill and Mueller (1928) conducted an RRT study with 16 college
seniors. The students were engaged in the training over a period of 3
months with three 40-min practice periods per week. These researchers
said that they emphasized the same factors as O'Brien (1926) did in his
training. Their rate measures from 2 min of reading were 252 wpm on
the pretest and 504 wpm on the posttest. Averill and Mueller reported
results from an unusual kind of comprehension measure based upon 2
min of reading, namely, number of words reproduced. It is not clear
exactly how this was measured but it seems to be a count of the number
of words covered that were subsequently recalled and written down.
They reported an 11% increase in the number of words reproduced
from pre to post (144.6 to 160) but this measure does not avoid the
Percent-Comprehension Pitfall because it was not converted into percentage comprehension; the 144.6 words reproduced from the 504
words read on the pretest is 29% while the 160 words reproduced out of
the 1004 read on the posttest is 16%. Thus, this index of the accuracy of
comprehension indicates that comprehension was cut in half while rate
was doubled. Additionally, a small drop occurred in a second measure of
comprehension, the Thorndike–McCall Reading Scale, from 58.8 to
56.0, pre to post.

This Averill and Mueller research appears to be the first to succumb
to the Efficiency-Index Pitfall. The comprehension score on the Thorndike–McCall Reading Scale is probably a roughly valid index of reading
efficiency and this index decreased as a result of the RRT, thus indicating
that the RRT was not effective in helping these students read more efficiently. Yet, these same data were interpreted by these researchers as
indicating that "marked increase in the speed of reading may be effected
without any impairment of the comprehension" (p. 129). Finally, this is
also the first known study of RRT that did not use a control group, thus
becoming the first to succumb to this pitfall. These data must be inter-

preted as providing no support for the efficiency of RRT, in direct opposition to the authors' interpretation of the same data.

Lauer (1936) studied the reading rates of college students before and after 20 practice sessions. Apparently, the subjects measured their own reading rates in their own textbooks during daily study periods. The mean reading rate of all 346 subjects was 248 wpm and the mean improvement from the beginning to the end of the 20 practice sessions was 35%. This research is notable because it appears to be the first published on the effect of RRT that did not include any measure of comprehension, the first that failed to avoid the No-Comprehension-Measurement Pitfall.

Weber (1939) gave RRT to college students; it involved 6 weeks of tachistoscopic exercises, among other treatments. The 25 students in the experimental group were selected to be comparable initially to the 25 in the control group. The scores on the comprehension section of the Iowa Advanced Silent Reading Test were almost identical after training, 130.4 versus 129.8, respectively. Yet, the data collected, presented in several tables, were interpreted by Weber as providing support for RRT. Acknowledging the Efficiency-Index Pitfall, these data can alternatively be interpreted as providing no support for RRT.

Bear (1939) provided a lengthy description of the Dartmouth program for diagnostic and remedial reading which he said was known on the campus as "speeded reading." The remedial group was mostly freshmen, one-half of which were officially requested to participate because of low test scores or low grades and the other half "did the work entirely on their own initiative" (p. 74). The control group was the remainder of the freshman class. Bear reported that when the mean gains between September and May for the remedial and control groups were compared, "the remedial group was found to score 7.8 points higher in comprehension, 7.9 points higher in rate, and 37.7 more words read per minute. Unfortunately, he did not report the actual rates pre and post. Even worse, these small gains could be due entirely to regression to the mean since a large portion of the remedial group was selected from the freshman class at the beginning of the year because of their low test scores. Therefore, it would not be prudent to interpret this small gain of 37.7 wpm as evidence for the efficacy of RRT.

Dearborn and Wilking (1941) reported upon three experiments involving RRT. Experiment 1 involved two groups of Harvard freshmen, 16 in the experimental group and 16 in the control group. Two standardized reading tests were administered but only percentile ranks on these tests were reported, i.e., no raw scores and no rates in wpm; the results favored the experimental group. It was also reported that "the photographic records of the experimental group showed an increased rate of reading from 251 to 382 wpm" (p. 669), but there were no comprehension scores associated with these measures. In Experiment 2, it was stated that "A control group was formed, and its members were paired with those who received remedial instruction" (p. 670), and this was the extent of the description of the control group. The results were favorable to the experimental group; reading rate increased from 248 to 333 wpm in the experimental group on the Nelson–Denny test, thereby illustrating the Rate-Measurement Pitfall. Experiment 3 had no control group. These data could be interpreted by some as supporting RRT but it could also be argued that the research did not meet minimum research standards.

Bridges (1941) performed an experiment with 129 students in grades 4, 5, and 6. This research appears to have avoided all the known pitfalls discussed earlier. Three comparable groups of 43 were each given a different treatment for 20 min each day for 40 days over a period from February to May. The speed group was told the tests showed they needed to read faster, and the treatment focused on getting them to read faster. The comprehension group was told the tests showed they needed to read more carefully, and the treatment focused on getting them to read more carefully. The control group was asked to read in their book each day. On the posttests, the speed group had the highest rate scores (GE = 7.7 compared to 6.7 and 6.4) and the lowest comprehension scores (GE = 5.4 compared 5.7 and 5.9). Bridges concluded that ". . . it seems likely that over-emphasis on speed not only does not improve comprehension in the group as a whole at this level, but may actually tend to retard the development of comprehension" (pp. 317–318). These data do not support RRT.

Goldstein and Justman (1942) reviewed prior research on RRT and noted that there had been no studies in a typical classroom ". . . where the necessity of covering a certain amount of course content makes extended experiments impossible, and where expensive apparatus is not available" (p. 510). They set out to remedy this by conducting two experiments. In the first experiment, they told their students that (a) most students can improve their reading, (b) whispering and lip movements tend to slow up reading, (c) rapid reading can be attained from few and short fixations, (d) students should try to see phrases, even entire sentences at a glance, (e) reading should not be a passive absorption of ideas but instead should anticipate what the author is going to say, and (f) students should try to read at a rate that is "faster-than-convenient." It should be noted again that this same advice could probably be found in any RRT instruction today. Ten minutes at the beginning of 14 class meetings were devoted to practice on these factors that were supposed to improve their reading. The students read passages and then answered questions. Goldstein and Justman reported that the average gain from the first practice to the last was 383 to 661 wpm, and the average comprehension score improved from 12.1 to 14.1. Disregarding the measurement problems involved in mixing multiple-choice questions and completion questions on the same tests, this appears to be the first published RRT study that failed to avoid the Test-Treatment Pitfall. There was no way of estimating the degree to which subjects simply learned how to answer these particular kinds of questions better from the first practice to the last. In the second experiment, students brought 1000-word passages of their own choosing for the class and then wrote ten true–false items. This time rate increased from 286 at the first practice session to 534 wpm at the 14th and last practice session, and the comprehension scores increased from 8.4 to 8.7. Again, there was no evidence that the Test-Treatment Pitfall has been avoided. Without any evidence that this pitfall had been avoided, it is impossible to consider these data as providing support for the efficacy of RRT. Furthermore, there was no control group in either of these two experiments.

Kilby (1945) investigated the effect of four types of college reading instruction: intensive reading, rapid reading with thorough comprehension, rapid reading, and skimming. Freshmen were invited to participate in the 16 one-hour training periods if they scored low on the Iowa Silent Reading Tests. The students were compared on their average grades in course work on a scale from 0 to 100. Each group was compared with each of the other groups and with controls who did not volunteer but had academically comparable scores prior to the training. One reason for reviewing this research is to point out that students who volunteer for such courses are ordinarily more motivated and are likely to study longer and harder so that they are not comparable to students matched on pretest scores. The average grade in all course work at the end of the semester in which the training took place, was 2–3 points higher than the matched controls, a rather small difference on a scale from 0 to 100. More important, however, was the fact that the first group who focused on practicing intensive, thorough, and careful reading had better average grades in all course work than either of the two groups that focused upon rapid reading, 3 points better than one group and 1 point better than the other. Kilby published a large amount of data, collected as part of his doctoral dissertation, but none were as important as that summarized above. Therefore, it seems reasonable to conclude that Kilby presented no sound evidence to support RRT as a method for improving the grades of college freshmen.

Lewis (1949) compared two methods of RRT, one that focused primarily upon eye movements and the other that focused primarily upon comprehension. There were 13 students who spent 1.5 hours per session using mechanical techniques designed to improve their eye movements: eye movement photography, flashmeter, metronome, and exercises designed to increase their fixation span. This group was also given some work assignments of two 15-min periods a day practicing their eye movements. In a separate group, there were 14 students who spent the same amount of time over an 8-week period reading selections of measured difficulty while attempting to increase their speed of comprehension. In this group, no mechanical devices were used and no mention of eye movements was made. This latter group also had more homework; they were required to read a full novel each week and keep records of the times they read. Furthermore, they were also required to submit book reports when they finished each book. The students were divided into the two matched groups so their pretest means were equal, about 284 wpm and 93% comprehension. At the end of the course, the eye movement group read at 340 wpm with 85% comprehension, and the comprehension group read at 478 wpm with 97% comprehension. Seemingly, these data eliminated any need for mechanical equipment or eye movement training because the comprehension group read at a rate that was 41% faster and had a higher comprehension score. However, there was absolutely no description of how comprehension was measured. Given this No-Test-Description Pitfall it is impossible to evaluate the results. Since the comprehension group spent a great deal of time discussing books, analyzing short stories, finding main ideas, etc., it seems more than possible that the instructor for the course taught the comprehension group how to go fast and still be able to answer the kinds of comprehension questions he wrote. Without even any indication that the questions were objective, these data must be disregarded.

Glock (1949) compared three RRT methods with each other. One method was the Harvard Films which projects material on to a screen in phrases at varying rates. Another method used the same Harvard Film material except it was projected two lines at a time. The third method was the same Harvard Film material presented in printed or typed form instead of by film. Glock administered many different tests, pre and post, and concluded that "The efficiency of the method varied with the criterion and teacher used," and "no single method was best for all teachers" (p. 105). Since there was no control group, these results cannot be used to evaluate the effectiveness of RRT.

Cosper and Mills (1953) reported data they had collected from several classes in developmental reading. They had administered the Diagnostic

Reading Tests, Survey Section (DRT). This test measures reading rate from a count of the number of words read in the first passage during the first 3 min of the test. There is no comprehension measure directly associated with the words read during this first 3 min so this research failed to avoid the Rate-Measurement Pitfall. This test seems to be a little worse than the Nelson–Denny for evaluating RRT because, as noted earlier, the comprehension score on the Nelson–Denny does provide a roughly valid index of reading efficiency. The DRT provides a similar comprehension score, but the DRT comprehension score comes from the sum of the number correct on two slightly different 20-item subtests so it is not as technically sound as the Nelson–Denny.

It should be noted that the above research of Cosper and Mills also succumbed to the Efficiency-Index Pitfall. The DRT comprehension score declined from the beginning to the end of three semesters and it improved trivially from 30.6 to 31.4 the fourth semester. Therefore, the rauding efficiency level of these students probably did not improve. However, the authors did not fail to conclude that: "the results of two years of instruction in reading at Purdue clearly demonstrate that students can learn to read much faster with the same amount of comprehension" (p. 360). There was no recognition that the rate measure had no corresponding measure of comprehension and there was no recognition that the comprehension score was a valid index indicating the students showed no improvement in reading efficiency.

It should also be noted that data from the Iowa Silent Reading Test was also reported by Cosper and Mills. It is admirable that this test makes an attempt to measure the comprehension that is associated with one minute reading rate measures. However, there is no correction for guessing on the items that cover the entire passage even though some students may only finish reading the first quarter. Without a correction for guessing it is quite possible and likely that the induced skimming process at the end of RRT will result in all the items being answered but a lower percentage of the items answered correctly. Therefore, the lowered accuracy of comprehension associated with a skimming process will not be detected by this test. Cosper and Mills report higher percentile ranks at the end of the course compared to the beginning of the course on six different scores taken from the Iowa test. However, the average gain of 21 they reported in percentile rank units could easily result from taking the test twice or from only the more motivated students staying in the course until the end. Without a control group these data cannot be taken seriously as support for the efficiency of RRT.

Kallen and Kyser (1956) evaluated a reading-improvement program for adults which involved an 18-hour course spread over 5 weeks; it was primarily devoted to increasing rate using the Harvard Reading Films and a tachistoscope. They used the Robinson–Hall Reading Tests.

Before reporting the results from Kallen and Kyser, it should be noted that use of the Robinson–Hall Test avoids the two major pitfalls associated with the Nelson–Denny and the Diagnostic Reading Test, namely the Rate-Measure Pitfall and the Efficiency-Index Pitfall. On the Robinson–Hall Test, students are given a lengthy article to read and after 10 min they are stopped. They record the line they were reading, and the number of words up to this point determines their reading rate. They are then given the test items, and asked to answer only the ones relevant to the material they have read. The score is the percentage of items answered correctly out of those attempted up to the point where the individual stopped reading. Therefore, this test measures percentage comprehension, and reading rate, in a manner that is theoretically ideal for indicating accuracy of comprehension, A, and rate of comprehension, R.

Kallen and Kyser reported the scores on the Robinson–Hall Test for 73 adults who participated in their program. On the pretest, they read at 231 wpm with a 75.5% accuracy of comprehension score. On the posttest, they read at 322 wpm with a 72.8% score. So, the rate score increased by 40% and the accuracy score *decreased* by 3%. It is possible that the accuracy score may have dropped further if there had not been a practice effect or a difference in forms of the test. A control group would help sort out these effects, and these researchers did mention rate scores on the Robinson–Hall for a control group. Unfortunately, they gave no description of the control group; it is a mystery as to how they got them, who they were, or even how many were in the group. Furthermore, they neglected to report the accuracy scores for the control group. Such data cannot be reasonably interpreted as supporting the efficiency of RRT training.

Morton (1959) conducted one of the most thorough investigations of RRT ever published; he avoided all of the pitfalls noted earlier. The subjects were 65 adults ranging from 21 to 63 years old who were executives in the headquarters of the General Post Office in England. The course is described below using excerpts from the report:

> The course investigated was a commercial Reading Efficiency course, based on the Harvard Reading Course, designed by Perry and Whitlock. . . . This series of films allow the projection on a screen of what is, in effect, the page of a book, revealing only a certain number of words on a line at a time so that, in principle, the reader's eye is led across each line in a series of regular jumps.
>
> The films act as pacing devices, forcing the reader to concentrate and preventing him from regressing. They are supposed to increase his perceptual span, i.e., the number of words absorbed at one fixation, and hence decrease

the number of fixations in a given time. For the most part, instruction in new techniques takes the form of exhortations to the students 'to press on' with their reading, to avoid regression and to try to take more at a single glance. Throughout the course students are urged to practice assiduously at home and in work and much of the effect of the course is thought to depend upon this practice. (p. 223)

Training exercises in skimming were also given and one 700-word passage was administered to each class with a comprehension test given after the timed reading. The course was taught twice a week for 6 weeks. The 65 subjects were divided into two matched groups. The experimental group was tested before the course and a week after completion. The control group was tested during the same interval but did not take the course until after a second testing. It may be noted that this is an excellent design but one that is seldom found in the literature; twice as many subjects are accepted as can be treated, with one-half put into a waiting list to take the course later and thereby acting as a control group.

Each subject in Morton's study was *individually* administered three different experimental tests, each with two matched passages that were counterbalanced. The passages for each test were over 1000 words in length. The questions on the passages were administered orally and answered orally. Excerpts below partially describe the testing.

The questions covered the whole of the passage in some detail, paying more attention to the ideas expressed than the facts. (p. 225) In a way it might be more accurate to say that the passage was discussed. This may seem to be highly subjective and inaccurate method of testing and was certainly more difficult than any other method since, for example, a subject might answer three of four questions at once, sometimes in an indirect way. (p. 225)

From the reading tests come two measures: the time taken to complete the passage, and the percentage comprehended and reproduced. . . . Comprehension was measured as the percentage of the ideas or facts in the article, relevant to the stated intention, which were correctly reproduced. . . . The most satisfactory and realistic measure would seem to be one of efficiency, this being defined as the product of speed and comprehension. . . . (p. 226)

The design and procedures used by Morton were exemplary, even though the testing was questionable due to the uncertain amount of subjectivity that could easily creep in, especially when the examiners probably knew at the time of testing which group each subject was in. Nonetheless, it is commendable that Morton would go to such great lengths to develop tests that had a great deal of external validity.

Many of Morton's experimental procedures were exquisite but his data analysis was frustratingly inadequate. First, he calculated his efficiency scores. Then, he submitted them to two conversions that camouflagged any direct interpretations of his results. One conversion involved the use of standard scores that had a mean of 100 and a standard deviation of 20. The other conversion involved calculating a ratio of the experimental group mean divided by the control group's mean. Any one or two of the above conversions could be followed with ease but all three left a mystery as to what the data represented. For example, he reported no reading rates. He reported a 54% improvement in each of all three tests as a result of taking the course. Two of the tests were also given 6 months after the course was over. There was still a 30% and 35% advantage to having taken the course, 6 months later.

Taken at face value, these data of Morton's seem to suggest that rauding rate can be increased 30–50% as a result of taking a 6-week course in RRT. Several factors temper this interpretation, however. First, we have no idea how fast these subjects read before the course. Suppose these subjects read at a typical rate of college students found by Taylor (1965), i.e., 280 wpm. A 30% increase would be 364 wpm. It is conceded that a 13% variation in rate is quite normal (see Carver, 1983). It is also conceded that 6 weeks of reading practice including an extra hour or two each day may have in fact increased the rauding rate of these subjects by 10–20%. It is also conceded that extra concentration on going a little faster can probably increase speed by 10–20% without any loss of comprehension. Second, even this amount of gain, 30%, is suspect given the following comments from Morton's report:

> Many of the students in the present course were hesitant in applying the new techniques to important, difficult or lengthy material. But when the new techniques amount primarily to little more than increased concentration and more 'active' reading, it is difficult to see any rational basis for their hesitancy. . . . (p. 234)

The above remarks suggest that even the long-term gain of 30% is suspect because the students were "hesitant" to read this way except under special circumstances. It seems quite likely that what is being taught is a skimming skill that involves concentrating upon moving the eyes a little faster without regressing even when sentence understanding suffers. If this is a reasonable explanation of what the students have learned, then it is easy to see why they would not want to use this skill when reading anything "important" because of the negative consequences associated with the failure to understand and remember "important" textual information. It is equally easy to see how they would not feel comfortable using this newly learned skimming process when the material was difficult because they would be comprehending such a small percentage of the materials. Finally, it is also easy to see why they would not want to apply this newly learned skimming process on lengthy material because they would fatigue fast when concentrating so intensely in order to operate this process. If you want to walk 5 miles, it is probably best if you do not concentrate on walking as fast as you possibly can. Instead, you will probably arrive at your destination faster and in better physical condition if you walk at your normal walking pace. Similarly, if you want to raud a lengthy article, it is probably best if you use your rauding process rather than a skimming process because you will probably understand all of the thoughts faster this way and you will also be in better physical condition when you have accomplished that goal.

In summary, the data collected by Morton suggest that RRT can induce subjects to move from their regular rauding process which operates at around 280 wpm to a skimming process which operates at around 364 Wpm. Morton's data taken at face value suggest that there is a permanent increase in reading efficiency of 30–50%. Yet, it seems difficult to believe that subjects have experienced a permanent increase in their rauding rate of 30–50%, especially when Morton reports that subjects are hesitant to use their newly learned skill when the material is important, difficult, or lengthy. Instead, it seems more likely that the increase in efficiency that Morton found is due solely to an increase in concentration associated with operating a skimming process that in fact is less efficient in terms of comprehending sentences but Morton's testing was not sensitive to this loss in efficiency. Finally, the subjective nature of Morton's testing was troublesome to say the least.

Laffitte (1964) compared the effects of perceptual training with skimming training. He gave 25 college students perceptual training that involved a tachistoscope and a reading accelerator. The skimming group of 17 was given practice in learning to skim or "pre-read." On the Diagnostic Reading Test, both groups gained approximately the same amount; the perceptual group increased their rate 21% from 219 to 264 wpm, and the skimming group increased their rate 29%, from 210 to 271 wpm. On the comprehension section of the test, each group changed very little. The perceptual group gained 1.5, from 26.6 to 28.1, and the skimming group gained 0.9 from 26.3 to 27.2, the two gains being 3% and 3%, respectively. Remember that this comprehension score is a roughly valid index of reading efficiency so the evidence indicated that neither group improved their reading efficiency more than trivially (3%) in spite of participating in three 50-min training sessions weekly for 8 weeks. In Laffitte's discussion of his results it was clear that he succumbed to the Efficiency-Index Pitfall. His research has been reviewed in some detail because he appears to be the first to recognize that RRT is really skimming training, and his results indicated that training which concentrated on the perceptual aspects of reading produced results that were no different from skimming training.

Maxwell (1965) investigated the effect of telling students to read faster. Her design provided controls for possible differences due to test forms, order of administration, and order of experimental condition. The Robinson–Hall Reading Test was administered to 104 college students under two conditions, normal and fast. Under the fast condition, the students were asked to "read as fast as possible without loss of comprehension" (p. 181). The rate scores under the normal and fast conditions were 219 and 256, respectively; the corresponding accuracy scores were 71% and 67%. Notice that simply asking these students to read faster resulted in a 17% increase in rate and a 4% decrease in accuracy.

After giving these 104 students two forms of the test, Maxwell then divided them into an experimental group and a control group. The experimental group was "given a handout describing techniques for improving reading speed and told to practice these techniques daily for one hour" (p. 184), during the next week. Both groups were tested again at the end of a week with a third form of the Robinson–Hall. At the posttest session, both groups were instructed to read the material as fast as they could. Compared to the scores under the original fast condition, the control group increased their rate 11% to 286 wpm, and the experimental group increased their rate 19% to 304 wpm. However, the control group increased their accuracy score 4% while the experimental group had a 0% gain in their accuracy score. It should also be noted that the control group increased its rate 31% over the original normal test condition while its accuracy score decreased 1% (from 71 to 70), and the corresponding changes for the experimental group were a 39% increase in rate with a 3% loss in accuracy (from 71 to 68).

These data, from one of the best reading tests available, indicate that college students can simply be asked to go faster on a test and they will increase their rate 17% with a loss in the accuracy score of only 4%. College students can be asked twice to go faster on the Robinson–Hall Test, and they can increase their rate 31% with only a 1% loss in the accuracy of comprehension score. Notice that these gains have been made without RRT on one of the best tests available. Furthermore, college students can be (a) asked to go fast, (b) given a handout describing techniques for reading fast, and (c) asked to practice reading fast, and they can make gains of 39% in rate with only a 3% loss in accuracy scores. These data suggest that the effectiveness of a program for RRT needs to be compared to these gains on the Robinson–Hall Reading Test when there was little or no training.

Maxwell and Mueller (1967) compared three groups that had been given different instructions relevant to increasing their reading rate. As background for their research, they noted that Laycock (1955) reported "that students requested to read a passage as fast as possible without 'sacrificing comprehension' showed a 40 percent gain over their previous tested reading rate" (p. 184). Maxwell and Mueller administered two forms of the Robinson–Hall Reading Tests 1 week apart to three separate groups of college students, 40 per group. After the first test had been administered each group was given different instructions. The techniques group was given a handout that described "causes of slow reading (regression, vocalization, etc.) and explained several techniques for improving rate (e.g., conscious forcing of one to read faster, using a card or one's finger as a pacer, using a Z-pattern in reading down a page, etc.)" and they were instructed to "practice these techniques and to return the following week" (p. 187). The placebo group was "given a handout designed to motivate them to read faster by extolling the benefits of rapid reading, but which did not describe specific techniques for them to follow in increasing their reading rate" (p. 186), and was told to return the following week. The control group was simply asked to return the following week. This research appears to have avoided all the pitfalls.

Maxwell and Mueller reported the following rate changes, pre to post, on the Robinson–Hall: techniques group, 240 to 328 wpm for a 37% gain; placebo group, 250 to 278 wpm for a 11% gain; control group, 268 to 290 wpm, for an 8% gain. The techniques group gained 37% by simply being given a handout on rapid reading theory and asked to practice during the subsequent week. This result replicated the 39% gain found by Maxwell (1965), discussed earlier. The pre and post percentage comprehension scores were as follows: techniques group, 69.8 to 68.2 for a 2% loss; placebo group, 71.8 to 71.5 for a 0% loss; control group, 73.0 to 73.6 for a 1% gain. Maxwell and Mueller further analyzed the data from the techniques group to see if those who practiced the technique more, gained more. Those who tried the methods once or twice during the week gained just as much as those who tried the methods every day.

These data suggest that students can be told a little of the theory behind RRT and that is enough to get some of them to try out a skimming process that is 37% faster. Furthermore, the best available test (at that time) showed no important loss in the accuracy of comprehension. However, this 37% increase in rate with a 2% loss in accuracy should be compared to earlier data collected by Maxwell (1965). She found a 31% increase in rate with a 1% loss in accuracy for a control group who was simply told to go read faster on this same test. When this comparison is made, the gain of the techniques group seems inconsequential.

There are several points that should be kept in mind when interpreting the Maxwell and Mueller data. First, the gain for these college students was from 240 to 328 wpm, but the 328 wpm was only 13% faster than the control group which read 290 wpm on the posttest. Second, both the 290 wpm for the control group and the 328 wpm for the group that received RRT are well within the range expected for the rauding process. Third, the techniques group read 13% faster than the control group on the posttest, but it also comprehended 5% less, 68.2 versus 73.6%. Fourth, it is expecting too much from the Robinson–Hall Test for it to register a 13% decrement in the accuracy of comprehension when there is a 13% increase in the rate of comprehension. Fifth, these gains in RRT resulted from training which consisted of a handout describing how to read fast and asking students to practice reading fast over a 1-week period.

In summary, these data from Maxwell and Mueller can be reasonably interpreted as indicating that students can be induced to read faster by telling them about the theory underlying RRT but their increase in rate and their loss in accuracy of comprehension is approximately equal to students who have simply taken the test twice and were asked to read fast each time.

Berger (1968a) compared four methods of improving reading rate, comprehension, and flexibility. The four methods were (a) tachistoscope, (b) controlled reader, (c) control pacing, and (d) paperback scanning. This study appeared to be well designed, given the accepted limitations of a quasi-experimental design. A reasonably comparable control group was included. Berger's primary conclusion was that "the paperback scanning method produced the most significant results over the other methods . . ." (p. 596). Unfortunately, the statistical significance pitfall was not avoided. Only tests of statistical significance were reported in four tables; there were no rates or comprehension scores reported.

Swalm and Kling (1973) gave RRT to pupils in grades 5 and 6. The 38 students in the experimental group were given timed reading drills and the 38 students in the control group were given free reading time equal to the amount of time devoted to rate instruction in the experimental group. The instruction covered a period of 10 weeks with three 30-min periods each week. The Diagnostic Reading Test, DRT, and the Van Wagenen Rate of Comprehension Scale were pre- and post-administered. On the DRT, the experimental group increased their rate from 153 to 403 wpm, for a 163% gain, while the control group increased their rate from 149 to 180 wpm for a 21% gain. Remember, these gains in rate on the DRT represent the Rate-Measurement Pitfall. On the comprehension part of the DRT, both groups gained 1% pre to post thereby indicating that the RRT had not been successful in improving reading efficiency. This is another example of the Efficiency-Index Pitfall. One reason for reviewing this study is that it used a type of reading rate test, the Van Wagenen, not discussed before. This test plus the Chapman–Cook and the Tinker Speed of Reading Test are all examples of tests that contain easy to read sentences with a word changed toward the end of very short paragraphs; the task for the examinee is to read as fast as possible and still be able to mark out correctly the anomalous word in as many items as possible during the time limit. These tests provide relatively good indices of reading rate but the scores are not in units of wpm but items correctly marked. In this Swalm and Kling study, the experimental group had a pre–post gain on the Van Wagenen of 21% and the control group had a corresponding gain of 14%. On another informal test that was given, the experimental group had a 15% *lower* comprehension score.

Swalm and Kling interpreted their data as follows: "No clear picture of the effect of rate training on comprehension emerged from the study" (p. 163). It is also possible to recognize the Efficiency-Index Pitfall and interpret these data as providing no support for the efficacy of RRT.

R. G. Graf (1973) investigated the speed and comprehension of a group of 31 students who took RRT from a private firm. Pre and post tests were administered to these students and also to 31 students in a control group. Fill-in and multiple-choice questions were developed on passages that ranged from 1683 to 1817 words in length. The passages were taken from *Doctor Zhivago*, a *Playboy* article, a *Redbook* article, and an experimental psychology book. Over the four articles, the speed readers increased their rate pre–post from 216 to 695 wpm for a 222% gain and the control group increased from 258 to 285 wpm for a 10% gain. On the comprehension tests, the speed readers went from 66% to 40% for a 26% loss in the accuracy of comprehension. This study appears to have avoided all the pitfalls associated with evaluating RRT, and it found a major loss in the accuracy of comprehension, *A*, associated with the major increase in rate, *R*.

Brown and McDowell (1979) reported upon the rate and accuracy of comprehension of 70 college students before and after they had taken a reading improvement course. The pre- and post-tests consisted of articles and questions taken from a reading improvement textbook. Rate increased tremendously from 257 to 1956 wpm while percentage comprehension dropped only from 63% to 57%. The main reason for reviewing this study is to illustrate the Skimming-Items Pitfall. There is no evidence that the test questions taken from this book, primarily used to induce people to read faster, are sensitive to the loss in the accuracy of comprehension that is ordinarily associated with increases in rate. Without such evidence, it must be assumed that the questions are skimming questions that can be answered just as well at 400–500 wpm as they can at 250–300 wpm.

CONCLUSIONS

Of all the studies of RRT reviewed, it appears that the only studies that met minimum standards and avoided all of the known pitfalls were the following: Bridges (1941); R. G. Graf (1973); Maxwell and Mueller (1967); Morton (1959). The Bridges study was notable because emphasizing speed in a group of elementary students in fact got them going faster but their comprehension scores went down considerably compared to the other groups. The Morton study was notable for its elaborate description of experimental details, its subjective testing, its hopelessly complicated data transformations, and its 30% long-term improvement in reading efficiency measures. The Maxwell and Mueller study was notable for finding a 37% improvement in rate after a treatment that consisted of a handout taken home; it was also notable that after the treatment the RRT group read 13% faster than the controls and comprehended 5% less. The Graf study was notable for its 26% loss in the accuracy of comprehension associated with taking a commercially available speed reading course.

If the four studies noted above were the only ones available, then it might be difficult to make a data-based decision about the efficacy of RRT. However, there were a large number of studies of RRT, referenced earlier, in connection with the Efficiency-Index Pitfall, that used the Nelson–Denny or the Diagnostic Reading Test and found no change or trivial differences in comprehension scores. Since these comprehension test scores do reflect reading efficiency, it is clear that there are a large amount of data that indicate that all types of RRT do not result in important gains in the efficiency of comprehension, E, or rauding efficiency level, E_L. The data that exist are exceptionally poor in quality but there has been enough research where the RRT groups did not do better on valid indices of reading efficiency to be reasonably confident that these RRT classes produce improvement in rauding rate that varies from zero to 5%, at best. There have also been enough data collected to be reasonably confident that most students can be easily induced to shift up to a skimming process, Gear 4, that operates about 50% faster than the rauding process, Gear 3. Furthermore, it appears that it is possible to induce students to adopt such a skimming process in a matter of minutes or a few hours; there is no evidence that it is necessary for college students to spend several hours on instruction or practice before they will adopt a skimming process that is 50% faster than their rauding process.

It should be possible to develop a screening test to locate individuals who need skimming training. Students would be asked to read at a rate that is about twice as fast as they normally read, just to get an overview, and then ask them both skimming-type questions and sentence-comprehension-type questions. Under these conditions, those students who do *not* read at least 50% faster, who do *not* answer at least 75% of the skimming items correctly, and who do answer more than 75% of the sentence comprehension questions correctly are likely candidates for skimming training.

In summary, rauding theory holds that rauding rate, R_r, is relatively constant and probably can only be improved by those people who do not regularly raud relatively easy materials. Some researchers, some theorists, and some laypersons seem to think that anyone can improve their rauding rate by 50–300% from RRT. There is no valid research evidence to support this claim despite the fact that there has been a great deal of research on RRT. Almost all of the published research is seriously flawed by one or more pitfalls that render the results invalid. However, since there have been many studies that found no gain in the comprehension section of standardized reading tests, this constitutes strong evidence against the efficacy of RRT because these measures actually indicate that RRT produced no gain in reading efficiency. If rate actually increased in these studies, then accuracy had to decrease, otherwise efficiency could not have remained constant.

Almost all RRT is really skimming training in disguise. Over 60 years ago, Judd and Buswell (1922) gave some salient advice that was quoted earlier and will be quoted again. They said "nor is there any more dangerous habit to acquire than that of skimming" (p. 152). It is dangerous to get into the habit of using a faster and less powerful skimming process when the rauding process is required to comprehend accurately the complete thoughts in sentences.

PART V

The Last Part

This final part of the book contains three unrelated chapters. In Chapter 19, which follows, the research relevant to speed readers and super readers will be reviewed. Chapter 20 contains methodological recommendations for conducting and reporting reading rate research. Chapter 21, the last chapter, contains answers to the questions posed in Chapter 1 and a summary of the most important conclusions drawn from all the research and theory reviewed in Chapters 2–20.

SPEED READERS AND SUPER READERS

INTRODUCTION

Are there individuals who can read at 1000 words per minute, or faster, and still comprehend 75% or more of the complete thoughts in relatively easy material? Can speed readers do this? How fast can individuals successfully operate their rauding process?

This chapter will review the research relevant to exceptionally good readers and speed readers, i.e., those who supposedly can read at very fast speeds and still accurately comprehend what they are reading. First, however, a section will be devoted to measuring the degree of individual differences in reading rate so that the subsequent research can be placed in context. Then, the review of relevant research will be presented, followed by conclusions.

INDIVIDUAL DIFFERENCES

Earlier, in Chapter 2, the average rate of rauding at each grade level was presented in Table 2.1. For example, the mean rate for college readers found by Taylor (1965) was 280 wpm which was estimated to be 286 Wpm. These data, however, do not reflect upon how much college students vary among themselves with respect to reading rate. Some measure of variation is needed.

In the 1981 *Examiner's Manual* for the Nelson–Denny Reading Test, the means and standard deviations (SDs) for rate are given for Form E and Form F from an equating study. The two means for college seniors were 300 wpm and 290 wpm, and the two SDs were 103 and 81, respectively. The SD is a measure of variability; it is a special way of averaging (i.e., the quadratic mean) the deviations around the arithmetic mean. Assuming a normal distribution with a mean of 300 Wpm and a SD of about 90 Wpm, 16% of the college seniors would read faster than 390 Wpm and 2% would read faster than 480 Wpm. From the normative data given for Form E, less than 1% of college seniors reported that they read faster than 600 wpm on the Nelson–Denny Reading Test.

As noted in Chapters 13 and 18, these reading rates on the Nelson–Denny are self-reported from the first one minute of reading and there is no comprehension check on what was read. Therefore, there is nothing to prevent a college senior who has a rauding rate of 300 Wpm from shifting up to a skimming process or a scanning process that operates at 600 Wpm during this first one minute. Also, there is nothing to prevent a lower ability college senior, for example, from shifting down to a learning process during this first one minute. So, the variability in these reading rates on the Nelson–Denny is probably larger than the variability in rauding rates because variability is exaggerated by some students operating in Gear 4 or Gear 5 with higher reading rates and by some students operating in Gear 1 or Gear 2 with lower reading rates.

With this background, it seems safe to conclude that individuals who have rauding rates that are 600 Wpm or higher are either nonexistent or exceptionally rare; if such individuals exist they can be called super readers. Yet, reported reading rates at 600 Wpm or higher would not provide evidence of a super reader because many individuals can operate a scanning process or a skimming process at 600 Wpm or higher. There must be some evidence that the individual was accurately comprehending ($A > 0.75$) the complete thoughts in the sentences of the passages. Stated differently, there must be some evidence that an individual has a rauding rate of 600 Wpm or higher before the existence of a super reader can be acknowledged. Simply reporting a reading rate higher than 600 Wpm, with no sound evidence that the rauding process was being successfully operated, should *not* be interpreted as evidence of a super reader.

The following quotation, taken from Morse *et al.* (1968), provides some interesting historical information regarding the fast reading speed of the distinguished educational psychologist, Professor Edward L. Thorndike, of Columbia University:

> Professor Thorndike has been credited by *Time* magazine with having read the *Cyclopedia of Education* as bedtime reading. Professor Walter F. Dearborn, of Harvard University, has recently obtained some eye-movement records of Professor Thorndike's reading by means of the electrical-potential technique. Dr. Dearborn has given the present writer permission to use the section of Professor Thorndike's electro-oculogram shown on Figure 8. The reading material in this case was a selection from Adam Smith's *Wealth of Nations*. A comprehension check was required. A rough estimate of Professor Thorn-

dike's performance, as illustrated on Figure 14, indicates that he was reading at about 560 words per minute and making an average of six fixations per line. With Professor Thorndike's record to supplement the eye-movement records obtained from the subjects of this investigation, it seems clear that even the most omnivorous of readers do not read with the lightning rates commonly reported, especially when they are asked to make good their performance on a comprehension check test. (p. 167)

It appears that Professor Thorndike was an exceptionally good reader, but there was no evidence that he could read faster than 600 Wpm and still accurately comprehend.

In summary, finding individuals who can consistently comprehend more than 75% of what they are reading while operating their rauding process at a rate higher than 600 Wpm would constitute evidence that super readers existed. Without sound evidence that the sentences in previously unread material were being accurately comprehended, the conclusion would have to be that the high rates reflected the operation of a skimming or a scanning relationship.

RESEARCH

Adelaide M. Abell (1894) collected reading rate data from 41 members of a Wellesley psychology class. She appears to be the first to conduct and publish an empirical study of how fast individuals read, and that is the primary reason for referring to her research. Unfortunately, she measured reading time and it was not possible to determine rate in wpm since she did not report the length of the "short story" she asked these students to read.

Dearborn (1906) published an extensive study of eye movements (over 130 pages in length), and he reported the reading rates of eight subjects in words per 20 seconds. These eight subjects were selected for this part of his research because they were the fastest four and slowest four out of a group of 30. Reading rates were given for nine different passages taken from *Robinson Crusoe*. The average reading rate for the fastest reader in this group was 654 wpm. Random samples of lines from *Robinson Crusoe* produced an average of 5.1 characters per word which is $D_L = 1.3$; Equation (2.1) was applied and the result was 546 Wpm. This means that the fastest reader that Dearborn could find read an easy and familiar children's book at a rate less than 600 Wpm. Dearborn also appears to be the first researcher to refer to the "rapid reader."

King (1916) appears to be the first to conduct an experiment that induced individuals to read faster than what he called their "natural rate." Out of 94 university students, he randomly assigned half to a group that was paced to cover more of an article while the other half was paced to cover less of the article. From his grading of the test questions relevant to the material they covered, the "fasts" answered 45.7% correctly and the "slows" answered 53.3% correctly. Thus, in 1916 we have the first evidence that rapid reading results in a *decrease* in accuracy of comprehension. This article is mostly of historical interest because (a) there was no measure of rate in wpm, (b) there was very little description of the test questions, and (c) the grading appeared to be very subjective.

W. R. Dixon (1951) reported upon the reading rate of 48 university professors and 48 graduate students as they read passages in three subject matter areas, education, physics, and history. (Note: This research was also reviewed earlier in Chapters 5 and 10 from a different perspective.) These readers should be among the best in the world since doing well in their chosen area of work in academics requires high reading proficiency. There were no important differences in rate between professors and graduate students. The 32 professors and graduate students in education read at a mean rate of 300.2 Wpm, the 32 in physics read at a mean rate of 300.5 Wpm, and those 32 in history read at a mean rate of 317.3 Wpm. From these data, it appears that the average college professor and average graduate student have a rauding rate level at about $R_L = 16$, from the equation presented in Chapter 11.

For the above research, the standard deviations were averaged from the data presented, and these resulting SDs were 89.0 Wpm for education, 77.1 Wpm for physics, and 92.2 Wpm for history. These SDs are approximately equal to the 81 and 103 presented earlier in this chapter for college seniors.

Out of these 96 exceptionally good readers, only five read at least one of the three eight grade level selections ($D_L = 8$) faster than 500 Wpm, and none read a passage faster than 600 Wpm. Of these five fastest readers, only one maintained a rate of 500 Wpm or faster on all three passages, on history, education, and physics. Dixon described this latter individual as follows:

> Case 13 happens to be the individual who has the reputation on the University of Michigan campus of being able to read a line or a paragraph at a glance. One will search the record shown for this case . . . in vain for evidence of single eye-fixations per line or paragraph. (p. 166)

These data from exceptionally good readers who are reading relatively easy material further corroborate the assumption made earlier that a rauding rate greater than 600 Wpm would be indicative of a super reader, yet none have been found.

Thomas (1962) studied the eye movements of a purported super reader while he was covering pages at about 10,000 wpm. A close reading of this report, however, reveals that there was no check on the accuracy of comprehension following reading. Since individuals can skip over words at almost any rate, the crucial question is whether such individuals can do what F. Smith (1971) claims they can do, namely, "comprehend an entire page from the same number of features that a normally skilled reader might require to read barely a tenth of the words" (p. 204). In the Thomas research, the only reference made to comprehension was the following statement: "No tests of comprehension were made . . . but S was tested on a later occasion by Dr. Russell Stauffer, and showed good comprehension" (p. 105). Such a lack of scientific rigor is breathtaking, and does not constitute satisfactory evidence of a super reader.

Taylor (1962) studied 41 trainees who had taken Evelyn Wood's speed reading course called Reading Dynamics. These individuals ". . . had an education background of what might be considered equivalent to a master's degree," and "had served in administrative or teaching capacities" (p. 41). The course was taught by Evelyn Wood herself. The eye movements of the group were photographed before and after the course. It was reported that "the trainees increased their average rate from 474 to 564 w.p.m., an increase of 90 w.p.m., or 20%" (p. 43). It was also reported that the average comprehension before the course was 78% and after the course it was 81%. Short passages were used in the collection of the preceding data. After the course, "the trainees were given an opportunity to read 'dynamically' in a book" (p. 45). Their average rates in this testing were above 1000 Wpm but the average comprehension reported was only about 50%. Taylor summarized his results as follows:

> In summary, an analysis of these eye-movements photographs shows that the gain exhibited by these seemingly above-average trainees was comparatively slight, and there are suggestions that their gain in performance could be, in part, attributed to drive and motivation during the testing, and that when they attempted to read "dynamically," they appeared to resort to a skimming and scanning-like process, with a substantial loss of comprehension. (p. 55)

These data leave little doubt that when individuals speed read at rates above 1000 wpm, they are operating a skimming process. However, the pre and post average rates of 474 Wpm and 564 Wpm with 78% and 81% comprehension scores respectively call into question the earlier assertion that rauding rates greater than 600 Wpm are exceptionally rare or nonexistent. Unfortunately, there was no SD reported as a measure of variability, and there was no description of the tests or procedures used to measure comprehension. Before accepting the idea that there are super readers who have rauding rates above 600 Wpm, it would be necessary to have a better description of the procedures and measures used for rate and comprehension.

Adams (1963) stated that out of 2000 individuals taking a standardized reading test, there were 12 who read at or above a rate of 1500 words per minute (wpm) and had comprehension at or above 70%. These 12 sound like super readers. In this research study, the individuals reported when they had finished reading a given passage. The reading rates were determined from their self-reported times. The individuals were also allowed to grade their own answer sheets. Adams urged scientists who doubted that anyone could read over 1000 wpm to accept these data as factual and to modify their theories accordingly. This is an ineffectual argument. Out of these 2000 studied by Adams, it is not unreasonable to assume that the 12 who were above 1500 wpm included the following: two outright forgers, two who copied from their neighbors, two who made honest mistakes in their grading, two who reported an early finish and then went back and actually finished, and four who reported lower scores but whose data were mistakenly recorded in the transfer of data from the test. These data leave much to be desired in terms of establishing the existence of super readers. One score reported by Adams was 90% reading comprehension at the rate of 17,040 wpm. One might have expected that there would have been a thorough search to find this individual because she or he would seem to have abilities that make the rest of us appear closer to apes in brain functioning. Again, these data cannot be interpreted as documenting the existence of super readers.

Carver (1972a) investigated the tests that have been used to measure comprehension during speed reading. The tests were used in a research study described by Evelyn Wood (1963) as follows:

> At the University of Delaware, a careful study of the Evelyn Wood Reading Dynamic technique was made by William Liddle, a Ph.D. candidate, using a control and an experimental group. In reading non-fiction, he found no significant differences in comprehension between the two groups, despite the fact that the experimental group read at 1300 Wpm—better than three times the speed of the control group. (p. 44)

Carver (1972a) noted that in this unpublished doctoral dissertation by Liddle, two kinds of material were used, nonfiction and fiction, and that the speed readers had lower comprehension scores than the controls on both nonfiction and fiction. For nonfiction, the control readers had a 72% comprehension score and the speed readers were lower at 68%; this was the difference that Wood (1963) mentioned as *not* being statistically significant. Carver hypothesized that the reason why the difference was not larger for the nonfiction materials was because the test was insensitive to comprehension decrements; the test was probably composed of skimming items as was discussed earlier in Chapter 18.

Carver investigated his hypothesis about the test containing skimming items by administering the questions to a small group ($N = 6$), who were not allowed to read the passages before they took the tests. He found that under this control condition, 57% of the nonfiction questions were answered correctly and 51% of the fiction questions were answered correctly. Notice that the speed readers were able to answer only 11% more of the nonfiction questions than this group which did not read the passages, and they were able to answer only 17% more of the fiction questions.

The above data collected by Carver invalidate the assertion by Wood (1963) that speed readers can read at 1300 wpm and still comprehend just as much as normal readers do when they read at rates well below 600 wpm. The speed readers were undoubtedly operating a skimming process and most of the test questions used to measure comprehension could be answered after skimming, or without reading at all. Again, these data cannot be interpreted as establishing the existence of super readers.

Cranney, Brown, Hansen, and Inouye (1982) compared a small group of speed readers ($N = 5$) to two control groups while reading chapters in a social psychology textbook. One control group consisted of six graduate students in social psychology, called the informed group, and the other control group consisted of six honors undergraduates who had no background in social psychology, called the uninformed group. Each of these three groups (experimental, informed, and uninformed) were tested three ways. Under the power condition, they were paced to read each page at an average rate of 260 wpm. Under the speed condition, they were paced to read each page at an average rate of 3000 wpm. Under the preferred rate condition, they read each page at their own preferred rate. After reading a chapter each of the above three ways (power, speed, and preferred) they were allowed to write down notes on what they could recall. Then, they were allowed to go back to the chapter again. Finally, they were allowed to take additional notes, without referring back. Then, they were asked to record on a cassette tape "an organized, detailed summary that reflected as much as they could recall about the chapter just read" (p. 528). It was pointed out that the speed readers in the experimental group had taken the Reading Dynamics course where they (a) had been taught to use the hand as a pacer, (b) had been taught a note-taking technique, called "mapping," and (c) had been taught to read faster using a technique called "add-a-page drill." After these data had been collected, the tape-recorded recalls were scored by having judges evaluate "comprehension as percent of the total material recalled" (p. 529).

The results of the above research by Cranney *et al.* will be presented for each of the three reading conditions; the reading rates to be reported have been adjusted to include the extra time spent reading after the first note-taking session. Under the power reading condition, the rates for the speed readers, informed readers, and uninformed readers were 198, 201, and 204 wpm, respectively, and the corresponding percentage comprehension scores were 74, 54, and 51. Notice that the average rates were almost exactly the same for all three groups, about 200 wpm, but the accuracy of comprehension for the speed readers, 74%, was much higher than the informed readers, 54%, which consisted of third and fourth year graduate students in social psychology who were reading a textbook in their field of social psychology. These recall data suggest that the speed readers were much better readers than the informed readers, since the speed readers could operate a learning process at the same rate as the informed readers and still comprehend 20% more even when the material was in the chosen field of study for the informed readers. The results for the uninformed readers were similar to the informed readers and did not add enough information to justify their inclusion. So, from this point on, this review will be simplified by disregarding the scores of the second control group, the uninformed readers.

The above data suggest that the speed readers were either much better readers in general than the informed group, or they were much better note takers, or they were much better at organizing and verbalizing their recalls, or they were much better at all of the above. The point is, when reading fast was not important but comprehending, remembering, writing notes, organizing notes, and verbalizing recalls at a very slow rate was important, the speed reader group was much better than the informed readers. The size of this difference can be measured using Cohen's *d* as an effect size measure (see Carver, 1984a), and it turns out to be 1.65. Cohen (1977) considers a *d* of 0.2 to be a small effect, 0.5 to be a medium effect, and 0.8 to be a large effect. Therefore, it can be seen that the speed readers were a great deal better at this task at 200 wpm than the informed readers since the difference between the two groups represented an extremely large effect size (1.65 compared to a large effect size of 0.80).

The five speed readers in this research were described as university students, with two being undergraduates, two being English honors students, and one being a graduate student in instructional psychology. Each of these five students had been nominated by teachers at the Reading Dynamics course because these students had successfully used the technique for at least one year. So, with these data from the power reading condition, it is clear that the speed readers were a great deal better at this task than the controls, probably because they were selected to be the best out of a large group of very good readers.

Under the speed condition in the Cranney *et al.* research, the adjusted rates for all three groups were the same, 1800 wpm; the speed readers had a mean percentage comprehension score of 62 and the corresponding score for the informed group was 45. Again, a very large difference showing the superiority of the speed readers. Cohen's *d* was calculated to be 1.55, which again indicates a very large effect size that is approximately equal to the effect size found under the power condition, 1.65. In both the power condition (about 200 wpm) and the speed condition (about 1800 wpm), the speed readers demonstrated that they were much better at performing these tasks of comprehending, remembering, taking notes, organizing notes, and verbalizing recalls. However, it seems entirely possible that the scoring of these recalls is heavily influenced by a production ability that (a) loads heavily on a skill at which these five students excel, (b) was further emphasized in this course, and (c) was steadily practiced by these five students so that they are much better at this particular task than most any other group, especially unpracticed students. It would be necessary to measure the ability of these speed readers to read other material at 1800 Wpm and show that they had comprehended over 75% of the complete thoughts before jumping to the conclusion that they were super readers who have rauding rates greater than 600 Wpm.

Under the preferred rate condition in this research, the speed readers and the informed readers read at 1134 wpm and 304 wpm, respectively, and the mean comprehension score for both groups was 65%. Cranney *et al.* interpreted this result as indicating that the speed readers can go faster (1134 versus 304) while maintaining respectable comprehension (65% versus 65%). However, the more reasonable way to interpret this result is to note that these five students who were exceptionally superior to the informed control group under both the power condition (200 wpm) and the speed condition (1800 wpm) lost all of their superiority when they read at 1134 wpm and the informed control group read at 304 wpm. If the speed readers had maintained their superiority in the preferred condition on the comprehension measure (with a Cohen's *d* of around 1.5) while reading at a rate of 1134 Wpm, then there would have been strong evidence that they had somehow learned to read at this high rate without sacrificing any comprehension. However, it is obvious that they sacrificed comprehension; otherwise why did they not show the same exceptional superiority on the comprehension score that they showed under the power and speed conditions when both groups read at the same rate?

The above research indicates that speed readers can operate a skimming process that helps them perform well under certain study conditions. Yet, their performance suffers greatly at rates over 1000 Wpm as compared to rates around 300 wpm. Good study skills require the use of various scanning, skimming, rauding, learning, and memorizing processes, as well as note taking. These data serve to showcase the kind of exceptionally good study skills that can be achieved by some exceptionally good readers, possibly with the help of a commercial course such as Reading Dynamics. However, these data do not provide sound evidence that there are individuals who can operate their rauding process at rates over 600 Wpm and still comprehend the complete thoughts in over 75% of the sentences.

Homa (1983) was asked by the American Speedreading Academy (ASA) to test two of its graduates who supposedly could read at rates exceeding 100,000 wpm. Together with ASA, they worked out three different tests that would be given to determine the unique abilities of these two men. Two of the tests involved visual perception, and Homa found that neither of the two speed readers were better than control subjects. He summarized the perceptual results as follows:

> Their perceptual extent was no different from the control subjects. Their accuracy on the paragraph perception test was comparable to that of control subjects, although they demonstrated a much greater tendency to guess at the words presented. (p. 126)

Homa also gave the speed readers a 20-item multiple choice test on a chapter from a book used in one of his university classes. He had already used the same book and test in one of his classes so it was possible to assign a grade on the test using the same criteria that he had used in his class. In a class of 52, he had assigned 10 A's, 10 B's, 15 C's, 7 D's, and 10 F's, with anyone scoring below 14 being given an F. The two speed readers were allowed to read at their own rate, and then they were given the test. They did poorly, below 14 for an F, so he repeated the testing again, 3–5 days later, and then a third time, 3–5 days later. He reported that one speed reader averaged about 30,000 wpm over the three exams, and the other averaged about 15,000 wpm. He also said that both speed readers would have been given F's because they failed the exam. He summarized his findings as follows: "In conclusion, the only noteworthy skill exhibited by the two speed-readers was a remarkable dexterity in page-turning" (p. 126). These data certainly do not support the existence of super readers.

Carver (1984b) investigated how much college students could comprehend under speed reading conditions. (Note: This research was reviewed earlier in Chapters 10 and 16 from a different perspective.) Passages were presented that were about 100 words in length and grade 10 in difficulty. Rate was varied from 62.5 to 100,000 Wpm using motion picture film to present a passage on the screen for a fixed amount of time. The time that a 100-word passage was on the screen under the 100,000 Wpm condition was about 1/18th of a second. So, the rates were actually average rates since the entire passage was on the screen for a fixed amount of time to produce a certain average reading rate in order to finish reading the passage. Four different measures of comprehension were used.

Carver found that at 250 Wpm and slower, accuracy of comprehension was estimated to be above 75%. At 500 Wpm, accuracy of comprehension was around 40–50%. At 1000 Wpm, accuracy of comprehension was around 20%. Above 1000 Wpm, accuracy of comprehension fluctuated around 0%. It should be noted again that accuracy of comprehension was around 20% at an average rate of 1000 Wpm, not an actual rate of 1000 Wpm. The passage was on the screen for a fixed amount of time and these college students could have operated their rauding process during this time at 300 Wpm and only finished about the first third of the passage. Instead, if each sentence had been presented at an average rate of 1000 Wpm, then none of the sentences could have been finished at the rauding rate and then the comprehension of complete thoughts in these passages would no doubt have been much closer to 0%. These data indicate that typical college students cannot comprehend 75% or more of relatively easy passages at rates greater than 500 Wpm. This research further documents the low probability of finding anyone with a rauding rate above 600 Wpm.

Carver (1985b) conducted a thorough investigation of some of the world's best readers. There were four speed readers, including a former demonstrator and teacher for Evelyn Wood Reading Dynamics. There were four professionals, including a writer for the *New Yorker* magazine. There were four college students who were selected because they scored the highest on screening tests. There were four in a test group, including one subject who had a perfect score on the SAT examination. These 16 subjects were individually administered a battery of tests that required about 8.5 hours spread over 2–3 days. Four different techniques were used to measure reading rate. On the two measures that required comprehension to be highly accurate, all four groups averaged around 300 Wpm. However, on the two measures where there was no check on comprehension, the speed reading group averaged over 800 Wpm. These data were interpreted as indicating that the speed readers automatically adopt a skimming process when there is nothing that requires them to comprehend 75% or more of the thoughts in the sentences. Thus, the apping rate (discussed in Chapter 9) of speed readers seem to have been set for a skimming or scanning process instead of the rauding process.

The speed readers in this research did *not* distinguish themselves by doing better than the other groups on the vocabulary and comprehension sections of the Nelson–Denny Reading Test. If their reading efficiency was better than the other groups, then they should have scored higher on the Comprehension section of the Nelson–Denny (see the Efficiency-Index Pitfall in Chapter 18). Also, on a skimming test that required choosing the best title for a passage, the speed readers were *not* best at 300 Wpm (they ranked third out of the four groups) and they were worst at 7500 Wpm. On this same skimming test, the scores of all four groups were approximately equal at 1500 Wpm, with the speed reading group slightly better than the other three groups. If the speed readers have a special ability to go fast and still obtain the gist, then they should have been the best group at 7500 Wpm, but they were the worst. In fact, they were the best at 1500 Wpm but their superiority was trivial.

In one series of tests given by Carver, short passages were presented for varying lengths of time and then accuracy of comprehension was measured. It was possible to estimate rauding rate from the curves that showed accuracy increasing as reading time increased, i.e., rate decreased from 1200 Wpm to 240 Wpm (see Carver, 1985a). The means of these estimated rauding rates varied from 268 Wpm with 86% comprehension for the college student group to 444 Wpm with 71% comprehension for the speed reader group. These data provided no evidence for rauding rates above 600 Wpm.

Carver also used book length articles of about 6000 words in length. A test measuring the recall of important details from these books was given under the following four average rates: 375 Wpm, 1500 Wpm, 6000 Wpm, and 24,000 Wpm. *The speed readers distinguished themselves by scoring the lowest of all four groups at every one of these four rates.* Under the 375 Wpm condition, the test group recalled more than 75% of the important details. The speed readers recalled about 40% at 375 Wpm, about 20% at 1500 Wpm, about 5% at 6000 Wpm, and about 5% at 24,000 Wpm. A control group of 36 college students recalled about 4% under the 24,000 Wpm condition so the speed readers were essentially equal to typical college students in their ability to recall important details at high reading rates.

Immediately after Carver had administered the above test for recalling the important details from a book, another test was administered that required the individuals to write a summary of the entire book in 100 words or less. The speed readers were no better than the other groups on this task under three of the four rates: 375 Wpm, 6000 Wpm, and 24,000 Wpm. However, the speed readers were clearly better than the other groups under the 1500 Wpm condition. It may be remembered that the speed readers were slightly better on the skimming tests under the 1500 Wpm condition, but no other condition. It seems likely that these speed readers have an apping rate that operates at around 1000 to 1500 Wpm; they are habitually operating a skimming process that focuses upon getting the gist or overview. The verbal production ability of these readers coupled with their apping rate of about 1200 Wpm allows them to write better summaries of what they have read at this rate. It should not go unnoticed, however, these speed readers remembered the least of the important details at every rate from 375 Wpm to 24,000 Wpm.

This research provides the most detailed evidence to date of what speed readers and other superior readers are capable of doing. There was no evidence that any of these superior readers had a rauding rate over 600 Wpm; therefore there was no evidence for the existence of super readers. The speed readers were different from the other readers in that they typically operated a skimming process at rates around 1000 Wpm or higher, unless there was a requirement that comprehension be relatively high, e.g., 75% or greater. By adopting a skimming process for their apping rate, they were able to show some superiority on gist or summary tasks at rates around 1000 Wpm. Yet, they showed no superiority at any other higher or lower rate, they showed no superiority for remembering important details at this rate, and they showed no superiority in any other tasks at higher or lower rates.

In summary, it appears that speed readers have adopted a skimming process as their normal or typical reading process and they will habitually operate this process unless the situation demands that they shift down to achieve the goals of the rauding process. There was no evidence that speed readers were super readers or that any super readers exist who have rauding rates over 600 Wpm.

Just and Carpenter (1987) reported on a lengthy and admirable investigation of speed readers which further clarifies their abilities. A group of 11 college students were studied who had just graduated from a 7-week Reading Dynamics course given by Evelyn Wood. During this period, the students had spent approximately 50 hours practicing rapid reading, including 17 hours in class. These speed readers were compared to 13 normal readers and 12 skimmers who were from the same college population. The normal group was asked to read normally and the skimmers were ". . . asked to read quickly, using whatever strategies they felt comfortable with" (p. 429). All three groups were asked to read two passages, one from *Reader's Digest* called Colter, and the other from *Scientific American* called Mars. After reading, they were given 20 comprehension questions, 10 gist questions and 10 detail questions.

Just and Carpenter found that overall, the normal readers averaged about 240 wpm, the skimmers averaged about 600 wpm, and the speed readers averaged about 700 wpm. On the four comprehension measures—gist and detail on the easier Colter passage and gist and detail on the harder Mars passage—the normal readers generally answered at least 15% more questions correctly than the speed readers; the exception was on the detail test for the harder Mars passage where the normal group answered about 24% correctly and the speed readers answered about 17% correctly, a 7% advantage for the normal readers. The skimmers generally answered almost exactly the same number of questions correctly as the speed readers; the exception was on the easier Colter passage where the speed readers answered around 10% more of the questions correctly compared to the skimmers. Just and Carpenter summarized these comprehension results as follows:

> The only advantage of the speed readers in the comprehension test occurred on high-level questions that interrogate the gist of familiar, easy passages. The speed readers were able to answer more questions than the skimmers about the gist of the Colter passage. Speed readers had no advantage in answering questions about details or answering questions about the more difficult Mars passage. Neither group . . . performed as well as the normal readers, showing that reading faster does lower comprehension. (p. 445)

These results prompted Just and Carpenter to offer this advice: ". . . readers can increase their reading speed by sacrificing the amount they understand from a text; faster speed usually implies lessened comprehension, a trade-off" (p. 425). Remember from Chapter 16, that Sisson (1939) gave similar advice 50 years ago. These data do not suggest that these college students have learned to read at rates over 600 Wpm while comprehending as accurately as they did before they took the speed reading course. These data do not suggest that these college students have been transformed into super readers who can operate their rauding process at rates over 600 Wpm and still comprehend over 75% of relatively easy material. These data do not provide evidence for the existence of individuals who have rauding rates over 600 Wpm.

Just and Carpenter also studied the eye movements of these three groups as they were reading. They reported that normal readers ordinarily fixated upon almost every word whereas the speed readers and skimmers ordinarily skip over words, seldom fixating upon two words in a row. With respect to an ability to skip over unimportant words, they concluded that:

> Neither speed readers nor skimmers are very selective about fixating the most important words of a text. The span over which rapid readers extract word meaning is relatively narrow. Rapid readers cannot answer questions about detail if they did not fixate directly on it or within three character spaces of it. (p. 448).

These data of Just and Carpenter seem to support the suggestion made by Carver (1985b) that speed reading is really skimming in disguise, with one minor qualification. According to Just and Carpenter, "the speed readers do not use an exotic scanning strategy except that their scanning is more uniform, which may free some attentional resources" (p. 448). By practicing these skipping or skimming eye movements, the speed readers probably become more natural or habitual, i.e., this skimming rate becomes their apping rate. This high-speed apping has minor advantages. In Carver's research, the speed readers had a slight advantage in getting the gist at 1500 Wpm, a bigger advantage in writing a summary at 1500 Wpm, but no advantage in remembering important details at any rate. The modest advantage found by Carver for speed readers did not generalize to other rates, such as 6000, 7500, or 24,000 Wpm. Again, this finding supports high-speed apping but not high-speed rauding.

In the Just and Carpenter research, the one advantage of speed readers over the skimmers was in answering gist questions on a relatively easy passage from *Reader's Digest*. This advantage did not hold up on a more difficult passage from *Scientific American* and it did not hold up when questions were asked about details. It appears that speed readers have practiced reading at a fast rate, such as 1000 Wpm, until their eye movements become rather habitual at this rate. They are automatically skipping words with less attention required than skimmers who do approximately the same thing but do it a little less well because they must direct more attention to moving their eyes so that less attention can be paid to extracting meaning from the words. These data from Just and Carpenter plus the earlier data from Carver (1985a) seem to support this apping interpretation.

Just and Carpenter also reported that normal readers fixated more upon content words and more upon low-frequency words even when word length was constant. However, it is important to remember that these college students were reading at about 240 wpm which is borderline between a learning process and the rauding process (see Chapter 2).

Since these readers knew that they would be given a 20-item test on what they read, it seems reasonable that many of them would shift down to a learning process. Therefore, it is quite likely that these results pertaining to fixations upon a certain type of word would probably evaporate if all of these college readers were using their rauding process on the *Reader's Digest* article. At a minimum, it seems important to find out if these results will replicate at rates closer to 260–300 Wpm, which are more typical for college students.

Nell (1988) reported the reading rates for 30 ludic readers, defined as reading at least one book of light fiction for pleasure each week. (Note: these data were reviewed earlier in Chapter 10 from a different perspective.) About half of these subjects were recruited from a newspaper advertisement for "bookworms." Since these individuals are avid readers of very easy materials, it would seem to be fertile ground for finding some of the world's fastest readers. Out of the rates reported for reading a book of their own choosing for 30 min, there were two of these ludic readers who had rates above 600 wpm (not Wpm). Subject 220 had a rate of 921 wpm and Subject 118 had a rate of 794 wpm. Thus, these two are potential candidates for being super readers. However, this measure of rate suffers from the No-Comprehension-Measure Pitfall, introduced in Chapter 18. Since there was no measure or test over what was read, it could be that these two individuals were skimming, with less than 75% of the complete thoughts being comprehended. Nell did provide some additional evidence regarding this possibility. He also administered a 1000-word passage with comprehension questions, with rate in wpm adjusted using an index of the accuracy of comprehension. Subject 220, with the 921 wpm rate noted earlier, had a Reading Comprehension Speed (RCS) of 472 wpm; no evidence of a super reader. Subject 118, with the 794 wpm rate noted earlier, had an RCS of 695 wpm. This individual appears to be a candidate for being a super reader. However, this is one small piece of evidence from a study that was not designed to provide reliable evidence regarding the existence of individuals who can accurately comprehend at rates above 600 Wpm. If such super readers exist they should be apparent among ludic readers since they are highly practiced in reading the easiest possible material, light fiction.

CONCLUSIONS

The facts associated with research on speed reading, rapid reading training, and super readers have been reviewed in this chapter and the previous one. In the previous chapter, there were only a few studies conducted on rapid reading training that would pass minimum standards for internal and external validity, and their results were mixed. However, there was a sizable number of studies that found no difference between pre and post training using the comprehension scores on standardized reading tests, and this constitutes evidence against any improvement in reading efficiency associated with the training.

With respect to the research on speed readers reviewed earlier in this chapter, there were only three studies that suggested the existence of super readers, and were also relatively sound methodologically: they were the ones conducted by Taylor (1962), Cranney et al. (1982), and Nell (1988). The Taylor research was positive because a highly educated group was reading at a rate of 474 Wpm with 78% comprehension before training and 564 Wpm with 81% comprehension after training. These high rates with such high mean scores for the accuracy of comprehension would indeed suggest the existence of some super readers who do have rauding rates over 600 Wpm. However, this positive aspect of the study was offset somewhat by a skimpy description of the procedures and comprehension tests. Also, the small 20% gain in rate from taking the Reading Dynamics course was not very supportive of rapid reading training, and Taylor's book length test given after the course indicated that the graduates were skimming at rates above 1000 wpm with mean comprehension scores around 50%.

The seemingly positive aspect of the Cranney et al. study was that the speed reading group read at 1134 wpm and scored as high on a comprehension test, 65%, as a group of graduate students reading at 304 Wpm who were highly informed about the material being read. However, the speed readers were much better than the graduate students at the skimming, note taking, organizing, and verbal recalling skills required on the same type of comprehension test when it was given at 200 Wpm. This means that the speed readers were much better at this task at any rate, probably because they were selected in a manner that assured that they were more successful at the studying skills being tested. Therefore, since the speed readers had more of this ability than the graduate students but scored no better on these studying tasks when they read at 1234 Wpm, this means that the speed readers were giving up a great deal of comprehension when they read at 1134 Wpm.

The Nell (1988) research was positive in that one of 30 people, selected because they were avid readers of light fiction, had a 695 wpm score on a test designed to measure reading rate adjusted for accuracy of comprehension. However, this was not a Wpm rate with an objective measure indicating greater than 75% accuracy of comprehension. So, these data provide a possible candidate for being a super reader, one who may just barely reach the criterion of 600 Wpm with 75% accuracy of comprehension. Yet, on the basis of these data alone, it would be presumptuous to assume that in fact this was a super reader. Thus, neither the Taylor (1962) research, nor the Cranney *et al.* (1982) research, nor the Nell research provided definitive evidence for the existence of super readers.

On the negative side, there were two studies that were exceptionally thorough in their investigation of speed readers, Carver (1985b) and Just and Carpenter (1987). In these studies, it was found that the exemplary speed readers were not super readers but were simply good readers who chose to read around 1000 Wpm whenever there was no requirement that the accuracy of comprehension be high. These speed readers were slightly better on tests that required gist, somewhat better at writing an overview at rates around 1000–1500 Wpm, and were better than skimmers in answering gist questions on easy passages. But, these speed readers were no better on these overview kinds of tasks at other rates such as 6000 Wpm, or 24,000 Wpm. These speed readers were consistently worse when recalling important details at all rates for both easy and hard passages. There was no evidence that speed readers have learned to skip the less important information. It does appear that the speed readers do have a slight and restricted advantage. They have practiced reading so much as a certain fast speed, that they have learned to move their eyes this way habitually. This means they have a little more attention left for cognition compared to unpracticed skimmers who still must devote attention to moving their eyes over words without stopping and without trying to comprehend the complete thoughts in sentences.

The preceding paragraphs have reviewed the theory and factual research evidence relevant to rapid reading training, speed reading, and super readers. A picture emerges which seems to fit the entire situation very well. There is no sound evidence that anyone exists who has a rauding rate higher than 600 Wpm. On the other hand, almost anyone can be trained to operate a skimming or scanning process at rates around 600 Wpm or higher. There is no limit to the rate at which various scanning and skimming processes can operate, such as 10,000 to 100,000 Wpm. And, if skimming-type questions are asked it can be made to appear that "comprehension" is high at these rates because over 75% of these easy questions can be answered at these high rates. Still, there is no sound evidence that an individual's rauding rate can be improved by rapid reading training.

Now that the factual evidence and the theoretical explanations have been thoroughly treated, it seems important to consider the body of opinion associated with speed reading. A search of scholarly journals yielded 50 articles that offered opinions about speed reading. Undoubtedly, some articles were missed, and this count does not include any of the articles from popular magazines, such as *Reader's Digest, Ladies Home Journal,* or *Forbes.* As noted in Chapter 18, there are many articles espousing fast reading or speed reading (e.g., Ahuja, 1977; McBride, 1981), and there are many articles debunking rapid reading (e.g., Carver, 1972b; Spache, 1962). Carver (1971f) devoted an entire book to debunking speed reading but there have been many more books published that extoll its virtues and explain in textbook detail how to do it (such as Brown, 1962; Klaeser, 1977; N. B. Smith, 1957). There have been television programs praising it (e.g., Siegel, 1979), and there are instructional video tapes available for purchase (e.g., Cavett, 1986). There are countless commercially available programs that charge hundreds of dollars to teach it (such as Reading Dynamics and the American Speedreading Academy), and there are courses being offered in many universities that also claim to teach it.

If speed reading advocates would concede that what they are teaching is a type of skimming process, instead of the rauding process that is used in normal reading, then there would not be any controversy about its merits. However, speed reading advocates have blurred the distinction among the different basic processes used in reading. This cultivated ambiguity, promoted by speed reading advocates, is often fueled by the opinions and pronouncements of highly respected theorists and researchers in psychology and education. For example, Gibson, Bishop, Schiff, and Smith (1964) stated that "it was not necessary for psychologists to point out that speedy readers do not dwell on every letter, but take in words, phrases, and conceivably even sentences at a glance" (p. 173). Later, Neisser (1967) said that "rapid reading is no more limited to 1200 or 600 words a minute than to 300" (p. 135), and that "rapid reading represents an achievement as impossible in theory as it is commonplace in practice" (p. 137). Then, Bower (1970) said that "a skilled reader can read with comprehension at rates of more than 1000 words per minute" and that this "presents an irresistible challenge to theoretical explanation" (p. 135). However, none of the above respected researchers offered any empirical data substantiating the existence of these super reading feats, and none provided any references to other research where such data had been collected. We researchers and educators need to get our houses in order with respect to opinions based on theory that has sound supporting empirical evidence. Until then, lay persons will probably continue to be misled by experts, who should know better, extolling the virtues of speed reading and rapid reading training.

Speed reading is 95% nonsense and 5% sense (see Carver, 1971f). The 95% nonsense involves claiming that some individuals can shift to a skimming process and still accurately comprehend 75% or more of the complete thoughts in the sentences of passages. The 5% sense involves teaching some individuals process flexibility by getting them to shift out of the rauding process to a skimming process when the goal justifies such gear shifting. Still, it should be remembered that individuals cannot shift up to fourth gear or higher without losing the power of sentence comprehension associated with third gear, the work horse of reading.

Speed readers are best regarded as experienced or expert skimmers. This was discerned earlier by Morse *et al.* (1968), as evidenced by the following quotation: "Cases of individuals who are supposed to read in 'gulps,' 'chunks,' or 'sections,' may be put down as masterful skimming" (p. 178).

METHODOLOGY

INTRODUCTION

Recommendations will be made for improving future research on reading rate, using the context of rauding theory and the research contained in earlier chapters. These recommendations will build upon those given in the past (Carver, 1975b).

From the standpoint of rauding theory, little can be learned about reading rate without information describing (a) the difficulty of the passage that was read, (b) the rauding ability of the individual, including rauding accuracy level and rauding rate level, and (c) the instructions and objective consequences designed to produce a certain type of reading process. The methodology associated with these situational variables will be addressed first. Then, various design, measurement, and data analysis factors will be considered, and examples given. Finally, a case will be made for conducting more research that is specifically designed to investigate the rauding process.

PASSAGE DESCRIPTION

Introduction

The passages used in research need to be around 100 words in length, or longer, and they need to be described in terms of their length, composition, and difficulty level.

Length

The length of the passage must be reported, preferably in standard length words, six character spaces per standard length word. Passages that are only one sentence in length may not be representative of the integrative component of the rauding process, for example. The length in actual words may also be reported. It is not uncommon for length information to be omitted (e.g., see Birkmire, 1985; Cirilo & Foss, 1980). Without knowing length in actual words or standard words, it is impossible for the researcher to determine rate in wpm or Wpm.

Composition

The composition of the passage should be briefly described. The number of sentences in a short passage could be given. The topic could be given. A description in terms of narrative versus expository text could be given. When the passages have already been published, such as the Bormuth passages (Carver, 1984c), then the ID number can be given so that the composition of the passage is entirely public information.

When it is desirable to study the rate at which the rauding process operates, it is highly desirable to use passages that are at least a few sentences long. There are many research studies that involve the reading of isolated sentences (e.g., P. Dixon, 1982; Garnham, 1981; Garrod & Sanford, 1977; Keenan & Brown, 1984); these are of quasi relevance to the rauding process, however, because they do not require the integration of the thought in the present sentence to the thoughts in prior sentences.

Difficulty Level

Some measure of material difficulty must be given, e.g., Dale–Chall, Fry, and Flesch (see Klare, 1963). However, the most valid measure of difficulty appears to be the Rauding Scale of Prose Difficulty (Carver, 1975a). This measure requires the judgments of qualified experts. Obtaining this measure can become troublesome since many people must be tested in order to find at least three qualified experts. A mechanical substitute for this Rauding Scale is the DRP-GE-Difficulty measure (Carver, 1985c) which is a rescaling of the Degrees of Reading Power (DRP) readability technique into GE units. This DRP measure can be obtained with the aid of a computer program.

Some estimate of rauding difficulty level, D_L, in GE units must be provided, and the best measures, at present, seem to be the Rauding Scale and the DRP, described above. The DRP and the Rauding Scale measures are both available for all of the 330 Bormuth passages, mentioned above. Examples of studies which failed to report a measure of the difficulty level of the material are as follows: Cirilo and Foss (1980); Kintsch and Kozminsky (1977).

DESCRIPTION OF INDIVIDUAL

Introduction

Any study of reading rate is not complete without a good estimate of the rauding ability of the readers. Rauding ability is summarized by a measure of rauding efficiency level, E_L, or better still, it can be divided into its two components: rauding accuracy level, A_L, and rauding rate level, R_L. Evidence was presented in Chapter 3 that these three variables describe almost all of the reliable variance involved in standardized tests that measure reading comprehension, vocabulary, and rate, and they will be discussed in turn.

Efficiency Level

"General reading ability is not a fiction" (p. 304), according to Gates (1921). It is commonly measured by standardized reading comprehension tests, such as the ones included in the batteries for the Iowa Test of Basic Skills (ITBS) or the Nelson–Denny Reading Test (NDRT). These reading comprehension measures provide scores that are correlates of individual differences in rauding efficiency level, E_L (see Carver, 1990d). As explained in earlier chapters, rauding efficiency level, E_L, is the highest difficulty level at which individuals can accurately comprehend 75% of the complete thoughts while reading at a rate commensurate with that level. So, E_L provides a more precise or refined way of defining and measuring general reading ability as it has traditionally been measured by reading comprehension tests.

Farr (1971) has provided an excellent review of early reading tests, including tests of reading rate. He notes that "reading comprehension was usually defined during the early 1920's as the process of thought-getting" (p. 190). Thus, the early tests of reading comprehension were designed to measure the efficiency of the rauding process. It is no accident, therefore, that reading comprehension tests today are still providing correlates of E_L.

Presently, the best indicant of E_L seems to be an average of the rauding accuracy level and the rauding rate level (Carver, 1990d), to be described in the next two subsections. The reading comprehension scores on most standardized reading tests, such as the ITBS or the NDRT, validly reflect individual differences in rauding efficiency level, even though their GE score may *not* provide valid absolute levels of E_L in GE units. Still, the GE scores on the ITBS are likely to be very close to E_L as estimated from the Accuracy Level Test and the Rate Level Test, mentioned above.

Accuracy Level

As explained in earlier chapters, an individual's rauding accuracy level, A_L, is the highest level of material difficulty, D_L, that can be accurately comprehended when it is read at the individual's rauding rate, R_r. Scores on vocabulary tests, such as those included in the ITBS and the NDRT, correlate highly with individual differences in A_L (Carver, 1990d). However, tests such as the ITBS and NDRT do not purport to provide criterion-referenced GE measures; this means that individuals who have 5.5 GE scores on the Vocabulary section of the ITBS are *not* purported to be able to comprehend about 75% or more of the complete thoughts in material at the GE = 5.5 difficulty. At present, the best measure of A_L appears to be provided by the Accuracy Level Test (Carver, 1987c). It is a vocabulary test that has been scaled to provide criterion-referenced GE units for A_L. Yet, the Vocabulary GE score on the ITBS is likely to be very close to A_L as estimated by the Accuracy Level Test.

It will be difficult to justify the omission of an indicator of A_L in future studies of reading rate, because $A_L - D_L$ is a measure of relative difficulty which indicates whether the material being read is relatively easy or relatively hard, and this is an important factor influencing what reading process is likely to be operating. For example, researchers who want to study the rauding process should make sure that $A_L > D_L$. If the material being read is relatively hard, $A_L < D_L$, then it is more likely that an individual will shift out of the rauding process into a learning process in order to be able to comprehend the material accurately. It should also be remembered that the constancy of reading rate is purported to hold under conditions wherein the rauding process is operating, and this also means that the materials should be relatively easy, $A_L > D_L$, when investigating the rauding process.

In summary, A_L needs to be estimated in research on reading so that it can be compared to D_L.

Rate Level

As was noted in earlier chapters, an individual's rauding rate, R_r, is the fastest rate at which the individual can accurately comprehend relatively easy material. This rate can be scaled into GE units, R_L, called rauding rate level. These units reflect the average rate of individuals at that A_L. For example, individuals at $R_L = 7$, have a rauding rate equal to the average rate of individuals at $A_L = 7$ (see Carver, 1987a).

There are few measures that reliably and validly reflect individual differences in R_L. For example, the ITBS has no correlate of rauding rate level and the rate measure on the NDRT is not very reliable or valid for this purpose (see Carver, 1987a). At present, it appears that the most reliable and valid measure of R_L can be obtained from the Rate Level Test (Carver, 1987a). It provides a criterion-referenced GE measure. Farr and Carey (1986) have provided examples of reading rate tests, and they note that there are still many tests, such as the NDRT, which measure rate on passages with "no concomitant assessment of whether the reader understands what is read" (p. 121). It should also be noted that at least three of the nine tests given as examples by Farr and Carey reflect both rate level and accuracy level concomitantly, so these tests are likely to provide a better correlate of rauding efficiency level, E_L, than R_L.

Providing an estimate of the R_r or R_L of experimental subjects would greatly improve most studies of reading rate. This estimate could be compared to the actual reading rates obtained in the research. If the obtained rates are not approximately equal to R_r, then it is less likely that the rauding process was involved. If the obtained rates are considerably higher than R_r, then it is more likely that a scanning or skimming process was operating. If the obtained rates are considerably lower than R_r, then it is more likely that a learning or memorizing process was operating.

Summary

Ideally, future studies of reading rate will provide a measure of A_L and R_L. E_L can then be estimated from an average of A_L and R_L, and R_r can be obtained from R_L using Appendix B. These measures describe the subjects in terms of their rauding ability so that generalizing from the results involving materials at known difficulty levels can be done with more validity. When studying the rauding process, it is more likely that the process was operating if the material was relatively easy, $A_L > D_L$, and the experimentally obtained reading rates were approximately equal to the measured rauding rate of the subjects, R_r.

PROCESS

Introduction

Basic information must be given relative to the type of reading process that was used in the research situation. Crucial to making inferences about the type of reading process is information about the relative difficulty of the material, instructions given to the subjects, the objective consequences of the reading, and the rate at which the process operated.

Relative Difficulty

Perhaps the most important variable to be measured in a study of reading rate is the relative difficulty of the material being read, $A_L - D_L$.

For example, if rauding rate is measured when the materials are relatively hard, $A_L < D_L$, then it is unlikely that the measure will be highly valid. As noted earlier, individuals are more likely to shift out of the rauding process when the material is relatively hard, $A_L < D_L$.

It is very difficult to interpret reading rate results when there is no estimate of A_L and D_L, so that no estimate of relative difficulty, $A_L - D_L$, is possible. Relative difficulty ordinarily influences the type of reading process used by the individuals. Furthermore, relative difficulty, $A_L - D_L$, has a major influence upon the accuracy of comprehension when the rauding process is operating (see Carver, 1975a). The relative difficulty, $A_L - D_L$, of a passage can be substituted into Equation (2.14) to get an estimate of the individual's rauding accuracy, A_r, for that passage.

Instructions

As noted earlier in Chapter 2, the instructions given to the subjects in an investigation ordinarily influence their reading rate via the process that they adopt. Instructions to read normally or naturally are likely to produce a rauding rate for most people as long as the materials are relatively easy ($A_L > D_L$) and the objective consequences of reading do not force the individuals to shift out of their natural third gear.

At a minimum, published reports must describe the instructions in detail. Ideally, the investigator would announce the type of reading process under investigation and would then describe the instructions that were designed to produce this process. The effects of instructions are likely to be attenuated after one or more practice trials involving the objective consequences, to be discussed next.

Objective Consequences

Individuals often have the opportunity to modify the process they operate on the basis of their evaluation of their success associated with the process. Therefore, the objective consequences of reading should be in harmony with the instructions. For example, telling individuals to read normally or naturally and then giving them a difficult test on what they have read is apt to force them to shift gears on subsequent passages, out of third gear into second or first gear. Administering multiple-choice questions that are not relatively easy is likely to force individuals to adopt a learning process. Asking individuals to recall everything they can remember is likely to force individuals to adopt a memorizing process.

Reporting some estimate of the accuracy of comprehension, A, is also ideal. When individuals are only 50%, or less, successful they are more likely to shift to a lower gear so as to improve their success rate. Or, if they are 90%, or more, successful they may shift to a higher gear to improve their efficiency in accomplishing the task. It is desirable, when possible, to convert empirical measures of the accuracy of comprehension into absolute measures of the accuracy of comprehension, A, using the rauding rescaling procedure (Carver, 1985a). When the Accuracy Level Test and the Rate Level Test have been administered to the subjects, and the difficulty level and length of the passages have been measured, then A_L, D_L, and R_r can be estimated so that the accuracy of comprehension, A, can be predicted for any length of time allowed for reading, $1/R$, using Equations (2.11), (2.12), (2.13), and (2.14).

When studying the rauding process, it is important that the task consequences not be so severe that individuals are forced to shift to a lower gear to get the power they need to be successful with respect to the objective consequences. Ideally, both the instructions and the objective consequences will be designed to produce a certain reading process. However, some researchers might want to study recall after individuals have executed the rauding process. In this latter situation, the objective consequences will not match the instructions by design.

Rate

The rate at which the reading process operated must be reported, as mentioned earlier. Ideally, this rate would be reported in standard words per minute, Wpm, as explained in Chapter 2. Without this rate information, it is difficult to be confident about the process that was operating. For example, it is easy to concede that the rauding process was probably operating when college students at $A_L = 14$ are given material to read normally at $D_L = 5$ and they read it at a rate of 300 Wpm. However, in this situation if the rate was 150 Wpm or 450 Wpm, then some explanation for this abnormality would be needed; it must be explained why a learning process or a skimming process was probably operating (see Table 2.2). The ideal in a research study is to have an estimate of the rauding rate, R_r, of the subjects (e.g., from the Rate Level Test) that can be compared to the rate at which the experimental passages were read.

Any study that compares the rates of passages at differing levels of difficulty must report rate in standard words per minute, Wpm, not wpm. Or, some other measure that controls for word length (see Chapter 2) must be used. It is quite possible to find different rates in wpm, using actual words, when in fact the rates in Wpm, using standard words, were exactly the same. Given the lawfully constant nature of the rate at which the rauding process operates in Wpm across material at different levels of difficulty (e.g., see Carver, 1983) there is no justification for a failure to measure rate properly in Wpm, or some other standardized measure such as those described in Chapter 2. Examples of recent studies that did not control for varying word length are as follows: Birkmire (1985); P. Graf and Levy (1984); Horowitz and Samuels (1985).

In summary, experimental reading rates in Wpm need to be compared to estimates of the rauding rates of the subjects, R_r, so that interpretations are more accurate about the type of rauding process that was actually being executed by the subjects.

Summary

Reading rate information is not very useful when it is impossible to identify the type of reading process that was operating. Any research on reading rate should report the relative difficulty of the materials, the instructions given to individuals, the objective consequences of their reading, the rauding rate of the subjects, and the rate at which the process operated because these items are crucially important for determining which reading process was actually being used in the research. When estimates of A_L, D_L, R_r, and R are provided, then Equations (2.11), (2.12), (2.13), and (2.14) can be used to predict the accuracy of comprehension, A.

DESIGN

In experimental studies where the dependent variable is reading rate, there are several important design considerations, many of which were discussed as pitfalls in Chapter 18. One of those will be repeated here to emphasize its importance. Too many studies administer some measure of comprehension or retention after the passage is read at a certain rate but never administer it under a control condition to see what the comprehension score would be when reading time was zero, or rate was infinite. This no-reading control condition is necessary to determine what score on the test represents 0% accuracy of comprehension. Under some conditions, these empirical measures can be rescaled to reflect absolute estimates of A (see Carver, 1985a).

In the design of the research, another extremely important consideration is how much the subjects know about the consequences of reading. Investigations of a memorizing process will need to give practice tests with feedback to assure that a memorizing process is being used during reading. Subjects who are told to read normally, and subsequently are asked to write down in detail everything they can recall about the passage are likely to use their rauding process on the first passage but not on subsequent passages. So, if the intent of the researcher is to study free recall after using the rauding process, then the best design would involve only one passage and no practice. This design would not allow the subjects to shift out of the rauding process into a memorizing process once they found out about the objective consequences. Indeed, this is a common pitfall in reading research. Subjects are asked to read normally but they quickly learn that they cannot do this and still satisfy the objective consequences of the researcher.

ORAL RATE

In some research, the dependent variable is oral reading rate (e.g., see Kolers, 1975a). The primary methodological pitfall associated with oral reading rate involves the failure to recognize the differences among maximum oral reading rate, MORR, performance oral reading rate, PORR, and rauding oral reading rate, RORR, as were discussed in Chapter 14. Another methodological problem surfaces when the purpose of the research is to study processes associated with reading and then oral reading is used to investigate one of the processes; this problem is compounded when it is not clear whether MORR, PORR, RORR, or some combination is involved (e.g., see P. Graf & Levy, 1984). It seems likely that only pure MORR and RORR will be lawfully related to rauding rate, and those relationships await future research.

RATE VERSUS TIME

In some research studies, mean reading time is reported and in other research studies, mean reading rate is reported. The relationship between the time to read a passage and rate of reading the passage is curvilinear, not linear. Therefore, the mean time to read a passage converted into average rate will not be the same as the mean rate for reading the passage. Furthermore, the distribution of reading times is likely to be highly skewed (see Gilhooly & Logie, 1981; Kershner, 1964) so that log transforms of reading time are often used in data analyses (e.g., see N. E. Jackson & Biemiller, 1985; Kolers, 1975b, 1976). Even though reading times are highly skewed, rates are not, i.e., the frequency distributions of rates are often symmetrical and approximately normally distributed. Therefore, when using the mean of individual differences as an average, it seems better to use the mean of rates instead of time.

The above problem was addressed recently by Walsh, Price, and Gillingham (1988). They argued for using the reciprocal of time in data analyses; Wpm is a reciprocal of a rauding time measure, as recommended for use above. Walsh *et al.* note that ". . . the reciprocal reaction times of an individual usually have a symmetrical, approximately normal distribution, which is aptly described by the mean, whereas untransformed reaction times usually have a strongly skewed distribution" (p. 113).

There seems to be no good reason to use the log of time to reduce skewness when rate, a reciprocal of time, can be used instead. Another advantage of rate in Wpm is that it is a standard measure that can meaningfully interpreted in any context whereas the use of time measures can only be meaningfully interpreted relative to the context of the study. For example, suppose it is reported that the mean time to read a passage was 37 seconds; this information would be more meaningfully interpreted if it was reported that the mean reading rate was 200 Wpm. Average rate can be made more meaningful by reference to the rates for each grade level presented in Table 2.1 or Appendix B, and to the model rates for various reading processes given in Table 2.2. The following studies are examples of those which reported reading times instead of reading rates: Aaronson and Ferres (1983a); Garrod and Sanford (1977); Haberlandt and Bingham (1978); Keenan and Brown (1984); Kieras (1978); Schwanenflugel and Shoben (1983); Townsend (1983).

In rauding theory, certain equations require rate (such as $E = AR$) and other equations work best with time, or $1/R$. For example, there is a linear relationship between the accuracy of comprehension, A, and the amount of time allowed for reading a passage, $1/R$, as long as the time allowed is less than that needed to finish the passage at the rauding rate [see Equation (2.11)]. After the time allowed for reading exceeds the time required to finish the passage once at the rauding rate, then the relationship between A and $1/R$ shifts from linear to curvilinear [see Equation (2.12)]. These latter relationships are fundamental to rauding theory and they have a great deal of empirical support. However, they are not well known in the research world even though many research results can be readily explained by them. For example, Masson (1983) studied the "proportion correct" (an indicant of accuracy) under rates of 375 and 500 wpm plus a no-reading control condition (these data were reviewed in Chapter 6). He plotted these data on a graph with rate on the horizontal axis and the control condition set apart to the far right. If he had known of the lawful relationship between accuracy, A, and time, $1/R$, he could have plotted time (in seconds per word) on the horizontal axis with the control condition at 0.0 msec per word on the far left. Then, he would have noted that a straight line fitted his data quite well; the more time allowed per word, then the proportionally higher the accuracy scores, at least as long as the rates were higher than the rauding rates of his subjects (see Figs. 16.4, 16.5, and 16.6).

In summary, when looking at the effects of varying rates, R, upon some indicant of accuracy, it is possible to detect highly lawful relationships when A is plotted as a function of a measure of time per unit, $1/R$, instead of a measure that uses units per time, such as Wpm.

STATISTICAL SIGNIFICANCE

The perils of statistical significance testing have already been discussed as a pitfall in Chapter 18. However, these dangers are great enough to deserve further comment in this chapter.

Statistical significance testing ordinarily involves a precise null hypothesis ($M_2 - M_1 = 0$) and a vague research hypothesis. This point estimate of zero (the null hypothesis) can usually be rejected when the sample size is large, thus permitting the claim for support of a vague research hypothesis. In the future, we need precise research hypotheses that can be tested by comparing a theoretically predicted value (e.g., using equations in Chapter 2) with an empirically determined value. The closer together these two values, the theoretical point and the empirical point, the more support there is for the theory. An example of a precise research hypothesis is that college seniors operate their rauding process at an average rate of 300 Wpm.

Testing a precise research hypothesis does not fit statistical significance testing because rejecting the precise null hypothesis implies support for a mutually exclusive but vague research hypothesis. The ideal in future reading research, however, is for the research hypothesis to be the same as the null hypothesis, that is, for there to be no difference between the theoretically predicted value and the empirically determined value. Yet, statistical significance testing was not designed to be of use when the research hypothesis and the null hypothesis are the same and not mutually exclusive. When the failure to reject the null hypothesis provides *support* for the research hypothesis, statistical significance testing is left standing on its head.

Continued reliance on statistical significance testing will impede progress because its normal use involves a corrupt form of the scientific method (Carver, 1978b). We will make better scientific decisions and we will make more progress in the area of research on reading, if we disregard tests of statistical significance and rely more upon effect size measures (see Carver, 1978a, 1984a). At a minimum, effect size measure must be reported. Never is it acceptable to report statistical significance without reporting the research data, as sometimes happens (e.g., see Fishman, 1978).

RESEARCH EXAMPLE

In this section, a hypothetical example will be given for writing a research report based upon the recommendations presented earlier in this chapter.

Title: The effect of random spacing between words upon reading rate during the operation of the rauding process.

Purpose: To determine if randomly inserted extra spaces between words, ranging from one to nine character spaces in length, lowers the rate at which the rauding process operates.

Subjects: There were 60 college students who were paid for their participation. From an earlier administration of the Accuracy Level Test and the Rate Level Test, their mean A_L was estimated to be 13.0, and their mean R_L was estimated to be 12.8; this R_L value was used to estimate R_r as 265 Wpm or 15.9 Spm. Students who did not score at least 10.6 on the Accuracy Level Test were ineligible to participate so that the relative difficulty of the passages used in the research was $+2.0$ or higher for all subjects.

Passages: The four passages used were sampled from the 33 Bormuth passages (see Carver, 1984c) which were at the eighth grade level of difficulty, according to the Rauding Scale of Prose Difficulty (Carver, 1975a); D_L was estimated as 8.5. The four passages varied in length from 102 to 105 standard words, and covered a range of topics. Their Bormuth ID numbers were 134, 432, 531, and 733.

The regular typing of a passage consisted of double spaced lines with regular spacing between words and sentences, one space between words and two spaces between sentences. The spaced typing of a passage consisted of one to nine spaces between words, randomly determined.

Procedures: The students were tested individually. They were told at the outset that (a) they would be asked to read passages at their normal reading rate, and (b) when they finished a passage they would be asked to rate it on a scale from 1 to 5 indicating how difficult it was for them to comprehend.

The students were given a loose leaf notebook with the passages and instructions on alternating pages. The last words on each page were "TURN THE PAGE." The time each student spent reading each passage was timed surreptitiously by observing when the page was turned to begin reading and when it was turned after finishing reading. From the standpoint of the student, they were simply reading at their normal rate in order to rate the difficulty of the passage afterwards. If these students had been told that they were being observed primarily to measure their reading rate, they probably would have been more self-conscious about their rate, and this may have decreased the external validity of the results.

Design: Each student was given four passages to read. The first two were the same for all students, and were considered practice. The first passage was regular and the second was spaced. The last two, passage A and passage B, were presented with A first for half the students and B first for the other half. Each passage was typed in two forms, regular and spaced. There were 15 students in each of four groups to control for passages, order, and form effects.

This study was designed to induce the rauding process in all the students by using relatively easy passages, by instructing the students to read normally, and by using objective consequences that were not likely to force shifts out of the rauding process which is typical and normal for most readers. The estimated values of A_L and D_L, given earlier, were used to estimate the mean rauding accuracy of these students as $A_r = 0.82$, using Equation (2.14). This means that it can be predicted that these students would be comprehending about 82% of the sentences in these passages.

Data Analysis: The time taken to read each passage, in minutes, was divided into the number of standard words in the sentence to obtain a rate in Wpm.

The results from the difficulty judgments will not be reported. This task was included solely to provide a plausible purpose for the students.

Results: The mean rate for the regular condition was 260 Wpm which was very close to the estimated mean rauding rate for these students, 265 Wpm, as was reported earlier. The mean rate for the spaced condition was 203 Wpm, which was 22% slower. The SDs under both conditions were 90. The standard error of the mean for the regular condition was 12, and for the spaced condition the standard error of the mean was also 12.

Discussion: This research was designed to elicit the rauding process, or normal reading. It seems likely that this was achieved since the mean rauding rate of these students for the standard text, 260 Wpm, was close to their mean rauding rate as estimated for the Rate Level Test, 265 Wpm. The difference between the standard text and the text that contained extra random spaces between words was 57 Wpm, or a 22% drop in rate. This drop appeared to be reliable since the standard errors associated with each mean were only 12 Wpm.

This detrimental effect on rauding rate, associated with the extra random spaces between words, appears to be substantial and reliable. Therefore, it seems reasonable to conclude that the rauding process of college level readers is slowed about 20% by extra random spaces placed between words.

This random spacing probably disrupts apping, the habitual movements of the eyes during reading. Ordinarily, the eyes move across a regular line of print in an habitual manner that requires no attention. These extra random spaces inserted between words probably require extra attention to the eye movements in order to perceive each word.

Conclusion: For college level readers, the rauding process operates slower than the rauding rate when extra random spaces are inserted between words, probably because apping is disrupted.

RAUDING

The most important methodological implication to be inferred from research reviewed in previous chapters is the necessity to discriminate between the rauding process and other reading processes when conducting and reporting research on rate. It is commonly asserted that reading speed depends on the purpose for reading and on the complexity or difficulty of the material being read (e.g., see Shores & Husbands, 1950). This is partly true but wholly misleading because it erroneously suggests that there is no constancy associated with reading rate. In rauding theory, the purpose is specified when the goal of the reader is to raud, i.e., understand the complete thoughts in sentences of passages, which is the normal or ordinary purpose of reading. Reading rate ordinarily will be constant in Wpm across varying levels of difficulty when the rauding process is operating, and this process is likely to be operating (a) when the goal of the reader is to raud, and (b) when the difficulty of the material is relatively easy, $A_L > D_L$.

The lawfulness and predictability of reading rate is often blurred. Research results are often interpreted as ambiguous or even conflicting when there is no recognition that the rauding process is importantly different from other reading processes. There is lawfulness to reading rate when it is recognized that the rauding process is one of five basic reading processes that operate at different rates. Research in reading is more likely to move upward from the unknown and fuzzily known to finding lawful relationships if researchers plan, conduct, and report research that focuses upon a particular type of reading process. When investigating reading, it helps tremendously to know whether or not third gear, the normal, natural, ordinary, and typical reading process, is involved.

There is a great deal of theory, and also data, beyond the confines of rauding theory to support the existence of different processes being involved in reading. As noted in an earlier chapter, Danks (1969) contended that the learning and comprehension processes are not necessarily isomorphic and that the variables identified as important in one process may have a minimal effect in the other process. Kinstch and Kozminsky (1977) stated that "summarization involves quite different psychological processes than recall" (p. 497). Kieras (1981) investigated the effect of three different reading tasks, free reading, topic choice, and recall, upon reading times, and found that the times varied with the component subprocesses involved in the task. Also in 1981, Cirilo asked students to read sentences under three conditions, namely, give verbatim recalls (Gear 1), take comprehension tests afterwards (Gear 2), and "read them as they would at home" (Gear 3), and found that the reading times decreased as the gear increased which is in accordance with rauding theory (see Table 2.2); it should be acknowledged that Cirilo did not use the term "gear," nor did he refer to rauding theory. Aaronson and Ferres (1983a) have stated that, "People read for many different purposes, and they read the same text very differently depending upon those purposes" (p. 675); they found that reading times were greater when reading for retention than when reading for comprehension, another result in accordance with the theorized differences between the first, second, and third gears of rauding theory. In another empirical study, Aaronson and Ferres (1983b) concluded that "reading strategies are influenced by text attributes, task demands, and individual abilities" (p. 700). Given the above acknowledgments of differing processes involved in reading, the present thesis is that the naturalness, pervasiveness, and lawfulness of the rauding process is being neglected at the expense of investigations of learning processes (e.g., see Cirilo & Foss, 1980; Schwanenflugel & Shoben, 1983) and memorizing processes (e.g., see Keenan & Brown, 1984; Kieras, 1978; Townsend, 1983).

In summary, researchers who seem to want to study the more normal or natural reading process could consider clarifying their intentions by saying that they are investigating the rauding process, and then design their research accordingly. And, those researchers who are not studying the rauding process could clarify their intentions by specifying which type of reading process they are investigating, e.g., scanning, skimming, learning, or memorizing (or some combination involved in studying), and then design the relative difficulty of the research materials, their instructions, and their objective consequences accordingly.

CONCLUSIONS

In the future, reading rate research can be improved by specifying which reading process is involved, preferably making it explicit whether the rauding process is involved or not. Research results involving a scanning, skimming, learning, or memorizing process should not be generalized to the rauding process. Once the process to be investigated is made explicit, then the design of the research must follow. The relative difficulty of the material to be read must fit that process (see Chapter 2). The instructions to the subjects must fit that process (see Chapter 2). The objective consequences, such as the comprehension measures, must fit that process (see Chapter 2).

Future research can also be improved by reporting upon the rauding ability of the subjects and the rauding difficulty of the materials, preferably using valid indicators of A_L, D_L, and R_r. This latter information makes it possible (a) to determine the relative difficulty of the material, $A_L - D_L$, and (b) to compare the reading rates found in the research with the rauding rate, R_r, of the subjects. Both relative difficulty, $A_L - D_L$, and rauding rate, R_r, help establish what reading process was likely to have been used by the readers. Furthermore, these estimated values can be substituted into Equations (2.11), (2.12), (2.13), and (2.14) to obtain predicted estimates of the accuracy of comprehension, A, for any rate, R.

Most research investigating the effect of rate, R, upon the accuracy of comprehension, A, could benefit from an analysis that relates A to $1/R$ because this relationship between accuracy and time is highly lawful. It would seem helpful for future research studies to specify the type of reading process being investigated, and to estimate A, R, E, A_r, R_r, E_r, A_L, R_L, E_L, and D_L These theoretical constructs seem to organize our knowledge in more fruitful ways, and allow us to make specific predictions about an individual's accuracy of comprehension.

21

CONCLUSIONS

INTRODUCTION

The questions that were raised at the end of Chapter 1 will now be answered from the perspective of the research and theory reviewed in Chapters 2–20. Then, a summary of the most important conclusions will be presented.

QUESTIONS AND ANSWERS

Question 1   Do most individuals read at a relatively constant rate?

Answer   Yes, most individuals do have a constant reading rate, in standard words per minute, Wpm. Most individuals operate their rauding process most of the time at their rauding rate, and this rate is constant. Other goals may sometimes force individuals to shift out of this third gear of reading, which involves lexical access, semantic encoding, and sentential integration. Individuals may shift into lower gears, such as memorizing (Gear 1) or learning (Gear 2) which are more powerful but slower, or they may shift into higher gears, such as skimming (Gear 4) or scanning (Gear 5) which are faster but less powerful. There is no evidence that reading rates at the higher gears, 3–5, are affected by the difficulty of the material. When operating the rauding process (Gear 3) and the material becomes relatively hard, individuals are likely to shift down to a learning process (Gear 2). So, reading rate during normal or typical reading is constant because the goal is to comprehend the complete thoughts contained in the successive sentences, and the process required to perform this task most successfully operates at a constant rate across varying levels of material difficulty, at least as long as the material is relatively easy.

The research reviewed in Chapter 3 provides a more detailed answer to Question 1. For example, the changes in rate due to differing experimental tasks (McConkie & Meyer, 1974; McConkie & Rayner, 1974; McConkie et al., 1973) have been relatively small in size, varying from a mean of about 150 wpm to about 250 wpm, and mainly involved various learning processes, Gear 2. The research reported by Carver (1971b), G. R. Miller and Coleman (1971), Coke (1974), and Carver (1976) established that college students tend to read at a constant rate even when the material varied in difficulty from the elementary level to the college level.

Question 2 Is silent speech (covertly talking to oneself) harmful to reading, and does it slow down reading rate?

Answer Silent speech during reading seems to be an inherent aspect of normal reading, i.e., the rauding process, Gear 3. It is definitely not harmful and the research evidence seems to indicate that it helps the rauding process operate at its top speed. Silent speech is an aid to the short-term memory required to perform successfully the components involved in the slower but more powerful reading processes, Gears 1–3. Whether silent speech is helpful to the operation of the two faster gears, skimming and scanning, is still not clear. However, there is no evidence that it is harmful or slows skimming and scanning. Educators who consider silent speech harmful, and try to get students to eliminate it, do not have the benefit of supporting evidence.

The research reviewed in Chapter 4 provides a more elaborate answer to Question 2. For example, the extensive research of Edfeldt (1960) established that it is impossible to consider silent speech as being harmful to reading, and the extensive research of Sokolov (1972) established that silent speech is the principal mechanism of thinking. There was a great deal of research conducted in the 1970s and early 1980s relevant to scanning, skimming, rauding, learning, and memorizing and none of it found that silent speech was harmful to reading.

Question 3 Is reading done by looking at each word, or can reading rate be increased by skipping the less informative words with no loss in comprehension?

Answer Eye movement studies leave no doubt that normal or typical reading involves looking at almost every word. The rauding process, Gear 3, and the two slower and more powerful processes, Gears 1 and 2, all involve fixations on almost every word at least once. There is no evidence that these processes can be operated successfully without a fixation on each word, or within about three character spaces of each word. Of course, certain skimming and scanning processes, Gears 4–5, can be successfully operated by skipping over words. But, there is no evidence from skimming research that individuals can predict which words are less informative when they skim. Furthermore, during the operation of the rauding process, Gear 3, individuals cannot skip over unimportant words and increase the rate at which they successfully comprehend the complete thoughts in sentences.

A more complete answer to Question 3 can be found in Chapter 5. For example, the research of Rayner (1975) and Rayner *et al.* (1981) established that the rauding process operates in a word for word manner because almost all words are fixated and no information is obtained from words that are not within about three character spaces of a fixation. McConkie and Hogaboam (1985) established that the rauding process does *not* involve the formation of hypotheses about upcoming text that allows unimportant words to be skipped or read more rapidly. With respect to the operation of a learning process during reading, the research of Just and Carpenter (1980) established that Gear 2 definitely involves looking at almost every word.

Question 4   When individuals read at their typical, normal, natural, or ordinary rate, is that their most efficient rate?

Answer   Yes, most individuals typically read at their rauding rate and it is their most efficient rate. This rate is optimal because when the rauding process is operated at faster or slower rates there will be fewer complete thoughts comprehended during each minute of reading. Individuals have a typical, normal, natural, and ordinary rate of reading, and they habitually operate their rauding process at this rate when they read; they read at this constant rate even when the material varies in difficulty because it maximizes their efficiency of comprehension. This third gear of reading is used by most individuals most of the time, and it is operated at the individual's rauding rate because it accomplishes the primary goal of reading most efficiently, i.e., understanding the complete thoughts the author intended to communicate in the least amount of time.

A more extensive answer to Question 4 can be found in the research reviewed in Chapter 6. For example, Carver (1982) established that college students comprehend the sentences in fifth grade material most efficiently at the same rate that they comprehend the sentences in college level material most efficiently, about 300 Wpm. Carver (1983) also established that college students typically read material at this same rate of 300 Wpm, even when the material varies in difficulty from grade 5 to grade 14.

Question 5 Is there only one reading process, or are there several different processes that can all be legitimately called reading processes?

Answer There are many different processes that involve reading and therefore can be called reading processes. It is a mistake to talk about "the" reading process as if there were only one process. When the goal is to understand the complete thoughts in relatively hard material, there are some components involved in this process that are quite different from the components involved in the process that is used to get the gist from a chapter or a book. Processes that involve different components or steps cannot be the same process. It is helpful to conceive of five basic reading processes that can be used to accomplish different goals, have different components, provide different results or consequences, and operate at different rates. These five basic processes have been called memorizing (Gear 1), learning (Gear 2), rauding (Gear 3), skimming (Gear 4), and scanning (Gear 5). There appears to be only one rauding process, Gear 3, whereas there may be many different variations of the other processes such as many types of skimming processes. Research results obtained during the operation of one reading process will not necessarily generalize to another reading process. For example, there is a large amount of data indicating that the results of research conducted during the execution of a memorizing process, Gear 1, the slowest but most powerful of all the reading processes, will not generalize to the operation of the rauding process, Gear 3.

A more complete answer to Question 5 is contained in Chapters 6, 7, and 8. The scanning research of Fisher and Lefton (1976) and Fisher *et al.* (1978) established that a target word can be correctly recognized by college students at a rate of about 600 wpm. Masson (1982) established that college students who skim at rates around 375 wpm, and higher, are not able to skip over the unimportant words and read only the important words. Carver's (1982, 1983) research established the existence of a rauding process that operates at a constant rate which is also a rate that is typical, threshold, and optimal. Research studies that involved a pure learning process were not easy to isolate, but the study conducted by Morasky and Willcox (1970) is an exemplary one. There has been a great deal of reading research conducted that involved a memorizing process (e.g., see Kintsch & Keenan, 1973; Kintsch *et al.*, 1975).

Question 6 What determines how fast individuals typically read?

Answer Most individuals typically read at the fastest rate at which they can comprehend the complete thoughts in the successive sentences of relatively easy material. This fastest rate has been called their rauding rate. Therefore, the most important determiner of typical reading rate for most individuals is their rauding rate. This is because most individuals typically operate their rauding process at its fastest rate. Some individuals have higher rauding rates than other individuals because they can think faster, or have a higher cognitive speed. However, there are other subsidiary determiners of the rauding process rate. Some individuals habitually operate their rauding process at a rate slower than their rauding rate because they typically operate a learning process instead of a rauding process. These habitual eye movements that comprise natural or normal reading are called apping, and apping rate is an important determiner of the rauding process rate. Practice, in terms of regularly reading relatively easy materials, helps maintain the apping rate at the rauding rate. So, the rate at which the rauding process operates for individuals is theorized to be determined by a host of interrelated factors, e.g., rauding rate, apping rate, cognitive speed, and practice, but individuals typically read at their rauding rate so the most important determiner of reading rate is rauding rate.

Chapter 9 contains a lengthy theoretical answer to Question 6. Other than the single correlational study of Carver (1986), little empirical evidence exists relevant to this question. Obviously, it is a fertile ground for future research.

Question 7 Are good readers also flexible readers because they automatically adjust their rate to the difficulty of the material and to their purpose for reading?

Answer No, good readers do not automatically adjust their rate to changes in the difficulty level of the materials they are reading (see Carver, 1971b, 1983; Coke, 1976; G. R. Miller & Coleman, 1971; Zuber & Wetzel, 1981). Contrary to conventional wisdom, good readers do not have difficulty flexibility. Good readers tend to read at the same rate even when the material varies widely in difficulty, at least as long as the material is relatively easy for them. It is true that if the material becomes relatively hard, then good readers may shift out of their rauding process, Gear 3, and into a different reading process such as a learning process, Gear 2. It is misleading to consider this latter change in rate associated with gearing down as difficulty flexibility; it is better to call this "process-flexibility," because there is a qualitative shift to a different reading process that involves different components. As for purpose flexibility, it is true that individuals sometimes change their purpose for reading. However, drastically different purposes do not always result in different reading processes, different reading rates, or different results or consequences (Carver, 1984b; Hill, 1964). Contrary to conventional wisdom, good readers often do not show purpose flexibility because different purposes can often be accomplished by the same reading process. Therefore, purpose flexibility is a misleading concept. Again, it seems best to replace this concept of purpose flexibility with process flexibility because good readers will shift from one reading process to another whenever a different process best accomplishes their desired goal. So, good readers are *not* flexible readers in the sense that they automatically adjust their rate to their purpose or to the difficulty level of the material. Instead, good readers are flexible readers in the sense that they are able to shift from one reading process to another when such gear shifting is needed to accomplish their desired goal. Good readers do *not* adjust their reading rates; instead, they adjust their reading processes which in turn involve different components that make the process operate at different rates. Different reading processes involve different components and this is the reason they operate at different rates. In summary, good readers do not have rate flexibility, difficulty flexibility, or purpose flexibility but good readers do have process flexibility.

Chapter 10 contains a great deal of research relevant to Question 7. For example, evidence against difficulty flexibility was found in the research of DiStefano *et al.* (1981), Letson (1959), Rankin (1978), Rankin and Kehle (1972), and Shebilske and Fisher (1981). Exemplary evidence against purpose flexibility was collected by Hill (1964) who found that good reading college students did not change their rate to accomplish certain purposes better, such as "prepare for exams," "identify key ideas," and "analyze author motives."

Question 8 Is there more growth in reading rate each year during the early grades of school as compared to the later grades?

Answer No, the growth in reading rate appears to be approximately the same each year from grades 2 to 12, i.e., about 14 Wpm each year on the average. The relationship between reading rate and grade in school is almost perfectly linear after grade 2. This relationship between rate and grade in school also is linear for tasks related to reading, such as visual word matching and oral reading.

Chapter 11 contains a large amount of research data relevant to Question 8. For example, the data presented by Taylor (1965) established that the growth in reading rate is steady at about 12–14 Wpm each year in school from grade 2 through grade 12. A reanalysis of the data collected by Doehring (1976) established that 35 reading-related tasks all had an almost perfect linear relationship to grade in school, from kindergarten to grade 10; these data suggest that the 14 Wpm growth in rauding rate each year in school is due to maturational factors rather than to education, practice, or experience.

Question 9 To what extent is rauding rate influenced by word recognition speed?

Answer The rate at which individuals can recognize words is one of the most important factors influencing rauding rate. Classical word recognition studies, however, have often been misinterpreted. Many of these studies have shown that words can be recognized faster when redundancy is provided by context. Yet, this relationship between redundancy and rate does not hold for rauding rate; the rauding process does not increase in speed as the reading material becomes easier, i.e., more redundant. Some studies have found differences between good and poor readers in word recognition speed but these individual differences appear to be explained by thinking rate, or cognitive speed, C_s.

Chapter 12 contains a great deal of research relevant to Question 9. For example, Hogaboam and Perfetti (1978) established that elementary school children require longer to recognize a two-syllable word compared to a one-syllable word, and that skilled readers required less time than less-skilled readers. M. D. Jackson and McClelland (1979) established that much of the variance between individuals in their reading efficiency could be explained by a simple measure of how fast the names of letters could be matched, and this factor seems to be more readily described as cognitive speed, C_s.

Question 10 What is the relationship between the rate of comprehension during reading and the rate of comprehension during auding?

Answer When the same passages are presented at the same rates during auding and reading, the accuracy of comprehension is the same; this fact is readily interpreted as evidence that the rauding process operates equally for most individuals whether the words are presented auditorily or visually. An individual's rauding rate is the same whether the words in passages are written or spoken. When the material is relatively easy, there is no superiority for reading passages over listening to them. The maximum efficiency of comprehension during reading is no higher than the maximum efficiency of comprehension during auding because both involve the same processes for comprehending the complete thoughts in sentences, only the stimulus mode is different.

The research reviewed in Chapter 13 provides a more thorough answer to Question 10. For example, the extensive research reviewed by Sticht *et al.* (1974) established the close connection between reading and auding for children. Carver's (1982) research with college students established that (a) when passages are presented at the same rate during reading and auding, then the accuracy of comprehension is the same, and (b) when passages are presented at different rates, the efficiency of comprehension is the highest at about 300 Wpm for both reading and auding, even when the material varies in difficulty from grade level 5 to grade level 14.

Question 11   What is the relationship between oral reading rate and rauding rate?

Answer   The answer to this question depends upon what is meant by oral reading rate. Oral reading rate varies with whether the individual is (a) performing for an audience, (b) attempting to comprehend the sentences in passages while reading aloud, or (c) reading aloud as fast as possible, called Maximum Oral Reading Rate, MORR. Only MORR appears to provide a reliable measure, and it is highly related to rauding rate. For example, it is likely that students who have a MORR of 150 Wpm also have a rauding rate around 150 Wpm. Adults and college students seem to have an average MORR around 200–250 Wpm. It seems likely that rauding rate causes MORR so that MORR can be used to provide an accurate and objective indicant of rauding rate.

Chapter 14 contains an extensive review of research relevant to Question 11. For example, Morton (1964) has established that MORR for college students increases from an average of 157 wpm for randomly ordered words to 216 wpm for normal text. Poulton and Brown (1967) established that the average MORR for housewives (245 wpm) was faster than reading aloud for comprehension (227 wpm) and faster than reading with expression for an audience (166 wpm).

Question 12   Can the rate at which the rauding process operates be increased by grouping the words in passages into more meaningful units or phrases?

Answer   No! There is no replicated evidence that most individuals can operate their rauding process at a higher rate, or more accurately, by somehow improving the standard way that text is presented. For example, putting extra blank spaces between phrases or putting one phrase on each line, does not improve the rate of comprehension, the accuracy of comprehension, or the efficiency of comprehension. However, there are many forms of textual presentation that slow the rate at which the rauding process operates. For example, presenting the words in all capital letters seems to slow this rate slightly, and putting 13 spaces between each word also slows rate for almost all readers. But, separating words with extra blank spaces improves the rate of comprehension for beginning level readers. Presenting the words in passages one word at a time in the center of a computer screen has no detrimental effect upon the accuracy of comprehension as compared to normal reading, and this suggests that individuals have learned to move their eyes from one word to the next in the most efficient manner during normal reading. It appears that individuals operate their rauding process at its fastest possible rate (about 300 Wpm for college students) which is limited by how fast they can think, not by the nature of the stimulus, whether it is a standard form of printed text, one word at a time on a computer screen, or an auditorily presented version.

Chapter 15 contains the research relevant to answering Question 12. For example, Carver (1970) established that spatially chunking words into meaningful units or phrases does not help the rauding process operate any faster. Patberg and Yonas (1978) established that putting large blank spaces around each word slows the rauding process about 20% for skilled readers. Also, Juola *et al.* (1982) established that presenting words one at a time on a computer screen, with no eye movements needed to read the text, was not detrimental to the accuracy of comprehension at rates ranging from about 200 to 600 wpm.

Question 13   What is the relationship between rate and comprehension?

Answer   This question has several answers because rate and comprehension have not been precisely defined by theory or research, and confusions have resulted. The question can be answered quite precisely when the concepts of rate and comprehension are replaced by three rauding theory constructs associated with a passage, namely accuracy of comprehension, A, rate of comprehension, R, and efficiency of comprehension, E, plus three constructs associated with the ability of the reader, namely rauding accuracy level, A_L, rauding rate level, R_L, and rauding efficiency level, E_L. As R is increased, then A will decrease, at least between about 100 and 1000 Wpm. This means that there is a high and negative, within-individual correlation between R and A. So, as individuals increase their rate, their accuracy will decrease because there is a rate–accuracy tradeoff. The relationship between the time allowed for reading passages, $1/R$, and A has been quantified and expressed quite precisely by mathematical equations. There is a great deal of empirical support for the validity of these equations indicating that (a) A is linearly related to $1/R$ as long as the time allowed does not exceed that required to finish reading the passage once at the individual's rauding rate, R_r, and (b) the relationship between A and $1/R$ becomes curvilinear after the passage has been read once at R_r.

If reading comprehension refers to individual differences in ability, then there is a different relationship between rate and comprehension that depends upon the constructs involved. Individual differences in rauding ability are reflected by (a) the GE of the most difficult material that an individual can raud, A_L, (b) the GE of the individual's rauding rate, R_L, and (c) the GE of an individual's rauding efficiency, E_L. For example, an individual may have scored at the sixth grade level on the Accuracy Level Test, $A_L = 6$, indicating that the most difficult material that this individual can accurately comprehend, $A > 0.75$, is at the sixth grade level. Other tests that reliably reflect individual differences in accuracy level, such as the Degrees of Reading Power test, have been called correlates of A_L because they do not purport to measure A_L in GE units. If the standardized measurement of rate involves some correlate of rauding rate level, R_L, and the standardized measurement of reading comprehension involves some correlate of rauding accuracy level, A_L, then the correlation between these two variables will *not* be highly negative as it was with R and A. The correlations between correlates of R_L and A_L have ranged from slightly negative to moderately positive. Furthermore, if comprehension is taken to mean some correlate of E_L, then most research has found a high positive correlation, up to 0.80, between correlates of R_L and E_L.

The relationship between rate and comprehension is also confused by the way rate has been measured. Previous research has not always restricted the measurement of rate to the rauding process, so variations in rate between individuals may also involve individuals shifting gears to a faster skimming process or a slower learning process. The lawfulness of the relationships among A, R, and E and among A_L, R_L, and E_L is restricted to the rauding process.

So, the relationship between rate and comprehension is ambiguous because more than two constructs are involved. If reading rate is restricted to the rauding process, then the relationships involved are lawful. In these situations, E depends upon A and R, so there will always be a high relationship between indicants of rate, R, and efficiency, E, and also between indicants of accuracy, A, and E. Since E_L depends upon A_L and R_L, then there will always be a high relationship between indicants of rate level, R_L, and efficiency level, E_L, and also between indicants of accuracy level, A_L, and E_L. In summary, the within-individual correlation between A and R is high and negative while the between-individual correlation between A_L and R_L is near zero to moderately positive; the relationship between rate and comprehension depends upon which aspects are involved, A, R, E, A_L, R_L, or E_L. The most lawful relationships known at present are between the time allowed to operate the rauding process on a passage, $1/R$, and the subsequent accuracy of comprehension, A.

Chapter 16 contains the research relevant to Question 13. For example, Carver (1982) established that increasing the rate, R, at which passages are presented results in a decrease in their accuracy of comprehension, A; Carver (1985a) established that the accuracy of comprehension, A, can be predicted quite precisely using mathematical equations.

Question 14 What does automaticity have to do with rauding rate?

Answer Automaticity refers to the ability to recognize a word rapidly with little attention required. Repeatedly practicing the recognition of a particular word is the best way to reach full automaticity for the word. The rauding process ordinarily operates on relatively easy materials so it seems likely that automaticity is a given condition for almost all the words involved in typical or normal reading. Rauding rate is a construct that inextricably involves automaticity because the lexical access of each word during the execution of the rauding process proceeds without any unnecessary or extra attention devoted to the recognition of these words. It has been theorized that there are still gains possible in how fast a word can be recognized even after it has reached automaticity. Therefore, it seems likely that words in relatively easy material need to be practiced by rauding the sentences that contain them, in order to maintain the operation of the rauding process at its highest rate, the rauding rate. Repeatedly reading the same passages probably does not maintain rauding rate at its highest level as much as spending this time reading many different passages once. Repeated readings, the educational treatment associated with automaticity, probably is more helpful in situations that do not involve the rauding process and do not involve automaticity; repeatedly reading the same passage is probably most helpful when beginning readers are just learning to associate the sound of a word with its shape, which is the pre-automaticity phase. It seems best to consider automaticity as a pre-condition of rauding rate. Practicing known words to increase their automaticity is not likely to improve rauding rate because automaticity involves improvement which takes place at rates much lower than the rauding rate. Improvements in rauding accuracy level, A_L, are likely to involve automaticity because the best way to increase this level is by reading a great many materials at a matched difficulty, $A_L = D_L$, and this practice with new words will eventually result in their reaching full automaticity. So, automaticity is indirectly involved in both the rauding rate level, R_L, and improvements in A_L. Practice, taking the form of reading relatively easy materials, is likely to maintain R_L at its highest level. Practice, taking the form of attempting to operate the rauding process on materials at a level equal to A_L in difficulty, is likely to be the best way to improve A_L. So, automaticity is involved in rauding ability because rauding rate involves full automaticity during lexical access, and improvement in rauding accuracy to higher levels requires that new words be practiced to full automaticity and beyond.

Chapter 17 contains the research relevant to Question 14. For example, a reanalysis of the data collected by Hogaboam and Perfetti (1978) seems to indicate that words proceed through a linear automaticity phase before they approach a curvilinear phase whose asymptote reflects individual differences in cognitive speed. And, the data collected by Rashotte and Torgesen (1985) suggest that repeatedly reading the same passage does not improve the rauding rate of beginning readers as much as spending this time reading different passages once.

Question 15 Does rapid reading training, RRT, increase rauding rate so that individuals can increase their rate of comprehension, R, on passages without any loss in their accuracy of comprehension, A?

Answer No! RRT is actually skimming training in disguise. RRT is often effective in inducing individuals to shift gears and operate a skimming process much of the time, but there will be an accompanying loss in the accuracy of comprehension at the higher rates. Almost all of the research conducted on the efficacy of RRT has not been designed to avoid well-known threats to internal and external validity. However, the weight of the existing evidence indicates that reading efficiency cannot be increased by RRT, i.e., standardized reading comprehension tests that provide correlates of rauding efficiency level, E_L, indicate no important increases pre to post RRT.

Chapter 18 contains the research relevant to Question 15. For example, R. G. Graf (1973) avoided all of the documented methodological pitfalls and found that RRT resulted in a 26% loss, pre to post, in a measure of the accuracy of comprehension. Morton (1959) also avoided all of the known methodological pitfalls prevalent in RRT research and found that this training resulted in a 30% long-term improvement in a measure of reading efficiency, but the measures were not objective and there was no report of the reading rates involved.

Question 16 Are there individuals who can successfully operate their rauding process at rates greater than 600 Wpm, or stated differently, are there speed readers or super readers who have rauding rates greater than 600 Wpm?

Answer NO! There is no sound empirical evidence that individuals exist who can operate their rauding process at rates higher than 600 Wpm and still consistently comprehend more than 75%, even on relatively easy material. The best available evidence indicates that rates higher than 600 Wpm are associated with skimming and scanning processes that result in an accuracy of comprehension, *A*, below 75%. Those studies that report scores on tests higher than 75% at rates higher than 600 wpm seem to have used skimming-type questions that are easy to answer at almost any rate. There is no sound evidence that super readers exist, that is, no speed readers or any other readers who have rauding rates higher than 600 Wpm.

Chapter 19 contains the research relevant to Question 16. For example, Carver (1985b) studied 16 of the world's best readers and found that none of them could comprehend 75% or more of relatively easy materials at rates over 600 Wpm; there was evidence that the four speed readers in the group habitually read at speeds around 1000 Wpm but they were obviously operating a skimming process because they could only recall about 20% of the important details in a relatively easy book at these high rates.

SUMMARY OF CONCLUSIONS

The content of this book has been organized around the five basic reading processes. A graphic summary of those processes is presented in Fig. 21.1. Notice that the five horizontal lines represent the five basic processes and length of these lines represents the relative importance of each process in terms of the amount of time spent on each process. For example, the rauding process has the longest line and this represents the assumption that the rauding process is used about 90% of the total time that all readers spend reading. For each of the five processes, a column has also been presented for gear number, process name, rate at which the process operates in Wpm, and the time, in accordance with the information given at the outset in Table 2.2. This figure summarizes the organizing framework of rauding theory. Even though the rauding process operates most frequently in the population of readers, college students are likely to operate a learning process most of the time. The primary way that we assimilate difficult knowledge from text is by using a learning process, so its importance should also be acknowledged.

The research and theory reviewed has left little or no doubt about the necessity for discriminating among the various reading processes (e.g., see Walker, 1933) because the facts and laws associated with the operation of one process will not necessarily generalize to another (e.g., see

GEAR	PROCESS	Wpm	msec/W	
5	A Scanning Process	600	100	
4	A Skimming Process	450	133	
3	The Rauding Process	300	200	
2	A Learning Process	200	300	
1	A Memorizing Process	138	433	

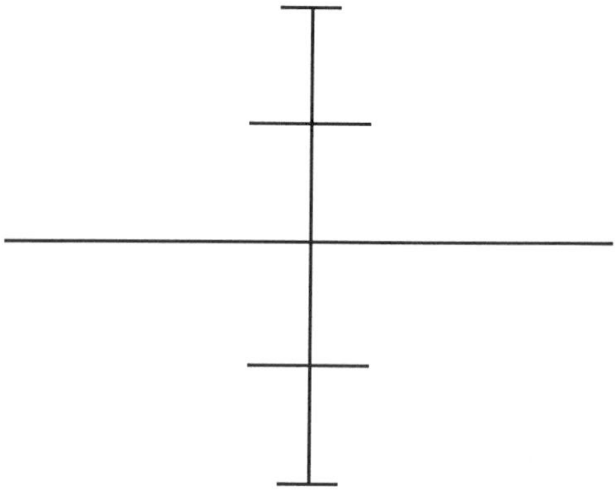

Figure 21.1 A graphic summary of the five basic reading processes.

Aaronson & Scarborough, 1976). The findings associated with the faster but less powerful skimming and scanning processes (Gears 4–5) will not necessarily generalize to the rauding process (Gear 3), and the findings associated with the slower but more powerful learning and memorizing processes (Gears 1–2) also will not necessarily generalize to the rauding process. For example, Just and Carpenter (1980) found that some words are fixated much longer than other words but this research involved a learning process and their results and conclusions will not generalize to the rauding process. The rauding process, third gear, is the most important of all reading processes because it involves the typical kind of reading that has traditionally been called normal, natural, or ordinary reading.

The fastest rate that the rauding process can operate, on relatively easy materials, is called the rauding rate. There appears to be no doubt that this rate is relatively constant within individuals because students from fourth grade to college level normally read material that varies in difficulty from grade level 2 to grade level 14 at approximately the same rate in standard words per minute, Wpm (Ballantine, 1951; Carver, 1976, 1983; Coke, 1974; G. R. Miller & Coleman, 1971; Morse, 1951; Zuber & Wetzel, 1981). The constancy of operating the rauding process is probably the most established fact associated with reading rate; it is Law I in rauding theory (Carver, 1981). This constancy of rate is purported to hold as long as (a) the material is relatively easy, $A_L > D_L$, (b) the instructions and objective consequences associated with the reading task are designed to induce the rauding process, and (c) rate is controlled for word length, such as using standard words per minute, Wpm. The empirical factual evidence supporting this law has been overwhelmingly disregarded by researchers; for example, it was never mentioned in the recently published *Handbook of Reading Research* (Pearson, 1984). Possibly this is because some research is seemingly contradictive (e.g., Kintsch & Keenan, 1973) but in fact involved a learning process or a memorizing process.

This rauding rate that is normal, natural, and typical is also the optimal rate because faster or slower rates for operating the rauding process are less efficient. For example, college students comprehend the most per unit of time when they read college level materials at about 300 Wpm, and they do not comprehend more of grade 5 materials, per unit of time, when they go faster than 300 Wpm. This is because 300 Wpm is their rauding rate, and it is the most efficient rate for operating the rauding process for both grade 5 and grade 14 materials. Those who recommend to students that they speed up their rate when they encounter easier materials are doing students a disservice because efficiency of comprehension will decrease when they do. Those who notice that college students typically read grade 5 material at the same rate at which they read grade 14 material are apt to lament that most students are not flexible. However, it is a credit to the intelligence of college students that they have learned to read at a constant rate because it is the most efficient rate for normal reading; changing or increasing that rate for easier materials would result in less efficient reading so students do not shift out of this highly efficient process with its constant rate. The fact that the optimal rate for auding is also around 300 Wpm for college students further supports the idea that an individual's rauding rate results in highest efficiency of comprehension (Carver, 1977, 1982; deHaan, 1977; Foulke, 1968; Jester & Travers, 1966). The fact that the rauding rate is the optimal rate, or most efficient rate, is expressed in rauding theory as the Third Law of Rauding (Carver, 1981), and there is strong empirical evidence supporting this law.

There have been a great many unnecessary confusions and contradictions surrounding previous research involving reading rate and reading comprehension simply because researchers have not discriminated among the accuracy of comprehension, A, the rate of comprehension, R, and the efficiency of comprehension, E. The Second Law of Rauding Theory is that $E = AR$, which holds that efficiency can be divided into the two components that have traditionally been recognized as the main ingredients of reading, speed and comprehension (e.g., see Gates, 1921; Perfetti, 1985; Pintner, 1913; Singer, 1965). Reading comprehension is sometimes measured in a way that reflects A, and other times it is measured in a way that reflects E (e.g., see Letson, 1958), and these two measures produce drastically different results. This confusion is compounded when there is also a failure to recognize that the within-subject relationships involving E, A, and R for passages are not the same as the between-subject relationships for ability involving rauding efficiency level, E_L, rauding accuracy level, A_L, and rauding rate level, R_L. For example, there is no doubt that A and R are negatively correlated within individuals so that increasing the rate at which a passage is presented for reading, R, will automatically result in a decrease in the accuracy of comprehension, A (Carver, 1973a, 1982, 1984b; Jester & Travers, 1966; Juola et al., 1982; Masson, 1982; Poulton, 1958). However, A_L and R_L are likely to be positively correlated between individuals indicating that those individuals within a group who can accurately comprehend the more difficult materials tend to be the same individuals who can raud the fastest (e.g., see Blommers & Lindquist, 1944; Eurich, 1930; Tinker, 1939). This failure to discriminate among E, A, R, E_L, A_L, and R_L when investigating the relationship between rate and comprehension has seldom been explicitly recognized. The concept of "reading comprehension" is often used in confusing ways because it is not clear which constructs are involved: E, A, E_L, or A_L. This conceptual confusion is exacerbated by standardized tests that are said to measure reading comprehension but in fact measure R_L about as much as they measure A_L because these measures of reading comprehension are in fact measuring reading efficiency not accuracy (Carver, 1977, 1990d). It would be helpful for researchers to discriminate among the constructs of E, A, R, E_r, A_r, R_r, E_L, A_L, and R_L whenever it is purported that reading rate and reading comprehension are being investigated.

Whenever researchers purport to study normal reading, or the rauding process, it would also be helpful to report the difficulty level, D_L, of the material. This will allow a determination of relative difficulty of the material, $A_L - D_L$. If the material is relatively hard, $A_L < D_L$, then the individual is likely to switch to a learning process. Also, comparing the reading rate found in a research study to the previously measured rauding rate, R_r, of the subjects will help determine whether a rauding process was likely to have been executed. Whenever rate, R, is measured it is best to report it in standard length words per minute, Wpm, because rate is not constant across passages varying in D_L when rate is measured in actual words per minute, wpm (e.g., see Carver, 1983).

The standard way of printing passages and typing passages on a page appears to be optimal for almost all readers. Spatially grouping words into more meaningful units, or phrases, does not increase the rate at which the rauding process operates. However, this standard text presentation is not optimal for beginning level readers who can operate their rauding process faster if there is more than one space between words.

The habitual eye movements of natural or normal reading are called apping (taken from *a*utomatic *p*ilot for *p*rose). Our eyes seem to be programmed to fixate upon every word (or within about three character spaces) so that every word can be lexically accessed, semantically encoded, and sententially integrated during the rauding process. There is no evidence that some words can be profitably skipped during this process because they are redundant; little words such as "the" or "a" are not inherently less important to comprehending the complete thoughts contained in sentences at the rauding rate. The eye movements of apping seem to represent an overlearned habit that allows the components of the rauding process to operate with little or no attention diverted to moving the eyes. Apping makes the rauding process operate with eye movements just as effectively as when there is no need to move the eyes, such as during auding and when the words are presented one at a time in the center of a computer screen. The factor limiting how fast the rauding process can operate does not appear to involve visual processes, such as eye movements or word recognition speed *per se*. Instead, rauding rate seems to be limited by a more central cognitive speed, which probably improves with maturity but varies greatly between individuals.

Rauding rate does increase each year during the school grades from 2 to 12, and the growth in rate each year is around 14 Wpm. This means that the relationship between rauding rate and grade in school is linear. Furthermore, this relationship is also linear for reading-related tasks, such as the visual matching of words, suggesting that this yearly growth in rate probably is not due to practice, experience, or education, but instead is due to maturation.

Silent speech ordinarily accompanies the rauding process. The words are internally articulated as they are being processed. This inner speech is an aid to the process, and it is not likely that the rauding process can operate at the rauding rate without the accompanying speech recoding.

There appears to be a high relationship between rauding rate and maximum oral reading rate, MORR. There is support for the hypothesis that MORR is caused by rauding rate, but more confirming research is needed. It appears that MORR is a direct, objective indicator of rauding rate, and a good predictor of typical silent reading rate, or apping rate.

Automaticity is ordinarily an inherent part of the rauding process because individuals typically read materials that are relatively easy for them, so they are recognizing the words without any unnecessary extra attention devoted specifically to word recognition. However, even after words reach full automaticity they still do not appear to have reached their maximum recognition speed, the speed associated with an individual's rauding rate. This rate is probably reached after a great deal of practice beyond full automaticity. The best way to maintain known words at their rauding rate is probably to read relatively easy materials regularly. Students who are trying to improve their rauding accuracy level, A_L, by attempting to raud materials that are not relatively easy will encounter new and unknown words that will have to be fully automatized before they can begin to be processed at the rauding rate. The best way to keep adding new words to the population that can be processed at the rauding rate probably is to read materials that are *not* relatively easy.

The concept of automaticity has spawned an educational treatment called repeated readings, but this treatment probably works best with beginning readers, e.g., first graders where automaticity is secondary to learning how to pronounce each word accurately. The best way to achieve automaticity, and eventually rauding rate, for the most words in the shortest period of time is probably to be reading new passages continually, not repeatedly reading old ones.

Rapid reading training, RRT, is usually effective in getting students to practice using a skimming process. However, there is no sound evidence that this training will increase the rauding rate of individuals. There is a great deal of evidence that RRT will *not* increase an individual's efficiency of comprehension, as measured by standardized reading comprehension tests. RRT probably should be replaced by reading process training (RPT) which would consist of training skilled readers (at $A_L = 8$ or higher) how and when to shift gears among the five basic reading processes, scanning, skimming, rauding, learning, and memorizing.

There appears to be no evidence that speed readers exist who can successfully operate their rauding process at 600 Wpm or higher. A search was made for evidence supporting the existence of these super readers but there was no supporting evidence that met minimum scientific standards. Speed readers are really skimmers in disguise; they are individuals who habitually operate a skimming process whereas most individuals habitually operate their rauding process. Speed readers have accepted the large drop in the accuracy of comprehension, A, associated with their skimming process; they can remember only a fraction of the important details when they skim at rates around 1000–1500 Wpm. Speed readers have not learned a skill that allows them to triple their reading rate with no loss in their accuracy of comprehension because tripling rate will cut the accuracy of comprehension to about one-third or less of that associated with the rauding rate. Instead, speed readers are individuals who typically read in fourth or fifth gear, sometimes shifting down to third gear. There appears to be no advantage to this habit, except for those atypical individuals who have goals that can ordinarily be met by a skimming process.

In the future, researchers need to consider seriously the advantages of making explicit the specific reading process they intend for their subjects to operate in their research. It seems obvious now that the results of studies wherein the subjects operated a learning process or a memorizing process will not necessarily generalize to the rauding process, in spite of any wishful thinking along these lines that may continue to exist. In order to study a particular reading process, it is necessary to administer appropriate instructions to the subjects, present passages of sufficient length and difficulty level, and then tailor the objective consequences to the process. The difficulty level of the materials should be reported, D_L, and the rauding ability of the subjects should also be reported, A_L and R_r. A calculation of the relative difficulty, $A_L - D_L$, can be used to determine whether the materials are relatively easy, a prerequisite for investigations involving the rauding process. Measuring the rate at which the subjects read the research materials, in Wpm, is imperative because this obtained rate can be compared to their estimated rauding rate, R_r, to provide confirming evidence relevant to which particular reading process was actually used by the subjects. Even research involving reading comprehension might be greatly improved by (a) using the constructs of A, R, E, A_r, R_r, E_r, A_L, R_L, E_L, D_L, and Wpm when the research is designed, and (b) reporting measurements of these constructs in the published research report.

With regard to the traditional concept of reading flexibility, it is wrong to suggest that good readers should be flexible with respect to the difficulty level of the material. Good readers should not automatically increase the rate at which the rauding process operates as the material becomes easier because the rauding process operates most efficiently at the rauding rate, no matter what the difficulty level. Also contrary to conventional wisdom, it is grossly misleading to suggest that good readers are flexible in the sense that they automatically change their rate or their process with every change in purpose. For example, the goals associated with many different purposes can be accomplished with the rauding process. The concepts of purpose flexibility and difficulty flexibility cause more heat and confusion than light and understanding; it seems better to replace them with the concept of process flexibility.

Good readers are flexible readers in the sense that they know how and when to shift gears from one reading process to another. They shift out of their rauding process, Gear 3, to a higher gear when a faster but less powerful process is needed and they shift down to a lower gear when a slower but more powerful process is needed. So, it can be said that good readers are process flexible, and that all skilled readers need to be process flexible.

Good readers do not show flexibility by simply adjusting their rate. They show flexibility by adjusting their reading process so the components associated with the process best accomplish their goals. Because the different components of each process require varying amounts of time to operate successfully, rate therefore varies with the particular process. Rate is a by-product of a process change. It is misleading to say that good readers adjust their rate; instead, they adjust their process which in turn causes a change in rate. Changing rate is not a cause of good reading; changing rate, and the lack thereof during the operation of the rauding process, are the effects of good reading.

The concept of process flexibility is perhaps the most important new idea resulting from this review of research and theory on reading rate. For most of the time spent reading, skilled readers will be operating their rauding process at a constant rate, their rauding rate. But, skilled readers must know when and how to shift up to scanning or skimming and shift down to learning or memorizing when their goals are better met using these atypical but basic reading processes. The concept of process flexibility seems to have potential for improving research and practice in reading.

It will be difficult to accept the concept of process flexibility without also accepting the rauding process as the most important of all the basic reading processes. In turn, this means that the concept of reading comprehension must be refined and replaced with constructs associated with the rauding process: accuracy of comprehension, A, rate of comprehension, R, efficiency of comprehension, E, rauding accuracy, A_r, rauding rate, R_r, rauding efficiency, E_r, rauding accuracy level, A_L, rauding rate level, R_L, and rauding efficiency level, E_L. Without these concepts and constructs from rauding theory, it would be almost impossible to make sense out of all the prior research that has been conducted on reading rate. These concepts and constructs of rauding theory can be used to reveal the order and lawfulness associated with reading rate and reading comprehension.

The constructs of rauding theory have been interrelated using mathematical equations. When the rauding ability of the individual has been estimated in the form of A_L and R_r and the rauding difficulty of the passage has been estimated in the form of D_L, then these equations can be used to predict A for any R. Empirical techniques now exist for objectively estimating all of these constructs, so it is now possible to make precise predictions regarding how much of a particular book, chapter, or passage will be comprehended by a particular individual, or group, given a knowledge of how much time is spent rauding it. These lawful and causal relationships can be used to describe, explain, predict, and control the reading rate and reading comprehension of individuals.

We now know a great deal about reading rate and its importance, thanks to those researchers who have been collecting empirical data during the past century. And, a framework has been erected for learning much more during the next century.

APPENDIX A
E. B. COLEMAN

JUST AND CARPENTER'S THEORY OF READING: LENGTH AND EYE FIXATIONS

Just and Carpenter (1980) published a cognitively oriented theory of reading comprehension based on the mechanics of eye movements. They cast their theory into the form of a multiple regression equation based on 17 (or 22) predictors, and it accounted for 72% (or 94%) of the variance in "gaze durations."

Below is an equation that accounts for essentially the same amount of variance, but requires one predictor only. To let you derive it for yourself, Table 1 has reordered the sectors of the Just–Carpenter Flywheel passage (their Table 3).

The first column of figures in Table 1 gives the observed gaze durations. Pause long enough to rank-order them and estimate their correlation with length of line. Column 2 gives gaze durations estimated from the complete J–C model (22 predictors). Column 3 gives them estimated from length alone [number of character spaces multiplied by 37.03; 37.03 = total milliseconds (29,809) divided by total character spaces (805)]. Correlations with the observed durations are 0.985 for predictions from the complete J–C model; 0.977 for predictions from length alone. Length can account for a lot of variance.

Length compares about as well in predicting gaze duration on individual words. Just and Carpenter (p. 347) gave gaze durations for two sentences of the Flywheel passage. Table 2 reorders their 43 words according to length. Column 2 gives mean observed duration for each word; Column 3 gives the J–C predictions; Column 4 the length predictions. Correlations with observed durations are 0.909 for the J–C predictions and 0.873 for the length predictions.

459

Table 1

Reordering of Just and Carpenter's Table 3

	Obs.	J–C	Length
known to man.	478	680	518
it is made from.	615	780	630
as in an automobile.	769	718	778
when space is unlimited.	1289	1252	926
any flywheel will fly apart.	1200	1304	1074
that powers the drive shaft.	1056	1264	1074
If it spins too fast for its mass,	1414	1502	1259
the more energy can be stored in it.	1270	1536	1370
This flywheel stores the maximum energy	1416	1596	1444
when the wheel is confined in a small space	1522	1448	1592
providing the maximum possible storage of energy	1799	1870	1777
Flywheels are one of the oldest mechanical devices	1921	1999	1852
Every internal-combustion engine contains a small flywheel	2316	2398	2148
The greater the mass of a flywheel and the faster it spins	2143	2304	2148
But its maximum spinning speed is limited by the strength of the material	2440	2553	2703
One type of flywheel consists of round sandwiches of fiberglass and rubber	2746	3064	2703
Another type, the "superflywheel," consists of a series of rimless spokes	2938	2830	2703
that converts the jerky motion of the pistons into the smooth flow of energy	2477	2807	2814

Table 2

Gaze Durations of Individual Words

Word	Obs.	J–C	Length
a	41	102	74
a	21	102	74
of	165	75	111
of	73	75	111
of	29	75	111
of	22	75	111
is	69	128	111
in	32	87	111
as	70	112	111
in	164	87	111
an	195	127	111
of	46	75	111
of	60	75	111
and	0	80	148
the	51	78	148
the	128	77	148
the	72	77	148
One	169	165	148
type	215	236	185
when	253	138	185
round	196	249	222
wheel	199	239	222
small	267	206	222
space	197	209	222
type,	182	236	222
rubber	328	338	259
energy	272	378	259
series	346	289	259
spokes	519	319	259
maximum	369	354	296
storage	308	297	296
Another	323	334	296
rimless	467	361	296
flywheel	295	409	333
consists	290	304	333
possible	326	318	333
confined	336	326	333
consists	276	304	333
fiberglass	482	413	370
providing	431	349	370
sandwiches	504	438	407
automobile.	340	465	481
"superflywheel,"	626	513	629

The length correlations, though a hairbreadth below these J–C correlations, happen to be a hairbreadth above the J–C correlations based on all 15 passages, but neither difference is large enough to wage theoretical war about. Besides, accuracy in prediction could be raised a trifle by taking the curvilinearity of the length effect into account. Accuracy could be raised a little more by adding other mechanical predictors such as the typical undershooting of the first word in a line, the effect of breaking and hyphenating a word at the end of a line, and the like. But that would be overkill; correlations of 0.873 or 0.977 are high enough to make the point: Mechanical effects may be accounting for almost all of the variance.

They *may* be. The conclusion has to be tentative because important cognitive predictors are correlated with length. To give only one example: Function words tend to be short (from one to three or four letters), and they make up about 50% of typical passages. There are elementary ways to tease the mechanical variance apart from the more interesting variance due to predictability, familiarity, functor versus contentor, and the rest. For example, plot gaze duration on individual words against their length in letters, but plot several curves such as one for function words versus one for content words. Or obtain cloze scores (or other predictability indices) on each word in the 15 passages and plot several curves representing different levels of predictability.

Perhaps there will be great differences between such curves, but until the variance due to these differences is computed, Tables 1 and 2 suggest that the following hypothesis should not be dismissed out of hand. In purposeful reading of long passages, most of the moment-by-moment, word-by-word variance may be due to mechanical effects.

APPENDIX B

Converting Rate in Wpm to
Grade Equivalents Expressed as R_L

Wpm	R_L
121	2.5
135	3.5
149	4.5
163	5.5
177	6.5
191	7.5
205	8.5
219	9.5
233	10.5
247	11.5
261	12.5
275	13.5
289	14.5
303	15.5
317	16.5
331	17.5
345	18.5

GLOSSARY

accuracy of comprehension: proportion of thoughts in a passage that were comprehended; symbolized as A; number of thoughts or sentences in a passage that were comprehended during reading or auding per the total number of thoughts or sentences in the passage.

actual rate: rate of comprehension, R, when the rate at which the words are presented are directly manipulated, e.g., by use of motion picture film or time-compressed speech; the rate that accompanies an attempt to manipulate directly the rauding process rate; contrast with average rate.

actual words: a count of the number of words in a passage when a word is defined as the letter string between two blank spaces except that two words separated by a hypen is counted as two words; contrast with standard word.

apping: automatic pilot for prose; eye movements during reading that have become habitual and rhythmic and therefore require little or no attention.

auding: listening to orally presented words, letters, or other language symbols to gain information or knowledge.

average rate: rate of comprehension, R, when presentation time is directly manipulated instead of rate, e.g. by allowing an individual to read a passage for a fixed amount of time; the passage presentation rate that accompanies an attempt to allow the rauding process to proceed at the rauding rate; contrast with actual rate.

basic reading processes: the five basic reading processes in rauding theory are scanning, skimming, rauding, learning, and memorizing; reading processes used on passages.

cognitive power: basic ability to solve intellectual problems; symbolized as C_p.

cognitive speed: basic rate of thinking about verbal material; symbolized as C_s.

complete thought: the meaning of a sentence or independent clause.

comprehending: understanding or grasping the meaning.

correlate: a variable that is related to a theoretical construct but has different units of measurement.

difficulty flexibility: the ability of an individual to decrease reading rate as the difficulty of the material increases.

difficulty level: rauding difficulty level of the passage; symbolized as D_L; a measurement of passage readability in GE units; rauding difficulty of a passage as indicated by the Rauding Scale of Prose difficulty, or some other readability technique such as the Dale–Chall formula or the Fry readability graph.

efficiency of comprehension: number of thoughts comprehended in a passage per the amount of time allowed for reading or auding; symbolized as E; product of accuracy of comprehension, A, and rate of comprehension, R.

fact recalling: finding a word in memory, recognizing its meaning within the sentence, integrating the word into the complete thought of the sentence, storing the thoughts well enough that they can be recognized later, and rehearsing the thoughts or factual information sufficiently that it can be freely recalled later.

gear shifting: changing from one reading process to another; changing from one of the five basic reading processes to another.

idea remembering: finding a word in memory, recognizing its meaning within the sentence, integrating the word into the complete thought of the sentence, and storing the thoughts well enough that there is a good probability that they can be recognized later.

indicant: an empirical measure of a theoretical construct that ordinarily has the same units of measurement as the construct.

inefficiency constant: index of the amount of inefficiency associated with having more than enough time to execute the rauding process once on a passage; symbolized by i; depends upon rauding rate and rauding accuracy (see Equation 2.12.).

learning process: one of the five basic reading processes; to read either relatively easy or relatively hard material and know its meaning at a later time, possibly by taking a multiple-choice test; involves the reading of sentences in passages that are relatively difficult in order to comprehend them; a model learning process can be described as involving lexical access, semantic encoding, sentential integration, idea remembering, and processing at a rate around 200 Wpm for college students.

lexical access: finding a word in memory; word identification; to recognize a word, except "word recognition" often means to pronounce a word correctly.

memorizing process: one of the five basic reading processes; a series of steps carried out on the words of a passage so as to increase the probability that the words, facts, ideas, or thoughts can be freely recalled on a subsequent occasion; implementation of those activities which are most likely to result in the recall of information; often involves the word-for-word recall of a passage either in written or oral form; a model memorizing process has been described as involving the components of lexical access, semantic encoding, sentential integration, idea remembering, fact recalling, and operating at about 138 Wpm for college students.

operating: carrying out the components or steps of a process.

optimal rate: the rate of comprehension, R, associated with the maximum efficiency of comprehension, E; the optimal rate of comprehension for most individuals is theorized to be their rauding rate, R_r; college students tend to average around 300 Wpm for their rauding rate, R_r, and their optimal rate tends to be this same rate.

passage: a set of connected thoughts usually in the form of related sentences and sometimes organized in paragraphs; a body of prose material either in spoken or written form.

presentation time: amount of reading time for a passage, either as allowed or spent depending upon whether time is fixed or free to vary; symbolized as t; usually measured in minutes.

process: a series of progressive and independent steps designed to accomplish a goal; a phenomenon that continuously changes with time, usually cyclic or algorithmic in nature.

process flexibility: the shifting of gears from one reading process to another in order to accomplish a goal that is best accomplished by the components of a certain reading process.

purpose flexibility: changing reading rate as the purpose for reading changes so as to be better able to accomplish the purpose.

rate of comprehension: rate of passage presentation; symbolized as R; number of complete thoughts in a passage that are encountered or presented per the amount of time allowed for reading or auding; measured by standard length sentences per minute, Sentences per minute (Spm); often reported as wpm or Wpm.

rate flexibility: continually changing rate as difficulty and purpose change.

raud: comprehension of all or almost all of the consecutively encountered thoughts during reading or auding; comprehending about 75% or more of the complete thoughts encountered during the operation of the rauding process.

rauder: one who rauds or attempts to raud; a person who is operating the rauding process.

rauding: attending to each consecutive word in sentences and comprehending each consecutively encountered complete thought in a passage; operating the rauding process and comprehending about 75% or more of the thoughts in a passage.

rauding accuracy: accuracy of comprehension, A, when the rauding process is operated on a passage at the rauding rate; symbolized as A_r.

rauding accuracy level: the highest level of passage difficulty, D_L, at which individuals can comprehend at least 75% of the thoughts when operating their rauding process at their rauding rate, R_r; symbolized as A_L; indicated by a GE score on the Accuracy Level Test (vocabulary tests are usually good correlates).

rauding efficiency: efficiency of comprehension, E, when the rauding process is operated on a passage at the rauding rate, R_r; symbolized as E_r.

rauding efficiency level: the highest level of passage difficulty, D_L, at which individuals can accurately comprehend ($A > 0.75$) when the passage is presented at a rate commensurate with that difficulty level; symbolized as E_L; traditional standardized tests of reading comprehension are correlates of E_L.

rauding process: the process used by an individual to comprehend each consecutively encountered complete thought in a passage; involves the components of lexical access, semantic encoding, and sentential integration; one of the five basic reading processes. (Note: according to rauding theory, when an individual operates the rauding process on a passage, it involves perceiving and internally articulating each consecutive word in a passage in an attempt to comprehend each consecutive sentence and thereby understand the thoughts in the passage that the author intended to communicate; during reading the rauding process also includes a fixation centered on almost every word in a passage.)

rauding rate: highest rate at which an individual can raud relatively easy passages; symbolized as R_r; highest rate, R, at which an individual can accurately operate the rauding process, $A > 0.75$, on relatively easy passages; highest rate at which all or almost all the consecutively encountered sentences in passages can be comprehended. (Note: according to rauding theory, rauding rate is also a constant rate, an optimal rate, a threshold rate, and the typical rate at which the rauding process operates.)

rauding rate level: the rauding rate, R_r, in grade equivalent units; symbolized as R_L; the average rauding rate of individuals at each rauding accuracy level, A_L; measured by the Rate Level Test.

reading: looking at visually presented words, letters, or other language symbols to gain information or knowledge.

reading comprehension: the comprehension or understanding associated with reading; could refer to one, some, or all of the following: (a) rauding accuracy level, A_L, (b) rauding efficiency level, E_L, (c) rauding accuracy, A_r, (d) rauding efficiency, E_r, (e) accuracy of comprehension, A, and (f) efficiency of comprehension, E.

reading process: any of a number of different processes used in reading to accomplish different goals.

reading rate: speed of reading under any reading process; could refer to rate of comprehension, R, or rauding rate, R_r.

relative difficulty: the rauding difficulty level of the material in relationship to the rauding accuracy level of the reader; symbolized as $A_L - D_L$.

relatively easy: passages that are at a difficulty level which are below the rauding accuracy level of the reader ($A_L > D_L$).

relatively hard: passages that are at a difficulty level that is above the rauding accuracy level of the reader ($A_L < D_L$).

scanning process: one of the five basic reading processes; a reading process which involves looking at each individual word simply to recognize it; involves only lexical access; a model scanning process can be described as involving a search for a target word in a passage, and for college students this process operates around 600 Wpm.

semantic encoding: finding a word in memory and also recognizing its meaning as it is used in the sentence; attaching a contextually relevant meaning to a word.

sentential integrating: finding a word in memory, recognizing its meaning as it is used in the sentence, and integrating the word with the prior words to form the complete thought represented by the sentence in the context of a passage.

Sentences per minute (Spm): rate determined from a count of the number of standard sentences in a passage divided by presentation time in minutes.

skimming process: one of the five basic reading processes; those reading processes which involve a sampling of the population of information to learn more about that body of information; involves skipping words when done in connection with passages; a series of steps carried out on the words in a passage so as to increase one's general knowledge about the information contained in the passage; involves sampling words or phrases and inferring about what was skipped; a model skimming process can be described as involving lexical access and semantic encoding in order to find two words in a passage whose order has been reversed, and this process can be successfully operated by college students at around 450 Wpm.

standard sentence: 100 character spaces; symbolized as S; sixteen and two-thirds standard length words; also signified by Sentence.

standard word: six character spaces; symbolized as W; six consecutive characters including letters and punctuation marks with one blank space after each word and two blank spaces after each sentence; also signified by Word; sometimes defined as five letters.

studying: activities involving the basic reading processes, possibly supplemented by productive activities such as note taking, underlining, reciting, and outlining which are used as part of a strategy for increasing one's understanding or future recall of the information in a passage.

word: any one of the thousands of entries in a dictionary; the letter strings between two blank spaces in a sentence (except for two words separated by a hyphen).

Word: a standard length word; a standard word; six character spaces counting each letter, punctuation mark, one character space after each word, and two character spaces after each sentence.

word for word reading: a reading process in which an attempt is made to lexically access, semantically encode, and sententially integrate every word in a passage; the rauding process is word for word reading and most learning processes and memorizing processes also involve word for word reading. (Note: This definition should not be confused with another usage that means a perfect oral rendition of a passage.)

words per minute (wpm): reading rate determined from a count of the actual number of words in a passage divided by the presentation time.

Words per minute (Wpm): rate determined from a count of the standard words in a passage divided by the presentation time.

REFERENCES

Aaronson, D. (1976). *Journal of Experimental Psychology: Human Perception and Performance,* **2**(1), 42–55.

Aaronson, D., & Ferres, S. (1983a). Lexical categories and reading tasks. *Journal of Experimental Psychology: Human Perception and Performance,* **9**(5), 675–699.

Aaronson, D., & Ferres, S. (1983b). Model for coding lexical categories during reading. *Journal of Experimental Psychology: Human Perception and Performance,* **9**(5), 700–725.

Aaronson, D., & Scarborough, H. S. (1976). Performance theories for sentence coding: Some quantitative evidence. *Journal of Experimental Psychology: Human Perception and Performance,* **2**(1), 56–70.

Aaronson, D., & Scarborough, H. S. (1977). Performance theories for sentence coding. *Journal of Verbal Learning and Verbal Behavior,* **16,** 277–303.

Abell, A. M. (1894). Rapid reading; advantages and methods. *Educational Review,* **8,** 283–286.

Adams, R. B. (1963). The phenomenon of supernormal reading ability. *Yearbook of the National Reading Conference,* **12,** 133–142.

Ahuja, P. (1977). Rapid reading programs, increased reading speed and good comprehension. *Psycho-lingua,* **7**(1–2), 7–10.

Allington, R. L. (1978). Effects of contextual constraints upon rate and accuracy. *Perceptual and Motor Skills,* **46,** 1318.

Allington, R. L. (1983). Fluency: The neglected reading goal. *Reading Teacher,* **36**(6), 556–561.

Anderson, I. H. (1937). Studies in the eye movements of good and poor readers. In *Studies in the psychology of reading. I.* University of Iowa Studies in Psychology No. 21. Psychological Monographs, Vol. XLVIII No. 3, p. 15. Princeton, NJ: Psychological Review Company.

Anderson, I. H., & Swanson, D. E. (1937). Common factors in eye-movements in silent and oral reading. *Psychology Monographs,* **48**(3), 61–69.

Anderson, T. H., & Armbruster, B. B. (1984). Studying. In P. D. Pearson (Ed.), *Handbook of reading research.* New York: Longman.

Aquino, M. R. (1969). The validity of the Miller-Coleman readability scale. *Reading Research Quarterly,* **4,** 352–357.

Atkinson, R. C., & Shiffrin, R. M. (1968). Human memory: A proposed system and its control processes. In K. W. Spence & J. T. Spence (Eds.), *The psychology of learning and motivation: Advances in research and theory* (Vol. 2, pp. 89–195). New York: Academic Press.

Averill, L. A., & Mueller, A. D. (1928). The effect of practice on the improvement of silent reading in adults. *Journal of Educational Research*, **17**, 125–129.

Backman, J., Lundberg, I., Nilsson, L., & Ohlsson, K. (1984). Reading skill and the processing of text structure. *Scandinavian Journal of Educational Research*, **29**(3), 113–128.

Baddeley, A. D., Eldridge, M., & Lewis, V. (1981). The role of subvocalisation in reading. *Quarterly Journal of Experimental Psychology: Human Experimental Psychology*, **33A**(4), 439–454.

Bain, J. W. (1971, April). Reading achievement gains of adults in Air-Force program. *Journal of Reading*, pp. 467–472, 500.

Ballantine, F. A. (1951). Age changes in measures of eye-movements in silent reading. In *Studies in the psychology of reading* (University of Michigan Monographs in Education No. 4, pp. 67–114). Ann Arbor: University of Michigan Press.

Bassin, C. B., & Martin, C. J. (1976). Effect of three types of redundancy reduction on comprehension, reading rate, and reading time of English Prose. *Journal of Educational Psychology*, **68**(5), 649–652.

Bayle, E. (1942). The nature and causes of regressive movements in reading. *Journal of Experimental Education*, **11**(1), 16–36.

Bear, R. M. (1939). The Dartmouth program for diagnostic and remedial reading with special reference to visual factors. *Educational Records Supplement*, **12**, 69–88.

Bear, R. M., & Odbert, H. S. (1940). Experimental studies of the relation between rate of reading and speed of association. *Journal of Psychology*, **10**, 141–147.

Belmore, S. M. (1985). Reading computer-presented test. *Bulletin of the Psychonomic Society*, **23**(1), 12–14.

Berger, A. (1966, December). Selected review of studies on the effectiveness of various methods of increasing reading efficiency. *Journal of the Reading Specialist*, pp. 74–87.

Berger, A. (1967). *Speed reading: An annotated bibliography* (No. 14). Newark, DE: International Reading Association.

Berger, A. (1968a). Effectiveness of four methods of increasing reading rate, comprehension, and flexibility. In J. A. Figurel (Ed.), *Forging ahead in reading* (pp. 588–596). Newark, DE: International Reading Association.

Berger, A. (1968b, February). Ten important sources of information on speed reading. *Journal of Reading*, pp. 359–361.

Berger, A. (1969). Are machines needed to increase reading rate? *Educational Technology*, **9**(8), 59–60.

Berger, A., & Peebles, J. D. (1976). *Rates of comprehension*. Newark, DE: International Reading Association.

Bergquist, L. (1984). Rapid silent reading: Techniques for improving rate in intermediate grades. *Reading Teacher*, **38**, 50–53.

Biemiller, A. (1977). Relationships between oral reading rates for letters, words, and simple text in the development of reading achievement. *Reading Research Quarterly*, **13**(2), 223–253.

Birkmire, D.P. (1985). The influence of text structure, background knowledge, and purpose. *Reading Research Quarterly*, **20**(3), 314–326.

Blommers, P., & Lindquist, E. F. (1944). Rate of comprehension of reading: Its measurement and its relation to comprehension. *Journal of Educational Psychology*, **35**(8), 449–473.

Boles, D. B., & Eveland, D. C. (1983). Visual and phonetic codes and the process of generation in letter matching. *Journal of Experimental Psychology: Human Perception and Performance*, **9**(5), 657–674.

Bostian, L. R. (1976). Effect of line width, reading speed and comprehension. *Journalism Quarterly*, **53**(2), 328–330.

Bouma, H., & deVoogd, A. H. (1974). On the control of eye saccades in reading. *Vision Research*, **14**, 273–284.

Bower, T. E. R. (1970). Reading by eye. In H. Levin & J. P. Williams (Eds.), *Basic studies on reading* (pp. 134–146). New York: Basic Books.

Boyd, R. (1966). Rate of comprehension in reading among sixth form pupils in New Zealand schools. *Reading Teacher*, **20**, 237–241.

Brandt, J. D. (1975). Internal versus external locus of control and performance in controlled and motivated reading-rate improvement instruction. *Journal of Counseling Psychology*, **22**(5), 377–382.

Breznitz, Z. (1987). Increasing first graders' reading accuracy and comprehension by accelerating their reading rates. *Journal of Educational Psychology*, **79**(3), 236–242.

Bridges, L. H. (1941). Speed versus comprehension in elementary reading. *Journal of Educational Psychology*, **32**(4), 314–320.

Brim, B. J. (1968). Impact of a reading improvement program. *Journal of Educational Research*, **62**(4), 177–182.

Britton, B. K., Glynn, S. M., Muth, D., & Penland, M. J. (1985). *Journal of Reading Behavior*, **17**(2), 101–113.

Britton, B. K., Holdredge, T. S., Curry, C., & Westbrook, R. D. (1979). Use of cognitive capacity in reading identical texts with different amounts of discourse level meaning. *Journal of Experimental Psychology: Human Learning and Human Memory*, **5**(3), 262–270.

Brown, J. I. (1962). *Efficient reading*. Boston, MA: D. C. Heath.

Brown, J. I. (1976). Techniques for increasing reading rate. In J. E. Merritt (Ed.), *New horizons in reading* (pp. 158–164). Newark, DE: International Reading Association.

Brown, J. I., & McDowell, E. E. (1979). The role of self-image on reading rate and comprehension achievement. *Reading Improvement*, **16**(1), 22–27.

Burge, P. D. (1983). Comprehension and rate: Oral v. silent reading for low achievers. *Reading Horizons*, **23**(3), 201–206.

Buros, O. K. (1965). *Sixth mental measurements yearbook*. Highland Park, NJ: Gryphon Press.

Buswell, G. T. (1922). *Fundamental reading habits: A study of their development*. Chicago, IL: University of Chicago.

Buswell, G. T. (1947). The subvocalization factor in the improvement of reading. *Elementary School Journal*, **48**, 190–196.

Buswell, G. T. (1951). The relationship between rate of thinking and rate of reading. *School Review*, **59**, 339–346.

Campbell, A. J., Marchetti, F. M., & Mewhort, D. J. K. (1981). Reading speed and text production: A note on right-justification techniques. *Ergonomics*, **24**(8), 633–640.

Campbell, D. T., & Stanley, J. C. (1963). Experimental and quasi-experimental designs for research on teaching. In N. L. Gage (Ed.), *Handbook of research on teaching*. Washington, DC: American Educational Research Association.

Carlson, T. R., (1949). The relationship between speed and accuracy of comprehension. *Journal of Educational Research*, **42**, 500–512.

Carpenter, T. W., & Jones, Y. (1975, December). Improving comprehension and rate gain at the college level. *Journal of Reading*, pp. 223–225.

Carver, R. P. (1970). Effect of a "chunked" typography upon reading rate and comprehension. *Journal of Applied Psychology*, **54**, 288–296.

Carver, R. P. (1971a). Pupil dilation and its relationship to information processing during reading and listening. *Journal of Applied Psychology*, **55**, 126–134.

Carver, R. P. (1971b). Evidence for the invalidity of Miller-Coleman readability scale. *Journal of Reading Behavior*, **4**(3), 42–47.

Carver, R. P. (1971c). *Manual for the Basic Reading Rate Scale.* Kansas City, MO: Revrac Publications.

Carver, R. P. (1971d). A computer model of reading and its implications for measurement and research. *Reading Research Quarterly*, **6**, 449–471.

Carver, R. P. (1971e). Development and evaluation of a test of information storage during reading. *Journal of Educational Measurement*, **8**(1), 33–44.

Carver, R. P. (1971f). *Sense and nonsense in speed reading.* Silver Spring, MD: Revrac Publications.

Carver, R. P. (1972a). Comparisons among normal readers, speed readers, and clairvoyant readers. *Yearbook of the National Reading Conference*, **21**, 150–155.

Carver, R. P. (1972b, August). Speed readers don't read; they skim. *Psychology Today*, pp. 22–30.

Carver, R. P. (1972c). Analysis of the Chunked Reading Test and reading comprehension. *Journal of Reading Behavior*, **5**(4), 282–296.

Carver, R. P. (1973a). Understanding information processing, and learning from prose materials. *Journal of Educational Psychology*, **64**(1), 76–84.

Carver, R. P. (1973b). Effect of increasing the rate of speech presentation upon comprehension. *Journal of Educational Psychology*, **65**(1), 118–126.

Carver, R. P. (1974). Two dimensions of tests: Psychometric and edumetric. *American Psychologist*, **29**, 512–518.

Carver, R. P. (1975a). Measuring prose difficulty using the Rauding Scale. *Reading Research Quarterly*, **11**, 660–685.

Carver, R. P. (1975b). Designing reading rate research. *Yearbook of the National Reading Conference Yearbook*, **24**, 241–245.

Carver, R. P. (1976). Word length, prose difficulty, and reading rate. *Journal of Reading Behavior*, **8**, 193–204.

Carver, R. P. (1977). Toward a theory of reading comprehension and rauding. *Reading Research Quarterly*, **13**, 8–63.

Carver, R. P. (1978a). Sense and nonsense about generalizing to a language population. *Journal of Reading Behavior*, **10**, 25–33.

Carver, R. P. (1978b). The case against statistical significance testing. *Harvard Educational Review*, **48**, 378–399.

Carver, R. P. (1981). *Reading comprehension and rauding theory.* Springfield, IL: Charles C. Thomas. (Reprint: Kansas City, MO: Revrac Publications, 1987).

Carver, R. P. (1982). Optimal rate of reading prose. *Reading Research Quarterly*, **18**, 56–88.

Carver, R. P. (1983). Is reading rate constant or flexible? *Reading Research Quarterly*, **18**, 190–215.

Carver, R. P. (1984a). *Writing a publishable research report.* Springfield, IL: Charles C. Thomas.

Carver, R. P. (1984b). Rauding theory predictions of amount comprehended under different purposes and speed reading conditions. *Reading Research Quarterly*, **19**, 205–218.

Carver, R. P. (1984c). *Manual for Bormuth's Reading Passages and Carver's Questions.* Kansas City, MO: Revrac Publications.

Carver, R. P. (1985a). Measuring absolute amounts of reading comprehension using the rauding rescaling procedure. *Journal of Reading Behavior*, **17**, 29–53.

Carver, R. P. (1985b). How good are some of the world's best readers? *Reading Research Quarterly*, **20**, 398–419.

Carver, R. P. (1985c). Measuring readability using DRP units. *Journal of Reading Behavior*, **17**, 303–316.

Carver, R. P. (1986). Validity of the Rate Test. *Yearbook of the National Reading Conference*, **35**, 382–386.

Carver, R. P. (1987a). *Technical manual for the Rate Level Test*. Kansas City, MO: Revrac Publications.

Carver, R. P. (1987b). *Manual for the Rauding Efficiency Level Test*. Kansas City, MO: Revrac Publications.

Carver, R. P. (1987c). *Technical manual for the Accuracy Level Test*. Kansas City, MO: Revrac Publications.

Carver, R. P. (1987d). Teaching rapid reading training in the intermediate grades: Helpful or harmful? *Reading Research and Instruction*, **26**(2), 65–76.

Carver, R. P. (1987e). Should reading comprehension skills be taught? *Yearbook of the National Reading Conference*, **36**, 115–126.

Carver, R. P. (1987f). *Manual for the Reading Efficiency Level Battery*. Kansas City, MO: Revrac Publications.

Carver, R. P. (1988). *Manual for the Cognitive Speed Battery*. Kansas City, MO: Revrac Publications.

Carver, R. P. (1989a). Relationship between maximum oral reading rate and rauding rate. *Yearbook of the National Reading Conference*, **38**, 421–425.

Carver, R. P. (1989b). Silent reading rates in grade equivalents. *Journal of Reading Behavior*, **21**(2), 155–166.

Carver, R. P. (1990a). *Reliability and validity of the speed of thinking test*. Unpublished manuscript.

Carver, R. P. (1990b). *Improving the ability to comprehend while reading using rauding theory*. Unpublished manuscript.

Carver, R. P. (1990c). *Predicting accuracy of comprehension from the time spent reading*. Unpublished manuscript.

Carver, R. P. (1990d). *What do standardized tests of reading comprehension measure in terms of efficiency, accuracy, and rate?* Unpublished manuscript.

Carver, R. P. (1990e). *Predicting accuracy of comprehension from the relative difficulty of the material*. Unpublished manuscript.

Carver, R. P. (1990f). Rescaling the Degrees of Reading Power test to provide valid scores for selecting materials at the instructional level. *Journal of Reading Behavior*, **12**(1), 1–18.

Carver, R. P., & Hoffman, J. V. (1981). The effect of practice through repeated readings on gain in reading ability using a computer based instructional system. *Reading Research Quarterly*, **16**(3), 374–390.

Cattell, R. B. (1971). *Abilities: Their structure, growth, and action*. Boston, MA: Houghton Mifflin.

Cavett, D. (1986). *Speed reading with Dick Cavett*. New York: Time-Life Video. (A video tape distributed by Ambrose Video, New York).

Cirilo, R. K. (1981). Referential coherence and text structure in story comprehension. *Journal of Verbal Learning and Verbal Behavior*, **20**, 358–367.

Cirilo, R. K., & Foss, D. J. (1980). Text structure and reading time for sentences. *Journal of Verbal Learning and Verbal Behavior*, **19**, 96–109.

Cloer, C. T., Jr. (1977). Subvocalization—asset, liability, or both? *Yearbook of the National Reading Conference*, **26**, 209–213.

Cohen, J. (1977). *Statistical power analysis for the behavioral sciences*. New York: Academic Press.

Coke, E. U. (1974). The effects of readability on oral and silent reading rates. *Journal of Educational Psychology*, **66**(3), 406–409.

Coke, E. U. (1976). Reading rate, readability, and variations in task-induced processing. *Journal of Educational Psychology*, **68**(2), 167–173.

Coke, E. U. (1977). The effect of altering context cues in prose on reading rate in a search task. *Journal of Reading Behavior*, **9**(4), 365–380.

Coke, E. U., & Rothkopf, E. Z. (1970). Note on a simple algorithm for a computer-produced reading ease score. *Journal of Applied Psychology*, **54**(3), 208–210.

Coleman, E. B. (1971). Developing a technology of written instruction: Some determiners of the complexity of prose. In E. Z. Rothkopf & P. E. Johnson (Eds.), *Verbal learning research and the technology of written instruction* (pp. 155–204). New York: Teachers College Press, Columbia University.

Coleman, E. B., & Hahn, S. C. (1966). Failure to improve readability with a vertical typography. *Journal of Applied Psychology*, **50**(5), 434–436.

Coleman, E. B., & Kim, I. (1961). Comparison of several styles of typography in English. *Journal of Applied Psychology*, **45**(4), 262–267.

Collins, C. (1979). Speedway: The action way to speed read to increase reading rate for adults. *Reading Improvement*, **16**(3), 225–229.

Combs, S. L. (1966). Reading for speed and comprehension. *Journal of Secondary Education*, **41**, 295–298.

Cosper, R., & Mills, B. (1953). Reading comprehension and speed. *School and Society*, **77**, 359–362.

Cranney, A. G., Brown, B. L., Hansen, D. M., & Inouye, D. K. (1982). Rate and Reading Dynamics reconsidered. *Journal of Reading*, **25**, 526–533.

Cunningham, J. W. (1979, January). An automatic pilot for decoding. *Reading Teacher*, pp. 420–424.

Cunningham, P. M. & Cunningham, J. W. (1978). Investigating the print to meaning hypothesis. *Yearbook of the National Reading Conference*, **27**, 116–120.

Cushman, W. H. (1986). Reading from microfiche, a VDT, and the printed page: Subjective fatigue and performance. *Human Factors*, **28**(1), 63–73.

Danks, J. H. (1969). Grammaticalness and meaningfulness in the comprehension of sentences. *Journal of Verbal Learning and Verbal Behavior*, **8**, 687–696.

Danks, J. H. (1980). Comprehension in listening and reading: Same or different? In F. B. Murray (Ed.), *Reading and understanding* (pp. 1–39). Newark, DE: International Reading Association.

Davis, F. B. (1962). Measurement of improvement in reading skill courses. *Yearbook of the National Reading Conference*, **11**, 30–40.

Dearborn, W. F. (1906). The psychology of reading. *Archives of Philosophy, Psychology and Scientific Methods*, **14**(1, No. 4), 4–135.

Dearborn, W. F. & Wilking, S. V. (1941). Improving the reading of college freshmen. *School Review*, **49**, 668–678.

Dee-Lucas, D. (1979). Reading speed and memory for prose. *Journal of Reading Behavior*, **11**(3), 221–233.

deHaan, H. J. (1977). A speech-rate intelligibility threshold for speeded and time-compressed connected speech. *Perception & Psychophysics*, **22**(4), 366–372.

DiStefano, P., Noe, M., & Valencia, S. (1981). Measurement of the effects of purpose and passage difficulty on reading flexibility. *Journal of Educational Psychology*, **73**(4), 602–606.

Dixon, P. (1982). Plans and written directions for complex tasks. *Journal of Verbal Learning and Verbal Behavior*, **21**, 70–84.

Dixon, W. R. (1951). Studies of the eye-movements in reading of university professors and graduate students. In *Studies in the psychology of reading* (University of Michigan Monographs in Education No. 4, pp. 113–178). Ann Arbor: University of Michigan Press.

Doehring, D. G. (1976). Acquisition of rapid reading responses. *Monographs of the Society for Research in Child Development*, **41**(2), 1–54.

DuBois, P. H. (1932). A speed factor in mental tests. *Archives of Psychology*, **141**, 1–38.

Edfeldt, A. W. (1960). *Silent speech and silent reading*. Chicago, IL: University of Chicago Press.

Ehri, L. C., & Wilce, L. S. (1974). Printed intonation cues and reading in children. *Visible Language*, **8**(3), 265–274.

Ehri, L. C., & Wilce, L. S. (1979). Does word training increase or decrease interference in a Stroop task? *Journal of Experimental Child Psychology*, **27**, 352–364.

Ehri, L. C., & Wilce, L. S. (1983). Development of word identification speed in skilled and less skilled beginning readers. *Journal of Educational Psychology*, **75**(1), 3–18.

Ekwall, E. E. (1969, October). The truth about speed reading. *Phi Delta Kappan*, pp. 97–98.

Ellis, N. C., & Miles, T. R. (1978). Visual information processing as a determinant of reading speed. *Journal of Research in Reading*, **1**(2), 108–120.

Eriksen, C. W., Pollack, M. D., & Montague, W. E. (1970). Implicit speech: Mechanism in perceptual encoding. *Journal of Experimental Psychology*, **84**, 502–507.

Eurich, A. C. (1930). The relation of speed of reading to comprehension. *School and Society*, **32**, 404–406.

Farr, R. (1971). Measuring reading comprehension: An historical perspective, *Yearbook of the National Reading Conference*, **20**, 187–197.

Farr, R., & Carey, R. F. (1986). *Reading: What can be measured?* Newark, DE: International Reading Association.

Favreau, M., & Segalowitz, N. S. (1982). Second language reading in fluent bilinguals. *Applied Psycholinguistics*, **3**, 329–341.

Favreau, M., & Segalowitz, N. S. (1983). Automatic and controlled processes in the first and second-language reading of fluent bilinguals. *Memory & Cognition*, **11**(6), 565–574.

Fisher, D. F. (1975). Reading and visual search. *Memory & Cognition*, **3**(2), 188–196.

Fisher, D. F., & Lefton, L. A. (1976). Peripheral information extraction: A developmental examination of reading processes. *Journal of Experimental Child Psychology*, **21**, 77–93.

Fisher, D. F., & Lefton, L. A., & Moss, J. H. (1978). Reading geometrically transformed text: A developmental approach. *Bulletin of the Psychonomic Society*, **11**(3), 157–160.

Fishman, A. S. (1978). The effect of anaphoric references and noun phrase organizers on paragraph comprehension. *Journal of Reading Behavior*, **10**(2), 159–170.

Fleisher, L. S., Jenkins, J. R., and Pany, D. (1979). Effects on poor readers' comprehension training in rapid decoding. *Reading Research Quarterly*, **15**(1), 30–48.

Fleming, J. T. (1968, December). Skimming: Neglected in research and teaching. *Journal of Reading*, pp. 211–214, 218.

Flesch, R. (1949). *The art of readable writing*. New York: Harper & Brothers.

Flynn, P. (1977, May). Speed is the carrot. *Journal of Reading*, pp. 683–687.

Forster, K. I. (1970). Visual perception of rapidly presented word sequences of varying complexity. *Perception & Psychophysics*, **8**, 215–221.

Foster, J. J., & Bruce, M. (1982). Reading upper and lower case on viewdata. *Applied Ergonomics*, **13**(2), 145–149.

Foulke, E. (1968). Listening comprehension as a function of word rate. *Journal of Communication*, **18**, 198–206.

Foulke, E., & Sticht, T. G. (1966). Listening preferences of college students for literary material of moderate difficulty. *Journal of Auditory Research*, **6**, 397–401.

Foulke, E., & Sticht, T. G. (1969). Review of research on the intelligibility and comprehension of accelerated speech. *Psychological Bulletin*, **72**(11), 50–62.

Francis, R. D., Collins, J. K. & Cassel, A. J. (1973). The effect of reading tuition on academic achievement: Volunteering and methods of tuition. *British Journal of Educational Psychology*, **43**, 298–300.

Frase, L. T, & Schwartz, B. J. (1979). Typographical cues that facilitate comprehension. *Journal of Educational Psychology*, **71**(2), 197–206.

Friedrich, F. J., Shadler, M., & Juola, J. F. (1979). Developmental changes in units of processing in reading. *Journal of Experimental Child Psychology*, **28**(2), 344–358.

Fry, E. B. (1978). *Skimming and scanning*. Providence, RI: Jamestown Publishers.

Garnham, A. (1981). Anaphoric references to instances, instantiated and non-instantiated categories: A reading time study. *British Journal of Psychology*, **72**, 377–384.

Garrod, S., & Sanford, A. (1977). Interpreting an aphoric relations: The integration of semantic information while reading. *Journal of Verbal Learning and Verbal Behavior*, **16**, 77–90.

Gates, A. I. (1921). An experimental and statistical study of reading and reading tests. *Journal of Educational Psychology*, **12**(6), 303–314.

Gates, A. I. (1926). A study of the role of visual perception, intelligence, and certain associative processes in reading and spelling. *Journal of Educational Psychology*, **19**, 433–445.

Geyer, J. J. (1968). Comprehensive and partial models related to the reading process. *Reading Research Quarterly*, **7**, 541–587.

Gibson, E. J., & Levin, H. (1975). *The psychology of reading*. Cambridge, MA: MIT Press.

Gibson, E. J., Bishop, C. H., Schiff, W., and Smith, J. (1964). *Journal of Experimental Psychology*, **67**(2), 173–182.

Gilbert, L. C. (1953). *Functional motor efficiency of the eyes and its relation to reading* (University of California Publications in Education, Vol. II, No. 3, pp. 159–231). Berkeley: University of California Press.

Gilbert, L. C., & Gilbert, D. W. (1942). Reading before the eye-movement camera versus reading away from it. *Elementary School Journal*, **42**, 443–447.

Gilhooley, K. J., & Logie, R. H. (1981). Word age-of-acquisition, reading latencies and auditory recognition. *Current Psychological Research*, **1**(4), 251–262.

Glock, M. D. (1949). The effects upon eye-movement and reading rate at the college level of three methods of training. *Journal of Educational Psychology*, **40**, 93–106.

Goldstein, H., & Justman, J. (1942). A classroom approach to the improvement of reading rate of college students. *Journal of Educational Psychology*, **33**, 506–516.

Goodman, K. S. (1966). A psycholinguistic view of reading comprehension. *Yearbook of the National Reading Conference*, **15**, 188–196.

Goodman, K. S. (1976). Behind the eye: What happens in reading. In H. Singer & R. B. Ruddel (Eds.), *Theoretical models and processes of reading*. Newark, DE: International Reading Association.

Gough, P. B. (1972). One second of reading. In J. F. Kavanagh & I. G. Mattingly (Eds.) *Language by ear and by eye* (pp. 331–358). Cambridge, MA: MIT Press.

Gough, P. B. (1984). Word recognition, In P. D. Pearson (Ed.), *Handbook of reading research* (pp. 225–254). New York: Longman.

Gould, J. D., Alfaro, L., Barnes, V., Finn, R., Grischkowsky, N., and Minuto, A. (1987). Reading is slower from CRT displays than from paper: Attempts to isolate a single-variable explanation. *Human Factors*, **29**(3), 269–299.

Gould, J. D., Alfaro, L., Finn, R., Haupt, E. J., & Minuto, A. (1987). Reading from CRT displays can be as fast as reading from paper. *Human Factors*, **29**(5), 497–517.

Gould, J. D., & Grischkowsky, N. (1984). Doing the same work with hard copy and with cathode-ray tube (CRT) computer terminals. *Human Factors*, **26**(3), 323–337.

Graesser, A. C., Hoffman, N. L., & Clark, L. F. (1980). Structural components of reading time. *Journal of Verbal Learning and Verbal Behavior*, **19**, 135–151.

Graf, P., & Levy, B. A. (1984). Reading and remembering: Conceptual and perceptual processing involved in reading rotated passages. *Journal of Verbal Learning and Verbal Behavior*, **23**(3), 405–424.

Graf, R. G. (1973, December). Speed reading: Remember the tortoise. *Psychology Today*, pp. 112–113.

Graham, H. L. (1975, Fall). The fetish of "reading rate." *Journal of Education*, pp. 18–23.

Granaas, M. M., McKay, T. D., Laham, R. D., Hurt, L. D. & Juola, J. F. (1984). Reading moving text of a CRT screen. *Human Factors*, **26**(1), 97–104.

Gray, W. S. (1922). Remedial cases in reading. *Supplementary educational monographs* (No. 22). Chicago, IL: University of Chicago Press.

Greene, E. B. (1931). Effectiveness of various rates of silent reading of college students. *Journal of Applied Psychology*, **15**, 214–227.

Gregory, M., & Poulton, E. C. (1970). Even versus uneven right-hand margins and the rate of comprehension in reading. *Ergonomics*, **13**(4), 427–434.

Guttentag, R. E., and Haith, M. M. (1978). Automatic processing as a function of age and reading ability. *Child Development*, **49**, 707–716.

Haber, L. R., & Haber, R. N. (1981). Perceptual processes in reading: An analysis-by-synthesis model. In F. I. Pirozzolo & M. C. Wittrock (Eds.), *Neuropsychological and cognitive processes in reading* (pp. 167–200) New York: Academic Press.

Haberlandt, K. F., & Bingham, G. (1978). Verbs contribute to the coherence of brief narratives: Reading related and unrelated sentence triples. *Journal of Verbal Learning and Verbal Behavior*, **17**, 419–425.

Haberlandt, K. F., Graesser, A. C., Schneider, N. J., & Kiely, J. (1986). Effects of task and new arguments on word reading times. *Journal of Memory and Language*, **25**(3), 314–322.

Hansen, D. M. (1977). A discourse structure analysis of the comprehension of rapid readers. *Yearbook of the National Reading Conference*, **26**, 221–226.

Hanson, E. (1968, April). Factors related to reading rates. *Journal of Reading*, pp. 663–669.

Hardyck, C. D., & Petrinovich, L. F. (1970). *Journal of Verbal Learning and Verbal Behavior*, **9**, 647–652.

Hardyck, C. D., Petrinovich, L. F., & Ellsworth, D. W. (1966). *Science*, **154**, 1467–1468.

Harris, A. J. (1968, December). Research on some aspects of comprehension: Rate, flexibility, and study skills. *Journal of Reading*, pp. 205–260.

Harris, A. J., & Sipay, E. R. (1985). *How to increase reading ability: A guide to developmental and remedial methods.* New York: Longman.

Hartley, J. (1980). Spatial cues in text. *Visible Language*, **14**(1), 62–79.

Hausfeld, S. (1981). Speeded reading and listening comprehension for easy and difficult materials. *Journal of Educational Psychology*, **73**(3), 312–319.

Hellebust, G. (1973). Speed-of-reading comprehension: Proceed with caution—but proceed. *Elementary English*, **50**(6), 897–899, 928.

Henney, M. (1983, Summer). The effect of all-capital vs. regular mixed print, as presented on a computer screen, on reading rate and accuracy. *AEDS Journal*, pp. 205–217.

Herculane, M. (1961). A survey of the flexibility of reading rates and techniques according to purpose. *Journal of Developmental Reading*, **4**, 207–210.

Herman, P. A. (1985). The effect of repeated readings on reading rate, speech pauses, and word recognition accuracy. *Reading Research Quarterly*, **20**(5), 553–565.

Hill, W. R. (1964). Influence of direction upon the flexibility of advanced college readers. *Yearbook of the National Reading Conference*, **13**, 119–125.

Himelstein, H. C., & Greenberg, G. (1974). the effect of increasing reading rate on comprehension. *Journal of Psychology*, **86**, 251–259.

Hoffman, J. V. (1978). Relationship between rate and reading flexibility. *Reading World*, **17**(4), 325–328.

Hoffman, J. V. (1979). Developing flexibility through ReFlex action. *Reading Teacher*, **33**(3), 323–329.

Hogaboam, T. W., & Perfetti, C. A. (1978). Reading skill and the role of verbal experience in decoding. *Journal of Educational Psychology*, **70**(5), 717–729.

Homa, D. (1983). An assessment of two extraordinary speed-readers. *Bulletin of the Pscyhonomic Society*, **21**(2), 123–126.

Horowitz, R., & Samuels, S. J. (1985). Reading and listening to expository text. *Journal of Reading Behavior*, **17**(3), 185–198.

Huey, E. B. (1908). *The psychology and pedagogy of reading*. New York: Macmillan. (Republished: Cambridge, MA: MIT Press, 1968).

Hunt, E. (1978). Mechanics of verbal ability. *Psychological Review*, **85**(2), 109–130.

Hunt, E., Frost, N., & Lunneborg, C. (1973). Individual differences in cognition: A new approach to intelligence. In G. H. Bower (Ed.), *The psychology of learning and motivation: Advances in research and theory* (Vol. 7). New York: Academic Press.

Jackson, M. D. (1980). Further evidence for a relationship between memory access and reading ability. *Journal of Verbal Learning and Verbal Behavior*, **19**, 683–694.

Jackson, M. D., & McClelland, J. L. (1975). Sensory and cognitive determinants of reading speed. *Journal of Verbal Learning and Verbal Behavior*, **14**, 575–589.

Jackson, M. D., & McClelland, J. L. (1979). Processing determinants of reading speed. *Journal of Experimental Psychology: General*, **108**(2), 151–181.

Jackson, N. E., & Biemiller, A. J. (1985). Letter, word, and text reading times of precocious and average readers. *Child Development*, **56**, 196–206.

Jacobowitz, T., & Haupt, E. J. (1984). Retrieval speed in reading comprehension: Failure to generalize. *Yearbook of the National Reading Conference*, **33**, 241–246.

Jandreau, S. M., Muncer, S. J., & Bever, T. G. (1986). Improving the readability of text with automatic phrase-sensitive formating. *British Journal of Educational Technology*, **17**(2), 128–133.

Jenkins, J. J. (1979). Four points to remember: A tetrahedral model of memory experiments. In L. S. Cermak & F. I. M. Craik (Eds.), *Levels of processing in human memory*. Hillsdale, NJ: Erlbaum.

Jensen, A. R. (1982). The chromometry of intelligence. In R. J. Sternberg (Ed.) *Advances in the psychology of human intelligence*. Hillsdale, NJ: Erlbaum.

Jester, R. E., & Travers, R. M. W. (1966). Comprehension of connected meaningful discourse as a function of rate and mode of presentation. *Journal of Educational Research*, **59**(7), 297–302.

Judd, C. H., & Buswell, G. T. (1922). *Silent reading: A study of the various types* (Supplementary Educational Monographs No. 23). Chicago, IL: University of Chicago.

Juel, C., & Holmes, B. (1981). Oral and silent reading of sentences. *Reading Research Quarterly*, **16**(4), 545–568.

Juola, J. F., Ward, N. J., & McNamara, T. (1982). Visual search and reading of rapid serial presentations of letter strings, words, and text. *Journal of Experimental Psychology: General*, **3**(2), 208–227.

Just, M. A., & Carpenter, P. A. (1980). A theory of reading: From eye fixations to comprehension. *Psychological Review*, **87**(4), 329–354.

Just, M. A., & Carpenter, P. A. (1987). *The psychology of reading and language comprehension*. Newton, MA: Allyn & Bacon.

Kail, R. V., Jr., & Marshall, C. V. (1978). Reading skill and memory scanning. *Journal of Educational Psychology*, **70**, 808–814.

Kallen, A. D., & Kyser, G. (1956). Organization and evaluation of a reading-improvement program. *Personnel*, **33**(2), 141–148.

Katz, L., & Wicklund, D. A. (1971). Word scanning rate for good and poor readers. *Journal of Educational Psychology*, **62**(2), 138–140.

Katz, L., & Wicklund, D. A. (1972). Letter scanning rate for good and poor readers in grades two and six. *Journal of Educational Psychology*, **63**(4), 363–367.

Kavanaugh, J. F., & Mattingly, I. G. (1972). *Language by ear and by eye*. Cambridge, MA: MIT Press.

Keenan, J. M., & Brown, P. (1984). Reading rate and retention as a function of the number of propositions in a text. *Child Development*, **55**, 1556–1569.

Keesey, J. C. (1973). Memory for logical structure and verbal units in prose material at increased rates of presentation. *Psychological Reports*, **33**, 419–428.

Kershner, A. M. (1964). Speed of reading in an adult population under differential conditions. *Journal of Applied Psychology*, **48**(1), 25–28.

Kieras, D. E. (1978). Good and bad structure in simple paragraphs: Effects on apparent theme, reading time, and recall. *Journal of Verbal Learning and Verbal Behavior*, **17**, 13–28.

Kieras, D. E. (1981). Component processes in the comprehension of simple prose. *Journal of Verbal Learning and Verbal Behavior*, **20**(1), 1–23.

Kilby, R. W. (1945). The relation of a remedial reading program to scholastic success in college. *Journal of Educational Psychology*, **36**(9), 513–534.

King, I. (1916). A comparison of slow and rapid reading. *School and Society*, **4**, 830–834.

Kintsch, W., & Keenan, J. (1973). Reading rate and retention as a function of the number of propositions in the base structure of sentences. *Cognitive Psychology*, **5**, 257–274.

Kintsch, W., & Kozminsky, E. (1977). Summarizing stories after reading and listening. *Journal of Educational Psychology*, **69**(5), 491–499.

Kintsch, W., Kozminsky, E., Streby, W. J., McKoon, G., & Keenan, J. M. (1975). Comprehension and recall of text as a function content variables. *Journal of Verbal Learning and Verbal Behavior*, **14**, 196–214.

Klaeser, B. M. (1977). *Reading improvement: A complete course for increasing speed*. Chicago, IL: Nelson-Hall.

Klapp, S. T., Anderson, W. G., & Berrian, R. W. (1973). Implicit speech in reading reconsidered. *Journal of Experimental Psychology*, **100**(2), 368–374.

Klare, G. R. (1963). *The measurement of readability*. Ames: Iowa State University Press.

Klare, G. R. (1984). Readability. In P. D. Pearson (Ed.), *Handbook of reading research* (pp. 681–744). New York: Longman.

Klare, G. R., Nichols, W. H., & Shuford, E. H. (1957). The relationship of typographical arrangement to the learning of technical training material. *Journal of Applied Psychology*, **41**(1), 41–45.

Kleiman, G. M. (1975). Speech recoding in reading. *Journal of Verbal Learning and Verbal Behavior*, **14**, 323–339.

Kliegl, R., Olson, R. K., & Davidson, B. J. (1982). Regression analyses as a tool for studying reading processes: Comment on Just and Carpenter's eye fixation theory. *Memory & Cognition*, **10**(3), 287–296.

Kolers, P. A. (1972). Experiments in reading. *Scientific American*, **227**(1), 84–91.

Kolers, P. A. (1975a). Memorial consequences of automatized encoding. *Journal of Experimental Psychology: Human Learning and Memory*, **1**(6), 689–701.

Kolers, P. A. (1975b). Specificity of operations in sentence recognition. *Cognitive Psychology*, **7**, 289–306.

Kolers, P. A. (1976). Reading a year later. *Journal of Experimental Psychology: Human Learning and Memory*, **2**(5), 554–565.

Kolers, P. A., Duchnicky, R. L., & Ferguson, D. C. (1981). Eye movement measurement of readability of CRT displays. *Human Factors*, **23**(5), 517–527.

Kolers, P. A., & Lewis, C. L. (1972). Bounding of letter sequences and the integration of visually presented words. *Acta Psychologica*, **36**, 112–124.

Kruk, R. S., & Muter, P. (1984). Reading of continuous text on video screens. *Human Factors*, **26**(3), 339–345.

LaBerge, D., & Samuels, S. J. (1974). Toward a theory of automatic information processing in reading. *Cognitive Psychology*, **6**, 293–323.

Labmeier, A. M., & Vockell, E. L. (1973). A reading development course. *Reading Horizons*, **13**(2), 64–71.

Laffitte, R. G., Jr. (1963). Analysis of increased rate of reading of college students. *Yearbook of the National Reading Conference*, **12**, 110–111.

Laffitte, R. G., Jr. (1964). Analysis of increased rate of reading of college students. *Journal of Developmental Reading*, **7**, 165–174.

Landauer, T. K. (1962). Rate of implicit speech. *Perceptual and Motor Skills*, **15**, 646.

Larsen, R. P., & Feder, D. D. (1940). Common and differential factors in reading and hearing comprehension. *Journal of Educational Psychology*, **31**(4), 241–252.

Lauer, A. R. (1936). An experimental study of the improvement in reading by college students. *Journal of Educational Psychology* **27**, 655–662.

Lauritzen, C. (1982, January). A modification of repeated readings for group instruction. *Reading Teacher*, pp. 456–458.

Laycock, F. (1955). Significant characteristics of college students with varying flexibility in reading rate: I. Eye-movements in reading prose. *Journal of Experimental Education*, **23**, 311–330.

Leeds, D. S. (1969). A summary of the research on the relationship between speed and comprehension in reading. *Journal of the Reading Specialist* **9**(2), 83–96.

Leslie, R., & Calfee, R. (1971). Visual search through word lists as a function of grade level, reading ability, and target repetition. *Perception & Psychophysics*, **10**, 169–171.

Letson, C. T. (1958). Speed and comprehension in reading. *Journal of Educational Research*, **52**(2), 49–53.

Letson, C. T. (1959). The relative influence of material and purpose on reading rates. *Journal of Educational Research*, **52**(6), 238–240.

Levy, B. A. (1977). Reading: Speech and meaning processes. *Journal of Verbal Learning and Verbal Behavior*, **16**, 623–638.

Lewis, N. (1949). An investigation into comparable results obtained from two methods of increasing reading speed among adults. *College English*, **11**, 152–156.

Lindquist, E. F. (1953). *Design and analysis of experiments in psychology and education*. Boston, MA: Houghton Mifflin.

Lopardo, G., & Sadow, M. W. (1982). Criteria and procedures for the method of repeated readings. *Journal of Reading*, **26**(2), 156–160.

Lorch, E. P., Lorch, R. F., Jr., Gretter, M. L., & Horn, D. G. (1987). On-line processing of topic structure by children and adults. *Journal of Experimental Child Psychology*, **43**, 81–95.

Lorch, R. F., Jr., & Lorch, E. P. (1986). On-line processing of summary and importance signals in reading. *Discourse Processes*, **9**, 489–496.

Lorch, R. F., Jr., Lorch, E. P., & Matthews, P. D. (1985). On-line processing of the topic structure of a text. *Journal of Memory and Language*, **24**, 350–362.

Mann, H. P. (1957). Some hypotheses on perceptual and learning processes with their applications to the process of reading: A preliminary note. *Journal of Genetic Psychology*, **90**, 167–202.

Margolin, C. M., Griebel, B., & Wolford, G. (1982). Effects of distraction on reading versus listening. *Journal of Experimental Psychology: Learning, Memory, & Cognition*, **8**(6), 613–618.

Martin, C. J., & Herndon, M. A. (1972). Development of telegraphic prose based upon a random word deletion scheme. *Yearbook of the National Reading Conference*, **21**, 30–34.

Martin, M. (1978). Speech recoding in silent reading. *Memory & Cognition*, **6**(2), 108–114.

Mason, M. (1980). Reading ability and the encoding of item and location information. *Journal of Experimental Psychology: Human Perception and Performance*, **6**(1), 89–98.

Masson, M. E. J. (1982). Cognitive processes in skimming stories. *Journal of Experimental Psychology: Learning, Memory, and Cognition*, **8**(5), 400–417.

Masson, M. E. J. (1983). Conceptual processing of text during skimming and rapid sequential reading. *Memory & Cognition*, **11**(3), 262–274.

Matthews, R. C., Coon, R. C., & Rosenthal, G. T. (1980, October). Broken text as a predictor of reading ability in the early grades. *Reading World*, pp. 57–64.

Maxwell, M. J. (1965). An experimental investigation of the effect of instructional set and information on reading rate. *Yearbook of the National Reading Conference*, **14**, 181–187.

Maxwell, M. J. (1969a). Assessing skimming and scanning skills improvement. *Yearbook of the National Reading Conference*, **18**, 229–233.

Maxwell, M. J. (1969b). *Skimming and scanning improvement.* New York: McGraw-Hill.

Maxwell, M. J. (1972). Skimming and scanning improvement: The needs, assumptions and knowledge base. *Journal of Reading Behavior*, **5**(1), 47–59.

Maxwell, M. J. (1978). Learning style and other correlates of performances on a scanning experiment. *Journal of Reading Behavior*, **10**(1), 49–55.

Maxwell, M. J., & Mueller, A. C. (1967, December). Relative effectiveness of techniques and placebo conditions in changing reading rates. *Journal of Reading*, pp. 184–191.

McBride, V. G. (1981, October). How fast can you read this? Learn how to see faster, read faster. *School and Community*, pp. 37–39, 58.

McClusky, H. Y. (1934). An experiment in the influence of preliminary skimming in reading. *Journal of Educational Psychology*, **25**, 521–529.

McConkie, G. W. (1982). Some perceptual aspects of reading. Chap. 3. *Bell Association for the Deaf*, pp. 35–42.

McConkie, G. W. (1983). Eye movements and perception during reading. In K. Rayner (Ed.), *Eye movements in reading: Perceptual and language processes* (pp. 69–86). New York: Academic Press.

McConkie, G. W., & Hogaboam, T. W. (1985). Eye position and word identification during reading. In R. Groner, G. W. McConkie, & C. Menz (Eds.), *Eye movements and information processing* (pp. 159–192). Amsterdam: Elsevier/North-Holland.

McConkie, G. W., Hogaboam, T. W., Wolverton, G. S., Zola, D., & Lucas, P. A. (1979). Toward the use of eye movements in the study of language processing. *Discourse Processes*, **2**, 157–177.

McConkie, G. W., & Meyer, B. J. F. (1974). Investigation of reading strategies: II. A replication of payoff condition effects. *Journal of Reading Behavior*, **6**(2), 151–158.

McConkie, G. W., & Rayner, K. (1973). An on-line computer technique for studying reading: Identifying the perceptual span. *Yearbook of the National Reading Conference*, **22,** 119–130.

McConkie, G. W., & Rayner, K. (1974). Reading strategies and payoff conditions, reading rate, and retention. *Journal of Reading Behavior*, **6**(1), 9–18.

McConkie, G. W., & Rayner, K. (1975). The span of the effective stimulus during a fixation in reading. *Perception & Psychophysics*, **17**(6), 578–586.

McConkie, G. W., Rayner, K., & Wilson, S. J. (1973). Experimental manipulation of reading strategies. *Journal of Educational Psychology*, **65**(1), 1–8.

McConkie, G. W., & Zola, D. (1984). Eye movement control during reading: The effect of word units. In W. Prinz & A. F. Sanders (Eds.), *Cognition and Motor Processes* (pp. 63–74). Berlin, Germany: Springer-Verlag.

McConkie, G. W., Zola, D., Blanchard, H. E., & Wolverton, G. S. (1982). Perceiving words during reading: Lack of facilitation from prior peripheral exposure. *Perception & Psychophysics*, **32**(3), 271–281.

McCracken, R. A. (1960). Accelerating the reading speed of sixth grade gifted children. *Exceptional Children*, **27,** 27–28.

McCracken, R. A. (1965, January). Internal versus external flexibility of reading rate. *Journal of Reading*, pp. 208–209.

McCutchen, D., and Perfetti, C. A. (1982). The visual tongue-twister effect: Phonological activation in silent reading. *Journal of Verbal Learning and Verbal Behavior*, **21,** 672–687.

McDade, J. E. (1937). An hypothesis for non-oral reading: Argument, experiment, and results. *Journal of Educational Research*, **30**(7), 489–503.

McDonald, A. S. (1963). The placebo response and reading research. *Yearbook of the National Reading Conference*, **12,** 220–229.

McDonald, A. S. (1971). Reading versatility twelve years later. *Yearbook of the National Reading Conference*, **20,** 168–173.

McGuigan, F. J. (1970). Covert oral behavior during the silent performance of reading tasks. *Psychological Bulletin*, **74**(5), 309–326.

McGuigan, F. J. (1973). Electrical movement of covert processes as an explication of "higher mental events." In F. J. McGuigan & R. A. Schoonover (Eds.), *The psychophysiology of thinking* (pp. 343–385). New York: Academic Press.

Mead, C. D. (1915). Silent versus oral reading with one hundred sixth-grade children. *Journal of Educational Psychology*, **6**(6), 345–348.

Mead, C. D. (1917). Results in silent versus oral reading. *Journal of Educational Psychology*, **8**(6), 367–368.

Mehler, J., Bever, T. G., & Carey, P. (1967). What we look at when we read. *Perception & Psychophysics*, **2,** 213–218.

Meyer, B. J. F. (1975). *The organization of prose and its effects on memory*. Amsterdam: North-Holland.

Meyer, D. E., Schvaneveldt, R. W., & Ruddy, M. C. (1974). Functions of graphemic and phonemic codes in visual word-recognition. *Memory & Cognition*, **2**(2), 309–321.

Miller, D. (1966). A review of speed-reading theory and techniques for the ophthalmologist. *American Journal of Ophthalmology*, **62,** 334–338.

Miller, G. R., & Coleman, E. B. (1967). A set of thirty-six passages calibrated for complexity. *Journal of Verbal Learning and Verbal Behavior*, **6,** 851–854.

Miller, G. R., & Coleman, E. B. (1971). The measurement of reading speed and the obligation to generalize to a population of reading materials. *Journal of Reading Behavior*, **4**(3), 48–56.

Miller, J. R., & Kintsch, W. (1980). Readability and recall of short prose passages: A theoretical analysis. *Journal of Experimental Psychology: Human Learning and Memory,* **6**(4), 335–354.

Miller, P. A. (1978). Considering flexibility of reading rate for assessment and development of efficient reading behavior. In S. J. Samuels (Ed.), *What research has to say about reading rate for assessment and development of efficient reading behavior* (pp. 72–83). Newark, DE: International Reading Association.

Mitchell, D. C. & Green, D. W. (1978). The effects of context and content on immediate processing in reading. *Quarterly Journal of Experimental Psychology,* **30**, 609–636.

Moore, H., & McLaughlin, L. (1934). *Reading and study aids.* Ann Arbor, MI: Edwards Brothers.

Morasky, R. L., & Willcox, H. H. (1970). Time required to process information as a function of question placement. *American Educational Research Journal,* **7**(4), 561–567.

Morse, W. C. (1951). A comparison of the eye-movements of average fifth- and seventh-grade pupils reading materials of corresponding difficulty. In *Studies in the psychology of reading* (University of Michigan Monographs in Education No. 4, pp. 1–64). Ann Arbor: University of Michigan Press.

Morse, W. C., Ballantine, F. A., & Dixon, W. R. (1968). *Studies in the psychology of reading.* New York: Greenwood Press.

Morton, J. (1959). An investigation into the effects of an adult reading efficiency course. *Occupational Psychology,* **33**, 222–238.

Morton, J. (1964). The effects of context upon speed of reading, eye movements and eye-voice span. *Quarterly Journal of Experimental Psychology,* **16**(4), 340–354.

Moss, M. J. (1980). The effect of a film aided coaching course on the rate of students reading of texts of varying difficulty. *Journal of Research in Reading,* **3**(1), 11–16.

Moyer, S. B. (1982). Repeated readings. *Journal of Learning Disabilities,* **15**(10), 619–623.

Mullins, C. J., & Mowry, H. W. (1953). Twenty-one top executives learn to read 216% faster. *Personnel Journal,* **31**, 336–338.

Muter, P. Latremouille, S. A., Treurniet, W. C., and Beam, P. (1982). Extended readings of continuous text on television screens. *Human Factors,* **24**(5), 501–508.

Naish, P. (1980). The effects of graphemic and phonemic similarity between targets and masks in a backward visual masking paradigm. *Quarterly Journal of Experimental Psychology,* **32**, 57–68.

Nania, F., & Moe, I. L. (1962, March). Rate flexibility training for able junior high pupils. *National Association of Secondary-School Principals,* pp. 82–86.

National Assessment of Educational Progress (NAEP) (1972). *Reading rate and comprehension* (Report 02-R-09). Denver, CO: Education Commission of the States.

Neisser, U. (1964). Visual search. *Scientific American,* **210**, 94–102.

Neisser, U. (1967). *Cognitive psychology.* New York: Appleton-Century-Crofts.

Nell, V. (1988). The psychology of reading for pleasure: Needs and gratifications. *Reading Research Quarterly,* **23**(1), 6–50.

Neville, M. H. (1975). Effectiveness of rate of aural message on reading and listening. *Educational Research,* **18**(1), 37–43.

North, A. J., & Jenkins, L. B. (1951). Reading speed and comprehension as a function of typography. *Journal of Applied Psychology,* **35**(4), 225–228.

O'Brien, J. (1926). *Silent reading.* New York: Macmillan.

O'Regan, K. (1979). Saccade size control in reading: Evidence for the linguistic control hypothesis. *Perception & Psychophysics,* **25**(6), 501–509.

O'Shea, L. J., Sindelar, P. T., & O'Shea, D. J. (1985). The effects of repeated readings and attentional cues on reading fluency and comprehension. *Journal of Reading Behavior,* **17**(2), 129–142.

Otto, W., Barrett, T. C., & Harris, T. L. (1968). Research in reading. *Journal of Experimental Education*, **37**, 65–77.

Palmer, J., MacLeod, C. M., Hunt, E., & Davidson, J. E. (1985). Information processing correlates of reading. *Journal of Memory and Language*, **24**, 59–88.

Patberg, J. P., & Yonas, A. (1978). The effects of the reader's skill and the difficulty of the text on the perceptual span in reading. *Journal of Experimental Psychology: Human Perception and Performance*, **4**(4), 545–552.

Patterson, D. G., & Tinker, M. A. (1940). *How to make type readable*. New York: Harper & Row.

Pearson, P. D. (Ed.). (1984). *Handbook of reading research*. New York: Longman.

Perfetti, C. A. (1985). *Reading ability*. New York: Oxford University Press.

Perfetti, C. A., & Hogaboam, T. (1975). Relationship between single word decoding and reading comprehension skill. *Journal of Educational Psychology*, **67**(4), 461–469.

Pintner, R. (1913). Inner speech during silent reading. *Psychological Review*, **20**, 129–153.

Posner, M., & Mitchell, R. F. (1967). Chronometric analysis of classification. *Psychological Bulletin*, **74**(5), 392–409.

Posner, M., Boies, S., Eichelman, W., & Taylor, R. (1969). Retention of visual and name codes of single letters. *Journal of Experimental Psychology Monographs*, **79**(1, Pt. 2).

Potter, M. C., Kroll, J. F., & Harris, C. (1980). Comprehension and memory in rapid sequential reading. In R. S. Nickerson (Ed.), *Attention and performance VIII* (pp. 395–418). Hillsdale, NJ: Erlbaum.

Poulton, E. C. (1958). Time for reading and memory. *British Journal of Psychology*, **49**(3), 230–245.

Poulton, E. C. (1961). British courses for adults on effective reading. *British Journal of Educational Psychology*, **31**, 128–137.

Poulton, E. C. (1969). Asymmetrical transfer in reading tests produced by teleprinter and by typewriter. *Journal of Applied Psychology*, **53**(3), 244–249.

Poulton, E. C., & Brown, C. H. (1967). Memory after reading aloud and reading silently. *British Journal of Psychology*, **58**, 219–222.

Pressey, L. C. (1928). *A manual of reading exercises for freshmen*. Columbus: Ohio State University Press.

Preston, R. C., & Botel, M. (1951, August). Reading comprehension tested under timed and untimed conditions. *School and Society*, p. 71.

Raduege, T. A. & Schwantes, F. M. (1987). Effects of rapid word recognition training on sentence context effects in children. *Journal of Reading Behavior*, **19**(4), 395–414.

Rankin, E. F. (1962). The relationship between reading rate and comprehension. *Yearbook of the National Reading Conference*, **11**, 1–5.

Rankin, E. F. (1963). Sequential emphasis upon speed and comprehension in a college reading improvement program. *Journal of Developmental Reading*, **7**, 46–54.

Rankin, E. F. (1970). How flexibly do we read? *Journal of Reading Behavior*, **3**(3), 34–38.

Rankin, E. F. (1978). Rate of comprehension flexibility—a new measurement procedure. *Yearbook of the National Reading Conference*, **27**, 266–273.

Rankin, E. F., & Kehle, T. J. (1972). A comparison of the reading performance of college students with conventional versus negative internal (intra-article) reading flexibility. *Yearbook of the National Reading Conference*, **21**, 51–58.

Rashotte, C. A., & Torgesen, J. K. (1985). Repeated reading and reading fluency in learning disabled children. *Reading Research Quarterly*, **20**(2), 180–188.

Raygor, A. L., Wark, D. M., & Warren, A. D. (1966, January). Operant conditioning of reading rate: The effect of a secondary reinforcer. *Journal of Reading*, pp. 147–156.

Rayner, K. (1975). The perceptual span and peripheral cues in reading. *Cognitive Psychology*, **7**, 65–81.

Rayner, K. (1986). Eye movements and the perceptual span in beginning and skilled readers. *Journal of Experimental Child Psychology*, **41**(2), 211–236.

Rayner, K., Inhoff, A. W., Morrison, R. E., Slowiaczek, M. L., & Bertera, J. H. (1981). *Journal of Experimental Psychology: Human Perception and Performance*, **7**(1), 167–179.

Rayner, K., & Pollatsek, A. (1981). Eye movement control during reading: Evidence for direct control. *Quarterly Journal of Experimental Psychology*, **33A**, 351–373.

Reinking, D. (1988). Computer-mediated text and comprehension differences: The role of reading time, reader preference, and estimation of learning. *Reading Research Quarterly*, **23**(4), 484–498.

Remmers, H. H., & Stalnaker, J. M. (1928). An experiment in remedial reading exercises at the college level. *School and Society*, **28**, 797–800.

Riley, J. A., & Lowe, J. D., Jr. (1981, October). A study of enhancing vs. reducing subvocal speech during reading. *Journal of Reading*, pp. 7–13.

Ring, C. C., & Bentley, I. M. (1930). The effect of training upon the rate of adult reading. *American Journal of Psychology*, **42**, 429–430.

Robinson, F. P. (1933). The role of eye-movements in reading with an evaluation of techniques for their improvements. *University of Iowa: Series on Aims and Progress of Research*, No. 39.

Robinson, F. P. (1940). "Speed versus comprehension in reading"—A discussion. *Journal of Educational Psychology*, **31**, 554–558.

Rothkopf, E. Z. (1972). Structural text features and the control of processes in learning from written materials. In J. B. Carroll & R. O. Freedle (Eds.), *Language comprehension and the acquisition of knowledge*. New York: Wiley.

Rothkopf, E. Z., & Coatney, R. P. (1974). Effects of context passages on subsequent inspection rates. *Journal of Applied Psychology*, **59**(6), 679–682.

Ruppel, G. (1979). Self-management and reading rate improvement. *Journal of Counseling Psychology*, **26**(5), 451–454.

Sailor, A. L., & Ball, S. E. (1975). Peripheral vision training in reading speed and comprehension. *Perceptual Motor Skills*, **41**, 761–762.

Salasoo, A. (1986). Cognitive processing in oral and silent reading. *Reading Research Quarterly*, **21**(1), 59–69.

Samuels, S. J. (1969). Effect of word associations on the recognition of flashed words. *Journal of Educational Psychology*, **60**(2), 97–102.

Samuels, S. J. (1979, January). The method of repeated readings. *Reading Teacher*, pp. 403–408.

Samuels, S. J. (1985). Toward a theory of automatic information processing in reading: Updated. In H. Singer & R. B. Ruddell (Eds.), *Theoretical models and processes of reading* (pp. 719–721). Newark, DE: International Reading Association.

Samuels, S. J., & Dahl, P. R. (1975). Establishing appropriate purpose for reading and its effect on flexibility of reading rate. *Journal of Educational Psychology*, **67**(1), 38–43.

Sanocki, T., Goldman, K., Waltz, J., Cook, C., Epstein, W., & Oden, G. C. (1985). Interaction of stimulus and contextual information during reading: Identifying words within sentences. *Memory & Cognition*, **13**(2), 145–157.

Schale, F. (1972). Measuring degree and rate of visual awareness during growth in rapid reading on television. *Yearbook of the National Reading Conference*, **21**, 167–171.

Schmalhofer, F., & Glavanov, D. (1986). Three components of understanding a programmers manual: Verbatim, propositional and situational representations. *Journal of Memory and Language*, **25**(3), 279–294.

Schmidt, D. L. (1972). Does rapid reading training work? *Training and Development Journal,* **26**(2), 26–29.

Schreiber, P. A. (1980). On the acquisition of reading fluency. *Journal of Reading Behavior,* **12**(3), 177–186.

Schwanenflugel, P. J., & Shoben, E. J. (1983). Differential context effects in the comprehension of abstract and concrete verbal materials. *Journal of Experimental Psychology: Learning, Memory, and Cognition,* **9**(1), 82–102.

Secor, W. B. (1899). Visual reading: A study in mental imagery. *American Journal of Psychology,* **11**, 225–236.

Seibert, E. W. (1943). Reading reactions for varied types of subject matter. *Journal of Experimental Education,* **12**, 37–44.

Sharon, A. T. (1973). What do adults read? *Reading Research Quarterly,* **9**(2), 148–169.

Shebilske, W. L., & Fisher, D. F. (1981). Eye movements reveal components of flexible reading strategies. *Yearbook of the National Reading Conference,* **30**, 51–56.

Shebilske, W. L., & Reid, L. S. (1979). Reading eye movements, macro-structure and comprehension processes. In P. A. Kolers, M. E. Wrolstad, & H. Bouma (Eds.) *Processing of visible language* (Vol. 1, pp. 99–112). New York: Plenum.

Sherer, P. (1975). Skimming and scanning: De-mything the process with a college student. *Journal of Reading,* **19**(1), 24–27.

Shores, J. H. (1961). Are fast readers the best readers? A second report. *Elementary English,* **37**, 236–245.

Shores, J. H., & Husbands, K. L. (1950). Are fast readers the best readers? *Elementary English,* **27**, 52–57.

Siegel, M. (1979). *The art of reading.* Washington, DC: Learn, Inc. (A television program).

Simpson, R. H. (1940). Improving reading and related study skills of college women. *College English,* **1**, 322–332.

Singer, H. (1965). A developmental model for speed of reading in grades three through six. *Reading Research Quarterly,* **1**(1), 29–49.

Sisson, E. D. (1937). Habits of eye movements in reading. *Journal of Educational Psychology,* **28**, 437–450.

Sisson, E. D. (1939). The causes of slow reading: An analysis. *Journal of Educational Psychology,* **30**, 206–214.

Slowiaczek, M. L., & Clifton, C., Jr. (1980). Subvocalization and reading for meaning. *Journal of Verbal Learning and Verbal Behavior,* **19**, 573–582.

Smiley, S. S., Oakley, D. D., Worthen, D., Campione, J. C., & Brown, A. L. (1977). Recall of thematically relevant material by adolescent good and poor readers as a function of written versus oral presentation. *Journal of Educational Psychology,* **69**(4), 381–387.

Smith, F. (1969). Familiarity of configuration vs discriminability of features in the visual identification of words. *Psychonomic Science,* **14**(6), 262–263.

Smith, F. (1971). *Understanding reading—A psycholinguistic analysis of reading and learning to read.* New York: Holt, Rinehart, & Winston.

Smith, F. (1972a). Phonology and orthography: Reading and writing. *Elementary English,* **49**, 1075–1088.

Smith, F. (1972b). *Psycholinguistics and reading.* New York: Holt, Rinehart, & Winston.

Smith, H. P., & Tate, T. R. (1953). Improvements in reading rate and comprehension of subjects training with the tachistoscope. *Journal of Educational Psychology,* **44**, 176–184.

Smith, N. B. (1957). *Speed reading made easy.* Englewood Cliffs, NJ: Prentice-Hall.

Snowling, M., & Frith, U. (1981). The role of sound, shape and orthographic cues in early reading. *British Journal of Psychology,* **72**, 83–87.

Sokolov, A. N. (1972). *Inner speech and thought.* New York: Plenum.

Spache, G. D. (1962, January). Is this a breakthrough in reading? *Reading Teacher*, pp. 258–263.

Spache, G. D. (1963). *Toward better reading*. Champaign, IL: Garrard.

Spiegel, M. R., & Bryant, N. D. (1978). Is speed of processing information related to intelligence and achievement? *Journal of Educational Psychology*, **70**(6), 904–910.

Spoehr, K., & Smith, E. E. (1973). The role of syllables in perceptual processing. *Cognitive Psychology*, **5**, 71–89.

Stanovich, K. E., Cunningham, A. E., & West, R. F. (1981). A longitudinal study of the development of automatic recognition skills in first graders. *Journal of Reading Behavior*, **13**(1), 57–73.

Stanovich, K. E., & West, R. F. (1981). The effect of sentence context on ongoing word recognition: Tests of a two-process theory. *Journal of Experimental Psychology: Human Perception and Performance*, **7**(3), 658–672.

Steinacher, R. (1971, November). Reading flexibility: Dilemma and solution. *Journal of Reading*, pp. 143–150.

Sticht, T. G., Beck, L. J., Hauke, R. N., Kleiman, G. M., & James, J. H. (1974). *Auding and reading: A developmental model*. Alexander, VA: Human Resources Research Organization.

Sticht, T. G., & James, J. H. (1984). Listening and reading. In P. D. Pearson (Ed.), *Handbook of reading research* (pp. 293–318). New York: Longman.

Stone, C. W. (1922). Improving the reading ability of college students. *Journal of Educational Method*, **2**, 8–23.

Stone, C. W., & Colvin, C. (1920, September). "How to study" as a source of motive in educational psychology. *Journal of Educational Psychology*, pp. 384–354.

Stroop, J. R. (1935). Studies of inference in serial verbal reactions. *Journal of Experimental Psychology*, **18**, 643–661.

Stroud, J. B. (1942). A critical note on reading. *Psychological Bulletin*, **39**, 173–178.

Stroud, J. B. (1945). Rate of visual perception as a factor in rate of reading. *Journal of Educational Psychology*, **36**, 487–498.

Stroud, J. B., & Henderson, M. (1943). Rate of reading and learning by reading. *Journal of Educational Psychology*, **34**(4), 193–205.

Swalm, J., & Kling, M. (1973). Speed reading in the elementary school. *Elementary School Journal*, **74**(3), 158–164.

Swanson, D. E. (1937). Common elements in silent and oral reading. *Psychological Monographs*, **48**(3), 36–60.

Sweiger, J. D. (1972). Designs and organizational structure of junior and community college reading programs across the country. *Yearbook of the National Reading Conference*, **21**, 1–7.

Taylor, S. E. (1962). An evaluation of forty-one trainees who had recently completed the "Reading Dynamics" program. *Yearbook of the National Reading Conference*, **11**, 41–56.

Taylor, S. E. (1965). Eye movements in reading: Facts and fallacies, *American Educational Research Journal*, **2**, 187–202.

Thames, K. H., & Rossiter, C. M., Jr. (1972). The effects of reading practice with compressed speech on reading rate and listening comprehension. *AV Communication Review*, **20**(1), 35–42.

Thomas, E. L. (1962). Eye movements in speed reading. In R. G. Stauffer (Ed.), *Speed reading: Practices and procedures* (pp. 104–117). Newark, DE: University of Deleware School of Education.

Thompson, M. R., & Whitehill, R. P. (1970). Relationships between reading flexibility and speed gains. *Journal of Educational Research*, **63**(5), 213–215.

Tinker, M. A. (1926). Reading reactions for mathematical formulae. *Journal of Experimental Psychology,* **9,** 444–467.

Tinker, M. A. (1932). The relation of speed to comprehension in reading. *School and Society,* **36,** 158–160.

Tinker, M. A. (1939). Speed versus comprehension in reading as affected by level of difficulty. *Journal of Educational Psychology,* **30**(2), 81–94.

Tinker, M. A. (1940). Dr. Robinson on speed versus comprehension in reading: A discussion. *Journal of Educational Psychology,* **32,** 559–560.

Tinker, M. A. (1945). Rate of work in reading performance as measured in standardized tests. *Journal of Educational Psychology,* **36,** 217–228.

Tinker, M. A. (1946). The study of eye movements in reading. *Psychological Bulletin,* **43**(2), 93–120.

Tinker, M. A. (1958). Recent studies of eye movements in reading. *Psychological Bulletin,* **55**(4), 215–231.

Tinker, M. A. (1963). *Legibility of print.* Ames: Iowa State University Press.

Tinker, M. A. (1965). *Bases for effective reading.* Minneapolis: University of Minnesota Press.

Tinker, M. A. (1969). The uses and limitations of eye-movement studies in reading. *Yearbook of the National Reading Conference,* **18,** 4–8.

Tinker, M. A., & Patterson, D. G. (1928). Influence of type form on speed of reading. *Journal of Applied Psychology,* **12,** 359–368.

Tirrell, F. J., Mount, M. K., & Scott, N. A. (1977). Self-reward and external reward: Methodological considerations and contingency instructions. *Psychological Reports,* **41,** 1103–1110.

Tousignant, J. P., Hall, D., & Loftus, E. F. (1986). Discrepancy detection and vulnerability to misleading postevent information. *Memory & Cognition,* **14**(4), 329–338.

Townsend, D. T. (1983). Thematic processing in sentences and texts. *Cognition,* **13,** 223–261.

Traxler, A. E. (1934). The relationships between rate of reading and speed of association. *Journal of Educational Psychology,* **25,** 357–365.

Trollip, S. R., & Sales, G. (1986). Readability of computer generated text. *Human Factors,* **28**(2), 159–163.

Tuckey, J. S. (1960). Seven years of acceleration. *Journal of Developmental Reading,* **3,** 221–231.

Tuinman, J. J. (1973). Determining the passage dependency of comprehension questions in five major tests. *Reading Research Quarterly,* **9**(2), 206–223.

Tulving, E., & Gold, C. (1963). Stimulus information and contextual information as determinants of tachistoscopic recognition of words. *Journal of Experimental Psychology,* **66,** 319–327.

Tzeng, O. J. L., & Wang, W. S.-Y. (1983). The first two r's. *American Scientist,* **71,** 238–243.

Underwood, N. R., & McConkie, G. W. (1985). Perceptual span for letter distinctions during reading. *Reading Research Quarterly,* **20**(2), 153–162.

Underwood, N. R., & Zola, D. (1986). The span of letter recognition of good and poor readers. *Reading Research Quarterly,* **21**(1), 6–19.

Walker, R. Y. (1933). The eye-movements of good readers. *Psychological Monographs,* **44**(3), 95–117.

Walsh, D. J., Price, G. G., & Gillingham, M. G. (1988). The critical but transitory importance of letter naming. *Reading Research Quarterly,* **23**(1), 108–122.

Waters, G. S., Komoda, M. K., & Arbuckle, T. Y. (1985). The effects of concurrent tasks on reading: Implications for phonological recoding. *Journal of Memory and Language,* **24,** 27–45.

Weber, C. O. (1939). The acquisition and retention of reading skills by college freshmen. *Journal of Educational Psychology*, **30**, 453–460.

Weintrab, S. (1967). Research. *Reading Teacher*, **21**, 169–173.

West, R. F., & Stanovich, K. E. (1978). Automatic contextual facilitation in readers of three ages. *Child Development*, **49**, 717–727.

West, R. F., & Stanovich, K. E. (1979). The development of automatic word recognition skills. *Journal of Reading Behavior*, **11**, 211–219.

Whipple, G. M., & Curtis, J. N. (1917). Preliminary investigation of skimming in reading. *Journal of Educational Psychology*, **8**, 336–349.

Wickens, C. D. (1974). Temporal limits of human information processing: A Developmental study. *Psychological Bulletin*, **81**, 739–755.

Wood, E. N. (1960). A breakthrough in reading. *Reading Teacher*, **14**, 115–117.

Wood, E. N. (1963). Opinions differ on speed reading. *NEA Journal*, Apr.; pp. 44, 46.

Woodworth, R. S. (1938). *Experimental psychology*. New York: Henry Holt.

Yoakam, G. A. (1928). *Reading and study: More effective study through better reading habits*. New York: Macmillan.

Zuber, B. L., & Wetzel, P. A. (1981). Eye movement determinants of reading rate. In B. L. Zuber (Ed.), *Models of oculomotor behavior and control* (pp. 193–208). Boca Raton, FL: CRC Press.

AUTHOR INDEX

SUBJECT INDEX